EXPLORING SOCIAL PSYCHOLOGY

CANADIAN EDITION

EXPLORING SOCIAL PSYCHOLOGY

DAVID G. MYERS
Hope College

STEVEN M. SMITH
Saint Mary's University

Toronto   Montréal   Boston   Burr Ridge, IL   Dubuque, IA   Madison, WI   New York
San Francisco   St. Louis   Bangkok   Bogotá   Caracas   Kuala Lumpur   Lisbon   London
Madrid   Mexico City   Milan   New Delhi   Santiago   Seoul   Singapore   Sydney   Taipei

Exploring Social Psychology
Canadian Edition

Statistics Canada information is used with the permission of the Minister of Industry, as Minister responsible for Statistics Canada. Information on the availability of the wide range of data from Statistics Canada can be obtained from Statistics Canada's Regional Offices, its World Wide Web site at <http://www.statcan.ca>, and its toll-free access number 1-800-263-1136.

ISBN-13: 978-0-07-097197-4
ISBN-10: 0-07-097197-8

1 2 3 4 5 6 7 8 9 10 TCP 0 9 8 7

Printed and bound in Canada.

Editorial Director: Joanna Cotton
Sponsoring Editor: Karen Ritcey
Marketing Manager: Marc Trudel
iLearning Sales Specialist: Joanne Barnett
Developmental Editor: Jodi Lewchuk
Editorial Associate: Marina Seguin
Copy Editor: Kelli Howey
Senior Production Coordinator: Madeleine Harrington
Cover and Interior Design: Dave Murphy, Valid Design & Layout
Cover Image Credit: © Ingram Publishing/SuperStock
Page Layout: Valerie Bateman, Valid Design & Layout
Printer: Transcontinental Printing Group

Library and Archives Canada Cataloguing in Publication

Myers, David G
    Exploring social psychology / David G. Myers, Steven M. Smith. — Canadian ed.

Includes bibliographical references and indexes.
ISBN-13: 978-0-07-097197-4
ISBN-10: 0-07-097197-8

1. Social psychology—Textbooks. I. Smith, Steven M. (Steven Michael), 1971-
II. Title.

HM1033.M94 2006   302   C2006-904929-7

About the Authors

David G. Myers is the John Dirk Werkman Professor of Psychology at Michigan's Hope College, where students have voted him "Outstanding Professor." Myers's love of teaching psychology is manifest in his writings for the lay public. His articles have appeared in two dozen magazines and he has authored or co-authored a dozen books, including *The Pursuit of Happiness* (Avon, 1993) and *Intuition: Its Powers and Perils* (Yale University Press, 2002).

Also an award-winning researcher, Myers received the Gordon Allport Prize from Division 9 of the American Psychological Association for his work on group polarization. His scientific articles have appeared in more than two dozen journals, including *Science, American Scientist, Psychological Science*, and the *American Psychologist*. He has served his discipline as consulting editor to the *Journal of Experimental Social Psychology* and the *Journal of Personality and Social Psychology*.

In his spare time he has chaired his city's Human Relations Commission, helped found a community action agency that assists impoverished families, and spoken to dozens of collegiate and religious groups. David and Carol Myers are parents of two sons and a daughter.

Steven M. Smith is an Associate Professor of Psychology at Saint Mary's University. He completed his B.A. (Honours) at Bishop's University in Lennoxville, Quebec, and his M.A. and Ph.D. in Social Psychology at Queen's University in Kingston, Ontario. Dr. Smith regularly teaches Social Behaviour, Attitudes and Persuasion, and Psychology and Law. His lectures are well received, and he has been nominated for the Saint Mary's University Student Association Faculty of Arts Teaching Award.

Dr. Smith is an active researcher. Not surprisingly, his research interests parallel his teaching interests, and he is dedicated to applying his theoretical work to real-world concerns. His research has been supported by the Social Sciences and Humanities Research Council, whose Psychology Adjudication committee he chaired in 2006. Along with colleagues, Dr. Smith has also received funding from the Canadian Institutes of Health Research, the Nova Scotia Health Research Foundation, and a number of private organizations. His work has appeared in journals such as the *Journal of Applied Psychology* and *Journal of Personality and Social Psychology*.

Dr. Smith has lent his expertise to a number of community organizations, particularly advising on communication and social marketing issues. Dr. Smith's wife, Isabel, is a clinical developmental psychologist, and together they have two heavily analyzed children, Sydney and Dylan.

Brief Contents

Table of Contents

PART FOUR
Social Relations

Preface

Welcome to the Canadian Edition of *Exploring Social Psychology*. I am very proud to be involved with the first Canadian edition of this book. As someone who has taught social psychology courses for a number of years, I am well aware of the breadth of choices available to instructors when choosing a text to accompany an introductory social psychology course. I am also aware of the challenges involved with teaching a comprehensive course in a single semester.

Most textbooks are simply too long and too expensive. Shorter books often fail to cover the topics instructors want, even in a one-semester course. That is why I have always been impressed with David Myers's *Exploring Social Psychology* text. It was short enough for a one-term course, yet was comprehensive enough to cover the most important topics. However, students would tell me that it was not "Canadian" enough.

A CANADIAN PERSPECTIVE ON SOCIAL PSYCHOLOGY

This shortcoming—that the book was not "Canadian" enough—is what this edition aims to address. Importantly, this book is not about dropping in a few Canadian names and changing the spelling of the word *behavior* to *behaviour*. Discussing the topic of social psychology in a Canadian context means exploring the extent to which certain psychological issues are different in Canada than in the rest of the world. We are very fortunate that many of world's leading social psychologists are Canadian. One only needs to look at the editorial boards of the major peer-reviewed journals in the field to verify this. Therefore, this book is about delving into social psychology in the Canadian context, addressing issues that are by their nature Canadian (topics such as acculturation, multiculturalism, and the challenges faced by Aboriginal Peoples in Canada), and, most importantly, illustrating why social psychology should be relevant to every student.

David Myers wrote *Exploring Social Psychology* from a very personal perspective. I have continued that tradition with my contributions to the Canadian Edition. The theme running through this book reflects what I feel is at the root of social psychological research: storytelling. When we tell a story, we talk not only about what the people did, but also about why they did it. Understanding the *why* of social behaviour is the basis of a great deal of research in the field of social psychology.

PEDAGOGICAL FEATURES OF THE CANADIAN EDITION

This book also reflects one of my core principles in the teaching of social psychology—one that is shared by most other teachers—that students learn better when they are engaged in the material. Therefore, one of my primary aims in this book is to engage you, the student, through the use of critical-thinking exercises, application tasks, and storytelling.

- **Critical-Thinking Approach.** Since I began teaching, I have found that one of the ways to engage students is to force them to think critically about questions (e.g., "Do opposites attract?") and ask them to commit to a predicted outcome by putting their hands up in class. I use these "thought experiments" to get students to think about the topic I am presenting. I have tried to incorporate this approach into the text by asking you, in each module, to think about one of the central issues covered. In many cases I ask you to commit to a response by answering a question or predicting an outcome. As an added bonus, responses to some of the questions can be tabulated so that students and instructors can learn how people in the course have responded. In some modules of the book, you are asked to think about a specific experiment or issue that has been described in the module, and to critique it from a methodological or ethical standpoint.

- **Application Tasks and Activities.** Another goal I have worked toward in my teaching is to make social psychology real for students. In each class I strive to engage students by incorporating what they have learned into their everyday lives. I have sought to incorporate this goal by designating specific activities for all of the modules that can be completed at the Online Learning Centre for this text (www.mcgrawhill.ca/olc/myers). Identified in the text's margins with an OLC icon, these activities will illustrate important topics so that you can get a better understanding of how social psychological principles apply to *your* world. Designed to complement both the text and in-class instruction, these web-based interactive tools are available to all students and instructors who use this book.

- **Storytelling.** As I mention above, I believe a central element to exploring social psychology is the stories we tell. I believe that using narratives is yet another way to engage people in the subject matter. Therefore, in each module of the book I have tried to incorporate at least one researcher's story about how they got involved in that topic, or how their research came up with a way to answer an important question in their area.

NEW IN THE CANADIAN EDITION: APPLYING SOCIAL PSYCHOLOGY

As with any revision, there are a number of elements of the book that have been updated or changed. Consistent with the above theme of applying social psychology in each chapter, I have added a new section to the book entitled "Applying Social

Psychology." In this section we address three areas where the principles of social psychology have been adapted to understand and/or respond to a particular applied concern. Specifically, we cover the topics of Media and Social Behaviour, Social Psychology and the Law, and Social Psychology and the Environment. To accomplish this addition of material, a number of modules have been carefully edited and amalgamated. Consequently, *Exploring Social Psychology*, Canadian Edition, though heavily revised and somewhat changed, is no longer than the previous edition of the book. Thus we have retained one of the key features of this text: its manageable length.

ACKNOWLEDGEMENTS

I am very grateful to those people who took the time to review the last edition of *Exploring Social Psychology* with an eye to a Canadian edition. In addition, I am very grateful to the reviewers who took the time to review early versions of modules for this Canadian edition. Without their help, this book would not have been possible. I express my heartfelt thanks to:

Gary Anderson, Camosun College
Gira Bhatt, Kwantlen University College
David Bourgeois, Saint Mary's University
Jim Cameron, Saint Mary's University
Stan Cameron, Centennial College
Rory Coughlan, Trent University
Roger Covin, King's College at University of Western Ontario
Ellen Domm, Capilano College
Richard Ennis, Wilfrid Laurier University
Ken Fowler, Memorial University of Newfoundland
Kris Gerhardt, Wilfrid Laurier University (Brantford)
Rosalie Hawrylko, Capilano College
Daniel Lagace-Seguin, Mount Saint Vincent University
Neil McGrenaghan, Humber Institute of Technology & Advanced Learning
Gregory McGuire, St. Francis Xavier University
Sara Pawson Herrington, Kwantlen University College
Maureen Roberts, Centennial College
Saba Safdar, Guelph University
Antoinette Semenya, Simon Fraser University
Fuschia Sirios, University of Windsor
Alwin Spence, John Abbott College
Jennifer Stamp, Dalhousie University
Amy Walther-Ford, Georgian College
Frank Winstan, Vanier College

Of course, this project would not have gotten off the ground were it not for a fortunate meeting between myself and James Buchanan, who was then the Executive Sponsoring Editor of this project. James, thanks for believing that this was a worthwhile project. My Developmental Editor at McGraw-Hill Ryerson, Jodi Lewchuk, was an invaluable resource in the production of this book. The constant feedback and support she gave me made the development of this book possible. In addition, the crash course in manuscript preparation was an absolute necessity.

However, from the day-to-day perspective of getting this project researched and written, I could not have produced this work in this book in such a short timeframe without the help of my dedicated and talented research assistant, Christine Hole. Christine, I give you my sincere thanks for all of the hard work and fantastic information that you were able to obtain and I was able to put into this book. I would also like to thank Karen Mitchell for her dedicated work tracking down references and sources for much of the information in the book.

Finally, I could never have accomplished this without the love and constant support of my wife, Isabel, my daughter, Sydney, and my son, Dylan, who tolerated many late nights while I worked on the book. Thanks, guys — I love you more than you know.

STEVEN M. SMITH

PART ONE

Introducing Social Psychology

"We cannot live for ourselves alone," remarked the novelist Herman Melville, "for our lives are connected by a thousand invisible threads." Social psychologists study those connections by scientifically exploring how we *think about*, *influence*, and *relate to* one another.

In the first two modules we explain how we do that exploring; how we play the social psychology game. As it happens, the ways we social psychologists form and test ideas can be carried into life itself, enabling us to think smarter as we analyze everyday social thinking, social influences, and social relations.

If intuition and common sense were utterly trustworthy, we would be less in need of scientific inquiry and critical thinking. But the truth, as Module 2 relates, is that whether we are reflecting on research results or everyday events we readily succumb to a powerful hindsight bias, also called the *I-knew-it-all-along phenomenon*.

Methods in Social Psychology

Imagine yourself in the following situation. You have just returned home from a trip to Winnipeg, where you were visiting family. You get a call from the RCMP, who want to drop by to "ask you a few questions." Being the innocent person that you are, you agree. Once the police arrive, they begin to question you about your trip and ask if you remember buying coffee at a donut shop before you left town. You reply, "Of course, I always need coffee before a long drive." Before leaving, the police ask permission to take your picture. Again, you believe you are innocent of any crime and agree to be photographed.

Much to your surprise, three days later the police are back and you are arrested. You are taken to a Winnipeg police station where you are fingerprinted and put in a cell. Later you are subjected to a humiliating strip search, and then you are questioned for 13 hours. The police show you pictures of a horrific murder that occurred at the donut shop you visited. The teenager who worked there had been strangled and left for dead. The police have an eyewitness who saw you running from the scene of the crime. They tell you your fingerprints were found at the scene. Your alibi for the time of the murder is now saying she doesn't remember seeing you that day. The police start to question your mental state. What would you do? Would you continue to deny your involvement? Would you confess and hope for a lenient sentence? Would you ask to see a lawyer? Would the police come to their senses and realize you are innocent? If someone else were in a similar situation and confessed, would you believe that they were guilty?

Social psychologists scientifically explore how we think about, influence, and relate to one another. Which of your everyday social connections might be studied scientifically by a social psychologist?

OLC
Activity 1.1

Implausible? This was Tom Sophonow's reality. He spent 4 years in prison for the murder of that Winnipeg teenager and another 16 years trying to clear his name. What would you have done in his situation? Many people believe that they would never confess to a crime they didn't commit, but doing so is much more likely than people imagine. Police are trained to create situations that encourage suspects to confess. This is very useful when suspects are actually criminals, but incredibly dangerous when suspects are innocent. Visit the Online Learning Centre to complete Activity 1.1 and learn more about this case.

The French philosopher-novelist Jean-Paul Sartre (1946) would have had no problem accepting this premise. We humans are "first of all beings in a situation," he believed. "We cannot be distinguished from our situations, for they form us and decide our possibilities" (pp. 59–60, paraphrased). Social psychology is a science that studies the influences of our situations, with special attention to how we view and affect one another. "Our lives are connected by a thousand invisible threads," said the novelist Herman Melville. Social psychology aims to illuminate those threads. It does so by asking questions that have intrigued us all:

- How and what do people *think* of one another? How reasonable are the ideas we form of ourselves? Of our friends? Of strangers? How tight are the links between what we think and what we do?
- How, and how much, do people *influence* one another? How strong are the invisible threads that pull us? Are we creatures of our gender roles? Our groups? Our cultures? How can we resist social pressure, or even sway the majority?
- What shapes the way we *relate to* one another? What leads people sometimes to hurt and sometimes to help? What kindles social conflict? And how might we transform the closed fists of aggression into the open arms of compassion?

A common thread runs through these questions: They all deal with how people view and affect one another. That is what the field of social psychology is all about: attitudes and beliefs, conformity and independence, love and hate. To put it formally, **social psychology** is *the scientific study of how people think about, influence, and relate to one another*.

Social psychology The scientific study of how people think about, influence, and relate to one another.

Unlike other scientific disciplines, social psychology has more than 6 billion amateur practitioners. People-watching is a universal hobby—in parks, at school, and at the mall. As we observe people, we form ideas about how human beings think about, influence, and relate to one another. Professional social psychologists do the same, only more systematically (by forming theories) and painstakingly (often with experiments that create miniature social dramas that pin down cause and effect).

FORMING AND TESTING THEORIES

We social psychologists have a hard time thinking of anything more fascinating than human existence. If, as Socrates counselled, "The unexamined life is not worth living," then simply "knowing thyself" seems a worthy enough goal.

As we wrestle with human nature to pin down its secrets, we organize our ideas and findings into theories. A **theory** is *an integrated set of principles that explain and predict* observed events. Theories are a scientific shorthand.

In everyday conversation, "theory" often means "less than fact"—a middle rung on a confidence ladder from guess to theory to fact. But to a scientist, facts and theories are apples and oranges. Facts are agreed-upon statements about what we observe. Theories are *ideas* that summarize and explain facts. "Science is built up with facts, as a house is with stones," said Jules Henri Poincaré, "but a collection of facts is no more a science than a heap of stones is a house."

Theories not only summarize—they also imply testable predictions, called **hypotheses**. Hypotheses serve several purposes. First, they allow us to test a theory by suggesting how we might try to falsify it. In making predictions, a theory puts its money where its mouth is. Second, predictions give *direction* to research. Any scientific field will mature more rapidly if its researchers have a sense of direction. Theoretical predictions suggest new areas for research; they send investigators looking for things they might never have thought of. Third, the predictive feature of good theories can also make them *practical*. A complete theory of aggression, for example, would predict when to expect aggression and how to control it. As Kurt Lewin, one of modern social psychology's founders, declared, "There is nothing so practical as a good theory."

Consider how this works. Say we observe that people sometimes explode violently when in crowds. We might therefore theorize that the presence of other people makes individuals feel anonymous and lowers their inhibitions. Let's play with this idea for a moment. Perhaps we could test it by constructing a laboratory experiment simulating an execution by electric chair. What if we asked individuals in groups to administer punishing shocks to a hapless victim without knowing which one of the group was actually shocking the victim? Would these individuals administer stronger shocks than individuals acting alone, as our theory predicts?

We might also manipulate anonymity: Would people deliver stronger shocks hiding behind masks? If the results confirm our hypothesis, they might suggest some practical applications. Perhaps police brutality could be reduced by having officers wear large name tags and drive cars identified with large numbers, or by videotaping their arrests—all of which have, in fact, recently become common practice in many cities.

But how do we conclude that one theory is better than another? A good theory (1) effectively summarizes a wide range of observations; and (2) makes clear predictions that we can use to (a) confirm or modify the theory, (b) generate new exploration, and (c) suggest practical application. When we discard theories, usually it's not because they have been proved false. Rather, like old cars, they get replaced by newer, better models.

Theory An integrated set of principles that explain and predict observed events.

Hypothesis A testable proposition that describes a relationship that might exist between events.

CORRELATIONAL RESEARCH: DETECTING NATURAL ASSOCIATIONS

Most of what you will learn about social-psychological research methods you will absorb as you read later chapters. But let us go backstage now and take a brief look at how social psychology is done. This glimpse behind the scenes will be just enough for you to appreciate the findings discussed later and to think critically about everyday social events.

Correlational research
The study of the naturally occurring relationships among the variables.

Social-psychological research varies by location. It can take place in the *laboratory* (a controlled situation) or in the *field* (everyday situations). And it varies by method—**correlational research** asks whether two or more factors are naturally associated, and **experimental research** manipulates some factor to see its effect on another. If you want to be a critical reader of psychological research reported in newspapers and magazines, it pays to understand the difference between correlational and experimental research.

Experimental research
Studies that seek clues to cause–effect relationships by manipulating one or more factors (independent variables) while controlling others (holding them constant).

Using some real examples, let's first consider the advantages of correlational research (often involving important variables in natural settings) and the disadvantages (ambiguous interpretation of cause and effect). Today's psychologists relate personal and social factors to human health.

In June 2005 an article appeared in a number of news sources indicating that drinking diet soft drinks resulted in weight gain. Soft drink companies have long argued that weight-conscious consumers could help control their weight by drinking diet soft drinks instead of their original high-calorie, sugar-laced beverages. The study, conducted by Sharon Fowler and her colleagues (see Fowler & others, 2005), found that consuming soft drinks was correlated with obesity—the more you drink, the more likely you are to be obese. Given their high sugar content, perhaps this finding was not surprising. However, what surprised the researchers even more was that consuming *diet* soft drinks was *even more* strongly related to obesity rates.

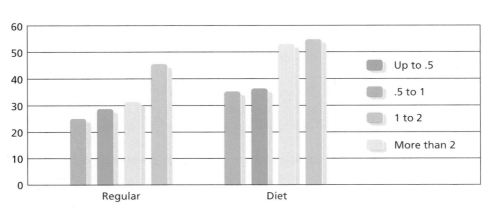

FIGURE 1–1
Percentage risk of becoming overweight by type and amount of pop consumed.

Data from Fowler & others, 2005.

As shown in Figure 1-1, a person's risk of being clinically overweight or obese increased with the amount of soft drinks they drank per day. More surprisingly, we can see that the risk was higher in every consumption category for diet soda drinkers over regular soda drinkers. Why was this the case? Could it be that drinking diet soda causes weight to increase in people who drink it? Should obese people who drink diet soft drinks switch to regular in order to lose weight? What are some of the alternative explanations for this effect? Visit the Online Learning Centre and complete Activity 1.2 to learn more about this topic.

**OLC
Activity 1.2**

Correlation versus Causation

The diet cola–weight gain question illustrates the most irresistible thinking error made by both amateur and professional social psychologists: When two things go together, it is terribly tempting to conclude that one is causing the other. Correlations indicate a relationship. Correlational research therefore allows us to *predict*, but it cannot tell us whether changing one variable will *cause* changes in another.

The correlation–causation confusion is behind much muddled thinking in popular psychology. Consider another very real correlation—between self-esteem and academic achievement. Children with high self-esteem tend also to have high academic achievement. (As with any correlation, we can also state this the other way around: High achievers tend to have high self-esteem.) Why do you suppose this is (see Figure 1-2 on page 8)?

Some people believe a "healthy self-concept" contributes to achievement. Thus, boosting a child's self-image may also boost school achievement. Believing so, 30 U.S. states have enacted more than 170 self-esteem–promoting statutes.

But others, including psychologists William Damon (1995), Robyn Dawes (1994), Mark Leary (1998), Martin Seligman (1994), and Roy Baumeister & others (2003), doubt that self-esteem is really "the armour that protects kids" from underachievement (or drug abuse and delinquency). Perhaps it's the other way around: Perhaps problems and failures cause low self-esteem. Perhaps self-esteem often reflects the reality of how things are going for us. Perhaps self-esteem grows from hard-won achievements. Do well and you will feel good about yourself; goof off and fail and you will feel like a schmuck. A study of 635 Norwegian schoolchildren suggests that a string of gold stars beside one's name on the spelling chart and constant praise from an admiring teacher can boost a child's self-esteem (Skaalvik & Hagtvet, 1990). It's also possible that self-esteem and achievement correlate because both are linked to underlying intelligence and family social status.

That possibility was raised in two studies—one a U.S. national sample of 1,600 young men, another of 715 Minnesota youngsters (Bachman & O'Malley, 1977; Maruyama & others, 1981). When the researchers statistically removed the effect of intelligence and family status, the correlation between self-esteem and achievement evaporated.

This man is drinking diet soda in his bathrobe for breakfast.

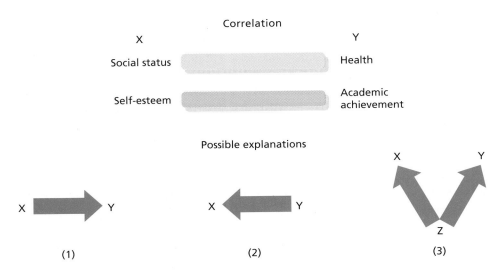

FIGURE 1–2
When two variables correlate, any combination of three explanations is possible.

Advanced correlational techniques can suggest cause–effect relations, for example by statistically extracting the influence of "confounded" (extraneous but associated) variables. Thus, the researchers just mentioned saw the correlation between self-esteem and achievement evaporate after extracting differences in intelligence and family status. (Among people of similar intelligence and family status, the self-esteem–achievement relationship was minimal.)

So, the great strength of correlational research is that it tends to occur in real-world settings where we can examine factors such as race, sex, and social status that we cannot manipulate in the laboratory. Its great disadvantage lies in the ambiguity of the results. The point is so important that, even if it fails to impress people the first 25 times they hear it, it is worth making a 26th time: Knowing that two variables change together enables us to predict one when we know the other; but *correlation does not specify cause and effect.*

EXPERIMENTAL RESEARCH: SEARCHING FOR CAUSE AND EFFECT

The near impossibility of discerning cause and effect among naturally correlated events prompts most social psychologists to create laboratory simulations of everyday processes whenever this is feasible and ethical. These simulations are roughly similar to aeronautical wind tunnels. Aeronautical engineers don't begin by observing how flying objects perform in a wide variety of natural environments. The variations in both atmospheric conditions and flying objects are so complex that they would surely find it difficult to organize and use such data to design better aircraft. Instead, they construct a simulated reality that is under their control. Then they can manipulate wind conditions and observe the precise effect of particular wind conditions on particular wing structures.

Control: Manipulating Variables

Like aeronautical engineers, social psychologists experiment by constructing social situations that simulate important features of our daily lives. By varying just one or two factors at a time—called **independent variables**—the experimenter pinpoints how changes in these one or two things affect us. As the wind tunnel helps the aeronautical engineer discover principles of aerodynamics, so the experiment enables the social psychologist to discover principles of social thinking, social influence, and social relations. The ultimate aim of wind tunnel simulations is to understand and predict the flying characteristics of complex aircraft. Social psychologists experiment to understand and predict complex human behaviours. They aim to understand why behaviour varies among people, across situations, and over time.

Independent variable The experimental factor that a researcher manipulates.

Social psychologists have used the experimental method in about three-fourths of their research studies (Higbee & others, 1982), and in two out of three studies the setting has been a research laboratory (Adair & others, 1985). To illustrate the laboratory experiment, consider an experiment that typifies a possible cause–effect explanation of correlational findings: the well-known correlation between television viewing and children's behaviour. Children who watch many violent television programs tend to be more aggressive than those who watch few. This suggests that children might be learning from what they see on the screen. As we hope you now recognize, this is a correlational finding. Figure 1-3 on page 10 reminds us that there are two other cause–effect interpretations that do not implicate television as the cause of the children's aggression. (What are they?)

Social psychologists have therefore brought television viewing into the laboratory, where they control the amount of violence the children see. By exposing children to violent and nonviolent programs, researchers can observe how the amount of violence affects behaviour. Chris Boyatzis and his colleagues (1995) showed some elementary schoolchildren, but not others, an episode of the 1990s' most popular—and violent—children's television program, *Power Rangers*. Immediately after viewing the episode, the viewers committed seven times as many aggressive acts per two-minute interval as the nonviewers. The observed aggressive acts we call the **dependent variable**. Such experiments indicate that television can be one cause of children's aggressive behaviour. This research, as well as reseach that examines the link between playing violent video games and aggression, will be discussed in greater detail in a later module.

Dependent variable The variable being measured, so-called because it may *depend* on manipulations of the independent variable.

So far we have seen that the logic of experimentation is simple: By creating and controlling a miniature reality, we can vary one factor and then another and discover how these factors, separately or in combination, affect people. Now let's go a little deeper and see how an experiment is done.

Every social-psychological experiment has two essential ingredients. We have just considered one—*control*. We manipulate one or two independent variables while trying to hold everything else constant. The other ingredient is *random assignment*.

Random Assignment: The Great Equalizer

Recall that we were reluctant, on the basis of a correlation, to assume that viewing violence *causes* aggressiveness. A survey researcher might measure and statistically extract other possibly pertinent factors and see if the correlations survive. But one can never control for all the factors that might distinguish violence viewers from nonviewers. Maybe violence viewers differ in education, culture, intelligence—or in dozens of ways the researcher hasn't considered.

In one fell swoop, **random assignment** eliminates all such extraneous factors. With random assignment, each person has an equal chance of viewing the violence or the nonviolence. Thus, the people in both groups would, in every conceivable way—family status, intelligence, education, initial aggressiveness—average about the same. Highly intelligent people, for example, are equally likely to appear in both groups. Because random assignment creates equivalent groups, any later aggression difference between the two groups must have something to do with the only way they differ—whether or not they viewed violence (Figure 1-3).

The Ethics of Experimentation

Our television example illustrates why some experiments are ethically sensitive. Social psychologists would not, over long time periods, expose one group of children to brutal violence. Rather, they briefly alter people's social experience and note the effects. Sometimes the experimental treatment is a harmless, perhaps even enjoyable, experience to which people give their knowing consent. Sometimes, however, researchers find themselves operating in a grey area between the harmless and the risky.

Social psychologists often venture into that ethical grey area when they design experiments that engage intense thoughts and emotions. Experiments need not have what Elliot Aronson, Marilynn Brewer, and Merrill Carlsmith (1985) call

Random assignment
The process of assigning participants to the conditions of an experiment such that all persons have the same chance of being in a given condition. (Note the distinction between random assignment in experiments and random sampling in surveys. Random *assignment* helps us infer cause and effect. Random *sampling* helps us generalize to a population.)

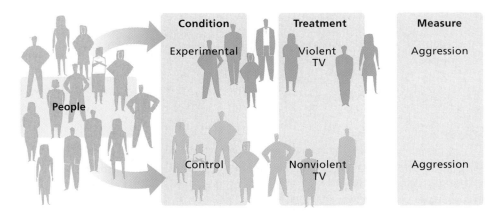

FIGURE 1-3
Random assignment. Experiments randomly assigning people either to a condition that receives the experimental treatment or to a control condition that does not. This gives the researcher confidence that any later difference is somehow caused by the treatment.

mundane realism. That is, laboratory behaviour (for example, delivering electric shocks as part of an experiment on aggression) need not be literally the same as everyday behaviour. For many researchers, that sort of realism is indeed mundane—not important. But the experiment *should* have **experimental realism**—it should absorb and involve the participants. Experimenters do not want their people consciously play-acting or ho-humming it; they want to engage real psychological processes. Forcing people to choose whether to give intense or mild electric shock to someone else can, for example, be a realistic measure of aggression. It functionally simulates real aggression.

Achieving experimental realism sometimes requires deceiving people with a plausible cover story. If the person in the next room actually is not receiving the shocks, the experimenter does not want the participants to know this. That would destroy the experimental realism. Thus, about one-third of social-psychological studies (though a decreasing number) have used deception in their search for truth (Korn & Nicks, 1993; Vitelli, 1988).

Researchers often walk a tightrope in designing experiments that will be involving yet ethical. To believe that you are hurting someone, or to be subjected to strong social pressure to see if it will change your opinion or behaviour, may be temporarily uncomfortable. Such experiments raise the age-old question of whether ends justify means. Do the insights gained justify deceiving and sometimes distressing people?

University research ethics boards now review all research that involves human participants. This includes issues such as medical research, as well as the type of research that is described in this book. In Canada, the three major federal granting councils have developed a Tri-Council Policy Statement on Ethical Conduct for Research Involving Humans (see Tri-Council Policy Statement, 2005, available at www.pre.ethics.gc.ca). Only those universities that certify compliance with this policy receive research funding from these agencies. Indeed, before any funding is released to researchers, they must prove they have ethical approval from their institution.

The Tri-Council Policy is based on some guiding ethical principles:

- Respect for human dignity
- Free and **informed consent** (that is, participants must know enough about what is being done in the study to make an informed decision)
- Concern for vulnerable persons (that is, people who cannot provide free and informed consent—for example, minors—must have appropriate representation—for example, parents or guardians)
- Privacy and confidentiality of any information collected from participants, and
- Justice and inclusiveness.

In addition, participants have the right to be completely debriefed at the end of any study and informed of its purpose. Finally, participants have the right to be told if they were deceived, and the reason for that deception.

The experimenter should be sufficiently informative *and* considerate so that people leave feeling at least as good about themselves as when they came in. Better yet, the participants should be repaid by having learned something about the nature of

Mundane realism
The degree to which an experiment is superficially similar to everyday situations.

Experimental realism
The degree to which an experiment absorbs and involves its participants.

OLC
Activity 1.3

Informed consent An ethical principle requiring that research participants be told enough to enable them to decide whether they wish to participate.

psychological inquiry. When treated respectfully, few participants mind being deceived (Epley & Huff, 1998; Kimmel, 1998). Indeed, say social psychology's defenders, professors evoke far greater anxiety and distress by giving and returning course exams than researchers now do in their experiments.

GENERALIZING FROM LABORATORY TO LIFE

As the research on children, television, and violence illustrates, social psychology mixes everyday experience and laboratory analysis. Throughout this book we will do the same by drawing our data mostly from the laboratory and our illustrations mostly from life. Social psychology displays a healthy interplay between laboratory research and everyday life. Hunches gained from everyday experience often inspire laboratory research, which deepens our understanding of our experience.

This interplay appears in the children's television experiment. What people saw in everyday life suggested experimental research. Network and government policymakers—those with the power to make changes—are now aware of the results. The consistency of findings on television's effects—in the lab and in the field—is true of research in many other areas, including studies of helping, leadership style, depression,

The Story Behind the Research

When Rod Lindsay was a graduate student at the University of Alberta in the late 1970s he met Gary Wells, a new faculty member who specialized in the accuracy of eyewitness identification. At the time, Lindsay did not know much about eyewitness identification research. However, together these researchers would eventually become two of the most recognized eyewitness researchers in the world. Lindsay and Wells preferred to enact their "crimes" live (other lab-based researchers frequently used videotapes or slide sequences to present staged crimes, leaving open the possibility that the research was not generalizable to the "real world" of live crimes).

Lindsay and Wells's participants were brought into a lab room and seated. The research assistant would then escort a second "participant" into the room and seat him or her nearer the door. After introducing the participants, the research assistant would

say she had to leave the room for a while. The second participant was actually a confederate of the experimenter. After engaging the participant in small talk, the confederate would suddenly "steal" something (for example a calculator or the research assistant's purse) and run out of the room.

Not surprisingly, this often left the participant shaken (as a real crime would). After the participant calmed down, he or she was asked to give a description of the criminal and to try to make an identification from a lineup. Dr. Lindsay's research typically found that witnesses in these "real" crimes were quite likely to make errors in their lineup identifications. More importantly, he began to test factors that affected eyewitness errors (poor instructions, poor lineup construction, sequential presentation) that eventually led to lineup procedures designed to reduce identification errors in the real world. |

and self-efficacy. The effects one finds in the lab have been mirrored by effects in the field. "The psychology laboratory has generally produced psychological truths rather than trivialities," note Craig Anderson and his colleagues (1999).

We need to be cautious, however, in generalizing from laboratory to life. Although the laboratory uncovers basic dynamics of human existence, it is still a simplified, controlled reality. It tells us what effect to expect of variable *X*, all other things being equal—which, in real life, they never are. Moreover, as you will see, the participants in many experiments are post-secondary students. Although this may help you identify with them, students are hardly a random sample of all humanity. Would we get similar results with people of different ages, educational levels, and cultures? This is always an open question.

Nevertheless, we can distinguish between the *content* of people's thinking and acting (their attitudes, for example) and the *process* by which they think and act (for example, how attitudes affect actions and vice versa). The content varies more from culture to culture than does the process. For example, Canadians and Americans have different views on a number of social issues (such as attitudes toward gay marriage; Bibby, 2004) and similar views on other topics (for example capital punishment; see Honeyman & Ogloff, 1996). However, even though Canadian and American attitudes can differ, *how* attitudes and behaviours change are likely to be the same. Our behaviours may differ, yet be influenced by the same social forces.

CONCEPTS TO REMEMBER

Social psychology   p. 4
Theory   p. 5
Hypothesis   p. 5
Correlational research   p. 6
Experimental research   p. 6
Independent variable   p. 9

Dependent variable   p. 9
Random assignment   p. 10
Mundane realism   p. 11
Experimental realism   p. 11
Informed consent   p. 11

Please visit the *Exploring Social Psychology* Online Learning Centre at **www.mcgrawhill.ca/college/myers** to participate in module activities, view module videos, access research and study tools, and test your knowledge with interactive quizzes, exercises, and scenarios.

Common Sense and the Hindsight Bias

*Residents of Kashechewan,
Ontario, protesting government
inaction over the problem of
contaminated water, which
forced an evacuation of the
town.* Do you agree with
commentators who claim
that government "should
have known" and prevented
the problem rather than
managing the resulting
crisis?

Anything seems commonplace, once explained.
DR. WATSON TO SHERLOCK HOLMES

Do social psychology's theories provide new insight into the human condition? Or do they only describe the obvious? Many of the conclusions presented in this book will probably have already occurred to you, for social psychology is all around you. We constantly observe people thinking about, influencing, and relating to one another. It pays to discern what that facial expression predicts, how to get someone to do something, or whether to regard another person as friend or foe. For centuries, philosophers, novelists, and poets have observed and commented upon social behaviour, often with keen insight. Social psychology is everybody's business.

Therefore, can we say that social psychology is only common sense expressed in different words? Social psychology faces two contradictory criticisms: One is that it is trivial because it documents the obvious; the second is that it is dangerous because its findings could be used to manipulate people. Is the first objection valid—does social psychology simply formalize what any amateur already knows intuitively?

Writer Cullen Murphy (1990) thinks so: "Day after day social scientists go out into the world. Day after day they discover that people's behavior is pretty much what you'd expect." Nearly a half-century earlier, historian Arthur Schlesinger, Jr. (1949) reacted with similar scorn to social scientists' studies of American World War II soldiers.

What did these studies find? Another reviewer, sociologist Paul Lazarsfeld (1949), offered a sample with interpretive comments, a few of which we paraphrase:

1. Better-educated soldiers suffered more adjustment problems than did less-educated soldiers. (Intellectuals were less prepared for battle stresses than were street-smart people.)

2. Southern soldiers coped better with the hot South Sea Island climate than did Northern soldiers. (Southerners are more accustomed to hot weather.)

3. White privates were more eager for promotion than were Black privates. (Years of oppression take a toll on achievement motivation.)

4. Southern Blacks preferred Southern to Northern White officers (because Southern officers were more experienced and skilled in interacting with Blacks).

One problem with common sense, however, is that we invoke it after we know the facts. Events seem far more obvious and predictable in hindsight. Experiments reveal that when people learn the outcome of an experiment, that outcome suddenly seems unsurprising—certainly less surprising than it is to people who are simply told about the experimental procedure and the possible outcomes (Slovic & Fischhoff, 1977). With new knowledge at hand, our efficient memory system purges its outdated presumption (Hoffrage & others, 2000).

You perhaps experienced this phenomenon when reading Lazarsfeld's summary of findings. For Lazarsfeld went on to say, "*Every one of these statements is the direct opposite of what was actually found.*" In reality, the book reported that less-educated soldiers adapted more poorly. Southerners were not more likely than Northerners to adjust to a tropical climate. Blacks were more eager than Whites for promotion, and so forth. "If we had mentioned the actual results of the investigation first [as Schlesinger experienced], the reader would have labeled these 'obvious' also."

Likewise, in everyday life we often do not expect something to happen until it does. *Then* we suddenly see clearly the forces that brought the event about and feel unsurprised. The deadly tainted water crisis at Walkerton, Ontario, the forced evacuation on the Kashechewan Reserve in the north of the province, the Swissair plane crash off Peggy's Cove in Nova Scotia, and Paul Martin's knowledge of the Sponsorship Program to promote federalism in Quebec are all events where numerous TV and newspaper commentators have argued that the principals involved "should have known."

If this **hindsight bias** (also called the I-knew-it-all-along phenomenon) is pervasive, you may now be feeling that you already knew about it. Indeed, almost any conceivable result of a psychological experiment can seem like common sense—*after* you know the result.

Before reading further, visit the Online Learning Centre and do Activity 2.1, an exercise in common sense. Steven regularly asks students in his classes to do a task similar to the one you just did on the OLC. Once students have responded to the items, he asks them to explain why they gave the answers they did. For example, let's explore the saying "Opposites attract." Do they? Many students invariably say yes.

Hindsight bias The tendency to exaggerate, *after* learning an outcome, one's ability to have foreseen how something turned out. Also known as the *I-knew-it-all-along phenomenon.*

OLC
Activity 2.1

When asked why, students will say it is because in relationships (romantic or otherwise) we look for people who "complete" or "complement" us. Other students say that "Birds of a feather flock together" is a better description, as we seek out people who are similar to us. As it turns out . . . it depends. Sometimes finding people who complement our skills can be quite useful, but typically we tend to marry people who are similar to us in terms of age, education, religiosity, and core values.

When Neal Roese was a student at the University of Western Ontario (he is now a professor at the University of Illinois), he began some research with Dr. James Olson on counterfactual thinking (for example when, after a particular event in our lives such as a failure on an exam, we think about what "could have been" or how things could have been different). Later, while reading about the hindsight bias, where people think the individuals involved "should have known" the outcome, Roese wondered how these two seemingly inconsistent patterns of thinking could be reconciled. He approached Dr. Olson with the problem, and together they devised a project to explain this apparent discrepancy (see Roese & Olson, 1996).

They realized that people engage in the hindsight bias when they have a sense of certainty around the specific set of conditions under which an event occurs: "given the way things were, the outcome was inevitable." However, people engage in counterfactual thinking (that is, thinking about alternatives) if they believe some of those conditions could have been changed. For example, if you fail an exam after a night of drinking you might think, "Well of course I failed; I was out drinking all night!" But you might also think, "If only I hadn't gone out drinking, I could have passed the exam." Thus, counterfactual thinking and the hindsight bias are not inconsistent at all.

The hindsight bias creates a problem for many psychology students. Sometimes results are genuinely surprising (for example, that Olympic *bronze* medalists take more joy in their achievement than do *silver* medalists). More often, when you read the results of experiments in your textbooks, the material seems easy, even obvious. When you later take a multiple-choice test on which you must choose among several plausible conclusions, the task may become surprisingly difficult. "I don't know what happened," the befuddled student later moans. "I thought I knew the material."

The I-knew-it-all-along phenomenon not only can make social science findings seem like common sense, but also can have pernicious consequences. It is conducive to arrogance—an overestimation of our own intellectual powers. Moreover, because outcomes seem as if they should have been foreseeable, we are more likely to blame decision makers for what are, in retrospect, "obvious" bad choices than to praise them for good choices, which also seem obvious. In 2003, after the seemingly successful invasion of Afghanistan, U.S. President George Bush made clear his intent to invade Iraq in order to depose Saddam Hussein. Across the U.S., many people were confident that the "coalition of the willing" could rapidly overwhelm the Iraqi defences and "liberate" the country. Within Canada, a debate raged as to whether we should become involved. At the time, joining the coalition was seen as "smart" and "neighbourly." Failing to get involved would hurt our relationship with the U.S. and incur costs in terms of trade relations. Many politicians argued that getting involved was the right thing to do. Now, several years later, after a long, expensive, and devastating war (both for coalition forces and for innocent civilians) with no end in sight,

OLC
Activity 2.2

most people would argue that they knew all along getting involved would be a bad idea and many deny they ever supported involvement.

Likewise, we sometimes blame ourselves for "stupid mistakes"—perhaps for not having handled a person or a situation better. Looking back, we see how we should have handled it. "I should have known how busy I would be at the semester's end and started that paper earlier." But sometimes we are too hard on ourselves. We forget that what is obvious to us *now* was not nearly so obvious at the time. Physicians who are told both a patient's symptoms and the cause of death (as determined by autopsy) sometimes wonder how an incorrect diagnosis could have been made. Other physicians, given only the symptoms, don't find the diagnosis nearly so obvious (Dawson & others, 1988). (Would juries be slower to assume malpractice if they were forced to take a foresight rather than a hindsight perspective?)

So what do we conclude—that common sense is usually wrong? Sometimes it is. Common sense and medical experience assured doctors that bleeding was an effective treatment for typhoid fever, until someone in the mid 1800s bothered to experiment— to divide patients into two groups: one bled, the other given mere bed rest.

Other times, conventional wisdom is right—or it falls on both sides of an issue: Does happiness come from knowing the truth, or preserving illusions? From being with others, or living in peaceful solitude? Opinions are a dime a dozen; no matter what we find, there will be someone who foresaw it. (Mark Twain jested that Adam was the only person who, when saying a good thing, knew that nobody had said it before.) But which of the many competing ideas best fit reality?

The point is not that common sense is predictably wrong. Rather. . . it depends. We easily deceive ourselves into thinking that we know and knew more than we do and did. And this is precisely why we need science—to help us sift reality from illusion and genuine predictions from easy hindsight.

CONCEPT TO REMEMBER

Hindsight bias   p. 15

Please visit the *Exploring Social Psychology* Online Learning Centre at **www.mcgrawhill.ca/college/myers** to participate in module activities, view module videos, access research and study tools, and test your knowledge with interactive quizzes, exercises, and scenarios.

Social Thinking

This book unfolds around its definition of social psychology: the scientific study of how we *think about* (Part Two), *influence* (Part Three), and *relate to* (Part Four) one another.

These modules on social thinking examine the interplay between our sense of self and our social worlds, by showing, for example, how self-interest colours our social judgments.

Succeeding modules explore the quite amazing and sometimes rather amusing ways in which we form beliefs about our social worlds. We have quite remarkable powers of intuition (or what social psychologists call *automatic information processing*), yet in at least a half-dozen ways, our intuition often fails us. Knowing these ways not only beckons us to humility, but also can help us sharpen our thinking, keeping it more closely in touch with reality.

We will explore the links between attitudes and behaviours: Do our attitudes determine our behaviours? Do our behaviours determine our attitudes? Or does it work both ways?

Defining and Expressing the Self-Concept

W ho are you? As a unique and complex creature, you have many ways to complete the sentence "I am . . . . " What answers might you give? Visit the Online Learning Centre to do Activity 3.1 and find out. Taken together, your answers define your **self-concept**.

In 2005, the word "self" appeared in 7,713 book and article summaries in *Psychological Abstracts*—nine times the number that appeared in 1970. Our sense of self organizes our thoughts, feelings, and actions. So, we begin our tour of social psychology with a look at self-concept (how we come to know ourselves) and at the self in action (how our sense of self drives our attitudes and actions).

Whatever we do in our years on this global spaceship, whatever we infer and interpret, whatever we conceive and create, whomever we meet and greet, will be filtered through our selves. How, and how accurately, do we know ourselves? What determines our self-concepts?

Self-concept affects how we perceive ourselves and others. What factors contribute to your sense of self?

OLC
Activity 3.1

Self-concept A person's answers to the question, "Who am I?"

AT THE CENTRE OF OUR WORLDS: OUR SENSE OF SELF

Self-schema Beliefs about self that organize and guide the processing of self-relevant information.

Schemas are mental templates by which we organize our worlds. Our *self*-schemas—our perceiving ourselves as athletic, overweight, smart, or whatever—powerfully affect how we process social information (Markus & Wurf, 1987). These self-defining beliefs influence how we perceive, remember, and evaluate other people and ourselves. If athletics is a central part of your self-concept (if being an athlete is one of your self-schemas), then you will tend to notice others' bodies and skills. You will quickly recall sports-related experiences. And you will welcome information that is consistent with your self-schema (Kihlstrom & Cantor, 1984). The self-schemas that make up our self-concepts operate like a mental Dewey Decimal System for cataloguing and retrieving information.

Self-reference effect The tendency to process efficiently and remember well information related to oneself.

Consider how the self influences memory, a phenomenon known as the **self-reference effect**: *When information is relevant to our self-concepts, we process it quickly and remember it well* (Higgins & Bargh, 1987; Kuiper & Rogers, 1979; Symons & Johnson, 1997).

The self-reference effect illustrates a basic fact of life: Our sense of self is at the centre of our worlds. Because we tend to see ourselves on centre stage, we overestimate the extent to which others' behaviour is aimed at us. We often see ourselves as responsible for events in which we played only a small part (Fenigstein, 1984). When judging someone else's performance or behaviour, we often spontaneously compare it with our own (Dunning & Hayes, 1996). And if, while talking to one person, we overhear our name spoken by another in the room, our auditory radar instantly shifts our attention.

From our self-focused perspectives we readily presume that others are noticing and evaluating us. Thomas Gilovich and his colleagues (2000) demonstrated this by having individual Cornell University students don Barry Manilow T-shirts before entering a room with other students. Feeling self-conscious, the T-shirt wearers guessed that nearly half their peers would notice the shirt (only 23 percent did). Keenly aware of our emotions, we often have an illusion that they are transparent to others. The same goes for our social blunders and public mental slips. What we agonize over, others may hardly notice and soon forget (Savitsky & others, 2001). The more self-conscious we are, the more we believe this "illusion of transparency" (Vorauer & Ross, 1999).

SELF AND CULTURE

How did you complete the item in Activity 3.1? If you have not done Activity 3.1 yet, please do so now (we'll wait).

That scale, developed by James Cameron at Saint Mary's University in Halifax, is designed to assess your overall feelings about who you are relative to a specific target group. In this case, we discussed your Canadian identity. Each person who lives in Canada has his or her own personal sense of "self." However, what is less clear is the extent to which our perception of self is dependent on those around us.

Individualism The concept of giving priority to one's own goals over group goals and defining one's identity in terms of personal attributes rather than group identifications.

For some people, especially those in industrialized Western cultures, **individualism** prevails. Identity is pretty much self-contained. Adolescence is a time of separating from parents, becoming self-reliant, and defining one's personal, *independent self*. Uprooted and placed in a foreign land, one's identity—as a unique individual with particular abilities, traits, values, and dreams—would remain intact. The psychology of Western cultures assumes that your life will be enriched by defining your possible selves and believing in your power of personal control. By the last century's end, individualism had become the dominant voice in popular culture.

Cultures native to Asia, Africa, and Central and South America place a greater value on **collectivism**. They nurture what Shinobu Kitayama and Hazel Markus (1995) call the *interdependent self*. People are more self-critical and have less need for positive self-regard (Heine & others, 1999). Identity is defined more in relation to others. Malaysians, Indians, Japanese, and traditional Kenyans such as the Maasai, for example, are much more likely than Australians, Americans, and the British to complete the "I am" statement with their group identities (Bochner, 1994; Dhawan & others, 1995; Ma & Schoeneman, 1997; Markus & Kitayama, 1991).

However, making general statements about a culture's individualistic or collectivist orientations is oversimplified. Even within Canada, there are regional and ethnic differences as well. For example, people in Quebec and Ontario tend to be more liberal, whereas people in Western Canada (particularly Alberta) tend to be more individualistic. Conservatives tend to be economic individualists ("don't tax or regulate me") and moral collectivists ("do legislate against immorality"). Liberals tend to be economic collectivists and moral individualists.

With an *inter*dependent self, one has a greater sense of belonging. Uprooted and cut off from family, colleagues, and loyal friends, interdependent people would lose the social connections that define who they are. They have not one self but many selves: self-with-parents, self-at-work, self-with-friends (Cross & others, 1992). As Figure 3-1 and Table 3-1 suggest, the interdependent self is embedded in social

Collectivism Giving priority to the goals of one's groups (often one's extended family or work group) and defining one's identity accordingly.

OLC
Video 3.1

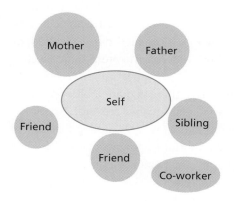

Independent view of self

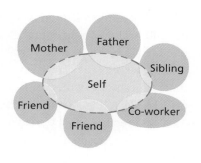

Interdependent view of self

FIGURE 3-1

Self-construal as independent or interdependent. The independent self acknowledges relationships with others. But the interdependent self is more deeply embedded in others.

From Markus & Kitayama, 1991.

TABLE 3-1 *Self-Concept: Independent or Interdependent*

	Independent	*Interdependent*
Identity is	*Personal*, defined by individual traits and goals	*Social*, defined by connections with others
What matters	*Me*—personal achievement and fulfillment; my rights and liberties	*We*—group goals and solidarity; our social responsibilities and relationships
Disapproves of	*Conformity*	*Egotism*
Illustrative motto	"To thine own self be true"	"No one is an island"
Cultures that support	Individualistic Western	Collectivistic Asian and Third World

memberships. Conversation is less direct and more polite (Holtgraves, 1997). The goal of social life is not so much to enhance one's individual self as to harmonize with and support one's communities. The individualized latté—"decaf, single shot, skinny, extra hot"—that seems just right at a North American espresso shop would seem a bit weird in Seoul, note Heejung Kim and Hazel Markus (1999). Their studies confirm that Korean people place less value on uniqueness and more on tradition and shared practices.

Self-esteem in collectivist cultures correlates closely with "what others think of me and my group." Self-concept is malleable (context-specific) rather than stable (enduring across situations). For those in individualistic cultures, "outside" appraisals of oneself and one's group matter somewhat less (Crocker, 1994; Kwan & others, 1997). Self-esteem is more personal and less relational. Threaten our *personal* identity and we'll feel angrier and gloomier than when someone threatens our collective identity (Gaertner & others, 1999).

But what is the Canadian identity? Interestingly, there is quite a bit of research that suggests one of the main ideals of being Canadian is that we are "not American" (see Hedley, 1994; Lalonde, 2002; MacGregor, 2003). A 1999 poll published in *Maclean's* reported that Canadians felt the most important elements of the Canadian identity were our flag, our climate and geography, the achievements of Canadians throughout the world, our healthcare system, our role in international politics, and our multicultural heritage. Interestingly, the same poll found that although 71 percent of Americans thought Canada and the United States were mainly the same, only 49 percent of Canadians agreed.

A popular reflection of the Canadian identity is Molson's award-winning international Molson Canadian beer ad campaign featuring "Joe Canadian." This ad, which first appeared during the Academy Awards in 2000, had the following text:

Hey. I'm not a lumberjack, or a fur trader...
I don't live in an igloo, or eat blubber, or own a dogsled...
and I don't know Jimmy, Sally, or Suzy from Canada,
although I'm certain they're really really nice.

I have a Prime Minister, not a president.
I speak English and French, not American.
And I pronounce it "about," not "a boot."

I can proudly sew my country's flag on my backpack.
I believe in peace keeping, not policing,
diversity, not assimilation,
and that the beaver is a truly proud and noble animal.
A toque is a hat, a chesterfield is a couch,
and it is pronounced "zed." Not "zee"—"zed"!!!!

Canada is the second largest landmass!
The first nation of hockey!
and the best part of North America!

My name is Joe!!
And I am Canadian!!!

Truro, Nova Scotia, native Jeff Douglas stands atop Citadel Hill in Halifax with the Canadian flag; Douglas portrays Joe Canadian in a Molson Canadian beer commercial.

This ad campaign was an instant hit and was parodied by numerous websites and comedians. Beyond that, however, politicians and pundits used the ad to make a point. For example, Sheila Copps, then Minister of Canadian Heritage, used the ad to open an address at an international conference in Boston, citing it as an example of our distinct identity. Other Members of Parliament parodied the ad in the House of Commons to point to differences in socio-political orientation. Interestingly, Richard Marceau, a Bloc Québécois MP, used the opportunity to make a distinction between Quebec and Canadian identities that read, in part: "We in Quebec have a real department of culture, not one for heritage. What we fear is not comparison with Americans, but assimilation with Canadians. In Quebec, when we say we are bilingual that does not mean we just know a few pick-up lines. Our objective is to make Quebec known throughout the world, not … put our foot in our mouths every chance we get." Although a TV ad and commentary from a few politicians do not define the Canadian identity, the flavour of these things does reflect distinctions within regional cultures in Canada.

SELF-KNOWLEDGE

"Know thyself," admonished the Greek philosopher Socrates. We certainly try. We readily form beliefs about ourselves, and we don't hesitate to explain why we feel and act as we do. But how well do we actually know ourselves?

"There is one thing, and only one in the whole universe which we know more about than we could learn from external observation," noted C. S. Lewis (1952, pp. 18–19). "That one thing is [ourselves]. We have, so to speak, inside information; we are in the know." Indeed. Yet, sometimes we *think* we know, but our inside information is wrong. This is the unavoidable conclusion of some fascinating research.

Explaining Our Behaviour

Why did you choose your university or college? Why did you lash out at your room-mate? Why did you fall in love with that special person? Sometimes we know. Sometimes we don't. Asked why we have felt or acted as we have, we produce plausible answers. Yet, when causes are subtle, our self-explanations are often wrong.

For example, Donald Dutton at the University of British Columbia conducted a clever study to explore how people misattributed fear responses as sexual attraction (1974). Men were interviewed by a female research assistant after crossing the fear-arousing Capilano Suspension Bridge, which goes across a gorge in Vancouver. These men, compared to men who crossed a more solid bridge, used more sexual imagery in a later projective test and they were more likely to phone the female research assistant for a "follow up." Although there has been some suggestion that it may not have been fear participants felt (see Kenrick & Cialdini, 1977), nonetheless these men were misattributing their arousal to attraction for the research assistant.

Sometimes people think they *have* been affected by something that has had no effect. Richard Nisbett and Timothy Wilson (1977) had University of Michigan students rate a documentary film. While some of them watched, a power saw roared just outside the room. Most people believed that this distracting noise affected their ratings. But it didn't; their ratings were similar to those of control subjects who viewed the film without distraction.

Even more thought-provoking are studies in which people recorded their moods—every day for two or three months (Stone & others, 1985; Weiss & Brown, 1976; Wilson & others, 1982). They also recorded factors that might affect their moods: the day of the week, the weather, the amount they slept, and so forth. At the end of each study, the people judged how much each factor had affected their moods. Remarkably (given that their attention was being drawn to their daily moods), there was little relationship between their perceptions of how important a factor was and how well the factor actually predicted a mood. These findings raise a disconcerting question: How much insight do we really have into what makes us happy or unhappy?

Predicting Our Behaviour

People also err when predicting their behaviour. If asked whether they would obey demands to deliver severe electric shocks or would hesitate to help a victim if several other people were present, people overwhelmingly deny their vulnerability to such influences. But, as we will see, experiments have shown that many of us are vulnerable. Moreover, consider what Sidney Shrauger (1983) discovered when he had college students predict the likelihood that they would experience dozens of different events during the ensuing two months (becoming romantically involved, being sick, and so forth): Their self-predictions were hardly more accurate than predictions based on the average person's experience.

People also err frequently when predicting the fate of their relationships. Dating couples predict the longevity of their relationships through rose-coloured glasses. Focusing on the positives, lovers may feel sure they will always be lovers.

The Story Behind the Research

As a student at the University of Waterloo, Dr. Tara MacDonald (now at Queen's University) was interested in understanding how people made important decisions and how well they could make predictions about themselves and their future. In her classes, she learned that sometimes groups can make better decisions than individuals. Thus, she wondered if there were times when it would probably be better to let others make important decisions for you. Indeed, in the real world, we do this all the time—we let magazines guide our purchase of cars, and we let bankers tell us how expensive a car we can afford.

Along with her supervisor at the time, Dr. Michael Ross, Dr. MacDonald developed a study to explore whether parents and friends of Waterloo students were better judges of the students' romantic relationships than were the students themselves (see MacDonald & Ross, 1999). She asked students to make predictions about their relationships (for example, how long they would last) and asked their roommates and parents to make the same predictions. The research found, surprisingly, that the outsiders were more accurate in their predictions than the people involved in the relationship! Drs. MacDonald and Ross concluded that this was likely because someone involved in the relationship is not able to make an objective assessment of the relationship and thus cannot accurately predict its outcome. It is likely that this is the case for many important decisions we make on a regular basis. I

When predicting negative behaviours such as crying or lying, self-predictions are more accurate than predictions by one's mother and friends (Shrauger & others, 1996). Nevertheless, the surest thing we can say about your individual future is that it is sometimes hard for even you to predict. When predicting your behaviour, the best advice is to consider your past behaviour in similar situations (Osberg & Shrauger, 1986, 1990).

Predicting Our Feelings

Many of life's big decisions involve predicting our future feelings. Would marrying this person lead to lifelong contentment? Would entering this profession make for satisfying work? Would going on this vacation produce a happy experience? Or would the likelier results be divorce, job burnout, and holiday disappointment?

Sometimes we know how we will feel—if we fail that exam, win that big game, or soothe our tensions with a half-hour jog. But often we don't. In recent studies, people have mispredicted how they would feel some time after a romantic breakup, or when receiving a gift, losing an election, winning a game, and being insulted (Gilbert & Jenkins, 2001). George Loewenstein and David Schkade (1999) offer some examples:

- When male youths are shown sexually arousing photographs, then exposed to a passionate date scenario in which their date asks them to "stop," they acknowledge the possibility that they might not stop. If they are not first shown sexually arousing pictures, they more often deny the possibility of their being sexually aggressive. When not aroused, one easily mispredicts how one will feel and act when aroused—a phenomenon that leads to many unintended pregnancies.

- Only one in seven occasional smokers (of less than one cigarette per day) predict they will be smoking in five years. But they underestimate the power of their drug cravings, for nearly half will still be smoking (Lynch & Bonnie, 1994).

- People overestimate how much their well-being would be affected by warmer winters, weight gain or loss, more television channels, or more free time. Even extreme events, such as winning a provincial lottery or suffering a paralyzing accident, affect long-term happiness less than most people suppose.

Our intuitive theory seems to be: We want. We get. We are happy. If that were true, this chapter would have fewer words. In reality, note Daniel Gilbert and Timothy Wilson (2000), we often "miswant." People who imagine an idyllic desert island holiday with sun, surf, and sand may be disappointed when they discover "how much they require daily structure, intellectual stimulation, or regular infusions of Pop Tarts." We think that if our candidate or team wins, we will be delighted for a long while. But study after study reveals that the emotional traces of such good tidings evaporate more rapidly than we expect.

And if we mispredict how enduring the positive impact of positive events will be, we are even more prone to such "durability bias" regarding negative events. Our capacity for coping with significant negative events is striking. When people being tested for HIV predict how they will feel five weeks after getting the results, they expect to be feeling misery over bad news and elation over good news. Yet, five weeks later, the bad news recipients are less distraught and the good news recipients are less elated than they anticipated (Sieff & others, 1999). And when Gilbert and his colleagues (1998) asked assistant professors to predict their happiness a few years after achieving tenure or not, most believed a favourable outcome was important for their future happiness. "Losing my job would crush my life's ambitions. It would be terrible." Yet, when surveyed several years after the event, those denied tenure were about as happy as those who received it.

Let's make this personal. Gilbert and Wilson invite us to imagine how we might feel a year after losing our nondominant hands. Compared to today, how happy would you be?

In thinking about this, you perhaps focused on what the calamity would mean: no clapping, no shoe tying, no competitive basketball, impeded keyboarding. Although you likely would forever regret the loss, your general happiness some time after the event would be influenced by "two things: (a) the event, and (b) everything else." In *focusing* on the negative *event*, we discount the importance of everything else that contributes to happiness and so overpredict our misery. Moreover, say Gilbert and Wilson, people neglect the speed and power of their psychological immune system, which includes their strategies for rationalizing, discounting, forgiving, and limiting emotional trauma. Being largely ignorant of our psychological immune system (a phenomenon Gilbert and Wilson call *immune neglect*), we accommodate to disabilities, romantic breakups, exam failures, tenure denials, and personal and team defeats more readily than we would expect. We are resilient.

SELF-PRESENTATION BIASES

Much of how we perceive ourselves depends on how we present ourselves to others. As we will see in the next module, we sometimes interpret our social world in a very self-serving way. Similarly, we spend a significant amount of time being careful to present ourselves in a positive light. However, are these self-enhancing presentations always sincere? Consider the last time you went for a job interview—how did you dress; how did you speak; what did you say? Think of a "first date" you may have had—did you show the "real you" right away?

False Modesty

There is significant evidence that people present a different self than the one they may be feeling. However, often people present themselves in a more negative light than a more positive one. For example, you probably have a friend who always says after an exam "I did terribly! I know I failed!" but consistently ends up with high grades. This is known as *false modesty*. Why might people do this? Such self-disparaging remarks can actually be self-serving: The comment "I look terrible in this outfit" is usually countered with "No, you look great!"

False modesty also appears in people's accounts of their successes in life. In acceptance speeches, people often thank all of those who have helped them achieve their successes. But do people really believe that others are the cause of their success? Interestingly, the audience of the speech makes a difference. Roy Baumiester and Stacy Ilko (1995) asked people to write a description of an important success experience in their life. Participants who signed their names and expected to present their description to an audience were much more likely to acknowledge the help and support of others than those participants who wrote anonymously. Indeed those who wrote anonymously were much more likely to attribute their successes to their own efforts—suggesting that the gratitude expressed by the non-anonymous writers was shallow and superficial.

Self-Handicapping

Sometimes, people can sabotage their own chances for success. Take for example the student who goes out drinking the night before a final exam. Surprisingly, this type of self-destructive behaviour often has a self-protective aim (see Arkin & others, 1986; Baumeister & Scher, 1988). Why? Because it allows the person to say "I'm really not a failure—if I hadn't gone out the night before, I would have done well on the exam." Thus self-handicapping protects both our self-esteem and our public image. If we fail, we have an outside factor to blame; if we succeed, we must really be competent. Researchers have documented a number of ways in which people will self-handicap. For example, fearing failure, people will:

- reduce their preparation for an upcoming athletic event (Rhodewalt & others, 1984)
- give their opponent an advantage (Shepperd & Arkin, 1991)
- report feeling depressed (Baumgardner, 1991)

Impression Management

Self-presentation Wanting to present a desired image both to an external audience (other people) and an internal audience (ourselves).

To varying degrees, we are continually managing the impressions we create. **Self-presentation** refers to our wanting to present a desired image both to an external audience (other people) and an internal audience (ourselves). We want others to perceive us as good, friendly, and competent people, and for the most part we want to see ourselves in that light as well. In familiar situations (such as with family) this may occur with little effort and we may be less modest. In unfamiliar situations (such as at a party) we are acutely aware of the impression we are creating (Leary & others, 1994; Tice & others, 1995) and will modify our behaviour accordingly.

For some people, conscious self-presentation is a way of life. Others are less concerned about how they are seen by others. To assess this individual difference in people's self-presentation style, Mark Snyder developed the self-monitoring scale (see Snyder, 1987). People who score high in self-monitoring act like a social chameleon, adapting easily to social situations. Interestingly, they may espouse attitudes that they don't really hold (for example, Zanna & Olson, 1982) and their new attitudes can help them adjust to new jobs, roles, and relationships (see Snyder & DeBono, 1989). People who are low in self-monitoring care less about what others think and are more focused on, and tend to act on, their internal thoughts and beliefs (McCann & Hancock, 1983). For example, when low-self-monitoring British university women answered questions about their gender-related attitudes, they were not affected by how the female interviewer dressed. However, high-self-monitoring women answered in more feminine ways if the interviewer was dressed in a feminine manner (Smith & others, 1997). Where do you fall on this continuum? Go to the Online Learning Centre and complete Activity 3.2 to find out.

OLC
Activity 3.2

Presenting oneself in such a way as to create a desired impression takes some skill. People want to be seen as able yet honest and modest (Carlston & Shovar, 1983). Modesty creates a good impression, and unsolicited boasting creates a bad impression (see Forsyth & others, 1981; Holtgraves & Srull, 1989). However, false modesty—"I did well, but it's no big deal"—can also be perceived negatively. Thus, making a good impression takes social skill. Overall, our self-concept is defined by how we perceive ourselves. Yet how we perceive ourselves is also dependent on how others perceive us. Thus our self-concept will always to some extent be influenced by others.

CONCEPTS TO REMEMBER

Self-concept   p. 21
Self-schema   p. 22
Self-reference effect   p. 22

Individualism   p. 23
Collectivism   p. 23
Self-presentation   p. 30

Please visit the *Exploring Social Psychology* Online Learning Centre at **www.mcgrawhill.ca/college/myers** to participate in module activities, view module videos, access research and study tools, and test your knowledge with interactive quizzes, exercises, and scenarios.

Self-Serving Bias

D o you like yourself? Or are you your worst critic?

It is widely believed that most of us suffer from low self-esteem. A generation ago, humanistic psychologist Carl Rogers (1958) concluded that most people he knew "despise themselves, regard themselves as worthless and unlovable." Many popularizers of humanistic psychology concurred. "All of us have inferiority complexes," contended John Powell (1989). "Those who seem not to have such a complex are only pretending." As Groucho Marx (1960) lampooned, "I don't want to belong to any club that would accept me as a member."

Actually, most of us have a good reputation with ourselves. In studies of self-esteem, even low-scoring people respond in the midrange of possible scores. (A low-self-esteem person responds to statements such as "I have good ideas" with a qualifying adjective, such as "somewhat" or "sometimes.") Moreover, one of social psychology's most provocative, yet firmly established, conclusions concerns the potency of **self-serving bias**: the tendency to perceive and present oneself favourably.

Self-serving bias may play a role in how a driver explains a car accident. Was the crash a result of the driver's ability or external factors?

OLC
Activity 4.1

Self-serving bias   The tendency to perceive and present oneself favourably.

EXPLAINING POSITIVE AND NEGATIVE EVENTS

Seventy experiments have found that people accept credit when told they have succeeded. They attribute the success to their ability and effort, but they attribute failure to external factors such as bad luck or the problem's inherent "impossibility" (Campbell & Sedikides, 1999). Similarly, in explaining their victories, athletes commonly credit themselves, but they attribute losses to something else: bad breaks, bad referee calls, or the other team's superior effort or dirty play (Grove & others, 1991; Lalonde, 1992; Mullen & Riordan, 1988). And how much responsibility do you suppose car drivers tend to accept for their accidents? On insurance forms, drivers have described their accidents in words such as these: "An invisible car came out of nowhere, struck my car, and vanished"; "As I reached an intersection, a hedge sprang up, obscuring my vision, and I did not see the other car"; "A pedestrian hit me and went under my car" (*Toronto News*, July 26, 1977).

The Story Behind the Research

Dr. Michael Ross, a professor at the University of Waterloo, and his colleagues (for example, Ross & Sicoly, 1979) have found that self-serving biases extend to all kinds of personal situations. Dr. Ross became interested in this issue, as he does with many of the topics he researches, because he was trying to explain the behaviour of the people around him. As a faculty member, he repeatedly found himself in situations where two colleagues would be arguing over order of authorship on academic papers (a situation graduate students and faculty members can certainly relate to). Obviously, the person who contributed most to the project ought to be the first author. However, he observed that often more than one person would believe they had contributed the most and deserved to be first author. Indeed, he found himself in conflict with his own student on just such an assessment. (Consistent with this anecdotal evidence, Steven Smith has found [see Parks & others, 2005] that if three authors provide a percentage estimate of how much they contributed to a published paper, the total percentage value

assigned by the first, second, and third authors combined adds up to 158 percent!)

Dr. Ross and his colleague Fiore Sicoly wanted to explore whether this self-serving bias extended to personal relations as well. They surveyed young married Canadians and found that they typically took more responsibility for activities such as cleaning the house and caring for the children than their spouse gave them credit for (indeed, this is a situation David Myers has found himself in as well). But *why* did this occur? Ross and Sicoly suggested that when people are allocating responsibility for a joint endeavour, people attempt to recall the contributions each made to the task. They suggested that people might recall a disproportionate share of their own contributions relative to their partner's contribution, and therefore claim greater responsibility than their partners would assign to them. Interestingly, this explanation for the effect suggests a cognitive, rather than motivational, explanation. In other words, we make these kinds of attributions not because we are trying to make ourselves look better, but simply because of the way we search for and process information. I

Such biases in allocating responsibility contribute to marital discord, dissatisfaction among workers, and impasses when bargaining (Kruger & Gilovich, 1999). Small wonder that divorced people usually blame their partner for the breakup (Gray & Silver, 1990), or that managers usually blame poor performance on workers' lack of ability or effort (Imai, 1994; Rice, 1985). (Workers are more likely to blame something external—inadequate supplies, excessive workload, difficult co-workers, ambiguous assignments.)

Students also exhibit self-serving bias. After receiving an exam grade, those who do well tend to accept personal credit. They judge the exam to be a valid measure of their competence (Arkin & Maruyama, 1979; Davis & Stephan, 1980; Gilmor & Reid, 1979; Griffin & others, 1983). Those who do poorly are much more likely to criticize the exam.

**OLC
Activity 4.2**

Reading this research, we can't resist a satisfied "knew-it-all-along" feeling. But consider teachers' ways of explaining students' good and bad performances. When there is no need to feign modesty, those assigned the role of teacher tend to take credit for positive outcomes and blame failure on the student (Arkin & others, 1980; Davis, 1979). Teachers, it seems, are likely to think, "With my help, Maria graduated with honours. Despite all my help, Melinda flunked out."

CAN WE ALL BE BETTER THAN AVERAGE?

Self-serving bias also appears when people compare themselves to others. If the sixth-century-B.C. Chinese philosopher Lao-tzu was right that "at no time in the world will a man who is sane over-reach himself, over-spend himself, over-rate himself," then most of us are a little insane. For on most *subjective* and *socially desirable* dimensions, most people see themselves as better than average. Consider the following illustrative examples:

- Dr. Lionel Standing at Bishop's University in Quebec has found that university and college students who were asked to judge the "accuracy" of a personality profile were more likely to rate the positive traits as accurately describing themselves than negative traits (MacDonald & Standing, 2002), and that students who smoke perceive themselves as smoking "less than" their friends (Standing, 2002).

- Ninety percent of business managers rate their performance as superior to that of their average peer (French, 1968). In Australia, 86 percent of people rate their job performance as above average, and 1 percent as below average (Headey & Wearing, 1987).

- Most drivers—even most drivers who have been hospitalized for accidents—believe themselves to be safer and more skilled than the average driver (Guerin, 1994; McKenna & Myers, 1997; Svenson, 1981).

- Most people perceive themselves as more intelligent than their average peer, as better looking, and as much less prejudiced (*Public Opinion*, 1984; Wylie, 1979). In a 1997 Gallup Poll, only 14 percent of White Americans rated their prejudice against Blacks as 5 or higher on a 0 to 10 scale. Yet, Whites perceived prejudice (5 or above) among 44 percent of *other* Whites.

- Los Angeles residents view themselves as healthier than most of their neighbours, and most college students believe they will outlive their actuarially predicted age of death by about 10 years (Larwood, 1978; C. R. Snyder, 1978).

Subjective behaviour dimensions (such as "disciplined") trigger greater self-serving bias than objective behavioural dimensions (such as "punctual"). Students are more likely to rate themselves superior in "moral goodness" than in "intelligence" (Allison & others, 1989; Van Lange, 1991). And community residents overwhelmingly see themselves as *caring* more than most others about the environment, about hunger, and about other social issues, though they don't see themselves as *doing* more, such as contributing time or money to those issues (White & Plous, 1995). Interestingly, a number of factors appear to moderate the occurrence of self-serving biases. Education doesn't eliminate self-serving bias; even social psychologists exhibit it, by believing themselves more ethical than most social psychologists (Van Lange & others, 1997). In addition, Nancy Higgins at St. Thomas University and Ghira Bhatt at Kwantlen University College in B.C. (for example, Higgins & Bhatt, 2001) have demonstrated that Canadian students are less likely to engage in self-serving biases than Indian students. Hildy Ross and her colleagues (for example, Ross & others, 2004) have demonstrated that as children get older they are more likely to engage in self-serving explanations for their behaviour.

Subjective qualities give us leeway in constructing our own definitions of success (Dunning & others, 1989, 1991). Rating my "athletic ability," you might ponder your basketball play, not the agonizing weeks you spent as a Little League baseball player hiding in right field. Assessing your "leadership ability," you might conjure up an image of a great leader whose style is similar to yours. By defining ambiguous criteria in our own terms, each of us can see ourselves as relatively successful. In one survey of 829,000 high school students, 0 percent rated themselves below average in "ability to get along with others" (a subjective, desirable trait), 60 percent rated themselves in the top 10 percent, and 25 percent saw themselves among the top 1 percent!

We also support our self-images by assigning importance to the things we're good at. Over a semester, those who ace an introductory computer science course come to place a higher value on being a computer-literate person in today's world. Those who do poorly are more likely to scorn computer geeks and to exclude computer skills as pertinent to their self-images (Hill & others, 1989).

UNREALISTIC OPTIMISM

Optimism predisposes a positive approach to life. "The optimist," notes H. Jackson Brown (1990, p. 79), "goes to the window every morning and says, 'Good morning, God.' The pessimist goes to the window and says, 'good god, morning.'" Many of us, however, have what researcher Neil Weinstein (1980, 1982) terms "an unrealistic optimism about future life events." At Rutgers University, for example, students perceive themselves as far more likely than their classmates to get a good job, draw a good salary, and own a home, and as far less likely to experience negative events, such as developing a drinking problem, having a heart attack before age 40, or being fired. In Scotland, most older teens think they are much less likely than their peers to become infected with HIV (Abrams, 1991; Pryor & Reeder, 1993). This type of thinking is apparent after disasters as well. For example, before Hurricane Juan struck Halifax in September 2003, residents did not believe that even if the hurricane struck it would do much damage. Of course, Juan did more than $100 million in damage. Interestingly, in the fall of 2005, as the remnants of Hurricane Katrina crept north from a devastated Louisiana, Nova Scotia residents predicted dire consequences. Of course, Katrina did not strike Nova Scotia at all. However, illusory optimism can rebound. For example, after the September 11, 2001 terrorist attacks in the United States, 80 percent of Canadians thought their lives would be deeply and permanently changed, but one year later only 16 percent still believed this (*Toronto Star*/EKOS, 2002).

Linda Perloff (1987) notes how illusory optimism increases our vulnerability. Believing ourselves immune to misfortune, we do not take sensible precautions. In one survey, 137 marriage licence applicants accurately estimated that half of marriages end in divorce, yet most assessed their chance of divorce as zero percent (Baker & Emery, 1993). Sexually active undergraduate women who don't consistently use contraceptives perceive themselves, compared to other women at their university, as much less vulnerable to unwanted pregnancy (Burger & Burns, 1988). Those who cheerfully shun seat belts, deny the effects of smoking, and stumble into ill-fated relationships remind us that blind optimism, like pride, may go before a fall.

Optimism definitely beats pessimism in promoting self-efficacy, health, and well-being (Armor & Taylor, 1996). Being natural optimists, most people believe they will be happier with various aspects of their lives in the future—a belief that surely helps create happiness in the present (Robinson & Ryff, 1999). Half of 18- to 19-year-old Americans believe that they are "somewhat" or "very likely" to "be rich"—a belief shared by progressively fewer people with age (Moore, 2003). Yet a dash of realism—or what Julie Norem (2000) calls "defensive pessimism"—can save us from the perils of unrealistic optimism. Self-doubt can energize students, most of whom—especially those destined for low grades—exhibit excess optimism about upcoming exams (Prohaska, 1994; Sparrell & Shrauger, 1984). (Such illusory optimism often disappears as the time approaches for receiving the exam back [Taylor & Shepperd, 1998].) Students who are overconfident tend to underprepare. Their equally able but more anxious peers, fearing that they are going to bomb on the upcoming exam, study furiously and get higher grades (Goodhart, 1986; Norem & Cantor, 1986; Showers & Ruben, 1987). The moral: Success in school and beyond requires enough optimism to sustain hope and enough pessimism to motivate concern.

FALSE CONSENSUS AND UNIQUENESS

We have a curious tendency to further enhance our self-images by overestimating or underestimating the extent to which others think and act as we do—a phenomenon called the **false consensus effect**. On matters of *opinion*, we find support for our positions by overestimating the extent to which others agree (Krueger & Clement, 1994; Marks & Miller, 1987; Mullen & Goethals, 1990). If we favour the Quebec sovereignty referendum or support New Zealand's National Party, we wishfully overestimate the extent to which others agree (Babad & others, 1992; Koestner, 1993).

When we behave badly or fail in a task, we reassure ourselves by thinking that such lapses are common. After one person lies to another, the liar begins to perceive the other as dishonest (Sagarin & others, 1998). They guess that others think and act

False consensus effect
The tendency to overestimate the commonality of one's opinions and one's undesirable or unsuccessful behaviours.

as they do: "I lie, but doesn't everyone?" If we cheat on our income taxes or smoke, we are likely to overestimate the number of other people who do likewise. If we harbour negative ideas about another racial group, we presume that many others also have negative stereotypes (Krueger, 1996). Thus, our perceptions of others' stereotypes may reveal something of our own.

False consensus might occur because we generalize from a limited sample, which prominently includes ourselves (Dawes, 1990). Lacking other information, why not "project" ourselves; why not impute our own knowledge to others and use our responses as a clue to their likely responses? Also, we're more likely to associate with people who share our attitudes and behaviours and then to judge the world from the people we know.

False uniqueness effect
The tendency to underestimate the commonality of one's abilities and one's desirable or successful behaviours.

On matters of *ability* or when we behave well or successfully, a **false uniqueness effect** more often occurs (Goethals & others, 1991). We serve self-image by seeing our talents and moral behaviours as relatively unusual. Thus, those who drink heavily but use seat belts will *over*estimate (false consensus) the number of other heavy drinkers and *under*estimate (false uniqueness) the commonality of seat belt use (Suls & others, 1988). Thus, we may see our failings as relatively normal and our virtues as less commonplace than they are. Remarkably, Cathy McFarland at Simon Fraser University in B.C. has found that people can demonstrate both false consensus and false uniqueness effects in the same context (see McFarland & Miller, 1990). She presented participants with two aversive situations and asked them to indicate which they would least like to be involved with. Participants were then asked to rate the percentage of other students who would choose to avoid that same situation, and predict their and the "typical student's" emotional reactions to the situation. Interestingly, students overestimated the percentage of students who would choose to avoid the situation they chose to avoid (demonstrating

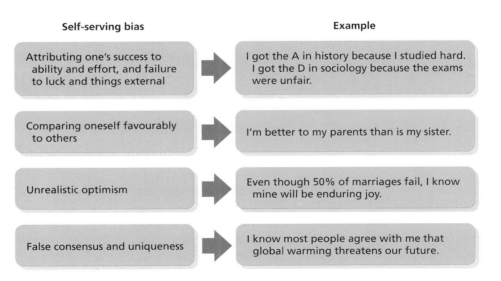

FIGURE 4-1
How self-serving bias works.

false consensus) and they predicted that their emotional reactions would be stronger than the typical student (demonstrating false uniqueness).

To sum up, these tendencies toward self-serving attributions, congratulatory comparisons, illusory optimism, and false consensus and uniqueness are major sources of self-serving biases (see Figure 4-1).

SELF-ESTEEM MOTIVATION

Why do people perceive themselves in self-enhancing ways? One explanation sees the self-serving bias as a by-product of how we process and remember information about ourselves. Recall the study in which married people gave themselves credit for doing more housework than did their spouses. Might this not be due, as Michael Ross and Fiore Sicoly (1979) believe, to our greater recall for what we've actively done and our lesser recall for what we've not done or merely observed others doing?

Are the biased perceptions, then, simply a perceptual error, an unemotional bent in how we process information? Or are self-serving *motives* also involved? It's now clear from research that we have multiple motives. Questing for self-knowledge, we're eager to assess our competence (Dunning, 1995). Questing for self-confirmation, we're eager to *verify* our self-conceptions (Sanitioso & others, 1990; Swann, 1996, 1997). Questing for self-affirmation, we're especially motivated to *enhance* our self-image (Sedikides, 1993).

One common way to enhance our self-esteem is to engage in *downward social comparison*—comparing yourself to someone who is worse than you on a particular trait (see Wood & others, 2000). Joanne Wood at the University of Waterloo and her colleagues (Wood & others, 1985) found that even breast cancer patients compare themselves to patients who are worse off in order to feel better.

So, does *upward social comparison*—comparing yourself to someone better than you on a particular trait—make you feel worse? As mentioned in an earlier module, it depends. Penelope Lockwood (now at the University of Toronto) and Ziva Kunda from the University of Waterloo (see Lockwood & Kunda, 1997, 1999, 2000) found that if people thought about their "usual" self before comparing themselves to a student "superstar," the comparison made them feel better about themselves as they were inspired by the comparison. However, if people thought about their "best" self before the social comparison, they were discouraged by their abilities relative to the "superstar." Thus social comparisons depending on the context can make us feel better or worse about ourselves—something we can all appreciate.

Self-esteem threats occur among friends and married partners, too. Although shared interests are healthy, *identical* career goals can produce tension or jealousy (Clark & Bennett, 1992). Similarly, people feel greater jealousy toward a romantic rival whose achievements are in the domain of their own aspirations (DeSteno & Salovey, 1996).

What underlies the motive to maintain or enhance self-esteem? Mark Leary (1998, 1999) believes that our self-esteem feelings are like a fuel gauge. As we noted earlier, relationships are conducive to our surviving and thriving. Thus, the self-esteem gauge alerts us to threatened social rejection, motivating us to act with greater sensitivity to others' expectations. Studies confirm that social rejection lowers our self-esteem, strengthening our eagerness for approval. Spurned or jilted, we feel unattractive or inadequate. Like a blinking dashboard light, this pain can motivate action—self-improvement and a search for acceptance and inclusion elsewhere.

REFLECTIONS ON SELF-SERVING BIAS

The Self-Serving Bias as Adaptive

Self-esteem has its dark side, but it also has a bright side. When good things happen, high- more than low-self-esteem people tend to savour and sustain the good feelings (Wood & others, 2003). Self-serving bias and its accompanying excuses also help protect people from depression (Snyder & Higgins, 1988). Nondepressed people excuse their failures on laboratory tasks or perceive themselves as being more in control than they are. Depressed people's self-appraisals are more accurate: sadder but wiser.

In their "terror management theory," Jeff Greenberg, Sheldon Solomon, and Tom Pyszczynski (1997) propose another reason why positive self-esteem is adaptive—it buffers anxiety, including anxiety related to our certain death. In childhood, we learn that when we meet the standards taught us by our parents, we are loved and protected; when we don't, love and protection may be withdrawn. We therefore come to associate viewing ourselves as good with feeling secure. Greenberg and his colleagues argue that positive self-esteem—viewing oneself as good and secure—even protects us from feeling terror over our eventual death. Their research shows that reminding people of their mortality (say, by writing a short essay on dying) motivates them to affirm their self-worth. Moreover, when facing threats, increased self-esteem leads to decreased anxiety.

As this new research on depression and anxiety suggests, there may be some practical wisdom in self-serving perceptions. It may be strategic to believe we are smarter, stronger, and more socially successful than we are. Cheaters may give a more convincing display of honesty if they believe themselves honourable. Belief in our superiority can also motivate us to achieve—creating a self-fulfilling prophecy—and can sustain a sense of hope in difficult times.

The Self-Serving Bias as Maladaptive

Although self-serving pride may help to protect us from depression, it can, at times, be maladaptive. People who blame others for their social difficulties are often unhappier than people who can acknowledge their mistakes (C. A. Anderson & others, 1983; Newman & Langer, 1981; Peterson & others, 1981). Moreover, the most self-enhancing people often come across to others as egotistical, condescending, and deceitful (Colvin & others, 1995). In human history, expansive egos have marked genocidal dictators, White supremacists, and drunken spouse-abusers (Baumeister & others, 1996). When someone's inflated self-esteem is challenged by others' criticisms or taunts, the result is sometimes an abusive or murderous rage.

Research by Barry Schlenker (1976; Schlenker & Miller, 1977a, 1977b) has also shown how self-serving perceptions can poison a group. As a rock band guitarist during his college days, Schlenker noted that "rock band members typically overestimated their contributions to a group's success and underestimated their contributions to failure. I saw many good bands disintegrate from the problems caused by these self-glorifying tendencies." In his later life as a University of Florida social psychologist, Schlenker explored group members' self-serving perceptions. Most presented themselves as contributing more than the others in their group when the group did well; few said they contributed less.

Self-serving biases also inflate people's judgments of their groups. When groups are comparable, most people consider their own group superior (Codol, 1976; Jourden & Heath, 1996; Taylor & Doria, 1981). Thus:

- Most university sorority members perceive those in their sorority as far less likely to be conceited and snobby than those in other sororities (Biernat & others, 1996).

- Fifty-three percent of Dutch adults rate their marriage or partnership as better than that of most others; only 1 percent rate it as worse than most (Buunk & van der Eijnden, 1997).

- Sixty-six percent of parents give their oldest child's public schools a grade of A or B. But nearly as many—64 percent—give the *nation's* public schools a grade of C or D (Whitman, 1996).

- Most corporation presidents and production managers overpredict their own firms' productivity and growth (Kidd & Morgan, 1969; Larwood & Whittaker, 1977).

That people see themselves with a favourable bias is hardly new—the tragic flaw portrayed in ancient Greek drama was *hubris*, or pride. Like the subjects of our experiments, the Greek tragic figures were not self-consciously evil; they merely thought too highly of themselves.

If pride is akin to the self-serving bias, then what is humility? Is it self-contempt? Or can we be self-affirming and self-accepting without a self-serving bias? True humility is more like self-forgetfulness than false modesty. It leaves people free to rejoice in their special talents and, with the same honesty, to recognize the talents of others.

CONCEPTS TO REMEMBER

Self-serving bias   p. 31
False consensus effect   p. 35
False uniqueness effect   p. 36

Please visit the *Exploring Social Psychology* Online Learning Centre at www.mcgrawhill.ca/college/myers to participate in module activities, view module videos, access research and study tools, and test your knowledge with interactive quizzes, exercises, and scenarios.

Self-Efficacy

Terry Fox during his Marathon of Hope to raise funds for cancer research. How would you characterize Terry Fox's sense of self-efficacy?

Self-efficacy A sense that one is competent and effective. Distinguished from self-esteem, a sense of one's self-worth.

We have considered a potent self-serving bias uncovered by social psychologists. When most people see themselves as more moral and deserving than others, conflict among people and nations is a natural result.

Studies of the self-serving bias expose deep truths about human nature. But single truths seldom tell the whole story because the world is complex. Indeed, there is an important complement to these truths. High self-esteem—a sense of self-worth—is adaptive. Compared to those with low self-esteem, people with high self-esteem are happier, less neurotic, less troubled by ulcers and insomnia, and less prone to drug and alcohol addictions (Brockner & Hulton, 1978; Brown, 1991). Many clinical psychologists report that underneath much human despair is an impoverished self-acceptance.

Additional research on "locus of control," optimism, and "learned helplessness" confirms the benefits of seeing oneself as competent and effective. Albert Bandura (1986), who was born in Northern Alberta, merges much of this research into a concept called **self-efficacy**, a scholarly version of the wisdom behind the power of positive thinking. An optimistic belief in our own possibilities pays dividends (Bandura & others, 1999; Maddux & Gosselin, 2003). People with strong feelings of self-efficacy are more persistent, less anxious and depressed, and more academically successful (Gecas, 1989; Maddux, 1991; Scheier & Carver, 1992).

Your self-efficacy is how competent you feel to do something; your self-esteem is your sense of self-worth. (A skilled burglar might feel high self-efficacy and low self-esteem.) If you believe you can do something, will this belief necessarily make a difference? That depends on a second factor: Do you have *control* over your outcomes? You may, for example, feel like an effective driver (high self-efficacy), yet feel endangered by drunken drivers (low control). You may feel like a competent student or worker; but fearing discrimination based on your age, gender, or appearance, you may think your prospects are dim.

LOCUS OF CONTROL

"I have no social life," complained a 40-something single man to student therapist Jerry Phares. At Phares's urging, the patient went to a dance, where several women danced with him. "I was just lucky," he later reported, "it would never happen again." When Phares reported this to his mentor, Julian Rotter, it crystallized an idea he had been forming. In Rotter's experiments and in his clinical practice, some people seemed to persistently "feel that what happens to them is governed by external forces of one kind or another, while others feel that what happens to them is governed largely by their own efforts and skills" (quoted by Hunt, 1993, p. 334).

What do you think? Are people more often captains of their destinies or victims of their circumstances? Are they the playwrights, directors, and actors of their own lives or prisoners of invisible situations? Rotter called this dimension **locus of control**. With Phares, he developed 29 paired statements to measure a person's locus of control. Imagine yourself taking their test. Which do you more strongly believe?

Go to the Online Learning Centre and complete Activity 5.1. Did your answers to the questions in Activity 5.1 indicate that you believe you control your own destiny (*internal* locus of control)? Or that chance or outside forces determine your fate (*external* locus of control)? Those who see themselves as internally controlled are more likely to do well in school, successfully stop smoking, wear seat belts, practise birth control, deal with marital problems directly, make lots of money, and delay instant gratification in order to achieve long-term goals (Findley & Cooper, 1983; Lefcourt, 1982; Miller & others, 1986).

Locus of control The extent to which people perceive outcomes as internally controllable by their own efforts and actions, or as externally controlled by chance or outside forces.

OLC
Activity 5.1

LEARNED HELPLESSNESS VERSUS SELF-DETERMINATION

The benefits of feelings of control also appear in animal research. Dogs taught that they cannot escape shocks while confined will learn a sense of helplessness. Later, these dogs cower passively in other situations when they *could* escape punishment. Dogs that learn personal control (by escaping their first shocks successfully) adapt easily to a new situation. Researcher Martin Seligman (1975, 1991) notes similarities to this **learned helplessness** in human situations. Depressed or oppressed people, for example, become passive because they believe their efforts have no effect. Helpless dogs and depressed people both suffer paralysis of the will, passive resignation, even motionless apathy (see Figure 5-1 on page 42).

Learned helplessness The hopelessness and resignation learned by humans or animals who perceive themselves as having no control over repeated bad events.

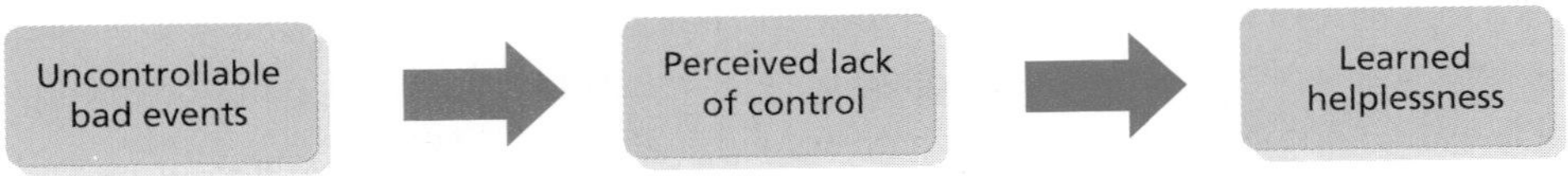

FIGURE 5-1
Learned helplessness. When animals and people experience uncontrollable bad events, they learn to feel helpless and resigned.

Here is a clue to how institutions—whether malevolent, like concentration camps, or benevolent, like hospitals—can dehumanize people. In hospitals, "good patients" don't ring bells, don't ask questions, don't try to control what's happening (Taylor, 1979). Such passivity may be good for hospital efficiency, but it is bad for people's health and survival. Losing control over what you do and what others do to you can make unpleasant events profoundly stressful (Pomerleau & Rodin, 1986). Several diseases are associated with feelings of helplessness and diminished choice. So is the rapidity of decline and death in concentration camps and nursing homes. Hospital patients who are trained to believe they can control stress require fewer pain relievers and sedatives and exhibit less anxiety (Langer & others, 1975).

Ellen Langer and Judith Rodin (1976) tested the importance of personal control by treating elderly patients in a highly rated nursing home in one of two ways. With one group, the benevolent caregivers stressed "our responsibility to make this

The Story Behind the Research

Dr. Daniel Bailis has done extensive research on how self-determinism and perceptions of control affect health outcomes. His line of research on the impact of control on stress and health was developed during a time of high stress for Dr. Bailis—a faculty strike at the University of Manitoba that began just a month after he arrived. Dr. Bailis was trying to get his research program started by accessing a Statistics Canada National Population Health Survey database containing responses from a representative sample of more than 12,000 Canadians. Fortunately, the strike allowed him to set up meetings in coffee shops with colleagues from sociology, social psychology, developmental psychology, and his own department of health, leisure, and human performance. During the time of the strike, Dr. Bailis and his team developed a successful grant application to the National Health Research and Development Program at Health Canada to work with the database.

Data from the study that Dr. Bailis and his colleagues conducted with the Statistics Canada data demonstrated that people who believe themselves to have control over their lives have more positive health outcomes. Interestingly, Dr. Bailis has also found evidence that having less perceived control over their lives could be an important reason why people with lower socioeconomic status have poorer physical and mental health overall.

a home you can be proud of and happy in." They gave the passive patients their normal well-intentioned, sympathetic care. Three weeks later, most patients were rated by themselves, by interviewers, and by nurses as further debilitated. Langer and Rodin's other treatment promoted personal control. It stressed opportunities for choice, the possibilities for influencing nursing-home policy, and the person's responsibility "to make of your life whatever you want." These patients were given small decisions to make and responsibilities to fulfill. Over the ensuing three weeks, 93 percent of this group showed improved alertness, activity, and happiness.

Studies confirm that systems of governing or managing people that promote personal control will indeed promote health and happiness (Deci & Ryan, 1987).

- Prisoners given some control over their environments—by being able to move chairs, control TV sets, and operate the lights—experience less stress, exhibit fewer health problems, and commit less vandalism (Ruback & others, 1986; Wener & others, 1987).

- Workers given leeway in carrying out tasks and making decisions experience improved morale (Miller & Monge, 1986).

- Institutionalized residents allowed choice in such matters as what to eat for breakfast, when to go to a movie, or whether to sleep late or get up early, may live longer and certainly are happier (Timko & Moos, 1989).

- Homeless shelter residents who perceive little choice in when to eat and sleep, and little control over their privacy, are more likely to have a passive, helpless attitude regarding finding housing and work (Burn, 1992).

Can there ever be too much of a good thing like freedom and self-determination? Barry Schwartz (2000, 2004) contends that individualistic modern cultures indeed have "an excess of freedom," causing decreased life satisfaction and increased clinical depression. Too many choices can lead to paralysis, or what Schwartz calls "the tyranny of freedom." After choosing from among 30 kinds of jams or chocolates, people express less satisfaction with their choices than those choosing among six options (Iyengar & Lepper, 2000). With more choice comes information overload and more opportunities for regret.

In other experiments, people have expressed greater satisfaction with irrevocable choices (like those made in an "all purchases final" sale) than with reversible choices (as when allowing refunds or exchanges). Ironically, people like and will pay for the freedom to reverse their choices. Yet, that freedom "can inhibit the psychological processes that manufacture satisfaction" (Gilbert & Ebert, 2002). Owning something irreversibly makes it feel better. This principle might help explain a curious social phenomenon (Myers, 2000): National surveys show that people expressed more satisfaction with their marriages back when marriage was more irrevocable ("all purchases final"). Today, despite greater freedom to escape bad marriages and try new ones, people tend to express somewhat less satisfaction with the marriage that they have.

REFLECTIONS ON SELF-EFFICACY

The Power of Positive Thinking

Although psychological research on perceived self-control is relatively new, the emphasis on taking charge of one's life and realizing one's potential is not. The you-can-do-it theme of Horatio Alger's rags-to-riches books is an enduring Western idea. We find it in Norman Vincent Peale's 1950s best-seller, *The Power of Positive Thinking*. ("If you think in positive terms you will get positive results. That is the simple fact.") We find it in the many self-help books and videos that urge people to succeed through developing positive mental attitudes.

We also see this on TV from popular self-help gurus. For example, Dr. Phil McGraw ("Dr. Phil") repeatedly advises viewers that "We teach people how to treat us" and "When you choose the behaviour, you choose the consequences" (the latter is a phrase Steven Smith uses repeatedly with his six-year-old—she hates it when he says that!). The underlying implication of all of these messages is that we have control over our behaviour and its outcomes. Yet, Bandura emphasizes that self-efficacy does not grow primarily by self-persuasion ("I think I can, I think I can") or by puffing people up like hot-air balloons ("You're terrific!"). Its chief source is the experience of success. If your initial efforts to lose weight, stop smoking, or improve your grades succeed, your self-efficacy increases.

After mastering the physical skills needed to repel a sexual assault, women feel less vulnerable, less anxious, and more in control (Ozer & Bandura, 1990). After experiencing academic success, students develop higher appraisals of their academic ability, which in turn often stimulate them to work harder and achieve more (Felson, 1984; Marsh & Young, 1997). To do one's best and achieve is to feel more confident and empowered.

So there is a power to positive thinking. But let us remember the point at which we began our consideration of self-efficacy: Any truth, separated from its complementary truth, is a half-truth. The truth embodied in the concept of self-efficacy can encourage us to not resign ourselves to bad situations, to persist despite initial failures, to exert effort without being overly distracted by self-doubts. But lest the pendulum swing too far toward *this* truth, we had best remember that it, too, is not the whole story. If positive thinking can accomplish *anything*, then if we are unhappily married, poor, or depressed, we have only ourselves to blame. For shame! If only we had tried harder, been more disciplined, less stupid. Failing to appreciate that difficulties sometimes reflect the oppressive power of social situations can tempt us to blame people for their problems and failures, or even to blame ourselves too harshly for our own. Ironically, life's greatest disappointments, as well as its highest achievements, are born of the highest expectations. The bigger we dream, the more we might attain—and the more we risk falling short.

The Dark Side of Self-Esteem

Critics question popular psychology's assumption that positive self-esteem is the secret to successful, happy living. Low self-esteem does predict increased risk of depression, drug abuse, and some forms of delinquency. High self-esteem fosters initiative, resilience, and pleasant feelings (Baumeister & others, 2003). Yet, teen males who engage in sexual activity at an "inappropriately young age" tend to have *higher* than average self-esteem. So do teen gang leaders, extreme ethnocentrists, and terrorists, notes Robyn Dawes (1994, 1998).

Steven Spencer at the University of Waterloo has demonstrated in numerous studies (for example, Fein & Spencer, 1997; Spencer & others, 1998) that when people's self-esteem is threatened, they tend to stereotype members of minority groups. In his studies, students are randomly assigned to receive positive or negative feedback about their own performance on a task, and then they are asked to evaluate a member of a stereotyped group (for example, Blacks, Asians). People who received negative feedback were more likely to demonstrate stereotypic attitudes and behaviours toward these group members.

In another experiment, Brad Bushman and Roy Baumeister (1998) had 540 undergraduate volunteers write a paragraph, in response to which another supposed student gave them either praise ("great essay!") or stinging criticism ("one of the worst essays I have read!"). Then each essay writer played a reaction-time game against the supposed other student. When the supposed opponent lost, the writer could assault him or her with noise of any intensity and for any duration. Among writers who had received criticism, those with the biggest egos—the highest self-esteem—were "exceptionally aggressive," delivering three times the auditory torture of those with normal self-esteem.

"The enthusiastic claims of the self-esteem movement mostly range from fantasy to hogwash," concludes Baumeister (1996), who suspects he has "probably published more studies on self-esteem than anybody else." "The effects of self-esteem are small, limited, and not all good." High-self-esteem folks, he reports, are more likely to be obnoxious, to interrupt, and to talk *at* people rather than *with* them (in contrast to the more shy, modest, self-effacing folks with low self-esteem). "My conclusion is that self-control is worth 10 times as much as self-esteem."

The dark side of high self-esteem exists in tension with the findings that people expressing low self-esteem are somewhat more vulnerable to assorted clinical problems including anxiety, loneliness, and eating disorders. When feeling bad or threatened, they are more likely to view everything through dark glasses—to notice and remember others' worst behaviours and to think their partners don't love them (Murray & others, 1998, 2002; Ybarra, 1999).

Unlike a fragile self-esteem, a secure self-esteem—one rooted more in feeling good about who one is than on grades, looks, money, or others' approval—is conducive to long-term well-being (Kernis, 2003; Schimel & others, 2001). Jennifer Crocker and her colleagues (2002, 2003, 2004) confirmed this in studies with

University of Michigan students. Those whose self-worth was most fragile—most contingent on external sources—experienced more stress, anger, relationship problems, drug and alcohol use, and eating disorders than did those whose worth was rooted more in internal sources, such as personal virtues. Ironically, note Crocker and Lora Park (2004), those who pursue self-esteem, perhaps by seeking to become beautiful, rich, or popular, may lose sight of what really makes for quality of life. Moreover, if feeling good about ourselves is our goal, then we may become less open to criticism, more likely to blame than empathize with others, and more pressured to succeed at activities rather than simply to enjoy them. Over time, such pursuit of self-esteem can fail to satisfy our deep needs for competence, relationship, and autonomy, note Crocker and Park. To focus less on one's self-image, and more on developing one's talents and relationships, eventually leads to greater well-being.

CONCEPTS TO REMEMBER

Self-efficacy   p. 40
Locus of control   p. 41
Learned helplessness   p. 41

Please visit the *Exploring Social Psychology* Online Learning Centre at **www.mcgrawhill.ca/college/myers** to participate in module activities, view module videos, access research and study tools, and test your knowledge with interactive quizzes, exercises, and scenarios.

The Fundamental Attribution Error

When the 2006 Canadian Olympic Men's Hockey Team roster was announced to the Canadian public, we had high hopes. People expected a repeat performance of the 2002 gold-medal win in the 2006 Turin games. Yet in 2006 the team didn't even make it into the medals round. Why do you think that happened? Many commentators argued that the team felt invincible and did not prepare enough, that they didn't try very hard, or that their coaching staff was wasting too much time trying to deal with the Janet Gretzky gambling scandal. However, it is also reasonable that they'd had a long flight, or uncomfortable rooms, or were influenced by other factors outside of their control such as simply having a weaker team than their competitors. Why did the commentators blame the team?

As later modules will reveal, social psychology's most important lesson concerns how much we are affected by our social environment. At any moment, our internal state, and therefore what we say and do, depends on the situation (as well as on what we bring to the situation). How does this affect you? Before you read on, go to the Online Learning Centre and complete the survey in Activity 6.1. We would like to get your impressions of your performance on a recent exam. Sometimes, how we do on an exam can be influenced by both situational as well as internal factors.

Attribution researchers—those who study how we explain (attribute) others' behaviour—have found that we often fail to appreciate this important lesson. When explaining someone's behaviour, we underestimate the impact of the situation and overestimate the extent to which it reflects the individual's traits and attitudes.

People are biased to assume that everyone's behaviour corresponds to their inner dispositions. Such assumptions are not always correct—some weekend bikers are weekday professionals. What are some other common examples of the fundamental attribution error?

OLC
Activity 6.1

Do you make these same kinds of mistakes? In Activity 6.1, you were asked to give reasons for why you did poorly on an exam. What reasons did you provide? Steven Smith has done this "thought experiment" with his class for many years, and you probably gave the some of the following reasons he hears often: "The exam was unfair"; "I didn't sleep well the night before"; "I had too much work to do"; "There were too many distractions in the class"—in other words, these reasons highlight the situational aspects of why you did poorly. Next, you were asked why a friend did poorly on a similar exam. You probably gave somewhat different reasons: "He would rather party than study"; "She doesn't study hard enough"; "He isn't that smart"; and so on. These reasons highlight your friend's internal attributes, and you probably ignored or discounted the situational reasons for his or her poor performance. Does this sound similar to what happened with the Olympic men's hockey team?

This discounting of the situation, dubbed by Lee Ross (1977) the **fundamental attribution error**, appears in many experiments. In the first such study, Edward Jones and Victor Harris (1967) had students read debaters' speeches supporting or attacking Cuba's leader, Fidel Castro. When the position taken was said to have been chosen by the debater, the students logically enough assumed it reflected the person's own attitude. But what happened when the students were told that the debate coach had assigned the position? People who were merely feigning a position wrote more forceful statements than you'd expect (Allison & others, 1993; Miller & others, 1990). Thus, even knowing that the debater had been told to take a pro-Castro position did not prevent students from inferring that the debater in fact had some pro-Castro leanings (Figure 6-1). People seemed to think, "Yeah, I know he was assigned that position, but to some extent I think he really believes it." In short, we tend to presume that others *are* the way they act.

Fundamental attribution error The tendency for observers to underestimate situational influences and overestimate dispositional influences upon others' behaviour. (Also called *correspondence bias*, because we so often see behaviour as corresponding to a disposition.)

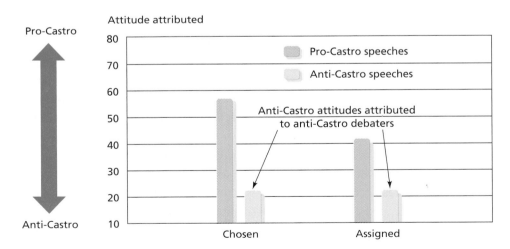

FIGURE 6-1
The fundamental attribution error. When people read a debate speech supporting or attacking Fidel Castro, they attributed corresponding attitudes to the speech writer, even when the debate coach assigned the writer's position.

Data from Jones & Harris, 1967.

We commit the fundamental attribution error when we explain *other people's* behaviour. We often explain *our own* behaviour in terms of the situation. So John might attribute his behaviour to the situation ("I was angry because everything was going wrong"), while Alice might think, "John was hostile because he is an angry person." When referring to ourselves, we typically use verbs that describe our actions and reactions ("I get annoyed when . . ."). Referring to someone else, we more often describe what that person is ("He is nasty") (Fiedler & others, 1991; McGuire & McGuire, 1986; White & Younger, 1988).

THE FUNDAMENTAL ATTRIBUTION ERROR IN EVERYDAY LIFE

If we know the checkout cashier is taught to say, "Thank you and have a nice day," do we nevertheless automatically conclude that the cashier is a friendly, grateful person? We certainly know how to discount behaviour that we attribute to ulterior motives (Fein & others, 1990). Yet consider what happened when students talked with a supposed clinical psychology graduate student who acted either warm and friendly or aloof and critical. Researchers David Napolitan and George Goethals (1979) told half the students beforehand that her behaviour would be spontaneous. They told the other half that for purposes of the experiment, she had been instructed to feign friendly (or unfriendly) behaviour. The effect of the information? None. If she acted friendly, they assumed she was really a friendly person; if she acted unfriendly, they assumed she was an unfriendly person. As when viewing a dummy on the ventriloquist's lap or a movie actor playing a "good-guy" or "bad-guy" role, we find it difficult to escape the illusion that the scripted behaviour reflects an inner disposition. Perhaps this is why Leonard Nimoy, who played Mr. Spock on the original *Star Trek*, entitled his book *I Am Not Spock*.

The discounting of social constraints was further revealed in a thought-provoking experiment by Lee Ross and his collaborators (Ross & others, 1977). The experiment recreated Ross's firsthand experience of moving from graduate student to professor. His doctoral oral exam had proved a humbling experience as his apparently brilliant professors quizzed him on topics they specialized in. Six months later, *Dr.* Ross was himself an examiner, now able to ask penetrating questions on *his* favourite topics. Ross's hapless student later confessed to feeling exactly as Ross had a half-year before—dissatisfied with his ignorance and impressed with the apparent brilliance of the examiners.

In the experiment, with Teresa Amabile and Julia Steinmetz, Ross set up a simulated quiz game. He randomly assigned some Stanford University students to play the role of questioner, some to play the role of contestant, and others to observe. The researchers invited the questioners to make up difficult questions that would demonstrate their wealth of knowledge. Any one of us can imagine such questions using one's own domain of competence: "Where is Bainbridge Island?" "How did Mary, Queen of Scots, die?" "Which has the longer coastline, Europe or Africa?" If even these few questions have you feeling a little uninformed, then you will appreciate the results of this experiment.*

* Bainbridge Island is across Puget Sound from Seattle. Mary, Queen of Scots, was beheaded while in the custody of her cousin, Queen Elizabeth I. Although the African continent is more than double the area of Europe, Europe's coastline is longer. (It is more convoluted, with lots of harbours and inlets, a geographical fact that contributed to its role in the history of maritime trade.)

Everyone had to know that the questioner would have the advantage. Yet, both contestants and observers (but not the questioners) came to the erroneous conclusion that the questioners *really were* more knowledgeable than the contestants (Figure 6-2). Follow-up research shows that these misimpressions are hardly a reflection of low social intelligence. If anything, intelligent and socially competent people are *more* likely to make the attribution error (Block & Funder, 1986).

In real life, those with social power usually initiate and control conversations, which often leads underlings to overestimate their knowledge and intelligence. Medical doctors, for example, are often presumed to be experts on all sorts of questions unrelated to medicine. Similarly, students often overestimate the brilliance of their teachers. (As in the experiment, teachers are questioners on subjects of their special expertise.) When some of these students later become teachers, they are usually amazed to discover that teachers are not so brilliant after all.

To illustrate the fundamental attribution error, most of us need look no further than our own experiences. Determined to make some new friends, Bev plasters a smile on her face and anxiously plunges into a party. Everyone else seems quite relaxed and happy as they laugh and talk with one another. Bev wonders to herself, "Why is everyone always so at ease in groups like this while I'm feeling shy and tense?" Actually, everyone else is feeling nervous, too, and making the same

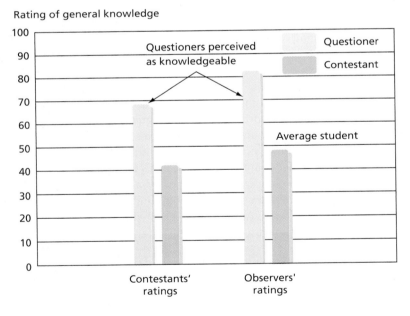

FIGURE 6-2
Both contestants and observers of a simulated quiz game assumed that a person who had been randomly assigned the role of questioner was actually far more knowledgeable than the contestant. Actually, the assigned roles of questioner and contestant simply made the questioner seem more knowledgeable. The failure to appreciate this illustrates the fundamental attribution error.

Data from Ross & others, 1977.

attribution error in assuming that Bev and the others *are* as they *appear*—confidently convivial.

Attributions of responsibility are at the heart of many judicial decisions (Fincham & Jaspars, 1980). For example, in the early 1990s the Scarborough rapist terrorized the area around Toronto with a series of rapes and murders. When it was revealed that Paul Bernardo was the rapist, and his wife Karla Homolka had participated in the kidnapping, rape, and murder of teenage girls (including her own sister), the Canadian public were horrified. Karla Homolka quickly made a deal with the prosecuting attorneys arguing that she was a victim of the situation and that her husband had beaten her and forced her to play a small part in the rapes and murders. Her plea bargain gave her a 12-year sentence for the crimes. Shortly thereafter videotaped evidence was turned over to the police that showed

she was a much more willing participant than she claimed. Clearly, the prosecutors exhibited a fundamental attribution error in deciding the cause of the crimes was her husband's evil inclinations, thus attributing the crimes to Paul Bernardo, rather than to her, while ignoring the possibility of the role of having a willing accomplice in Homolka (a situational factor) as a factor in the crimes. (However, it raises the interesting question of why prosecutors were so willing to accept situational reasons as an excuse for *her* behaviour.) Ironically, now that Homolka has been released from prison (while her former husband remains incarcerated as a "dangerous offender"), the public has called the prosecutor's office incompetent for having failed to make the right decision—another example of the fundamental attribution error. Visit the Online Learning Centre to do Activity 6.2, an analysis of defence lawyer behaviour in the Bernardo case.

Karla Homolka after her release from prison in 2005. Can you identify other high-profile legal cases where the fundamental attribution error has come into play?

OLC
Activity 6.2

WHY DO WE MAKE THE ATTRIBUTION ERROR?

So far we have seen a bias in the way we explain other people's behaviour: We often ignore powerful situational determinants. Why do we tend to underestimate the situational determinants of others' behaviour but not of our own?

Perspective and Situational Awareness

Differing Perspectives

Attribution theorists point out that our perspective differs when we observe others than when we act (Jones, 1976; Jones & Nisbett, 1971), often referred to as the *actor–observer bias*. When we act, the environment commands our attention. When we watch another person act, that person occupies the centre of our attention and the situation becomes relatively invisible. To use the perceptual analogy of figure and ground, the person is the figure that stands out from the surrounding environmental ground. So the person seems to cause whatever happens. If this theory is true, what might we expect if the perspectives were reversed? What if we could see ourselves as others see us and if we saw the world through their eyes? Shouldn't this eliminate or reverse the typical attribution error?

See if you can predict the result of a clever experiment conducted by Michael Storms (1973). Picture yourself as a subject in Storms's experiment. You are seated facing another student with whom you are to talk for a few minutes. Beside you is a TV camera that shares your view of the other student. Facing you from alongside the other student are an observer and another TV camera. Afterward, both you and the observer judge whether your behaviour was caused more by your personal characteristics or by the situation.

Question: Which of you—subject or observer—will attribute the least importance to the situation? Storms found it was the observer (another demonstration of the fundamental attribution tendency). What if we reverse points of view by having you and the observer each watch the videotape recorded from the other's perspective? (You now view yourself, while the observer views what you saw.) This reverses the attributions: The observer now attributes your behaviour mostly to the situation you faced, while you now attribute it to your person. *Remembering* an experience from an observer's perspective—by "seeing" oneself from the outside—has the same effect (Frank & Gilovich, 1989). For another example of this, remember the attributions you made about your own and a friend's performance on exams. Most people focus on the situation to explain their own poor performance and personal attributes to explain another's performance.

In another experiment, people viewed a videotape of a suspect confessing during a police interview. If they viewed the confession through a camera focused on the suspect, they perceived the confession as genuine. If they viewed it through a camera focused on the detective, they perceived it as more coerced (Lassiter & Irvine, 1986). In courtrooms, most confession videotapes focus on the confessor. As we might expect, note Daniel Lassiter and Kimberly Dudley (1991), such tapes yield a nearly 100-percent conviction rate when played by prosecutors. Perhaps a more impartial videotape would show both interrogator and suspect.

Perspectives Change with Time

As the once-visible person recedes in their memory, observers often give more and more credit to the situation. Immediately after hearing someone argue an assigned position, people assume that's how the person really felt. A week later they are much more ready to credit the situational constraints (Burger, 1991). The day after a U.S. presidential election, Jerry Burger and Julie Pavelich (1994) asked voters why the election turned out as it did. Most attributed the outcome to the candidates' personal traits and positions (the winner from the incumbent party was likeable). When they asked other voters the same question a year later, only a third attributed the verdict to the candidates. More people now credited circumstances, such as the country's good mood and the robust economy.

Circumstances can also shift our perspective on ourselves. Seeing ourselves on television redirects our attention to ourselves. Seeing ourselves in a mirror, hearing our tape-recorded voices, having our pictures taken, or filling out biographical questionnaires similarly focus our attention inward, making us *self*-conscious instead of *situation*-conscious. Looking back on ill-fated relationships that once seemed like the unsinkable *Titanic*, people can see the icebergs (Berscheid, 1999). All these experiments point to a reason for the attribution error: *We find causes where we look for them.*

To see this in your own experience, consider: Would you say your social psychology instructor is a quiet or a talkative person? Our guess is you inferred that he or she is fairly outgoing. But consider the situation further: Your attention focuses on your instructor while he or she behaves in a public context that demands speaking. The instructor also observes his or her own behaviour in many different situations—in the classroom, in meetings, at home. "Me talkative?" your instructor might say. "Well, it all depends on the situation. When I'm in class or with good friends, I'm rather outgoing. But at conventions and in unfamiliar situations I feel and act rather shy." Because we are acutely aware of how our behaviour varies with the situation, we see ourselves as more variable than other people (Baxter & Goldberg, 1987; Kammer, 1982; Sande & others, 1988). "Nigel is uptight, Fiona is relaxed. With me it varies."

The less opportunity we have to observe people's behaviour in contexts, the more we attribute to their personalities. Thomas Gilovich (1987) explored this by showing people a videotape of someone and then having them describe the person's actions to other people. The secondhand impressions were more extreme, partly because retellings focus attention on the person rather than on the situation (Baron & others, 1997). Similarly, people's impressions of someone they have heard about from a friend are typically more extreme than their friend's firsthand impressions (Prager & Cutler, 1990).

The Story Behind the Research

Dr. Robert Gifford and his colleagues at the University of Victoria (for example, Gifford & Hine, 1997) wanted to understand the extent to which people's biased cognitions (for example, the fundamental attribution error, the actor–observer bias, false-consensus effect, self-serving biases) occur when we are trying to allocate resources. They argued that although we often engage in the fundamental attribution error when explaining others' behaviours in general, it was not clear if these types of cognitions would also occur when people are competing for scant resources. In order to assess this, they exposed participants to a "Commons Dilemma" whereby two people or groups are vying for the same limited resource (this procedure is discussed in detail in a later module). Participants were seated in groups and told they had to try to maximize their gains (by harvesting as many trees and

fish as they could) while preserving the resource (that is, not depleting the trees and fish to zero).

Next, the researchers asked participants to describe the reasons for their own behaviour (for example, how much of the resource they took for themselves), as well as provide potential explanations for their competitor's behaviour. Gifford and Donald Hine (1997) found that the fundamental attribution error was strong—participants were more likely to attribute their competitor's behaviour to his or her personal characteristics (for example, personality, traits, character, mood) than to the situational aspects (for example, such as the effect of being in the experiment or the competitive nature of the task). Thus the fundamental attribution error can occur in a number of settings. Interestingly, the authors also confirmed a number of other biases (for example, self-serving biases, false-consensus effects) in the same context. |

Cultural Differences

Cultures also influence the attribution error (Ickes, 1980; Watson, 1982). A Western worldview predisposes people to assume that people, not situations, cause events. Internal explanations are more socially approved (Jellison & Green, 1981). "You can do it!" we are assured by the pop psychology of positive-thinking Western culture.

The assumption here is that, with the right disposition and attitude, anyone can surmount almost any problem: You get what you deserve and deserve what you get. Thus, we often explain bad behaviour by labelling a person "sick," "lazy," or "sadistic." As children grow up in Western culture, they learn to explain behaviour in terms of the other's personal characteristics (Rholes & others, 1990; Ross, 1981). As a first-grader, one of David Myers's sons brought home an example. He unscrambled the words, "gate the sleeve caught Tom on his," into "The gate caught Tom on his sleeve." His teacher, applying the Western cultural assumptions of the curriculum materials, marked this wrong. The "right" answer located the cause within Tom: "Tom caught his sleeve on the gate."

The fundamental attribution error occurs across all cultures studied (Krull & others, 1999). Yet, people in Eastern Asian cultures are somewhat more sensitive to the importance of situations. Thus, they are less inclined to assume that others' behaviour corresponds to their traits (Choi & others, 1999; Farwell & Weiner, 2000; Masuda & Kitayama, 2004).

Some languages promote external attributions. Instead of "I was late," Spanish idiom allows one to say, "The clock caused me to be late." In collectivist cultures, people less often perceive others in terms of personal dispositions (Lee & others, 1996; Zebrowitz-McArthur, 1988). They are less likely to spontaneously interpret a behaviour as reflecting an inner trait (Newman, 1993). When told of someone's actions, Hindus in India are less likely than Americans to offer dispositional explanations ("She is kind") and more likely to offer situational explanations ("Her friends were with her") (Miller, 1984).

HOW FUNDAMENTAL IS THE FUNDAMENTAL ATTRIBUTION ERROR?

Like most provocative ideas, the presumption that we're all prone to a fundamental attribution error has its critics. Granted, say some, there is an attribution *bias*. But in any given instance, this may or may not produce an "error," just as parents who are biased to believe their child does not use drugs may or may not be correct (Harvey & others, 1981). We can be biased to believe what is true. Moreover, some everyday circumstances, such as being in church or on a job interview, are like the experiments we have been considering: They involve clear constraints. Actors realize the constraints more than observers—hence, the attribution error. But in other settings—in one's room, at a park—people exhibit their individuality. In such settings, people may see their own behaviour as *less* constrained than do observers (Monson & Snyder, 1977; Quattrone, 1982; Robins & others, 1996). So it's an overstatement to say that at all times and in all settings observers underestimate situational influences. For this

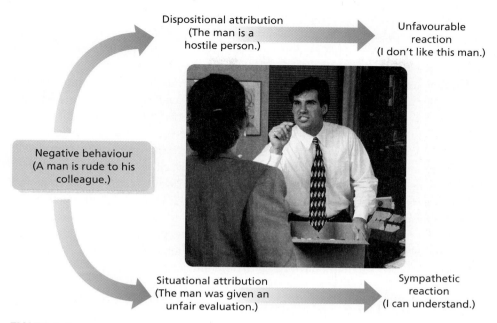

Dispositional attribution
(The man is a
hostile person.)

Unfavourable
reaction
(I don't like this man.)

Negative behaviour
(A man is rude to his
colleague.)

Situational attribution
(The man was given an
unfair evaluation.)

Sympathetic
reaction
(I can understand.)

FIGURE 6-3

Attributions and reactions. How we explain someone's negative behaviour determines how we feel about it.

reason, many social psychologists follow Edward Jones in referring to the fundamental attribution error—seeing behaviour as corresponding to an inner disposition—as the *correspondence bias*.

Nevertheless, experiments reveal that the bias occurs even when we are aware of the situational forces—when we know that an assigned debate position is not a good basis for inferring someone's real attitudes (Croxton & Miller, 1987; Croxton & Morrow, 1984; Reeder & others, 1989) or that the questioners' role in the quiz game gives the questioners an advantage (Johnson & others, 1984). It is sobering to think that we can know about a social process that distorts our thinking and still be susceptible to it. Perhaps that's because it takes more mental effort to assess social effects on people's behaviour than it does merely to attribute it to their dispositions (Gilbert & others, 1988, 1992; Webster, 1993). It's as if the busy person thinks, "This isn't a very good basis for making a judgment, but it's easy and all I've got time to look at."

The attribution error is, however, *fundamental* because it colours our explanations in basic and important ways. Researchers in Britain, India, Australia, and the United States have found that people's attributions predict their attitudes toward the poor and unemployed (Furnham, 1982; Pandey & others, 1982; Skitka, 1999; Wagstaff, 1983; Zucker & Weiner, 1993). Those who attribute poverty and unemployment to personal dispositions ("They're just lazy and undeserving") tend to adopt political positions unsympathetic to such people (Figure 6-3). Their views differ from those who make external attributions ("If you or I were to live with the same overcrowding, poor education, and discrimination, would we be any better off?"). French investigators Jean-Leon Beauvois and

Nicole Dubois (1988) report that "relatively privileged" middle-class people are more likely than less-advantaged people to assume that people's behaviours have internal explanations. (Those who have made it tend to assume that you get what you deserve.)

Can we benefit from being aware of the attribution error? As faculty members, the authors of this textbook are frequently called upon to participate in the hiring of new faculty members at our respective institutions. David Myers once assisted with some interviews for a faculty position. One candidate was interviewed by six of us at once; each of us had the opportunity to ask two or three questions. David came away thinking, "What a stiff, awkward person he is." He met the second candidate privately over coffee, and they immediately discovered they had a close, mutual friend. As they talked, he became increasingly impressed by what a "warm, engaging, stimulating person she is." Only later did he remember the fundamental attribution error and reassess his analysis. He had attributed his stiffness and her warmth to their dispositions; in fact, he later realized, such behaviour resulted partly from the difference in their interview situations. Had he viewed these interactions through their eyes instead of his own, he might have come to different conclusions.

CONCEPT TO REMEMBER

Fundamental attribution error   p. 48

Please visit the *Exploring Social Psychology* Online Learning Centre at **www.mcgrawhill.ca/college/myers** to participate in module activities, view module videos, access research and study tools, and test your knowledge with interactive quizzes, exercises, and scenarios.

7

Heuristics and Errors in Reasoning

What good fortune for those in power that people do not think.

ADOLF HITLER

Defaced posters of the Conservative and Liberal party leaders in the 2006 federal election. How might supporters of the Conservatives, Liberals, NDP, and Bloc Québécois react differently to seeing the graffiti on these campaign signs?

What species better deserves the name *Homo sapiens*—wise humans? Our cognitive powers outstrip the smartest computers in recognizing patterns, handling language, and processing abstract information. Our information processing is also wonderfully efficient. With such precious little time to process so much information, we specialize in mental shortcuts. Scientists marvel at the speed and ease with which we form impressions, judgments, and explanations. In many situations, our snap generalizations—"That's dangerous!"—are adaptive. They promote our survival.

But our adaptive efficiency has a trade-off: snap generalizations sometimes err. Our helpful strategies for simplifying complex information can lead us astray. To enhance our own powers of critical thinking, let's consider five reasons for unreason—common ways in which people form or sustain false beliefs:

1. Our preconceptions control our interpretations.
2. We ignore base-rate information.
3. We are more swayed by memorable events than by facts.
4. We misperceive correlation and control.
5. Our beliefs can generate their own confirmation.

OUR PRECONCEPTIONS CONTROL OUR INTERPRETATIONS

A significant fact about the human mind is that our preconceptions guide how we perceive and interpret information. We construe the world through theory-tinted glasses. Your attitude toward the Prime Minister is largely determined by whether you support the Conservatives, the Liberals, the NDP, or the Bloc Québécois. People will grant that preconceptions influence social judgments, yet fail to realize how great the effect is. Consider recent experiments. Some examine how *prejudg-*ments affect the way people perceive and interpret information. Others plant a judgment in people's minds *after* they have been given information to study how after-the-fact ideas bias recall. The overarching point: *We respond not to reality as it is but to reality as we construe it.*

An experiment by Robert Vallone, Lee Ross, and Mark Lepper (1985) reveals just how powerful preconceptions can be. They showed pro-Israeli and pro-Arab students six network news segments describing the 1982 killing of civilian refugees at two camps in Lebanon. As Figure 7-1 illustrates, each group perceived the networks as hostile to its side. The phenomenon is commonplace: Political candidates and their supporters nearly always view the news media as unsympathetic to their cause. Sports fans perceive referees as partial to the other side—for example, after the 2002 Olympic women's hockey final in Salt Lake City, where the Canadian team was assessed many more penalties than the U.S. team, fans in Canada (an author of this textbook included) were outraged by the "bias" shown by the referees. Indeed, people continued to feel slighted for years. At the 2006 Olympic women's hockey final in Turin, commentators were still referring to the "unfair" penalty calling in the 2002 game. Consistent with this, people in conflict

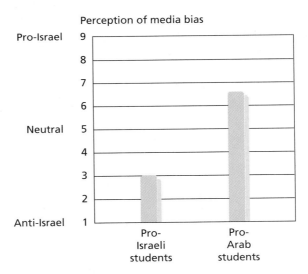

FIGURE 7-1

Pro-Israeli and pro-Arab students who viewed network news descriptions of the "Beirut massacre" believed the coverage was biased against their point of view.

(married couples, labour and management, opposing racial groups) see impartial mediators as biased against them.

Our shared assumptions about the world can even make contradictory evidence seem supportive. For example, Ross and Lepper assisted Charles Lord (1979) in asking students to evaluate the results of two supposedly new research studies. Half the students favoured capital punishment and half opposed it. One study confirmed and the other disconfirmed the students' beliefs about the deterrent effect of the death penalty. The results: Both proponents and opponents of capital punishment readily accepted evidence that confirmed their belief but were sharply critical of disconfirming evidence. Showing the two sides an *identical* body of mixed evidence had therefore not lessened their disagreement but *increased* it.

Is this why, in politics, religion, and science, ambiguous information often fuels conflict? As mentioned above, how we react to politicians and government policies depends largely on our existing attitudes. Polling has consistently demonstrated that supporters of the Conservative Party have positive attitudes toward Stephen Harper. Conservative supporters also accept the arguments made by the Conservative Party on a number of issues (for example, same-sex marriage legislation; crime and punishment). However, Conservative supporters are likely to counterargue information if it comes from other political parties and it disagrees with their existing attitudes. These effects are not limited by party affiliation—New Democrat, Bloc Québécois, and Liberal supporters will do the same thing. Thus, it is not surprising that research has demonstrated that presidential TV debates in the United States have mostly reinforced pre-debate opinions. By nearly a 10 to 1 margin, those who already favoured one candidate or the other in the 1960, 1976, and 1980 debates perceived their candidate as having won (Kinder & Sears, 1985).

Filmmakers can control people's perceptions of emotion by manipulating the setting in which they see a face. They call this the "Kulechov effect," after a Russian film director who would skillfully guide viewers' inferences by manipulating their assumptions. Kulechov demonstrated the phenomenon by creating three short films that presented the face of an actor with a neutral expression after viewers had first been shown a dead woman, a dish of soup, or a girl playing—making the actor seem sad, thoughtful, or happy. The moral: There is a reality out there, but our minds actively construe it. Other people might construe reality differently and might, therefore, behave differently.

WE IGNORE BASE-RATE INFORMATION

Imagine we tell you about the 100 people that work at JMS Building Supplies. We tell you that 20 of them are in sales, and 80 of them are engineers. Next, we ask you to consider "Rick":

> Rick works at JMS Building Supplies. Rick is a happy-go-lucky guy. He enjoys sports. He drives a nice car. Although he has been divorced, he tries to see his two children as frequently as he can. However, his hectic schedule keeps him busy. His friends would describe him as outgoing, energetic, and the life of the party. *Question:* What are the chances that Rick is one of the salespeople at JMS?

You probably guessed that there is a high likelihood Rick is one of the salespeople, even though there is only a 20-percent chance that this is true (if 80 percent of the employees are engineers, there is an 80-percent chance Rick is an engineer).

Baruch Fischhoff and his colleagues (1984) have demonstrated that people are more likely to judge a person like Rick as a salesperson, regardless of the base rates, because he seems more *representative* of salespeople in general. When we judge someone or something by comparing it to our mental representations it is called using a *representativeness heuristic*. These heuristics, or mental shortcuts, are very useful. Typically, they provide us with easy and simple decision criteria for which to guide our decisions and behaviour. However, sometimes they can lead us astray (as it probably did for you above).

WE ARE MORE SWAYED BY MEMORABLE EVENTS THAN BY FACTS

Consider: Does the letter *k* appear in print more often as the first letter of a word or as the third letter? Do more people live in Cambodia or in Tanzania?

Availability heuristic
An efficient but fallible rule of thumb that judges the likelihood of things in terms of their availability in memory. If instances of something come readily to mind, we presume it to be commonplace.

You probably answered in terms of how readily instances of *k*'s, Cambodians, and Tanzanians come to mind. If examples are readily *available* in our memory—as words beginning with *k* and as Cambodians tend to be—then we presume that such are commonplace. Usually it is, so we are often well served by this cognitive rule of thumb, called the **availability heuristic**. (For the actual answers to these questions, see this chapter's Conclusions.) For example, most marketing surveys ask us how often we take trips or use products. The ease with which instances of these types of actions come to mind is usually an excellent estimate of our behaviour.

But sometimes the rule deludes us. Stuart McKelvie, a professor at Bishop's University in Lennoxville, Quebec, has explored how the availability heuristic can affect our judgments. If people hear a list of famous people of one sex (Mother Teresa, Oprah Winfrey, and Madonna) intermixed with an equal size list of unfamous people of the other sex (Donald Scarr, William Wood, Mel Jasper), the famous names will later be more cognitively available. Most people will therefore recall having heard more (in this instance) women's than men's names (McKelvie, 1995, 1997; Tversky & Kahneman, 1973). Vivid, easy-to-imagine events, such as diseases with easy-to-picture symptoms, may likewise seem more likely to occur than harder-to-picture events (MacLeod & Campbell, 1992; Sherman & others, 1985). Even fictional happenings in novels, television, and movies leave images that later penetrate our judgments (Gerrig & Prentice, 1991).

Our use of the availability heuristic highlights a basic principle of social thinking: People are slow to deduce particular instances from a general truth, but they are remarkably quick to infer general truth from a vivid instance. No wonder that after hearing and reading stories of rapes, robberies, and beatings, 9 out of 10 Canadians overestimate—usually by a considerable margin—the percentage of crimes that involve violence (Doob & Roberts, 1988).

The availability heuristic explains why powerful anecdotes are often more compelling than statistical information and why perceived risk is therefore often badly out of joint with real risks (Allison & others, 1992). Because news footage of airplane crashes is a readily available memory for most of us, we often suppose we are more at risk travelling in commercial airplanes than in cars. Actually, recent figures released on 2004 airline accidents data by the International Civil Aviation Administration demonstrate that it has never been safer to fly. The airline fatality rate for 100 million kilometres travelled was 0.005 (ICAO, 2005). In other words, 1 person dies for every 20 billion kilometres flown. This can be compared to a rate of 1.00 (or one death) per 100 million kilometres travelled in cars (and a frightening 17.5 for motorcycles; ATSB, 2005). Thus, by distance travelled, you are 200 times more likely to die in a car crash than in a plane crash. Even after terrorists crashed four airplanes into U.S. targets on September 11, 2001, Americans were much safer on planes than in cars. Not surprisingly, however, the 9/11 attacks on the World Trade Center and the Pentagon dramatically influenced people's assessments of their risk of being the victim of a terrorist attack. Perhaps as we would expect, although both Canadians and Americans perceive themselves to be at risk, Americans perceive a greater risk of such an attack than Canadians (see Bailis & others, 2005).

The horrific images of September 11 are still cognitively available as influences on our perceptions of the risk of flying (which, even in 2001, was actually far safer than driving).

WE MISPERCEIVE CORRELATION AND CONTROL

Another influence on everyday thinking is our search for order in random events, a tendency that can lead us down all sorts of wrong paths.

Illusory Correlation

It's easy to see a correlation where none exists. When we expect to find significant relationships, we easily associate random events, perceiving an **illusory correlation**. An excellent example of this is the perceived relationship between sugar consumption and hyperactivity in children. Although there is no evidence that sugar causes "bad" behaviour in children, David DiBattista, a professor at Brock University in St. Catharines, Ontario, found that many teachers believe it does. He found that

Illusory correlation
Perception of a relationship where none exists, or perception of a stronger relationship than actually exists.

80 percent of 389 primary school teachers surveyed believed that consuming sugar resulted in behavioural problems in hyperactive children and increased activity levels in children overall. Further, 55 percent of the teachers had counselled parents to reduce their child's sugar intake in order to control activity level. Regardless of the scientific evidence, many teachers continue to believe sugar consumption has an adverse affect on behaviour.

Other experiments confirm that people easily misperceive random events as confirming their beliefs (Crocker, 1981; Jennings & others, 1982; Trolier & Hamilton, 1986). If we believe a correlation exists, we are more likely to notice and recall confirming instances. If we believe that premonitions correlate with events, we notice and remember the joint occurrence of the premonition and the event's later occurrence. We seldom notice or remember all the times unusual events do not coincide with a premonition. If, after we think about a friend, the friend calls us, we notice and remember this coincidence. We don't notice all the times we think of a friend without any ensuing call or receive a call from a friend about whom we've not been thinking.

Illusion of Control

Illusion of control
Perception of uncontrollable events as subject to one's control or as more controllable than they are.

Our tendency to perceive random events as related feeds an **illusion of control**— *the idea that chance events are subject to our influence.* This is what keeps gamblers going and what makes the rest of us do all sorts of unlikely things.

Gambling

Ironically, the illusion of control is important in games of chance. Gambling is a major money-maker in North America. In Canada alone there are currently 87,000 slot machines and video lottery terminals (VLTs), 60 casinos, 250 race tracks, and 25,000 licences for bingo-type games. Provincial government–run gambling revenues in 2003–2004 were $12.7 billion, $6.3 billion of which was profit (Azmier, 2005). A group of Saint Mary's University researchers has found that although family income is a s gnificant predictor of gambling (that is, the more we make the more likely we are to gamble), lower-income households are overrepresented among high-spending gamblers, and they tend to spend a greater percentage of their income on gambling products (for example games and lotteries; Macdonald & Perrier, 2004). Less educated people are also overrepresented among the "big spenders." In addition, the games (and the casinos) themselves are designed to increase spending and time playing the games. Robert Ladouceur and his colleagues at Université Laval (for example, Ladouceur & Sévigny, 2005) have demonstrated that putting a device on a VLT that allows the player to stop the machine actually increases the player's illusion of control, resulting in gamblers playing for a longer time (and thus spending more money).

The Story Behind the Research

It is within the context of the illusion of control that Dr. Michael Wohl, now a faculty member at Carleton University in Ottawa, began his research into the role of luck in gambling. Interestingly, this research began when Dr. Wohl visited a casino while he was a graduate student at the University of Alberta. While watching a game of craps, he noticed that many of the players performed certain rituals before they threw the dice (for example, blowing on the dice or shaking them a certain way), and he wondered why. He discussed this question with Dr. Mike Enzle, his research supervisor, and they developed a series of studies to examine the illusion of control and how people's personal perception of "luck" can influence their gambling (see Wohl & Enzle, 2002). They found that, indeed, some people perceive themselves as personally lucky and try to use whatever luck they believe themselves to possess to maximize gambling-related outcomes.

Expanding on these initial results, Wohl and Enzle (2003) assessed whether situational factors could promote perceptions of personal luck, and whether such self-perceptions would influence betting behaviour. Participants were seated in front of a "slot machine" that was rigged to provide certain outcomes. Each player started with 5 tokens that were worth 20 cents each. Players would be able to remit their tokens for cash at the end of the experiment, thus they were motivated to maximize their winnings. The researchers manipulated people's success on the slot machine by creating a situation where participants either just missed a big win ($14), or just missed a big loss (bankruptcy). Although people in both conditions won an equal amount of money ($2), the people who avoided bankruptcy felt luckier, and they were more likely to continue to play the game (ultimately losing more money) than people who had missed a big win. Ultimately, in a real casino, slot machines are among the worst games because of the high loss-to-win ratio (craps and roulette offer the best chances of winning, approximately 49 percent). Players who continue to play will ultimately end up with less money. ∎

Regression Toward the Average

Amos Tversky and Daniel Kahneman (1974) noted another way by which an illusion of control can arise: We fail to recognize the statistical phenomenon of **regression toward the average**. Because an individual's exam scores fluctuate partly by chance, most students who get extremely high scores on an exam will get lower scores on the next exam. Because their first score is at the ceiling, their second score is more likely to fall back ("regress") toward their own average than to push the ceiling even higher. (This is why a student who does consistently good work, even if never the best, will sometimes end a course at the top of the class.) Conversely, the lowest-scoring students on the first exam are likely to improve. If those who scored lowest go for tutoring after the first exam, the tutors are likely to feel effective when the student improves, even if the tutoring had no effect.

Regression toward the average The statistical tendency for extreme scores or extreme behaviour to return toward one's average.

Indeed, when things reach a low point, we will try anything, and whatever we try—going to a psychotherapist, starting a new diet and exercise plan, reading a self-help book—is more likely to be followed by improvement than by further deterioration. Events are not likely to continue at an unusually good or bad extreme. (When we're extremely high or low, we tend to fall back toward our normal average.)

OUR BELIEFS CAN GENERATE THEIR OWN CONFIRMATION

Self-fulfilling prophecy
The tendency for one's expectations to evoke behaviour in others that confirms the expectations.

There's one additional reason why our intuitive beliefs resist reality: They sometimes lead us to act in ways that produce their apparent confirmation. Our beliefs about other people can therefore become **self-fulfilling prophecies**.

In his well-known studies of "experimenter bias," Robert Rosenthal (1985) found that research subjects sometimes live up to what is expected of them. In one study, experimenters asked subjects to judge the success of people in various photographs. The experimenters read the same instructions to all their subjects and showed them the same photos. Nevertheless, experimenters led to expect high ratings obtained higher ratings than did those who expected their subjects to see the photographed people as failures. Even more startling—and controversial—are reports that teachers' beliefs about their students similarly serve as self-fulfilling prophecies.

Do Teacher Expectations Affect Student Performance?

Teachers do have higher expectations for some students than for others. Perhaps you have detected this after having a brother or sister precede you in school, after receiving a label such as "gifted" or "learning disabled," or after being tracked with "high-ability" or "average-ability" students. Perhaps conversation in the teachers' lounge sent your reputation ahead of you. Or perhaps your new teacher scrutinized your school file or discovered your family's social status. Do such teacher expectations affect student performance? Before you read on, visit the Online Learning Centre to complete Activity 7.1 on why teachers' expectations may influence student performance.

OLC
Activity 7.1

By Rosenthal's own count, in only 39 percent of the 448 published experiments do expectations significantly affect performance (Rosenthal, 1991). Low expectations do not doom a capable child, nor do high expectations magically transform a slow learner into a valedictorian. Human nature is not so pliable. High expectations do seem to influence low achievers, for whom a teacher's positive attitude may be a hope-giving breath of fresh air (Madon & others, 1997). How are expectations transmitted? Rosenthal and other investigators report that teachers look, smile, and nod more at "high-potential students." Teachers also may teach more to their "gifted" students, set higher goals for them, call on them more, and give them more time to answer (Cooper, 1983; Harris & Rosenthal, 1985, 1986; Jussim, 1986).

Do Students' Expectations Affect Teachers?

Reading the experiments on teacher expectations makes us wonder about the effect of *students'* expectations upon their teachers. You no doubt begin many of your courses having heard "Professor Brown is interesting" and "Professor Jones is a bore."

A research team led by David Jamieson (1987) experimented with four Ontario high school classes taught by a newly transferred teacher. During individual interviews, they told students in two of the classes that both other students and the research team rated the teacher very highly. Compared to the control classes, the students given positive expectations paid better attention during class. At the end of the teaching unit, they also got better grades and rated the teacher as clearer in her teaching. The attitudes that a class has toward its teacher are as important, it seems, as the teacher's attitude toward the students.

Do We Get What We Expect from Others?

So the expectations of experimenters and teachers, though usually reasonably accurate assessments, occasionally act as self-fulfilling prophecies. How general is this effect? Do we get from others what we expect of them? Studies show that self-fulfilling prophecies also operate in work settings (with managers who have high or low expectations), in courtrooms (as judges instruct juries), and in simulated police contexts (as interrogators with guilty or innocent expectations interrogate and pressure suspects) (Kassin & others, 2003; Rosenthal, 2003). There are times when negative expectations of someone lead us to be extra nice to that person, which induces them to be nice in return—thus *dis*confirming our expectations. But a more common finding in studies of social interaction is that, yes, we do, to some extent, get what we expect (Olson & others, 1996).

In laboratory games, hostility nearly always begets hostility: People who perceive their opponents as noncooperative will readily induce them to be noncooperative (Kelley & Stahelski, 1970). Self-confirming beliefs abound when there is conflict. Each party's perception of the other as aggressive, resentful, and vindictive induces the other to display these behaviours in self-defence, thus creating a vicious, self-perpetuating circle. Whether I expect my wife to be in a bad mood or in a warm, loving mood may affect how I relate to her, thereby inducing her to confirm my belief.

So do intimate relationships prosper when partners idealize one another? Are positive illusions of the other's virtues self-fulfilling? Or are they more often self-defeating, by creating expectations that can't be met and that ultimately spell doom? Among University of Waterloo dating couples followed by Sandra Murray and her associates (1996, 2000), positive ideals of one's partner were good omens. Idealization helped buffer conflict, bolster satisfaction, and turn self-perceived frogs into princes or princesses. When someone loves and admires us, it helps us become more the person he or she imagines us to be. Among married couples, too, those who worry that their partner doesn't love and accept them interpret slight hurts as rejections, which motivates them to devalue the partner and distance themselves. Those who presume their partner's love and acceptance respond less defensively, and even may be closer to their partner (Murray & others, 2003). Love helps create its presumed reality.

Several experiments conducted by Mark Snyder (1984) at the University of Minnesota show how, once formed, erroneous beliefs about the social world can induce others to confirm those beliefs, a form of self-fulfilling prophecy called **behavioural confirmation**. In a now-classic study, Snyder, Elizabeth Tanke, and Ellen Berscheid (1977) had men students talk on the telephone with women they thought (from having been shown a picture) were either attractive or unattractive. Analysis of just the women's comments during the conversations revealed that the supposedly attractive women spoke more warmly than the supposedly unattractive women. The men's erroneous beliefs had become a self-fulfilling prophecy by leading them to act in a way that influenced the women to fulfill the men's stereotype that beautiful people are desirable people.

> **Behavioural confirmation**
> A type of self-fulfilling prophecy whereby people's social expectations (based more on social beliefs than personal expectation) lead them to act in ways that cause others to confirm the expectations.

Expectations influence children's behaviour, too. After observing the amount of litter in three classrooms, Richard Miller and his colleagues (1975) had the teacher and others repeatedly tell one class that it should be neat and tidy. This persuasion increased the amount of litter placed in wastebaskets from 15 to 45 percent, but only temporarily. Another class, which also had been placing only 15 percent of its litter in wastebaskets, was repeatedly congratulated for being so neat and tidy. After eight days of hearing this, and still two weeks later, these children were fulfilling the expectation by putting more than 80 percent of their litter in wastebaskets. Tell children they are hard-working and kind (rather than lazy and mean), and they may live up to their labels.

These experiments help us understand how social beliefs, such as stereotypes about people with disabilities or about people of a particular race or sex, may be self-confirming. We help construct our own social realities. How others treat us reflects how we and others have treated them.

CONCLUSIONS

We have reviewed some reasons why people sometimes come to believe what may be untrue. We cannot easily dismiss these experiments: Most of their participants were intelligent people, often students at leading universities. Moreover, these predictable distortions and biases occurred even when payment for right answers motivated people to think optimally. As one researcher concluded, the illusions "have a persistent quality not unlike that of perceptual illusions" (Slovic, 1972).

Research in cognitive social psychology thus mirrors the mixed review given humanity in literature, philosophy, and religion. Many research psychologists have spent lifetimes exploring the awesome capacities of the human mind. We are smart enough to have cracked our own genetic code, to have invented talking computers, to have sent people to the moon. Three cheers for human reason.

Well, two cheers—because the mind's premium on efficient judgment makes our intuition more vulnerable to misjudgment than we suspect. With remarkable ease, we form and sustain false beliefs. Led by our preconceptions, overconfident, persuaded by vivid anecdotes, perceiving correlations and control even where none may exist, we construct our social beliefs and then influence others to confirm them. "The naked intellect," observed novelist Madeleine L'Engle, "is an extraordinarily inaccurate instrument."

Answer to Question 1:   The letter *k* appears in print two to three times more often as the third letter. Yet most people judge that *k* appears more often at the beginning of a word. Words beginning with *k* are more readily available to memory, surmise Tversky and Kahneman (1974), and ease of recall—availability—is our heuristic for judging the frequency of events.

Answer to Question 2:   Tanzania's 35 million people greatly outnumber Cambodia's 12 million. Most people, having more vivid images of Cambodians, guess wrong.

CONCEPTS TO REMEMBER

Availability heuristic   p. 60
Illusory correlation   p. 61
Illusion of control   p. 62

Regression toward the average   p. 63
Self-fulfilling prophecy   p. 64
Behavioural confirmation   p. 66

Please visit the *Exploring Social Psychology* Online Learning Centre at **www.mcgrawhill.ca/college/myers** to participate in module activities, view module videos, access research and study tools, and test your knowledge with interactive quizzes, exercises, and scenarios.

Understanding Attitudes and Behaviour

Victims of the Rwandan genocide in a mass grave. Can changing the way people think about one another help to prevent violence and human catastrophe in regions such as Rwanda, South Africa, and Darfur?

Imagine you are in the following situation. You are part of a research study. You are sitting in a researcher's office and he tells you that you have been randomly assigned to be one of the "guards" in an experiment about prison life. What kind of guard would you be? Would you be "tough but fair"? Would you be strict? Would you be sadistic and cruel? How would you behave? How do you think you *should* behave? Philip Zimbardo wanted to know, and that's why he constructed a mock prison in the basement of a Stanford University building. How do you think his participants behaved?

For years, social psychologists have been asking themselves the following question: which comes first, belief or behaviour? Inner attitude or outer action? Character or conduct? What is the relationship between who we *are* (on the inside) and what we *do* (on the outside)?

Opinions on this chicken-and-egg question vary. "The ancestor of every action is a thought," wrote American essayist Ralph Waldo Emerson in 1841. To the contrary, said British Prime Minister Benjamin Disraeli, "Thought is the child of Action." Most people side with Emerson. Underlying our teaching, preaching, and counselling is the assumption that private beliefs determine public behaviour: If we want to alter people's actions, we therefore need to change their hearts and minds.

DO ATTITUDES INFLUENCE BEHAVIOUR?

Attitudes are beliefs and feelings that can influence our reactions. If we *believe* that someone is threatening, we might *feel* dislike and therefore *act* unfriendly. "Change the way people think," said South African civil rights martyr Steve Biko (echoing Emerson), "and things will never be the same."

Believing this, social psychologists during the 1940s and 1950s studied factors that influence attitudes. However, numerous studies showed that attitudes did not always predict behaviour. For example, Stephen Corey (1937) asked his students to report their attitudes toward cheating (which were negative) and then provided the opportunity to cheat in class. He found a correlation of .00 between their attitudes and their cheating behaviour. More damaging to attitude–behaviour researchers was the Wicker (1971) meta-analysis. Allan Wicker found that the overall relationship between attitudes and behaviour was weak to nonexistent. At the time attitudes were among the most studied topics in social psychology—but if attitudes did not predict behaviour, what was the point in studying them?

So, do attitudes predict behaviour? As with many other psychological questions, the answer is … it depends. In response to these studies and others, attitudes researchers devised a three-pronged approach to the problem:

1. *Specificity:* Corey had measured general attitudes toward cheating and then assessed cheating behaviours. General attitudes do not predict specific behaviour well. To predict specific behaviours, one must ask specific questions. For example, James Olson and Mark Zanna (1981) found that attitudes toward jogging predicted jogging behaviour well. Diane Morrison (1989) found that attitudes toward contraceptive use predicted contraceptive use. Interestingly, general attitudes can predict classes of behaviour as well: Russell Weigel and Lee Newman (1976) found that general attitudes toward the environment can predict classes of pro-environmental behaviours.

2. *Mathematical models:* Martin Fishbein and Icek Ajzen (1980) developed the *theory of reasoned action,* and later Ajzen (1990) proposed the *theory of planned behaviour* to explain when attitudes would predict behaviour. As shown in Figures 8-1 and 8-2 on page 70, the models both have attitudes and behaviour in them, but also include a number of factors external to the attitudes themselves (that is, perceived social norms, perceived behavioural control, behavioural intentions). For example, most smokers have negative attitudes toward smoking and want to quit, yet they do not. They feel they do not have control over their behaviour. When combined, these factors have been found to be excellent predictors of behaviour in a variety of domains.

3. *Attitude strength:* A final approach to understanding the sometimes tricky attitude–behaviour relation was to explore the role of attitude strength. Strong attitudes (those we feel passionately about) are persistent over time, resistant to change, and they influence perception and judgment of attitude-relevant information. Most importantly, strong attitudes consistently predict behaviour. Weak attitudes are less likely to do so (see Krosnick & Petty, 1995).

Attitude A belief and feeling that can predispose our response to something or someone.

FIGURE 8–1
Theory of reasoned action.

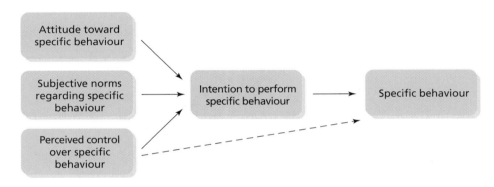

FIGURE 8–2
Theory of planned behaviour.

Thus, early research that explored the attitude–behaviour relationship often looked at attitudes that were poorly assessed, did not take external factors into account, or examined both strong and weak attitudes. So, do attitudes predict behaviour? The answer is, quite clearly, yes—under certain conditions.

DOES BEHAVIOUR INFLUENCE ATTITUDES?

Do we also come to believe in what we've stood up for? Indeed. One of social psychology's big lessons is that we are likely not only to think ourselves into a way of acting but also to act ourselves into a way of thinking. Many streams of evidence confirm that *attitudes follow behaviour*.

Role-Playing

Role A set of norms that define how people in a given social position ought to behave.

The word **role** is borrowed from the theatre and, as in the theatre, refers to actions expected of those who occupy a particular social position. When enacting new social roles, we may at first feel phony. But our unease seldom lasts.

Think of a time when you stepped into some new role—perhaps your first days on a job, or at university, or in a sorority or fraternity. That first week on campus, for example, you may have been supersensitive to your new social situation and tried valiantly to act appropriately and to root out your high school behaviour. At such times we feel self-conscious. We observe our new speech and actions because they aren't natural to us. Then one day we notice something amazing: Our sorority enthusiasm or our pseudo-intellectual talk no longer feels forced. The role has begun to fit as comfortably as our old jeans and T-shirt.

As mentioned in this chapter's introduction, in one study college men volunteered to spend time in a simulated prison constructed in Stanford's psychology department by Philip Zimbardo (1971; Haney & Zimbardo, 1998). Zimbardo was wondering whether prison brutality is a product of evil prisoners and malicious guards or whether the institutional roles of guard and prisoner would embitter and harden even compassionate people. Do the people make the place violent? Or does the place make the people violent?

So, by a flip of a coin, Zimbardo designated some students as guards. He gave them uniforms, billy clubs, and whistles and instructed them to enforce the rules. The other half, the prisoners, were locked in cells and made to wear humiliating outfits. After a jovial first day of "playing" their roles, the guards and prisoners, and even the experimenters, got caught up in the situation. The guards began to disparage the prisoners, and some devised cruel and degrading routines. The prisoners broke down, rebelled, or became apathetic. There developed, reported Zimbardo (1972), a "growing confusion between reality and illusion, between role-playing and self-identity. . . . This prison which we had created . . . was absorbing us as creatures of its own reality." Observing the emerging social pathology, Zimbardo was forced to call off the planned two-week simulation after only six days.

The take-home lesson: What is unreal (an artificial role) can evolve into what is real. Take on a new role—as sorority member, teacher, soldier, or salesperson—and it may shape your attitudes.

OLC
Activity 8.1
Video 8.1

Saying Becomes Believing

People induced to support something about which they have real doubts will often feel bad about their deceit. Just think about the last time a friend asked to you to lie for him or her. Did you do it? Did you feel bad about it? Interestingly, when people lie, they begin to believe what they are saying—*provided* they weren't bribed or coerced into doing so. When there is no compelling external explanation for one's words, saying becomes believing (Klaas, 1978).

Tory Higgins and his colleagues (Higgins & McCann, 1984; Higgins & Rholes, 1978) illustrated how saying becomes believing. They had university students read a personality description of someone and then summarize it for someone else, who was believed either to like or dislike this person. The students wrote a more positive description when the recipient liked the person. Having said positive things, they also then liked the person more themselves. Asked to recall what they had read, they remembered the description as more positive than it was. In short, it seems that we are prone to adjust our messages to our listeners, and, having done so, to believe the altered message.

The Foot-in-the-Door Phenomenon

Foot-in-the-door phenomenon The tendency for people who have first agreed to a small request to comply later with a larger request.

Most of us can recall times when, after agreeing to help out with a project or an organization, we ended up more involved than we ever intended, vowing that in the future we would say no to such requests. How does this happen? Experiments suggest that if you want people to do a big favour for you, an effective strategy is this: Get them to do a small favour first. In the best-known demonstration of this **foot-in-the-door** principle, researchers posing as drive-safely volunteers asked Californians to permit the installation of huge, poorly lettered "Drive Carefully" signs in their front yards. Only 17 percent consented. Others were first approached with a small request: Would they display 3-inch "Be a safe driver" window signs? Nearly all readily agreed. When approached two weeks later to allow the large, ugly signs in their front yards, 76 percent consented (Freedman & Fraser, 1966). One project helper who went from house to house later recalled that, not knowing who had been previously visited, "I was simply stunned at how easy it was to convince some people and how impossible to convince others" (Ornstein, 1991).

The Story Behind the Research

Dr. Lee Fabrigar, a faculty member at Queen's University, has been very interested in persuasion research since he began his psychological education at Miami University of Ohio. Shortly after he began his post at Queen's, he was approached by a student who wanted to develop more effective ways of obtaining donations, as she was responsible for soliciting contributions from Queen's University alumni over the phone. When he began to look into the literature on compliance tactics, he quickly realized that the theory explaining why the effects occurred was incomplete.

Specifically, Dr. Fabrigar noticed that the explanation for why the foot-in-the-door effect occurred was because the initial request changed people's self-perception and activated commitment and consistency principles (see Fabrigar & others, 2002). However, the evidence for this mechanism was lacking. Dr. Fabrigar suspected that this could be because although self-perception was likely involved it probably had to do specifically with self-perception relevant to the behaviour at hand (see our discussion of specificity in attitudes earlier in this module). To test this idea he constructed a study on alcohol awareness. After coming into the lab, participants were told that the researchers were interested in learning about students' views on alcohol consumption. Half of the participants were asked if they would be willing to sign a petition asking the University to start an alcohol awareness program (the small initial request). All of the participants were then asked about their general self-perceptions, as well as their self-perceptions about the target issue of alcohol awareness. Next, all of the participants were asked if they would be interested in signing up for a series of one-hour workshops on alcohol awareness being held on campus (the large request). As expected, those students who had initially agreed to sign the petition were much more likely to sign up for the workshops. Further analyses demonstrated that this effect could be explained by participants' specific perceptions about their own attitudes toward university programs promoting responsible drinking, but not by their general perceptions of how helpful people saw themselves as being. Thus this research provides some solid evidence for the mechanisms underlying the foot-in-the-door effect. ❙

Other researchers have confirmed the foot-in-the-door phenomenon with altruistic behaviours.

- Patricia Pliner and her collaborators (1974) found 46 percent of Toronto suburbanites willing to give to the Cancer Society when approached directly. Others, asked a day ahead to wear a lapel pin publicizing the drive (which all agreed to do), were nearly twice as likely to donate.

- Anthony Greenwald and his co-researchers (1987) approached a sample of registered voters the day before the 1984 U.S. presidential election and asked them a small question: "Do you expect that you will vote or not?" All said yes. Compared to other voters not asked their intentions, they were 41 percent more likely to vote.

- Angela Lipsitz and others (1989) report that ending blood-drive reminder calls with, "We'll count on seeing you then, OK? [pause for response]" increased the show-up rate from 62 to 81 percent.

Note that in these experiments the initial compliance—signing a petition, wearing a lapel pin, stating one's intention—was voluntary. We will see again and again that when people commit themselves to public behaviours *and* perceive these acts to be their own doing, they come to believe more strongly in what they have done.

Social psychologist Robert Cialdini is a self-described "patsy." "For as long as I can recall, I've been an easy mark for the pitches of peddlers, fund-raisers, and operators of one sort or another." To better understand why one person says yes to another, he spent three years as a trainee in various sales, fund-raising, and advertising organizations, discovering how they exploit "the weapons of influence." He also put these weapons to the test in simple experiments. In one, Cialdini and his collaborators (1978) explored a variation of the foot-in-the-door phenomenon by experimenting with the **low-ball technique**, a tactic used by some car dealers. Some salespeople are extremely well versed in the use of these tactics. For example, Steven Smith likes to shop for cars (although he has only ever purchased one) and has experienced how automobile dealers use these tactics. For example, when he helped his sister-in-law buy a new car, the salesman prepared the bill of sale, which the sister-in-law signed. When he returned, an additional $375 had been added to the cost for "tire fees" and "processing" (a clear example of the low-ball technique). His sister-in-law still purchased the car. When he shopped for a vehicle for himself, a saleswoman gave him a car to drive home for the night (an example of employing the commitment and consistency principle—"I am already taking the car home, I must want it"). Have you ever fallen prey to one of these tactics? Go to the Online Learning Centre and complete Activity 8.2 to find out.

Marketing researchers and salespeople have found that these principles work even when we are aware of a profit motive (Cialdini, 1988). A harmless initial commitment—returning a card for more information and a gift, agreeing to listen to an investment possibility—often moves us toward a larger commitment. Salespeople sometimes exploit the power of small commitments by trying to bind people to purchase agreements. Many places now have laws that allow customers of door-to-door salespeople

Low-ball technique
A tactic for getting people to agree to something. People who agree to an initial request will often still comply when the requester ups the ante. People who receive only the costly request are less likely to comply with it.

OLC
Activity 8.2

a few days to think over their purchases and cancel. To combat the effect of these laws, many companies have the customer, rather than the salesperson, fill out the agreement. Having written it themselves, people usually live up to their commitment.

The foot-in-the-door phenomenon is well worth learning about. Someone trying to seduce us—financially, politically, or sexually—usually will try to create a momentum of compliance. The practical lesson: Before agreeing to a small request, think about what may follow.

Evil Acts and Attitudes

The attitudes-follow-behaviour principle works with immoral acts as well. Evil sometimes results from gradually escalating commitments. A trifling evil act can make a worse act easier. Evil acts gnaw at the actor's moral sensitivity. To paraphrase La Rochefoucauld's *Maxims* (1665), it is not as difficult to find a person who has never succumbed to a given temptation as to find a person who has succumbed only once.

For example, cruel acts corrode the consciences of those who perform them. Harming an innocent victim—by uttering hurtful comments or delivering electric shocks—typically leads aggressors to disparage their victims, thus helping them justify their behaviour (Berscheid & others, 1968; Davis & Jones, 1960; Glass, 1964). We tend not only to hurt those we dislike but also to dislike those we hurt. In studies establishing this, people would justify an action especially when coaxed into it, not coerced. When we agree to a deed voluntarily, we take more responsibility for it.

The phenomenon appears in wartime. Concentration camp guards would sometimes display good manners to inmates in their first days on the job, but not for long. Soldiers ordered to kill may initially react with revulsion to the point of sickness over their act, but not for long (Waller, 2002). Often they will denigrate their enemies with dehumanizing nicknames. Actions and attitudes feed one another, sometimes to the point of moral numbness. The more one harms another and adjusts one's attitudes, the easier harm-doing becomes. Conscience mutates.

Evil acts shape the self, but so, thankfully, do moral acts. Researchers have tested this by giving children temptations when it seems no one is watching. Consider what happens when children resist the temptation. In a dramatic experiment, Jonathan Freedman (1965) introduced elementary school children to an enticing battery-controlled robot, instructing them not to play with it while he was out of the room. Freedman used a severe threat with half the children and a mild threat with the others. Both were sufficient to deter the children.

Several weeks later a different researcher, with no apparent relation to the earlier events, left each child to play in the same room with the same toys. Of the 18 children who had been given the severe threat, 14 now freely played with the robot; but two-thirds of those who had been given the mild deterrent still resisted playing with it. The mildly deterred children apparently internalized their decisions. This new attitude controlled their subsequent actions. Moral action, especially when chosen rather than coerced, affects moral thinking.

Can Change in Behaviour Change Attitudes?

If moral action feeds moral attitudes, will positive interracial behaviour reduce racial prejudice—much as mandatory seatbelt use has produced more favourable seatbelt attitudes? This was part of social scientists' testimony before the U.S. Supreme Court's 1954 decision to desegregate schools. Their argument ran like this: If we wait for the heart to change—through preaching and teaching—we will wait a long time for racial justice. But if we legislate moral action, we can, under the right conditions, indirectly affect heartfelt attitudes.

This idea runs counter to the presumption that "you can't legislate morality." Yet, attitude change has, in fact, followed desegregation. Consider some correlational findings from this mammoth social experiment:

- Following the Supreme Court decision, the percentage of White Americans favouring integrated schools more than doubled and now includes nearly everyone.

- In the 10 years after the Civil Rights Act of 1964, the percentage of White Americans who described their neighbourhoods, friends, co-workers, or other students as all-White declined by about 20 percent for each of these measures. Interracial behaviour was increasing. During the same period, the percentage of White Americans who said that Blacks should be allowed to live in any neighbourhood increased from 65 percent to 87 percent (*ISR Newsletter,* 1975). Attitudes were changing, too.

- More uniform national standards against discrimination were followed by decreasing differences in racial attitudes among people of differing religions, classes, and geographic regions. As Americans came to act more alike, they came to think more alike (Greeley & Sheatsley, 1971; Taylor & others, 1978).

Considering the objections some people had before same-sex marriage legislation was introduced here in Canada, it is worth considering what people's views will be in 10 years. One Liberal Member of Parliament has been quoted as saying that in 10 years same-sex marriage will not be an issue. Given the information above, although objections may not disappear entirely, attitudes may change dramatically over the next 10 years. In other words, maybe behaviour can change attitudes.

WHY DOES BEHAVIOUR AFFECT ATTITUDES?

Social psychologists agree: Our actions influence our attitudes, sometimes turning foes into friends, captives into collaborators, and doubters into believers. Social psychologists debate: Why?

One idea is that, wanting to make a good impression, people might merely express attitudes that *appear* consistent with their actions. Let's be honest with ourselves. We do care about appearances—why else would we spend so much on clothes, cosmetics, and weight control? To manage the impression we're creating, we might adjust what we say to please rather than offend. To appear consistent we might, at times, feign attitudes that harmonize with our actions.

But this isn't the whole story. Experiments suggest that some genuine attitude change follows our behaviour commitments. Cognitive dissonance theory and self-perception theory offer two explanations.

Cognitive dissonance theory, developed by the late Leon Festinger (1957), proposes that we feel tension ("dissonance") when two simultaneously accessible thoughts or beliefs ("cognitions") are psychologically inconsistent—as when we decide to say or do something we have mixed feelings about. Festinger argued that to reduce this unpleasant arousal, we often adjust our thinking.

Dissonance theory pertains mostly to discrepancies between behaviour and attitudes. We are aware of both. Thus, if we sense some inconsistency, perhaps some hypocrisy, we feel pressure for change. That helps explain why, in a British survey, half of cigarette smokers disagreed with the near-consensus among non-smokers that smoking is "really as dangerous as people say" (Eiser & others, 1979) and why the perception of risk among those who have quit declines after relapsing (Gibbons & others, 1997). Before the 2003 U.S. invasion of Iraq, the main justification provided for such a war was because Saddam Hussein had weapons of mass destruction. Consistent with this, only 38 percent of Americans said that a war would be justified if no weapons of mass destruction were found (Gallup, 2003). Overall, four in five Americans believed that U.S. troops would find such weapons, and a similar percentage supported the war (Duffy, 2003; Newport & others, 2003). However, when no such weapons were found, many Americans experienced dissonance. Consistent with dissonance theory, people's attitudes changed. Now 58 percent felt the war was justified regardless of whether weapons of mass destruction were found, as the purpose of the war was to liberate the Iraqi people and provide stability in the Middle East.

So if we can persuade others to adopt a *new* attitude, their behaviour should change accordingly; that's common sense. Or if we can induce people to behave differently, their attitude should change (that's the self-persuasion effect we have been reviewing). How does cognitive dissonance work? Well, imagine yourself as a subject in Festinger and James Carlsmith's classic (1959) study on the topic. For an hour you perform a series of mind-numbing tasks, such as repeatedly turning wooden knobs. At the end of the hour, the experimenter tells you that he is in a bind. The study he is conducting is about expectations and performance. In order for the experiment to work, he tells you, participants have to believe they are going to be doing a fun task. Unfortunately, the confederate he usually has who would normally brief the next participant can't make the session. Would you be willing to fill in? He agrees to pay you, so you go ahead and lie to the next participant and tell him that it was a very enjoyable and interesting task. Finally, as you are leaving, the secretary asks you to fill out a form, where you are asked how much you really enjoyed the knob-turning task. Festinger and Carlsmith paid participants either $1 or $20 to lie. When do you think you would end up with the more positive attitude toward the experiment?

Steven Smith has performed this thought experiment in a number of classes, and the prediction is always the same—participants paid $20 (a lot of money in 1959) would have the more positive attitudes. Is that what you predicted? Perhaps surprisingly, Festinger and Carlsmith predicted that when participants had insufficient justification

Cognitive dissonance theory Cognitive dissonance is tension that arises when one is simultaneously aware of two inconsistent cognitions, as when we realize that we have, with little justification, acted contrary to our attitudes. Cognitive dissonance theory proposes that we act to reduce such tension, as when we adjust our attitudes to correspond with our actions.

OLC
Activity 8.3

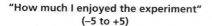

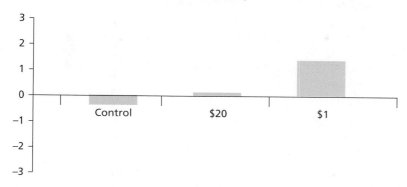

FIGURE 8-3

Dissonance theory predicts that when we have insufficient justification for our behaviour our attitudes will shift accordingly. When given insufficient justification ($1), participants' attitudes toward the tasks became more positive, whereas when people were given sufficient justification ($20) their attitudes remained similar to the control condition.

Data from Festinger & Carlsmith, 1959.

for their behaviour, their attitudes toward the task would become more positive. Much to the amazement of many people, consistent with their predictions, when participants were induced to lie for $1 (an insufficient justification) participants' attitudes toward the task became more positive, whereas when participants were provided with sufficient justification ($20), their attitudes remained similar to the attitudes of those in the control condition (who were not asked to lie; see Figure 8-3).

Cognitive dissonance theory assumes that our need to maintain a consistent and positive self-image motivates us to adopt attitudes that justify our actions. Assuming no such motive, **self-perception theory** says simply that when our attitudes are unclear to us, we observe our behaviours and then infer our attitudes from them. As Anne Frank wrote in her diary, "I can watch myself and my actions just like an outsider." Having done so—having noted how we have treated others—we infer how we felt about them.

Dissonance theory best explains what happens when our actions openly contradict our well-defined attitudes. When, say, we hurt someone we like, we feel tension, which we might reduce by viewing the other as a jerk. Self-perception theory best explains what happens when we are unsure of our attitudes: We infer them by observing ourselves. If we lend our new neighbours, whom we neither like nor dislike, a cup of sugar, our helpful behaviour can lead us to infer that we like them.

In proposing self-perception theory, Daryl Bem (1972) assumed that when we're unsure of our attitudes, we infer them, much as we make inferences about others' attitudes. So it goes as we observe our own behaviour. What we freely say and do can be self-revealing. To paraphrase an old saying, How do I know what I think until I hear what I say or see what I do?

Self-perception theory
The theory that when unsure of our attitudes, we infer them much as would someone observing us—by looking at our behaviour and the circumstances under which it occurs.

The debate over how to explain the attitudes-follow-behaviour effect has inspired hundreds of experiments that reveal the conditions under which dissonance and self-perception processes operate. As often happens in science, each theory provides a partial explanation of a complex reality. If only human nature were simple, one simple theory could describe it. Alas, but thankfully, we are not simple creatures, and that is why there are many miles to go before psychological researchers can sleep.

CONCEPTS TO REMEMBER

Attitude p. 69	**Low-ball technique** p. 73
Role p. 70	**Cognitive dissonance theory** p. 76
Foot-in-the-door phenomenon p. 72	**Self-perception theory** p. 77

Please visit the *Exploring Social Psychology* Online Learning Centre at **www.mcgrawhill.ca/college/myers** to participate in module activities, view module videos, access research and study tools, and test your knowledge with interactive quizzes, exercises, and scenarios.

PART THREE

Social Influence

Social psychologists study not only how we think about one another—our topic in the preceding modules—but also how we influence and relate to one another. In Modules 9 through 16 we therefore probe social psychology's central concern: the powers of social influence.

What are these unseen social forces that push and pull us? How powerful are they? Research on social influence helps illuminate the invisible strings by which our social worlds move us about. This unit reveals these subtle powers, especially the cultural sources of gender attitudes, the forces of social conformity, the routes to persuasion, and the consequences of being with others and participating in groups.

When we see how these influences operate in everyday situations, we can better understand why people feel and act as they do. And we can ourselves become less vulnerable to unwanted manipulation, and more adept at pulling our own strings.

The Role of Gender, Genes, and Culture in Social Behaviour

There are many obvious dimensions of human diversity—height, weight, hair colour, to name just a few. But for people's self-concepts and social relationships, the two dimensions that matter most, and that people first attune to, are race and, especially, sex (Stangor & others, 1992).

Later, we will consider how race and sex affect the way others regard and treat us. For now, let's consider **gender**—the characteristics people associate with male and female. What behaviours *are* universally characteristic and expected of males? Of females? We frequently read about gender differences in popular magazines like *Cosmopolitan* and *Men's Health.* We see these gender differences and stereotypes portrayed on countless TV shows.

"Of the 46 chromosomes in the human genome, 45 are unisex," notes Judith Rich Harris (1998). Females and males are therefore similar in many physical traits, such as age of sitting, teething, and walking. They also are alike in many psychological traits, such as overall vocabulary, creativity, intelligence, self-esteem, and happiness. So shall we conclude that men and women are essentially the same, except for a few anatomical oddities that hardly matter apart from special occasions?

Actually, there are some differences, and it is these differences, not the many similarities, that capture attention and make news. In both science and everyday life, differences excite interest. Compared to the average man, the average woman has 70 percent

There are many dimensions to human diversity. How might gender play a role in how the woman and the man pictured here experience their neighbourhood differently?

Gender In psychology, the characteristics, whether biological or socially influenced, by which people define male and female.

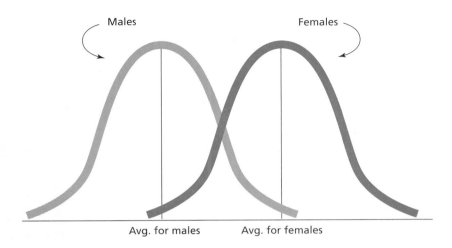

FIGURE 9-1
Hypothetical distribution of "nuturing" behaviour by gender.

more fat, possesses 40 percent less muscle, and is 12 cm shorter. Men enter puberty two years later, are 20 times more likely to have colour-deficient vision, and die five years sooner. Women are twice as vulnerable to anxiety disorders and depression. Women have a slightly better sense of smell. They more easily become re-aroused immediately after orgasm. Men are three times more likely to commit suicide, and five times more likely to become alcoholic. Men also are much more likely to suffer hyperactivity or speech disorders as children, to display antisocial personalities as adults, and to be able to wiggle their ears.

During the 1970s, many scholars worried that studies of such gender differences might reinforce stereotypes. Would gender differences be construed as women's deficits? Although the findings confirm some stereotypes of women—as less aggressive, more nurturant, and more sensitive—those are traits that many feminists celebrate and most people prefer (Swim, 1994). Small wonder, then, that most people rate their feelings regarding "women" as more *favourable* than their feelings regarding "men" (Eagly, 1994; Haddock & Zanna, 1994). One of the authors of this textbook regularly discusses the research on gender differences in his classes. Interestingly, although most students smile and nod as he describes these differences, there are always a handful of people who object and say: "But this is wrong! This doesn't describe me!" This is quite possible. It is important to remember when we talk about gender differences we are talking about average differences—the distribution of traits for males and females definitely overlaps. For example, Figure 9-1 describes a hypothetical distribution of how nurturing men and women are.

GENDER DIFFERENCES

Let's compare men's and women's social connections, dominance, aggressiveness, and sexuality. Having described these differences, we can then consider how the evolutionary and cultural perspectives might explain them. Do gender differences reflect tendencies predisposed by natural selection? Or are they culturally constructed—a reflection of the roles that men and women often play and the situations in which they act?

Independence versus Connectedness

Individual men display outlooks and behaviours that vary from fierce competitiveness to caring nurturance. So do individual women. Without denying that, psychologists Nancy Chodorow (1978, 1989), Jean Baker Miller (1986), and Carol Gilligan (1982) and her colleagues (1990) have contended that women, more than men, give priority to close, intimate relationships.

The difference surfaces in childhood. Boys tend to strive for independence; they define their identities in separation from the caregiver, usually their mother. Girls tend to welcome *inter*dependence; they define their identities through their social connections. Boys' play often involves group activity. Girls' play occurs in smaller groups, with less aggression, more sharing, more imitation of relationships, and more intimate discussion (Lever, 1978). Perhaps this is because, even from a young age, girls are also more talkative than boys and use more affiliative speech, whereas boys use more assertive speech (although these differences are small; Leaper & Smith, 2004).

Adult relationships extend this gender difference. Women describe themselves in more relational terms, experience more relationship-linked emotions, and are more attuned to others' relationships (Gabriel & Gardner, 1999; Tamres & others, 2002). In conversation, men more often focus on tasks and on connections with large groups; women focus on personal relationships (Tannen, 1990). In groups, men talk more to give information; women talk more to share lives, give help, or show support (Dindia & Allen, 1992; Eagly, 1987). Among first-year American college students, 5 in 10 males and 2 in 3 females say it is *very* important to "help others who are in difficulty" (Sax & others, 1999). In an interesting study conducted by Debbie Moskowitz and her colleagues at McGill University in Montreal, women and men, across a 20-day period, monitored their interpersonal behaviour (Moskowitz & others, 1994; Suh & others, 2004). Moskowitz found that women were in general more communal and agreeable than men, but especially when they were interacting with other women. Men interacting with men were more likely to show dominance-oriented behaviours.

In general, report Felicia Pratto and her colleagues (1997), men gravitate disproportionately to jobs that enhance inequalities (prosecuting attorney, corporate advertising); women gravitate to jobs that reduce inequalities (public defender, advertising work for a charity). Studies of 640,000 people's job preferences reveal some tendency for men more than women to value earnings, promotion, challenge, and power, and for women more than men to value good hours, personal relationships, and opportunities to help others (Konrad & others, 2000). Indeed, in most of the North American caregiving professions, such as social worker, teacher, and nurse, women outnumber men. Women also seem more charitable: Among individuals leaving estates worth more than $5 million, 48 percent of women and 35 percent of men make a charitable bequest, and women's colleges have unusually supportive alumni (National Council for Research on Women, 1994).

Women's connections as mothers, daughters, sisters, and grandmothers bind families (Rossi & Rossi, 1990). Women spend more time caring for both preschoolers and aging parents (Eagly & Crowley, 1986). Compared to men, they buy three times as many gifts and greeting cards, write two to four times as many personal letters, and make 10 to 20 percent more long distance calls to friends and family (Putnam, 2000). Asked to provide photos that portray who they are, women include more photos of parents and of themselves with others (Clancy & Dollinger, 1993). For women, especially, a sense of mutual support is crucial to marital satisfaction (Acitelli & Antonucci, 1994).

Empathy The vicarious experience of another's feelings; putting oneself in another's shoes.

When surveyed, women are far more likely to describe themselves as having **empathy**, or being able to feel what another feels—to rejoice with those who rejoice and weep with those who weep. To a lesser extent, the empathy difference extends to laboratory studies. Shown slides or told stories, girls react with more empathy (Hunt, 1990). Given upsetting experiences in the laboratory or in real life, women more than men express empathy for others enduring similar experiences (Batson & others, 1996). Women are more likely to cry or report feeling distressed at another's distress (Eisenberg & Lennon, 1983). This helps explain why, compared to friendships with men, both men and women report friendships with women to be more intimate, enjoyable, and nurturing (Rubin, 1985; Sapadin, 1988). When they want empathy and understanding, someone to whom they can disclose their joys and hurts, both men and women usually turn to women.

One explanation for this male–female empathy difference is that women tend to outperform men at reading others' emotions. In her analysis of 125 studies of men's and women's sensitivity to nonverbal cues, Judith Hall (1984) discerned that women are generally superior at decoding others' emotional messages. For example, shown a two-second silent film clip of the face of an upset woman, women guess more accurately whether she is criticizing someone or discussing her divorce.

Women also are more skilled at *expressing* emotions nonverbally, reports Hall. This is especially so for positive emotion, report Erick Coats and Robert Feldman (1996). They had people talk about times they had been happy, sad, and angry. When shown five-second silent video clips of these reports, observers could much more accurately discern women's than men's emotions when recalling happiness. Men, however, were slightly more successful in conveying anger. Ursula Hess at l'Université du Québec à Montréal conducted some interesting research on why this might be the case. She has found some evidence that the facial cues for certain emotions (for example, anger and happiness) may naturally differ between genders. Indeed, when she used men's and women's faces that had been equated for these cues, the gender stereotype was reversed—women were rated as more angry and men as more happy (Hess, 2004).

SOCIAL DOMINANCE

Imagine two people: One is "adventurous, autocratic, coarse, dominant, forceful, independent, and strong." The other is "affectionate, dependent, dreamy, emotional, submissive, and weak." If the first person sounds more to you like a man and the second like a woman, you are not alone, report John Williams and Deborah Best (1990a, p. 15). The world around, from Asia to Africa and Europe to Australia, people *rate* men as more dominant, driven, and aggressive.

These perceptions and expectations correlate with reality. In essentially every society, men *are* socially dominant. In no known societies do women dominate men (Pratto, 1996). As we will see, gender differences vary greatly by culture, and gender differences are shrinking over time as women assume more managerial and leadership positions. Yet consider:

- Women in 2005 were but 16 percent of the world's legislators and 5 percent of prime ministers and presidents (IPU, 2005). Women are 1 percent of the chief executives of the world's 500 largest corporations (Eagly & others, 2003).

- Men more than women are concerned with social dominance and are more likely to favour conservative political candidates and programs that preserve group inequality (Eagly & others, 2003; Sidanius & Pratto, 1999).

- Men have been half of all jurors but 90 percent of elected jury leaders and most of the leaders of ad hoc laboratory groups (Davis & Gilbert, 1989; Kerr & others, 1982).

As is typical of those in higher-status positions, men still initiate most of the inviting for first dates, do most of the driving, and pick up most of the tabs (Laner & Ventrone, 1998, 2000).

Men's style of communicating undergirds their social power. As leaders in situations where roles aren't rigidly scripted, men tend to be directive; women to be democratic (Eagly & Johnson, 1990). Men tend to excel as directive, task-focused leaders; women as social leaders who build team spirit (Eagly & Karau, 1991; Eagly & others, 1995; Wood & Rhodes, 1991). Men more than women place priority on winning, getting ahead, and dominating others (Sidanius & others, 1994). They also take more risks (Byrnes & others, 1999). When they lead democratically, women leaders are evaluated as favourably as men. When they lead autocratically, women are evaluated less favourably than men (Eagly & others, 1992). People will accept a man's "strong, assertive" leadership more readily than a woman's "pushy, aggressive" leadership.

Men's conversational style reflects their concern for independence; women's for connectedness. Men are more likely to act as powerful people often do—talking assertively, interrupting intrusively, touching with the hand, staring more, smiling less (Anderson & Leaper, 1998; Carli, 1991; Ellyson & others, 1991). Stating the results from a female perspective, women's influence style tends to be more indirect—less interruptive, more sensitive, more polite, less cocky.

So is it right to declare (in the title words of one 1990s bestseller), *Men Are from Mars, Women Are from Venus*? Actually, note Kay Deaux and Marianne LaFrance

(1998), men's and women's conversational styles vary with the social context. Much of the style we attribute to men is typical of people (men *and* women) in positions of status and power. Moreover, individuals vary; some men are characteristically hesitant and deferential, some women direct and assertive. Clearly, it oversimplifies to suggest that women and men are from different emotional planets.

Aggression

Aggression Physical or verbal behaviour intended to hurt. In laboratory experiments, this might mean delivering electric shocks or saying something likely to hurt another's feelings. By this social psychological definition, one can be socially assertive without being aggressive.

By **aggression**, psychologists mean behaviour intended to hurt. Throughout the world, hunting, fighting, and warring are primarily male activities. In surveys, men admit to more aggression than do women. In laboratory experiments, men indeed exhibit more physical aggression; for example, by administering what they believe are hurtful electric shocks (Knight & others, 1996). In Canada, the male-to-female arrest rate is 7 to 1 for murder and 6 to 1 for assault (Statistics Canada, 2000). Across the world, murder rates vary. Yet, in all regions, men are roughly 20 times more likely to murder men than women are to murder women (Daly & Wilson, 1989).

But as with communication styles, the gender difference fluctuates with the context. When there is provocation, the gender gap shrinks (Bettencourt & Miller, 1996). And, within less assaultive forms of aggression—say, slapping a family member, throwing something, or verbally attacking someone—women are no less aggressive than men (Björkqvist, 1994; White & Kowalski, 1994). Indeed, says John Archer (2000) from a statistical digest of 82 studies, women are slightly more likely to commit an aggressive act. But men are more likely to inflict an injury; 62 percent of those injured by a partner are women.

So why are there differences in aggressive behaviour? One explanation that has been suggested is that in many social situations men and women differ in status. If that status is controlled for, the differences may be reduced or eliminated. Michael Conway and his colleagues (for example, Conway & Schaller, 2005) at Concordia University in Montreal have explored this question and found that status could (to some extent) account for these differences.

Sexuality

There is also a gender gap in sexual attitudes and assertiveness. It's true that, in their physiological and subjective responses to sexual stimuli, women and men are "more similar than different" (Griffitt, 1987). Yet, consider:

- "I can imagine myself being comfortable and enjoying 'casual' sex with different partners," agreed 48 percent of men and 12 percent of women in an Australian survey (Bailey & others, 2000).
- The American Council on Education's recent survey of a quarter million first-year college students offers a similar finding. "If two people really like each other, it's all right for them to have sex even if they've known each other for only a very short time," agreed 53 percent of men but only 30 percent of women (Sax & others, 2002).

OLC
Activity 9.1

- In a survey of 3,400 randomly selected 18- to 59-year-old Americans, half as many men (25 percent) as women (48 percent) cited affection for the partner as a reason for first intercourse. How often do they think about sex? "Every day" or "several times a day," said 19 percent of women and 54 percent of men (Laumann & others, 1994).

- Lily Tsui and Elena Nicoladis (2004) from the University of Alberta interviewed Canadian university students about their first intercourse experience. Although women typically rated the experience as more painful and less physically satisfying than men did, they did not differ in terms of how emotionally satisfying they found the experience.

The gender difference in sexual attitudes carries over to behaviour. "With few exceptions anywhere in the world," report cross-cultural psychologist Marshall Segall and his colleagues (1990, p. 244), "males are more likely than females to initiate sexual activity." Moreover, among people of both sexual orientations, "men without women have sex more often, with more different partners, than women without men" (Baumeister, 1991, p. 151; Bailey & others, 1994). Compared to lesbians, gay men also report more interest in uncommitted sex, more responsiveness to visual stimuli, and more concern with partner attractiveness (Bailey & others, 1994). "It's not that gay men are oversexed," observes Steven Pinker (1997). "They are simply men whose male desires bounce off other male desires rather than off female desires."

Indeed, observe Roy Baumeister and Kathleen Vohs (2004; Baumeister & others, 2001), men not only fantasize more about sex, have more permissive attitudes, and seek more partners, they also are more quickly aroused, desire sex more often, masturbate more frequently, are less successful at celibacy, refuse sex less often, take more risks, expend more resources to gain sex, and prefer more sexual variety. One survey asked 16,288 people from 52 nations how many sexual partners they desired in the next month. Among those unattached, 29 percent of men and 6 percent of women wanted more than one partner (Schmitt, 2003). These results were nearly identical for both straight and gay people (29 percent of gay men and 6 percent of lesbians desired more than one partner).

Sexual fantasies express the gender difference (Ellis & Symons, 1990). In male-oriented erotica, women are unattached and lust driven. In romance novels, whose primary market is women, a tender male is emotionally consumed by his devoted passion for the heroine. Social scientists aren't the only ones to have noticed. "Women can be fascinated by a four-hour movie with subtitles wherein the entire plot consists of a man and a woman yearning to have, but never actually having a relationship," observes humorist Dave Barry (1995). "Men HATE that. Men can take maybe 45 seconds of yearning, and they want everybody to get naked. Followed by a car chase. A movie called 'Naked People in Car Chases' would do really well among men."

EVOLUTION AND GENDER: DOING WHAT COMES NATURALLY?

"What do you think is the main reason men and women have different personalities, interests, and abilities?" asked the Gallup Organization (1990) in a national survey. "Is it mainly because of the way men and women are raised, or are the differences part of their biological makeup?" Among the 99 percent who answered the question (apparently without questioning its assumptions), nearly equal numbers answered "upbringing" and "biology."

There are, of course, those salient biological sex differences. Men have the muscle mass to hunt game; women can breast-feed. Are biological sex differences limited to such obvious distinctions in reproduction and physique? Or do men's and women's genes, hormones, and brains differ in ways that also contribute to behavioural differences?

Gender and Mating Preferences

Noting the worldwide persistence of gender differences in aggressiveness, dominance, and sexuality, evolutionary psychologist Douglas Kenrick (1987) suggested, as have many others since, that "we cannot change the evolutionary history of our species, and some of the differences between us are undoubtedly a function of that history." Evolutionary psychology predicts no gender differences in all those domains in which the sexes faced similar adaptive challenges (Buss, 1995). Both sexes regulate heat with sweat, have similar taste preferences to nourish their bodies, and grow calluses where the skin meets friction. But evolutionary psychology does predict gender differences in behaviours relevant to dating, mating, and reproduction.

**OLC
Video 9.1**

Consider, for example, the male's greater sexual initiative. The average male produces many trillions of sperm in his lifetime, making sperm cheap compared to eggs. Moreover, while a female brings one fetus to term and then nurses it, a male can spread his genes by fertilizing many females. Thus, say evolutionary psychologists, females invest their reproductive opportunities carefully, by looking for signs of health and resources. Males compete with other males for chances to win the genetic sweepstakes by sending their genes into the future. They seek fertile soil in which to plant their seed; women seek men who will help them tend the garden—resourceful and monogamous dads rather than wandering cads.

Moreover, evolutionary psychology suggests, physically dominant males gained more access to females, which over generations enhanced male aggression and dominance. Whatever genetically influenced traits enabled Montezuma II to become Aztec king were also perpetuated through offspring from some of his 4,000 women (Wright, 1998). If our ancestral mothers benefitted from being able to read their infants' and suitors' emotions, then natural selection may have similarly favoured emotion-detecting ability in females. Underlying all these presumptions is the principle that *nature selects traits that help send one's genes into the future.*

The Story Behind the Research

Dr. Maryanne Fisher, an evolutionary psychologist at Saint Mary's University in Halifax, has always been interested in how people compete for romantic partners. Although there has been a great deal of research on how men compete with each other, there has been little on how women compete for partners. One day, while at a conference in Italy, she stopped by an art gallery. As it was her day off, she was dressed rather casually. While she was admiring the paintings a group of well-dressed women walked by her, openly looked at her, and began to snicker. Dr. Fisher thought they were probably ridiculing her clothes, but it occurred to her (tongue planted firmly in cheek) that it could be because they felt threatened by her beauty and were derogating her in order to feel better about themselves and their ability to compete with her for romantic partners.

To test the theory that derogating other women may be one way women compete for partners, she devised a study (see Fisher, 2005). She presented women with pictures of men and women, and asked the participants to rate the pictures on attractiveness. When women were in the most fertile time of their menstrual cycle, they rated the women as less attractive than when they rated the same pictures in a less fertile time of their cycle. Interestingly, their ratings of the male pictures were not similarly affected. Thus, Fisher provided clear evidence that women devalue the attractiveness of other women at the time of the month when (from an evolutionary standpoint) they are most likely to be seeking a mate. I

Little of this process is conscious. No one stops to calculate, "How can I maximize the number of genes I leave to posterity?" Rather, say evolutionary psychologists, our natural yearnings are our genes' way of making more genes.

Evolutionary psychology also predicts that men will strive to offer what women will desire—external resources and physical protection. Male peacocks strut their feathers, and male humans their abs, Audis, and assets. "Male achievement is ultimately a courtship display," says Glenn Wilson (1994). Women, sometimes assisted by cosmetic surgery, strive to offer men the youthful, healthy appearance (connoting fertility) that men desire. Sure enough, note Buss (1994) and Alan Feingold (1992), women's and men's mate preferences confirm these predictions. Consider:

> Studies in 37 cultures, from Australia to Zambia, reveal that men everywhere feel attracted to women whose physical features, such as youthful faces and forms, suggest fertility. Women everywhere feel attracted to men whose wealth, power, and ambition promise resources for protecting and nurturing offspring. Men's greater interest in physical form also makes them the consumers of most of the world's visual pornography. But there are gender similarities, too: Whether residing on an Indonesian island or in urban San Paulo, both women and men desire kindness, love, and mutual attraction.

Reflecting on these findings, Buss (1999) reports feeling somewhat astonished "that men and women across the world differ in their mate preferences in precisely the ways predicted by the evolutionists. Just as our fears of snakes, heights, and spiders provide a window for viewing the survival hazards of our evolutionary ancestors, our mating desires provide a window for viewing the resources our ancestors needed for reproduction. We all carry with us today the desires of our successful forebearers."

THE ROLE OF CULTURE

Culture The enduring behaviours, ideas, attitudes, and traditions shared by a large group of people and transmitted from one generation to the next.

Culture is what's shared by a large group and transmitted across generations—ideas, attitudes, behaviours, and traditions. The diversity of our languages, customs, and expressive behaviours suggests that much of our behaviour is socially programmed, not hardwired. Genes are not fixed blueprints: their expression depends on the environment (Lickliter & Honeycutt, 2003). Thus, the genetic leash is long. As sociologist Ian Robertson (1987) has noted:

> Americans eat oysters but not snails. The French eat snails but not locusts. The Zulus eat locusts but not fish. The Jews eat fish but not pork. The Hindus eat pork but not beef. The Russians eat beef but not snakes. The Chinese eat snakes but not people. The Jalé of New Guinea find people delicious. (p. 67)

If we all lived as homogeneous ethnic groups in separate regions of the world, as some people still do, cultural diversity would be less relevant to our daily living. In Japan, where there are 127 million people, of whom 126 million are Japanese, internal cultural differences are minimal compared with those found in Los Angeles, where the public schools have coped with 82 different languages (Iyer, 1993).

Increasingly, cultural diversity surrounds us. More and more we live in a global village, connected to our fellow villagers by e-mail, jumbo jets, and international trade. Cultural diversity exists within nations, too. The United Kingdom, Canada, the United States, and Australia each offer a national culture, with a prevalent language, national media, national holidays, and a democratic political system. But they also offer distinct regional cultures marked by clustered immigrant populations, various languages, and distinct climates, dialects, and values.

Migration and refugee evacuations are mixing cultures more than ever. "East is East and West is West, and never the twain shall meet," wrote the nineteenth-century British author Rudyard Kipling. But today, East and West, and North and South, meet all the time. Italy is home to many Albanians, Germany to Turks, England to Pakistanis, and the result is both friendship and hate crimes. For North Americans and Australians, too, one's country is more and more a mingling of cultures. One in six Canadians is an immigrant. As we work, play, and live with people from diverse cultural backgrounds, it helps to understand how our cultures influence us and to appreciate important ways in which cultures differ. In a world divided by conflicts, genuine peace requires respect for differences and appreciation for similarities.

To realize the impact of our own culture, we need only confront another one. A German student, accustomed to speaking rarely to "Herr Professor," considers it strange that at our institutions most faculty office doors are open and students stop by freely. An Iranian student on her first visit to a McDonald's restaurant fumbles around in her paper bag looking for the eating utensils until she sees the other customers eating their french fries with, of all things, their hands. In many areas of the globe, your best manners are serious breaches of etiquette. Foreigners visiting Japan often struggle to master the rules of the social game—when to take their shoes off, how to pour the tea, when to give and open gifts, how to act toward someone higher or lower in the social hierarchy.

As etiquette rules illustrate, all cultures have their accepted ideas about appropriate behaviour. We often view these social expectations, or norms, as a negative force that imprisons people in a blind effort to perpetuate tradition. Norms do restrain and control us—so successfully and so subtly that we hardly sense their existence. Like fish in the ocean, each of us is so immersed in our culture that we must leap out of it to understand its influence. "When we see other Dutch people behaving in what foreigners would call a Dutch way," note Dutch psychologists Willem Koomen and Anton Dijker (1997), "we often do not realize that the behavior is typically Dutch."

To those who don't accept them, such norms may seem arbitrary and confining. To most in the Western world, the Muslim woman's veil seems arbitrary and confining, but not to most in Muslim cultures. But just as a play moves smoothly when the actors know their lines, so social behaviour occurs smoothly when people know what to expect. Norms grease the social machinery. In unfamiliar situations, when the norms may be unclear, we monitor others' behaviour and adjust our own accordingly. An individualist visiting a collectivist culture, or vice versa, may at first feel anxious and self-conscious. In familiar situations, our words and acts come effortlessly.

Cultures also vary in their norms for expressiveness and personal space. To someone from a relatively formal northern European culture, a person whose roots are in an expressive Mediterranean culture may seem "warm, charming, inefficient, and time-wasting." To the Mediterranean person, the northern European may seem "efficient, cold, and overconcerned with time" (Triandis, 1981). Latin American business executives who arrive late for a dinner engagement may be mystified by how obsessed their North American counterparts are with punctuality.

Personal space is a sort of portable bubble or buffer zone that we like to maintain between ourselves and others. As the situation changes, the bubble varies in size. With strangers we maintain a fairly large personal space, keeping a distance of a metre or more between us. On uncrowded buses, or in restrooms or libraries, we protect our space and respect others' space. We let friends come closer, often within a metre.

Individuals differ: Some people prefer more personal space than others (Smith, 1981; Sommer, 1969; Stockdale, 1978). Groups differ, too: Adults maintain more distance than children. Men keep more distance from one another than do women. For reasons unknown, cultures near the equator prefer less space and more touching and hugging. Thus the British and Scandinavians prefer more distance than the French and Arabs; North Americans prefer more space than Latin Americans.

Personal space A portable bubble or buffer zone that we like to maintain between ourselves and others.

Culture and Gender

We can see the shaping power of culture in ideas about how men and women should behave—and in the scorn that they endure when violating expectations (Kite, 2001). In countries everywhere, girls spend more time helping with housework and child care, while boys spend more time in unsupervised play (Edwards, 1991). Even in contemporary, dual-career, North American marriages, men do most of the household repairs and women arrange the child care (Bianchi & others, 2000; Biernat & Wortman, 1991). In fact, women do most household work "everywhere," reports the United Nations (1991). And "everywhere, cooking and dishwashing are the least shared household chores." Such behaviour expectations for males and females define **gender roles**.

Gender role A set of behavioural expectations (norms) for males or females.

In an experiment with Princeton University undergraduate women, Mark Zanna and Susan Pack (1975) showed the impact of gender-role expectations. The women answered questionnaires on which they described themselves to a tall, unattached, male senior student they expected to meet. Those led to believe the man's ideal woman was home-oriented and deferential to her husband presented themselves as more traditionally feminine than did women expecting to meet a man who liked strong, ambitious women. Moreover, given a problem-solving test, those expecting to meet the nonsexist man behaved more intelligently: They solved 18 percent more problems than those expecting to meet the man with the traditional views. This adapting of themselves to fit the man's image was much less pronounced if the man was less desirable—a short, already attached freshman. In a companion experiment by Dean Morier and Cara Seroy (1994), men similarly adapted their self-presentations to meet desirable women's gender-role expectations.

But does culture construct gender roles? Or do gender roles merely reflect behaviour naturally appropriate for men and women? The variety of gender roles across cultures and over time shows that culture, indeed, constructs our gender roles.

Is life more satisfying when both spouses work and share child care, or when women stay home and care for the children while the husband provides? When the Pew Global Attitudes (2003) survey posed that question to 38,000 people, majorities in 41 of 44 countries said the more satisfying way of life was when both spouses worked in both domains. But as Figure 9-2 shows, the country-to-country differences were considerable. Egyptians disagreed with the world majority opinion by 2 to 1, whereas Vietnamese concurred by 11 to 1. In industrialized societies, roles vary enormously. Women fill 1 in 10 managerial positions in Japan and Germany and nearly 1 in 2 in Australia and the United States (ILO, 1997; Wallace, 2000). In North America, most doctors and dentists are men; in Russia most doctors are women, as are most dentists in Denmark.

CONCLUSIONS: BIOLOGY *AND* CULTURE

We needn't think of evolution and culture as competitors. Cultural norms subtly but powerfully affect our attitudes and behaviour, but they don't do so independent of biology. Everything social and psychological is ultimately biological. If others' expectations influence us, that is part of our biological programming. Moreover, what our biological heritage initiates, culture may accentuate. If genes and hormones predispose males to be more physically aggressive than females, culture may amplify this difference through norms that expect males to be tough and females to be the kinder, gentler sex.

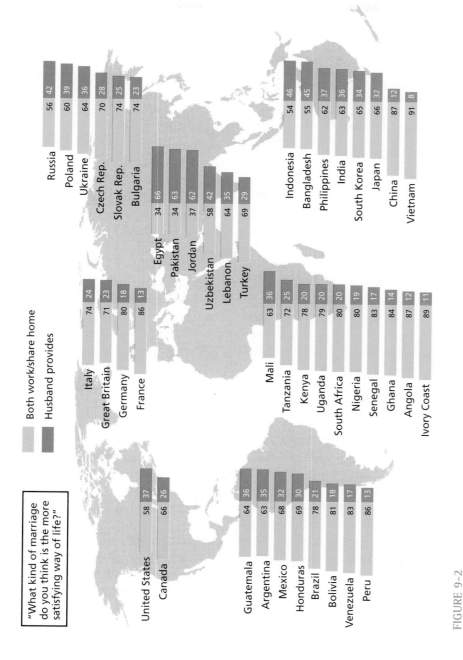

FIGURE 9–2

Approved gender roles vary with culture.

Data from the 2003 Pew Global Attitudes Survey.

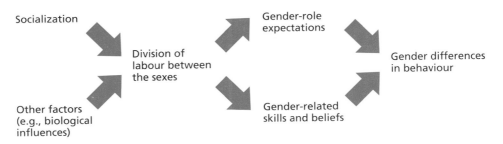

FIGURE 9-3
A social-role theory of gender differences in social behaviour. Various influences, including childhood experiences and factors, bend males and females toward differing roles. It is the expectations and the skills and beliefs associated with these differing roles that affect men's and women's behaviour.

Adapted from Eagly, 1987 and Eagly & Wood, 1991.

Interaction The effect of one factor (such as biology) depends on another factor (such as environment).

OLC
Video 9.2

Biology and culture may also **interact.** Today's genetic science indicates how experience uses genes to change the brain (Quartz & Sejnowski, 2002). Environmental stimuli can turn on genes that produce new brain cell branching receptors. Visual experience turns on genes that develop the brain's visual area. Parental touch turns on genes that help offspring cope with future stressful events. Genes don't just constrain us; they respond adaptively to our experiences.

Biology and experience interact as biological traits influence how the environment reacts. People respond differently to a David Beckham than to a Woody Allen. Men, being 8 percent taller and averaging almost double the proportion of muscle mass, may likewise have different experiences than women. Or consider this: A very strong cultural norm dictates that males should be taller than their female mates. In one study, only 1 in 720 married couples violated this norm (Gillis & Avis, 1980). With hindsight, we can speculate a psychological explanation: Perhaps being taller (and older) helps men perpetuate their social power over women. But we can also speculate evolutionary wisdom that might underlie the cultural norm: If people preferred partners of the same height, tall men and short women would often be without partners. As it is, evolution dictates that men tend to be taller than women, and culture dictates the same for couples. So the height norm might well be a result of biology *and* culture.

In *Sex Differences in Social Behavior*, Alice Eagly (1987, 1997) and Wendy Wood (1991) theorize how biology and culture interact (Figure 9-3). They believe that a variety of factors, including biological influences and childhood socialization, predispose a sexual division of labour. In adult life, the immediate causes of gender differences in social behaviour are the *roles* that reflect this sexual division of labour. Men, because of their strength and speed, tend to be found in roles demanding physical power. Women's capacity for childbearing and nursing inclines them to more nurturant roles.

Each gender then tends to exhibit the behaviours expected of those who fill such roles and to have their skills and beliefs shaped accordingly. Although biology predisposes men to strength tasks and women to infant care, Wood and Eagly (2000) conclude that "the behavior of women and men is sufficiently malleable that individuals of both genders are fully capable of effectively carrying out organizational roles at all levels."

CONCEPTS TO REMEMBER

Gender   p. 81
Empathy   p. 84
Aggression   p. 86
Culture   p. 90

Personal space   p. 91
Gender role   p. 92
Interaction   p. 94

Please visit the *Exploring Social Psychology* Online Learning Centre at **www.mcgrawhill.ca/college/myers** to participate in module activities, view module videos, access research and study tools, and test your knowledge with interactive quizzes, exercises, and scenarios.

Conformity and Obedience

Muslim women gather to pray en masse. How comfortable are you behaving differently from others?

Imagine you are standing alone on the corner of a busy intersection. You want to cross the street. The Don't Walk signal is clearly flashing. There is a lull in the traffic. Do you cross? (Students living in Nova Scotia may be saying "Absolutely not!" while students living in Montreal may be asking "What's a Don't Walk signal?") Now, let's change the situation a little bit. What if you are not alone on the corner? What if another person crosses in front of you? Would that change your behaviour? What if there were a group of people standing on the corner, all waiting for the Walk signal? Chances are you will conform to what the rest of the group is doing, even if this is very different than what you would normally do. It is not easy to be different.

In this module we will address the topics of conformity and obedience. In a previous module we covered compliance—agreeing to simple requests—and how different techniques such as the *foot-in-the-door* and *low-balling* techniques can increase compliance. In the next module we will discuss persuasion—a direct attempt to change people's attitudes and beliefs. Here, however, we deal with conformity and obedience. Conformity is distinct from compliance and persuasion because it involves a change in behaviour that does not involve an attempt at persuasion or a direct request. For example, when you go to class, you sit down like everyone else. Why? How would you feel if in the middle of class you simply stood up? Would you feel awkward? In order to fit in with society and our peer groups, we frequently conform—we look to others to see what we should do. Obedience is engaging in behaviour because we are given a direct order. It does not involve "convincing" or persuading anyone—you are simply told to do something and you do it.

Researchers who study conformity and obedience construct miniature social worlds—laboratory microcultures that simplify and simulate important features of everyday social influence. Consider two noted sets of experiments. Each provides a method for studying conformity and obedience—and some startling findings.

ASCH'S STUDIES OF CONFORMITY

From his boyhood, Solomon Asch (1907–1996) recalls a traditional Jewish seder at Passover:

> I asked my uncle, who was sitting next to me, why the door was being opened. He replied, "The prophet Elijah visits this evening every Jewish home and takes a sip of wine from the cup reserved for him."
>
> I was amazed at this news and repeated, "Does he really come? Does he really take a sip?"
>
> My uncle said, "If you watch very closely, when the door is opened you will see—you watch the cup—you will see that the wine will go down a little."
>
> And that's what happened. My eyes were riveted upon the cup of wine. I was determined to see whether there would be a change. And to me it seemed it was tantalizing, and of course, it was hard to be absolutely sure—that indeed something was happening at the rim of the cup, and the wine did go down a little. (Aron & Aron, 1989, p. 27)

Years later, social psychologist Asch recreated his boyhood experience in his laboratory. Imagine yourself as one of Asch's volunteer subjects. You are seated sixth in a row of seven people. After explaining that you will be taking part in a study of perceptual judgments, the experimenter asks you to say which of the three lines shown in Figure 10-1 on page 98 matches the standard line. You can easily see that it's line 2. So it's no surprise when the five people responding before you all say, "Line 2."

OLC
Activity 10.1

The next comparison proves as easy, and you settle in for what seems a simple test. But the third trial startles you. Although the correct answer seems just as clear-cut, the first person gives a wrong answer. When the second person gives the same wrong answer, you sit up in your chair and stare at the cards. The third person agrees with the first two. Your jaw drops; you start to perspire. "What is this?" you ask yourself. "Are they blind? Or am I?" The fourth and fifth people agree with the others. Then the experimenter looks at you. Now you are experiencing an epistemological dilemma: "How am I to know what is true? Is it what my peers tell me or what my eyes tell me?"

Dozens of college students experienced this conflict during Asch's experiments. Those in a control condition who answered alone were correct more than 99 percent of the time. Asch wondered: If several others (confederates coached by the experimenter) gave identical wrong answers, would people declare what they

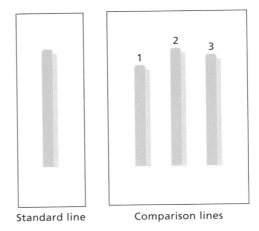

Standard line   Comparison lines

FIGURE 10-1
Sample comparison from Solomon Asch's conformity procedure. The participants judged which of three comparison lines matched the standard.

would otherwise have denied? Although some people never conformed, three-quarters did so at least once. All told, 37 percent of the responses were conforming (or should we say "*trusting* of others"?). Of course, that means 63 percent of the time people did not conform. Despite the independence shown by many of his subjects, Asch's (1955) feelings about the conformity were as clear as the correct answers to his questions: "That reasonably intelligent and well-meaning young people are willing to call white black is a matter of concern. It raises questions about our ways of education and about the values that guide our conduct."

Asch's results are startling because they involved no obvious pressure to conform—there were no rewards for "team play," no punishments for individuality. If people are this compliant in response to such minimal pressure, how much more compliant will they be if they are directly coerced? Could someone force the average American or British Commonwealth citizen to perform cruel acts? One would guess not: Their humane, democratic, individualistic values would make them resist such pressure. Besides, the easy verbal pronouncements of these experiments are a giant step away from actually harming someone; you and I would never yield to coercion to hurt another. Or would we? Social psychologist Stanley Milgram wondered.

MILGRAM'S OBEDIENCE EXPERIMENTS

Milgram's (1965, 1974) experiments testing what happens when the demands of authority clash with the demands of conscience have become social psychology's most famous and controversial experiments. "Perhaps more than any other empirical contributions in the history of social science," notes Lee Ross (1988), "they have become part of our society's shared intellectual legacy—that small body of historical incidents, biblical parables, and classic literature that serious thinkers feel free to draw on when they debate about human nature or contemplate human history."

In one of Asch's conformity experiments (top), subject number 6 experienced uneasiness and conflict after hearing five people before him give a wrong answer.

Here is the scene staged by Milgram, a creative artist who wrote stories and stage plays: Two men come to Yale University's psychology laboratory to participate in a study of learning and memory. A stern experimenter in a grey technician's coat explains that this is a pioneering study of the effect of punishment on learning. The experiment requires one of them to teach a list of word pairs to the other and to punish errors by delivering shocks of increasing intensity. To assign the roles, they draw slips out of a hat. One of the men, a mild-mannered, 47-year-old accountant who is the experimenter's confederate, pretends that his slip says "learner" and is ushered into an adjacent room. The "teacher" (who has come in response to a newspaper ad) takes a mild sample shock and then looks on as the experimenter straps the learner into a chair and attaches an electrode to his wrist.

Teacher and experimenter then return to the main room (see Figure 10-2 on page 100), where the teacher takes his place before a "shock generator" with switches ranging from 15 to 450 volts in 15-volt increments. The switches are labelled "Slight Shock," "Very Strong Shock," "Danger: Severe Shock," and so forth. Under the 435- and 450-volt switches appears "XXX." The experimenter tells the teacher to "move one level higher on the shock generator" each time the learner gives a wrong answer. With each flick of a switch, lights flash, relay switches click, and an electric buzz sounds.

OLC
Video 10.1

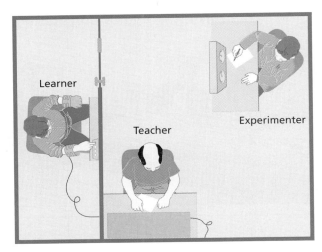

FIGURE 10-2
Milgram's obedience experiment.
Milgram, 1974.

If the participant complies with the experimenter's requests, he hears the learner grunt at 75, 90, and 105 volts. At 120 volts, the learner shouts that the shocks are painful. And at 150 volts, he cries out, "Experimenter, get me out of here! I won't be in the experiment anymore! I refuse to go on!" By 270 volts, his protests have become screams of agony, and he continues to insist to be let out. At 300 and 315 volts, he screams his refusal to answer. After 330 volts, he falls silent. In answer to the "teacher's" inquiries and pleas to end the experiment, the experimenter states that the nonresponses should be treated as wrong answers. To keep the participant going, he uses four verbal prods:

Prod 1: Please continue (*or* Please go on).
Prod 2: The experiment requires that you continue.
Prod 3: It is absolutely essential that you continue.
Prod 4: You have no other choice; you *must* go on.

How far would you go? Milgram described the experiment to 110 psychiatrists, college students, and middle-class adults. People in all three groups guessed that they would disobey by about 135 volts; none expected to go beyond 300 volts. Recognizing that self-estimates might reflect self-serving bias, Milgram asked them how far they thought *other* people would go. Virtually no one expected anyone to proceed to XXX on the shock panel. (The psychiatrists guessed about one in a thousand.)

But when Milgram conducted the experiment with 40 men—a vocational mix of 20- to 50-year-olds—26 of them (65 percent) went to 450 volts. In fact, all who reached 450 volts complied with a command to *continue* the procedure until, after two further trials, the experimenter called a halt.

Having expected a low rate of obedience, and with plans to replicate the experiment in Germany and assess the culture difference, Milgram was disturbed (A. Milgram, 2000). So instead of going to Germany, Milgram next made the learner's

Percentage of subjects still obedient

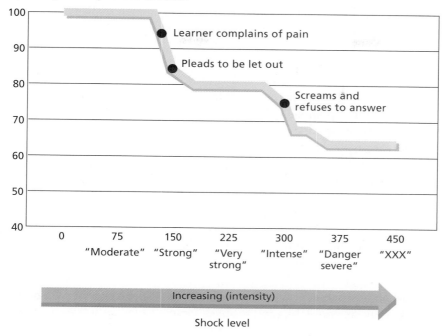

FIGURE 10-3
The Milgram obedience experiment. Percentage of subjects complying despite the learner's cries of protest and failure to respond.

From Milgram, 1965.

protests even more compelling. As the learner was strapped into the chair, the teacher heard him mention his "slight heart condition" and heard the experimenter's reassurance that "although the shocks may be painful, they cause no permanent tissue damage." The learner's anguished protests were to little avail; of 40 new men in this experiment, 25 (63 percent) fully complied with the experimenter's demands (Figure 10-3).

The obedience of his subjects disturbed Milgram. The procedures he used disturbed many social psychologists (Miller, 1986). The "learner" in these experiments actually received no shock (he disengaged himself from the electric chair and turned on a tape recorder that delivered the protests). Nevertheless, some critics said that Milgram did to his participants what they did to their victims: He stressed them against their will. Indeed, many of the "teachers" did experience agony. They sweated, trembled, stuttered, bit their lips, groaned, or even broke into uncontrollable nervous laughter. A *New York Times* reviewer complained that the cruelty inflicted by the experiments "upon their unwitting subjects is surpassed only by the cruelty that they elicit from them" (Marcus, 1974). Critics also argued that the participants' self-concepts might have been altered. One participant's wife told him, "You can call yourself Eichmann" (referring to Nazi death camp administrator Adolf Eichmann). CBS television depicted the results and the controversy in a two-hour dramatization starring

OLC
Activity 10.2

William Shatner, of *Star Trek* fame, as Milgram. So, should Milgram have done his experiments? Visit the Online Learning Centre to complete Activity 10.2, a critical analysis of the Milgram experiments, and come to your own conclusions.

What Breeds Obedience?

Milgram did more than reveal the extent to which people will obey an authority; he also examined the conditions that breed obedience. In further experiments, he varied the social conditions and got compliance ranging from 0 to 93 percent fully obedient. Four factors that determined obedience were the victim's emotional distance, the authority's closeness and legitimacy, whether or not the authority was institutionalized, and the liberating effects of a disobedient fellow subject.

Emotional Distance of the Victim

Milgram's subjects acted with least compassion when the "learners" could not be seen (and could not see them). When the victim was remote and the "teachers" heard no complaints, nearly all obeyed calmly to the end. When the learner was in the same room, "only" 40 percent obeyed to 450 volts. Full compliance dropped to 30 percent when teachers were required to force the learner's hand into contact with a shock plate.

In everyday life, too, it is easiest to abuse someone who is distant or depersonalized. People will be unresponsive even to great tragedies. Executioners often depersonalize those being executed by placing hoods over their heads. The ethics of war allow one to bomb a helpless village from 40,000 feet but not to shoot an equally helpless villager. In combat with an enemy they can see, many soldiers either do not fire or do not aim. Such disobedience is rare among those given orders to kill with the more distant artillery or aircraft weapons (Padgett, 1989).

On the positive side, people act most compassionately toward those who are personalized. That is why appeals for the unborn, for the hungry, or for animal rights are nearly always personalized with a compelling photograph or description. Perhaps even more compelling is an ultrasound picture of one's own developing fetus. When queried by John Lydon and Christine Dunkel-Schetter (1994), expectant women expressed more commitment to their pregnancies if they had seen ultrasound pictures of their fetuses that clearly displayed body parts.

Closeness and Legitimacy of the Authority

The physical presence of the experimenter also affected obedience. When Milgram gave the commands by telephone, full obedience dropped to 21 percent (although many lied and said they were obeying). Other studies confirm that when the one making the request is physically close, compliance increases. Given a light touch on the arm, people are more likely to lend a dime, sign a petition, or sample a new pizza (Kleinke, 1977; Smith & others, 1982; Willis & Hamm, 1980).

The authority, however, must be perceived as legitimate. In another twist on the basic experiment, the experimenter received a rigged telephone call that required him to leave the laboratory. He said that since the equipment recorded data automatically, the "teacher" should just go ahead. After the experimenter left, another person, who had been assigned a clerical role (actually a second confederate), assumed command. The clerk "decided" that the shock should be increased one level for each wrong answer and instructed the teacher accordingly. Now 80 percent of the teachers refused to comply fully. The confederate, feigning disgust at this defiance, sat down in front of the shock generator and tried to take over the teacher's role. At this point, most of the defiant participants protested. Some tried to unplug the generator. One large man lifted the zealous confederate from his chair and threw him across the room. This rebellion against an illegitimate authority contrasted sharply with the deferential politeness usually shown the experimenter.

It also contrasts with the behaviour of hospital nurses who, in one study, were called by an unknown physician and ordered to administer an obvious drug overdose (Hofling & others, 1966). The researchers told one group of nurses and nursing students about the experiment and asked how they would react. Nearly all said they would not have

The Story Behind the Research

Interestingly, people can deviate from authority and go against group consensus, given the right conditions. Lucian Conway and Mark Schaller (2005) conducted a study at the University of British Columbia where they had participants making decisions about which of two computer systems should be adopted by a hypothetical company. Participants were asked to play the role of the vice-president of the company in charge of purchasing decisions. Participants were told that they were the person in the company who would be in charge of making the final decision about which new computer system the company should purchase. Supposedly, the initial recommendation had been made by a committee, but the vice-president had to give final approval.

Next, the researchers manipulated the behaviour of the company's president. Half of the participants discovered that the president of the company had issued an order that a particular system *must* be chosen. All of the committee members had then chosen that system (that is, they made a unanimous decision for one computer system). For the other half of the participants, the president gave no such order but the committee's decision was still unanimous. Next, half of the participants were told

that the president was no longer with the company and half were told he was still with the company. Finally, participants were asked to decide which computer system to adopt for the company.

As the authors predicted, participants who believed the president had given an order about which system to choose no longer believed that the selected computer system was the best system for the company. However, if the president was still with the company, the participants still chose the computer system selected by the committee (that is, the participants obeyed the authority). However, if the president was no longer with the company (that is, they had a new boss) they went against the committee's selection and chose the competing computer system.

What does this tell us about obeying authority? Clearly, there are many situations where disobeying authority is the right thing to do. It is not always obvious how we can encourage disobedience when the situation warrants it. However, this study suggests one relevant factor—the presence or absence of the authority figure. It is easier to disobey when the person giving the orders is no longer around. When do you think you are most likely to disobey an order? I followed the order. One said she would have replied, "I'm sorry, sir, but I am not authorized to give any medication without a written order, especially one so large over the usual dose and one that I'm unfamiliar with. If it were possible, I would be glad to do it, but this is against hospital policy and my own ethical standards." Nevertheless, when 22 other nurses were actually given the phoned-in overdose order, all but one obeyed without delay (until being intercepted on their way to the patient). Although not all nurses are so compliant (Krackow & Blass, 1995; Rank & Jacobson, 1977), these nurses were following a familiar script: Doctor (a legitimate authority) orders; nurse obeys.

Compliance with legitimate authority was also apparent in the strange case of the "rectal ear ache" (Cohen & Davis, 1981, cited by Cialdini, 1988). A doctor ordered ear drops for a patient suffering infection in the right ear. On the prescription, the doctor abbreviated "place in right ear" as "place in R ear." Reading the order, the compliant nurse put the required drops in the compliant patient's rectum.

Institutional Authority

If the prestige of the authority is this important, then perhaps the institutional prestige of Yale University legitimized the Milgram experiment commands. In postexperimental interviews, many participants said that had it not been for Yale's reputation, they would not have obeyed. To see whether this was true, Milgram moved the experiment to Bridgeport, Connecticut. He set himself up in a modest commercial building as the "Research Associates of Bridgeport." When the usual "heart disturbance" experiment was run with the same personnel, what percentage of the men do you suppose fully obeyed? Though reduced, the rate remained remarkably high—48 percent.

The Liberating Effects of Group Influence

These classic experiments give us a negative view of conformity. Can conformity be constructive? Perhaps you can recall a time you felt justifiably angry at an unfair teacher, or with someone's offensive behaviour, but you hesitated to object. Then one or two others objected, and you followed their example. Milgram captured this liberating effect of conformity by placing the teacher with two confederates who were to help conduct the procedure. During the experiment, both confederates defied the experimenter, who then ordered the real subject to continue alone. Did he? No. Ninety percent liberated themselves by conforming to the defiant confederates.

REFLECTIONS ON THE CLASSIC STUDIES

The common response to Milgram's results is to note their counterparts in recent history: the "I was only following orders" defences of Adolf Eichmann in Nazi Germany; of Lieutenant William Calley, the U.S. soldier who in 1968 directed the unprovoked slaughter of hundreds of Vietnamese in the village of My Lai; and of the "ethnic cleansing" occurring more recently in Iraq, Rwanda, Bosnia, and Kosovo.

U.S. soldiers have recently been charged (and some have been court-martialled) for the torture and humiliation of numerous prisoners in Abu Ghraib prison in Iraq. They

An inmate of Camp X-Ray is escorted by two guards while other inmates are seen in their cells in Guantanamo Bay Naval Base, Cuba.

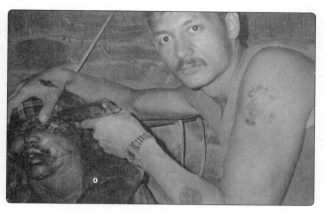

A Canadian soldier posing with 16-year-old Somali Shidane Arone.

have been accused of similar crimes by human rights group Amnesty International at the U.S. detention centre for "unlawful combatants" in Guantanamo Bay, Cuba.

However, this is not solely an American issue. In 1992 Canadian soldiers of the Airborne Regiment (which has since been disbanded) shot and killed two Somalis, one execution-style. A few days later soldiers captured, tortured, and killed a 16-year-old, taking pictures of themselves with the dead Somali boy as souvenirs.

What compels people to commit these horrible acts? Soldiers are trained to obey superiors, and often do, even when carrying out clearly unethical and immoral orders. How is this different from the experiments described here?

The "safe" scientific contexts of the obedience experiments differ from the wartime contexts. Moreover, much of the mockery and brutality of war and genocide goes beyond obedience (Miller, 2004). The obedience experiments differ from the other conformity experiments in the strength of the social pressure: Compliance is explicitly commanded. Without the coercion, people did not act cruelly. Yet, both the Asch and Milgram experiments share certain commonalities. They showed how compliance can take precedence over moral sense. They succeeded in pressuring people to go against their own consciences. They did more than teach an academic lesson; they sensitized us to moral conflicts in our own lives. And they illustrated and affirmed some familiar social psychological principles: the link between behaviour and attitudes, the power of the situation, and the strength of the fundamental attribution error.

Behaviour and Attitudes

In Module 8 we noted that attitudes fail to determine behaviour when external influences override inner convictions. These experiments vividly illustrate this principle. When responding alone, Asch's subjects nearly always gave the correct answer. It was another matter when they stood alone against a group. In the obedience experiments, a powerful social pressure (the experimenter's commands) overcame a weaker one (the remote victim's pleas). Torn between the pleas of the victim and the orders of the experimenter, between the desire to avoid doing harm and the desire to be a good subject, a surprising number of people chose to obey. Level of personal responsibility is clearly an issue here. Milgram created an experiment where participants were only indirectly involved. In conditions where someone else triggered the shock and participants simply recorded events, 95 percent of participants continued in the experiment to the full 450-volt level.

Recall the step-by-step entrapment of the foot-in-the-door phenomenon (Module 8) as we compare this hypothetical experiment to what Milgram's subjects experienced. Their first commitment was mild—15 volts—and it elicited no protest. You, too, would agree to do that much. By the time they delivered 75 volts and heard the learner's first groan, they already had complied five times. On the next trial, the experimenter asked them to commit an act only slightly more extreme than what they had already repeatedly committed. By the time they delivered 330 volts, after 22 acts of compliance, the subjects had reduced some of their dissonance. They were therefore in a different psychological state from that of someone beginning the experiment at that point. As we saw in Module 8, external behaviour and internal disposition can feed one another, sometimes in an escalating spiral. Thus, reported Milgram (1974, p. 10):

> Many subjects harshly devalue the victim *as a consequence* of acting against him. Such comments as, "He was so stupid and stubborn he deserved to get shocked," were common. Once having acted against the victim, these subjects found it necessary to view him as an unworthy individual, whose punishment was made inevitable by his own deficiencies of intellect and character.

During the early 1970s, the military junta then in power in Greece used this "blame-the-victim" process to train torturers (Haritos-Fatouros, 1988, 2002; Staub, 1989, 2003).

As a Holocaust survivor, University of Massachusetts social psychologist Ervin Staub knows too well the forces that can transform citizens into agents of death. From his study of human genocide across the world, Staub (2003) shows where this process can lead. Too often, criticism produces contempt, which licenses cruelty, which, when justified, leads to brutality, then killing, then systematic killing. Evolving attitudes both follow and justify actions. Staub's disturbing conclusion: "Human beings have the capacity to come to experience killing other people as nothing extraordinary" (1989, p. 13).

The Power of the Situation

The most important lesson of Module 9 (that culture is a powerful shaper of lives) and this module's most important lesson—that immediate situational forces are just as powerful—reveal the strength of the social context. For example, new immigrants to Canada frequently find themselves in new social contexts that can affect their conformity behaviour. Consistent with this, Romin Tafarodi and his colleagues at the University of Toronto (Tafarodi & others, 2002) have found that people from ethnic minorities (in this case Chinese-Canadians) trying to assimilate into new cultures may be more likely to conform to the majority group when their physical appearance is made salient. They asked participants to judge artwork while either standing in front of a mirror (that is, making their appearance salient) or without a mirror present. Participants were provided with normative ratings of the paintings supposedly given by the majority group. Participants who were made aware of their appearance judged the artwork in a manner consistent with the norm. Thus culture, and one's position within it, can influence the extent to which one conforms.

So, how comfortable are you with being different from the group? To feel this for yourself, imagine violating some minor norms: standing up in the middle of a class; singing out loud in a restaurant; greeting senior professors by their first names; playing golf in a suit; munching Cracker Jacks at a piano recital; shaving half your head. In trying to break with social constraints, we suddenly realize how strong they are.

Some of Milgram's own students learned this lesson when he and John Sabini (1983) asked for their help in studying the effects of violating a simple social norm: asking riders on the New York City subway system for their seats. To their surprise, 56 percent gave up their seats, even when no justification was given. The students' own reactions to making the request were as interesting: Most found it extremely difficult. Often, the words got stuck in their throats, and they had to withdraw. Once having made their requests and gotten seats, they sometimes justified their norm violation by pretending to be sick. Such is the power of the unspoken rules governing our public behaviour.

The students in a Pennsylvania State University experiment found it similarly difficult to get challenging words out of their mouths. Some students imagined themselves discussing with three others whom to select for survival on a desert island. They were asked to imagine one of the others, a man, injecting three sexist comments, such as, "I think we need more women on the island to keep the men satisfied." How would they react to such sexist remarks? Only 5 percent predicted they would ignore each of the comments or wait to see how others reacted. But when Janet Swim and Lauri Hyers (1999) engaged other students in discussions where such comments were actually made by a male confederate, 55 percent (not 5 percent) said nothing. This, once again, demonstrates the power of normative pressures and how hard it is to predict behaviour, even our own behaviour.

The Fundamental Attribution Error

Why do the results of these classic experiments so often startle people? Is it not because we expect people to act in accord with their dispositions? It doesn't surprise us when a surly person is nasty, but we expect those with pleasant dispositions to be kind. Bad people do bad things; good people do good things.

When you read about Milgram's experiments, what impressions did you form of the subjects? Most people attribute negative qualities to them. When told about one or two of the obedient subjects, people judge them to be aggressive, cold, and unappealing—even after learning that their behaviour was typical (Miller & others, 1973). Cruelty, we presume, is inflicted by the cruel at heart.

Günter Bierbrauer (1979) tried to eliminate this underestimation of social forces (the fundamental attribution error). He had university students observe a vivid reenactment of the experiment or play the role of obedient teacher themselves. They still predicted that their friends would, in a repeat of Milgram's experiment, be only minimally compliant. Bierbrauer concluded that although social scientists accumulate evidence that our behaviour is a product of our social histories and current environments, most people continue to believe that people's inner qualities reveal themselves—that only good people do good and that only evil people do evil.

It is tempting to assume that Eichmann and the Auschwitz death camp commanders were uncivilized monsters. But after a hard day's work, the commanders would relax by listening to Beethoven and Schubert. Like most other Nazis, Eichmann himself was outwardly indistinguishable from common people with ordinary jobs (Arendt, 1963; Zillmer & others, 1995).

Or consider the German police battalion responsible for shooting nearly 40,000 Jews in Poland, many of them women, children, and elderly people who were shot in the backs of their heads. Christopher Browning (1992) portrays the "normality" of these men. Like the many, many others who ravaged Europe's Jewish ghettos, operated the deportation trains, and administered the death camps, they were not Nazis, SS members, or racial fanatics. They were labourers, salesmen, clerks, and artisans—family men who were too old for military service, but who, when directly ordered to kill, were unable to refuse.

Milgram's conclusion also makes it hard to attribute the Holocaust to unique character traits in the German people: "The most fundamental lesson of our study," he noted, is that "ordinary people, simply doing their jobs, and without any particular hostility on their part, can become agents in a terrible destructive process" (Milgram, 1974, p. 6). As Mister Rogers often reminded his preschool television audience, "Good people sometimes do bad things." Perhaps then, we should be more wary of political leaders whose charming dispositions lull us into supposing they would never do evil. Under the sway of evil forces, even nice people sometimes get corrupted, as they construct moral rationalizations for immoral behaviour (Tsang, 2002).

Please visit the *Exploring Social Psychology* Online Learning Centre at **www.mcgrawhill.ca/college/myers** to participate in module activities, view module videos, access research and study tools, and test your knowledge with interactive quizzes, exercises, and scenarios.

Two Routes to Persuasion

A street advertisement for the Apple iPod. How often are you persuaded by product advertising?

Think of the best advertisement you have ever seen. What made it good? Was it artistic? Was it funny? Was it sad? Was it informative? What was the ad for? Did you buy the product? Most people, when asked about their favourite advertisement, probably think about a very poignant ad, or a very funny one. Interestingly, most people cannot remember what the ad was for, and most never bought the product. Regardless, the advertisement was trying to persuade you to buy the product. Persuasion is everywhere—at the heart of politics, marketing, courtship, parenting, negotiation, conflict resolution, and courtroom decision making. Social psychologists therefore seek to understand what leads to effective, long-lasting attitude change. What factors affect persuasion? And how, as persuaders, can we most effectively "educate" others?

Imagine that you are a marketing or advertising executive, one of those responsible for the more than $400 billion spent annually worldwide on advertising (Brown & others, 1999). Or imagine that you want to promote energy conservation, to encourage breast-feeding, or to campaign for a political candidate. What could you do to make yourself and your message persuasive? If you are wary of being manipulated by such appeals, to what tactics should you be alert?

To answer such questions, social psychologists usually study persuasion the way some geologists study erosion—by observing the effects of various factors in brief, controlled experiments. The effects are small and are most potent on weak attitudes that don't touch our values (Johnson & Eagly, 1989; Petty & Krosnick, 1995). Yet they enable us to understand how, given enough time, such factors could produce big effects.

THE TWO ROUTES

OLC
Video 11.1

Central-route persuasion
Persuasion that occurs when interested people focus on the arguments and respond with favourable thoughts.

Peripheral-route persuasion Persuasion that occurs when people are influenced by incidental cues, such as a speaker's attractiveness.

In choosing tactics, you must first decide: Should you focus mostly on building strong *central arguments*? Or should you make your message appealing by associating it with favourable *peripheral cues*, such as sex appeal? Persuasion researchers Richard Petty and John Cacioppo (Cass-ee-OH-poh) (1986; Petty & Wegener, 1999) and Alice Eagly and Shelly Chaiken (1993) report that persuasion is likely to occur by either a central or a peripheral route. When people are motivated and able to think systematically about an issue, they are likely to take the **central route to persuasion**—focusing on the arguments. If those arguments are strong and compelling, persuasion is likely. If the message contains only weak arguments, thoughtful people will notice that the arguments aren't very compelling and will counterargue.

But sometimes the strength of the arguments doesn't matter. Sometimes we're not all that motivated or able to think carefully. If we're distracted, uninvolved, or just plain busy, we might not take the time to think carefully about the message content. Rather than noticing whether the arguments are particularly compelling, we might follow the **peripheral route to persuasion**—focusing on cues that trigger acceptance without much thinking. Billboards and television commercials—media that consumers are able to take in for only brief amounts of time—typically use visual images as peripheral cues. Our opinions regarding food, clothing, TV shows, and a wide range of products are often based more on feelings than on logic. Instead of providing arguments in favour of smoking, cigarette ads associate the product with images of beauty and pleasure. So do soft-drink ads that promote "the joy of cola" or "the real thing" with images of youth, vitality, and happy polar bears. On the other hand, computer ads, which interested, logical consumers might pore over for some time, seldom feature Hollywood stars or great athletes; instead, they offer customers information on competitive features and prices. Matching the type of message to the route that message recipients are likely to follow can greatly increase the likelihood that any attention will be paid to the persuasive message at all (Petty & others, 2000; Shavitt, 1990).

Even people who like to think sometimes form tentative opinions using the peripheral route to persuasion. We all make snap judgments using other rule-of-thumb heuristics: If a speaker is articulate and appealing, has apparently good motives, and has several arguments (or better, if the different arguments come from different sources), we usually take the easy peripheral route and accept the message without much thought (Figure 11-1).

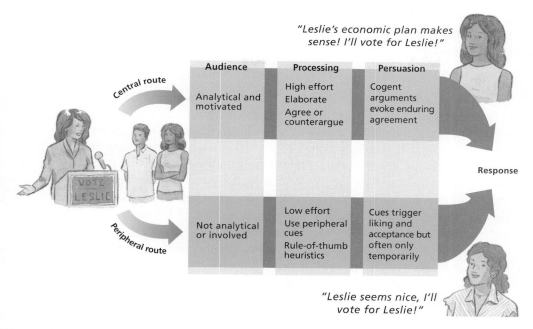

FIGURE 11-1

The central and peripheral routes to persuasion. Computer ads typically take the central route by assuming their audience wants to systematically compare features and prices. Soft-drink ads usually take the peripheral route, by merely associating their product with glamour, pleasure, and good moods. Central route processing more often produces enduring attitude change.

THE ELEMENTS OF PERSUASION

Among the primary ingredients of persuasion explored by social psychologists are these three: (1) the communicator, (2) the message content and how the message is communicated, and (3) the audience. In other words, who says what by what means to whom?

Who Says? The Communicator

Imagine you are talking to a car salesperson, who tells you that the car you are interested in is the most fuel-efficient in its class, has the best handling, and is cheaper than the competition. The salesperson also tells you all her customers have loved the car—no one has complained. Would you believe the salesperson? Would you buy the car? Now, what if you read the same information in *Consumer Reports* magazine? Most people would believe the magazine but not the salesperson. The salesperson clearly has something to gain, whereas the magazine does not.

Social psychologists have found that who is saying something affects how the message gets received. In one experiment, when the Socialist and Liberal leaders in the Dutch parliament argued identical positions using the same words, each was most effective with members of his own party (Wiegman, 1985). It's not just the message that matters, but also who says it. What makes one communicator more persuasive than another?

Credibility

Any of us would find a statement about the costs of smoking more believable if it came from Health Canada rather than a tobacco company. Credible communicators seem both *expert* (confidently knowledgeable) and *trustworthy.* They speak unhesitatingly and without any selfish motive. Some television ads are obviously constructed to make the communicator appear both expert and trustworthy. Drug companies peddle pain relievers using a white-coated speaker who declares confidently that most doctors recommend their ingredient (the ingredient, of course, is aspirin). Given such peripheral cues, people who don't care enough to analyze the evidence might reflexively infer that the product has value.

Credibility Believability. A credible communicator is perceived as both expert and trustworthy.

The effects of source **credibility** often diminish after a month or so. If a credible person's message is persuasive, its impact can fade as soon as the credible source is forgotten or dissociated from the message. On the other hand, the impact of a noncredible person can *increase* over time, if people remember the message better than the reason for discounting it (Cook & Flay, 1978; Gruder & others, 1978; Pratkanis & others, 1988). This delayed persuasion, after people forget the source or its connection with the message, is called the **sleeper effect**.

Sleeper effect A delay in the impact of a message; occurs when we remember the message but forget a reason for discounting it.

Attractiveness

Most people deny that endorsements by star athletes and entertainers affect them. Most people know that stars are seldom knowledgeable about the product they endorse. Besides, we know the intent is to persuade us; we don't just accidentally eavesdrop on Tiger Woods talking about why Buicks are so great, or Britney Spears talking about why drinking Pepsi makes her feel younger. Such ads are based on another characteristic of an effective communicator: attractiveness. We may think we are not influenced by attractiveness or likability, but researchers have found otherwise. Even something as simple as a fleeting conversation is enough to increase our liking for someone and our responsiveness to their influence (Burger & others, 2001). Our liking might open us up to the communicator's arguments (central-route persuasion), or it might trigger positive associations when we see the product later (peripheral-route persuasion).

Attractiveness Having qualities that appeal to an audience. An appealing communicator (often someone similar to the audience) is most persuasive on matters of subjective preference.

Attractiveness varies in several ways. *Physical appeal* is one. Arguments, especially emotional ones, are often more influential when they come from beautiful people (Chaiken, 1979; Dion & Stein, 1978; Pallak & others, 1983). *Similarity* is another. As Module 21 will emphasize, we tend to like people who are like us. We also are influenced by them. As a general rule, people respond better to a message that comes from someone in their "own" group (Van Knippenberg & Wilke, 1992; Wilder, 1990). Salespeople use this similarity-based approach as often as possible. Salespeople act in a friendly manner and try to convince you that they are similar to you—being from the same area, having a sibling who went to your school, or liking the same hobbies as you like.

What Is Said? The Message Content

It matters not only who says something, but also *what* that person says. If you were to help organize an appeal to get people to vote for school taxes or to stop smoking or to give money to world hunger relief, you might wonder how to concoct a recipe for central-route persuasion. Common sense could lead to arguments for both sides of these questions:

- Is a purely logical message most persuasive—or one that arouses emotion?
- Is persuasion based on what mood you are in?
- Do fear-based approaches work?
- Do you need to be aware of the process? In other words, do **subliminal messages** work?

Subliminal messages
Messages presented in such a manner as to be below a person's threshold of conscious awareness.

Reason versus Emotion

Suppose you were campaigning in support of world hunger relief. Would it be best to itemize your arguments and cite an array of impressive statistics? Or would you be more effective presenting an emotional approach—the compelling story of one starving child, for example? Of course, an argument can be both reasonable and emotional. You can marry passion and logic. Still, which is more influential—reason or emotion?

The answer: It depends on the audience. Well-educated or analytical people are more responsive to rational appeals than are less-educated or less-analytical people (Cacioppo & others, 1983, 1996; Hovland & others, 1949). Thoughtful, involved audiences travel the central route; they are most responsive to reasoned arguments. Disinterested audiences travel the peripheral route; they are more affected by how much they like the communicator (Chaiken, 1980; Petty & others, 1981).

The Effect of Good Feelings

Messages also become more persuasive through association with good feelings. Irving Janis and his colleagues (1965; Dabbs & Janis, 1965) found that Yale students were more convinced by persuasive messages if they were allowed to enjoy peanuts and Pepsi while reading them. Similarly, Mark Galizio and Clyde Hendrick (1972) found that Kent State University students were more persuaded by folk-song lyrics accompanied by pleasant guitar music than they were by unaccompanied lyrics. Those who like conducting business over sumptuous lunches with soft background music can celebrate these results.

Good feelings often enhance persuasion—partly by enhancing positive thinking (when people are motivated to think) and partly by linking good feelings with the message (Petty & others, 1993). As noted previously, people in a good mood view the world through rose-coloured glasses. They also make faster, more impulsive decisions; they rely more on peripheral cues (Bodenhausen, 1993; Schwarz & others, 1991). Unhappy people ruminate more before reacting, so they are less easily swayed by weak arguments. Thus, if you can't make a strong case, you might want to put your audience in a good mood and hope they'll feel good about your message without thinking too much about it. This is why many advertisers use humour in their approaches. The idea is this: If I make you laugh, you will associate your good mood with my product and you are more likely to buy it. Indeed, there is research that suggests this can work. For example, Jim Lyttle (2001) at the University of Toronto has shown that speakers who use humour (such as cartoons or self-effacing humour) are more persuasive, presumably because people who use humour are seen as more likeable or credible.

The Story Behind the Research

In marketing circles, there is one study that receives a great deal of attention, even today. In 1957, James Vicary claimed to have increased concession-stand sales at a movie theatre by introducing *subliminal messages* during the movie—messages that were flashed on the screen so quickly people couldn't actually see them. Vicary reported that popcorn sales increased by 50 percent and Coke sales increased by 18 percent after the messages were shown on the screen. Although this study has been accepted, quoted, and marketers have even tried to develop subliminal ads, there is no evidence that subliminal priming actually works. Indeed, Vicary fabricated the whole study in a desperate attempt to save his cash-strapped advertising firm (the ploy worked—even though the study was fake).

Drs. Erin Strahan (now at Wilfrid Laurier University), Steven Spencer, and Mark Zanna at the University of Waterloo decided to find out if subliminal advertising really does work. The idea began after Dr. Zanna had attended a talk in California while on sabbatical. The person giving the talk made a convincing argument that subliminal priming could not affect persuasion. Later, driving through the California mountains on the way to Santa Cruz, Dr. Zanna began thinking about a particular Michelin tire commercial (you might know the one, where the baby is sitting inside the tire and

the announcer says "You've got a lot riding on your tires"). Dr. Zanna wondered if he could increase sales by subliminally priming the emotional images of a crying child before the tire commercial. Thus, he wondered if subliminal priming could be used to create a psychological state that a persuasive communicator could take advantage of.

Once he was back in Waterloo, where Erin Strahan was just beginning her graduate studies, he, Dr. Spencer, and Strahan began to research the issue. In their studies subliminal priming did work, under certain conditions. Specifically, they found that subliminal priming worked when people were already motivated to engage in the behaviour. For example, in a pair of studies (see Strahan & others, 2002, 2005 for details), they found that people who had thirst-related words subliminally flashed in front of them on a screen (e.g., *thirst, dry*) drank more than participants who did not receive the primes, and were more persuaded by an ad for "SuperQuencher" that claimed to be the best thirst-quenching sports drink on the market. However, these differences were apparent only if the participants came into the study thirsty. Thus, this research suggests that subliminal priming works only if one is already predisposed to the behaviour. So, maybe Vicary's study would have worked after all—on the hungry moviegoers, anyway. I

The Effect of Arousing Fear

Messages can also be effective by evoking negative emotions. When trying to convince people to cut down on smoking, brush their teeth more often, get a tetanus shot, or drive carefully, a fear-arousing message can be potent (Muller & Johnson, 1990). The Canadian government is counting on the fact that showing cigarette smokers the horrible things that can happen to people who smoke adds to persuasiveness by requiring cigarette makers to include graphic representations of the hazards of smoking on each new pack of cigarettes (Newman, 2001). But how much fear should you arouse? Should you evoke just a little fear, lest people become so frightened that they tune out your painful message? Or should you try to scare the daylights out of them? Experiments by Howard Leventhal (1970) and his collaborators at the University of Wisconsin and by Ronald Rogers and his collaborators at the University of Alabama (Robberson & Rogers, 1988) show that, often, the more frightened people are the more they respond.

The effectiveness of fear-arousing communications is being applied in ads discouraging smoking, drinking and driving, and risky sexual behaviours. When Claude Levy-Leboyer (1988) found that attitudes toward alcohol and drinking habits among French youth were changed effectively by fear-arousing pictures, the French government incorporated this kind of information into its TV spots. To have one's fears aroused is to become more intensely interested in information about a disease and in ways to prevent it (Das & others, 2003; Ruiter & others, 2001). Fear-arousing communications are also increasing people's detection behaviours, such as getting mammograms, doing breast or testicular self-exams, and checking for signs of skin cancer. Indeed, all indications are that the Health Canada anti-smoking ads depicting diseased lungs and gums may be working. A study conducted by the Canadian Cancer Society in 2002 found that 58 percent of smokers interviewed said the new ads made them think about the health effects of smoking. Thirty-eight percent of smokers who attempted to quit in 2001 said the new warnings were a factor in their motivations to quit. Importantly, 21 percent of smokers who had been tempted to have a cigarette decided not to because of the new warnings. Finally, Statistics Canada reports that overall cigarette smoking rates declined from 24.3 percent of all Canadians in 1994 to 17.8 percent in 2003. The biggest declines have been with teenagers and young adults, suggesting that many people are simply not starting. Overall, anti-smoking campaigns over the decades have clearly had an effect. In 1965, a remarkable 50 percent of Canadians smoked, almost three times more than today.

However, people may engage in denial because, when they aren't told how to avoid the danger, frightening messages can be overwhelming (Leventhal, 1970; Rogers & Mewborn, 1976). Fear-arousing messages are more effective if you lead people not only to fear the severity and likelihood of a threatened event but also to perceive a solution (Devos-Comby & Salovey, 2002; Maddux & Rogers, 1983). Many ads aimed at reducing sexual risks aim both to arouse fear—"AIDS kills"—and to offer a protective strategy: Abstain or wear a condom or save sex for a committed relationship. During the 1980s, fear of AIDS did persuade many men to alter their behaviour. One study of 5,000 gay men found that, as the AIDS crisis mushroomed between 1984 and 1986, the number saying they were celibate or monogamous rose from 14 to 39 percent (Fineberg, 1988). However, more recent data suggest that these trends may be reversing. Some research by Ted Myers at the University of Toronto (Myers & others, 2004) found that the number of gay men who reported having unprotected homosexual sex in 2002 is double that of a decade earlier.

To Whom Is It Said? The Audience

It also matters who *receives* a message. Let's consider two other characteristics of those who receive a message: their age and their thoughtfulness.

How Old Are They?

People tend to have different social and political attitudes depending on their age. Social psychologists give two explanations for the difference. One is a *life-cycle explanation*: Attitudes change (for example, become more conservative) as people grow older. The other is a *generational explanation*: The attitudes older people adopted when they were young persist largely unchanged; because these attitudes are different from those being adopted by young people today, a generation gap develops.

The evidence mostly supports the generational explanation. In surveys and resurveys of groups of younger and older people over several years, the attitudes of older people usually show less change than do those of young people. As David Sears (1979, 1986) puts it, researchers have "almost invariably found generational rather than life cycle effects." However, recent research by Penny Visser and Jon Krosnick (1998) suggests that older adults, near the end of the life cycle, may become more susceptible to attitude change, due to a decline in the strength of their attitudes.

Older adults are not inflexible; most people in their fifties and sixties have more liberal sexual and racial attitudes than they had in their thirties and forties (Glenn, 1980, 1981). Few of us are utterly uninfluenced by changing cultural norms. The teens and early twenties are important formative years (Krosnick & Alwin, 1989), and the attitudes formed then tend to remain stable through middle adulthood. Young people might therefore be advised to choose their social influences—the groups they join, the media they imbibe, the roles they adopt—carefully.

Adolescent and early adult experiences are formative partly because they make deep and lasting impressions. We may therefore expect that today's young adults will include phenomena such as the explosion of e-mail, the Web, and September 11, 2001 as the memorable turning points in world history.

What Are They Thinking?

The crucial aspect of central route persuasion is not the message itself but the responses it evokes in a person's mind. Our minds are not sponges that soak up whatever pours over them. If the message summons favourable thoughts, it persuades us. If it provokes us to think of contrary arguments, we remain unpersuaded.

Forewarned is forearmed—If you care enough to counterargue. What circumstances breed counterargument? One is a warning that someone is going to try to persuade you. If you had to tell your family that you wanted to drop out of school, you would likely anticipate their pleading with you to stay. So you might develop a list of arguments to counter every conceivable argument they might make. Jonathan Freedman and David Sears (1965) demonstrated the difficulty of trying to persuade people under such circumstances. They warned one group of California high schoolers that they were going to hear a talk: "Why Teenagers Should Not Be Allowed to Drive." Those forewarned did not budge in their opinions. Others, not forewarned, did. In courtrooms, too, defence attorneys sometimes forewarn juries about prosecution evidence to come. With mock juries, such "stealing thunder" neutralizes its negative impact (Dolnik & others, 2003).

Sneak attacks on attitudes are especially useful with involved people. Given several minutes' forewarning, involved people will prepare defences (Chen & others, 1992; Petty & Cacioppo, 1977, 1979). When forewarned people regard an issue as trivial, however, they may agree even before receiving the message, to avoid later seeming gullible (Wood & Quinn, 2003).

Distraction disarms counterarguing.   Verbal persuasion is also enhanced by distracting people with something that attracts their attention just enough to inhibit counterarguing (Festinger & Maccoby, 1964; Keating & Brock, 1974; Osterhouse & Brock, 1970). Political ads often use this technique. The words promote the candidate, and the visual images keep us occupied so we don't analyze the words. Distraction is especially effective when the message is simple (Harkins & Petty, 1981; Regan & Cheng, 1973).

Uninvolved audiences use peripheral cues.   Analytical people—those with a high *need for cognition*—enjoy thinking carefully and prefer central routes (Cacioppo & others, 1996). People who like to conserve their mental resources—those with a low need for cognition—are quicker to respond to such peripheral cues as the communicator's attractiveness and the pleasantness of the surroundings. In addition, we also need to be motivated and able to understand the message. Carolyn Hafer and her colleagues (Hafer & others, 1996) at Brock University have demonstrated that when the message is complex, people are less likely to attend to it, and any persuasion that occurs will work through peripheral processes. However, if the message is simple, the strength of the argument is what matters.

But the issue matters, too. All of us actively struggle with issues that involve us while making snap judgments about things that matter little (Johnson & Eagly, 1990). As we mentally elaborate upon an important issue, the strength of the arguments and of our own thoughts determines our attitudes.

This basically simple theory—that *what we think in response to a message is crucial,* especially if we are motivated and able to think about it—helps us understand several findings. For example, we more readily believe trustworthy, expert communicators if we're following the peripheral route. When we trust the source, we think favourable thoughts and are less likely to counterargue. But mistrusting an expert source makes us more likely to follow the central route. Because of our careful thought about the message content, we may end up refuting a weak message (Priester & Petty, 1995).

The theory has also generated many predictions, most of which have been confirmed by Petty, Cacioppo, and others (Axsom & others, 1987; Harkins & Petty, 1987;

Leippe & Elkin, 1987). Many experiments have explored ways to stimulate people's thinking—by using *rhetorical questions*, by presenting *multiple speakers* (for example, having each of three speakers give one argument instead of one speaker giving three), by making people *feel responsible* for evaluating or passing along the message, by using *relaxed postures* rather than standing ones, by *repeating* the message, and by getting people's *undistracted attention*. With each of these techniques, they consistently found that *stimulating thinking makes strong messages more persuasive and* (because of counterarguing) *weak messages less persuasive.*

The theory also has practical implications. Effective communicators care not only about their images and their messages but also about how their audience is likely to react. The best instructors tend to get students to think actively. They ask rhetorical questions, provide intriguing examples, and challenge students with difficult problems. All of these techniques are likely to foster a process that moves information through the central route to persuasion. In classes where the instruction is less engaging, you can provide your own central processing. If you think about the material and elaborate on the arguments, you are likely to do better in the course.

CONCEPTS TO REMEMBER

Central-route persuasion   p. 110
Peripheral-route persuasion   p. 110
Credibility   p. 112

Sleeper effect   p. 112
Attractiveness   p. 112
Subliminal messages   p. 113

Please visit the *Exploring Social Psychology* Online Learning Centre at **www.mcgrawhill.ca/college/myers** to participate in module activities, view module videos, access research and study tools, and test your knowledge with interactive quizzes, exercises, and scenarios.

Understanding Indoctrination Tactics

This 1933 propaganda painting is entitled "Es lebe Deutschland" and commemorates the year Hitler came to power. Can you think of contemporary examples of political public-relations materials that employ the power of persuasion?

Joseph Goebbels, Germany's minister of "popular enlightenment" and propaganda from 1933 to 1945, understood the power of persuasion. Given control of publications, radio programs, motion pictures, and the arts, he undertook to persuade Germans to accept Nazi ideology. Julius Streicher, another member of the Nazi group, published *Der Stürmer*, a weekly anti-Semitic (anti-Jewish) newspaper with a circulation of 500,000 and the only paper read cover to cover by his intimate friend, Adolf Hitler. Streicher also published anti-Semitic children's books and, with Goebbels, spoke at the mass rallies that became part of the Nazi propaganda machine.

How effective were Goebbels, Streicher, and other Nazi propagandists? Did they, as the Allies alleged at Streicher's Nuremberg trial, "inject poison into the minds of millions and millions" (Bytwerk, 1976)? Most Germans were not persuaded to feel raging hatred for the Jews. But many were. Others became sympathetic to anti-Semitic measures. And most of the rest became either sufficiently uncertain or sufficiently intimidated to staff the huge genocidal program, or at least to allow it to happen. Without the complicity of millions of people, there would have been no Holocaust (Goldhagen, 1996).

The powers of persuasion were more recently apparent in what a Pew survey (2003) called the "rift between Americans and Western Europeans" over the Iraq War. Surveys shortly before the war, for example, revealed that Europeans (and Canadians) opposed military action against Iraq by about two to one, while Americans favoured it by the same margin (Burkholder, 2003; Moore, 2003; Pew, 2003). Once the war began, Americans' support for the war rose to more than three to one (Newport & others, 2003). Except for Israel, people surveyed in all other countries were opposed to the attack.

Without taking sides regarding the wisdom of the war—that debate we can leave to history—the huge rift between Americans and their distant cousins in other countries points to persuasion at work. What persuaded Americans to favour the war? What persuaded most people elsewhere to oppose it? (Tell us where you live and we will guess whether you view the United States more as protector or predator.)

In addition to possible rationalization of "my country's" actions, attitudes were also being shaped by persuasive messages that led half of Americans to believe that Saddam Hussein was directly involved in the 9/11 attacks and four in five to believe that weapons of mass destruction would be found (Duffy, 2003; Gallup, 2003; Newport & others, 2003). Sociologist James Davison Hunter (2002) notes that culture-shaping usually occurs top-down, as cultural elites control the dissemination of information and ideas. Thus, Americans and people elsewhere learned about and watched a different war (della Cava, 2003; Friedman, 2003b; Goldsmith, 2003; Krugman, 2003; Tomorrow, 2003). Depending on where you lived, you may have heard and read about

- "America's liberation of Iraq" or "America's invasion of Iraq."
- "Operation Iraqi Freedom" or "The War in Iraq."
- the Iraqi "death squads" or the "Fedayeen" irregulars.
- headlines such as "Tense Standoff Between Troops and Iraqis Erupts in Bloodshed" (ambiguous passive-voice headline of *Los Angeles Times*) or "U.S. Troops Fire on Iraqis; 13 Reported Dead" (active-voice headline of the same incident by Canada's CBC).
- scenes of captured and dead Iraqis or scenes of captured and dead Americans.
- brief clips of "the usual protestors" (Fox News) or features on massive antiwar rallies.

To many Americans, the media of other nations appeared to combine a pervasive anti-American bias with a blindness to the threat posed by Saddam Hussein. To many people elsewhere, the "embedded" American war journalists seemed to feel it their patriotic duty to sell the war. Regardless of where bias lay or whose perspective was better informed, this much seems clear: Depending on where they lived, people were fed (and discussed and believed) somewhat differing information. Persuasion matters.

As mentioned in the previous module, persuasive forces also have been harnessed to promote healthier living. Thanks partly to health promotion campaigns, the Canadian and American cigarette smoking rate has plunged to about 23 percent, barely more than half the rate of 40 years ago. Nonetheless, persuasion tactics can be used among a wide variety of groups.

CULT INDOCTRINATION

On an early-October evening in 1994, firefighters were called to the scene of a chalet fire in Moran Heights, near Montreal. Inside, they found two dead bodies, badly burned. In an adjoining chalet they found three more dead bodies, clearly murdered, including a three-month-old child. Authorities were shocked. However, they quickly realized that these bodies were linked to the Order of the Solar Temple.

The Solar Temple was started by Luc Jouret and Joseph Di Mambro. Jouret, the more charismatic of the two, became the spiritual leader of the group. They believed that they were the reincarnations of the Knights Templar, the protectors of the Holy Grail. Shortly after the fire in Moran Heights, 43 additional victims were found in Switzerland (16 more victims were found in France the following year). The leaders of the Order of the Solar Temple had ordered its members to commit ritualistic suicide (although many members appeared to have been killed before their bodies were burned) as the end of the world was upon them. Members of the Order believed that burning would purify their souls and prepare them for the spiritual transformation they would achieve when they reached the star Sirius. Members of the cult were prominent business people, journalists, and even the mayor of a small town. What would drive these people to kill themselves and others? For additional information about the Solar Temple, visit the Online Learning Centre and complete Activity 12.1.

The question on many minds: What persuades people to leave behind their former beliefs and join these groups? Shall we attribute their apparently strange behaviours to strange personalities? Or do their experiences illustrate the common dynamics of social influence and persuasion?

Bear three things in mind. First, this is hindsight analysis. It uses persuasion principles as categories for explaining, after the fact, a fascinating and sometimes disturbing social phenomenon. Second, explaining *why* people believe something says nothing about the *truth* of their beliefs. That is a logically separate issue. A psychology of religion might tell us *why* a theist believes in God and an atheist disbelieves, but it cannot tell us who is right. Explaining either belief does not explain it away. So if someone tries to discount your beliefs by saying, "You just believe that because . . . ," you might recall Archbishop William Temple's reply to a questioner who challenged: "Well, of course, Archbishop, the point is that you believe what you believe because of the way you were brought up." To which the archbishop replied: "That is as it may be. But the fact remains that you believe I believe what I believe because of the way I was brought up, because of the way you were brought up." Third, we must bear in mind that indoctrination tactics are used by a wide variety of groups, from mainstream religious groups, to biker and other gangs, to corporations, to governments trying to win over the hearts and minds of their citizens. Persuasion tactics are ubiquitous in our social world, and we must be able to recognize them when we encounter them if we are to successfully resist them. Cults provide a useful case study to explore because these groups are often intently studied. Therefore, we will focus here on some of the tactics they use.

Luc Jouret, one of the founders of the Order of the Solar Temple.

OLC
Activity 12.1

Cult (also called new religious movement) A group typically characterized by (1) distinctive rituals and beliefs related to its devotion to a god or a person, (2) isolation from the surrounding "evil" culture, and (3) a charismatic leader. (A sect, by contrast, is a spinoff from a major religion.)

In recent decades, several **cults**—which some social scientists call *new religious movements*—have gained much publicity: Sun Myung Moon's Unification Church, Jim Jones's People's Temple, David Koresh's Branch Davidians, Marshall Applewhite's Heaven's Gate, and the Solar Temple. Typically, the leader of the group is believed to be the new messiah.

In 1978 in Guyana, 914 disciples of Jim Jones, who had followed him there from San Francisco, shocked the world when they died by following his order to down a grape drink laced with tranquilizers, painkillers, and a lethal dose of cyanide.

In 1993, high-school dropout David Koresh used his talent for memorizing Scripture and mesmerizing people to seize control of a faction of a sect called the Branch Davidians. Over time, members were gradually relieved of their bank accounts and possessions. Koresh also persuaded the men to live celibately while he slept with their wives and daughters, and he convinced his 19 "wives" that they should bear his children. Under siege after a shootout that killed six members and four federal agents, Koresh told his followers they would soon die and go with him straight to heaven. In a botched raid attempt, U.S. federal agents rammed the compound with tanks, hoping to inject tear gas, and, by the end of the assault, 86 people were consumed in a fire that engulfed the compound.

Luc Jouret also began to demand the sexual submission of his followers. This type of behaviour is not atypical in cults, and is often considered an early warning sign (by people outside of the group) that the new religion is unhealthy.

Marshall Applewhite was not similarly tempted to command sexual favours. Having been fired from two music teaching jobs for homosexual affairs with students, he sought sexless devotion by castration, as had 7 of the other 17 Heaven's Gate men who died with him (Chua-Eoan, 1997; Gardner, 1997). While in a psychiatric hospital in 1971, Applewhite had linked up with nurse and astrology dabbler Bonnie Lu Nettles, who gave the intense and charismatic Applewhite a cosmological vision of a route to "the next level." Preaching with passion, he persuaded his followers to renounce families, sex, drugs, and personal money with promises of a spaceship voyage to salvation.

How could such things happen? What persuaded these people to give such total allegiance? Shall we make dispositional explanations—by blaming the victims? Shall we dismiss them as gullible kooks or dumb weirdos? Or can familiar principles of conformity, compliance, dissonance, persuasion, and group influence explain their behaviour—putting them on common ground with the rest of us who, in our own ways, are shaped by such forces?

Attitudes Follow Behaviour

Compliance Breeds Acceptance

As we saw in Module 8's discussion of behaviour and belief, people usually internalize commitments made voluntarily, publicly, and repeatedly. Cult leaders seem to know this. New converts soon learn that membership is no trivial matter. They are quickly made active members of the team. Rituals within the cult community, and public canvassing and fundraising, strengthen the initiates' identities as members. As those in social-psychological experiments come to believe in what they bear witness to (Aronson & Mills, 1959; Gerard & Mathewson, 1966), so cult initiates become committed advocates. The greater the personal commitment, the more the need to justify it.

The Foot-in-the-Door Phenomenon

How are we induced to make commitments? Seldom by an abrupt, conscious decision. One does not just decide, "I'm through with mainstream religion. I'm gonna find a cult." Nor do cult recruiters approach people on the street with, "Hi. I'm a Moonie. Care to join us?" Rather, the recruitment strategy exploits the foot-in-the-door principle. As an example of how groups use the foot-in-the-door technique to persuade you, let's consider one man's encounter with a new religious group in Montreal. Craig Silverman (2004) described his first meeting with members of the Raelians, who believe that their leader, Rael, was visited by aliens and is the "brother of Jesus" sent to save us by telling us our true origins and preparing us for the visit from our creators. In the Raelian philosophy, life on Earth was created by extraterrestrials and they will come back once an extraterrestrial embassy is built on Earth.

At the meeting Silverman attended, the people were very polite and friendly. They watched a video that asked all of the questions to which we want answers: Why are we here? What is the meaning of life? Where do we come from? The video answered some (but not all) of these questions and the newcomers were encouraged to buy the movement's books and DVDs to learn more and to obtain more answers to their questions. At the end of the session they were invited to sign up for additional lectures. This is an excellent example of the foot-in-the-door technique. Presumably, once you have bought the book or agreed to a new meeting, you have committed (albeit in a small way) to find out more.

Consistent with their approach at individual meetings, the Raelians operate a visitor's centre in the Eastern Townships of Quebec that is designed to work in a similar way. One of the authors of this textbook (Steven) has a brother (interestingly also a psychologist) who with his wife was visiting the Eastern Townships and saw a sign for a "UFO museum." On a whim, they decided to visit. Upon paying the entry fee, they gained entry to a building (intriguingly, billed as the largest building made of hay bales in the world) and started to wander through. They found themselves being shadowed by one of the group members, who offered information about the group and asked if they had questions. The couple were given several opportunities to purchase information, and soon found that the path they were on was deliberately complex with no obvious exits—so that they had to go through all of the exhibits and "sales pitches" before they could leave.

Persuasive Elements

We can also analyze cult persuasion using the factors discussed in Module 11: *Who* (the communicator) said *what* (the message) to *whom* (the audience)?

The Communicator

Successful cults have a charismatic leader—someone who attracts and directs the members. As in experiments on persuasion, a credible communicator is someone the audience perceives as expert and trustworthy; for example, Luc Jouret would perform "miracles." He arranged a sophisticated sound and light apparatus when he gave his speeches, and at the appointed time he would perform a miracle (making images of Jesus appear, and so on). These often convinced audiences that he was indeed whom he claimed to be, and led to many people joining the group.

Trust is another aspect of credibility. Cult researcher Margaret Singer (1979) noted that middle-class Caucasian youths are more vulnerable to recruitment because they are more trusting. They lack the "street smarts" of lower-class youths (who know how to resist a hustle) and the wariness of upper-class youths (who have been warned of kidnappers since childhood). Many cult members have been recruited by friends or relatives—people they trust (Stark & Bainbridge, 1980).

The Message

The vivid, emotional messages and the warmth and acceptance with which the group showers lonely or depressed people can be strikingly appealing: Trust the master, join the family; we have the answer, the "one way." The message echoes through channels as varied as lectures, small-group discussions, and direct social pressure.

The Audience

Recruits are often young—people under 25 and still at that comparatively open age before attitudes and values stabilize. Some, such as the followers of Jim Jones, are less-educated people who like the simplicity of the message and find it difficult to counterargue. But most are educated, middle-class people.

Potential converts are often at turning points in their lives, facing personal crises, or vacationing or living away from home. They have needs; the cult offers them an answer (Lofland & Stark, 1965; Singer, 1979). Gail Maeder joined Heaven's Gate after her T-shirt shop had failed. David Moore joined when he was 19, just out of high school, and searching for direction. Times of social and economic upheaval are especially conducive to someone who can make apparent simple sense out of the confusion (O'Dea, 1968; Sales, 1972).

As you read in the description of the Raelians above, members of these groups do not appear scary and intimidating. They are friendly, gentle, and pleasant people. People who join these groups often feel alienated from the larger society, and are looking for a group to provide acceptance. Similar processes work with youth and street gangs and religious organizations. Humans are social beings and we want to be accepted and liked by people. These groups (gangs, cults, religious groups) provide the social acceptance and sometimes provide (for example, as explicitly offered by the Raelians and other religious groups) the answers to life's important questions.

Group Effects

Cults also illustrate the next module's theme: the power of a group to shape members' views and behaviour. The cult typically separates members from their previous social support systems and isolates them with other cultists. There may then occur what Rodney Stark and William Bainbridge (1980) call a "social implosion": External ties weaken until the group collapses inward socially, each person engaging only with other group members. Cut off from families and former friends, they lose access to counterarguments. The group now offers identity and defines reality. Because the cult frowns on or punishes disagreements, the apparent consensus helps eliminate any lingering doubts. Moreover, stress and emotional arousal narrow attention, making people "more susceptible to poorly supported arguments, social pressure, and the temptation to derogate nongroup members" (Baron, 2000).

Marshall Applewhite and Bonnie Nettles (who died of cancer in 1985) at first formed their own group of two, reinforcing each other's aberrant thinking—a phenomenon that psychiatrists call *folie à deux* (French for "insanity of two"). As others joined them, the group's social isolation facilitated more peculiar thinking. As conspiracy-theory Internet discussion groups illustrate (Heaven's Gate was skilled in Internet recruiting), virtual groups can likewise foster paranoia.

Contrary to the idea that cults turn hapless people into mindless robots, these techniques—increasing behavioural commitments, persuasion, and group isolation—do not have unlimited power. Toward the end, the leaders of the Solar Temple became increasingly eccentric, and many of the members began to leave. One of the leaders' own sons exposed the frauds of the "religion experiences." Many of the members left, and some demanded their "contributions" of money be returned. The Unification Church has successfully recruited fewer than 1 in 10 people who attend its workshops (Ennis & Verrilli, 1989). Most who joined Heaven's Gate had left before that fateful day. David Koresh ruled with a mix of persuasion, intimidation, and violence. As Jim Jones made his demands more extreme, he, too, increasingly had to control people with intimidation. He used threats of harm to those who fled the community, beatings for noncompliance, and drugs to neutralize disagreeable members.

It is important to recognize cult influence techniques are in some ways similar to techniques used by groups more familiar to us. Fraternity and sorority members have reported that the initial "love bombing" of potential cult recruits is not unlike their own "rush" period. Members lavish prospective pledges with attention and make them feel special. During the pledge period, new members are somewhat isolated, cut off from old friends who did not pledge. They spend time studying the history and rules of their new group. They suffer and commit time on its behalf. They are expected to comply with all its demands. Not surprisingly, the result is usually a committed new member. These same techniques are used in sports teams and in the military. Any group that wants cohesion among its members will likely use some form of these tactics.

Much the same is true of some therapeutic communities for recovering drug and alcohol abusers. Zealous self-help groups form a cohesive "social cocoon," have intense beliefs, and exert a profound influence on members' behaviour (Galanter, 1989, 1990).

We use the examples of fraternities, self-help groups, and teams not to disparage them but to illustrate two concluding observations. First, if we attribute new religious movements to the leader's mystical force or to the followers' peculiar weaknesses, we may delude ourselves into thinking we are immune to social control techniques. In truth, our own groups—and countless salespeople, political leaders, and other persuaders—successfully use many of these tactics on us. Between education and indoctrination, enlightenment and propaganda, conversion and coercion, therapy and mind control, there is but a blurry line.

Second, the fact that Luc Jouret and other leaders abuse the power of persuasion does not mean persuasion is intrinsically bad. Nuclear power enables us to light up homes or wipe out cities. Persuasive power enables us to enlighten or deceive. Knowing that these powers can be harnessed for evil purposes should alert us, as scientists and as citizens, to guard against their immoral use. But the powers themselves are neither inherently evil nor inherently good; how we use them determines whether their effect is destructive or constructive. Condemning persuasion because of deceit is like condemning eating because of gluttony.

OLC
Activity 12.2

The Story Behind the Research

As we have outlined before, these techniques are not unique to cults; other organizations use them as well. Importantly, how the techniques are viewed is dependent on who is using them. During your reading of this module so far most of you probably said, "A team isn't the same thing as a cult!" From a psychological standpoint the techniques are the same, but they are perceived differently. Although most analyses focus on the leader as the communicator, perceptions of the group are important as well. Dr. Jeffrey Pfeifer at the University of Regina became interested in the cult phenomenon as an undergraduate when he read a book about how companies employ the same tactics with employees as cults do with new members. A few years later, one of Dr. Pfeifer's friends left Canada to train as an officer in the U.S. Marine Corps. Although he did not finish the training, once he returned to Canada he told Dr. Pfeifer about the techniques the Marines used (social isolation, sleep deprivation, mindless repetitive tasks) during training to develop group cohesion.

Dr. Pfeifer realized that these tactics, as well as those used by companies and mainstream religious groups, were exactly the same as tactics used by cults. Clearly, how acceptable the tactics are depends on who uses them. Dr. Pfeifer has demonstrated this phenomenon in a number of studies. In one study, Dr. Pfeifer (1992) asked participants to read a vignette about the experiences of a young man who joined a group. In each vignette the group used techniques to "convert" the young man. All of the vignettes were identical except for the name given to the group. The group was described either as the Moonies, the Catholic Seminary, or the U.S. Marines. Participants were asked to label the technique used by the group in each condition. *Brainwashing* was the term most used to describe the Moonie technique, whereas *re-socialization* and *conversion* were used to describe the Church and the Marines.

Interestingly, Dr. Pfeifer found that participants would develop negative evaluations of people who joined cults. For example, in one study he found that defendants in criminal cases were more likely to be found guilty if they had been or were alleged to be in a cult (see Pfeifer, 1999). Similarly, participants did not return a child to her mother's custody if they were told the mother belonged to or was suspected of being in a cult (Pfeifer, 2006). This is why these "new religions" do not identify themselves as "cults"—this label would destroy their credibility. However, the techniques they use are the same. ▌

RESISTING PERSUASION: ATTITUDE INOCULATION

This consideration of persuasive influences has perhaps made you wonder if it is possible to resist unwanted persuasion.

Blessed with logic, information, and motivation, we do resist falsehoods. If, because of an aura of credibility, the repair person's uniform and doctor's title have intimidated us into unquestioning agreement, we can rethink our habitual responses to authority. We can seek more information before committing time or money. We can question what we don't understand.

Stimulate Commitment

There is another way to resist: Before encountering others' judgments, make a public commitment to your position. Having stood up for your convictions, you will become less susceptible (or should we say less "open"?) to what others have to say.

Challenge Beliefs

How might we stimulate people to commit themselves? From his experiments, Charles Kiesler (1971) offers one possible way: Mildly attack their position. Kiesler found that when committed people were attacked strongly enough to cause them to react, but not so strongly as to overwhelm them, they became even more committed. Kiesler explains: "When you attack committed people and your attack is of inadequate strength, you drive them to even more extreme behaviors in defense of their previous commitment. Their commitment escalates, in a sense, because the number of acts consistent with their belief increases" (p. 88). Perhaps you can recall a time when this happened in an argument, as those involved escalated their rhetoric, committing themselves to increasingly extreme positions.

Develop Counterarguments

There is a second reason why a mild attack might build resistance. When someone attacks one of our cherished attitudes, we typically feel some irritation and contemplate counterarguments. Counterarguing helps people resist persuasion (Jacks & Cameron, 2003). Refute someone's persuasion, and know that you have done so, and you will feel more certain than ever (Tormala & Petty, 2002). Like inoculations against disease, even weak arguments will prompt counterarguments, which are then available for a stronger attack. William McGuire (1964) documented this in a series of experiments. McGuire wondered: Could we inoculate people against persuasion much as we inoculate them against a virus? Is there such a thing as **attitude inoculation**?

To test this, McGuire started with cultural truisms, such as, "It's a good idea to brush your teeth after every meal if at all possible." He then showed that people were vulnerable to a massive, credible assault upon these truisms (for example, prestigious authorities were said to have discovered that too much toothbrushing can damage one's gums). If, however, before having their belief attacked, they were "immunized" by first receiving a small challenge to their belief, *and* if they read or

Attitude inoculation
Exposing people to weak attacks upon their attitudes so that when stronger attacks come, they will have refutations available.

A "poison parasite" ad.

wrote an essay in refutation of this mild attack, then they were better able to resist the powerful attack.

Robert Cialdini and his colleagues (2003) agree that appropriate counterarguments are a great way to resist persuasion but wondered how to bring them to mind in response to a political opponent's ads, especially when the opponent (like most political incumbents) has a huge spending advantage. The answer, they suggest, is a "poison parasite" defence—one that combines a poison (strong counterarguments) with a parasite (retrieval cues that bring those arguments to mind when seeing the opponent's ads). In their studies, participants who viewed a familiar political ad were least persuaded by it when they had earlier seen counterarguments overlaid on a replica of the ad. Seeing the ad again thus also brought to mind the puncturing counterarguments. Antismoking ads have effectively done this, for example, by re-creating a "Marlboro Man" commercial set in the rugged outdoors but now showing a coughing, decrepit cowboy.

Case Studies: Large-Scale Inoculation Programs

Inoculating Children Against Peer Pressure to Smoke

In a clear demonstration of how laboratory research findings can lead to practical applications, a research team led by Alfred McAlister (1980) had high school students "inoculate" Grade 7 students against peer pressures to smoke. The Grade 7 students were taught to respond to advertisements implying that liberated women smoke by saying, "She's not really liberated if she is hooked on tobacco." They also acted in role-plays in which, after being called "chicken" for not taking a cigarette, they answered with statements like, "I'd be a real chicken if I smoked just to impress you." After several such sessions during Grades 7 and 8, the inoculated students were half as likely to begin smoking as uninoculated students at another junior high school that had an identical parental smoking rate (Figure 12-1).

Other research teams have confirmed that such inoculation procedures, sometimes supplemented by other life-skill training, reduce teen smoking (Botvin & others, 1995; Evans & others, 1984; Flay & others, 1985). Most newer efforts emphasize strategies for resisting social pressure. One study exposed Grade 6 to 8 students to antismoking films or to information about smoking, together with role-plays of student-generated ways of refusing a cigarette (Hirschman & Leventhal, 1989). A year and a half later, 31 percent of those who watched the antismoking films had taken up smoking. Among those who role-played refusing, only 19 percent had begun smoking. Another study involved the Grade 7 classes in a diverse sample of 30 junior high schools. It warned students about pressures to smoke and use drugs and offered them strategies for resisting (Ellickson & Bell, 1990). Among nonusers of marijuana, the training curbed initiation by one-third; among users, it reduced usage by half.

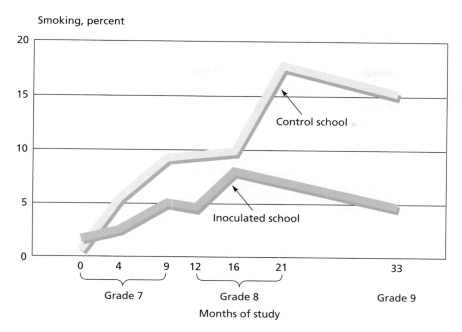

FIGURE 12-1

The percentage of cigarette smokers at an "inoculated" junior high school was much less than the percentage at a matched control school using a more typical smoking education program.

Data from McAlister & others, 1980; Telch & others, 1981.

Antismoking and drug education programs apply other persuasion principles, too. They use attractive peers to communicate information. They trigger the students' own cognitive processing ("Here's something you might want to think about"). They get the students to make a public commitment (by making a rational decision about smoking and then announcing it, along with their reasoning, to their classmates). Some of these smoking-prevention programs require only two to six hours of class, using prepared printed materials or videotapes. Today, any school district or teacher wishing to use the social-psychological approach to smoking prevention can do so easily, inexpensively, and with the hope of significant reductions in future smoking rates and associated health costs.

Inoculating Children Against the Influence of Advertising

Researchers have also studied how to immunize young children against the effects of television commercials. Sweden, Italy, Greece, Belgium, Denmark, and Ireland all restrict advertising that targets children, and other European countries have been discussing doing the same (McGuire, 2002). In the United States, notes Robert Levine in *The Power of Persuasion: How We're Bought and Sold*, the average child sees more than 10,000 commercials a year. "Two decades ago," he notes, "children drank twice as much milk as soda. Thanks to advertising, the ratio is now reversed" (2003, p. 16). Smokers often develop an "initial brand choice" in their teens, said a 1981 report from researchers at Philip Morris, a major player in the $11.2 billion spent annually on tobacco advertising and promotion (FTC, 2003). "Today's teenager is tomorrow's potential regular customer, and the overwhelming majority of smokers first begin to smoke while still in their teens" (Lichtblau, 2003). This research was prompted partly by studies showing that children, especially those under 8 years old, (1) have trouble distinguishing commercials from programs and fail to grasp their persuasive intent, (2) trust television advertising rather indiscriminately, and (3) desire and badger their parents for advertised products (Adler & others, 1980; Feshbach, 1980; Palmer & Dorr, 1980). Children, it seems, are an advertiser's dream: gullible, vulnerable, an easy sell. Moreover, half the 20,000 ads the typical child sees in a year are for low-nutrition, often sugary foods.

Armed with this data, citizens' groups have given the advertisers of such products a chewing out (Moody, 1980): "When a sophisticated advertiser spends millions to sell unsophisticated, trusting children an unhealthy product, this can only be called exploitation. No wonder the consumption of dairy products has declined since the start of television, while soft-drink consumption has almost doubled." On the other side are the commercial interests, who claim that such ads allow parents to teach their children consumer skills and, more importantly, finance children's television programs.

Meanwhile, researchers have wondered whether children can be taught to resist deceptive ads. In one such effort, a team of investigators led by Norma Feshbach (1980; Cohen, 1980) gave small groups of elementary schoolchildren three half-hour lessons in analyzing commercials. The children were inoculated by viewing ads and discussing them. For example, after viewing a toy ad, they were immediately given the toy and challenged to make it do what they had just seen in the commercial. Such experiences helped breed a more realistic understanding of commercials.

IMPLICATIONS

Indoctrination A process, used by a number of social groups, to teach members a partisan and uncritical acceptance of the group's perspective on issues.

It is important to recognize that although we have focused on cults in this module, it is not only cults that employ these tactics. Cults simply provide some of the more vivid examples of these approaches. We encounter persuasive tactics every single day—from simple advertising to requests for financial and personal contributions to a variety of groups. The best way to build resistance to persuasion probably isn't stronger **indoctrination** into your existing beliefs. If you are worried that you or one of your friends might be influenced by such a group, you should become aware of the different groups out there and become a critical thinker about what the purposes of the groups are. In order to resist persuasion, you need to prepare yourself to counter persuasive appeals. Groups apply this principle by forewarning members of how families and friends will attack their beliefs. When the expected challenge comes, the member is armed with counterarguments.

Another implication is that, for the persuader, an ineffective appeal can be worse than none. Can you see why? Those who reject an appeal are inoculated against further appeals. Consider an experiment in which Susan Darley and Joel Cooper (1972) invited students to write essays advocating a strict dress code. Because this was against the students' own positions and the essays were to be published, all chose *not* to write the essay—even those offered money to do so. After turning down the money, they became even more extreme and confident in their anti-dress-code opinions. Having made an overt decision against the dress code, they became even more resistant to it. Those who have rejected initial appeals to quit smoking may likewise become immune to further appeals. Ineffective persuasion, by stimulating the listener's defences, may be counterproductive. It may "harden the heart" against later appeals.

To be critical thinkers, we might take a cue from inoculation research. Do you want to build your resistance to persuasion without becoming closed to valid messages? Be an active listener and a critical thinker. Force yourself to counterargue. After hearing a political speech, discuss it with others. In other words, don't just listen—react. If the message cannot withstand careful analysis, so much the worse for it. If it can, its effect on you will be the more enduring.

OLC
Activity 12.3

CONCEPTS TO REMEMBER

Cult (also called new religious movement)   p. 122
Attitude inoculation   p. 127
Indoctrination   p. 130

Please visit the *Exploring Social Psychology* Online Learning Centre at www.mcgrawhill.ca/college/myers to participate in module activities, view module videos, access research and study tools, and test your knowledge with interactive quizzes, exercises, and scenarios.

How the Presence of Others Affects Our Behaviour

In the late nineteenth century, Norman Triplett discovered that cyclists' times were faster when they raced together rather than alone. Do you perform at your best when there are other people around you?

OLC
Activity 13.1

Co-actors Co-participants working individually on a noncompetitive activity.

magine yourself in front of a crowd. You are preparing to give a speech to a class of 150 students. How would you feel? You might suffer from some performance anxiety—you might be afraid of performing badly. Do you think you would feel differently if you were speaking in front of three friends instead of 150 strangers? Would your performance anxiety go away? When do you think you would perform your best? Do you perform best on your own, or when there are other people around you? Before you read the rest of this module, go to the Online Learning Centre and complete Activity 13.1, which explores how the presence of others might affect your performance.

THE PRESENCE OF OTHERS

Our world contains not only 6.4 billion individuals but also 200 nation-states, 4 million local communities, 20 million economic organizations, and hundreds of millions of other formal and informal groups—couples on dates, families, churches, housemates in bull sessions. How do these groups influence individuals?

Let's begin with social psychology's most elementary question: Are we affected by the mere presence of another person? "Mere presence" means people are not competing, do not reward or punish, and, in fact, do nothing except be present as a passive audience or as **co-actors**. Would the mere presence of others affect a person's jogging, eating, typing, or exam performance? The search for the answer is a scientific mystery story.

More than a century ago, Norman Triplett (1898), a psychologist interested in bicycle racing, noticed that cyclists' times were faster when racing together than when racing alone against the clock. Before he peddled his hunch (that others' presence boosts performance), Triplett conducted one of social psychology's first laboratory experiments. Children told to wind string on a fishing reel as rapidly as possible wound faster when they worked with co-actors than when they worked alone.

Ensuing experiments found that others' presence also improves the speed with which people do simple multiplication problems and cross out designated letters. It also improves the accuracy with which people perform simple motor tasks, such as keeping a metal stick in contact with a dime-sized disk on a moving turntable (called a "pursuit-rotor apparatus"; F. W. Allport, 1920; Dashiell, 1930; Travis, 1925). This **social facilitation** effect, as it came to be called, also occurs with animals. In the presence of others of their species, ants excavate more sand and chickens eat more grain (Bayer, 1929; Chen, 1937). In the presence of other sexually active rat pairs, mating rats exhibit heightened sexual activity (Larsson, 1956).

But wait: Other studies revealed that on some tasks, the presence of others *hinders* performance. In the presence of others, cockroaches, parakeets, and green finches learn mazes more slowly (Allee & Masure, 1936; Gates & Allee, 1933; Klopfer, 1958). This disruptive effect also occurs with people. Others' presence diminishes efficiency at learning nonsense syllables, completing a maze, and performing complex multiplication problems (Dashiell, 1930; Pessin, 1933; Pessin & Husband, 1933).

Saying that the presence of others sometimes facilitates performance and sometimes hinders it is about as satisfying as the typical Nova Scotia weather forecast—predicting that it might be sunny but then again it might rain. By 1940, research activity in this area had ground to a halt, and it lay dormant for 25 years until awakened by the touch of a new idea.

Social psychologist Robert Zajonc (pronounced *Zy-ence*, rhymes with *science*) wondered whether these seemingly contradictory findings could be reconciled. As often happens at creative moments in science, Zajonc (1965) used one field of research to illuminate another. In this case, the illumination came from a well-established principle in experimental psychology: Arousal enhances whatever response tendency is dominant (see Figure 13-1). Increased arousal enhances

Social facilitation
(1) Original meaning—the tendency of people to perform simple or well-learned tasks better when others are present.
(2) Current meaning—the strengthening of dominant (prevalent, or likely) responses in the presence of others.

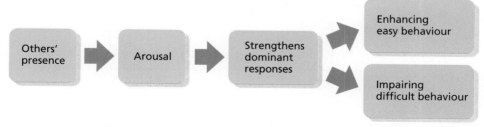

FIGURE 13-1
The effects of social arousal. Robert Zajonc reconciled apparently conflicting findings by proposing that arousal from others' presence strengthens dominant responses (the correct responses only on easy or well-learned tasks).

performance on easy tasks for which the most likely—"dominant"—response is the correct one. People solve easy anagrams, such as *akec*, fastest when they are anxious. On complex tasks, for which the correct answer is not dominant, increased arousal promotes *incorrect* responding. On harder anagrams, people do worse when anxious.

Could this principle solve the mystery of social facilitation? It seemed reasonable to assume what evidence now confirms—that others' presence will arouse or energize people (Mullen & others, 1997). (We can all recall feeling more tense or excited in front of an audience.) If social arousal facilitates dominant responses, it should *boost performance on easy tasks and hurt performance on difficult tasks*. Now the confusing results made sense. Winding fishing reels, doing simple multiplication problems, and eating were all easy tasks for which the responses were well learned or naturally dominant. Sure enough, having others around boosted performance. Learning new material, doing a maze, and solving complex math problems were more difficult tasks for which the correct responses were initially less probable. In these cases, the presence of others increased the number of incorrect responses on these tasks. The same general rule—*arousal facilitates dominant responses*—worked in both cases (refer to Figure 13-1). Suddenly, what had looked like contradictory results no longer seemed contradictory.

Zajonc's solution, so simple and elegant, left other social psychologists thinking what Thomas H. Huxley thought after first reading Darwin's *Origin of the Species*: "How extremely stupid not to have thought of that!" It seemed obvious—

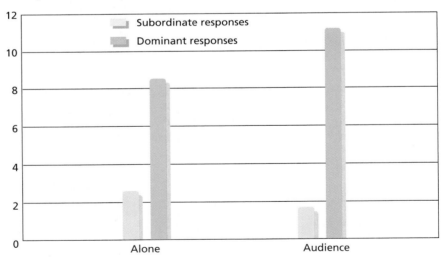

Average number of responses

FIGURE 13–2
Social facilitation of dominant responses. People responded with dominant words (practised 16 times) more frequently, and subordinate words (practised but once) less frequently when observers were present.

Data from Zajonc & Sales, 1966.

once Zajonc had pointed it out. Perhaps, however, the pieces appeared to merge so neatly only through the spectacles of hindsight. Would the solution survive direct experimental tests?

After almost 300 studies, conducted with the help of more than 25,000 volunteer subjects, the solution has survived (Bond & Titus, 1983; Guerin, 1993, 1999). Several experiments in which Zajonc and his associates manufactured an arbitrary dominant response confirmed that an audience enhanced this response. In one, Zajonc and Stephen Sales (1966) asked people to pronounce various nonsense words between 1 and 16 times. Then they told the people that the same words would appear on a screen, one at a time. Each time, they were to guess which had appeared. When the people were actually shown only random black lines for a hundredth of a second, they "saw" mostly the words they had pronounced most frequently. These words had become the dominant responses. People who took the same test in the presence of two others were even more likely to guess the dominant words (Figure 13-2).

The Story Behind the Research

Social facilitation has sometimes been found where we might not expect it. Drs. Peter Herman, Janet Polivy, and their colleagues at the University of Toronto have been working on a line of research for the last 25 years, trying to understand what factors are most predictive of when and how much people eat. Early on (for example, Polivy & others, 1979), Drs. Polivy and Herman realized that, contrary to popular belief, hunger and satiety were not the best predictors of people's eating behaviour. Their research focused primarily on eating patterns in dieters and non-dieters, but it soon became apparent that other influences were also important. They recognized that social context (that is, were other people in the room eating? what and how much were these others eating?) is a much better predictor of whether and how much people will eat than whether or not they are hungry.

More recently Herman, Polivy, and Deborah Roth, one of their graduate students (Herman & others, 2003) wrote a review and theoretical analysis of the literature on the role of the presence of others on food intake. Do you eat more when you are in a group, or do you eat less? Like performance on other tasks, the presence of others will affect us—it can either make us eat more or less depending on the situation. In their paper they discussed the existing research, which has found both inhibition and facilitation and tried to reconcile, as Zajonc did in other contexts, how these divergent effects could both be correct. They suggested that the behaviour of the other people is the key. If the other people in the room with you are eating, this may prompt you to eat more. In other words, you observe their behaviour and model your behaviour after them: you are observing what the "norm" for the group is and you act to fit in. This occurs for both men and women. However, the presence of others can lead to inhibition if you feel these people are evaluating you in some way. If you want to portray a good impression, you might eat less, so that people do not develop any negative evaluation of you. Again, for both men and women, behaviour depends on the behaviour of others and their evaluation of the situation.

In various ways, later experiments confirmed that social arousal facilitates dominant responses, whether right or wrong. Peter Hunt and Joseph Hillery (1973) found that in others' presence, students took less time to learn a simple maze and more time to learn a complex one (just as the cockroaches do!). And James Michaels and his collaborators (1982) found that good pool players in a student union (who had made 71 percent of their shots while being unobtrusively observed) did even better (80 percent) when four observers came up to watch them play. Poor shooters (who had previously averaged 36 percent) did even worse (25 percent) when closely observed.

Athletes perform well-practised skills, which helps explain why they often perform best when energized by the responses of a supportive crowd. Studies of more than 80,000 college and professional athletic events in Canada, the United States, and England reveal that home teams win about 6 in 10 games (somewhat fewer for baseball and football, somewhat more for basketball and soccer). Interestingly, some recent research by Stephen Bray and his colleagues at the University of Lethbridge (see Bray & others, 2003) suggests that home-field advantage is not always an advantage. In this research the authors found that home field was more of an advantage for good teams than for poor-performing teams. More specifically, they found that British professional soccer teams were more likely to tie their home games if they were poor-performing teams. Higher-quality teams were less likely to tie home games. The home advantage may, however, also stem from the players' familiarity with their home environment, less travel fatigue, feelings of dominance derived from territorial control, or increased team identity when cheered by fans (Zillmann & Paulus, 1993).

CROWDING: THE PRESENCE OF MANY OTHERS

So people do respond to others' presence. But does the presence of observers really arouse people? In times of stress, a comrade can be comforting. But with others present, people perspire more, breathe faster, tense their muscles more, and have higher blood pressure and a faster heart rate (Geen & Gange, 1983; Moore & Baron, 1983). Even a supportive audience may elicit poorer performance on challenging tasks (Butler & Baumeister, 1998). Having mom and dad at your first piano recital likely won't boost your performance.

The effect of other people increases with their number (Jackson & Latané, 1981; Knowles, 1983). Sometimes the arousal and self-conscious attention created by a large audience interferes even with well-learned, automatic behaviours, such as speaking. Given *extreme* pressure, we're vulnerable to failure. Stutterers tend to stutter more in front of larger audiences than when speaking to just one or two people (Mullen, 1986b). College basketball players become slightly *less* accurate in their free-throw shooting when very highly aroused by a packed rather than a near empty fieldhouse (Sokoll & Mynatt, 1984). In fact, Larry Leith at the University of Toronto has demonstrated that, in a sports context, just thinking about failure can cause you to fail. Leith had 80 students try to complete 25 basketball free throws. He randomly assigned participants to a condition where they were asked to think about missing the free throw, or not. He found that simply thinking about failing actually caused participants to miss more free throws.

Being *in* a crowd also intensifies positive or negative reactions. When they sit close together, friendly people are liked even more, and *un*friendly people are *dis*liked even more (Schiffenbauer & Schiavo, 1976; Storms & Thomas, 1977). In experiments with Columbia University students and with Ontario Science Centre visitors, Jonathan Freedman and his colleagues (1979, 1980) had an accomplice listen to a humorous tape or watch a movie with other subjects. When they all sat close together, the accomplice could more readily induce the subjects to laugh and clap. As theatre directors and sports fans know, and as researchers have confirmed, a "good house" is a full house (Aiello & others, 1983; Worchel & Brown, 1984).

Perhaps you've noticed that a class of 35 students feels more warm and lively in a room that seats just 35 than when spread around a room that seats 100. This occurs partly because when others are close by, we are more likely to notice and join in their laughter or clapping. But crowding also enhances arousal, as Gary Evans (1979) found. He tested 10-person groups of University of Massachusetts students, either in a room 20 by 30 feet or in one 8 by 12 feet. Compared to those in the large room, those densely packed had higher pulse rates and blood pressure (indicating arousal). Though their performance on simple tasks did not suffer, on difficult tasks they made more errors. In a study of university students in India, Dinesh Nagar and Janak Pandey (1987) similarly found that crowding hampered performance only on complex tasks, such as solving difficult anagrams. So, crowding enhances arousal, which facilitates dominant responses.

WHY ARE WE AROUSED IN THE PRESENCE OF OTHERS?

To this point we have seen that what you do well, you will be energized to do best in front of others (unless you become hyperaroused and self-conscious). What you find difficult may seem impossible in the same circumstances. What is it about other people that causes arousal? There is evidence to support three possible factors: evaluation apprehension, distraction, and mere presence.

Evaluation Apprehension

Nickolas Cottrell surmised that observers make us apprehensive because we wonder how they are evaluating us. To test whether **evaluation apprehension** exists, Cottrell and his associates (1968) repeated Zajonc and Sales' nonsense-syllable study at Kent State University and added a third condition. In this "mere presence" condition, they blindfolded observers, supposedly in preparation for a perception experiment. In contrast to the effect of the watching audience, the mere presence of these blindfolded people did *not* boost well-practised responses.

Other experiments confirmed Cottrell's conclusion: The enhancement of dominant responses is strongest when people think they are being evaluated. In one experiment, joggers on a University of California at Santa Barbara jogging path sped

Evaluation apprehension
Concern for how others are evaluating us.

up as they came upon a woman seated on the grass—*if* she was facing them rather than sitting with her back turned (Worringham & Messick, 1983).

Evaluation apprehension also helps explain:

- why people perform best when their co-actor is slightly superior (Seta, 1982).
- why arousal lessens when a high-status group is diluted by adding people whose opinions don't matter to us (Seta & Seta, 1992).
- why people who worry most about others' evaluations are the ones most affected by their presence (Gastorf & others, 1980; Geen & Gange, 1983).
- why social-facilitation effects are greatest when the others are unfamiliar and hard to keep an eye on (Guerin & Innes, 1982).

The self-consciousness we feel when being evaluated can also interfere with behaviours that we perform best automatically (Mullen & Baumeister, 1987). If self-conscious basketball players analyze their body movements while shooting critical free throws, they are more likely to miss.

Distraction

Glenn Sanders, Robert Baron, and Danny Moore (1978; Baron, 1986) carried evaluation apprehension a step further. They theorized that when people wonder how co-actors are doing or how an audience is reacting, they get distracted. This *conflict* between paying attention to others and paying attention to the task overloads the cognitive system, causing arousal. Evidence that people are indeed "driven by distraction" comes from experiments that produce social facilitation, not just by the presence of another person, but even by a nonhuman distraction, such as bursts of light (Sanders, 1981a,b).

Mere Presence

Zajonc, however, believes that the mere presence of others produces some arousal even without evaluation apprehension or arousing distraction. For example, people's colour preferences are stronger when they make judgments with others present (Goldman, 1967). On such a task, there is no "good" or "right" answer for others to evaluate and, thus, no reason to be concerned with their reactions. Still, others' presence is energizing.

Recall that facilitation effects also occur with nonhuman animals. This hints at an innate social arousal mechanism common to much of the zoological world. (Animals probably are not consciously worrying about how other animals are evaluating them.) At the human level, most joggers are energized when jogging with someone else, even one who neither competes nor evaluates.

This is a good time to remind ourselves of the purpose of a theory. A good theory is a scientific shorthand: It simplifies and summarizes a variety of observations. Social-facilitation theory does this well. It is a simple summary of many research findings. A good theory also offers clear predictions that (1) help confirm or modify the theory, (2) guide new exploration, and (3) suggest practical applications. Social-facilitation theory has definitely generated the first two types of prediction: (1) The basics of the theory (that the presence of others is arousing and that this social arousal enhances dominant responses) have been confirmed, and (2) the theory has brought new life to a long-dormant field of research.

Does it also suggest (3) some practical applications? We can make some educated guesses about possible applications. Many new office buildings have replaced private offices with large, open areas divided by low partitions. Might the resulting awareness of others' presence help boost the performance of well-learned tasks, but disrupt creative thinking on complex tasks? Can you think of other possible applications?

SOCIAL LOAFING

Think back to what we asked you at the beginning of this module: When do you perform best? Do you perform best on your own, or when there are other people around you? Think about the last time you worked on a group project (many of you may be doing one right now!). Have you ever been in a group where one person was not pulling his or her weight? Have you ever been that person, slacking off a bit because you know you can get away with it? We all do it, under certain conditions. In some situations this can be particularly frustrating, such as when you are working on a class project with a group of students. Sometimes a person who has done little or no work will get the same credit as you receive. What can you do in these situations to make that person work harder? Does the culture you come from make a difference? Social psychologists have been asking very similar questions. Will a group of berry pickers whose pickings go into a common pot work as hard as those paid for their individual pickings? In a team tug-of-war, will eight people on a side exert as much force as the sum of their best efforts in individual tugs of war? If not, why not?

Social facilitation usually occurs when people work toward individual goals and when their efforts, whether winding fishing reels or solving math problems, can be individually evaluated. These situations parallel some everyday work situations, but not those in which people pool their efforts toward a *common* goal and where individuals are *not* accountable for their efforts. A team tug-of-war provides one such example. Organizational fundraising—pooling candy sale proceeds to pay for the class trip—provides another. So does a class project in which all get the same grade. On such "additive tasks"—tasks wherein the group's achievement depends on the sum of the individual efforts—will team spirit boost productivity? Will bricklayers lay bricks faster when working as a team than when working alone? One way to attack such questions is with laboratory simulations.

Many Hands Make Light Work

Nearly a century ago, French engineer Max Ringelmann (reported by Kravitz & Martin, 1986) found that the collective effort of such teams was but half the sum of the individual efforts. This suggests, contrary to the common notion "in unity there is

FIGURE 13-3

The rope-pulling apparatus. People in the first position pulled less hard when they thought people behind them were also pulling.

(Data from Ingham, Levinger, Graves, & Peckham, 1974. Photo by Alan G. Ingham.)

strength," that group members may actually be *less* motivated when performing additive tasks. Maybe, though, poor performance stemmed from poor coordination—people pulling a rope in slightly different directions at slightly different times. A group of Massachusetts researchers led by Alan Ingham (1974) cleverly eliminated this problem by making individuals think others were pulling with them, when in fact they were pulling alone. Blindfolded participants were assigned the first position in the apparatus shown in Figure 13-3 and told, "Pull as hard as you can." They pulled 18 percent harder when they knew they were pulling alone than when they believed that behind them two to five people were also pulling. While completing his Ph.D. at Carleton University, Frederick Lichacz replicated the original Ringlemann study and added a couple of other twists (see Lichacz & Partington, 1996). He found that giving feedback to the participants on their performance was effective at increasing their individual efforts. In addition, he found that if people had experience with the task, they exerted a greater effort than if the task were a novel one for them.

Researchers Bibb Latané, Kipling Williams, and Stephen Harkins (1979; Harkins & others, 1980) kept their ears open for other ways to investigate this phenomenon, which they labelled social loafing. They observed that the noise produced by six people shouting or clapping "as loud as you can" was less than three times that produced by one person alone. Like the tug-of-war task, however, noisemaking is vulnerable to group inefficiency. So Latané and his associates followed Ingham's example by leading their Ohio State University participants to believe others were shouting or clapping with them, when in fact they were doing so alone.

Social loafing The tendency for people to exert less effort when they pool their efforts toward a common goal than when they are individually accountable.

Their method was to blindfold six people, seat them in a semicircle, and have them put on headphones, over which they were blasted with the sound of people shouting or clapping. People could not hear their own shouting or clapping, much less that of others. On various trials they were instructed to shout or clap either alone or along with the group. People who were told about this experiment guessed the subjects would shout louder when with others, because they would be less inhibited (Harkins, 1981). The actual result? Social loafing: When the participants believed five others were also either shouting or clapping, they produced one-third less noise than when they thought themselves alone. Social loafing occurred even when the subjects were high school cheerleaders who believed themselves to be cheering together or alone (Hardy & Latané, 1986).

John Sweeney (1973), a political scientist interested in the policy implications of social loafing, observed the phenomenon in an experiment at the University of Texas. Students pumped exercise bicycles more energetically (as measured by electrical output) when they knew they were being individually monitored than when they thought their output was being pooled with that of other riders. In the group condition, people were tempted to **free-ride**; they benefited from the group but gave little in return.

In this and 160 other studies (Karau & Williams, 1993), we see a twist on one of the psychological forces that makes for social facilitation: evaluation apprehension. In the social loafing experiments, individuals believe they are evaluated only when they act alone. The group situation (rope pulling, shouting, and so forth) *decreases* evaluation apprehension. When people are not accountable and cannot evaluate their own efforts, responsibility is diffused across all group members (Harkins & Jackson, 1985; Kerr & Bruun, 1981). By contrast, the social-facilitation experiments *increased* exposure to evaluation. When made the centre of attention, people self-consciously monitor their behaviour (Mullen & Baumeister, 1987). So the principle is the same: When being observed *increases* evaluation concerns, social facilitation occurs; when being lost in a crowd *decreases* evaluation concerns, social loafing occurs (see Figure 13-4 on page 142).

To motivate group members, one strategy is to make individual performance identifiable. Some football coaches do this by filming and evaluating each player individually. The Ohio State researchers had group members wear individual microphones while engaged in group shouting (Williams & others, 1981). Whether in a group or not, people exert more effort when their outputs are individually identifiable: University swim team members swim faster in intrasquad relay races when someone monitors and announces their individual times (Williams & others, 1989). Even without pay consequences, actual assembly line workers in one small experiment produced 16 percent more product when their individual output was identified (Faulkner & Williams, 1996).

Free riders People who benefit from the group but give little in return.

Social Loafing in Everyday Life

How widespread is social loafing? In the laboratory, the phenomenon occurs not only among people who are pulling ropes, cycling, shouting, and clapping but also among those who are pumping water or air, evaluating poems or editorials,

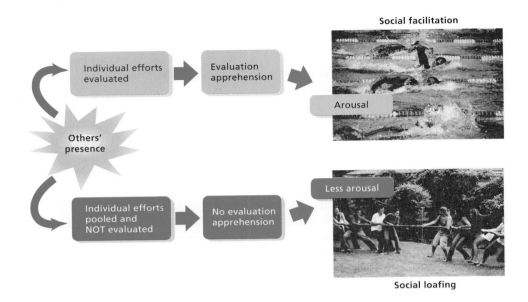

FIGURE 13-4

Social facilitation or social loafing? When individuals cannot be evaluated or held accountable, loafing becomes more likely. An individual swimmer is evaluated on her ability to win the race. In tug-of-war, no single person on the team is held accountable, so any one member might relax or loaf.

producing ideas, typing, and detecting signals. Do these results generalize to everyday worker productivity?

On their collective farms under communism, Russian peasants worked one field one day, another field the next, with little direct responsibility for any given plot. For their own use, they were given small, private plots. One analysis found that the private plots occupied 1 percent of the agricultural land, yet produced 27 percent of the Soviet farm output (H. Smith, 1976). In Hungary, private plots accounted for only 13 percent of the farmland but produced one-third of the output (Spivak, 1979). When China began allowing farmers to sell food grown in excess of that owed to the state, food production jumped 8 percent per year—2.5 times the annual increase in the preceding 26 years (Church, 1986).

In North America, workers who do not pay dues or volunteer time to their unions or professional associations nevertheless are usually happy to accept their benefits. This hints at another possible explanation of social loafing. When rewards are divided equally, regardless of how much one contributes to the group, any individual gets more reward per unit of effort by free-riding on the group. So people may be motivated to slack off when their efforts are not individually monitored and rewarded.

But surely collective effort does not always lead to slacking off. Sometimes the goal is so compelling and maximum output from everyone is so essential that team spirit maintains or intensifies effort. In an Olympic crew race, will the individual rowers in an eight-person crew pull their oars with less effort than those in a one- or two-person crew?

The evidence assures us they will not. People in groups loaf less when the task is *challenging, appealing,* or *involving* (Karau & Williams, 1993). On challenging tasks, people may perceive their efforts as indispensable (Harkins & Petty, 1982; Kerr, 1983; Kerr & Bruun, 1983). When people see others in their group as unreliable or as unable to contribute much, they work harder (Plaks & Higgins, 2000; Williams & Karau, 1991). Adding incentives or challenging a group to strive for certain standards also promotes collective effort (Harkins & Szymanski, 1989; Shepperd & Wright, 1989).

Groups also loaf less when their members are *friends* or identified with their group, rather than strangers (Davis & Greenlees, 1992; Karau & Williams, 1997; Worchel & others, 1998). Even just expecting to interact with someone again serves to increase effort on team projects (Groenenboom & others, 2001). Latané notes that Israel's communal kibbutz farms have actually outproduced Israel's noncollective farms (Leon, 1969). Cohesiveness intensifies effort. So will there be social loafing in group-centred cultures? To find out, Latané and his co-researchers (Gabrenya & others, 1985) headed for Asia, where they repeated their sound production experiments in Japan, Thailand, Taiwan, India, and Malaysia. Their findings? Social loafing was evident in all these countries, too.

Seventeen later studies in Asia reveal that people in collectivist cultures do, however, exhibit less social loafing than do people in individualist cultures (Karau & Williams, 1993; Kugihara, 1999). As we noted earlier, loyalty to family and work groups runs strong in collectivist cultures. Likewise, women tend to be less individualistic than men—and to exhibit less social loafing.

Some of these findings parallel those from studies of everyday work groups. When groups are given challenging objectives, when they are rewarded for group success, and when there is a spirit of commitment to the "team," group members work hard (Hackman, 1986). Keeping work groups small and forming them with equally competent people can also help members believe their contributions are indispensable (Comer, 1995). So while social loafing is a common occurrence when group members work collectively and without individual accountability, many hands need not always make light work. So, how do you get other students to do their share of the work when you are working on a joint task? Take a look at the principles outlined in this chapter and write down a few ideas. Then, visit the Online Learning Centre and complete Activity 13.2 to see if your ideas would work.

OLC
Activity 13.2

CONCEPTS TO REMEMBER

Co-actors   p. 132
Social facilitation   p. 133
Evaluation apprehension   p. 137

Social loafing   p. 140
Free riders   p. 141

Please visit the *Exploring Social Psychology* Online Learning Centre at www.mcgrawhill.ca/college/myers to participate in module activities, view module videos, access research and study tools, and test your knowledge with interactive quizzes, exercises, and scenarios.

Deindividuation

On November 14, 1997, under a bridge in Saanich on Vancouver Island, a 14-year-old girl was beaten bloody. Reena Virk, having survived the initial attack, struggled to get across the bridge and escape her attackers. Two of the original attackers caught up to her, and dragged her back under the bridge to finish her off. One of the attackers later bragged of standing on Reena's head to hold it under water—all while smoking a cigarette. The murder of Reena Virk stunned the nation. One of the most shocking elements of this case was that the group that did this to Reena was a group of teenagers who knew her from school, six girls and one boy. Eventually, all of the people involved were convicted for their crimes, but this case brought a number of issues to the attention of Canadians, including bullying, the role of Reena's ethnic and family background, and the potential role of the foster care system. But another question that people asked themselves was, "How could these kids have done this?" Would they have committed the same crime if they had been on their own, or did being in the group influence their behaviour?

Social facilitation experiments show that groups can arouse people. Social loafing experiments show that groups can diffuse responsibility. When arousal and diffused responsibility combine and normal inhibitions diminish, the results may be startling. People may commit acts that range from a mild lessening of restraint (throwing food in the dining hall, snarling at a referee, screaming during a rock concert) to impulsive self-gratification (group vandalism, orgies, thefts) to destructive social explosions (police brutality, soccer riots, lynchings). In a 1967 incident, 200 university students gathered to watch a disturbed fellow student threatening to jump from a tower. They began to chant "Jump. Jump. . . ." The student jumped to his death (UPI, 1967). Of course, deindividuation does not always have to be negative. We cheer loudly in support of our teams at sporting events, and protesting crowds can lead to positive social change.

However, these unrestrained behaviours have something in common: They are somehow provoked by the power of a group. Groups can generate a sense of excitement, of being caught up in something bigger than one's self. It is harder to imagine a single rock fan screaming deliriously at a private rock concert, a single student trying to coax someone to suicide, or even a single police officer beating a defenceless motorist. In certain kinds of group situations, people are more likely to abandon normal restraints, to lose their sense of individual identity, to become responsive to group or crowd norms—in a word, to become what Leon Festinger, Albert Pepitone, and Theodore Newcomb (1952) labelled **deindividuated**. What circumstances elicit this psychological state?

Deindividuation Loss of self-awareness and evaluation apprehension; occurs in group situations that foster responsiveness to group norms, good or bad.

The Craigflower Bridge, the site of the notorious murder of Reena Virk, who was swarmed by a gang of teenagers.

GROUP SIZE

After the Montreal Canadiens won the Stanley Cup in 1993, Montrealers celebrated in a rather unexpected way—they rioted. Similar riots have broken out in cities after local sports teams have won championships (for example, Chicago, Detroit). During the 2006 playoffs fans of the Edmonton Oilers rioted after the Oilers moved ahead in their series during the division finals! Riots such as these, as well as the string of riots that occurred in Paris in October 2005, can cause millions of dollars in damage and sometimes cost people their lives. Why does this happen? Perfectly normal and respectable people can find themselves involved in and participating in rioting. Indeed, one of Steven Smith's colleagues—now a tenured faculty member at a Canadian university—actually participated in the Toronto riot that occurred after the Blue Jays won the World Series.

A group has the power not only to arouse its members but also to render them unidentifiable. The snarling crowd hides the snarling basketball fan. A lynch mob enables its members to believe they will not be prosecuted; they perceive the action as the *group's*. Rioters, made faceless by the mob, are freed to loot. In an analysis of 21 instances in which crowds were present as someone threatened to jump from a building or bridge, Leon Mann (1981) found that when the crowd was small and exposed by daylight, people usually did not try to bait the person. But when a large crowd or the cover of night gave people anonymity, the crowd usually baited and

OLC
Video 14.1

Edmonton Oilers fans celebrate the NHL team's playoff series win in May 2006 by climbing onto a bus shelter. Riot police had to be called in to contain some of the crowd revelry that got out of hand.

jeered. Brian Mullen (1986a) reports a similar effect of lynch mobs: The bigger the mob, the more its members lose self-awareness and become willing to commit atrocities, such as burning, lacerating, or dismembering the victim. In each of these examples, from sports crowds to lynch mobs, evaluation apprehension plummets. Because "everyone is doing it," all can attribute their behaviour to the situation rather than to their own choices.

PHYSICAL ANONYMITY

We can experiment with anonymity to see if it actually lessens inhibitions. In one creative experiment, Philip Zimbardo (1970, 2002) dressed women in identical white coats and hoods, rather like Ku Klux Klan members (Figure 14-1). He got the idea for the experiment from his undergraduate students, who wondered how the "good boys" depicted in William Golding's *Lord of the Flies* could so suddenly become monstrous after painting their faces. Women in the experiment who were wearing the coats and hoods, when asked to deliver electric shocks to a woman, pressed the shock button twice as long as did women who were visible and wearing large name tags.

A research team led by Ed Diener (1976) cleverly demonstrated the effects of being in a group *and* being physically anonymous. At Halloween, they observed 1,352 children trick-or-treating. As the children, either alone or in groups, approached 1 of 27 homes, an experimenter greeted them warmly, invited them to "take *one* of the candies," and then left the room. Hidden observers noted that children in groups were more than twice as likely to take extra candy as solo children. Also, those who were left anonymous were more than twice as likely to transgress as children who had

FIGURE 14-1
Anonymous women delivered more shock to helpless victims than did identifiable women.

The Story Behind the Research

When computers and computer-mediated communication (e-mail, chat rooms, and so on) started to become commonplace, news shows and magazines predicted dire consequences for the future of interpersonal interaction. Although the computer age would lead to paperless offices and allow people the freedom to work from home, it would undoubtedly cause people to become isolated from one another. Isolation would lead to feelings of anonymity and deindividuation, and common courtesy would disappear. Pundits pointed to the proliferation of "flame" e-mails (rude, mean, or inappropriate messages) as an example.

While Dr. Kimberly Matheson was an undergraduate and master's student at Carleton University (she is now a faculty member there), she began to program and work with computers in her research. Far from feeling anonymous and isolated, she found using computers—and communicating through them—to be entertaining and engaging. Many of the news media presented an image of computer hackers: socially isolated individuals who kept to themselves and lost social contacts. However, Dr. Matheson did not believe it could be that simple. She proposed that computer-mediated

communications are very self-involving—even if you are isolated from other people, you are still (on one level at least) interacting with them.

When Dr. Matheson began her Ph.D. research at the University of Waterloo, she and Dr. Mark Zanna began to examine this issue in a more systematic way. Specifically, they experimentally manipulated whether participants engaged in computer-mediated versus face-to-face interactions. Next, participants were assessed on both public and private self-consciousness (see Matheson & Zanna, 1988, 1990). They found that in face-to-face communications both private self-consciousness and public self-consciousness were high. Conversely, computer-mediated communications reduced public self-consciousness (in other words, participants felt less inhibited), but private self-consciousness remained high (that is, deindividuation did not occur). Therefore, their research demonstrated that computer-mediated interactions are no more socially isolating than face-to-face communications. Both methods are self-involving. Dr. Matheson has suggested that inappropriate behaviour (such as sending flame e-mails) is much more likely to be the result of poor judgment rather than a deindividuation process. ∎

been asked their names and where they lived. As Figure 14-2 shows, the transgression rate varied dramatically with the situation. When they were deindividuated by group immersion combined with anonymity, most children stole extra candy.

These experiments make us wonder about the effect of wearing uniforms. Preparing for battle, warriors in some tribal cultures (like rabid fans of some sports teams) depersonalize themselves with body and face paints or special masks. After the battle, some cultures kill, torture, or mutilate any remaining enemies; other cultures take prisoners alive. Robert Watson (1973) scrutinized anthropological files and discovered that the cultures with depersonalized warriors were also the cultures that brutalized their enemies. But does this have a consequential impact on behaviour? In Northern Ireland, 206 of 500 violent attacks studied by Andrew Silke (2003) were conducted by attackers who wore masks, hoods, or other facial disguises. Compared with undisguised attackers, these anonymous attackers inflicted more serious injuries, attacked more people, and committed more vandalism.

Percent transgressing

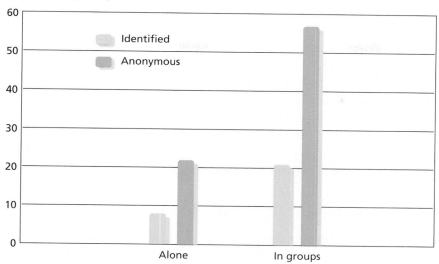

FIGURE 14-2

Children were more likely to transgress by taking extra Halloween candy when in a group, when anonymous, and, especially, when deindividuated by the combination of group immersion and anonymity.

Data from Diener & Wallbom, 1976.

Does becoming physically anonymous *always* unleash our worst impulses? Fortunately, no. In all these situations, people were responding to clear antisocial cues. Robert Johnson and Leslie Downing (1979) point out that the Klan-like outfits worn by Zimbardo's subjects may have encouraged hostility. In an experiment at the University of Georgia, women put on nurses' uniforms before deciding how much shock someone should receive. When those wearing the nurses' uniforms were made anonymous, they became *less* aggressive in administering shocks than when their names and personal identities were stressed. From their analysis of 60 deindividuation studies, Tom Postmes and Russell Spears (1998; Reicher & others, 1995) conclude that being anonymous makes one less self-conscious, more group-conscious, and more responsive to cues present in the situation, whether negative (Klan uniforms) or positive (nurses' uniforms). Given altruistic cues, deindividuated people even give more money (Spivey & Prentice-Dunn, 1990).

This helps explain why wearing black uniforms—which are traditionally associated with evil and death and worn by medieval executioners, Darth Vader, and Ninja warriors—have an effect opposite to that of wearing nurses' uniforms. Mark Frank and Thomas Gilovich (1988) report that, led by the Los Angeles Raiders and the Philadelphia Flyers, black-uniformed teams consistently ranked near the top of the National Football and Hockey Leagues in penalties assessed between 1970 and 1986. Follow-up laboratory research suggests that just putting on black jerseys can trigger wearers to behave more aggressively.

Being part of a team can have other effects as well. As mentioned in Module 12, sports teams frequently use tactics to increase group cohesion among its members. Another tactic sports teams use at times is the "hazing" of new players. New players are picked on, degraded, and even physically assaulted. Presumably, if it is difficult to become a member of the team, you will like it more once you become a member. The more effort we put into something, the more we appreciate it. However, sometimes hazing rituals go too far. There are a number of well-publicized hazing incidents in sports. For example, in the fall of 2005, the McGill Redmen football team had its season cancelled after a number of rookies were gagged, forced into degrading positions, and sexually assaulted with a broomstick. Although these behaviours are widely condemned, they are still disturbingly frequent.

AROUSING AND DISTRACTING ACTIVITIES

Aggressive outbursts by large groups often are preceded by minor actions that arouse and divert people's attention. Group shouting, chanting, clapping, or dancing serve both to hype people up and to reduce self-consciousness.

An excellent example of this is the well publicized behaviour of a group of fans at a Detroit Pistons game in November 2004. It started innocently enough when Ron Artest of the Indiana Pacers fouled a Pistons player. A fight broke out between the two players and the crowd quickly got involved, throwing beer cups, trash, and other debris onto the Pacers players. Remarkably, Ron Artest and two other teammates waded into the crowd and began fighting with the fans. This behaviour likely occurred because the fans believed that they could not be individually identified in the large crowd. Interestingly, many of the fans who caused the trouble were identified shortly after the fight, as television cameras had continued to roll. Many of the fans were subsequently featured in news stories and identified by the public. A similar approach was used to identify Guns N' Roses fans who rioted in Vancouver after the band cancelled a show at the last minute. The website the police set up received 12,000 hits per day in the first week, producing more than 80 useful tips.

Ed Diener's experiments (1976, 1979) have shown that such activities as throwing rocks and group singing can set the stage for more disinhibited behaviour. There is a self-reinforcing pleasure in acting impulsively while observing others doing likewise. When we see others act as we are acting, we think they feel as we do, which reinforces our own feelings (Orive, 1984). Moreover, impulsive group action absorbs our attention. When we yell at the referee, we are not thinking about our values; we are reacting to the immediate situation. Later, when we stop to think about what we have done or said, we sometimes feel chagrined. Sometimes. At other times we seek deindividuating group experiences—dances, worship experiences, group encounters—where we can enjoy intense positive feelings and closeness to others.

DIMINISHED SELF-AWARENESS

Group experiences that diminish self-consciousness tend to disconnect behaviour from attitudes. Dawn Mewhinney at the University of Guelph has found that one situation that may influence this phenomenon is people's expectations of a situation. For example, Mewhinney and her colleagues (1995) found that Canadian students going on spring break in Daytona Beach, Florida felt anonymous and believed that casual sex was both common and accessible. Perhaps not surprisingly, then, combining the perceptions of anonymity and perceived social norms, these students were more likely to engage in unplanned sexual activity. Consistent with this, experiments by Ed Diener (1980) and Steven Prentice-Dunn and Ronald Rogers (1980, 1989) reveal that unself-conscious, deindividuated people are less restrained, less self-regulated, more likely to act without thinking about their own values, and more responsive to the situation. These findings complement and reinforce the experiments on *self-awareness*.

Self-awareness is the opposite of deindividuation. Those made self-aware by acting in front of a mirror or TV camera exhibit *increased* self-control, and their actions more clearly reflect their attitudes. In front of a mirror, people taste-testing cream cheese varieties eat less of the high-fat variety (Sentyrz & Bushman, 1998).

People made self-aware are also less likely to cheat (Beaman & others, 1979; Diener & Wallbom, 1976). So are those who generally have a strong sense of themselves as distinct and independent (Nadler & others, 1982). People who are self-conscious, or who are temporarily made so, exhibit greater consistency between their words outside a situation and their deeds in it. Circumstances that decrease self-awareness, as alcohol consumption does, therefore increase deindividuation (Hull & others, 1983). And deindividuation decreases in circumstances that increase self-awareness: mirrors and cameras, small towns, bright lights, large name tags, undistracted quiet, individual clothes and houses (Ickes & others, 1978). When a teenager leaves for a party, a parent's parting advice could well be, "Have fun, and remember who you are." In other words, enjoy being with the group, but be self-aware; maintain your personal identity; don't become deindividuated.

CONCEPT TO REMEMBER

Deindividuation   p. 145

Please visit the *Exploring Social Psychology* Online Learning Centre at **www.mcgrawhill.ca/college/myers** to participate in module activities, view module videos, access research and study tools, and test your knowledge with interactive quizzes, exercises, and scenarios.

How Groups Intensify Decisions

Two Catholic pilgrims hold candles while listening to the late Pope John Paul II at World Youth Day in Toronto, Ontario, in July 2002. How might have participating in World Youth Day events strengthened the religious identities of the thousands of Catholics in attendance?

Group polarization
Group-produced enhancement of members' preexisting tendencies; a strengthening of the members' *average* tendency, not a split within the group.

Which effect—good or bad—does group interaction more often have? Police brutality and mob violence demonstrate its destructive potential. Yet, support-group leaders, management consultants, and educational theorists proclaim its benefits, and social and religious movements urge their members to strengthen their identities by fellowship with like-minded others.

Research helps clarify our understanding of such effects. Studies of people in small groups have produced a principle that helps explain both bad and good outcomes: *Group discussion often strengthens members' initial inclinations.* The research on this topic, called **group polarization**, illustrates the process of inquiry—how an interesting discovery often leads researchers to hasty and erroneous conclusions, which ultimately get replaced with more accurate conclusions. This is one scientific mystery David Myers can discuss firsthand, having been one of the detectives.

THE CASE OF THE "RISKY SHIFT"

A research literature of more than 300 studies began with a surprising finding by James Stoner (1961), then an MIT graduate student. For his master's thesis in industrial management, Stoner tested the commonly held belief that groups are more cautious than individuals. He posed decision dilemmas in which the participant's task was to advise imagined characters how much risk to take. Put yourself in the participant's shoes: What advice would you give the character in this situation?

> Helen is a writer who is said to have considerable creative talent but who so far has been earning a comfortable living by writing cheap westerns. Recently she has come up with an idea for a potentially significant novel. If it could be written and accepted, it might have considerable literary impact and be a big boost to her career. On the other hand, if she cannot work out her idea or if the novel is a flop, she will have expended considerable time and energy without remuneration.

Imagine that you are advising Helen. Please check the *lowest* probability that you would consider acceptable for Helen to attempt to write the novel.

Helen should attempt to write the novel if the chances that the novel will be a success are at least:

1 in 10

2 in 10

3 in 10

4 in 10

5 in 10

6 in 10

7 in 10

8 in 10

9 in 10

10 in 10 (Place a check here if you think Helen should attempt the novel only if it is certain that the novel will be a success.)

After making your decision, guess what this book's average reader would advise.

Having marked their advice on a dozen such items, five or so individuals would then discuss and reach agreement on each item. How do you think the group decisions compared to the average decision before the discussions? Would the groups be likely to take greater risks, be more cautious, or stay the same?

To everyone's amazement, the group decisions were usually riskier. Dubbed the "risky shift phenomenon," this finding set off a wave of group risk-taking studies. These revealed that risky shift occurs not only when a group decides by consensus; after a brief discussion, individuals, too, will alter their decisions. What is more, researchers successfully repeated Stoner's finding with people of varying ages and occupations in a dozen nations.

During discussion, opinions converged. Curiously, however, the point toward which they converged was usually a lower (riskier) number than their initial average. Here was a delightful puzzle. The small risky shift effect was reliable, unexpected, and without any immediately obvious explanation. What group influences produce such an effect? And how widespread is it? Do discussions in juries, business committees, and military organizations also promote risk taking? Does this explain why teenage reckless driving, as measured by death rates, nearly doubles when a 16- or 17-year-old driver has two passengers rather than none (Chen & others, 2000)? For this reason and others, most provinces issue new drivers *graduated* drivers' permits. These drivers must observe strict limitations (for example, a 0.00 blood alcohol level, no driving alone after midnight, and no infractions) for a period of years before they obtain an unrestricted licence.

After several years of study, as methodology and approach evolved, we learned that the risky shift was not universal. Sometimes people became *more cautious* after discussion. One of these featured "Roger," a young married man with two school-age children and a secure but low-paying job. Roger can afford life's necessities but few of its luxuries. He hears that the shares of a relatively unknown company may soon triple in value if its new product is favourably received or decline considerably if it does not sell. Roger has no savings. To invest in the company, he is considering selling his life insurance policy.

Can you see a general principle that predicts both the tendency to give riskier advice after discussing Helen's situation and more cautious advice after discussing Roger's?

If you are like most people, you would advise Helen to take a greater risk than Roger, even before talking with others. It turns out there is a strong tendency for discussion to accentuate these initial leanings.

We therefore realized that this group phenomenon was not a consistent shift to risk, but rather a tendency for group discussion to *enhance* group members' initial leanings. This idea led investigators to propose what Serge Moscovici and Marisa Zavalloni (1969) called a group polarization: Discussion typically strengthens the average inclination of group members.

DO GROUPS INTENSIFY OPINIONS?

Group Polarization Experiments

This new view of the changes induced by group discussion prompted experimenters to have people discuss statements that most of them favoured or most of them opposed. Would talking in groups enhance their initial inclinations, as it did with the decision dilemmas? In groups, would risk takers not only become riskier, but bigots also become despisers, and givers also become more philanthropic? That's what the group polarization hypothesis predicts (Figure 15-1).

Dozens of studies confirm group polarization. Moscovici and Zavalloni (1969) observed that discussion enhanced French students' initially positive attitude toward their president and negative attitude toward Americans. Mititoshi Isozaki (1984) found that Japanese university students gave more pronounced judgments of "guilty" after discussing a traffic case. And Glen Whyte (1993) reported that groups exacerbate the "too much invested to quit" phenomenon that has cost many businesses huge sums of money. Canadian business students imagined

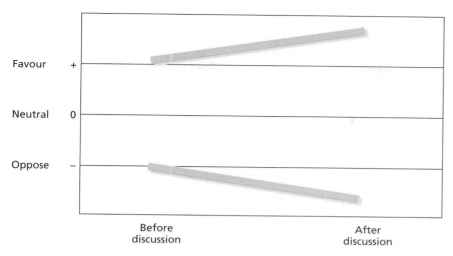

FIGURE 15-1

The group polarization hypothesis predicts that discussion will strengthen an attitude shared by group members. If people initially tend to favour something (say, risk on a life dilemma question), they tend to favour it even more after discussion. If they tend to oppose something, they tend to oppose it even more after discussion.

themselves having to decide whether to invest more money in the hope of preventing losses in various failing projects (for example, whether to make a high-risk loan to protect an earlier investment). They exhibited the typical effect: Seventy-two percent reinvested money they would seldom have invested if they were considering it as a new investment on its own merits. When making the same decision in groups, 94 percent opted for reinvestment.

Another research strategy has been to pick issues on which opinions are divided and then isolate people who hold the same view. Does discussion with like-minded people strengthen shared views? Does it magnify the attitude gap that separates the two sides?

George Bishop and David Myers wondered. So, they set up groups of relatively prejudiced and unprejudiced high school students and asked them to respond—before and after discussion—to issues involving racial attitudes, such as property rights versus open housing (Myers & Bishop, 1970). They found that the discussions among like-minded students did indeed increase the initial gap between the two groups.

Naturally Occurring Group Polarization

In everyday life, people associate mostly with others whose attitudes are similar to their own. (Look at your own circle of friends.) Does everyday group interaction with like-minded friends intensify shared attitudes? Do nerds become nerdier and jocks jockier? It happens. The self-segregation of boys into all-male groups and of girls into all-female groups accentuates over time their initially modest gender differences, notes Eleanor Maccoby (2002). Boys with boys become gradually more competitive and action oriented in their play and fictional fare, while girls with girls become more relationally oriented.

Group Polarization in Schools

One real-life parallel to the laboratory phenomenon is what education researchers have called the "accentuation phenomenon": Over time, initial differences among groups of college students become accentuated. If the students at college X are initially more intellectual than the students at college Y, that gap is likely to grow during college. Likewise, compared to fraternity and sorority members, independents tend to have more liberal political attitudes, a difference that grows with time in college (Pascarella & Terenzini, 1991). Researchers believe this results partly from group members reinforcing shared inclinations.

Group Polarization in Communities

Polarization also occurs in communities. During community conflicts, like-minded people associate increasingly with one another, amplifying their shared tendencies. Gang delinquency emerges from a process of mutual reinforcement within neighbourhood gangs, whose members share attributes and hostilities (Cartwright, 1975). If, on your block, "a second out-of-control 15-year-old moves in," surmises David Lykken (1997), "the mischief they get into as a team is likely to be more than merely double what the first would do on his own. . . . A gang is more dangerous than the sum of its individual parts." Indeed, "unsupervised peer groups" are "the strongest predictor" of a neighbourhood's crime victimization rate, report Bonita Veysey and Steven Messner (1999). Moreover, experimental interventions that group delinquent adolescents with other delinquents actually—no surprise to any group polarization researcher—*increase* the rate of problem behaviour (Dishion & others, 1999).

From their analysis of terrorist organizations around the world, Clark McCauley and Mary Segal (1987; McCauley, 2002) note that terrorism does not erupt suddenly. Rather, it arises among people whose shared grievances bring them together. As they interact in isolation from moderating influences, they become progressively more extreme. The social amplifier brings the signal in stronger. The result is violent acts that the individuals, apart from the group, would never have committed. Massacres are group phenomena, enabled by the killers egging each other on (Zajonc, 2000).

Group Polarization on the Internet

E-mail and electronic chat rooms offer a potential new medium for group interaction. By the beginning of the new century, 85 percent of Canadian teens were using the Internet for an average of 9.3 hours weekly (TGM, 2000). Its countless virtual groups enable peacemakers and neo-Nazis, geeks and goths, conspiracy theorists and cancer survivors, to isolate themselves with one another and find support for their shared concerns, interests, and suspicions (McKenna & Bargh, 1998, 2000).

The Story Behind the Research

The September 11, 2001 terrorist attacks on the World Trade Center and the Pentagon in the United States had a major impact on people around the world. One of the questions that people repeatedly asked was, "How could someone do this?" Most people (including U.S. President George W. Bush) called these terrorists "sick" and "evil" and said the attacks were the result of the actions of a few "extremists."

Dr. Don Taylor, a professor at McGill University in Montreal, has been conducting research on intergroup relations for many years. Early in his career, he noticed that psychologists exploring race relations (particularly in the U.S.) tended to focus on the negative behaviour of a few "extremists." Racism cannot be merely the problem of a few; otherwise, racism would not be a pervasive social problem. Clearly, racism involves widespread stereotyping and discrimination—it is everybody's problem. In Montreal, Dr. Taylor conducted research on Aboriginal peoples, a group in our culture whose members are discriminated against and are often marginalized by Canadian society. In 1990, Mohawks from Montreal-area reserves blocked access to the Mercier Bridge, one of the main arteries into and out of the city. During this blockade, Dr. Taylor was teaching on one of the reserves and was shuttled back and forth across police lines by a group of Mohawks with a speedboat. It was during this high-tension time that he became interested in what drove people to commit terrorist acts.

Dr. Taylor has argued that how most people approach the issue of extreme behaviour (such as terrorism) is too simplistic. He believes that if we label extremists as *sick* or *evil* it minimizes these acts and labels them as the unpredictable behaviour of madmen who must be hunted down and destroyed. Dr. Taylor and his colleagues (for example, Louis & Taylor, 2002; Taylor & Louis, 2004) have described the behaviour of extremists as very predictable from basic social psychological theory. We have to understand that people in groups tend to conform to the group, tend to polarize their beliefs, and tend to make decisions that are riskier and more extreme than individuals would on their own. When these existing tendencies are combined with real conflict and threats from outgroups, violence is really not all that surprising. In order to stop the extreme behaviour, we must understand why people are engaging in that behaviour in the first place. Dr. Taylor and his colleagues argue that if we can understand behaviour in this context, then we are in a better position to stop it from happening again in the future. Indeed, marginalizing these people (calling them sick and evil) and trying to hunt them down will only exacerbate the problem. Perhaps not surprisingly, efforts to fight terrorism head-on rarely meet with success. I

EXPLAINING GROUP POLARIZATION

Why do groups adopt stances that are more exaggerated than the average opinions of their individual members? Researchers hoped that solving the mystery of group polarization might provide some insights. Solving small puzzles sometimes provides clues for solving larger ones.

Among several proposed theories of group polarization, two survived scientific scrutiny. One deals with the arguments presented during a discussion, the other with how members of a group view themselves vis-à-vis the other members. The first idea is an example of informational influence (influence that results from accepting evidence about reality). The second is an example of normative influence (influence based on a person's desire to be accepted or admired by others).

Informational Influence

As we learned in Module 10, sometimes we agree with others because we think they have information we need to make the right decision—thus, group members are said to be having an *informational influence* on us. According to the best-supported explanation, group discussion elicits a pooling of ideas, most of which favour the dominant viewpoint. Ideas that were common knowledge to group members will often be brought up in discussion or, even if unmentioned, will jointly influence their discussion (Gigone & Hastie, 1993; Larson & others, 1994; Stasser, 1991). Other ideas may include persuasive arguments that some group members had not previously considered. When discussing Helen the writer, someone may say, "Helen should go for it, because she has little to lose. If her novel flops, she can always go back to writing cheap westerns." Such statements often entangle information about the person's *arguments* with cues concerning the person's *position* on the issue. But when people hear relevant arguments without learning the specific stands other people assume, they still shift their positions (Burnstein & Vinokur, 1977; Hinsz & others, 1997). *Arguments*, in and of themselves, matter.

Normative Influence

Social comparison
Evaluating one's opinions and abilities by comparing oneself to others.

Sometimes, people exert a *normative influence* on us—that is, we change our opinions or actions because we want to fit in with the group (be normal). Thus, a second explanation of polarization involves comparison with others. As Leon Festinger (1954) argued in his influential theory of **social comparison**, it is human nature to want to evaluate our opinions and abilities, something we can do by comparing our views with those of others. We are most persuaded by people in our "reference groups"—groups we identify with (Abrams & others, 1990; Hogg & others, 1990). Moreover, wanting people to like us, we may express stronger opinions after discovering that others share our views.

Perhaps you can recall a time when you and others were guarded and reserved in a group, until someone broke the ice and said, "Well, to be perfectly honest, I think . . ." Soon you were all surprised to discover strong support for your shared views.

Social comparison theory prompted experiments that exposed people to others' positions but not to their arguments. This is roughly the experience we have when reading the results of an opinion poll or of exit polling on election day. When people learn others' positions—without discussion—will they adjust their responses to maintain a socially favourable position? When people have made no prior commitment to a particular response, seeing others' responses does stimulate a small polarization (Goethals & Zanna, 1979; Sanders & Baron, 1977). This comparison-based polarization is usually less than that produced by a lively discussion. Still, it's surprising that, instead of simply conforming to the group average, people often go it one better.

GROUPTHINK

Do the social-psychological phenomena we have been considering in these first 15 modules occur in sophisticated groups like corporate boards or organizations such as NASA? Is there likely to be self-justification? Self-serving bias? A cohesive "we feeling" provoking conformity and rejection of dissent? Public commitment producing resistance to change? Group polarization? Social psychologist Irving Janis (1971, 1982) wondered whether such phenomena might help explain good and bad group decisions made by some twentieth-century American presidents and their advisers. To find out, he analyzed the decision-making procedures that led to several major fiascos, such as the lack of preparation for the World War II attack on Pearl Harbor, the ill-fated Bay of Pigs Invasion of Cuba by U.S.–sponsored forces, and the U.S. involvement in the Vietnam War.

More recently NASA has suffered through the loss of two space shuttles—the *Challenger*, which exploded shortly after takeoff in 1986, and the *Columbia*, which broke up over Texas on February 1, 2003, after heat shields that had been damaged during takeoff failed.

Janis believed blunders such as these were bred by the tendency of decision-making groups to suppress dissent in the interests of group harmony, a phenomenon he called **groupthink**. In work groups, camaraderie boosts productivity (Mullen & Copper, 1994). Moreover, team spirit is good for morale. But when making decisions, close-knit groups may pay a price. Janis believed that the soil from which groupthink sprouts includes an amiable, *cohesive* group; relative *isolation* of the group from dissenting viewpoints; and a *directive leader* who signals what decision he or she favours.

Groupthink "The mode of thinking that persons engage in when concurrence-seeking becomes so dominant in a cohesive in-group that it tends to override realistic appraisal of alternative courses of action."—Irving Janis (1971)

Symptoms of Groupthink

From historical records and the memoirs of participants and observers, Janis identified eight groupthink symptoms. These symptoms are a collective form of dissonance reduction that surface as group members try to maintain their positive group feeling when facing a threat (Turner & others, 1992, 1994).

The first two groupthink symptoms lead group members to *overestimate their group's might and right*:

- **An illusion of invulnerability**: The groups Janis studied all developed an excessive optimism that blinded them to warnings of danger.

- **Unquestioned belief in the group's morality:** Group members assume the inherent morality of their group and ignore ethical and moral issues.

Group members also become *closed-minded*:

- **Rationalization:** The groups discount challenges by collectively justifying their decisions.

- **Stereotyped view of opponent:** Participants in these groupthink tanks consider their enemies too evil to negotiate with or too weak and unintelligent to defend themselves against the planned initiative.

Finally, the group suffers from *pressures toward uniformity*:

- **Conformity pressure:** Group members rebuffed those who raised doubts about the group's assumption and plans, at times not by argument but by personal sarcasm.
- **Self-censorship:** Since disagreements were often uncomfortable and the groups seemed in consensus, members withheld or discounted their misgivings.
- **Illusion of unanimity:** Self-censorship and pressure not to puncture the consensus create an illusion of unanimity. What is more, the apparent consensus confirms the group's decision.
- **Mindguards:** Some members protect the group from information that would call into question the effectiveness or morality of its decisions.

Groupthink in Action

Groupthink symptoms can produce a failure to seek and discuss contrary information and alternative possibilities (Figure 15-2). When a leader promotes an idea and when a group insulates itself from dissenting views, groupthink may produce defective decisions (McCauley, 1989).

Groupthink was tragically evident in the decision process by which NASA decided to launch the space shuttle *Challenger* in January 1986 (Esser & Lindoerfer, 1989). Engineers at Morton Thiokol, which made the shuttle's rocket boosters, and at

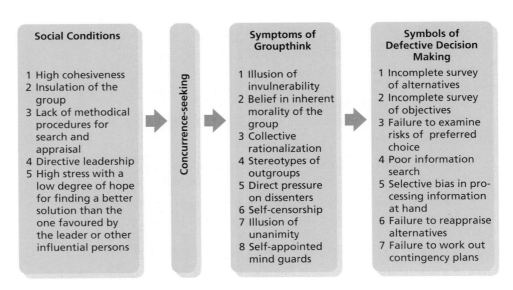

FIGURE 15-2
Theoretical analysis of groupthink.

Data from Janis & Mann, 1977, p. 132.

Rockwell International, which manufactured the orbiter, opposed the launch because of dangers posed to equipment by the subfreezing temperatures. The Thiokol engineers feared the cold would make the rubber seals between the rocket's four segments too brittle to contain the superhot gases. Several months before the doomed mission, the company's top expert had warned in a memo that it was a "jump ball" whether the seal would hold and that if it failed, "the result would be a catastrophe of the highest order" (Magnuson, 1986).

In a telephone discussion the night before the launch, the engineers argued their case with their uncertain managers and with NASA officials, who were eager to proceed with the already delayed launch. One Thiokol official later testified: "We got ourselves into the thought process that we were trying to find some way to prove to them [the booster] wouldn't work. We couldn't prove absolutely that it wouldn't work." The result was an *illusion of invulnerability*.

Conformity pressures also operated. One NASA official complained, "My God, Thiokol, when do you want me to launch, next April?" The top Thiokol executive declared, "We have to make a management decision," and then asked his engineering vice-president to "take off his engineering hat and put on his management hat."

To create an *illusion of unanimity*, this executive then proceeded to poll only the management officials and ignore the engineers. The go-ahead decision made, one of the engineers belatedly pleaded with a NASA official to reconsider: "If anything happened to this launch," he said prophetically, "I sure wouldn't want to be the person that had to stand in front of a board of inquiry to explain why I launched."

Thanks, finally, to *mindguarding*, the top NASA executive who made the final decision never learned about the engineers' concerns, nor about the reservations of the Rockwell officials. Protected from disagreeable information, he confidently gave the go-ahead to launch the *Challenger* on its tragic flight.

In 2003, tragedy struck again after NASA removed five members of an expert panel that warned of safety troubles for its aging shuttle fleet (Broad & Hulse, 2003). NASA said it was only bringing in fresh blood, but some of the panelists said the agency was trying to suppress their criticism, and that NASA was discounting their concerns, which, alas, gained credence when the *Columbia* disintegrated during its return to earth on February 1. Amazingly, when a report on the *Columbia* disaster was released in the summer of 2003, little seemed to have changed at NASA. Seventeen years after the *Challenger* explosion, another shuttled was destroyed, and the report on that disaster was eerily similar to the previous one.

British psychologists Ben Newell and David Lagnado (2003) believe groupthink symptoms may also have contributed to the invasion of Iraq by the U.S. and its allies. These authors and others contend that both Saddam Hussein and George W. Bush surrounded themselves with like-minded advisers, intimidated opposing voices into silence, and received filtered information that mostly supported their assumptions—Iraq's expressed assumption that the invading force could be resisted, and the U.S. assumption that a successful invasion would be followed by a short, peaceful occupation and a soon-thriving democracy.

Preventing Groupthink

Flawed group dynamics help explain many failed decisions; sometimes too many cooks spoil the broth. Given open leadership, however, a cohesive team spirit can improve decisions. Sometimes two or more heads *are* better than one. So, what can you do to avoid groupthink? Janis's (1982) recommendations for preventing groupthink incorporate many of the effective group procedures you can use in group situations:

- Be impartial—do not endorse any position.
- Encourage critical evaluation; assign a "devil's advocate."
- Occasionally subdivide the group, then reunite to air differences.
- Welcome critiques from outside experts and associates.
- Before implementing, call a "second-chance" meeting to air any lingering doubts.

OLC
Activity 15.1

When such steps are taken, group decisions may take longer to make yet ultimately prove less defective and more effective.

CONCEPTS TO REMEMBER

Group polarization   p. 152
Social comparison   p. 158
Groupthink   p. 159

Please visit the *Exploring Social Psychology* Online Learning Centre at **www.mcgrawhill.ca/college/myers** to participate in module activities, view module videos, access research and study tools, and test your knowledge with interactive quizzes, exercises, and scenarios.

Resisting Social Pressure

At this point in the book, some of you may be thinking, "I guess I don't really control my behaviour; it is all about the group!" Others among you are probably thinking the opposite: "This social psychology stuff is all nonsense—I make my own decisions!"

Which assessment is right? Do you have the most control over your own behaviour, or do forces outside you have the most control? You might suspect that, as with most psychological questions, the answer is "it depends." The last few modules have highlighted that the social context in which we find ourselves can clearly have an influence on our behaviour. However, that influence is definitely not universal. For example, not all of Milgram's participants obeyed; groups sometimes make excellent decisions; and we are not convinced by every advertisement we are exposed to. We can resist the social situation and sometimes even change it. Thus, each of these "social influence" modules concludes by calling attention to the opposite: the power of the person.

Perhaps stressing the power of culture leaves you somewhat uncomfortable. Most of us resent any suggestion that external forces determine our behaviour; we see ourselves as free beings, as the originators of our actions (well, at least of our good actions). We sense that believing in social determinism can lead to what philosopher Jean-Paul Sartre called "bad faith"—evading responsibility by blaming something or someone for one's fate.

The power of the social situation can have a powerful influence on our personal behaviour. What controls your behaviour: you or forces external to you?

Actually, social control (the power of the situation) and personal control (the power of the person) no more compete with one another than do biological and cultural explanations. Social and personal explanations of our social behaviour are both valid, for at any moment we are both the creatures and the creators of our social worlds. We may well be the products of our genes and environment. But it is also true that the future is coming, and it is our job to decide where it is going. Our choices today determine our environment tomorrow.

INTERACTING PERSONS AND SITUATIONS

Social situations do profoundly influence individuals. But individuals also influence social situations. The two *interact*.

The interaction occurs in at least three ways (Snyder & Ickes, 1985). First, a given social situation often *affects different people differently*. Because our minds do not see reality identically, each of us responds to a situation as we construe it. And some people are more sensitive and responsive to social situations than are others (Snyder, 1983). The Japanese, for example, are more responsive to social expectations than are the British (Argyle & others, 1978).

Second, interaction between persons and situations occurs because people often *choose their situations* (Ickes & others, 1997). Given a choice, sociable people select situations that evoke social interaction. When you chose your university or college, you were also choosing to expose yourself to a specific set of social influences. Ardent political liberals are unlikely to settle in Alberta and join the local Chamber of Commerce. They are more likely to live in Toronto and join Greenpeace (or to read *The Globe and Mail* rather than the *National Post*)—in other words, to choose a social world that reinforces their inclinations.

Third, people often *create their situations*. Recall again that our preconceptions can be self-fulfilling: If we expect someone to be extraverted, hostile, feminine, or sexy, our actions toward the person may induce the very behaviour we expect. What, after all, makes a social situation but the people in it? The social environment is not like the weather—something that just happens to us. It is more like our homes—something we make for ourselves.

The reciprocal causation between situations and persons allows us to see people as either *reacting to* or *acting upon* their environment. Each perspective is correct, for we are both the products and the architects of our social worlds. Is one perspective wiser, however? In one sense, it is wise to see ourselves as the creatures of our environments and to see others as free actors.

Perhaps we would do well more often to assume the reverse, however—to view ourselves as free agents and to view others as influenced by their environments. We would then assume self-efficacy as we view ourselves and seek understanding and social reform as we relate to others. (If we view others as influenced by their situations, we are more likely to understand and empathize than to smugly judge unpleasant behaviour as freely chosen by "immoral," "sadistic," or "lazy" persons.)

Most religions encourage us to take responsibility for ourselves but to refrain from judging others. Does religion teach this because our natural inclination is to excuse our own failures while blaming others for theirs?

RESISTING SOCIAL PRESSURE

Social psychology offers other reminders of the power of the person. We are not just billiard balls; we act in response to the forces that push upon us. Knowing that someone is trying to coerce us may even prompt us to react in the *opposite* direction. For example, think back to some of your early romantic relationships. Did you ever have a relationship with someone your parents did not like? Most of us have had this experience. You bring home the new love of your life, only to discover that your mother or father (or both) absolutely despises him or her. If your parents were social psychologists, they probably said nothing. However, if they were like most parents, they probably told you how they felt about your new *amour*. How did you react to this information? If you are like many of the students in the authors' classes, you probably liked your new love interest *even more* after you discovered your parents' true feelings. This is called *reactance*.

Reactance

Individuals value their sense of freedom and self-efficacy. So when social pressure becomes so blatant that it threatens their sense of freedom, they often rebel: think of children asserting their freedom and independence by doing the opposite of what their parents ask. Savvy parents, therefore, offer their children choices instead of commands: "It's time to clean up: Do you want a bath or a shower?"

The theory of psychological **reactance**—that people do indeed act to protect their sense of freedom—is supported by experiments showing that attempts to restrict a person's freedom often produce an anticonformity "boomerang effect" (Brehm & Brehm, 1981; Nail & others, 2000). After today's university women from Western cultures give thought to how traditional culture expects women to behave, they become *less* likely to exhibit traditional feminine modesty (Cialdini & others, 1998). Or suppose someone stops you on the street and asks you to sign a petition advocating something you mildly support. While considering the petition, you are told someone else believes "people absolutely should not be allowed to distribute or sign such petitions." Reactance theory predicts that such blatant attempts to limit freedom will actually increase the likelihood of your signing. When Madeline Heilman (1976) staged this experiment on the streets of New York City, that is precisely what she found.

Reactance may also contribute to underage drinking. A survey of 18- to 24-year-olds by the Canadian Centre on Substance Abuse (1997) revealed that 69 percent of those over the legal drinking age (21) had been drunk in the last year, as had 77 percent of those *under* 21. In the United States, a survey of students on 56 campuses revealed a 25-percent rate of abstinence among students of legal drinking age (21) but only a 19-percent abstinence rate among students under 21. The researchers, Ruth Engs and David Hanson (1989), also found that 15 percent of the legal-age students and 24 percent of the underage students were heavy drinkers. They suspect this

OLC
Activity 16.1

Reactance   A motive to protect or restore one's sense of freedom. Reactance arises when someone threatens our freedom of action.

reflects a reactance against the restriction. It probably also reflects peer influence. With alcohol use, as with drugs, peers influence attitudes, provide the substance, and offer a context for its use. This helps explain why postsecondary students, living in a peer culture that often supports alcohol use, drink more alcohol than their non-student peers (Atwell, 1986; Reitman & others, 2006).

Reactance may also play a role in more antisocial behaviours as well. Baumeister and colleagues (2002) have suggested that reactance processes may have an impact on sexual assault. They argue that when a woman refuses to comply with a man's desire for sex, he may react with frustration over his restricted freedom and increased desire for the forbidden activity. Mix reactance with narcissism—a self-serving sense of entitlement and low empathy for others—and the unfortunate result can be forced sex.

Reactance can occur in some rather unexpected situations as well. It may surprise you that in the 2001 census 20,000 Canadians indicated their religion as "Jedi." The Jedi, as you may know, are the guardians of peace and justice who manipulate the force to maintain order in the blockbuster *Star Wars* movies. Is this actually a religion 20,000 Canadians follow? Not likely. The move to choose Jedi as a religion was begun by Denis Dion, a man living outside Vancouver, as a protest (that is, reactance) against what he believed to be an intrusive Statistics Canada question. On the census, which Canadians are required to complete, one of the questions is concerning religion. Dion felt this question was none of the government's business and began an e-mail campaign to encourage others to defy the government by giving a bogus response: Jedi. Obviously, many others had a similar reaction, and indicated Jedi as their religion. Interestingly, this reaction has been seen in other countries as well—apparently there were 400,000 Jedi followers in the UK in 2001 (compared with 260,000 self-identified Jews), and 70,000 Australians listed themselves as Jedi in 2002.

Asserting Uniqueness

Imagine a world of complete conformity, where there were no differences among people. Would such a world be a happy place? If nonconformity can create discomfort, can sameness create comfort?

People feel uncomfortable when they appear too different from others. But, at least in Western cultures, they also feel uncomfortable when they appear exactly like everyone else. As experiments by C. R. Snyder and Howard Fromkin (1980) have shown, people feel better when they see themselves as unique. Moreover, they act in ways that will assert their individuality. In one experiment, Snyder (1980) led students to believe that their "10 most important attitudes" were either distinct from or nearly identical to the attitudes of 10,000 other students. When they then participated in a conformity experiment, those deprived of their feeling of uniqueness were most likely to assert their individuality by nonconformity. In another experiment, people who heard others express attitudes identical to their own altered their positions to maintain their sense of uniqueness.

Seeing oneself as unique also appears in people's "spontaneous self-concepts." William McGuire and his Yale University colleagues (McGuire & Padawer-Singer,

1978; McGuire & others, 1979) report that when children are invited to "tell us about yourself," they are most likely to mention their distinctive attributes. Foreign-born children are more likely than others to mention their birthplace. Redheads are more likely than black- and brown-haired children to volunteer their hair colour. Light and heavy children are the most likely to refer to their body weight. Minority children are the most likely to mention their race. Likewise, we become more keenly aware of our gender when we are with people of the other sex (Cota & Dion, 1986).

The principle, says McGuire, is that "one is conscious of oneself insofar as, and in the ways that, one is different." Thus, "If I am a Black woman in a group of White women, I tend to think of myself as a Black; if I move to a group of Black men, my blackness loses salience and I become more conscious of being a woman" (McGuire & others, 1978). This insight helps us understand why any minority group tends to be conscious of its distinctiveness and how the surrounding culture relates to it. The majority group, being less conscious of race, may see the minority group as hypersensitive. As another example, imagine you are sitting in your social psychology class and the person next to you asks you where you live. What would you say? You would probably give the name of the part of the city or the residence you live in. That is what identifies you. However, let's imagine you are visiting Stonehenge in England and someone asks you the same question. What is the most identifying information for you then? Probably that you live in Canada.

When the people of two cultures are nearly identical, they still will notice their differences, however small. Even trivial distinctions may provoke scorn and conflict. Jonathan Swift satirized the phenomenon in *Gulliver's Travels* with the story of the Little-Endians' war against the Big-Endians. Their difference: The Little-Endians preferred to break their eggs on the small end, the Big-Endians on the large end. On a world scale, the differences may not seem great between Scots and English, Hutus and Tutsis, Serbs and Croatians, or Canadians and Americans. But small differences can mean big conflicts (Rothbart & Taylor, 1992). Rivalry is often most intense when the other group most closely resembles you.

It seems that, while we do not like being greatly deviant, we are, ironically, all alike in wanting to feel distinctive and in noticing how we are distinctive. But as research on the self-serving bias (Module 4) makes clear, it is not just any kind of distinctiveness we seek, but distinctiveness in the right direction. Our quest is not merely to be different from the average, but *better* than average.

MINORITY INFLUENCE

We have seen that:

- Cultural situations mould us, but we also help create and choose these situations;

- Pressures to conform sometimes overwhelm our better judgment, but blatant pressure can motivate us to assert our individuality and freedom;

- Persuasive forces are indeed powerful, but we can resist persuasion by making public commitments and by anticipating persuasive appeals.

Consider, finally, how individuals can influence their groups.

At the beginning of most social movements, a small minority will sometimes sway, and then even become, the majority. "All history," wrote Ralph Waldo Emerson, "is a record of the power of minorities, and of minorities of one." Think of Copernicus and Galileo; of Martin Luther King, Jr. The American civil rights movement was ignited by the refusal of one African American woman, Rosa Parks, to relinquish her seat on a Montgomery, Alabama, bus. In Manitoba, one man's stand changed the course of constitutional reform in Canada. In 1990, the Meech Lake Accord was billed as the solution to Canada's constitutional crisis, but many people were disenchanted with the process through which it had been developed. Nonetheless, it appeared the Accord would pass. However, with time running short before the Accord expired, in order for debate to begin the Manitoba Legislature needed to unanimously waive the formality of a waiting period. Elijah Harper, a Manitoba MLA and an Aboriginal, was frustrated that the Meech Lake Accord had not taken Aboriginal peoples' views or concerns about constitutional reform into account. Therefore, he alone—against tremendous pressure from federal and provincial parties—voted against the waiver. Shortly after this vote, Newfoundland and Labrador Premier Clyde Wells announced he would not be putting the Accord forward for discussion in the Newfoundland and Labrador Legislature. These two actions effectively killed the Meech Lake Accord.

Small groups of people can also have an important impact on the larger group. In the early 1900s women did not have the right to vote in Canada. In 1914, Nellie McClung presided over a mock Parliament of women who presented arguments about the disasters that would befall society if men got the vote ("Politics unsettle men, and unsettled men mean unsettled bills, broken furniture, broken vows and divorce. Men's place is on the farm"). This event was key to turning the public tide in favour of granting women the vote in Canada.

What makes a minority persuasive? Experiments initiated by Serge Moscovici in Paris have identified several determinants of minority influence: consistency, self-confidence, and defection from the majority.

Consistency

More influential than a minority that wavers is a minority that sticks to its position. Moscovici and his associates (1969, 1985) have found that if a minority consistently judges blue slides as green, members of the majority will occasionally agree. But if the minority wavers, saying "blue" to one-third of the blue slides and "green" to the rest, virtually no one in the majority will ever agree with "green."

Still debated is the nature of this influence (Clark & Maass, 1990; Levine & Russo, 1987). Moscovici believes that a minority's following the majority usually reflects just public compliance, but a majority's following a minority usually reflects genuine acceptance—really recalling the blue slide as greenish. In public, people may wish not to align themselves with a deviant, minority view (Wood & others, 1994, 1996). A majority can also give us a rule of thumb for deciding truth ("All those smart cookies can't be wrong"); a minority influences us by making us think more deeply (Burnstein & Kitayama, 1989; Mackie, 1987). Minority influence is therefore more likely to take the thought-filled central route to persuasion. Experiments show—and experience confirms—that nonconformity, especially persistent nonconformity, is often painful (Levine, 1989). If you set out to be Ralph Waldo Emerson's minority of one, prepare yourself for ridicule—especially when you argue an issue that's personally relevant to the majority and when the group wants to settle an issue by reaching consensus (Kameda & Sugimori, 1993; Kruglanski & Webster, 1991; Trost & others, 1992). People may attribute your dissent to psychological peculiarities (Papastamou & Mugny, 1990). When Charlan Nemeth (1979) planted a minority of two within a simulated jury and had them oppose the majority's opinions, the duo was inevitably disliked. Nevertheless, the majority acknowledged that the persistence of the two did more than anything else to make them rethink their positions.

A persistent minority is influential, even if not popular, partly because it soon becomes the focus of debate (Schachter, 1951). Being the centre of conversation allows one to contribute a disproportionate number of arguments. And Nemeth reports that in minority influence experiments, as in the group polarization studies, the position supported by the most arguments usually wins. Talkative group members are usually influential (Mullen & others, 1989).

Self-Confidence

Consistency and persistence convey self-confidence. Furthermore, Nemeth and Joel Wachtler (1974) reported that any behaviour by a minority that conveys self-confidence—for example, taking the head seat at the table—tends to raise self-doubts among the majority. By being firm and forceful, the minority's apparent self-assurance may prompt the majority to reconsider its position. This is especially so on matters of opinion rather than fact. In her research at Italy's University of Padova, Anne Maass and her colleagues (1996) report that minorities are less persuasive regarding fact ("from which country does Italy import most of its raw oil?") than regarding attitude ("from which country should Italy import most of its raw oil?").

Defections from the Majority

A persistent minority punctures any illusion of unanimity. When a minority consistently doubts the majority wisdom, majority members become freer to express their own doubts and may even switch to the minority position. In research with university students, John Levine (1989) found that a minority person who had defected from the majority was more persuasive than a consistent minority voice. In her jury-simulation experiments, Nemeth found that once defections begin, others often soon follow, initiating a snowball effect.

Are these factors that strengthen minority influence unique to minorities? Sharon Wolf and Bibb Latané (1985; Wolf, 1987) and Russell Clark (1995) believe not. They argue that the same social forces work for both majorities and minorities. Informational and normative influence fuels both group polarization and minority influence. And if consistency, self-confidence, and defections from the other side strengthen the minority, such variables also strengthen a majority. The social impact of any position depends on the strength, immediacy, and number of those who support it. Minorities have less influence than majorities simply because they are smaller.

Anne Maass and Russell Clark (1984, 1986) agree with Moscovici, however, that minorities are more likely to convert people to *accepting* their views. And from their analyses of how groups evolve over time, John Levine and Richard Moreland (1985) conclude that new recruits to a group exert a different type of minority influence than do longtime members. Newcomers exert influence through the attention they receive and the group awareness they trigger in the old-timers. Established members feel freer to dissent and to exert leadership.

There is a delightful irony in this new emphasis on how individuals can influence the group. Until recently, the idea that the minority could sway the majority was itself a minority view in social psychology. Nevertheless, by arguing consistently and forcefully, Moscovici, Nemeth, Maass, Clark and others have convinced the majority of group influence researchers that minority influence is a phenomenon worthy of study. And the way that several of these minority influence researchers came by their interests should, perhaps, not surprise us. Anne Maass (1998) became interested in how minorities could effect social change after growing up in post-war Germany and hearing her grandmother's personal accounts of fascism. Charlan Nemeth (1999) developed her interest while she was a visiting professor in Europe "working with Henri Tajfel and Serge Moscovici. The three of us were 'outsiders'—I an American Roman Catholic female in Europe, they having survived World War II as Eastern European Jews. Sensitivity to the value and the struggles of the minority perspective came to dominate our work."

IS LEADERSHIP MINORITY INFLUENCE?

Leadership The process by which certain group members motivate and guide the group.

OLC
Activity 16.2

One example of the power of individuals is **leadership**, the process by which certain individuals mobilize and guide groups. Leadership matters, note Robert Hogan and associates (1994). In 1910, the Norwegians and English engaged in an epic race to the South Pole. The Norwegians, effectively led by Roald Amundsen, made it. The English, ineptly led by Robert Falcon Scott, did not; Scott and three team members died. Some coaches move from team to team, transforming losers into winners each time.

Some leaders are formally appointed or elected; others emerge informally as the group interacts. What makes for good leadership often depends on the situation—the best person to lead the engineering team may not make the best leader of the sales force. Some people excel at *task leadership*—at organizing work, setting standards, and focusing on goal attainment. Others excel at *social leadership*—at building teamwork, mediating conflicts, and being supportive.

Task leaders often have a directive style—one that can work well if the leader is bright enough to give good orders (Fiedler, 1987). Being goal oriented, such leaders also keep the group's attention and effort focused on its mission. Experiments show that the combination of specific, challenging goals and periodic progress reports helps motivate high achievement (Locke & Latham, 1990).

Social leaders often have a democratic style—one that delegates authority, welcomes input from team members, and, as we have seen, helps prevent groupthink.

The Story Behind the Research

Dr. Steven Spencer, a professor at the University of Waterloo, has been interested in the effect of stereotypes on people's attitudes and behaviour for a number of years. His recent work has focused on the role of stereotype threat and how this influences people's behaviours and judgments. Although we will focus on the issue of stereotypes, stereotype threat, and prejudice in later modules, one element of Dr. Spencer's research is particularly relevant to women in leadership positions. Dr. Spencer and his colleagues (Davies & others, 2005) explored how priming gender stereotypes can influence women's decisions whether to get involved in leadership roles.

In their experiment they exposed women to a set of TV commercials. In the experimental condition, women saw a set of ads that included two commercials with women in gender-stereotypic roles. In one commercial a teenager jumped up and down on her bed to express delight with a new acne medication. Another had a postsecondary-aged woman dreaming of becoming the homecoming queen. The control condition had women watching a set of non-gender-related commercials. Later in the study, the women were given the opportunity to indicate their preference for being a leader in a problem-solving task (directing the work of a group of problem solvers) or being one of the workers. Women who had been exposed to the gender-stereotypic commercials were more likely to indicate a preference for subordinate roles over leadership roles. This research demonstrates that leadership, which is key on so many issues, may be a role women avoid if they are afraid that they may be judged by others in a stereotypic way.

Many experiments reveal that such leadership is good for morale. Group members usually feel more satisfied when they participate in making decisions (Spector, 1986; Vanderslice & others, 1987). Given control over their tasks, workers also become more motivated to achieve (Burger, 1987). People who value good group feeling and take pride in achievement therefore thrive under social leadership.

Social leadership can be seen in the move by many businesses toward participative management, a management style common in Sweden and Japan (Naylor, 1990; Sundstrom & others, 1990). Ironically, a major influence on this "Japanese-style" management was M.I.T. social psychologist Kurt Lewin. In laboratory and factory experiments, Lewin and his students demonstrated the benefits of inviting workers to participate in decision making. Shortly before World War II, Lewin visited Japan and explained his findings to industrial and academic leaders (Nisbett & Ross, 1991). Japan's collectivist culture provided a receptive audience for Lewin's ideas about teamwork. Eventually, his influence circled back to North America.

The once-popular "great person" theory of leadership—that all great leaders share certain traits—has fallen into disrepute. Effective leadership styles, we now know, vary with the situation. People who know what they are doing may resent task leadership, while those who don't may welcome it. Recently, however, social psychologists have again wondered if there might be qualities that mark a good leader in many situations (Hogan & others, 1994). British social psychologists Peter Smith and Monir Tayeb (1989) report that studies done in India, Taiwan, and Iran have found that the most effective supervisors in coal mines, banks, and government offices score high on tests of *both* task and social leadership. They are actively concerned with how work is progressing *and* sensitive to the needs of their subordinates.

Studies also reveal that many effective leaders of laboratory groups, work teams, and large corporations exhibit the behaviours that help make a minority view persuasive. Such leaders engender trust by *consistently* sticking to their goals. And they often exude a *self-confident* charisma that kindles the allegiance of their followers (Bennis, 1984; House & Singh, 1987). Charismatic leaders typically have a compelling *vision* of some desired state of affairs, an ability to *communicate* this to others in clear and simple language, and enough optimism and faith in their group to *inspire* others to follow.

To be sure, groups also influence their leaders. Sometimes those at the front of the herd have simply sensed where it is already heading. Political candidates know how to read the opinion polls. Someone who typifies the group's views is more likely to be selected as a leader; a leader who deviates too radically from the group's standards may be rejected (Hogg & others, 1998). Smart leaders usually remain with the majority and spend their influence prudently. Nevertheless, effective individual leaders can sometimes exhibit a type of minority influence by mobilizing and guiding their group's energy.

In rare circumstances, the right traits matched with the right situation yield history-making greatness, notes Dean Keith Simonton (1994). To have a Winston Churchill or a Margaret Thatcher, a Mackenzie King or a Martin Luther King, Jr., takes the right person in the right place at the right time. When an apt combination of intelligence, skill, determination, self-confidence, and social charisma meets a rare opportunity, the result is sometimes a championship, a Nobel Prize, or a social revolution. Just ask Nellie McClung or Rosa Parks.

CONCEPTS TO REMEMBER

Reactance   p. 165
Leadership   p. 170

Please visit the *Exploring Social Psychology* Online Learning Centre at **www.mcgrawhill.ca/college/myers** to participate in module activities, view module videos, access research and study tools, and test your knowledge with interactive quizzes, exercises, and scenarios.

PART FOUR

Social Relations

Having explored how we do social psychology (Part One), and how we think about (Part Two) and influence (Part Three) one another, we come to social psychology's fourth facet—how we relate to one another. Our feelings and actions toward other people are sometimes negative, sometimes positive.

The upcoming modules on aggression, bias, and prejudice examine the unpleasant aspects of human relations: Why do we dislike, even despise, one another? Why and when do we hurt one another?

Then in the modules on conflict resolution, helping, liking, and loving, we explore the more pleasant aspects: How can social conflicts be justly and amicably resolved? When will we offer help to others? Why do we like or love particular people?

Understanding Aggression

I n February 1996, Jean Chrétien, then the prime minister of Canada, was wading through a crowd celebrating Flag Day in Hull, Quebec. Suddenly, the PM was confronted by an anti-poverty protester yelling insults into his face. Canadians were shocked by what happened next—the Prime Minister grabbed the protestor by the throat and angrily threw him aside. Although the protestor did not resist them, the RCMP officers who came to the PM's aid knocked out two of the protester's teeth. Who was the aggressor in this situation? Was there more than one aggressor?

How do you define *aggression*? Was the protester being the aggressor? Was it the PM? Or was it the RCMP? Is it aggression if someone gives you the finger after you cut them off in traffic? Is it aggression when you check an opposing player into the boards during a hockey game? How about if you suckerpunch another player from behind (like Vancouver Canucks player Todd Bertuzzi did to the Colorado Avalanche's Steve Moore, apparently ending his career)? Go to the Online Learning Centre and complete Activity 17.1 to judge whether the actions described constitute aggression.

As you will have noticed in Activity 17.1, aggression is not limited to individual-on-individual behaviour. Aggression can be perpetrated by the collective as well. In his 2003 book *Shake Hands with the Devil*, Canadian Lt-Gen. Romeo Dallaire describes

While some theorize that aggression is a fundamental part of human nature, others believe that society teaches humans to be violent. What are some variables that might affect our tolerance of aggression?

OLC
Activity 17.1

War-related deaths over the centuries (millions)

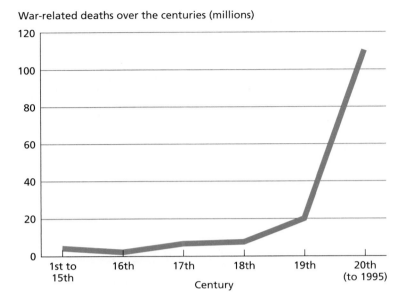

FIGURE 17-1

The bloodiest century. Twentieth-century humanity was the most educated, and homicidal, in history (data from Renner, 1999). Adding in genocides and human-made famines, there were approximately 182 million "deaths by mass unpleasantness" (White, 2000).

in horrific detail the slaughter of 800,000 Tutsis by rival Hutus in the 1994 "ethnic cleansing" of Rwanda. Although General Dallaire was in charge of the United Nations mission sent to the area to maintain order, the UN group was not authorized to intervene when the slaughter began. It took only a short 100 days to accomplish the killings. Unfortunately, even this level of violence is not unique.

During the last 100 years, 250 wars have killed 110 million people (see Figure 17-1). These tolls have come not only from the two World Wars, but also from countless genocides such as the Ottoman Empire genocide of Armenians, the Pakistani genocide of 3 million Bangladeshis, and the 1.5 million Cambodians murdered in a reign of terror that began in 1975 (Sternberg, 2003). As Hitler's genocide of millions of Jews, Stalin's genocide of millions of Russians, Mao's genocide of millions of Chinese, and the early North Americans' genocide of Aboriginal peoples attest, the human potential for cruelty knows no geographical or ethnic bounds.

Aggression Physical or verbal behaviour intended to hurt someone.

To a social psychologist, **aggression** is *any physical or verbal behaviour intended to hurt someone.* This excludes auto accidents, dental treatments, and sidewalk collisions. It includes slaps, direct insults, even gossipy "digs."

THEORIES OF AGGRESSION

Is Aggression an Instinct?

Philosophers have long debated whether our human nature is fundamentally that of a benign, contented, "noble savage" or that of a potentially explosive brute. The first view, argued by the eighteenth-century French philosopher Jean-Jacques Rousseau (1712–1778), blames society, not human nature, for social evils. The second idea, associated with the English philosopher Thomas Hobbes (1588–1679), sees society's laws as necessary to restrain and control the human brute. In the last century, the "brutish" view—that aggressive drive is inborn and thus inevitable—was argued by Sigmund Freud in Vienna and Konrad Lorenz in Germany.

Freud speculated that human aggression springs from a self-destructive impulse. It redirects toward others the energy of a primitive death urge (which, loosely speaking, he called the "death instinct"). Lorenz, an animal behaviour expert, saw aggression as adaptive rather than self-destructive. Both agreed that aggressive energy is instinctual (unlearned and universal). If not discharged, it supposedly builds up until it explodes or until an appropriate stimulus "releases" it, like a mouse releasing a mousetrap. Although Lorenz (1976) also argued that we have innate mechanisms for inhibiting aggression (such as making ourselves defenceless), he feared the implications of arming our "fighting instinct" without arming our inhibitions.

The idea that aggression is an instinct collapsed as the list of supposed human instincts grew to include nearly every conceivable human behaviour, and scientists became aware how much behaviour varies from person to person and culture to culture. Yet, biology clearly does influence behaviour just as nurture works upon nature. Our experiences interact with the nervous system engineered by our genes.

Neural Influences

Because aggression is a complex behaviour, no one spot in the brain controls it. But researchers have found neural systems in both animals and humans that facilitate aggression. When the scientists activate these areas in the brain, hostility increases; when they deactivate them, hostility decreases. Docile animals can thus be provoked into rage, and raging animals into submission.

In one experiment, researchers placed an electrode in an aggression-inhibiting area of a domineering monkey's brain. One small monkey, given a button that activated the electrode, learned to push it every time the tyrant monkey became intimidating. Brain activation works with humans, too. After receiving painless electrical stimulation in her amygdala (a part of the brain core), one woman became enraged and smashed her guitar against the wall, barely missing her psychiatrist's head (Moyer, 1976, 1983).

So, are violent people's brains in some way abnormal? To find out, Adrian Raine and his colleagues (1998, 2000) used brain scans to measure brain activity in murderers whose violence could not be attributed to childhood abuse or neglect and to measure the amount of grey matter in men with antisocial conduct disorder. They found that the prefrontal cortex, which acts like an emergency brake on deeper brain areas involved in aggressive behaviour, was 14 percent less active than normal in the nonabused murderers and 15 percent smaller in the antisocial men. Did the brain abnormality by itself predispose violence? Possibly not, but for some violent people it likely is a factor (Davidson & others, 2000).

Genetic Influences

Heredity influences the neural system's sensitivity to aggressive cues. It has long been known that animals of many species can be bred for aggressiveness. Sometimes this is done for practical purposes (the breeding of fighting cocks). Sometimes, breeding is done for research. Finnish psychologist Kirsti Lagerspetz (1979) took normal albino mice and bred the most aggressive ones together and the least aggressive ones. After repeating the procedure for 26 generations, she had one set of fierce mice and one set of placid mice.

Aggressiveness naturally varies among primates and humans (Asher, 1987; Olweus, 1979). Our temperaments—how intense and reactive we are—are partly brought with us into the world, influenced by our sympathetic nervous system's reactivity (Kagan, 1989). Identical twins, when asked separately, are more likely than fraternal twins to agree on whether they have "a violent temper" or have gotten in fights (Rowe & others, 1999; Rushton & others, 1986). Yet a person's temperament, observed in infancy, usually endures (Larsen & Diener, 1987; Wilson & Maheny, 1986). A child who is non-aggressive at age 8 will very likely still be non-aggressive at age 48 (Huesmann & others, 2003).

Blood Chemistry

Blood chemistry also influences neural sensitivity to aggressive stimulation. Both laboratory experiments and police data indicate that when people are provoked, alcohol unleashes aggression (Bushman, 1993; Bushman & Cooper, 1990; Taylor & Chermack, 1993; Testa, 2002). Violent people are more likely (1) to drink, and (2) to become aggressive when intoxicated (White & others, 1993). Consider:

- Tara MacDonald (at Queen's University) and her colleagues (MacDonald & others, 2000; Ortner & others, 2003) found that when intoxicated, people administer more painful electric shocks and are angrier.

- Peter Hoaken at McGill University has found (Hoaken & Pihl, 2000) that both men and women are more susceptible to provocation when intoxicated.

- Statistics Canada reports that in 2004 half of homicide victims and three-quarters of accused persons had consumed alcohol or drugs at the time of the crime.

The Story Behind the Research

Dr. Kathryn Graham, a senior scientist and Head of Social Factors and Prevention Interventions at the Centre for Addiction and Mental Health and an adjunct professor at the University of Western Ontario, has been exploring the role of alcohol in aggressive behaviour for more than 25 years. As a graduate student in social psychology at Simon Fraser University, Dr. Graham earned extra money as a bartender/waitress in a number of bars and clubs in Vancouver. As part of a course on aggression, she completed a project on alcohol and aggression where it became apparent that most of the research focused on a simplistic causal relationship between alcohol and aggression—namely, that alcohol consumption leads to aggressive behaviour. This simplistic relationship was not consistent with the wide range of behaviours that she had observed while working in the bars, specifically that the barroom environment had a large impact on the alcohol–aggression relationship. She was able to demonstrate this effect as part of an observational study of more than 200 bars and clubs in Vancouver conducted for her master's thesis and funded by the Nonmedical Use of Drugs Directorate of Health Canada (Graham & others, 1980).

Along with her colleagues, Dr. Graham has demonstrated a number of important findings regarding the relationship between alcohol and aggression. For example, a survey of 1,753 Ontario residents (Graham & Wells, 2001) found important gender differences in aggression, with women being more likely than men to be involved in aggression with someone of the opposite sex, often a romantic partner; men were more likely than women to engage in aggression with a same-sex opponent, often a stranger and often when both had been drinking, and frequently occurring in a bar or club. Moreover, the emotional impact of aggression appeared to be greater for women than for men (see Module 9 for a discussion of gender and aggression).

The higher rate of violence and violent crime among men, especially for physical violence in bars and clubs, led Graham and her colleague Samantha Wells to conduct a qualitative interview study with young men (Graham & Wells, 2003). This study found that fighting in bars and clubs was generally seen as normative and acceptable among young men. In terms of the role of alcohol in these incidents, it was seen as contributing to aggression by making people less aware of risks and more likely to take risks even when they were aware of them, increasing feelings of power and invincibility and increasing emotional responses to frustration and provocation. A later study examining aggression among adolescents found that drinking in public locations (bars, cars) was especially associated with increased risk of aggression for young men (Graham & others, 2005).

Dr. Graham and her colleagues have applied their extensive research on alcohol and aggression to the prevention of violence and injury in public drinking establishments. During the late 1990s they developed the *Safer Bars* program, which consists of two main components: (1) a workbook to help the bar owner/manager assess factors in the barroom environment that can contribute to aggressive behaviour (for example, bar layout factors such as bottlenecks; aggressive or poorly trained staff); and (2) a three-hour training session for bar staff and managers on how to prevent and reduce aggression, including issues such as assessing the situation before intervening, working as a team, not losing your temper with frustrating customers, using effective problem-solving skills and body language, and knowing your legal responsibilities. The program was evaluated in a randomized controlled trial conducted in large-capacity bars and clubs in Toronto. This large-scale study, funded by the U.S. National Institute on Alcohol Abuse and Alcoholism, employed more than 150 researchers who conducted unobtrusive observations before and after the intervention. The evaluation suggested that the program was working. Dr. Graham and her colleagues found significant improvements in knowledge and attitudes among staff who participated in the program, as well as significantly lower rates of moderate and severe physical aggression among bars and clubs that received the Safer Bars program compared with bars and clubs in the control group (Graham & others, 2004).

Alcohol enhances aggressiveness by reducing people's self-awareness and by reducing their ability to consider consequences (Hull & Bond, 1986; Ito & others, 1996; Steele & Southwick, 1985). Alcohol deindividuates, and it disinhibits.

Aggressiveness also correlates with the male sex hormone, testosterone. Although hormonal influences appear much stronger in lower animals than in humans, drugs that diminish testosterone levels in violent human males will subdue their aggressive tendencies.

After people reach age 25, their testosterone levels and rates of violent crime decrease together. Testosterone levels tend to be higher among prisoners convicted of unprovoked violent crimes than of nonviolent crimes (Dabbs, 1992; Dabbs & others, 1995, 1997). And among the normal range of teen boys and adult men, those with high testosterone levels are more prone to delinquency, hard drug use, and aggressive responses to provocation (Archer, 1991; Dabbs & Morris, 1990; Olweus & others, 1988). Testosterone, says James Dabbs (2000), "is a small molecule with large effects." Injecting a man with testosterone won't automatically make him aggressive, yet men with low testosterone are somewhat less likely to react aggressively when provoked (Geen, 1998).

PSYCHOLOGICAL INFLUENCES ON AGGRESSION

There exist important neural, genetic, and biochemical influences on aggression. Biological influences predispose some people more than others to react aggressively to conflict and provocation. But there is more to the story.

Frustration and Aggression

Frustration The blocking of goal-directed behaviour.

One of the first psychological theories of aggression is the popular frustration-aggression theory. "Frustration always leads to some form of aggression," said John Dollard and his colleagues (1939, p. 1). **Frustration** is anything (such as the malfunctioning vending machine) that blocks our attaining a goal. Frustration grows when our motivation to achieve a goal is very strong, when we expected gratification, and when the blocking is complete. When Rupert Brown and his colleagues (2001) surveyed British ferry passengers heading to France, they found much higher aggressive attitudes on a day when French fishing boats blockaded the port, preventing their travel. Blocked from obtaining their goal, the passengers became more likely (in responding to various vignettes) to agree with, for example, an insult toward a French person who had spilled coffee.

Displacement The redirection of aggression to a target other than the source of the frustration. Generally, the new target is a safer or more socially acceptable target.

As Figure 17-2 suggests, the aggressive energy need not explode directly against its source. We learn to inhibit direct retaliation, especially when others might disapprove or punish; instead, we *displace* our hostilities to safer targets. **Displacement** occurs in the old anecdote about a man who, humiliated by his boss, berates his wife, who yells at their son, who kicks the dog, which bites the mail carrier. In experiments and in real life, however, displaced aggression is most likely when the target shares some similarity to the instigator and does some minor irritating act that unleashes the displaced aggression (Marcus-Newhall & others, 2000; Miller & others, 2003;

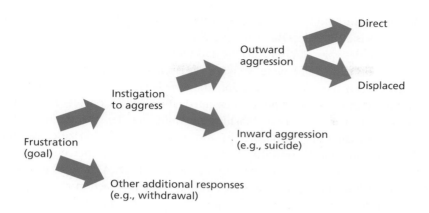

FIGURE 17-2

The classic frustration-aggression theory. Frustration creates a motive to aggress. Fear of punishment or disapproval for aggressing against the source of frustration may cause the aggressive drive to be displaced against some other target or even redirected against oneself.

Source: Based on Dollard & others, 1939; and Miller, 1941.

Pedersen & others, 2000). When a person harbours anger, even a trivial offence may elicit an explosive overreaction.

Laboratory tests of the frustration-aggression theory produced mixed results: Sometimes frustration increased aggressiveness, sometimes not. For example, if the frustration were understandable—if, as in one experiment by Eugene Burnstein and Philip Worchel (1962), a confederate disrupted a group's problem solving because his hearing aid malfunctioned (rather than just because he paid no attention)—then frustration led to irritation, not aggression.

Leonard Berkowitz (1978, 1989) realized that the original theory overstated the frustration-aggression connection, so he revised it. Berkowitz theorized that frustration produces *anger*, an emotional readiness to aggress. Anger arises when someone who frustrates us could have chosen to act otherwise (Averill, 1983; Weiner, 1981). A frustrated person is especially likely to lash out when aggressive cues pull the cork, releasing bottled-up anger. Sometimes the cork will blow without such cues. But, as we will see, cues associated with aggression amplify aggression (Carlson & others, 1990).

Berkowitz (1968, 1981, 1995) and others have found that the sight of a weapon is such a cue, especially when perceived as an instrument of violence rather than recreation. In one experiment, children who had just played with toy guns became more willing to knock down another child's blocks. In another, angered University of Wisconsin men gave more electric shocks to their tormenter when a rifle and a revolver (supposedly left over from a previous experiment) were nearby than when badminton racquets had been left behind (Berkowitz & LePage, 1967). Guns prime hostile thoughts and punitive judgments (Anderson & others, 1998; Dienstbier & others, 1998). Perhaps it is no surprise, then, that in 2003 two-thirds of U.S. murders were committed with firearms. As a comparison, in 2004 in Canada, only 28 percent of murders were committed using firearms—less than half the U.S. proportion. However, this is only part of the story: in 2002 in the U.S. there were 12,129 firearms-related homicides (plus 17,108 suicides and more than 1,000 accidental shootings), whereas in Canada there were 152 firearms-related homicides that same year. Although the U.S. has 10 times the population of Canada (298 million versus 30 million), it has 80 times the number of firearms deaths. Why? Consider that Vancouver, British Columbia, and Seattle, Washington, have similar populations, climates, economies, and rates of criminal activity and assault—except that Vancouver has had one-fifth as many handgun murders as Seattle and thus a 40-percent lower overall murder rate (Sloan & others, 1988). Can this have to do with the law? At the time of this writing, Canada has recently been through a federal election campaign. After a series of handgun-related deaths in Toronto, then–prime minister Paul Martin promised to ban handguns in Canada and maintain the billion-dollar firearms registry. Stephen Harper, since becoming prime minister, has argued the registry should be banned. Would such a ban have had an effect on handgun violence in the country? When Washington, D.C. adopted a law restricting handgun possession, the numbers of gun-related murders and suicides each abruptly dropped about 25 percent (Loftin & others, 1991).

Guns not only serve as aggression cues, they also put psychological distance between aggressor and victim. As Milgram's obedience studies taught us, remoteness from the victim facilitates cruelty. A knife can kill someone, but a knife attack is more difficult than pulling a trigger from a distance.

The Learning of Aggression

Theories of aggression based on instinct and frustration assume that hostile urges erupt from inner emotions, which naturally "push" aggression from within. Social psychologists contend that learning also "pulls" aggression out of us.

The Rewards of Aggression

By experience and by observing others, we learn that aggression often pays. Experiments have transformed animals from docile creatures into ferocious fighters. Severe defeats, on the other hand, create submissiveness (Ginsburg & Allee, 1942; Kahn, 1951; Scott & Marston, 1953).

People, too, can learn the rewards of aggression. A child whose aggressive acts successfully intimidate other children will likely become increasingly aggressive (Patterson & others, 1967). Aggressive hockey players—the ones sent most often to the penalty box for rough play—score more goals than nonaggressive players (McCarthy & Kelly, 1978a,b). Canadian teenage hockey players whose fathers applaud physically aggressive play show the most aggressive attitudes and style of play (Ennis & Zanna, 1991).

Collective violence can also have its rewards. For example, in January and February of 2006 Muslims in a number of European and Middle Eastern countries held sometimes-violent protests over offensive depictions of the Muslim prophet Mohammed in Danish and other newspapers. Although all newspapers in the

Western world insisted that they had the right to publish those caricatures, almost none did. Many cited fear of reprisals as a reason for not re-publishing the caricatures. The point is not that people consciously plan riots for their instrumental value, but that aggression sometimes has payoffs. If nothing more, it gets attention.

The same is true of terrorist acts, which enable powerless people to garner widespread attention. "Kill one, frighten ten thousand," asserts an ancient Chinese proverb. In this age of global communications, killing only a few can frighten tens of millions, as happened after the September 11, 2001 attacks in the U.S., when many Western democracies—including Canada, the United Kingdom, and the United States—spent billions of dollars on security and passed draconian legislation limiting the human rights of their citizens. These knee-jerk reactions can have serious consequences to individuals. No one knows this better than Maher Arar, a Canadian citizen who was deported to Syria after being stopped by U.S. customs agents in New York. Maher Arar spent almost a year in Syria, during which time he was tortured before finally being released. This could not have happened if the anti-terrorism laws did not exist. Deprived of what Margaret Thatcher called "the oxygen of publicity," terrorism would surely diminish, concluded Jeffrey Rubin (1986). It's like the 1970s incidents of naked spectators "streaking" onto football fields for a few seconds of television exposure. Once the networks decided to ignore the incidents, the phenomenon ended.

Observational Learning

Albert Bandura (1997) proposed a **social learning theory** of aggression. He believes that we learn aggression not only by experiencing its payoffs but also by observing others. As with most social behaviours, we acquire aggression by watching others act and noting the consequences.

Bandura (1979) believes that everyday life exposes us to aggressive models in the family, the subculture, and the mass media. Children of physically punitive parents tend to use aggression when relating to others. Their parents often disciplined them by screaming, slapping, and beating—modelling aggression as a method of dealing with problems (Patterson & others, 1982). These parents often had parents who were physically punitive (Bandura & Walters, 1959; Straus & Gelles, 1980). Although most abused children do not become criminals or abusive parents, 30 percent do later abuse their own children (Kaufman & Zigler, 1987; Widom, 1989).

The social environment outside the home also provides models. In communities where "macho" images are admired, aggression is readily transmitted to new generations (Cartwright, 1975; Short, 1969). The violent subculture of teenage gangs, for instance, provides its junior members with aggressive models. At sporting events such as soccer games, player violence precedes most incidents of fan violence (Goldstein, 1982). Gordon Russell at the University of Lethbridge found that watching boxing increased aggression in men, especially if they tended to perceive themselves as "macho" (1992).

So, people learn aggressive responses both by experience and by observing aggressive models. But when will aggressive responses actually occur? Bandura (1979) contended that aggressive acts are motivated by a variety of aversive experiences—

Social learning theory
The theory that we learn social behaviour by observing and imitating and by being rewarded and punished.

frustration, pain, insults. Such experiences arouse us emotionally. But whether we act aggressively depends upon the consequences we anticipate. Aggression is most likely when we are aroused *and* it seems safe and rewarding to aggress.

Environmental Influences

Social learning theory offers a perspective from which we can examine specific influences on aggression. Under what conditions do we aggress? What environmental influences pull our trigger?

Painful Incidents

Researcher Nathan Azrin (1967) wanted to know if switching off foot shocks would reinforce two rats' positive interactions with each other. Azrin planned to turn on the shock and then, once the rats approached each other, cut off the pain. To his great surprise, the experiment proved impossible. As soon as the rats felt pain, they attacked each other before the experimenter could switch off the shock. The greater the shock (and pain), the more violent the attack.

Is this true of rats alone? The researchers found that with a wide variety of species, the cruelty the animals imposed upon each other matched zap for zap the cruelty imposed upon them. As Azrin (1967) explained, the pain-attack response occurred with many types of animals. The animals would attack animals of their own species and also those of a different species, or stuffed dolls, or even tennis balls.

The researchers also varied the source of pain. They found that not just shocks induced attack; intense heat and "psychological pain"—for example, suddenly not rewarding hungry pigeons that have been trained to expect a grain reward after pecking at a disk—brought the same reaction as shocks. "Psychological pain" is, of course, what we call frustration.

Pain heightens aggressiveness in humans, also. Many of us can recall such a reaction after stubbing a toe or suffering a headache. Leonard Berkowitz and his associates demonstrated this by having University of Wisconsin students hold one hand in lukewarm water or painfully cold water. Those whose hands were submerged in the cold water reported feeling more irritable and more annoyed, and they were more willing to blast another person with unpleasant noise. In view of such results, Berkowitz (1983, 1989, 1998) now believes that aversive stimulation rather than frustration is the basic trigger of hostile aggression. Frustration is certainly one important type of unpleasantness. But any aversive event, whether a dashed expectation, a personal insult, or physical pain, can incite an emotional outburst. Even the torment of a depressed state increases the likelihood of hostile aggressive behaviour.

Heat

An uncomfortable environment also heightens aggressive tendencies. Offensive odours, cigarette smoke, and air pollution have all been linked with aggressive behaviour (Rotton & Frey, 1985). But the most-studied environmental irritant is heat. William Griffitt (1970; Griffitt & Veitch, 1971) found that compared to students who answered questionnaires in a room with a normal temperature, those who did so in an uncomfortably hot room (more than 32°C) reported feeling more tired and aggressive and expressed more hostility toward a stranger. Follow-up experiments revealed that heat also triggers retaliative actions (Bell, 1980; Rule & others, 1987).

Does uncomfortable heat increase aggression in the real world as well as in the laboratory? Consider:

- Brendan Rule and her colleagues (Rule & others, 1987) at the University of Alberta found that adults were more likely to finish stories with an aggressive ending if the temperature were hot (33°C) versus cool (21°C). They also displayed more negative emotions.
- Ehor Boyanowsky (1999) from Simon Fraser University found that people in hot conditions felt both aggressive and threatened relative to people in very cool conditions. Interestingly, the coldest condition led participants to feel the most romantic arousal.
- In heat-stricken Phoenix, Arizona, drivers without air conditioning are more likely to honk at a stalled car (Kenrick & MacFarlane, 1986).
- During the 1986 to 1988 major league baseball seasons, the number of batters hit by a pitch was two-thirds greater for games played when the temperature was in the 90s than for games played below 80 degrees (Reifman & others, 1991). Pitchers weren't wilder on hot days—they had no more walks and wild pitches. They just clobbered more batters.
- The riots occurring in 79 U.S. cities between 1967 and 1971 were more likely on hot than on cool days.
- When the weather is hot, violent crimes are more likely (Cotton, 1981; Rotton & Frey, 1985).
- Across the Northern Hemisphere, not only do hotter days have more violent crimes, but so do hotter seasons of the year, hotter summers, hotter years, hotter cities, and hotter regions (Anderson & Anderson, 1998; Anderson & others, 2000). If a 4-degree global warming occurs, Anderson and his colleagues project that the United States alone would annually see at least 50,000 more serious assaults.

Attacks

Being attacked or insulted by another is especially conducive to aggression. Numerous experiments (Dengerink & Myers, 1977; Ohbuchi & Kambara, 1985; and Taylor & Pisano, 1971) confirm that intentional attacks breed retaliatory attacks. In most of these experiments, one person competes with another in a reaction-time contest. After each test trial, the winner chooses how much shock to give the loser. Actually, each subject is playing a programmed opponent, who steadily escalates the amount of shock. Do the real subjects respond charitably? Hardly. Extracting "an eye for an eye" is the more likely response.

Crowding

Crowding—the subjective feeling of not having enough space—is stressful. Crammed in the back of a bus, trapped in slow-moving freeway traffic, or living three

Crowding A subjective feeling that there is not enough space per person.

to a small room in residence diminishes one's sense of control (Baron & others, 1976; McNeel, 1980). Might such experiences also heighten aggression?

The stress experienced by animals allowed to overpopulate a confined environment does heighten aggressiveness (Calhoun, 1962; Christian & others, 1960). But it is a rather large leap from rats in an enclosure or deer on an island to humans in a city. Nevertheless, it's true that dense urban areas do experience higher rates of crime and emotional distress (Fleming & others, 1987; Kirmeyer, 1978). Even when they don't suffer higher crime rates, residents of crowded cities may *feel* more fearful. Toronto's crime rate has been four times higher than Hong Kong's. Yet, compared to Toronto people, people from safer Hong Kong—which is four times more densely populated—have reported feeling more fearful on their city's streets (Gifford & Peacock, 1979).

REDUCING AGGRESSION

We have examined instinct, frustration-aggression, and social learning theories of aggression, and we have scrutinized influences on aggression. How, then, can we reduce aggression? Do theory and research suggest ways to control aggression?

Catharsis?

"Youngsters should be taught to vent their anger." So advised Ann Landers (1969). If a person "bottles up his rage, we have to find an outlet. We have to give him an opportunity of letting off steam." So asserted the prominent psychiatrist Fritz Perls (1973). Both statements assume the "hydraulic model"—accumulated aggressive energy that, like dammed-up water, needs a release.

The concept of catharsis is usually credited to Aristotle. Although Aristotle actually said nothing about aggression, he did argue that we can purge emotions by experiencing them and that viewing the classic tragedies therefore enabled a catharsis ("purgation") of pity and fear. To have an emotion excited, he believed, is to have that emotion released (Butcher, 1951).

The near consensus among social psychologists is that contrary to what Freud, Lorenz, and their followers supposed, catharsis also does *not* occur with violence (Geen & Quanty, 1977). For example, Robert Arms and his associates report that Canadian and American spectators of football, wrestling, and hockey games exhibit *more* hostility after viewing the event than before (Arms & others, 1979; Goldstein & Arms, 1971; Russell, 1983). Not even war seems to purge aggressive feelings. After a war, a nation's murder rate tends to jump (Archer & Gartner, 1976).

In laboratory tests of catharsis, Brad Bushman (2002) invited angered participants to hit a punching bag while either ruminating about the person who angered them or thinking about becoming physically fit. A third group did not hit the punching bag. Then, when given a chance to administer loud blasts of noise to the person who angered them, people in the punching bag plus rumination condition felt angrier and were most aggressive. Doing nothing at all more effectively reduced aggression than "blowing off steam."

In some real-life experiments too, aggressing has led to heightened aggression. Ebbe Ebbesen and his co-researchers (1975) interviewed 100 engineers and technicians shortly after they were angered by layoff notices. Some were asked questions that gave them an opportunity to express hostility against their employer or supervisors—for example, "What instances can you think of where the company has not been fair with you?" Afterward, they answered a questionnaire assessing attitudes toward the company and the supervisors. Did the previous opportunity to "vent" or "drain off" their hostility reduce it? To the contrary, their hostility increased. Expressing hostility bred more hostility.

Should we therefore bottle up anger and aggressive urges? Silent sulking is hardly more effective, because it allows us to continue reciting our grievances as we conduct conversations in our head. Fortunately, there are nonaggressive ways to express our feelings and to inform others how their behaviour affects us. Across cultures, those who reframe accusatory "you" messages as "I" messages—"I'm angry," or, "When you leave dirty dishes I get irritated"—communicate their feelings in a way that better enables the other person to make a positive response (Kubany & others, 1995). We can be assertive without being aggressive.

A Social Learning Approach

If aggressive behaviour is learned, then there is hope for its control. Let us briefly review factors that influence aggression and speculate on how to counteract them.

Anticipated rewards and costs influence instrumental aggression. This suggests that we should reward cooperative, nonaggressive behaviour. In experiments, children become less aggressive when caregivers ignore their aggressive behaviour and reinforce their nonaggressive behaviour (Hamblin & others, 1969).

Moreover, there are limits to punishment's effectiveness. Most mortal aggression is impulsive, hot aggression—the result of an argument, an insult, or an attack. Thus, we must *prevent* aggression before it happens. We must teach nonaggressive conflict-resolution strategies.

To foster a gentler world, we could model and reward sensitivity and cooperation from an early age. Training programs encourage parents to reinforce desirable behaviours and to frame statements positively ("When you finish cleaning your room you can go play," rather than, "If you don't clean your room, you're grounded.") One "aggression-replacement program" has reduced re-arrest rates of juvenile offenders and gang members by teaching the youths and their parents communication skills, training them to control anger, and raising their level of moral reasoning (Goldstein & Glick, 1994).

If observing aggressive models lowers inhibitions and elicits imitation, then we might also reduce brutal, dehumanizing portrayals in films and on television—steps comparable to those already taken to reduce racist and sexist portrayals. We can also inoculate children against the effects of media violence. In a recent study, Stanford University used 18 classroom lessons to persuade children to simply reduce their TV watching and video game playing (Robinson & others, 2001). They did—reducing their TV viewing by a third—and their aggressive behaviour at school dropped 25 percent compared to that of children in a control school.

Aggressive stimuli also trigger aggression. This suggests reducing the availability of weapons such as handguns. Jamaica in 1974 implemented a sweeping anticrime program that included strict gun control and censorship of gun scenes from television and movies (Diener & Crandall, 1979). In the following year, robberies dropped 25 percent, nonfatal shootings 37 percent.

Suggestions such as these can help us minimize aggression. But given the complexity of aggression's causes and the difficulty of controlling them, who can feel the optimism expressed by Andrew Carnegie's forecast that, in the twentieth century, "To kill a man will be considered as disgusting as we in this day consider it disgusting to eat one." Since Carnegie uttered those words in 1900, some 200 million human beings have been killed. It is a sad irony that although today we understand human aggression better than ever before, humanity's inhumanity is hardly diminished.

CONCEPTS TO REMEMBER

Aggression   p. 176
Frustration   p. 180
Displacement   p. 180

Social learning theory   p. 183
Crowding   p. 185

Please visit the *Exploring Social Psychology* Online Learning Centre at **www.mcgrawhill.ca/college/myers** to participate in module activities, view module videos, access research and study tools, and test your knowledge with interactive quizzes, exercises, and scenarios.

18

Understanding Outgroup Bias

Overweight people protesting against attitudes towards them. What forms of prejudice can you identify in your day-to-day experience in the world?

Prejudice comes in many forms—against "northeastern liberals" or "southern rednecks," against Arab "terrorists" or Christian "fundamentalists," against people who are short, or fat, or homely. Consider a few actual examples:

- As we learned in an earlier module, prejudice against girls and women is sometimes subtle, sometimes devastating. Nowhere in the modern world is it an accepted practice to leave female infants on a hillside to die of exposure, as was the occasional practice in ancient Greece. Yet, due to sex-selective abortions, China and India have millions of "missing women."

- When men seek roles traditionally associated with women, discrimination can run in the other direction. Elizabeth Turner and Anthony Pratkanis (1994) sent identical job-inquiry letters, which pretended to be from a community-college student in a child-care program, to 56 child-care centres and preschools in seven cities. When the letter was signed "Mary E. Johnson," nearly half the centres returned a stamped postcard, checking "we would be interested in discussing a position." When the letter was signed "David E. Johnson," only 1 in 10 replied with similar encouragement.

- Guy Shahan, an Israeli native who moved to Halifax, sent his résumé out for many different jobs and never received an offer for an interview. Convinced his credentials were good, he decided his last name was the barrier. After changing the name on his résumé to a more "Canadian"-sounding name (Graham), he received numerous interview offers.

- A group of homosexual students at the University of Illinois announced that the motto for one spring day would be: "If you are gay, wear blue jeans today." When the day dawned, many students who usually wore jeans woke up with an urge to dress up in a skirt or slacks. The gay group had made its point—that attitudes toward homosexuals are such that many students would rather give up their usual clothes than be suspected of being gay (*RCAgenda*, 1979).
- Shortly after September 11, 2001, hostilities flared against people perceived to be of Arab descent. In suburban New York City, a man tried to run down a Pakistani woman while shouting that he was "doing this for my country" (Brown, 2001). In Denton, Texas, a mosque was firebombed (Thompson, 2001). At Boston University, a Middle Eastern student was stabbed, and at the University of Colorado, students spray-painted the library with "Arabs Go Home." These were not isolated events. The American Arab Anti-Discrimination Committee catalogued more than 250 acts of violence against Arab American students on college campuses in the week following the attacks (CNN.com, 2001). Negative views of Middle Eastern immigrants have persisted. In one U.S. survey six months after the attacks, Pakistanis and Palestinians were rated as negatively as drug dealers (Fiske, 2002).

When seeking love and employment, overweight people—especially overweight White women—face slim prospects. In both correlational studies and in experiments (in which people are made to appear overweight or not), overweight people marry less often, gain entry to less desirable jobs, make less money, and are perceived as less attractive, intelligent, happy, self-disciplined, and successful (Gortmaker & others, 1993; Hebl & Heatherton, 1998; Pingitore & others, 1994). Weight discrimination is, in fact, notably greater than race or gender discrimination and occurs at every employment stage—hiring, placement, promotion, compensation, discipline, and discharge (Roehling, 2000). A recent Ipsos-Reid poll of 1,500 Canadians revealed that 54 percent of Canadians believe that people who are seriously overweight should pay more for employee health benefits. Clearly, people who are overweight are seen as responsible for their situation.

OLC
Activity 18.1

Prejudice A negative prejudgment of a group and its individual members.

WHAT IS PREJUDICE?

Prejudice, stereotyping, discrimination, racism, sexism—the terms often overlap. Let's clarify them. Each of the situations just described involved a negative evaluation of some group. And that is the essence of **prejudice**: a negative prejudgment of a group and its individual members. Prejudice biases us against a person based on the person's perceived group.

Prejudice is an attitude. An attitude is a distinct combination of feelings, inclinations to act, and beliefs. This combination is the ABC of attitudes: *affect* (feelings), *behaviour* tendency (inclination to act), and *cognition* (beliefs). A prejudiced person might *dislike* those different from self and *behave* in a discriminatory manner, *believing* them ignorant and dangerous.

The negative evaluations that mark prejudice can stem from emotional associations, from the need to justify behaviour, or from negative beliefs, called **stereotypes**. To stereotype is to generalize. To simplify the world, we generalize: The British are reserved. The French are arrogant. Professors are absentminded.

A problem with stereotypes arises when they are *overgeneralized* or just plain wrong. The presumption that jocks prefer sports-related courses to economics contains a germ of truth, but is overblown. Individuals within the stereotyped group vary more than expected (Brodt & Ross, 1998).

Prejudice is a negative *attitude*; **discrimination** is negative *behaviour*. Discriminatory behaviour often has its source in prejudicial attitudes (Dovidio & others, 1996). As Module 8 emphasized, however, attitudes and behaviour are often loosely linked, partly because our behaviour reflects more than our inner convictions. Prejudiced attitudes need not breed hostile acts, nor does all oppression spring from prejudice. **Racism** and **sexism** are institutional practices that discriminate, even when there is no prejudicial intent. If word-of-mouth hiring practices in an all-White business have the effect of excluding potential non-White employees, the practice could be called racist—even if an employer intended no discrimination.

HOW PERVASIVE IS PREJUDICE?

Is prejudice inevitable? Let's look at the most heavily studied examples—racial and gender prejudice.

Racial and Ethnic Prejudice

In the context of the world, every race is a minority. Non-Hispanic Whites, for example, are but one-fifth of the world's people and will be but one-eighth within another half-century. Thanks to mobility and migration during the past two centuries, the world's races now intermingle, in relations that are sometimes hostile, sometimes amiable.

To a molecular biologist, skin colour is a pretty trivial human characteristic, one controlled by a minuscule genetic difference between races. Moreover, nature doesn't cluster races in neatly defined categories. It is we, not nature, who label Tiger Woods "African American" (his ancestry is 25 percent African) or "Asian American" (he is also 25 percent Thai and 25 percent Chinese)—or even as Native American or Dutch (he is one-eighth each).

Racial and Ethnic Attitudes in Canada

Historically, there has always been some level of conflict among ethnic groups in Canada. Since before Confederation, conflict between French and English Canadians has been a source of concern for the country. It is no secret that some French Canadians (especially in Quebec) have had concerns about their treatment at the hands of an anglophone-dominated rest of Canada. Indeed, two close separation votes in Quebec

Stereotype A belief about the personal attributes of a group of people. Stereotypes are sometimes overgeneralized, inaccurate, and resistant to new information.

Discrimination Unjustifiable negative behaviour toward a group or its members.

Racism (1) An individual's prejudicial attitudes and discriminatory behaviour toward people of a given race, or (2) institutional practices (even if not motivated by prejudice) that subordinate people of a given race.

Sexism (1) An individual's prejudicial attitudes and discriminatory behaviour toward people of a given gender, or (2) institutional practices (even if not motivated by prejudice) that subordinate people of a given gender.

(the second which Steven Smith voted in and spent many hours watching the results of) have highlighted many of these issues. As an early attempt to deal with these issues, in the 1960s Prime Minister Lester Pearson officially made Canada a bilingual nation, and thus began a tradition of recognizing cultural uniqueness that has continued in the support and development of multiculturalism in Canada.

Importantly, today Canada is a multicultural society. More than 13 percent of Canadians identify themselves as visible minorities and 18 percent of people in Canada are immigrants (CRIC, 2005). When people living in Canada are asked to self-identify their ethnic identity on the Census, it becomes clear we are a diverse group. As shown in Figure 18-1, after we remove the 11 million people who simply identify themselves as "Canadian" a very multicultural population remains (although the two single largest groups are English and French). Furthermore, when surveys of Canadians are conducted, multiculturalism is one of the core values that we identify for our society. Indeed, to support this multicultural ideal, Parliament passed the Multiculturalism Policy in 1971 (the formal Act was passed in 1987). The stated purpose of the policy was to encourage people from all cultural backgrounds in Canada to share their unique cultural heritage with all members of Canadian society. The main aim was to promote tolerance and understanding among all cultural groups in Canada.

Multiculturalism has been highlighted as a distinctive element of Canadian society, making us distinct from other countries. More than 50 percent of Canadians are

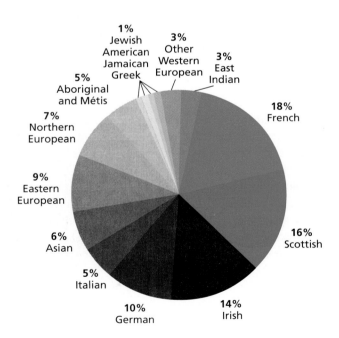

FIGURE 18-1
Self-Identified Ethnic Origin—("Canadian" responses omitted)

Source: Data from 2001 Census, courtesy of Statistics Canada. 29,239,035 total responses (of which 11,682,680 self-identified as "Canadian")

proud of Canada's multicultural identity, and almost 80 percent see a moderate to strong benefit from immigration in terms of benefits to cultural, cognitive, and intellectual resources (Parkin & Mendelsohn, 2003). This stands in interesting contrast to the U.S. policy on the integration of immigrants and minorities: the United States has a specific policy of assimilation. When you move to the U.S. you become part of the "great melting pot," and it is assumed you will assimilate into the existing culture and society. However, in Canada, immigrants are expected to become Canadian but also to maintain and share their unique cultural heritage with the rest of the country. However, attempting to maintain multiple identities during this process of *acculturation* (that is, when a person from one culture tries to re-establish his or her life in a new culture) can lead to personal conflict (see Berry, 1997). Sir Wilfrid Laurier, a French Canadian and our second prime minister, expressed this well when he said of his experience while trying to deal with issues surrounding full independence from Great Britain: "I am branded in Quebec as a traitor to the French, and in Ontario as a traitor to the English. In Quebec I am branded as a Jingo, in Ontario as a Separatist … I am neither. I am Canadian" (as quoted in Bliss, 2004, p. 46).

Nonetheless, to a great extent the multiculturalism policy seems to have been successful. John Berry and Rudolf Kalin, both at Queen's University, conducted an analysis of a national survey of attitudes toward different ethnic groups in Canada. For the most part their results were positive. People's overall comfort levels with ethnic-group members were very positive. Interestingly however, ethnic Canadians (people born and raised in Canada, regardless of ethnic origin) were rated more positively than immigrant Canadians (those born outside of Canada). Furthermore, people with European and Aboriginal backgrounds were rated more positively than people from other ethnic backgrounds.

As a counterpoint to this research, Douglas Palmer (1996), a social psychologist who works for Citizenship and Immigration Canada, found that Canadians, particularly younger Canadians, were often opposed to immigration. Interestingly, he found that prejudice was not a good predictor of attitudes toward immigration. He found that people's expectations about how immigrants are related to increases in crime and how immigrants affect their employment opportunities were a better predictor of people's attitudes toward immigration than their level of prejudice.

In a survey of students at 390 U.S. colleges and universities, 53 percent of African American students felt excluded from social activities (Hurtado & others, 1994). (Such feelings were reported by 24 percent of Asian Americans, 16 percent of Mexican Americans, and 6 percent of European Americans.) Such majority-minority relationships transcend race. On NBA basketball teams, minority players (in this case, Whites) feel similarly detached from their group's socializing (Schoenfeld, 1995).

This phenomenon of *greatest prejudice in the most intimate social realms* seems universal. In India, people who accept the caste system will typically allow someone from a lower caste into their homes but would not consider marrying such a person (Sharma, 1981). In a national survey of Americans, 75 percent said they would "shop at a store owned by a homosexual," but only 39 percent would "see a homosexual doctor" (Henry, 1994).

The Story Behind the Research

Dr. Victoria Esses, a professor at the University of Western Ontario, has been at the forefront of research on stereotyping and prejudice for a number of years. Her most recent work has focused on perceptions of immigrants. Dr. Esses became interested in this topic during her frequent visits to Toronto. On her travels, she frequently encountered immigrants and ethnic minorities and would talk to them about their personal experiences in the greater Toronto area.

Dr. Esses was surprised to learn that even though Canadians report that multiculturalism is an important value, immigrants perceived themselves as not always being welcome in Canada. Her subsequent research demonstrated that one reason for prejudice toward immigrants is that they are at times seen as competing with Canadians for resources, particularly jobs. In addition, Dr. Esses found that immigrants often felt that their skills were being undervalued in the Canadian job market (think back to the Guy Shahan anecdote at the beginning of this module). Economists and sociologists call this *skill discounting*. Although the Canadian immigration program allots more "points" to a potential immigrant based on education level and work experience (more points means a greater likelihood of being allowed to immigrate to Canada), immigrants find that once they have arrived in Canada they often cannot obtain jobs in their field.

Although her colleagues in other disciplines had identified skill discounting as an issue, they had not been able to address the cause of this behaviour. Dr. Esses wanted to understand if attitudes toward immigrants predicted people's assessment of job applicants. Thus, along with a colleague in organizational behaviour, Joerg Dietz, Dr. Esses decided to explore this issue using a multidisciplinary approach; she proceeded to use attitudes toward immigrants as a predictor of people's attitudes toward job applicants. Dr. Esses experimentally manipulated the country of origin (Canada, the United Kingdom, or India) of a potential job applicant but held education and ethnic background constant. In the study (see Esses & others, in press), they manipulated the résumé of a potential job applicant. All résumés were for an applicant with the name "Anita Singh," who was described as speaking French, English, and Hindi. Interestingly, if the applicant were described as being from Canada or the UK, participants' attitudes toward immigrants (positive or negative) had no impact on their ratings of the applicant's fit to the position or fit to the organization (two key evaluations made of any job applicant). However, if the applicant were described as being from India, attitudes were a significant predictor of evaluations—the more negative people's attitudes toward immigrants, the less the applicant was seen to "fit" the job and the organization. This suggested to Dr. Esses and her colleagues that people may feel more comfortable exhibiting prejudicial behaviours when they feel they can "get away" with it by appealing to the uncertainty of credentials obtained in India. |

Subtle Forms of Prejudice

Much prejudice remains hidden, until evoked by circumstance. When White students indicate racial attitudes while hooked up to a supposed lie detector, they admit to prejudice. Other researchers have invited people to evaluate someone's behaviour, that someone being either White or Black. Birt Duncan (1976) had White students at the University of California–Irvine observe a videotape of one man lightly shoving another during a brief argument. When a White man shoved a Black man, only 13 percent of

The Story Behind the Research

Since the early days of social psychology, researchers have been interested in prejudice and discrimination. Traditional research has focused on the attitudes and behaviours of the majority group (usually Whites) toward minorities. However, Ken Dion (1944–2004) realized that at least as important is the issue of how the target of the prejudice is affected. Dr. Dion spent more than 30 years (most of that time at the University of Toronto) researching prejudice and discrimination. His research was truly revolutionary and it changed the way prejudice research was conducted in Canada, in the United States, and around the world (Esses & others, 2005).

Dr. Dion grew up working in mills in a small New Hampshire town, and this was where he became aware that the people he knew did not have the money or opportunities other people had. This made him realize what it meant to be a member of a disadvantaged group (Earn & Adair, 2005). In his research he wanted to understand what it meant to the individual to be the subject of discrimination—what were the social-psychological and emotional consequences of perceiving one's self or one's group as the focus of prejudice?

It was no surprise to Dr. Dion that being the subject of prejudice and discrimination could have deleterious effects for an individual. However, what was particularly interesting to him, and what has spawned literally hundreds of research papers on the topic, was the finding that being discriminated against could actually have positive effects as well. In some of his early studies (for example, Dion, 1975), the victims of prejudice and discrimination actually bolstered their self-concepts (that is, had positive self-esteem) after the discrimination (for a review, see Dion, 2002). Interestingly, minority group members typically perceive more prejudice and discrimination against their ethnic group, put perceive little or no discrimination directed against themselves—this is called *personal/group discrimination discrepancy* (see Dion & Kawakami, 1996; Taylor & others, 1990). |

the observers rated the act as "violent behaviour." They interpreted the shove as "playing around" or "dramatizing." Not so when a Black man shoved a White man: Then, 73 percent said the act was "violent."

Experiments have assessed people's *behaviour* toward Blacks and Whites. Whites are equally helpful to any person in need—except when the needy person is remote (say, a wrong-number caller with a Black accent who needs a message relayed). Likewise, when asked to use electric shocks to "teach" a task, White people give no more (if anything, less) shock to a Black person than to a White person—except when they are angered or when the recipient can't retaliate or know who did it (Crosby & others, 1980; Rogers & Prentice-Dunn, 1981).

Although things may seem more rosy in Canada for minorities, a Gallup poll conducted in the early 1990s indicated that one in four Canadians felt they had been discriminated against. In 2005, an Ipsos-Reid poll reported that 1 in 6 Canadian adults (approximately 4 million people) felt they had been the victim of racism. Another national poll indicated that more than half of Canadians were aware of someone who had been discriminated against. In other words, although blatant and overt racism and

Dissimilarity breeds dislike: Like ethnic minorities elsewhere, Muslims living in France have encountered hostility. Here, protestors react against the law forbidding the wearing of veils in schools.

discrimination are on the decline, at minimum perceived discrimination is still an issue (see Dion, 2002).

Thus, if prejudice and discrimination is less obvious, how is it manifested in society? As blatant prejudice subsides, automatic emotional reactions linger. Recent research indicates that conscious prejudice can affect our instant reactions (Macrae & Bodenhausen, 2000). But Patricia Devine and her colleagues (1989, 2000) report that those low and high in prejudice sometimes have similar automatic reactions. They differ because low-prejudice people consciously try to suppress prejudicial thoughts and feelings. It's like breaking a bad habit, says Devine. Try as we might to suppress unwanted thoughts—thoughts about food, thoughts about romance with a friend's partner, judgmental thoughts about another group—they sometimes refuse to go away (Macrae & others, 1994; Wegner & Erber, 1992). The result for all of us: unwanted (dissonant) thoughts and feelings often persist.

All of this illustrates again our *dual attitude system* (Module 2). We can have differing explicit (conscious) and implicit (automatic) attitudes toward the same target. Thus, we may retain from childhood a habitual, automatic fear or dislike of people for whom we now express respect and appreciation. Although explicit attitudes may change dramatically with education, implicit attitudes may linger, changing only as we form new habits through practice (Kawakami & others, 2000).

A raft of new experiments (for example, Banaji & Bhaskar, 2000; Bargh & Chartrand, 1999; Fazio & others, 1995; Greenwald & others, 2000; Nosek & others, 2005; Olson & Fazio, 2004) have confirmed the phenomenon of automatic stereotyping and prejudice. These studies briefly flash words or faces that "prime" (automatically activate) stereotypes of some racial, gender, or age group. Without their awareness, the subjects' activated stereotypes may then bias their behaviour. Having been primed with images associated with African Americans, for example, they may then react with more hostility to an experimenter's annoying request. In clever experiments by Anthony Greenwald and his colleagues (1998, 2000), 9 in 10 White people took longer to identify pleasant words (such as peace and paradise) as "good" when associated with Black rather than White faces. The subjects, mind you, typically expressed little or no prejudice, only an unconscious, unintended response. Moreover, Hugenberg and Bodenhausen (2003) have demonstrated that the more strongly people exhibit such implicit prejudice, the readier they are to perceive anger in Black faces. However, there are a number of problems with the IAT methodology that are still being addressed by researchers in the field. To get a better understanding of this issue, and to find out if an IAT would label you as prejudiced, visit the Online Learning Centre and complete Activity 18.2.

OLC
Activity 18.2

In separate experiments, Joshua Correll and his co-workers (2002) and Anthony Greenwald and his co-workers (2003) invited people to press buttons quickly to "shoot" or "not shoot" men who suddenly appeared on-screen holding either a gun or a harmless object such as a flashlight or bottle. The participants (both Blacks and Whites, in one of the studies) more often mistakenly shot targets who were Black. In a related series of studies, Keith Payne (2001), and Charles Judd and colleagues (2004), found that when primed with a Black rather than a White face, people think guns: They more quickly recognize a gun and they more often mistake tools, such as

Automatic prejudice. When Joshua Correll and his colleagues invited people to react quickly to people holding either a gun or a harmless object, race influenced perceptions and reactions.

a wrench, for a gun. These studies help explain why Amadou Diallo (a Black immigrant in New York City) was shot 41 times by police officers for removing his wallet from his back pocket.

Gender Prejudice

How pervasive is prejudice against women? In Module 9, we examined gender-role norms—people's ideas about how women and men *ought* to behave. Here we consider gender *stereotypes*—people's beliefs about how women and men *do* behave. Norms are *pre*scriptive, stereotypes are *de*scriptive.

Gender Stereotypes

From research on stereotypes, two conclusions are indisputable: Strong gender stereotypes exist, and, as often happens, members of the stereotyped group accept the stereotypes. Men and women agree that you *can* judge the book by its sexual cover. In one survey, Mary Jackman and Mary Senter (1981) found that gender stereotypes were much stronger than racial stereotypes. For example, only 22 percent of men thought the two genders equally "emotional." Of the remaining 78 percent, those who believed females were more emotional outnumbered those who thought males were by 15 to 1. And what did the women believe? To within 1 percentage point, their responses were identical.

Consider, too, a study by Natalie Porter, Florence Geis, and Joyce Jennings Walstedt (1983). They showed students pictures of "a group of graduate students working as a team on a research project." Then they gave them a test of "first impressions," asking them to guess who contributed most to the group. When the group was either all male or all female, the students overwhelmingly chose the person at the head of the table. When the group was of mixed gender, a man occupying that position was again overwhelmingly chosen. But a woman at the head of the table was usually ignored. Each of the men received more of the leadership choices than all three women combined! This stereotype of men as leaders was true not only of women as well as men but also of feminists as well as nonfeminists. Newer research

Traditional gender stereotyping assumes that a father leaves a mother at home to perform child care while he goes to work (left) rather than other way around (right).

reveals that behaviours associated with leadership are perceived less favourably when enacted by a woman (Eagly & Karau, 2000). Assertiveness can seem less becoming in a woman than in a man (making it harder for women to become and succeed as leaders). How pervasive are gender stereotypes? Very.

Remember that stereotypes are generalizations about a group of people and may be true, false, or overgeneralized from a kernel of truth. (They may also be self-fulfilling.) In Module 9, we noted that the average man and woman do differ somewhat in social connectedness, empathy, social power, aggressiveness, and sexual initiative (though not in intelligence). Do we then conclude that gender stereotypes are accurate? Often they are, observed Janet Swim (1994). She found that students' stereotypes of men's and women's restlessness, nonverbal sensitivity, aggressiveness, and so forth were reasonable approximations of actual gender differences. Moreover, such stereotypes have persisted across time and culture. Averaging data from 27 countries, John Williams and his colleagues (1999, 2000) found that folks everywhere perceive women as more agreeable, men as more outgoing. The persistence and omnipresence of gender stereotypes leads some evolutionary psychologists to believe they reflect innate, stable reality (Lueptow & others, 1995).

But individuals' accuracy varies widely, and stereotypes are sometimes misapplied (Hall & Carter, 1999). Moreover, gender stereotypes sometimes exaggerate small differences, as Carol Lynn Martin (1987) concluded after surveying visitors to the University of British Columbia. She asked them to check which of several traits described them and to estimate what percentage of North American males and females had each trait. Males were indeed slightly more likely than females to describe themselves as assertive and dominant and were slightly less likely to describe themselves as tender and compassionate. But stereotypes of these differences were exaggerated: The people perceived North American males as almost twice as likely as females to be assertive and dominant and roughly half as likely to be tender and compassionate. By leading to exaggerated perceptions that become self-fulfilling prophecies, small differences may grow.

Stereotypes (beliefs) are not prejudices (attitudes). Stereotypes may support prejudice. Yet, one might believe, without prejudice, that men and women are "different yet equal." Let us therefore see how researchers probe for gender prejudice.

Gender Attitudes

Alice Eagly and her associates (1991) and Geoffrey Haddock and Mark Zanna (1994) also report that people don't respond to women with gut-level, negative emotions as they do to certain other groups. Most people like women more than men. They perceive women as more understanding, kind, and helpful. Thus, a *favourable* stereotype, which Eagly (1994) dubs the *women-are-wonderful effect*, results in a favourable attitude.

Is gender bias fast becoming extinct in Western countries? Has the women's movement nearly completed its work? As with race prejudice, blatant gender prejudice is dying, but subtle bias lives. The "bogus-pipeline method," for example, exposes bias: Men who believe an experimenter can read their true attitudes with a sensitive lie detector express less sympathy toward women's rights. Even on paper-and-pencil questionnaires, Janet Swim and her co-researchers (1995, 1997) have found a subtle ("modern") sexism that parallels subtle ("modern") racism. Both forms appear in denials of discrimination and in antagonism toward efforts to promote equality.

We can also detect bias in behaviour. That's what a research team led by Ian Ayres (1991) did. Team members visited 90 Chicago-area car dealers, using a uniform strategy to negotiate the lowest price on a new car that cost the dealer about $11,000. White males were given a final price that averaged $11,362; White females were given an average price of $11,504; Black males were given an average price of $11,783; and Black females were given an average price of $12,237.

Most women know that gender bias exists. They believe that sex discrimination affects most working women, as shown by the lower salaries for women and especially for jobs, such as child care, that are filled mostly by women. Garbage haulers (mostly men) make more than preschool teachers (mostly women). Consistent with research on prejudice, however, Faye Crosby and her colleagues (1989) have repeatedly found that most women deny feeling personally discriminated against. Discrimination, they believe, is something *other* women face. Their employers are not villainous. They are doing better than the average woman. Hearing no complaints, managers—even in discriminatory organizations—can persuade themselves that justice prevails.

In the world beyond democratic Western countries, gender discrimination looms even larger:

- Two-thirds of the world's unschooled children are girls (United Nations, 1991).

- In Saudi Arabia, women are forbidden to drive (Beyer, 1990).

- Around the world, people tend to prefer having baby boys. In the United States in 1941, 38 percent of expectant parents said they preferred a boy if they could only have one child; 24 percent preferred a girl; and 23 percent said they didn't care. In 2003, the answers were virtually unchanged with 38 percent still preferring a boy (Lyons, 2003; Simmons, 2000). With the widespread use of ultrasound to determine the sex of a fetus and the growing availability of abortion, these preferences are affecting the number of boys and girls. The 2000 China census revealed 119 newborn boys for every 100 girls (Walfish, 2001). The 2001 India census reported that Punjab Province had 126 newborn boys for every 100 girls (Dugger, 2001).

To conclude, overt prejudice is far less common today than it was four decades ago. The same is true of prejudice against homosexual people. Nevertheless, techniques that are sensitive to subtle prejudice still detect widespread bias. And in parts of the world, gender prejudice is literally deadly. We therefore need to look carefully and closely at the problem of prejudice and its causes.

CONCEPTS TO REMEMBER

Prejudice   p. 190
Stereotype   p. 191
Discrimination   p. 191

Racism   p. 191
Sexism   p. 191

Please visit the *Exploring Social Psychology* Online Learning Centre at **www.mcgrawhill.ca/college/myers** to participate in module activities, view module videos, access research and study tools, and test your knowledge with interactive quizzes, exercises, and scenarios.

Prejudice and Discrimination

I magine you are driving your car (a new Lexus, perhaps?) through downtown Vancouver. It is late at night, the streets are empty, and you are slowly making your way home. Suddenly, looking in your rearview mirror, you notice you are being followed by a police cruiser. How likely is it that you are going to be pulled over? Go to the Online Learning Centre and complete Activity 19.1 to enter your answer.

Interestingly, your response probably depends on your ethnic background. If you are Caucasian, you probably rated the likelihood lower than if you were non-Caucasian. Minorities expect to be the subject of discrimination. People perceive that the police engage in *racial profiling*—stopping people based on ethnic background rather than probable cause. Some Black Canadians have labelled this practice as being pulled over for a "DWB": Driving While Black. Is there any truth to these perceptions? Data released from the Kingston, Ontario police found that Black motorists were 3.7 times more likely to be stopped, and Aboriginals were 1.4 times more likely to be stopped than Whites. Both the Toronto and Halifax police have come under fire recently for perceived racial profiling. This is not limited to Canada, with similar statistics being reported in the United States, United Kingdom, and other countries. Racial profiling also seems to be a concern for people of Arabic descent at airports worldwide, as a consequence of the New York, London, and Madrid terrorist attacks. It remains to be

This sign for a Whites-only beach in South Africa during the Apartheid era of the 1980s is an example of the unequal status of Blacks in that country, a status that bred flagrant prejudice and racism. What forms does racism take in today's society?

OLC
Activity 19.1

seen if the June 2006 arrests of 17 terrorism suspects near Toronto will have an effect on how people of Arabic descent are treated in this country.

There have been severe criticisms of these practices, as they are cited as obvious examples of prejudice. Indeed, in a well-publicized 2003 ruling, the Nova Scotia Human Rights Commission found that heavyweight boxer Kirk Johnson was discriminated against by the Halifax Regional Police when he was pulled over and had his car impounded. Johnson received an apology and $10,000, and police had to revise their sensitivity training practices. However, some people argue this practice is *not* discrimination—these groups are more likely to commit crimes and therefore increased attention is appropriate. Why is it that something that is so blatantly ethnically based can be perceived by many normal, rational, and non-prejudiced people as acceptable?

Prejudice springs from several sources because it serves several functions. Prejudice may express our sense of who we are and gain us social acceptance. It may defend our sense of self against anxiety that arises from insecurity or inner conflict. And it may promote our self-interest by supporting what brings us pleasure and opposing what doesn't. Consider first how prejudice can function to defend self-esteem and social position.

SOCIAL SOURCES OF PREJUDICE

Unequal Status

A principle to remember: *Unequal status breeds prejudice.* Masters view slaves as lazy, irresponsible, lacking ambition—as having just those traits that justify the slavery. Historians debate the forces that create unequal status. But once these inequalities exist, prejudice helps justify the economic and social superiority of those who have wealth and power. Stereotypes rationalize unequal status (Yzerbyt & others, 1997).

Gender stereotypes, too, help rationalize gender roles. After studying these stereotypes worldwide, John Williams and Deborah Best (1990a) noted that if women provide most of the care to young children, it is reassuring to think women are naturally nurturant. If males run the businesses, hunt, and fight wars, it is comforting to suppose that men are aggressive, independent, and adventurous. In experiments, people perceive members of unknown groups as having traits that suit their roles (Hoffman & Hurst, 1990).

Discrimination's Impact: The Self-Fulfilling Prophecy

Attitudes may coincide with the social hierarchy not only as a rationalization for it but also because discrimination affects its victims. "One's reputation," wrote Gordon Allport, "cannot be hammered, hammered, hammered into one's head without doing something to one's character" (1958, p. 139). If we could snap our fingers and end all discrimination, it would be naive then to say, "The tough times are all over, folks! You can now put on suits or dresses and be attaché-carrying executives and professionals." When the oppression ends, its effects linger, like a societal hangover.

In *The Nature of Prejudice*, Allport catalogued 15 possible effects of victimization. Allport believed these reactions were reducible to two basic types—those that involve blaming oneself (withdrawal, self-hate, aggression against one's own group) and those that involve blaming external causes (fighting back, suspiciousness, increased group pride). If the net results are negative—say, higher rates of crime—people who discriminate can use them to justify their discrimination that helps maintain them.

Nevertheless, social beliefs *can* be self-confirming, as demonstrated in a clever pair of experiments by Carl Word, Mark Zanna, and Joel Cooper (1974). In the first experiment, Princeton University White men interviewed White and Black research assistants posing as job applicants. When the applicant was Black, the interviewers sat farther away, ended the interview 25 percent sooner, and made 50 percent more speech errors than when the applicant was White. Imagine being interviewed by someone who sat at a distance, stammered, and ended the interview rather quickly. Would it affect your performance or your feelings about the interviewer?

To find out, the researchers conducted a second experiment in which trained interviewers treated students in the same manner that the interviewers in the first experiment had treated either the White or Black applicants. When videotapes of the interviews were later rated, those who were treated like the Blacks in the first experiment seemed more nervous and less effective. Moreover, the interviewees could themselves sense a difference; those treated as were the Blacks judged their interviewers to be less adequate and less friendly. The experimenters concluded part of "the 'problem' of Black performance resides. . . within the interaction setting itself." As with other self-fulfilling prophecies prejudice affects its targets (Swim & Stangor, 1998). One vehicle for its doing so is "stereotype threat."

Stereotype Threat

Placed in a situation in which others expect you to perform poorly, your anxiety may cause you to confirm the belief. Claude Steele and his colleagues call this phenomenon **stereotype threat** (which we briefly discussed in Module 17)—a self-confirming apprehension that one will be evaluated based on a negative stereotype.

In several experiments, Steven Spencer, Steele, and Diane Quinn (1999) gave a very difficult math test to men and women students who had similar math backgrounds. When told that there were *no* gender differences on the test and no evaluation of any group stereotype, the women's performance consistently equalled the men's. Told that there *was* a gender difference, the women dramatically confirmed the stereotype (see Figure 19-1 on page 204). Frustrated by the extremely difficult test questions, they apparently felt added apprehension, which undermined their performances.

On the other hand, threat can motivate people to stereotype as well. For example, Lisa Sinclair (at the University of Winnipeg) and Ziva Kunda (at the University of Waterloo) found that when our self-worth is threatened, we may devalue the source of that threat. For example, they found that people rated women as less competent

OLC
Video 19.1

Stereotype threat
A disruptive concern, when facing a negative stereotype, that one will be evaluated based on a negative stereotype. Unlike self-fulfilling prophecies that hammer one's reputation into one's self-concept, stereotype threat situations have immediate effects.

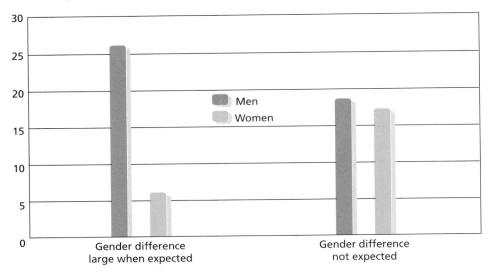

FIGURE 19-1

Stereotype vulnerability and women's math performance. Steven Spencer, Claude Steele, and Diane Quinn (1999) gave equally capable men and women a difficult math test. When subjects were led to expect inferior performance by women, women fulfilled the stereotype by scoring lower.

than men when they had recently been negatively evaluated by a woman (see Sinclair & Kunda, 2000). These people activated and used a gender stereotype to protect their self-concept. However, people who were positively evaluated did not exhibit that stereotype. Interestingly, Sinclair and Kunda (1999) have also demonstrated that we can actively inhibit our stereotypes (if, for example, we receive praise from a group we hold a negative stereotype toward). Thus the use and activation of stereotypes can depend on how the situation motivates our behaviour.

Might racial stereotypes be self-fulfilling? Steele and Joshua Aronson (1995) confirmed that they are when Whites and Blacks take difficult verbal abilities tests. Blacks underperformed Whites only when taking the tests under conditions high in stereotype threat. Jeff Stone and his colleagues (1999) report that stereotype threat affects athletic performance, too. Blacks did worse than usual when a golf task was framed as a test of "sports intelligence," and Whites did worse when it was a test of "natural athletic ability." "When people are reminded of a negative stereotype about themselves—'White men can't jump' or 'Black men can't think'—it can adversely affect performance," Stone (2000) surmised.

If you tell students they are at risk of failure (as is often suggested by minority support programs), the stereotype may erode their performance, says Steele (1997), and cause them to "disidentify" with school and seek self-esteem elsewhere (Figure 19-2). Moreover, students led to think they have benefitted from gender- or race-based preferences in gaining admission to a postsecondary institutuion or an academic group tend to underperform those who are led to feel competent (Brown & others, 2000). Better, therefore, to challenge students to believe in their potential, observes Steele.

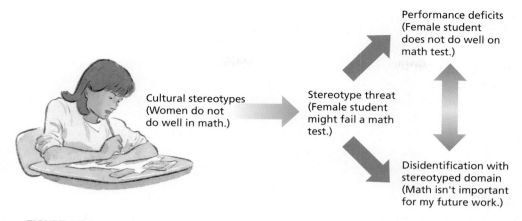

FIGURE 19-2

Stereotype threat. Threat from facing a negative stereotype can produce performance deficits and disidentification.

But how does stereotype threat undermine performance? One route is cognitive. Stereotype threat is distracting: The effort it takes to dismiss its allegations increases mental demands and decreases working memory (Croizet & others, 2004; Schmader & Johns, 2003; Steele & others, 2002). Another effect is motivational: Worrying about mistakes under stereotype threat can impair a person's performance (Keller & Dauenheimer, 2003; Seibt & Forster, 2004), and the physiological arousal that accompanies stereotype threat can impair performance on hard tests (Ben-Zeev, Fein, & Inzlicht, 2005; O'Brien & Crandall, 2003). (Recall from Module 13 the effect of arousal from others: Presence tends to strengthen performance on easy tasks and disrupt performance on hard tasks.)

If stereotype threats can disrupt performance, could *positive* stereotypes enhance it? Margaret Shih, Todd Pittinsky, and Nalini Ambady (1999) confirmed this possibility. When Asian American females were asked biographical questions that reminded them of their gender identity before taking a math test, their performance plunged (compared to that of a control group). When similarly reminded of their Asian identity, their performance rose. Negative stereotypes disrupt performance and positive stereotypes, it seems, facilitate performance.

SOCIAL IDENTITY

We humans are a group-bound species. Our ancestral history prepares us to feed and protect ourselves—to live—in groups. Humans cheer for their groups, kill for their groups, die for their groups. Not surprisingly, we also define ourselves by our groups, note Australian social psychologists John Turner (1981, 1987, 1991), Michael Hogg (1992, 1996, 2003), and their colleagues. Self-concept—our sense of who we are—contains not just a *personal identity* (our sense of our personal attributes and attitudes) but a **social identity**. What is your social identity?

Social identity The "we" aspect of our self-concept. The part of our answer to "Who am I?" that comes from our group.

The Story Behind the Research

Intergroup relations are an essential part of Canadian social and political life, so it is perhaps not surprising that intergroup relations have provided a distinctive research focus for Canadian social psychologists. As an honours student working with Dr. John Berry at Queen's University, Jim Cameron (now at Saint Mary's University in Halifax) discovered early on that social identity theory (Tajfel & Turner, 1979) is a useful framework for understanding perennial Canadian issues, such as immigration and multiculturalism. Later, in graduate school at York University, he became interested in the construct at the heart of the theory: social identity. He was especially intrigued by the fact that while researchers agreed that social identity reflects various contributions of social group membership to the self-concept, they didn't always agree on what exactly those contributions are. As a result, measures of social identification—which are crucial for testing the hypotheses of social identity theory and other theories of intergroup relations—were often based on imprecise definitions of the construct.

One of the primary aims of Dr. Cameron's graduate research, which he conducted with Dr. Richard Lalonde, was to determine whether they could capture the various meanings of social identification in a single, multidimensional measure. They found, looking first at gender-derived social identity, that it was indeed possible to distinguish among different ways in which gender contributes to the self (Cameron & Lalonde, 2001). The research suggested dimensions of social identity corresponding to three types of questions: "How important is this group to who I am?"; "How does being a member of this group make me feel?"; and "Do I feel like I belong with other members of this group?"

In subsequent research, Dr. Cameron found that the three-factor model of social identity applied to other group memberships as well, including ethnicity, nationality, and university (Cameron, 2004). Measuring the three dimensions should aid future research on the many ways that group membership contributes to psychological functioning (for example, in terms of self-esteem and well-being) and shapes social behaviour (for example, in terms of engaging in, and responding to, prejudice and discrimination). Go back to Activity 3.1 to explore your social identity. ∎

Working with the late British social psychologist Henri Tajfel, Turner proposed *social identity theory.* Turner and Tajfel [pronounced TOSH-fel] observed that:

- *We categorize:* We find it useful to put people, ourselves included, into categories. To label someone as a Hindu, a Scot, or a bus driver is a shorthand way of saying some other things about the person.
- *We identify:* We associate ourselves with certain groups (our **ingroups**), and gain self-esteem by doing so.
- *We compare:* We contrast our groups with other groups (**outgroups**), with a favourable bias toward our own group.

Ingroup "Us"—a group of people who share a sense of belonging, a feeling of common identity.

Outgroup "Them"—a group that people perceive as distinctively different from or apart from their ingroup.

We evaluate ourselves partly by our group memberships. Having a sense of "we-ness" strengthens our self-concepts. It *feels* good. We seek not only *respect* for ourselves but also *pride* in our groups (Smith & Tyler, 1997). Moreover, seeing our groups as superior helps us feel even better.

Ingroup Bias

The group definition of who you are—your ethnic background, religion, gender, academic major—implies a definition of who you are not. The circle that includes "us" (the ingroup) excludes "them" (the outgroup). Thus, the mere experience of being formed into groups may promote **ingroup bias**. Ask children, "Which are better, the children in your school or the children at [another school nearby]?" Virtually all will say their own school has the better children. For adults, too, the closer to home, the better things seem. Merely sharing a birthday with someone creates enough of a bond to evoke heightened cooperation in a laboratory experiment (Miller & others, 1998).

Ingroup bias The tendency to favour one's own group.

Ingroup bias is one more example of the human quest for a positive self-concept. We are so group conscious that, given any excuse to think of ourselves as a group, we will do so—and will then exhibit ingroup bias. Cluster people into groups defined by nothing more than their driver's licence number's last digit, and they'll feel a certain kinship with their number mates. In a series of experiments, Tajfel and Michael Billig (1974; Tajfel, 1970, 1981, 1982) discovered how little it takes to provoke favouritism toward *us* and unfairness toward *them*. In one study, Tajfel and Billig had British teenagers evaluate modern abstract paintings and then told them that they and some others had favoured the art of Paul Klee over that of Wassily Kandinsky. Finally, without ever meeting the other members of their "Klee" group, the teens divided some money among members of both groups.

In this and other experiments, defining groups even in this trivial way produced ingroup favouritism. David Wilder (1981) summarized the typical result: "When given the opportunity to divide 15 points [worth money], subjects generally award 9 or 10 points to their own group and 5 or 6 points to the other group." This bias occurs with both genders and with people of all ages and nationalities, though especially with people from individualist cultures (Gudykunst, 1989). (People in communal cultures identify more with all their peers and so treat everyone more the same.)

We also are more prone to ingroup bias when our group is small and lower in status relative to the outgroup (Ellemers & others, 1997; Mullen & others, 1992). To be a foreign student, to be gay or lesbian, or to be of a minority race or gender at some social gathering is to feel one's social identity more keenly and to react accordingly.

Even forming conspicuous groups on *no* logical basis—say, merely by composing groups X and Y with the flip of a coin—will produce some ingroup bias (Billig & Tajfel, 1973; Brewer & Silver, 1978; Locksley & others, 1980). In Kurt Vonnegut's novel *Slapstick*, computers gave everyone a new middle name; all "Daffodil-11s" then felt unity with one another and distance from "Raspberry-13s." The self-serving bias (Module 4) rides again, enabling people to achieve a more positive social identity: "We" are better than "they," even when "we" and "they" are defined randomly!

Conformity

Once established, prejudice is maintained largely by inertia. If prejudice is socially accepted, many people will follow the path of least resistance and conform to the fashion. They will act not so much out of a need to hate as out of a need to be liked and accepted.

Thomas Pettigrew's (1958) studies of Whites in South Africa and the American south revealed that, during the 1950s, those who conformed most to other social norms were also most prejudiced; those who were less conforming mirrored less of the surrounding prejudice. Prejudice may not be a manifestation of "sick" personalities but simply of the social norms.

Conformity also maintains gender prejudice. "If we have come to think that the nursery and the kitchen are the natural sphere of a woman," wrote George Bernard Shaw in an 1891 essay, "we have done so exactly as English children come to think that a cage is the natural sphere of a parrot—because they have never seen one anywhere else." Children who *have* seen women elsewhere—children of employed women—have less stereotyped views of men and women (Hoffman, 1977).

In all this, there is a message of hope. If prejudice is not deeply ingrained in personality, then as fashions change and new norms evolve, prejudice can diminish. And so it has.

EMOTIONAL SOURCES OF PREJUDICE

Although prejudice is bred by social situations, emotional factors often add fuel to the fire: Frustration can feed prejudice, as can personality factors like status needs and authoritarian tendencies. Let's see how.

Frustration and Aggression: The Scapegoat Theory

Pain and frustration (the blocking of a goal) often evoke hostility. When the cause of our frustration is intimidating or unknown, we often redirect our hostility. This phenomenon of "displaced aggression" may have contributed to the lynchings of African Americans in the south after the Civil War. Between 1882 and 1930, there were more lynchings in years when cotton prices were low and economic frustration was therefore presumably high (Hepworth & West, 1988; Hovland & Sears, 1940).

Targets for this displaced aggression vary. Following their defeat in World War I and their country's subsequent economic chaos, many Germans saw Jews as villains. Long before Hitler came to power, one German leader explained: "The Jew is just convenient. . . . If there were no Jews, the anti-Semites would have to invent them" (quoted by G. W. Allport, 1958, p. 325). In earlier centuries, people vented their fear and hostility on witches, whom they sometimes burned or drowned in public.

A famous experiment by Neal Miller and Richard Bugelski (1948) confirmed the scapegoat theory. They asked college-age men working at a summer camp to state their attitudes toward Japanese and Mexicans. Some did so before, and then after, being forced to stay in camp to take tests rather than attend a long-awaited free evening at a local theatre. Compared to a control group that did not undergo this frustration, the deprived group afterward displayed increased prejudice. As new studies confirm, people who are put in unhappy moods often think and act more negatively toward outgroups (Esses & Zanna, 1995; Forgas & Fiedler, 1996). Passions provoke prejudice.

One source of frustration is competition. When two groups compete for jobs, housing, or social prestige, one group's goal fulfillment can become the other group's frustration. Thus, the **realistic group conflict theory** suggests that prejudice arises when groups compete for scarce resources. This is consistent with the work of Victoria Esses, described in the previous module. Consistent with this, in Canada, opposition to immigration since 1975 has gone up and down with the unemployment rate (Palmer, 1996). When interests clash, prejudice—for some people—pays.

> **Realistic group conflict theory** The theory that prejudice arises from competition among groups for scarce resources.

Personality Dynamics

Any two people with equal reason to feel frustrated or threatened will often not be equally prejudiced. This suggests that prejudice serves other functions besides advancing competitive self-interest.

Need for Status, Self-Regard, and Belonging

Status is relative: To perceive ourselves as having status, we need people below us. Thus, one psychological benefit of prejudice, or of any status system, is a feeling of superiority. Most of us can recall a time when we took secret satisfaction in another's failure—perhaps seeing a brother or sister punished or a classmate failing a test. In Europe and North America, prejudice is often greater among those low or slipping on the socioeconomic ladder and among those whose positive self-image is being threatened (Lemyre & Smith, 1985; Pettigrew & others, 1997; Thompson & Crocker, 1985). In one study, members of lower-status sororities were more disparaging of other sororities than were members of higher-status sororities (Crocker & others, 1987). Perhaps people whose status is secure have less need to feel superior.

But other factors associated with low status could also account for prejudice. Imagine yourself as one of the Arizona State University students who took part in an experiment by Robert Cialdini and Kenneth Richardson (1980). You are walking alone across campus. Someone approaches you and asks your help with a five-minute survey. You agree. After the researcher gives you a brief "creativity test," he deflates you with the news that "you have scored relatively low on the test." The researcher then completes the survey by asking you some evaluative questions about either your school or its traditional rival, the University of Arizona. Would your feelings of failure affect your ratings of either school? Compared with those in a control group whose self-esteem was not threatened, the students who experienced failure gave higher ratings to their own school and lower ratings to their rival. Apparently, asserting one's social identity by boasting about one's own group and denigrating outgroups can boost one's ego.

James Meindl and Melvin Lerner (1984) at the University of Waterloo found that a humiliating experience—accidentally knocking over a stack of someone's important materials—provoked English-speaking Canadian students to express increased hostility toward French-speaking Canadians. And Teresa Amabile and Ann Glazebrook

(1982) found that Dartmouth College men who were made to feel insecure judged others' work more harshly.

In study after study, thinking about your own mortality—by writing a short essay on dying and the emotions aroused by thinking about death—also provokes enough insecurity to intensify ingroup favouritism and outgroup prejudice (Greenberg & others, 1990, 1994; Harmon-Jones & others, 1996; Schimel & others, 1999; Solomon & others, 2000).

The Authoritarian Personality

The emotional needs that contribute to prejudice are said to predominate in the "authoritarian personality." In the 1940s, University of California Berkeley researchers—two of whom had fled Nazi Germany—set out on an urgent research mission: to uncover the psychological roots of an anti-Semitism so poisonous that it caused the slaughter of millions of Jews and turned many millions of Europeans into indifferent spectators. In studies of American adults, Theodor Adorno and his colleagues (1950) discovered that hostility toward Jews often coexisted with hostility toward other minorities. Prejudice appeared to be less an attitude specific to one group than a way of thinking about those who are different. Moreover, these judgmental, **ethnocentric** people shared authoritarian tendencies—an intolerance for weakness, a punitive attitude, and a submissive respect for their ingroup's authorities, as reflected in their agreement with such statements as, "Obedience and respect for authority are the most important virtues children should learn."

Ethnocentrism A belief in the superiority of one's own ethnic and cultural group, and a corresponding disdain for all other groups.

As children, authoritarian people often were harshly disciplined. This supposedly led them to repress their hostilities and impulses and to "project" them onto outgroups. The insecurity of authoritarian children seemed to predispose them toward an excessive concern with power and status and an inflexible right-wrong way of thinking that made ambiguity difficult to tolerate. Such people therefore tended to be submissive to those with power over them and aggressive or punitive toward those beneath them.

Scholars criticized the research for focusing on right-wing authoritarianism and overlooking dogmatic authoritarianism of the left. Still, its main conclusion has survived: Authoritarian tendencies, sometimes reflected in ethnic tensions, surge during threatening times of economic recession and social upheaval (Doty & others, 1991; Sales, 1973). In Russia, individuals scoring high in authoritarianism have tended to support a return to communist ideology and to oppose democratic reform (McFarland & others, 1992, 1996).

Moreover, contemporary studies of right-wing authoritarians by University of Manitoba psychologist Bob Altemeyer (1988, 1992, 2004) confirm that there *are* individuals whose fears and hostilities surface as prejudice. Feelings of moral superiority may go hand in hand with brutality toward perceived inferiors.

Different forms of prejudice—toward Blacks, gays and lesbians, women, old people, fat people, AIDS victims, the homeless—*do* tend to coexist in the same individuals (Bierly, 1985; Crandall, 1994; Peterson & others, 1993; Snyder & Ickes, 1985). As Altemeyer concludes, right-wing authoritarians tend to be "equal opportunity bigots." The same is true of those with a *social dominance orientation*—who view people in terms of hierarchies of merit or goodness. Further, in an analysis of 6,600 Canadian students and their parents, Bob Altemeyer (2004) has found that people who are both high in authoritarianism and high in social dominance orientation are some of the most prejudiced individuals in society. Further, they tend to hold the economic and social power to influence public policy. By contrast, those with a more communal or universal orientation—who attend to people's similarities and presume "universal human rights" enjoyed by "all God's children"—are more welcoming of affirmative action and accepting of those who differ (Phillips & Ziller, 1997; Pratto & others, 1994, 2000; Sidanius & others, 1996; Whitley, 1999).

COGNITIVE SOURCES OF PREJUDICE

Much of the explanation of prejudice so far could have been written in the 1960s—but not what follows. This new look at prejudice, fuelled in the 1990s by more than 2,100 articles on stereotyping, applies the new research on social thinking. The basic point is this: Stereotyped beliefs and prejudiced attitudes exist not only because of social conditioning and because they enable people to displace hostilities, but also as by-products of normal thinking processes. Many stereotypes spring less from malice of the heart than the machinery of the mind. Like perceptual illusions, which are by-products of our knack for interpreting the world, stereotypes can be by-products of how we simplify our complex worlds.

Categorization

One way we simplify our environment is to *categorize*—to organize the world by clustering objects into groups (Macrae & Bodenhausen, 2000). A biologist classifies plants and animals. A human classifies people. Having done so, we think about them more easily. If persons in a group share some similarities—if most MENSA members are smart, most basketball players tall—knowing their group memberships can provide useful information with minimal effort (Macrae & others, 1994). Stereotypes sometimes offer "a beneficial ratio of information gained to effort expended" (Sherman & others, 1998). Customs inspectors and airplane antihijack personnel are therefore given "profiles" of suspicious individuals (Kraut & Poe, 1980).

We find it especially easy and efficient to rely on stereotypes when:

- pressed for time (Kaplan & others, 1993),
- preoccupied (Gilbert & Hixon, 1991),
- tired (Bodenhausen, 1990),
- emotionally aroused (Esses & others, 1993b; Stroessner & Mackie, 1993), and
- too young to appreciate diversity (Biernat, 1991).

Ethnicity and gender are, in our current world, powerful ways of categorizing people. We label people of widely varying ancestry as simply "Black," "White," "Indian," or "Asian." When subjects view different people making statements, they often forget who said what, yet they remember the race of the person who made each statement (Hewstone & others, 1991; Stroessner & others, 1990; Taylor & others, 1978). By itself, such categorization is not prejudice, but it does provide a foundation for prejudice.

The Story Behind the Research

Does how we expect other people to view us affect how we view them? Of course it does. If we think someone likes us, we will tend to like them. Dr. Jacquie Vorauer wondered if this also applied to how we view other groups in society. Do our expectations of how another ethnic group views us influence our perceptions of them as a group? Dr. Vorauer became interested in this topic while conducting research on "transparency"—how easy we believe it is for others to understand what we might be thinking in a situation. People tend to believe that it should be easy for people to understand what they are thinking about. (Most of us in relationships can appreciate how wrong people can be about this—how many of us have had a partner say "you *should have known* how I would feel"?) Dr. Vorauer was interested in understanding the limits of these beliefs. Are there situations where we do not expect people to understand us? To answer this question, Dr. Vorauer and her colleagues decided to investigate people's beliefs about how other people perceive us in intergroup situations.

Meta-stereotypes are beliefs people hold about how they are stereotyped by outgroup members. In order to understand how these work, Dr. Vorauer first needed to demonstrate their existence. In one of her early studies, she and her colleagues (Vorauer & others, 1998) demonstrated that White Canadians collectively hold a negative meta-stereotype about Aboriginals. In other words, White Canadians believe that Aboriginals hold negative stereotypes toward Whites. Vorauer and colleagues demonstrated that Whites further extend these beliefs to the individuals in the group. In a second paper, they demonstrated that Whites' concerns about being judged in light of stereotypes may often be unwarranted and that members of lower-status groups (Aboriginals) as well as higher-status groups (Whites) tend to take an outgroup member's behaviour personally, as reflecting an evaluation of themselves, during intergroup interaction (see Vorauer & Kumhyr, 2001). However, the implications seem clear. If Whites presume that outgroups are perceiving *them* negatively, this may result in Whites interpreting ambiguous behaviour from members of the outgroup as negative, which could result in negative feelings *toward* these groups, and could perpetuate negative stereotypes and beliefs in the long run. |

Perceived Similarities and Differences

Picture the following objects: apples, chairs, pencils.

There is a strong tendency to see objects within a group as being more uniform than they really are. Were your apples all red? Your chairs all straight-backed? Your pencils all yellow? It's the same with people. Once we assign people to groups—athletes, drama majors, math professors—we are likely to exaggerate the similarities within the groups and the differences between them (S. E. Taylor, 1981; Wilder, 1978). Mere division into groups can create an **outgroup homogeneity effect**—a sense that *they* are "all alike" and different from "us" and "our" group (Ostrom & Sedikides, 1992). Because we generally like people we think are similar to us and dislike those we perceive as different, the natural result is ingroup bias (Byrne & Wong, 1962; Rokeach & Mezei, 1966; Stein & others, 1965).

Outgroup homogeneity effect Perception of outgroup members as more similar to one another than are ingroup members. Thus "they are alike; we are diverse."

When the group is our own, we are more likely to see diversity:

- Many non-Europeans see the Swiss as a fairly homogeneous people. But to the people of Switzerland, the Swiss are diverse, encompassing French-, German-, and Italian-speaking groups.

- Many Anglo-Americans lump "Latinos" together. Mexican Americans, Cuban Americans, and Puerto Ricans see important differences, especially between their own subgroup and the others (Huddy & Virtanen, 1995).

- Sorority sisters perceive the members of any other sorority as less diverse than the mix in their own (Park & Rothbart, 1982). And business majors and engineering majors overestimate the uniformity of the other group's traits and attitudes (Judd & others, 1991).

In general, the greater our familiarity with a social group, the more we see its diversity (Brown & Wootton-Millward, 1993; Linville & others, 1989). The less our familiarity, the more we stereotype.

Perhaps you have noticed: *They*—the members of any racial group other than your own—even *look* alike. Many of us can recall embarrassing ourselves by confusing two people of another racial group, prompting the person we've misnamed to say, "You think we all look alike." Experiments by John Brigham, June Chance, Alvin Goldstein, and Roy Malpass in the United States and by Hayden Ellis in Scotland reveal that people of other races do in fact *seem* to look more alike than do people of one's own race (Chance & Goldstein, 1981, 1996; Ellis, 1981; Meissner and Brigham, 2001). When White students are shown faces of a few White and a few Black individuals and then asked to pick these individuals out of a photographic lineup, they more accurately recognize the White faces than the Black, and they often falsely recognize Black faces never before seen. See Module 26 for further discussion of this topic.

Blacks more easily recognize another Black than they do a White (Bothwell & others, 1989). And Hispanics more readily recognize another Hispanic whom they saw a couple of hours earlier than they do an Anglo (Platz & Hosch, 1988).

It's true outside the laboratory as well, as Daniel Wright and his colleagues (2001) found after either a Black or a White researcher approached Black and White people in South African and English shopping malls. When later asked to identify the researcher from lineups, people better recognized those of their own race. It's not that we cannot perceive differences among faces of another race. Rather, when looking at a face from another racial group we often attend first to race ("that man is Black"), rather than to individual features. When viewing someone of our own race, we are less race conscious and more attentive to individual details (Levin, 2000).

Distinctiveness

Other ways we perceive our worlds also breed stereotypes. Distinctive people and vivid or extreme occurrences often capture attention and distort judgments. As with the outgroup homogeneity effect, this innocent-seeming phenomenon sometimes breeds stereotypes.

Distinctive People Draw Attention

Have you ever found yourself in a situation where you were the only person present of your gender, race, or nationality? If so, your difference from the others probably made you more noticeable and the object of more attention. A Black in an otherwise White group, a man in an otherwise female group, or a woman in an otherwise male group seems more prominent and influential and to have exaggerated good and bad qualities (Crocker & McGraw, 1984; S. E. Taylor & others, 1979). This occurs because when someone in a group is made salient (conspicuous), we tend to see that person as causing whatever happens (Taylor & Fiske, 1978).

Have you noticed that people also define you by your most distinctive traits and behaviours? Tell people about someone who is a sky diver and a tennis player, report Lori Nelson and Dale Miller (1997), and they will think of the person as a sky diver. People also take note of those who violate expectations (Bettencourt & others, 1997). "Like a flower blooming in winter, intellect is more readily noticed where it is not expected," reflected Stephen Carter (1993, p. 54) on his experience as an African American intellectual. Such perceived distinctiveness makes it easier for highly capable job applicants from low-status groups to get noticed, though they also must work harder to prove that their abilities are genuine (Biernat & Kobrynowicz, 1997).

Ellen Langer and Lois Imber (1980) cleverly demonstrated the attention paid distinctive people. They asked Harvard students to watch a video of a man reading. The students paid closer attention when they were led to think he was out of the ordinary—a cancer patient, a millionaire, or a homosexual. They detected characteristics that other viewers ignored, and their evaluation of him was more extreme.

Sometimes we perceive others as reacting to our distinctiveness when actually they aren't. At Dartmouth College, researchers Robert Kleck and Angelo Strenta (1980) discovered this when they led college women to feel disfigured. The women thought the purpose of the experiment was to assess how someone would react to a facial scar created with theatrical makeup; the scar was on the right cheek, running from the ear to the mouth. Actually, the purpose was to see how the women themselves, when made to feel deviant, would perceive others' behaviour toward them. After applying the makeup, the experimenter gave each subject a small hand mirror so she could see the authentic-looking scar. When she put the mirror down, he then applied some "moisturizer" to "keep the makeup from cracking." What the "moisturizer" really did was remove the scar.

The scene that followed was poignant. A young woman, feeling terribly self-conscious about her supposedly disfigured face, talked with another woman who sees no such disfigurement and knows nothing of what has gone on before. If you have ever felt similarly self-conscious—perhaps about a physical handicap, acne, even just a bad hair day—then perhaps you can sympathize with the self-conscious woman. Compared to women who were led to believe their conversational partners merely thought they had an allergy, the "disfigured" women became acutely sensitive to how their partners were looking at them. They rated their partners as more tense, distant, and patronizing. In fact, observers who later analyzed videotapes of how the partners treated "disfigured" persons could find no such differences in treatment. Self-conscious about being different, the "disfigured" women misinterpreted mannerisms and comments they would otherwise not have noticed.

Vivid Cases

Our minds also use distinctive cases as a shortcut to judging groups. Are Blacks good athletes? "Well, there's Venus and Serena Williams and Shaquille O'Neal. Yeah, I'd say so." Note the thought processes at work here: Given limited experience with a particular social group, we recall examples of it and generalize from those (Sherman, 1996). Moreover, encountering examplars of negative stereotypes (say, a hostile Black person) can prime such stereotypes, leading people to minimize contact with the group (Henderson-King & Nisbett, 1996). Such generalizing from single cases can cause problems. Vivid instances, though more available in memory, are seldom representative of the larger group. Exceptional athletes, though distinctive and memorable, are not the best basis for judging the distribution of athletic talent among an entire group.

Those in a numerical minority, being more distinctive, also may be numerically overestimated by the majority. Consider a 1990 Gallup poll conducted in the United States. In the poll, American respondents estimated that the Black and Hispanic populations of the U.S. were 30 and 19 percent of the total population, respectively. Yet the actual numbers are significantly lower (see Figure 19-3). A 2002 Gallup poll found that the average person thought 21 percent of men are gay and 22 percent of women are lesbians. Yet actual numbers suggest that only 3 or 4 percent of men and 1 to 2 percent of women have a same-sex orientation (National Center for Health Statistics, 1991; Smith, 1998; Tarmann, 2002).

Myron Rothbart and his colleagues (1978) showed how distinctive cases also fuel stereotypes. Students read descriptions of the actions of 50 men, 10 of whom had committed either nonviolent crimes, such as forgery, or violent crimes, such as rape. Of those shown the list with the violent crimes, most overestimated the number of criminal acts.

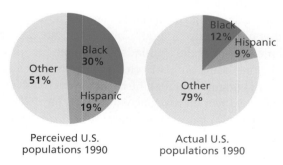

FIGURE 19-3
Overestimating minority populations.
Source: 1990 Gallup Poll (Gates, 1993).

The attention-getting power of distinctive, extreme cases helps explain why middle-class people so greatly exaggerate the dissimilarities between themselves and the underclass. The less we know about a group, the more we are influenced by a few vivid cases (Quattrone & Jones, 1980).

Attribution: Is It a Just World?

In explaining others' actions, we frequently commit the fundamental attribution error. We attribute their behaviour so much to their inner dispositions that we discount important situational forces. The error occurs partly because our attention focuses on the persons, not the situation. A person's race or sex is vivid and gets attention; the situational forces working upon that person are usually less visible. Until recently, the same was true of how we explained the perceived differences between women and men. Because gender-role constraints were hard to see, we attributed men's and women's behaviour solely to their innate dispositions. The more people assume that human traits are fixed dispositions, the stronger are their stereotypes (Levy & others, 1998). In a series of experiments conducted at the Universities of Waterloo and Kentucky, Melvin Lerner and his colleagues (Lerner & Miller, 1978; Lerner, 1980) discovered that merely *observing* another innocent person being victimized is enough to make the victim seem less worthy. Imagine that you, along with some others, are participating in one of Lerner's studies—supposedly on the perception of emotional cues (Lerner & Simmons, 1966). One of the participants, a confederate, is selected by lottery to perform a memory task. This person receives painful shocks whenever she gives a wrong answer. You and the others note her emotional responses.

After watching the victim receive these apparently painful shocks, the experimenter asks you to evaluate her. How would you respond? When observers were powerless to alter the victim's fate, they often rejected and devalued the victim. Juvenal, the Roman satirist, anticipated these results: "The Roman mob follows after Fortune . . . and hates those who have been condemned."

Linda Carli and her colleagues (1989, 1999) report that this **just-world phenomenon** colours our impressions of rape victims. Carli had people read detailed descriptions of interactions between a man and a woman. For example, a woman and her boss meet for dinner, go to his home, and each have a glass of wine. Some read a scenario that has a happy ending: "Then he led me to the couch. He held my hand and asked me to marry him." In hindsight, people find the ending unsurprising and admire the man's and woman's character traits. Others read the same scenario with a different ending: "But then he became very rough and pushed me onto the couch. He held me down on the couch and raped me." Given this ending, people see it as inevitable and blame the woman for behaviour that seems faultless in the first scenario.

Lerner (1980) noted that such disparaging of hapless victims results from the need of each of us to believe, "I am a just person living in a just world, a world where people get what they deserve." This suggests that people are indifferent to social injustice not because they have no concern for justice but because they see no injus-

OLC
Activity 19.2

Just-world phenomenon
The tendency of people to believe the world is just and that people therefore get what they deserve and deserve what they get.

tice. Those who assume a just world believe that rape victims must have behaved seductively (Borgida & Brekke, 1985), that battered spouses must have provoked their beatings (Summers & Feldman, 1984), that poor people don't deserve better (Furnham & Gunter, 1984), and that sick people are responsible for their illnesses (Gruman & Sloan, 1983). Such beliefs enable successful people to reassure themselves that they, too, deserve what they have. The wealthy and healthy can see their own good fortune, and others' misfortune, as justly deserved. Linking good fortune with virtue and misfortune with moral failure enables the fortunate to feel pride and to avoid responsibility for the unfortunate.

Social psychologists have been more successful in explaining prejudice than in alleviating it. Because prejudice results from many interrelated factors, there is no simple remedy. Nevertheless, we can now anticipate techniques for reducing prejudice (discussed further in modules to come): If unequal status breeds prejudice, then we can seek to create cooperative, equal-status relationships. If prejudice often rationalizes discriminatory behaviour, then we can mandate nondiscrimination. If outgroups seem more unlike one's own group than they really are, then we can make efforts to personalize their members. These are some of the antidotes for the poison of prejudice.

A number of these antidotes have been applied, and racial and gender prejudices have indeed diminished. It now remains to be seen whether, during this new century, progress will continue . . . or whether, as could easily happen in a time of increasing population and diminishing resources, antagonisms will again erupt into open hostility.

CONCEPTS TO REMEMBER

Stereotype threat   p. 203
Social identity   p. 205
Ingroup   p. 206
Outgroup   p. 206
Ingroup bias   p. 207

Realistic group conflict theory   p. 209
Ethnocentrism   p. 210
Outgroup homogeneity effect   p. 212
Just-world phenomenon   p. 216

Please visit the *Exploring Social Psychology* Online Learning Centre at **www.mcgrawhill.ca/college/myers** to participate in module activities, view module videos, access research and study tools, and test your knowledge with interactive quizzes, exercises, and scenarios.

Intergroup Conflict

T here is a speech that has been spoken in many languages by the leaders of many countries. It goes like this: "The intentions of our country are entirely peaceful. Yet, we are also aware that other nations, with their new weapons, threaten us. Thus we must defend ourselves against attack. By so doing, we shall protect our way of life and preserve the peace" (Richardson, 1960). Almost every nation claims concern only for peace but, mistrusting other nations, arms itself in self-defence. Considering that the above quote was written in 1960, at the height of the nuclear arms race, it is eerily similar to the arguments used by U.S. President George W. Bush to invade Iraq in 2003. He argued that Saddam Hussein's "weapons of mass destruction" were a clear and present danger to the United States and therefore justified the U.S.–imposed "regime change." Since the U.S.–led coalition forces invaded Iraq, more than 2,700 Coalition soldiers, 6,300 Iraqi soldiers, and at least 38,000 civilians have been killed (CBC, 2006). Although these numbers are staggering, they are a drop in the bucket compared to other major conflict regions in the world, such as Darfur and Rwanda, where hundreds of thousands have died.

Conflict A perceived incompatibility of actions or goals.

The elements of such **conflict** (a perceived incompatibility of actions or goals) are similar at all levels—from civil wars, to national conflicts where ethnic or cultural groups compete for access to natural resources, to international conflicts, to corporations vying for market share, to executives fighting for jobs within a company, to people's troubled relationships with their spouse or partner. Let's consider these conflict elements.

SOCIAL DILEMMAS

Several of the problems that most threaten our human future—nuclear arms, global warming, overpopulation, natural resource depletion—arise as various parties pursue their self-interests, ironically, to their collective detriment. Anyone can think, "It would cost me a lot to buy expensive pollution controls. Besides, by itself my pollution is trivial." Many others reason similarly, and the result is unclean air and water.

Thus, choices that are individually rewarding become collectively punishing. We therefore have an urgent dilemma: How can we reconcile individuals' well-being, including their right to pursue their personal interests, with communal well-being?

To isolate and illustrate this dilemma, social psychologists have used laboratory games that expose the heart of many real social conflicts. By showing us how well-meaning people become trapped in mutually destructive behaviour, they illuminate some fascinating, yet troubling, paradoxes of human existence. "Social psychologists who study conflict are in much the same position as the astronomers," notes conflict researcher Morton Deutsch (1999). "We cannot conduct true experiments with large-scale social events. But we can identify the conceptual similarities between the large scale and the small, as the astronomers have between the planets and Newton's apple. That is why the games people play as subjects in our laboratory may advance our understanding of war, peace, and social justice." Consider two examples: the Prisoners' Dilemma and the Tragedy of the Commons.

The Prisoners' Dilemma

One dilemma derives from an anecdote concerning two suspects questioned separately by the district attorney (DA) (Rapoport, 1960). They are jointly guilty; however, the DA has only enough evidence to convict them of a lesser offence. So the DA creates an incentive for each to confess privately: If one confesses and the other doesn't, the DA will grant the confessor immunity (and will use the confession to convict the other of a maximum offence). If both confess, each will receive a moderate sentence. If neither confesses, each will receive a light sentence. The matrix of Figure 20-1 on page 220 summarizes the choices. Faced with such a dilemma, would you confess?

To minimize their own sentences, many would confess, despite the fact that mutual confession elicits more severe sentences than mutual nonconfession. Note from the matrix that no matter what the other prisoner decides, each is better off confessing. If the other also confesses, one then gets a moderate sentence instead of a severe one. If the other does not confess, one goes free. Of course, each prisoner understands this. Hence, the social trap.

In some 2,000 studies (Dawes, 1991), university students have faced variations of the Prisoners' Dilemma with the outcomes being not prison terms but chips, money, or course points. How do you think you would do with the prisoners' dilemma? Visit the Online Learning Centre and complete Activity 20.1 to find out, then continue reading to see how others did. As Figure 20-2 on page 220 illustrates, on any given decision, a person is better off defecting (because such behaviour exploits the other's cooperation or protects against the other's exploitation). However—and here's the

OLC
Activity 20.1

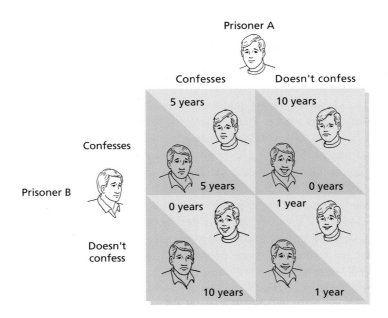

FIGURE 20-1

The Prisoners' Dilemma. In each box, the number above the diagonal is prisoner A's outcome. Thus, if both prisoners confess, both get five years. If neither confesses, each gets a year. If one confesses, that prisoner is set free in exchange for evidence used to convict the other of a crime, bringing a 10-year sentence. If you were one of the prisoners, unable to communicate with your fellow prisoner, would you confess?

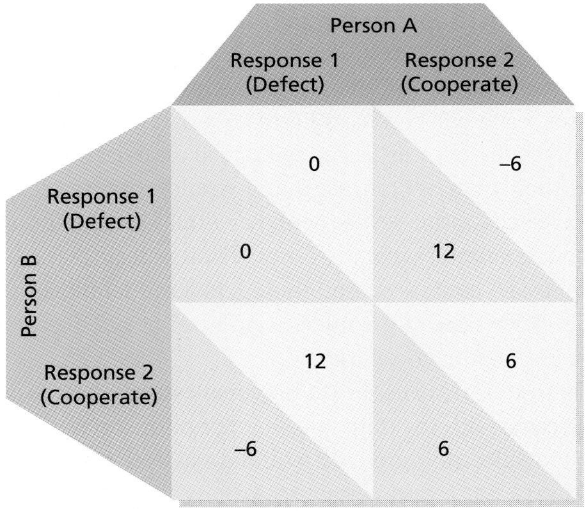

	Person A	
	Response 1 (Defect)	Response 2 (Cooperate)
Response 1 (Defect)	0 / 0	−6 / 12
Response 2 (Cooperate)	12 / −6	6 / 6

FIGURE 20-2

Laboratory version of the Prisoners' Dilemma. The numbers represent some reward, such as money. In each box, the number above the diagonal lines is the outcome for person A.

rub—by not cooperating, both parties end up far worse off than if they had trusted each other and thus had gained a joint profit. This dilemma often traps each one in a maddening predicament in which both realize they *could* mutually profit but, unable to communicate and mistrusting one another, become "locked in" to not cooperating.

The Tragedy of the Commons

Many social dilemmas involve more than two parties. Global warming stems from widespread deforestation and from the carbon dioxide emitted by the world's cars, oil furnaces, and coal-fired power plants. Each gas-guzzling car contributes infinitesimally to the problem, and the harm each does is diffused over many people. In an attempt to reduce worldwide greenhouse gas emissions, the United Nations sponsored a multi-nation agreement brokered at a conference in Kyoto, Japan. The agreement, which was then labelled the Kyoto Accord, promised to significantly reduce greenhouse gas emissions by 2012 and was signed by more than 100 countries worldwide. However, the United States, seen as a key signatory, withdrew from the accord, citing economic reasons. Under Prime Minister Stephen Harper, Canada is also considering scrapping the plan, claiming the potential for economic hardship (CBC, 2006). Perhaps not surprisingly, Canada and the United States are among the worst offenders when it comes to greenhouse gas emissions. To model such social predicaments, researchers have developed laboratory dilemmas that involve multiple people.

A metaphor for the insidious nature of social dilemmas is what ecologist Garrett Hardin (1968) called the "tragedy of the commons." He derived the name from the centrally located pasture area in old English towns, but the "commons" can be air, water, whales, cookies, or any shared and limited resource. If all use the resource in moderation, it may replenish itself as rapidly as it's harvested. The grass will grow, the whales will reproduce, and the cookie jar will get restocked. If not, there occurs a tragedy of the commons.

Imagine 100 farmers surrounding a commons capable of sustaining 100 cows. When each grazes one cow, the common feeding ground is optimally used. But then someone reasons, "If I put a second cow in the pasture, I'll double my output, minus the mere 1 percent overgrazing." So this farmer adds a second cow. So do each of the other farmers. The inevitable result? The Tragedy of the Commons—a grassless mud field.

Many real predicaments parallel this story. Environmental pollution is the sum of many minor pollutions, each of which benefits the individual polluters much more than they could benefit themselves (and the environment) if they stopped polluting. We deplete our natural resources because the immediate personal benefits of, say, taking a long, hot shower outweigh the seemingly inconsequential costs. Whalers knew others would exploit the whales if they didn't and that taking a few whales would hardly diminish the species. Therein lies the tragedy. Everybody's business (conservation) became nobody's business.

The Prisoners' Dilemma and the Tragedy of the Commons games have several similar features. First, both tempt people to explain their own behaviour situationally ("I had to protect myself against exploitation by my opponent") and to explain their partners' behaviour dispositionally ("She was greedy" "He was untrustworthy").

Most never realize that their counterparts are viewing them with the same fundamental attribution error (Gifford & Hine, 1997; Hine & Gifford, 1996).

Second, motives often change. At first, people are eager to make some easy
money, then to minimize their losses, and finally to save face and avoid defeat
(Brockner & others, 1982; Teger, 1980).

Third, most real-life conflicts, like the Prisoners' Dilemma and the Tragedy of the
Commons, are **non-zero-sum games**. The two sides' profits and losses need not add
up to zero. Both can win; both can lose. Each game pits the immediate interests of individuals against the well-being of the group. Each is a diabolical social trap that shows
how, even when individuals behave "rationally," harm can result. No malicious person
planned for the earth's atmosphere to be warmed by a blanket of carbon dioxide.

Not all self-serving behaviour leads to collective doom. In a plentiful commons—as
in the world of the eighteenth-century capitalist economist Adam Smith (1776, p. 18)—
individuals who seek to maximize their own profit may also give the community what
it needs: "It is not from the benevolence of the butcher, the brewer, or the baker, that we
expect our dinner," he observed, "but from their regard to their own interest."

> **Non-zero-sum games**
> Games in which outcomes
> need not sum to zero. With
> cooperation, both can win;
> with competition, both can
> lose. (Also called *mixed-
> motive situations*.)

Resolving Social Dilemmas

In those situations that are indeed social traps, how can we induce people to cooperate for their mutual betterment? Research with the laboratory dilemmas reveals
several ways (Gifford & Hine, 1997).

Regulation

If taxes were entirely voluntary, how many would pay their full share? Surely, many
would not, which is why modern societies do not depend on charity to pay for
schools, parks, and social and military security. We also develop laws and regulations
for our common good. An International Whaling Commission sets an agreed-upon
"harvest" that enables whales to regenerate.

Small Is Beautiful

There is another way to resolve social dilemmas: Make the group small. In a small
commons, each person feels more responsible and effective (Kerr, 1989). As a group
grows larger, people more often think, "I couldn't have made a difference anyway"—
a common excuse for noncooperation (Kerr & Kaufman-Gilliland, 1997). In small
groups, people also feel more identified with a group's success. Anything else that
enhances group identity will also increase cooperation. Even just a few minutes of
discussion or just believing that one shares similarities with others in the group can
increase "we feeling" and cooperation (Brewer, 1987; Orbell & others, 1988).

Communication

To escape a social trap, people must communicate. Although group communication
sometimes degenerates into threats and name calling (Deutsch & Krauss, 1960), more
often communication enables groups to cooperate—much more (Bornstein & others,
1988, 1989). Discussing the dilemma forges a group identity, which enhances con-

cern for the group's welfare. It devises group norms and consensus expectations and puts pressure on members to follow them. And especially when people are face-to-face, it enables them to commit themselves to cooperation (Bouas & Komorita, 1996; Drolet & Morris, 2000; Kerr & others, 1994, 1997; Pruitt, 1998).

Without communication, those who expect others not to cooperate will usually refuse to cooperate themselves (Messé & Sivacek, 1979; Pruitt & Kimmel, 1977). One who mistrusts almost has to be uncooperative (to protect against exploitation). Noncooperation, in turn, feeds further mistrust ("What else could I do? It's a dog-eat-dog world"). In experiments, communication reduces mistrust, enabling people to reach agreements that lead to their common betterment.

Changing the Payoffs

Cooperation rises when experimenters change the payoff matrix to make cooperation more rewarding and exploitation less rewarding (Komorita & Barth, 1985; Pruitt & Rubin, 1986). Changing payoffs also helps resolve actual dilemmas. In some cities, freeways clog and skies smog because people prefer the convenience of driving themselves directly to work. Each knows that one more car does not add noticeably to the congestion and pollution. To alter the personal cost–benefit calculations, many cities now give carpoolers incentives, such as designated freeway lanes or reduced tolls.

Appeals to Altruistic Norms

When cooperation obviously serves the public good, one can usefully appeal to the social-responsibility norm (Lynn & Oldenquist, 1986). When, for example, people believe public transportation can save time, they will be more likely to use it if they also believe it reduces pollution (Van Vugt & others, 1996). In the struggle for civil rights, many marchers willingly agreed, for the sake of the larger group, to suffer harassment, beatings, and jail. In wartime, people make great personal sacrifices for the good of their group. As Winston Churchill said of the Battle of Britain, the actions of the Royal Air Force pilots were genuinely altruistic: A great many people owed a great deal to those who flew into battle knowing there was a high probability—70 percent for those on a standard tour of duty—they would not return (Levinson, 1950).

To summarize, we can minimize destructive entrapment in social dilemmas by establishing rules that regulate self-serving behaviour, by keeping groups small, by enabling people to communicate, by changing payoffs to make cooperation more rewarding, and by invoking altruistic norms.

COMPETITION

In the module on prejudice, we noted that racial hostilities often arise when groups compete for jobs and other benefits. When interests clash, conflict erupts.

As Canadians, we are collectively no stranger to these types of conflicts. There are perpetual negotiations ongoing in an attempt to resolve centuries-old land claim issues between the federal government and numerous Aboriginal groups, with no resolution at hand. Some French Canadians in Quebec have perceived themselves to be so ill-treated that the Parti Québécois has held two referendums to decide whether Quebec should separate from the rest of Canada. Both of these conflicts have led to open hostility in the past (for example, the Oka Crisis and the FLQ bombings).

But does competition by itself provoke hostile conflict? Real-life situations are so complex that it is hard to be sure. If competition is indeed responsible, then it should be possible to provoke in an experiment. We could randomly divide people into two groups, have the groups compete for a scarce resource, and note what happens. This is precisely what Muzafer Sherif (1966) and his colleagues did in a dramatic series of experiments with typical 11- and 12-year-old boys. The inspiration for these experiments dated back to Sherif's witnessing, as a teenager, Greek troops invading his Turkish province in 1919:

> They started killing people right and left. [That] made a great impression on me. There and then I became interested in understanding why these things were happening among human beings. . . . I wanted to learn whatever science or specialization was needed to understand this intergroup savagery. (quoted by Aron & Aron, 1989, p. 131)

After studying the social roots of savagery, Sherif introduced the seeming essentials into several three-week summer camping experiences. In one such study, he divided 22 unacquainted boys into two groups, took them to a Boy Scout camp in separate buses, and settled them in bunkhouses about a kilometre apart at Oklahoma's Robber's Cave State Park. For most of the first week, they were unaware of the other group's existence. By cooperating in various activities—preparing meals, camping out, fixing up a swimming hole, building a rope bridge—each group soon became close-knit. They gave themselves names: "Rattlers" and "Eagles." Typifying the good feeling, a sign appeared in one cabin: "Home Sweet Home."

Group identity thus established, the stage was set for the conflict. Toward the end of the first week, the Rattlers "discovered the Eagles on 'our' baseball field." When the camp staff then proposed a tournament of competitive activities between the two groups (baseball games, tugs-of-war, cabin inspections, treasure hunts, and so forth), both groups responded enthusiastically. This was win–lose competition. The spoils (medals, knives) would all go to the tournament victor.

The result? The camp gradually degenerated into open warfare. It was like a scene from William Golding's novel *Lord of the Flies*, which depicts the social disintegration of boys marooned on an island. In Sherif's study, the conflict began with each side calling the other names during the competitive activities. Soon it escalated to dining hall "garbage wars," flag burnings, cabin ransackings, even fistfights. Asked to describe the other group, the boys said "they" were "sneaky," "smart alecks," "stinkers," while referring to their own group as "brave," "tough," "friendly."

The win–lose competition had produced intense conflict, negative images of the outgroup, and strong ingroup cohesiveness and pride. However, we cannot forget the impact that the groups and social identity forces may have (for example, Tajfel & Turner, 1979), which we discussed in the context of the previous two modules. Group polarization no doubt exacerbated the conflict. In experiments, groups behave more competitively than individuals in competition-fostering situations (see Wildschut & others, 2003). All this occurred without any cultural, physical, or economic differences between the two groups and with boys who were their communities' "cream of the crop." Sherif noted that, had we visited the camp at this point, we would have concluded these "were wicked, disturbed, and vicious bunches of youngsters" (1966, p. 85). Actually, their evil behaviour was triggered by an evil situation. Fortunately, as we will see in Module 21, Sherif not only made strangers into enemies; he then, as we will see, made the enemies into friends.

PERCEIVED INJUSTICE

"That's unfair!" "What a ripoff!" "We deserve better!" Such comments typify conflicts bred by perceived injustice. But what is justice? According to some social-psychological theorists, people perceive justice as equity—the distribution of rewards in proportion to individuals' contributions (Walster & others, 1978). If you and I have a relationship (employer–employee, teacher–student, husband–wife, colleague–colleague), it is equitable if:

$$\frac{\text{My outcomes}}{\text{My inputs}} = \frac{\text{Your outcomes}}{\text{Your inputs}}$$

If you contribute more and benefit less than I do, you will feel exploited and irritated; I may feel exploitative and guilty. Chances are, though, that you, more than I, will be sensitive to the inequity (Greenberg, 1986; Messick & Sentis, 1979).

We may agree with the equity principle's definition of justice yet disagree on whether our relationship is equitable. If two people are colleagues, what will each consider a relevant input? The one who is older may favour basing pay on seniority, the other on current productivity. Given such a disagreement, whose definition is likely to prevail? More often than not, those with social power convince themselves and others that they deserve what they're getting (Mikula, 1984). This has been called a "golden rule": Whoever has the gold makes the rules.

As this suggests, the exploiter can relieve guilt by valuing or devaluing inputs to justify the existing outcomes. Men may perceive the lower pay of women as equitable, given women's "less important" inputs. Those who inflict harm may blame the victim and thus maintain their belief in a just world.

And how do those who are exploited react? Elaine Hatfield, William Walster, and Ellen Berscheid (1978) detected three possibilities. They can accept and justify their inferior position ("We're poor; it's what we deserve, but we're happy"). They can demand compensation, perhaps by harassing, embarrassing, even cheating their exploiter. If all else fails, they may try to restore equity by retaliating.

An interesting implication of equity theory—an implication that has been confirmed experimentally—is that the more competent and worthy people feel (the more they value their inputs), the more they will feel underbenefited and thus eager to retaliate (Ross & others, 1971). Intense social protests generally come from those who believe themselves worthy of more than they are receiving.

Since 1970, professional opportunities for women have increased significantly. However, true equity has not been attained. The Canadian Department of Justice (2004) reports that women are consistently paid less than men (see Table 20-1 on page 226). But how are these inequities perceived? So long as women compared their

TABLE 20-1 *Average Salaries of Women Working Full Time as a Percentage of Average Salaries of Men*

Banking	64.4%
Transportation	73.6%
Communications	86.9%
Other sectors	78.1%
All sectors	**77.6%**

Source: Adapted from Canadian Human Rights Commission, 2004 Employment Equity Annual Report.

opportunities and earnings with those of other women, they felt generally satisfied—as they still do with their disproportionate share of family labour (Jackson, 1989; Major, 1989, 1993). Research by Serge Desmarais and his colleagues at the University of Guelph has found that since women are now more likely to see themselves as men's equals, their sense of relative deprivation has grown (see Desmarais & Curtis, 2001). If secretarial work and truck driving have "comparable worth" (for the skills required), then they deserve comparable pay; that's equity, say advocates of gender equality (Lowe & Wittig, 1989).

MISPERCEPTION

Recall that conflict is a *perceived* incompatibility of actions or goals. Many conflicts contain but a small core of truly incompatible goals; the bigger problem is the misperceptions of the other's motives and goals. The Eagles and the Rattlers did indeed have some genuinely incompatible aims. But their perceptions subjectively magnified their differences.

In earlier modules we considered the seeds of such misperception. The *self-serving bias* leads individuals and groups to accept credit for their good deeds and shuck responsibility for bad deeds, without according others the same benefit of the doubt. A tendency to *self-justify* further inclines people to deny the wrong of their evil acts that cannot be shucked off. Thanks to the *fundamental attribution error*, each side sees the other's hostility as reflecting an evil disposition. One then filters the information and interprets it to fit one's *preconceptions*. Groups frequently *polarize* these self-serving, self-justifying, biasing tendencies. One symptom of *groupthink* is the tendency to perceive one's own group as moral and strong, the opposition as evil and weak. Terrorist acts that are despicable brutality to most people are "holy war" to others. Indeed, the mere fact of being in a group triggers an *ingroup bias*. And negative *stereotypes*, once formed, are often resistant to contradictory evidence.

So it should not surprise us, though it should sober us, to discover that people in conflict form distorted images of one another. Even the types of misperception are intriguingly predictable.

Mirror-Image Perceptions

To a striking degree, the misperceptions of those in conflict are mutual. People in conflict attribute similar virtues to themselves and vices to the other. When American psychologist Urie Bronfenbrenner (1961) visited the former Soviet Union in 1960 and conversed with many ordinary citizens in Russian, he was astonished to hear them saying the same things about America that Americans were saying about Russia. The Russians said that the U.S. government was militarily aggressive; that it exploited and deluded the American people; that in diplomacy it was not to be trusted. "Slowly and painfully, it forced itself upon one that the Russians' distorted picture of us was curiously similar to our view of them—a mirror image."

When the two sides have clashing perceptions, at least one of the two is misperceiving the other. And when such misperceptions exist, noted Bronfenbrenner, "It is a psychological phenomenon without parallel in the gravity of its consequences . . . for *it is characteristic of such images that they are self-confirming.*" If A expects B to be hostile, A may treat B in such a way that B fulfills A's expectations, thus beginning a vicious circle.

Negative **mirror-image perceptions** have been an obstacle to peace in many places:

- Both sides of the Arab–Israeli conflict insisted that "we" are motivated by our need to protect our security and our territory, while "they" want to obliterate us and gobble up our land. "We" are the indigenous people here, "they" are the invaders. "We" are the victims, "they" are the aggressors" (Heradstveit, 1979; Rouhana & Bar-Tal, 1998). Both sides in this conflict feel that the land has been promised to them by God. This is obviously a difficult claim to verify and leaves the different sides firmly entrenched in their positions. Given such intense mistrust, negotiation is difficult.

- At Northern Ireland's University of Ulster, J. A. Hunter and his colleagues (1991) showed Catholic and Protestant students videos of a Protestant attack at a Catholic funeral and a Catholic attack at a Protestant funeral. Most students attributed the other side's attack to "bloodthirsty" motives but their own side's attack to retaliation or self-defence.

- Muslims and Hindus in Bangladesh exhibit the same ingroup-favouring perceptions (Islam & Hewstone, 1993).

- As the United States and Iraq prepared for war, each repeatedly spoke of the other as "evil." To George W. Bush, Saddam Hussein was a "murderous tyrant" and "madman" who was threatening the civilized world with weapons of mass destruction. To Iraq's government, the Bush government was a "gang of evil" that lusted for Middle Eastern oil.

Such conflicts, notes Philip Zimbardo (2004), engage "a two-category world—of good people, like US, and of bad people, like THEM." Opposing sides in a conflict tend to exaggerate their differences, note David Sherman, Leif Nelson, and Lee Ross (2003). On issues such as abortion, immigration, and affirmative action, proponents

Mirror-image perceptions
Reciprocal views of one another often held by parties in conflict; for example, each may view itself as moral and peace-loving and the other as evil and aggressive.

aren't as liberal and opponents aren't as conservative as their adversaries suppose. To resolve conflicts, it helps to understand the other's mind. But it isn't easy, notes Robert Wright (2003): "Putting yourself in the shoes of people who do things you find abhorrent may be the hardest moral exercise there is."

Destructive mirror-image perceptions also operate in conflicts between small groups and between individuals. As we saw in the dilemma games, both parties may say, "We want to cooperate. But their refusal to cooperate forces us to react defensively." In a study of executives, Kenneth Thomas and Louis Pondy (1977) uncovered such attributions. Asked to describe a significant recent conflict, only 12 percent felt the other party was cooperative; 74 percent perceived themselves as cooperative. The executives explained that they had "suggested," "informed," and "recommended," while their antagonist had "demanded," "disagreed with everything I said," and "refused."

Conflicts are often fuelled by an illusion that the enemy's top leaders are evil but their people, though controlled and manipulated, are pro-us. This *evil leader–good people* perception was clear in U.S. propaganda regarding the invasion of Iraq. Indeed, the name the U.S. gave to the invasion was "Operation Iraqi Freedom," suggesting that the U.S. was freeing the Iraqi people from an evil dictator and that they would be welcomed with open arms. This belief appears to have been wishful thinking.

Another type of mirror-image perception is each side's exaggeration of the other's position. People with opposing views on issues such as abortion, capital punishment, and government budget cuts often differ less than they suppose. Each side overestimates the extremity of the other's views, especially those of the group seeking change. And each presumes that "our" beliefs follow from the facts while "their" ideology dictates their interpretation of facts (Keltner & Robinson, 1996; Robinson & others, 1995). From such exaggerated perceptions arise culture wars. Ralph White (1996, 1998) reports that the Serbs started the war in Bosnia partly out of an exaggerated fear of the relatively secularized Bosnian Muslims, whose beliefs they wrongly associated with Middle Eastern Islamic fundamentalism and fanatical terrorism.

Shifting Perceptions

If misperceptions accompany conflict, then they should appear and disappear as conflicts wax and wane. They do, with startling regularity. The same processes that create the enemy's image can reverse that image when the enemy becomes an ally.

The Germans, who after two world wars were hated, then admired, and then again hated, were once again admired—apparently no longer plagued by what earlier was presumed to be cruelty in their national character. So long as Iraq was attacking Iran, even while using chemical weapons and massacring its own Kurds, many nations supported it. Our enemy's enemy is our friend. When Iraq ended its war with Iran and invaded oil-rich Kuwait in 1990, Iraq's behaviour suddenly became "barbaric." Images of our enemies change with amazing ease.

The extent of misperceptions during conflict provides a chilling reminder that people need not be insane or abnormally evil to form these distorted images of their antagonists. When we experience conflict with another nation, another group, or simply a roommate or parent, we readily misperceive our own motives and actions as wholly good and the other's as totally evil. Our antagonists usually form a mirror-image perception of us. So, trapped in a social dilemma, competing for scarce resources, or perceiving injustice, the conflict continues until something enables both parties to peel away their misperceptions and work at reconciling their actual differences. Good advice, then, is this: When in conflict, do not assume that the other fails to share your values and morality. Rather, compare perceptions, assuming that the other is likely perceiving the situation differently.

CONCEPTS TO REMEMBER

Conflict   p. 218
Non-zero-sum games   p. 222
Mirror-image perceptions   p. 227

Please visit the *Exploring Social Psychology* Online Learning Centre at **www.mcgrawhill.ca/college/myers** to participate in module activities, view module videos, access research and study tools, and test your knowledge with interactive quizzes, exercises, and scenarios.

MODULE TWENTY-ONE

Mediation and Dispute Resolution

The flag of the United Nations, an international body dedicated to achieving world peace and security. UN representatives and groups are often involved negotiating peace treaties and bringing stability to areas of the world experiencing conflict. How could you apply the approaches to mediation and dispute resolution described in this chapter in your life?

We have seen how conflicts are ignited by social traps, competition, perceived injustices, and misperceptions. Although the picture is grim, it is not hopeless. Sometimes closed fists become open arms as hostilities evolve into friendship. Social psychologists have focused on four strategies for helping enemies become comrades. We can remember these as the four Cs of peacemaking: contact, cooperation, communication, conciliation.

CONTACT

Might putting two conflicting individuals or groups into close contact enable them to know and like each other? We have seen why it might. We have seen that proximity—and the accompanying interaction, anticipation of interaction, and mere exposure—boosts liking. In the United States until 1954, schools were segregated such that Blacks and Whites went to separate schools. A 1954 Supreme Court decision (strongly influenced by the input of social scientists) desegregated the schools. Thus Blacks and Whites were forced to share space. Was this effective? Since 1954 overt prejudice has declined.

Was interracial contact the *cause* of these improved attitudes? Were those who actually experienced desegregation affected by it?

School desegregation has produced measurable benefits, such as leading more Blacks to attend and succeed in college (Stephan, 1988). Does desegregation of schools, neighbourhoods, and workplaces also produce favourable *social* results? The evidence is mixed.

On the one hand, many studies conducted during and shortly after the desegregation following World War II found Whites' attitudes toward Blacks improving markedly. Whether the people were department-store clerks and customers, merchant marines, government workers, police officers, neighbours, or students, racial contact led to diminished prejudice (Amir, 1969; Pettigrew, 1969).

Contact predicts tolerant attitudes in nonracial realms as well. In a painstakingly complete analysis, Linda Tropp and Thomas Pettigrew (2004) assembled data from 515 studies of 250,513 people in 38 nations. In 94 percent of studies, *increased contact predicted decreased prejudice*. The correlation holds not only for interracial contacts, but also contacts with the elderly, psychiatric patients, gays, and children with disabilities, notes Miles Hewstone (2003).

Findings such as these influenced the Supreme Court's 1954 decision to desegregate U.S. schools and helped fuel the civil rights movement of the 1960s (Pettigrew, 1986). Yet, studies of the effects of school desegregation have been less encouraging. After reviewing all the available studies, Walter Stephan (1986) concluded that White racial attitudes had been little affected by desegregation. For Blacks, the more noticeable consequences of desegregated schooling were behavioural—their increased likelihood of attending integrated (or predominantly White) colleges, living in integrated neighbourhoods, and working in integrated settings.

When Does Contact Improve Ethnic Attitudes?

There are clear issues associated with simple contact. Indeed, in a recent review of the impact of contact on racial attitudes, John Dixon, Kevin Durrheim, and Colin Tredoux (2005) have pointed out that contact is not always a good thing. The context in which that contact occurs is very important.

Canada has had its share of racial and ethnic tensions both in the past and today (recall our discussion of perceptions of discrimination from previous modules). Although there was never an official segregation policy, many would argue the federal government policy of relocating Aboriginals to reserves was a *de facto* segregation policy. Nonetheless, Canada has worked hard for many years to promote its multiculturalism policy. Yet ethnic groups choose to segregate themselves. Most large cities have neighbourhoods that are dominated by specific ethnic groups— many new immigrants choose to move into areas where they are surrounded by people similar to themselves.

Self-imposed segregation was evident in a South African desegregated beach, as Dixon and Durrheim (2003) discovered when they recorded the location of Black, White, and Indian beachgoers one midsummer (December 30) afternoon (see Figure 21-1 on page 232). Efforts to facilitate contact sometimes help, but sometimes fall flat. "We had one day when some of the Protestant schools came over," explained one Catholic youngster after a Northern Ireland school exchange (Cairns & Hewstone, 2002). "It was supposed to be like . . . mixing, but there was very little mixing. It wasn't because we didn't want to; it was just really awkward."

FIGURE 21-1
Desegregation needn't mean contact. After this Scottburgh, South Africa, beach became "open" and desegregated in the new South Africa, Blacks (represented by black circles), Whites (grey circles), and Indians (white circles) tended to cluster with their own race.

From Dixon & Durrheim, 2003.

Studies involving prolonged, personal contact—between Black and White prison inmates and between Black and White girls in an interracial summer camp, for example—show benefits (Clore & others, 1978; Foley, 1976). Among North American students who studied in Germany or Britain, the more their contact with host country people, the more positive their attitudes (Stangor & others, 1996). In experiments, those who form *friendships* with outgroup members develop more positive attitudes toward the outgroup (Pettigrew & Tropp, 2000; Wright & others, 1997). It is not just knowledge of other people that matters, however—it is also the emotional ties that form with intimate friendships and that serve to reduce anxiety (Hewstone, 2003; Pettigrew & Tropp, 2000).

Surveys of nearly 4,000 Europeans reveal that friendship is a key to successful contact: If you have a minority-group friend, you become much more likely to express sympathy and support for the friend's group, and even somewhat more support for immigration by that group. It's true of Germans' attitudes toward Turks, French people's attitudes toward Asians and North Africans, Netherlanders' attitudes toward Surinamers and Turks, and Britishers' attitudes toward West Indians and Asians

(Brown & others, 1999; Hamberger & Hewstone, 1997; Pettigrew, 1997). Likewise, anti-gay feeling is lower among people who know gays personally (Herek, 1993). Additional studies of attitudes toward the elderly, the mentally ill, AIDS patients, and those with disabilities confirm that contact often predicts positive attitudes (Pettigrew, 1998).

The social psychologists who advocated contact never claimed that contact of *any* sort would improve attitudes. They expected poor results when contacts were competitive, unsupported by authorities, and unequal (Pettigrew, 1988; Stephan, 1987). For many years in South Africa under apartheid, Blacks and Whites had extensive contact—yet Whites invariably were in dominant positions and Blacks were in menial ones. Such unequal contacts breed attitudes that merely justify the continuation of inequality. So it's important that the contact be **equal-status contact**, like that between the store clerks, the soldiers, the neighbours, the prisoners, and the summer campers.

COOPERATION

Although equal-status contact can help, it is sometimes not enough. It didn't help when Muzafer Sherif stopped the Eagles versus Rattlers competition and brought the groups together for noncompetitive activities, such as watching movies, shooting off fireworks, and eating. By this time, their hostility was so strong that mere contact only provided opportunities for taunts and attacks. When an Eagle was bumped by a Rattler, his fellow Eagles urged him to "brush off the dirt." Obviously, desegregating the two groups had hardly promoted their social integration.

Consider too the competitive situation in the typical classroom. Is the following scene familiar (Aronson, 1980, 2000)? Students compete for good grades, teacher approval, and various honours and privileges. The teacher asks a question. Several students' hands shoot up; other students sit, eyes downcast, trying to look invisible. When the teacher calls on one of the eager faces, the others hope for a wrong answer, giving them a chance to display their knowledge. The losers in this academic sport often resent the "nerds" or "geeks" who succeed. The situation abounds with both competition and painfully obvious status inequalities; we could hardly design it better to create divisions among the children.

Does competitive contact divide and *cooperative* contact unite? Consider what happens to people who together face a common predicament.

Common External Threats

Have you ever been in a natural disaster that has shut down your town? When the ice storm of 1997 hit Southern Ontario and Quebec, hundreds of thousands of people were left without power for days. A massive power failure struck Ontario and eight U.S. states in August 2003, leaving 50 million people without power. When Hurricane Juan hit Halifax in 2003, most of the city was without power for the better part of a week. What happened? News reports were filled with stories of people helping others in their communities—often, people they had never met. The Canadian Forces moved in, not to enforce law and order but to help remove downed trees and repair power poles. Such friendliness and camaraderie is common among

Equal-status contact
Contact made on an equal basis. Just as a relationship between people of unequal status breeds attitudes consistent with their relationship, so do relationships between those of equal status. Thus, to reduce prejudice, interracial contact should be between persons equal in status.

Team captain Mario Lemieux and goalie Martin Brodeur are surrounded by their teammates as the Canadian men's hockey team celebrates a gold-medal win over Team USA at the 2002 Salt Lake City Winter Olympics.

people who have experienced a shared threat (see Lanzetta, 1955).

Having a common enemy unified the groups of competing boys in Sherif's camping experiments—and in many subsequent experiments (Dion, 1979). Membership in civic organizations "has historically grown rapidly during and immediately after major wars," reports Robert Putnam (2000, p. 267). North Americans and Britishers' feelings of patriotism and unity were aroused by World War II, later by conflicts with the former Soviet Union during the Cold War, and by the September 11 terrorist attacks. Soldiers who together face combat often maintain lifelong ties with their comrades (Elder & Clipp, 1988). And nothing sparked Canadian pride and unity as much as Wayne Gretzky's assertion in the 2002 Winter Olympics that "the rest of the world" wanted the Canadian Men's Hockey team to lose. Few things so unite a people as having a common enemy.

Times of interracial strife may therefore be times of heightened group pride. For Chinese university students in Toronto, facing discrimination heightens a sense of kinship with other Chinese (Pak & others, 1991). Just being reminded of an outgroup (say, a rival school) heightens people's responsiveness to their own group (Wilder & Shapiro, 1984). When keenly conscious of who "they" are, we also know who "we" are.

However, we cannot forget that external threats can cause real conflict as well. In the aftermath of Hurricane Katrina in New Orleans in the fall of 2005, looting, murders, and roving gangs of gun-toting vigilantes were a frequent sight on the evening news. Residents had little support, and real threats and conflicts were present. These issues combined with the lack of law enforcement and the situation rapidly descended into anarchy.

Superordinate Goals

Superordinate goal
A shared goal that necessitates cooperative effort; a goal that overrides people's differences from one another.

Closely related to the unifying power of an external threat is the unifying power of **superordinate goals**—goals that compel all in a group and require cooperative effort. To promote harmony among his warring campers, Sherif introduced such goals. He created a problem with the camp water supply, necessitating the cooperation of both groups to restore the water. Given an opportunity to rent a movie, one expensive enough to require the joint resources of both groups, they again cooperated. When a truck "broke down" on a camping trip, a staff member casually left the tug-of-war rope nearby, prompting one boy to suggest that they all pull the truck to get it started. When it started, a backslapping celebration ensued over their victorious "tug-of-war against the truck."

After working together to achieve such superordinate goals, the boys ate together and enjoyed themselves around a campfire. Friendships sprouted across group lines. Hostilities plummeted. On the last day, the boys decided to travel home together on one bus. During the trip they no longer sat by groups. As the bus approached Oklahoma City and home, they, as one, spontaneously sang "Oklahoma" and then bade their friends farewell. With isolation and competition, Sherif made strangers into bitter enemies. With superordinate goals, he made enemies into friends.

Are Sherif's experiments mere child's play? Or can pulling together to achieve superordinate goals be similarly beneficial with adults in conflict? Robert Blake and Jane Mouton (1979) wondered. So, in a series of two-week experiments involving more than 1,000 executives in 150 different groups, they recreated the essential features of the situation experienced by the Rattlers and Eagles. Each group first engaged in activities by itself, then competed with another group, and then cooperated with the other group in working toward jointly chosen superordinate goals. Their results provided "unequivocal evidence that adult reactions parallel those of Sherif's younger subjects."

Extending these findings, Samuel Gaertner, John Dovidio, and their collaborators (1993, 2000) report that working cooperatively has especially favourable effects under conditions that lead people to define a new, inclusive group that dissolves their former subgroups. Old feelings of bias against another group diminish when members of the two groups sit alternately around a table (rather than on opposite sides), give their new group a single name, and then work together under conditions that foster a good mood. "Us" and "them" become "we."

Cooperative Learning

So far we have noted the apparently meagre social benefits of typical school desegregation (especially if unaccompanied by friendship formation and equal-status relationships) and the apparently dramatic social benefits of successful, cooperative contacts between members of rival groups. Could putting these two findings together suggest a constructive alternative to traditional desegregation practices? Several independent research teams speculated yes. Each wondered whether, without compromising academic achievement, we could promote interracial friendships by replacing competitive learning situations with cooperative ones. Given the diversity of their methods—all involving students on integrated study teams, sometimes in competition with other teams—the results are striking and very heartening.

One research team, led by Elliot Aronson (1978, 2000, 2002; Aronson & Gonzalez, 1988), elicited similar group cooperation with a "jigsaw" technique. In experiments in Texas and California elementary schools, the researchers assigned children to racially and academically diverse, six-member groups. The subject was then divided into six parts, with each student becoming the expert on his or her part. In a unit on Chile, one student might be the expert on Chile's history, another on its geography, another on its culture. First, the various "historians," "geographers," and so forth got together to master their material. Then they returned to the home groups to teach it to their classmates. Each group member held, so to speak, a piece of the jigsaw. The self-confident students therefore had to listen to and learn from the reticent students, who in turn soon realized they had something important to offer their peers.

OLC
Video 21.1

With cooperative learning, students learn not only the material but other lessons as well. Cross-racial friendships also begin to blossom. The exam scores of minority

Two young hockey fans send a message to NHL Commissioner Gary Bettman as Canada plays Slovakia in the World Cup in September 2004. Weeks later a labour dispute shut the NHL down for an entire season.

Bargaining Seeking an agreement through direct negotiation between parties to a conflict.

Mediation An attempt by a neutral third party to resolve a conflict by facilitating communication and offering suggestions.

Arbitration Resolution of a conflict by a neutral third party who studies both sides and imposes a settlement.

students improve (perhaps because academic achievement is now peer-supported). After the experiments are over, many teachers continue using cooperative learning (D. W. Johnson & others, 1981; Slavin, 1990). "It is clear," wrote race-relations expert John McConahay (1981), that cooperative learning "is the most effective practice for improving race relations in desegregated schools that we know of to date."

So, cooperative, equal-status contacts exert a positive influence on boy campers, industrial executives, and schoolchildren. Does the principle extend to all levels of human relations? Are families unified by pulling together to farm the land, restore an old house, or sail a sloop? Are communal identities forged by barn raisings, group singing, or cheering on the football team? Is international understanding bred by international collaboration in science and space, by joint efforts to feed the world and conserve resources, by friendly personal contacts between people of different nations? Indications are that the answer to all these questions is yes (Brewer & Miller, 1988; Desforges & others, 1991, 1997; Deutsch, 1985, 1994). Thus, an important challenge facing our divided world is to identify and agree on our superordinate goals and to structure cooperative efforts to achieve them.

COMMUNICATION

Conflicting parties have other ways to resolve their differences. When husband and wife, or labour and management, or nation X and nation Y disagree, they can **bargain** with one another directly. They can ask a third party to **mediate** by making suggestions and facilitating their negotiations. Or they can **arbitrate** by submitting their disagreement to someone who will study the issues and impose a settlement.

Bargaining

If you or I want to buy or sell a new car, are we better off adopting a tough bargaining stance—opening with an extreme offer so that splitting the difference will yield a favourable result? Or are we better off beginning with a sincere "good-faith" offer?

Experiments suggest no simple answer. On the one hand, those who demand more will often get more. Tough bargaining can lower the other party's expectations, making the other side willing to settle for less (Yukl, 1974). But toughness can sometimes backfire. Many a conflict is not over a pie of fixed size but over a pie that shrinks if the conflict continues. When a strike is prolonged, both labour and management lose. Both the National Hockey League and Major League Baseball learned this the hard way while enduring labour disputes. In the 2004–2005 lockout, the NHL and the players lost hundreds of millions of dollars of income, as well as public support, when the season was cancelled. When a similar strike crippled baseball in 1994, it took almost 10 years for the league to recover. Being tough can also diminish the chances of actually reaching an agreement. If the other party responds with an equally extreme stance, both may be locked into positions from which neither can back down without losing face.

Mediation

A third-party mediator may offer suggestions that enable conflicting parties to make concessions and still save face (Pruitt, 1998). If my concession can be attributed to a mediator, who is gaining an equal concession from my antagonist, then neither of us will be viewed as caving in to the other's demands.

The Story Behind the Research

Although most of the research on conflict resolution is conducted with adults, it all started with children and Muzafer Sherif's Robber's Cave experiment. Dr. Hildy Ross and her colleagues and students in the Family Studies Lab at the University of Waterloo are also interested in how children settle disputes. A great deal of their research over the years has involved observing children interacting. Dr. Ross and her colleagues started to notice patterns in children's behaviours, specifically in how they dealt with disputes over property (for example, toys; Hay & Ross, 1982). This led Dr. Ross and her colleagues to conduct research specifically examining how children behave when they have to resolve disputes among themselves.

Dr. Ross and her colleagues (Ross & others, 2004) have found that, similar to what we see in adults, children as young as four-and-a-half exhibit self-serving biases when they describe disputes they've had with their siblings. Specifically, the children attribute positive behaviours to themselves more frequently than to their brothers or sisters. Younger children outright denied their negative behaviours, whereas older children would admit to them but would immediately justify their harmful actions. You can probably remember yourself doing these sorts of things in conflicts with your siblings.

Dr. Avigail Ram completed her Ph.D. research in the Family Studies Lab, and found that a number of factors influenced siblings' conflict resolution styles (Ram, 2004). She brought siblings together in the lab and asked children to negotiate the division of some toys. Interestingly, she found that as children aged they were more likely to be considerate of their siblings' wants and desires. She also found that younger children could become more "other-oriented" if both siblings were explicitly asked to talk about why they wanted their favourites among the toys before they began negotiations. Thus, her research suggests that as we age our conflict-resolution skills may develop naturally, to some extent. But even when we are young we can benefit from mediation training.

Dr. Ross has also explored how parents (that is, an external mediator) can influence the outcomes of sibling disputes (Siddiqui & others, 2004). In naturalistic observations, she found that although parents generally support the idea of children working out their problems on their own, when they intervene in children's disputes they rarely encourage independent conflict resolution by their children; in only 2 percent of cases did parents suggest that their children could find a solution to their own disputes. Therefore, these researchers decided to explore whether parents could facilitate children's conflict management by introducing formal mediation procedures for parents to use in their interventions. In their study they trained mothers to act as mediators in children's disputes. They found that children responded very positively to the mediation, and felt empowered to solve their own conflicts. Younger siblings were particularly empowered. When their mothers mediated the conflicts children were more likely to suggest resolutions and to have those resolutions accepted by their siblings. When mothers intervened as they normally would, only the older siblings and the mothers suggested resolutions that were adopted to end disputes. Both mothers and children preferred mediation strategies as a way to solve their disputes. Thus, it is clear that children's disputes can be resolved much like adult disputes, and there is much to be learned in terms of finding appropriate ways of resolving conflicts. I

Turning Win–Lose into Win–Win

Mediators also help resolve conflicts by facilitating constructive communication. Their first task is to help the parties rethink the conflict and gain information about others' interests (Thompson, 1998). Typically, people on both sides have a competitive "win–lose" orientation: They are successful if their opponent is unhappy with the result, and unsuccessful if their opponent is pleased (Thompson & others, 1995). The mediator aims to replace this win–lose orientation with a cooperative "win–win" orientation, by prodding both sides to set aside their conflicting demands and instead to think about each other's underlying needs, interests, and goals. In experiments, Leigh Thompson (1990a,b) found that, with experience, negotiators become better able to make mutually beneficial trade-offs and thus to achieve win–win resolutions.

A classic story of such a resolution concerns the two sisters who quarrelled over an orange (Follett, 1940). Finally they compromised and split the orange in half, whereupon one sister squeezed her half for juice while the other used the peel to make a cake. In experiments at the State University of New York at Buffalo, Dean Pruitt and his associates induced bargainers to search for **integrative agreements**. If the sisters had agreed to split the orange, giving one sister all the juice and the other all the peel, they would have hit on such an agreement, one that integrates both parties' interests (Kimmel & others, 1980; Pruitt & Lewis, 1975, 1977). Compared to compromises, in which each party sacrifices something important, integrative agreements are more enduring. Because they are mutually rewarding, they also lead to better ongoing relationships (Pruitt, 1986).

Integrative agreements
Win–win agreements that reconcile both parties' interests to their mutual benefit.

Unravelling Misperceptions with Controlled Communications

Communication often helps reduce self-fulfilling misperceptions. Perhaps you can recall experiences similar to that of this college student:

> Often, after a prolonged period of little communication, I perceive Martha's silence as a sign of her dislike for me. She, in turn, thinks that my quietness is a result of my being mad at her. My silence induces her silence, which makes me even more silent . . . until this snowballing effect is broken by some occurrence that makes it necessary for us to interact. And the communication then unravels all the misinterpretations we had made about one another.

The outcome of such conflicts often depends on *how* people communicate their feelings to one another. Roger Knudson and his colleagues (1980) invited married couples to come to the University of Illinois psychology laboratory and relive, through role-playing, one of their past conflicts. Before, during, and after their conversation (which often generated as much emotion as the actual previous conflict), the couples were observed closely and questioned. Couples who evaded the issue—by failing to make their positions clear or failing to acknowledge their spouse's position—left with the illusion that they were more in harmony and agreement than they really were. Often, they came to believe they now agreed more when actually they agreed less. In contrast, those who engaged the issue—by making their positions clear and by taking one another's views into account—achieved more actual agreement and gained more accurate information about one another's perceptions. That helps explain why couples who communicate their concerns directly and openly are usually happily married (Grush & Glidden, 1987).

Conflict researchers report that a key factor is *trust* (Ross & Ward, 1995). If you believe the other person is well-intentioned, you are then more likely to divulge your needs and concerns. Lacking such trust, you may fear that being open will give the other party information that might be used against you.

When the two parties mistrust each other and communicate unproductively, a third-party mediator—a marriage counsellor, a labour mediator, a diplomat—sometimes helps. Often the mediator is someone trusted by both sides. The ongoing Palestinian–Israeli conflict has been an excellent example of what can happen when two sides are completely entrenched. For a number of years an international cooperative of countries has been attempting to act as a mediator in the dispute. To date, while some advances have been made, a lasting peace has not been achieved. Indeed, the agreements that have been brokered are largely due to the intervention of third parties.

After coaxing the conflicting parties to rethink their perceived win–lose conflict, the mediator often has each party identify and rank its goals. When goals are compatible, the ranking procedure makes it easier for each to concede on less important goals so that both achieve their chief goals (Erickson & others, 1974; Schulz & Pruitt, 1978). South Africa achieved internal peace when White and Black South Africans granted each other's top priorities—replacing apartheid with majority rule and safeguarding the security, welfare, and rights of Whites (Kelman, 1998).

Once labour and management both believe that management's goal of higher productivity and profit is compatible with labour's goal of better wages and working conditions, they can begin to work for an integrative win–win solution.

When the parties then convene to communicate directly, they are usually *not* set loose in the hope that, eyeball to eyeball, the conflict will resolve itself. In the midst of a threatening, stressful conflict, emotions often disrupt the ability to understand the other party's point of view. Communication may become most difficult just when it is most needed (Tetlock, 1985). The mediator will therefore often structure the encounter to help each party understand and feel understood by the other. The mediator may ask the conflicting parties to restrict their arguments to statements of fact, including statements of how they feel and how they respond when the other acts in a given way: "I enjoy having music on. When you play it loud, I find it hard to concentrate. That makes me crabby." Also, the mediator may ask people to reverse roles and argue the other's position or to imagine and explain what the other person is experiencing. Experiments show that inducing empathy decreases stereotyping and increases cooperation (Batson & Moran, 1999; Galinsky & Moskowitz, 2000). Or the mediator may have them restate one another's positions before replying with their own: "My turning up the stereo bugs you."

Neutral third parties may also suggest mutually agreeable proposals that would be dismissed—"reactively devalued"—if offered by either side. Constance Stillinger and her colleagues (1991) found that a nuclear disarmament proposal that Americans dismissed when attributed to the former Soviet Union seemed more acceptable when attributed to a neutral third party. Likewise, people will often reactively devalue a concession offered by an adversary ("they must not value it"); the same concession may seem more than a token gesture when suggested by a third party.

These peacemaking principles, based partly on laboratory experiments, partly on practical experience, have helped mediate both international and industrial conflicts (Blake & Mouton, 1962, 1979; Fisher, 1994; Wehr, 1979). One small team of Arab and Jewish Americans, led by social psychologist Herbert Kelman (1997), has conducted workshops bringing together influential Arabs and Israelis, and Pakistanis and Indians. Another social psychologist team, led by Ervin Staub and Laurie Ann Pearlman (2004), worked in Rwanda between 1999 and 2003 by training facilitators and journalists to understand and write about Rwanda's traumas in ways that promote healing and reconciliation. Using methods such as those we've considered, we can counter misperceptions and have participants seek creative solutions for their common good. Isolated, the participants are free to speak directly to their adversaries without fear that their constituents are second-guessing what they are saying. The result? Those from both sides typically come to understand the other's perspective and how the other side responds to their own group's actions.

Arbitration

Some conflicts are so intractable, the underlying interests so divergent, that a mutually satisfactory resolution is unattainable. In Bosnia and Kosovo Serbs and Muslims could not both have jurisdiction over the same homelands. In a divorce dispute over custody of a child, both parents cannot enjoy full custody. In these and many other cases (disputes over tenants' repair bills, athletes' wages, and national territories), a third-party mediator may—or may not—help resolve the conflict.

If not, the parties may turn to *arbitration* by having the mediator or another third party *impose* a settlement. Disputants usually prefer to settle their differences without arbitration so they retain control over the outcome. Neil McGillicuddy and others (1987) observed this preference in an experiment involving disputants coming to a dispute settlement centre. When people knew they would face an arbitrated settlement if mediation failed, they tried harder to resolve the problem, exhibited less hostility, and thus were more likely to reach agreement.

In cases where differences seem large and irreconcilable, the prospect of arbitration may have an opposite effect (Pruitt, 1986). The disputants may freeze their positions, hoping to gain an advantage when the arbitrator chooses a compromise. To combat this tendency, some disputes, such as those involving salaries of individual baseball players, are settled with "final-offer arbitration" in which the third party chooses one of the two final offers. Final-offer arbitration motivates each party to make a reasonable proposal.

Typically, however, the final offer is not as reasonable as it would be if each party, free of self-serving bias, saw its own proposal through others' eyes. Negotiation researchers report that most disputants are made stubborn by "optimistic overconfidence" (Kahneman & Tversky, 1995). Successful mediation is hindered when, as often happens, both parties believe they have a two-thirds chance of receiving the settlement their side has requested in a final-offer arbitration (Bazerman, 1986, 1990).

CONCILIATION

Sometimes tension and suspicion run so high that communication, much less resolution, becomes all but impossible. Each party may threaten, coerce, or retaliate against the other. Unfortunately, such acts tend to be reciprocated, escalating the conflict. So, would a strategy of appeasing the other party by being unconditionally cooperative produce a satisfying result? Often not. In laboratory games, those who are 100-percent cooperative often get exploited. Politically, a one-sided pacifism is out of the question anyway.

GRIT

Social psychologist Charles Osgood (1962, 1980) advocated a third alternative, one that is conciliatory rather than retaliatory, yet strong enough to discourage exploitation. Osgood called it "*g*raduated and *r*eciprocated *i*nitiatives in *t*ension reduction." He nicknamed it **GRIT**, a label that suggests the determination it requires. GRIT aims to reverse the "conflict spiral" by triggering reciprocal de-escalation. GRIT requires one side to initiate a few small de-escalatory actions, after *announcing a conciliatory intent*. The initiator states its desire to reduce tension, declares each conciliatory act prior to making it, and invites the adversary to reciprocate. Such announcements create a framework that helps the adversary correctly interpret what otherwise might be seen as weak or tricky actions. They also bring public pressure on the adversary to follow the reciprocity norm.

> **GRIT** Acronym for "*g*raduated and *r*eciprocated *i*nitiatives in *t*ension reduction"—a strategy designed to de-escalate international tensions.

Next, the initiator establishes credibility and genuineness by carrying out, exactly as announced, several verifiable *conciliatory acts*. This intensifies the pressure to reciprocate. Making conciliatory acts diverse—perhaps offering medical information, closing a military base, and lifting a trade ban—keeps the initiator from making a significant sacrifice in any one area and leaves the adversary freer to choose its own means of reciprocation. If the adversary reciprocates voluntarily, its own conciliatory behaviour may soften its attitudes.

GRIT *is* conciliatory. But it is not "surrender on the instalment plan." The remaining aspects of the plan protect each side's self-interest by *maintaining retaliatory capability*. The initial conciliatory steps entail some small risk but do not jeopardize either one's security; rather, they are calculated to begin edging both sides down the tension ladder. Morton Deutsch (1993) captures the spirit of GRIT in advising negotiators to be "'firm, fair, and friendly': *firm* in resisting intimidation, exploitation, and dirty tricks; *fair* in holding to one's moral principles and not reciprocating the other's immoral behavior despite his or her provocations; and *friendly* in the sense that one is willing to initiate and reciprocate cooperation."

Does GRIT really work? In laboratory dilemma games, a successful strategy has proved to be simple "tit-for-tat," which begins with a cooperative opening play and thereafter matches the other party's last response (Axelrod & Dion, 1988; Komorita & others, 1992; Van Lange & Visser, 1999). Cooperate-unless-you've-just-been-exploited is another successful strategy that tries to cooperate and is forgiving, yet does not tolerate exploitation (Nowak & Sigmund, 1993). Repeated conciliatory acts *do* breed greater trust (although self-serving biases often make one's own acts seem more conciliatory and less hostile than those of the adversary). Maintaining an equality of power *does* protect against exploitation.

GRIT-like strategies have occasionally been tried outside the laboratory, with promising results. For example, U.S. President George H. Bush in 1991 ordered the elimination of all land-based U.S. tactical nuclear warheads and took strategic bombers off high alert, putting their bombs in storage. Although leaving intact his least vulnerable and most extensive nuclear arsenal—submarine-based missiles—he invited the USSR's Mikhail Gorbachev to reciprocate. Eight days later Gorbachev did, taking his bombers off alert, storing their bombs, and announcing the removal of nuclear weapons from short-range rockets, ships, and submarines.

Might conciliatory efforts also help reduce tension between individuals? There is every reason to expect so. When a relationship is strained and communication non-existent, it sometimes takes only a conciliatory gesture—a soft answer, a warm smile, a gentle touch—for both parties to begin easing down the tension ladder, to a rung where contact, cooperation, and communication again become possible.

CONCEPTS TO REMEMBER

Equal-status contact   p. 233
Superordinate goal   p. 234
Bargaining   p. 236
Mediation   p. 236

Arbitration   p. 236
Integrative agreements   p. 238
GRIT   p. 241

Please visit the *Exploring Social Psychology* Online Learning Centre at www.mcgrawhill.ca/college/myers to participate in module activities, view module videos, access research and study tools, and test your knowledge with interactive quizzes, exercises, and scenarios.

Helping

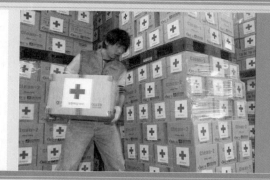

A South Korean Red Cross worker carries an aid supply kit for victims of a train explosion in North Korea on April 26, 2004. What are some of the factors that motivate people to act altruistically in times of crisis?

I magine yourself in the following situation. You are walking through town with a couple of your friends from university. You are having a good time, joking around and enjoying the weather. As you are crossing a bridge, you see a naked man (about your age) running toward you from the other side of the bridge. Cars slow down, people are staring, a few people are honking, but no one is stopping. Suddenly the man jumps up onto the railing of the bridge, which has a 15-metre drop into running water. What would you do? Would you say something to the man? Would you run up and try to stop him? Would you think it was all a joke? Would you encourage him to jump? In situations such as this, all of these things have happened. Sometimes people help; sometimes people encourage the person to jump. If you were in that situation, what would you do?

What do people do when faced with emergencies? It all depends. Would you risk your life to save someone else? In November of 1998, passengers on a Toronto subway platform saw a man behaving oddly with two small children. At first many were not sure what was going on, but it became clear that he was trying to push one of the kids onto the subway track. The bystanders acted quickly, jumping on the man and restraining him until police arrived. Had they not intervened, at least one, if not both, of the children would have been killed by a speeding subway train.

People can sometimes be incredibly generous. For example, after the South Asian tsunami killed more than 200,000 people in 2004, Canadians donated over $145 million to relief efforts (CBC News Online, 2005). However, people do not always help those in need.

THE CASE THAT STARTED IT ALL

On March 13, 1964, bar manager Kitty Genovese was set upon by a knife-wielding rapist as she returned to her Queens, New York, apartment house at 3:00 a.m. Her screams of terror and pleas for help—"Oh my God, he stabbed me! Please help me! Please help me!"—aroused 38 of her neighbours. Many came to their windows and watched while, for 35 minutes, she struggled to escape her attacker. Not until her attacker departed did anyone so much as call the police. Soon after, she died.

Eleanor Bradley tripped and broke her leg while shopping. Dazed and in pain, she pleaded for help. For 40 minutes, the stream of shoppers simply parted and flowed around her. Finally, a cab driver helped her to a doctor (Darley & Latané, 1968). What is shocking is not that in these cases some people failed to help, but that in each of these groups almost 100 percent of those involved failed to respond. Why? In the same or similar situations, would you react as they did? Or would you be a hero?

Acts of comforting, caring, and helping abound: Without asking anything in return, people offer directions, donate money, give blood, volunteer time. Why, and when, will people perform altruistic acts? And what can be done to lessen indifference and increase altruism? **Altruism** is selfishness in reverse. An altruistic person is concerned and helpful even when no benefits are offered or expected in return.

WHY DO PEOPLE HELP?

What motivates altruism? One idea, called **social-exchange theory**, is that we help after doing a cost–benefit analysis. As part of an exchange of benefits, helpers aim to maximize their rewards and minimize their costs. When donating blood, we weigh the costs (the inconvenience and discomfort) against the benefits (the social approval and noble feeling). If the anticipated rewards exceed the costs, we help.

You might object: Social-exchange theory takes the selflessness out of altruism. It seems to imply that a helpful act is never genuinely altruistic; we merely call it "altruistic" when the rewards are inconspicuous. If we know people are tutoring only to alleviate guilt or gain social approval, we hardly credit them for a good deed. We laud people for their altruism only when we can't otherwise explain it.

From babyhood onward, however, people sometimes exhibit a natural **empathy**, by feeling distress when seeing others in distress and relief when their suffering ends. Loving parents (unlike child abusers and other perpetrators of cruelty) suffer when their children suffer and rejoice over their children's joys (Miller & Eisenberg, 1988). Although some helpful acts are indeed done to gain rewards or relieve guilt, experiments suggest that other helpful acts aim simply to increase another's welfare, producing satisfaction for oneself merely as a byproduct (Batson, 1991). In these experiments, empathy often produces helping only when helpgivers believe the other will actually receive the needed help and regardless of whether the recipient knows who helped.

Social norms also motivate helping. They prescribe how we *ought* to behave. We learn the **reciprocity norm**—that we should return help to those who have helped

---

OLC
Activity 22.1

Altruism A motive to increase another's welfare without conscious regard for one's self-interests.

Social-exchange theory The theory that human interactions are transactions that aim to maximize one's rewards and minimize one's costs.

Empathy The vicarious experience of another's feeling; putting oneself in another's shoes.

Reciprocity norm An expectation that people will help, not hurt, those who have helped them.

us. Thus, we expect that those who receive favours (gifts, invitations, help) should later return them. The reciprocity norm is qualified by our awareness that some people are incapable of reciprocal giving and receiving. Thus, we also feel a **social-responsibility norm**—that we should help those who really need it, without regard to future exchanges. When we pick up the dropped books for the person on crutches, we expect nothing in return. But what happens when the potential costs of the situation conflict with these perceived norms? Sometimes the actual cost of a seemingly simple act (picking up a dropped object) is not what we expected. Sometimes we may be too embarrassed to help. In a clever study, Stuart McKelvie and James MacDonald (MacDonald & McKelvie, 1992) from Bishop's University explored helping in a real-world situation. In a shopping centre, they dropped either a mitten or a box of condoms in full view of people walking through the mall. The mitten was returned to the dropper 43 percent of the time, but the condoms were returned only 17 percent of the time. Thus, helping was avoided when the situation could cause embarrassment. Nonetheless, social-exchange theory and social norms can explain some helping.

In addition, these suggested reasons for helping make biological sense. The empathy that parents feel for their children and other relatives promotes the survival of their shared genes. Likewise, say evolutionary psychologists, reciprocal altruism in small groups boosts everyone's survival.

Social-responsibility norm
An expectation that people will help those dependent upon them.

WHEN DO PEOPLE HELP?

Social psychologists were curious and concerned about bystanders' lack of involvement during such events as the Kitty Genovese rape-murder. So they undertook experiments to identify when people will help in an emergency. Then they broadened the question to, Who is likely to help in nonemergencies—by such deeds as giving money, donating blood, or contributing time? Among their answers is that helping often increases among people who are:

- feeling guilty, thus providing a way to relieve the guilt or restore self-image;
- in a good mood; or
- deeply religious (evidenced by higher rates of charitable giving and volunteerism).

Social psychologists also study the *circumstances* that enhance helpfulness. The odds of our helping someone increase in these circumstances:

- We have just observed a helpful model.
- We are not hurried.
- The victim appears to need and deserve help.
- The victim is similar to ourselves.
- We are in a small town or rural area.
- There are few other bystanders.

The Story Behind the Research

Dr. John Holmes at the University of Waterloo is best known for his extensive research on relationships (you will learn of his work in the section on relationship maintenance in Module 24). However, in some of his research Dr. Holmes and his colleagues (Holmes & others, 2002) wanted to better understand the role of social exchange in altruism and charitable behaviour. Dr. Holmes and his colleagues proposed that people may *want* to be compassionate, but find it easier to do so when they can convince themselves that their charitable act actually conforms to their own self-interest. The researchers also believed it was important to test these hypotheses in real-world settings.

In two field studies they tested the hypothesis that people's willingness to help a charitable organization is greater when the act is presented as an economic transaction than when it is presented as an act of charity. In other words, they expected that people would be more willing to help when they thought they were getting something out of it. In

their first study, college students were approached and asked to donate money to a charity. Half of the participants were offered a product that was somewhat attractive, but not needed by most people (a decorative candle) in return for their donation, and half were not. As expected, participants donated more money to the charity when they were offered a product. In the second study, Holmes and his colleagues wanted to get a better understanding of how other contextual issues might influence participants' willingness to donate to a charity. They manipulated how much of a bargain the candles were. Consistent with their theory, participants were more likely to purchase the candles when they were reported to be a "bargain price" than if they were described as a "fair price." However, this occurred only when participants were told that the victims' need was high. Thus, one way to increase charitable donations is to create a situation where potential contributors feel they are getting a good deal out of the exchange. |

NUMBER OF BYSTANDERS

Bystander passivity during emergencies has prompted social commentators to lament people's "alienation," "apathy," "indifference," and "unconscious sadistic impulses." By attributing the nonintervention to the bystanders' dispositions, we can reassure ourselves that, as caring people, we would have helped. But were the bystanders such inhuman characters?

Social psychologists Bibb Latané and John Darley (1970) were unconvinced. They staged ingenious emergencies and found that a single situational factor—the presence of other bystanders—greatly decreased intervention. By 1980, four dozen experiments had compared help given by bystanders who perceived themselves to be either alone or with others. In about 90 percent of these comparisons, involving nearly 6,000 people, lone bystanders were more likely to help (Latané & Nida, 1981).

The victim was actually less likely to get help when many people were around. When Latané, James Dabbs (1975), and 145 collaborators "accidentally" dropped coins or pencils during 1,497 elevator rides, they were helped 40 percent of the time when one other person was on the elevator and less than 20 percent of the time when there were six passengers. Why? Latané and Darley surmised that as the number of bystanders increases, any given bystander is less likely to *notice* the incident, less likely to *interpret* the incident as a problem or emergency, and less likely to *assume responsibility* for taking action (Figure 22-1).

Noticing

In another study, Latané and Darley (1968) had Columbia University men fill out a questionnaire in a room, either by themselves or with two strangers. While they were working (and being observed through a one-way mirror), there was a staged emergency: Smoke poured into the room through a wall vent. Solitary students, who often glanced idly about the room while working, noticed the smoke almost immediately—usually in less than five seconds. Those in groups kept their eyes on their work. It typically took them about 20 seconds to notice the smoke.

Interpreting

Imagine you were one of the bystanders on the Toronto subway platform that day. You are staring straight ahead, just like the other 200 waiting people, thinking about your day. You hear a child crying and an angry man yelling and struggling with his son. What would you do? No one else seems to be noticing or caring. Would you?

Once we notice an ambiguous event, we must interpret it. Put yourself in the room filling with smoke. Though worried, you don't want to embarrass yourself by getting flustered. You glance at the others. They look calm, indifferent. Assuming everything must be okay, you shrug it off and go back to work. Then one of the others notices the smoke and, noting your apparent unconcern, reacts similarly. This is yet another example of informational influence. Each person uses others' behaviour as clues to reality.

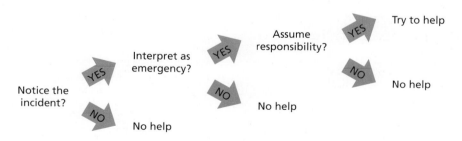

FIGURE 22-1

Latané and Darley's decision tree. Only one path up the tree leads to helping. At each fork of the path, the presence of other bystanders may divert a person down a branch toward not helping.

Adapted from Darley & Latané, 1968.

So it happened in Latané and Darley's experiment. When those working alone noticed the smoke, they usually hesitated a moment, then got up, walked over to the vent, felt, sniffed and waved at the smoke, hesitated again, and then went to report it. In dramatic contrast, those in groups of three did not move. Among the 24 men in eight groups, only one person reported the smoke within the first four minutes (Figure 22-2). By the end of the six-minute experiment, the smoke was so thick it was obscuring the men's vision and they were rubbing their eyes and coughing. Still, in only three of the eight groups did even a single person leave to report the problem.

Equally interesting, the group's passivity affected its members' interpretations. What caused the smoke? "A leak in the air conditioning." "Chemistry labs in the building." "Steam pipes." "Truth gas." Not one said, "Fire." The group members, by serving as nonresponsive models, influenced each other's interpretation of the situation.

This experimental dilemma parallels dilemmas we all face. Are the shrieks outside merely playful antics or the desperate screams of someone being assaulted? Is the boys' scuffling a friendly tussle or a vicious fight? Is the person slumped in the doorway sleeping, high on drugs, or seriously ill, perhaps in a diabetic coma? That surely was the question confronting those who passed by Sidney Brookins (AP, 1993). Brookins, who had suffered a concussion when beaten, died after lying near the door to a Minneapolis apartment house for two days. That may also have been the question for those who in 2003 watched Brandon Vedas overdose and die online. As his life ebbed, his audience, which was left to wonder whether he was putting on an act, failed to decipher available clues to his whereabouts and to contact police (Nichols, 2003).

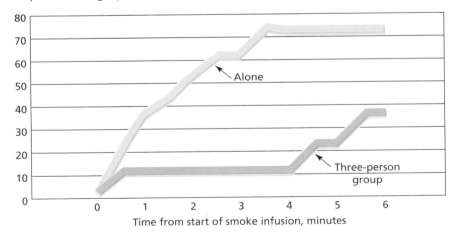

FIGURE 22-2

The smoke-filled-room experiment. Smoke pouring into the testing room was much more likely to be reported by individuals working alone than by three-person groups.

Data from Latané & Darley, 1968.

Assuming Responsibility

Misinterpretation is not the only cause of **bystander effect**—the inaction of strangers faced with ambiguous emergencies. And what about those times when an emergency is obvious? Those who saw and heard Kitty Genovese's pleas for help correctly interpreted what was happening. But the lights and silhouetted figures in neighbouring windows told them that others were also watching. This diffused the responsibility for action.

Few of us have observed a murder. But all of us have at times been slower to react to a need when others were present. Passing a stranded motorist on a highway, we are less likely to offer help than on a country road. To explore bystander inaction in clear emergencies, Darley and Latané (1968) simulated the Genovese drama. They placed people in separate rooms from which the participants would hear a victim crying for help. To create this situation, Darley and Latané asked some New York University students to discuss their problems with university life over a laboratory intercom. The researchers told the students that to guarantee their anonymity, no one would be visible, nor would the experimenter eavesdrop. During the ensuing discussion, when the experimenter turned his microphone on, the participants heard one person lapse into an epileptic seizure. With increasing intensity and speech difficulty, he pleaded for someone to help.

Of those led to believe there were no other listeners, 85 percent left their room to seek help. Of those who believed four others also overheard the victim, only 31 percent went for help. Were those who didn't respond apathetic and indifferent? When the experimenter came in to end the experiment, she did not find this response. Most immediately expressed concern. Many had trembling hands and sweating palms. They believed an emergency had occurred but were undecided whether to act.

After the smoke-filled room and the seizure experiments, Latané and Darley asked the participants whether the presence of others had influenced them. We know the others had a dramatic effect. Yet the participants almost invariably denied the influence. They typically replied, "I was aware of the others, but I would have reacted just the same if they weren't there." This response reinforces a familiar point: *We often do not know why we do what we do.* That is why experiments are revealing. A survey of uninvolved bystanders following a real emergency would have left the bystander effect hidden.

These experiments raise again the issue of research ethics. Were the researchers in the seizure experiment ethical when they forced people to decide whether to abort the discussion to report the problem? Would you object to being in such a study? Note that it would have been impossible to get your "informed consent" without destroying the cover for the experiment.

In defence of the researchers, they were always careful to debrief the laboratory participants. After explaining the seizure experiment, probably the most stressful, the experimenter gave the participants a questionnaire. One hundred percent said the deception was justified and that they would be willing to take part in similar

Bystander effect The finding that a person is less likely to provide help when there are other bystanders.

experiments in the future. None reported feeling angry at the experimenter. Other researchers confirm that the overwhelming majority of participants in such experiments say that their participation was both instructive and ethically justified (Schwartz & Gottlieb, 1981). In field experiments, an accomplice assisted the victim if no one else did, thus reassuring bystanders that the problem was being dealt with.

Remember that the social psychologist has a twofold ethical obligation: to protect the participants and to enhance human welfare by discovering influences upon human behaviour. Such discoveries can alert us to unwanted influences and show us how we might exert positive influences. The ethical principle seems to be: After protecting participants' welfare, social psychologists fulfill their responsibility to society by doing such research.

Will learning about the factors that inhibit altruism reduce their influence? Sometimes, such "enlightenment" is not our problem but one of our goals. We have heard of a number of cases where people ignored situations or even refused to help when people were in need. But could something as simple as a psychology class change people's behaviours in such situations? Recall the vignette at the beginning of the chapter of the man standing on the bridge railing. That very scenario unfolded in Ithaca, New York, in 1993. Pablo Salanova, Rob Lee, and Gretchen Goldfarb were walking through town when they saw a naked man leap onto the railing of a bridge. Initially they thought it was all a joke, but Gretchen, whose introductory psychology class had recently covered helping and prosocial behaviour, realized that it might be an emergency. At Gretchen's prompting, her two friends grabbed the man and kept him from jumping (likely to his death) from the bridge.

Experiments with University of Montana students by Arthur Beaman and his colleagues (1978) revealed that once people understand why the presence of bystanders inhibits helping, they become more likely to help in group situations. The researchers used a lecture to inform some students how bystander inaction can affect the interpretation of an emergency and feelings of responsibility. Other students heard either a different lecture or no lecture at all. Two weeks later, as part of a different experiment in a different location, the participants found themselves walking (with an unresponsive confederate) past someone slumped over or past a person sprawled beneath a bicycle. Of those who had not heard the helping lecture, a fourth paused to offer help; twice as many of those "enlightened" did so.

Having read this module, you, too, perhaps have changed. As you come to understand what influences people's responses, will your attitudes and your behaviour be the same? Coincidentally, a similar thing has happened to David Myers. A former student, now living in Washington, D.C., stopped by his office one day. She mentioned that she recently found herself part of a stream of pedestrians striding past a man lying unconscious on the sidewalk. "It took my mind back to our social psych class and the accounts of why people fail to help in such situations. Then I thought, 'Well, if I just walk by, too, who's going to help him?'" So she made a call to an emergency help number and waited with the victim—and other bystanders who then joined her—until help arrived.

So, how will learning about social influences upon helping affect you? Will the knowledge you've gained affect your actions? We hope so.

CONCEPTS TO REMEMBER

Altruism   p. 244
Social-exchange theory   p. 244
Empathy   p. 244

Reciprocity norm   p. 244
Social-responsibility norm   p. 245
Bystander effect   p. 249

Please visit the *Exploring Social Psychology* Online Learning Centre at **www.mcgrawhill.ca/college/myers** to participate in module activities, view module videos, access research and study tools, and test your knowledge with interactive quizzes, exercises, and scenarios.

Interpersonal Attraction

There are many theories to explain why one person is attracted to another. What factors—proximity? similarity? complementarity? belonging?—have contributed to your closest relationships?

Think back to your first romantic relationship. How did you meet him or her? What was it like? Was that person the only one you could think about? Did you agonize over what you would say when you saw him or her? Did you lose sleep? Now compare this to your relationship with your best friend. How did you meet him or her? How did you become friends? Is this someone who lived near you? Someone you met at school, at work, or in residence?

What predisposes one person to like, or to love, another? So much has been written about liking and loving that almost every conceivable explanation—and its opposite—has already been proposed. For most people—for you—what factors nurture liking and loving? Does absence make the heart grow fonder? Or is someone who is out of sight also out of mind? Is it likes that attract? Or opposites?

Consider a simple but powerful *reward theory of attraction:* We like those whose behaviour is rewarding to us, or whom we associate with rewarding events. Friends reward each other. Without keeping score, they do favours for one another. Likewise, we develop a liking for those whom we associate with pleasant happenings and surroundings. Thus, surmised researchers Elaine Hatfield and William Walster (1978), "romantic dinners, trips to the theatre, evenings at home together, and vacations never stop being important. . . . If your relationship is to survive, it's important that you *both* continue to associate your relationship with good things."

But as with most sweeping generalizations, the reward theory of attraction leaves many questions unanswered. What, precisely, *is* rewarding? Is it usually more rewarding to be with someone who differs from us or someone who is similar to us? To be lavishly flattered or constructively criticized? What factors have fostered *your* close relationships? Do we have an innate need to belong?

PROXIMITY

One of the most powerful predictors of whether any two people are friends is sheer proximity. Proximity can also breed hostility; most assaults and murders involve people living close together. But far more often, proximity kindles liking. Though it may seem trivial to those pondering the mysterious origins of romantic love, sociologists have found that most people marry someone who lives in the same neighbourhood, or works at the same company or job, or sits in the same class (Bossard, 1932; Burr, 1973; Clarke, 1952; Katz & Hill, 1958). Look around. If you marry, it will likely be to someone who has lived or worked or studied within walking distance.

Proximity Geographical nearness. Proximity (more precisely, "functional distance") powerfully predicts liking.

Interaction

Actually, it is not geographical distance that is critical but "functional distance"—how often people's paths cross. This was nicely illustrated in research by Leon Festinger and his colleagues (1952) in a study of married couples living in student apartments at MIT. They examined the relationships among couples who lived in an apartment building. They found that people were most likely to be friends with next-door neighbours, and people who lived in apartments in high-traffic areas (centrally located apartments, or people whose apartment doors were near stairwells) were more likely to be listed by others as "friends." Thus, proximity is important. Consistent with this, we frequently become friends with those who use the same entrances, parking lots, and recreation areas as we do. Randomly assigned college roommates, who of course can hardly avoid frequent interaction, are far more likely to become good friends than enemies (Newcomb, 1961). Such interaction enables people to explore their similarities, to sense one another's liking, and to perceive themselves as a social unit (Arkin & Burger, 1980). So if you're new in town and want to make friends, try to get an apartment near the mailboxes, a desk near the coffee pot, a parking spot near the main buildings. Such is the architecture of friendship.

Why does proximity breed liking? One factor is availability; obviously there are fewer opportunities to get to know someone who attends a different school or lives in another town. But there is more to it than that. Most people like their roommates, or those one door away, better than those two doors away. Those just a few doors away, or even a floor below, hardly live at an inconvenient distance. Moreover, those close by are potential enemies as well as friends. So why does proximity encourage affection more often than animosity?

Anticipation of Interaction

Already we have noted one answer: Proximity enables people to discover commonalities and exchange rewards. What is more, merely *anticipating* interaction boosts liking. John Darley and Ellen Berscheid (1967) discovered this when they gave University of Minnesota women ambiguous information about two other women, one of whom they expected to talk with intimately. Asked how much they liked each one, the women preferred the person they expected to meet. Expecting to date someone similarly boosts liking (Berscheid & others, 1976). Even voters on the losing side of an election will find their opinions of the winning candidate—whom they are now stuck with—rising (Gilbert & others, 1998).

The phenomenon is adaptive. Anticipatory liking—expecting that someone will be pleasant and compatible—increases the chance of forming a rewarding relationship (Klein & Kunda, 1992; Knight & Vallacher, 1981; Miller & Marks, 1982). And how good that we are biased to like those we often see. Our lives are filled with relationships with people whom we may not have chosen but with whom we need to have continuing interactions—roommates, siblings, grandparents, teachers, classmates, co-workers. Liking such people is surely conducive to better relationships with them, which in turn makes for happier, more productive living.

Mere Exposure

Mere-exposure effect
The tendency for novel stimuli to be liked more or rated more positively after the rater has been repeatedly exposed to them.

Proximity leads to liking not only because it enables interaction and anticipatory liking, but also for another reason: More than 200 experiments reveal that, contrary to the old proverb, familiarity does not breed contempt. Rather, it breeds fondness (Bornstein, 1989, 1999). **Mere exposure** to all sorts of novel stimuli—nonsense syllables, Chinese characters, musical selections, faces—boosts people's ratings of them. Do the supposed Turkish words *nansoma, saricik,* and *afworbu* mean something better or something worse than the words *iktitaf, biwojni,* and *kadirga*? University of Michigan students tested by Robert Zajonc (1968, 1970) preferred whichever of these words they had seen most frequently. The more times they had seen a meaningless word or a Chinese ideograph, the more likely they were to say it meant something good (Figure 23-1). Or consider: What are your favourite letters of the alphabet? People of differing nationalities, languages, and ages prefer the letters appearing in their own names and those that frequently appear in their own languages (Hoorens & others, 1990, 1993; Kitayama & Karasawa, 1997; Nuttin, 1987). French students rate capital *W*, the least frequent letter in French, as their least favourite letter. Japanese students prefer not only letters from their names, but also numbers corresponding to their birthdates.

The mere-exposure effect violates the commonsense prediction of boredom—*decreased* interest in—repeatedly heard music or tasted foods (Kahneman & Snell, 1992). Unless the repetitions are incessant ("Even the best song becomes tiresome if heard too often," says a Korean proverb), liking usually increases. When completed in 1889, the Eiffel Tower in Paris was mocked as grotesque (Harrison, 1977). Today it is the beloved symbol of Paris. Such changes make one wonder about initial reactions to new things. Do visitors to the Louvre in Paris really adore the *Mona Lisa*, or are they simply delighted to find a familiar face? It might be both: To know her is to like her.

The mere-exposure effect. If he is like most of us, Canadian Prime Minister Stephen Harper might prefer his familiar mirror-image (left), which he sees each morning while brushing his teeth, to his actual image (right).

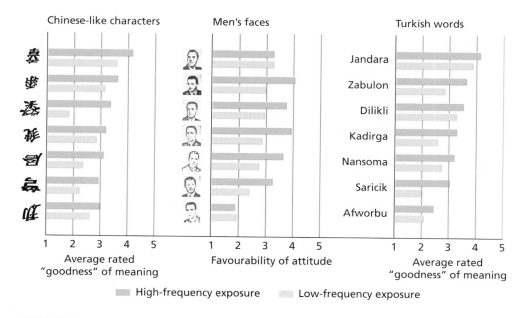

FIGURE 23–1

The mere-exposure effect. Students rated stimuli more positively after being shown them repeatedly.

Source: From Zajonc, 1968.

The mere-exposure effect has "enormous adaptive significance," notes Zajonc (1998). It is a "hard-wired" phenomenon that predisposes our attractions and attachments. It helped our ancestors categorize things and people as either familiar and safe, or unfamiliar and possibly dangerous. Of course, the phenomenon's darker side is our wariness of the unfamiliar—which may explain the primitive, automatic prejudice people often feel when confronting those who are different.

The mere-exposure effect colours our evaluations of others: We like familiar people (Swap, 1977). We even like ourselves better when we are the way we're used to seeing ourselves. In a delightful experiment, Theodore Mita, Marshall Dermer, and Jeffrey Knight (1977) photographed women and later showed each one her actual picture along with a mirror image of it. Asked which picture they liked better, most preferred the mirror image—the image *they* were used to seeing. (No wonder our photographs never look quite right.) When close friends of the subjects were shown the same two pictures, they preferred the true picture—the image *they* were used to seeing.

Advertisers and politicians exploit this phenomenon. When people have no strong feelings about a product or a candidate, repetition alone can increase sales or votes (McCullough & Ostrom, 1974; Winter, 1973). After endless repetition of a commercial, shoppers often have an unthinking, automatic, favourable response to the product. If candidates are relatively unknown, those with the most media exposure usually win (Patterson, 1980; Schaffner & others, 1981). Political strategists who understand the mere-exposure effect have replaced reasoned argument with brief ads that hammer home a candidate's name and sound-bite message.

PHYSICAL ATTRACTIVENESS

What do (or did) you look for in a potential date? Sincerity? Good looks? Character? Humour? Conversational ability? Sophisticated, intelligent people are unconcerned with such superficial qualities as good looks; they know "beauty is only skin deep" and "you can't judge a book by its cover." At least they know that's how they *ought* to feel. As Cicero counselled, "Resist appearance."

The belief that looks matter little may be another instance of how we deny real influences upon us, for there is now a file cabinet full of research studies showing that appearance *does* matter. The consistency and pervasiveness of this effect is disconcerting. Good looks are a great asset.

Attractiveness and Dating

Like it or not, a young woman's physical attractiveness is a moderately good predictor of how frequently she dates. A young man's attractiveness is slightly less a predictor of how frequently he dates (Berscheid & others, 1971; Krebs & Adinolfi, 1975; Reis & others, 1980, 1982; Walster & others, 1966). Does this imply, as many have surmised, that women are better at following Cicero's advice? Or does it merely reflect the fact that men more often do the inviting? If women were to indicate their preferences among various men, would looks be as important to them as to men?

Philosopher Bertrand Russell (1930, p. 139) thought not: "On the whole women tend to love men for their character while men tend to love women for their appearance."

To see whether men are indeed more influenced by looks, researchers have provided male and female students with various pieces of information about someone of the other sex, including a picture of the person. Or they have briefly introduced a man and a woman and later asked each about their interest in dating the other. In such experiments, men do put somewhat more value on opposite-sex physical attractiveness (Feingold, 1990, 1991; Sprecher & others, 1994). Perhaps sensing this, women worry more about their appearance and constituted nearly 90 percent of cosmetic surgery patients in the 1980s and 1990s (Crowley, 1996; Dion & others, 1990). But women, too, respond to a man's looks, and men appear to be noticing this. By 2001, the number of men having cosmetic surgery had increased significantly. The American Society of Plastic Surgeons reported that in that year 20 percent of all cosmetic surgeries were performed on men.

In one ambitious study, Elaine Hatfield and her co-workers (1966) matched 752 first-year students for a "Welcome Week" dance. The researchers gave each student personality and aptitude tests but then matched the couples randomly. On the night of the dance, the couples danced and talked for 2.5 hours and then took a brief intermission to evaluate their dates. How well did the personality and aptitude tests predict attraction? Did people like someone better who was high in self-esteem, or low in anxiety, or different from themselves in outgoingness? The researchers examined a long list of possibilities. But so far as they could determine, only one thing mattered: how physically attractive the person was (as previously rated by the researchers). The more attractive a woman was, the more he liked her and wanted to date her again. And the more attractive the man was, the more she liked him and wanted to date him again. Pretty pleases.

To say that attractiveness is important, other things being equal, is not to say that physical appearance always outranks other qualities. Some people more than others judge people by their looks (Livingston, 2001). Moreover, attractiveness probably most affects first impressions. But first impressions are important—and are becoming more so as societies become increasingly mobile and urbanized and as contacts with people become more fleeting (Berscheid, 1981).

Though interviewers may deny it, attractiveness and grooming affect first impressions in job interviews (Cash & Janda, 1984; Mack & Rainey, 1990; Marvelle & Green, 1980). This helps explain why attractive people have more prestigious jobs and make more money (Umberson & Hughes, 1987). Patricia Roszell and her colleagues (1990) looked at the attractiveness of a national sample of Canadians whom interviewers had rated on a 1 (homely) to 5 (strikingly attractive) scale. They found that for each additional scale unit of rated attractiveness, people earned, on average, an additional $1,988 annually. Irene Hanson Frieze and her associates (1991) did the same analysis with 737 MBA graduates after rating them on a similar 1 to 5 scale using student picture book photos. For each additional scale unit of rated attractiveness, men earned an added $2,600 and women earned an added $2,150.

The Matching Phenomenon

Not everyone can end up paired with someone stunningly attractive. So how do people pair off? Judging from research by Bernard Murstein (1986) and others, they pair off with people who are about as attractive as they are. Several studies have found a strong correspondence between the attractiveness of husbands and wives, of dating partners, and even of those within particular fraternities (Feingold, 1988). People tend to select as friends and especially to marry those who are a "good match" not only to their level of intelligence but also to their level of attractiveness.

Matching phenomenon
The tendency for men and women to choose as partners those who are a "good match" in attractiveness and other traits.

Experiments confirm this **matching phenomenon**. When choosing whom to approach, knowing the other is free to say yes or no, people usually approach someone whose attractiveness roughly matches their own (Berscheid & others, 1971; Huston, 1973; Stroebe & others, 1971). Good physical matches may also be conducive to good relationships, as Gregory White (1980) found in a study of UCLA dating couples. Those who were most similar in physical attractiveness were most likely, nine months later, to have fallen more deeply in love.

So who might we expect to be most closely matched for attractiveness—married couples or couples casually dating? White found, as have other researchers, that married couples are better matched.

Perhaps this research prompts you to think of happy couples who are not equally attractive. In such cases, the less attractive person often has compensating qualities. Each partner brings assets to the social marketplace, and the value of the respective assets creates an equitable match. Personal advertisements exhibit this exchange of assets (Cicerello & Sheehan, 1995; Koestner & Wheeler, 1988; Rajecki & others, 1991). Men typically offer wealth or status and seek youth and attractiveness; women more often do the reverse: "Attractive, bright woman, 26, slender, seeks warm, professional male." Moreover, men who advertise their income and education, and women who advertise their youth and looks, receive more responses to their ads (Baize & Schroeder, 1995). The asset-matching process helps explain why beautiful young women often marry older men of higher social status (Elder, 1969).

The Physical-Attractiveness Stereotype

Does the attractiveness effect spring entirely from sexual attractiveness? Clearly not, as Vicky Houston and Ray Bull (1994) discovered when they used a make-up artist to give an accomplice an apparently scarred, bruised, or birth-marked face. When riding on a Glasgow commuter rail line, people of *both* sexes avoided sitting next to the accomplice when she appeared facially disfigured. Moreover, much as adults are biased toward attractive adults, young children are biased toward attractive children (Dion, 1973; Dion & Berscheid, 1974; Langlois & others, 2000). To judge from how long they gaze at someone, even babies prefer attractive faces (Langlois & others, 1987).

Adults show a similar bias when judging children. Margaret Clifford and Elaine Hatfield (Clifford & Walster, 1973) gave Missouri Grade 5 teachers identical information about a boy or girl, but with the photograph of an attractive or unattractive child attached. The teachers perceived the attractive child as more intelligent and successful in school. Think of yourself as a playground supervisor having to discipline an unruly child. Might you, like the women studied by Karen Dion at the University of Toronto (1972), show less warmth and tact to an unattractive child? The sad truth is that most of us assume what we might call a "Bart Simpson effect"—that homely children are less able and socially competent than their beautiful peers.

What is more, we assume that beautiful people possess certain desirable traits. Other things being equal, we guess beautiful people are happier, sexually warmer, and more outgoing, intelligent, and successful—though not more honest or concerned for others (Eagly & others, 1991; Feingold, 1992b; Jackson & others, 1995). In collectivist Korea, honesty and concern for others are highly valued and *are* traits people associate with attractiveness (Wheeler & Kim, 1997).

Added together, the findings define a physical-attractiveness stereotype: What is beautiful is good. Children learn the stereotype quite early. Snow White and Cinderella are beautiful—and kind. The witch and the stepsisters are ugly—and wicked. "If you want to be loved by somebody who isn't already in your family, it doesn't hurt to be beautiful," surmised one 8-year-old girl. Or as one kindergarten girl put it when asked what it means to be pretty, "It's like to be a princess. Everybody loves you" (Dion, 1979). Think Princess Diana.

If physical attractiveness is this important, then permanently changing people's attractiveness should change the way others react to them. But is it ethical to alter someone's looks? Such manipulations are performed millions of times a year by plastic surgeons and orthodontists. With nose and teeth straightened, hair replaced and dyed, face lifted, fat liposuctioned, and breasts enlarged, can a self-dissatisfied person now find happiness? It must have some effect. Approximately 200,000 Canadian women have had breast augmentation surgery. In 2004 in the United States, 264,000 women had breast augmentation surgery in that year alone! Right now in Beverly Hills, there are twice as many cosmetic surgeons as pediatricians (*People*, 2003).

To examine the effect of such alterations, Michael Kalick (1977) had Harvard students rate their impressions of eight women based on profile photographs taken before or after cosmetic surgery. Not only did they judge the women as more physically attractive after the surgery but also as kinder, more sensitive, more sexually warm and responsive, more likable, and so on.

Do beautiful people indeed have desirable traits? Or was Leo Tolstoy correct when he wrote that it's "a strange illusion . . . to suppose that beauty is goodness"? There is some truth to the stereotype. Attractive children and young adults are somewhat more relaxed, outgoing, and socially polished (Feingold, 1992b; Langlois & others, 2000). William Goldman and Philip Lewis (1977) demonstrated this by having men call and talk for five minutes with each of three women students. Afterward the men and women rated their unseen telephone partners who happened to be most attractive as somewhat more socially skillful and likable. Physically attractive individuals tend also to be more popular, more outgoing, and more gender-typed (more traditionally masculine if male, more feminine if female) (Langlois & others, 1996).

These small average differences between attractive and unattractive people probably result from self-fulfilling prophecies. Attractive people are valued and

Physical-attractiveness stereotype The presumption that physically attractive people possess other socially desirable traits as well: What is beautiful is good.

favoured, and so many develop more social self-confidence. (Recall from Module 8 an experiment in which men evoked a warm response from unseen women they *thought* were attractive.) By this analysis, what's crucial to your social skill is not how you look but how people treat you and how you feel about yourself—whether you accept yourself, like yourself, feel comfortable with yourself.

Despite all the advantages of being beautiful, attraction researchers Elaine Hatfield and Susan Sprecher (1986) report there is also an ugly truth about beauty. Exceptionally attractive people may suffer unwelcome sexual advances and resentment from those of their own gender. They may be unsure whether others are responding to their performance, inner qualities, or just their looks, which in time will fade (Satterfield & Muehlenhard, 1997).

Who Is Attractive?

We have described attractiveness as if it were an objective quality like height, which some people have more of, some less. Strictly speaking, attractiveness is whatever the people of any given place and time find attractive. This, of course, varies. We learned earlier that culture influences the traits we find attractive, but do perceptions of beauty differ according to culture as well? Perhaps not as much as we might think. Recent research by Karen Dion (2002) suggests that although facial features may differ across cultures, what is considered attractive is surprisingly similar. Nonetheless, the beauty standards by which Miss Universe is judged hardly apply to the whole planet. People in various places and times have pierced noses, lengthened necks, dyed hair, painted skin, gorged themselves to become voluptuous, starved to become thin, and bound themselves with leather garments to make their breasts seem small and used silicone and padded bras to make them seem big.

Despite such variations, there remains "strong agreement both within and across cultures about who is and who is not attractive," notes Judith Langlois and her colleagues (2000). People's agreement about others' attractiveness is especially high when men rate women, and less so for men rating men (Marcus & Miller, 2003).

To be really attractive is, ironically, to be perfectly average. Research teams led by Judith Langlois and Lorri Roggman (1990, 1994) at the University of Texas and Anthony Little and David Perrett (2002), working with Ian Penton-Voak at the University of St. Andrews, have digitized multiple faces and averaged them using a computer. Inevitably, people find the composite faces more appealing than almost all the actual faces (see Figure 23-2).

Computer-averaged faces also tend to be perfectly symmetrical—another characteristic of strikingly attractive people (Gangestad & Thornhill, 1997; Mealey & others, 1999; Shackelford & Larsen, 1997). Research teams led by Gillian Rhodes (1999) and by Ian Penton-Voak (2001) have shown that if you could merge either half of your face with its mirror image—thus forming a perfectly symmetrical new face—you would boost your looks a tad. Averaging a number of such symmetrical faces produces an even better looking face. So, in some respects, perfectly average is quite attractive. It's even true for dogs, birds, and wristwatches, report Jamin Halberstadt and Rhodes (2000). For example, what people perceive as your average dog they also rate as attractive.

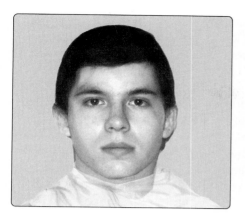

FIGURE 23-2

Is beauty merely in the eye of the beholder? Which of these faces is most attractive? People everywhere agree that the symmetrical face on the right (a composite of 32 male faces) is better looking, note Judith Langlois and her collaborators (1996). To evolutionary psychologists, such agreement suggests some universal standards of beauty rooted in our ancestral history.

What do you think is important? Visit the Online Learning Centre and complete Activity 23.1 to rate how important you find certain traits to be.

OLC
Activity 23.1

Evolution and Attraction

Psychologists working from the evolutionary perspective explain these gender differences in terms of reproductive strategy. They assume that beauty signals biologically important information: health, youth, and fertility. Over time, men who preferred fertile-looking women outreproduced those who were as happy to mate with prepubescent or postmenopausal females. They also assume evolution predisposes women to favour male traits that signify an ability to provide and protect resources. That, David Buss (1989) believes, explains why the males he studied in 37 cultures—from Australia to Zambia—did indeed prefer female characteristics that signify reproductive capacity. And it explains why physically attractive females tend to marry high-status males and why men compete with such determination to achieve fame and fortune.

So, in every culture the beauty business is big business that shows no signs of abating. Where money abounds, so does cosmetic surgery. We are, evolutionary psychologists suggest, driven by primal attractions. Like eating and breathing, attraction and mating are too important to leave to the whims of culture.

OLC
Video 23.1

The Contrast Effect

Although our mating psychology has biological wisdom, attraction is not all hardwired. What's attractive to you also depends on your comparison standards. Douglas Kenrick and Sara Gutierres (1980) had male confederates interrupt men in their residence rooms and explain, "We have a friend coming to town this week and we want to fix him up with a date, but we can't decide whether to fix him up with her or not, so we decided to conduct a survey. . . . We want you to give us your vote on how attractive you think she is . . . on a scale of 1 to 7." Shown a picture of an average young woman, those who had just been watching *Charlie's Angels*, a television show featuring three beautiful women, rated her less attractive than those who hadn't.

Laboratory experiments confirm this "contrast effect." To men who have recently been gazing at centrefolds, average women or even their own wives tend to seem less attractive (Kenrick & others, 1989). Viewing pornographic films simulating passionate sex similarly decreases satisfaction with one's own partner (Zillmann, 1989). Being sexually aroused may *temporarily* make a person of the other sex seem more attractive to heterosexuals. But the lingering effect of exposure to perfect "10s," or of unrealistic sexual depictions, is to make one's own partner seem less appealing—more like a "6" than an "8." It works the same way with our self-perceptions. After viewing a superattractive person of the same sex, people feel *less* attractive than after viewing a homely person (Brown & others, 1992; Thornton & Maurice, 1997).

The Attractiveness of Those We Love

Let's conclude our discussion of attractiveness on an upbeat note. Not only do we perceive attractive people as likable, we also perceive likable people as attractive. Perhaps you can recall individuals who, as you grew to like them, became more attractive. Their physical imperfections were no longer so noticeable. Alan Gross and Christine Crofton (1977) had students view someone's photograph after reading a favourable or unfavourable description of the person's personality. When portrayed as warm, helpful, and considerate, people *looked* more attractive. Discovering someone's similarities to us also makes the person seem more attractive (Beaman & Klentz, 1983; Klentz & others, 1987).

Moreover, love sees loveliness: The more in love a woman is with a man, the more physically attractive she finds him (Price & others, 1974). And the more in love people are, the less attractive they find all others of the other sex (Johnson & Rusbult, 1989; Simpson & others, 1990). "The grass may be greener on the other side," note Rowland Miller and Jeffry Simpson (1990), "but happy gardeners are less likely to notice."

SIMILARITY VERSUS COMPLEMENTARITY

Do opposites attract? Many of you probably know a couple who are completely different yet completely in love. Yet sometimes the saying "birds of a feather flock together" is more apt—you can probably easily come up with examples of friends who seem almost identical to each other in terms of attitudes, personalities, and preferences. What do *you* find more important in a relationship, similarity or complementarity? Visit the Online Learning Centre and complete Activity 23.2 to find out for yourself.

OLC
Activity 23.2

Do Birds of a Feather Flock Together?

Of this much we may be sure: Birds that flock together are of a feather. Friends, engaged couples, and spouses are far more likely than people randomly paired to share common attitudes, beliefs, and values. Furthermore, the greater the similarity between husband and wife, the happier they are and the less likely they are to divorce (Byrne, 1971; Caspi & Herbener, 1990). Such correlational findings are intriguing. But cause and effect remain an enigma. Does similarity lead to liking? Or does liking lead to similarity?

The Story Behind the Research

Dr. Marian Morry at the University of Manitoba has been interested in determining if similarity leads to attraction or if the opposite is true—that attraction leads to perceptions of similarity. When Dr. Morry began her first academic position, she got along well with many of her new colleagues. She at first felt that her new workmates were very similar to her. However, as she got to know them better, she realized that there were a number of areas where she and her colleagues were quite different. She began to suspect that in many situations attraction leads to perceptions of similarity, rather than the other way around.

To test her hypothesis, Dr. Morry designed a set of studies to explore how people perceived the traits, beliefs, and attitudes of the people they liked (see Morry, 2003, 2005). In one study (Morry, 2003), participants were asked to rate their and their friends' locus of control and friendship satisfaction. As Dr. Morry expected, participants perceived their friends to be similar to themselves on locus of control and satisfaction, but these perceptions did not match the friends' self-ratings. Instead, participants' perceptions reflected a belief in their friends' similarity to themselves. In a later study (Morry, 2005), she manipulated participants' relationship satisfaction and found similar effects—more satisfied individuals rated their friends as more similar. This provides clear evidence that attraction can lead to perceptions of similarity. |

Likeness Begets Liking

The likeness-leads-to-liking effect has been tested in real-life situations by noting who comes to like whom. At the University of Michigan, Theodore Newcomb (1961) studied two groups of 17 unacquainted, male transfer students. After 13 weeks of boardinghouse life, those whose agreement was initially highest were most likely to have formed close friendships. One group of friends was composed of five liberal arts students, each a political liberal with strong intellectual interests. Another was made up of three conservative veterans who were all enrolled in the engineering college. William Griffitt and Russell Veitch (1974) compressed the getting-to-know-you process by confining 13 unacquainted men in a fallout shelter. (The men were paid volunteers.) Knowing the men's opinions on various issues, the researchers could predict with better-than-chance accuracy those each man would most like and most dislike. As in the boardinghouse, the men liked best those most like themselves. Similarity breeds content. Birds of a feather *do* flock together.

Do Opposites Attract?

Are we not also attracted to people who are in some ways *different* from ourselves, in ways that complement our own characteristics? Researchers have explored this question by comparing not only friends' and spouses' attitudes and beliefs but also their ages, religions, races, smoking behaviours, economic levels, educations, height, intelligence, and appearance. In all these ways and more, similarity still prevails (Buss, 1985; Kandel, 1978). Smart birds flock together. So do rich birds, Protestant birds, tall birds, pretty birds.

Still we resist: Are we not attracted to people whose needs and personalities complement our own? Would a sadist and a masochist find true love? Even the *Reader's Digest* has told us that "opposites attract.... Socializers pair with loners, novelty-lovers with those who dislike change, free spenders with scrimpers, risk-takers with the very cautious" (Jacoby, 1986). Sociologist Robert Winch (1958) reasoned that the needs of someone who is outgoing and domineering would naturally complement those of someone who is shy and submissive. The logic seems compelling, and most of us can think of couples who view their differences as complementary: "My husband and I are perfect for each other. I'm Aquarius—a decisive person. He's Libra—can't make decisions. But he's always happy to go along with arrangements I make."

Complementarity
The popularly supposed tendency, in a relationship between two people, for each to complete what is missing in the other.

Some **complementarity** may evolve as a relationship progresses (even a relationship between two identical twins). Yet people seem slightly more prone to like and to marry those whose needs and personalities are *similar* (Botwin & others, 1997; Buss, 1984; Fishbein & Thelen, 1981a, b; Nias, 1979). Perhaps we shall yet discover some ways (other than heterosexuality) in which differences commonly breed liking. Dominance/submissiveness may be one such way (Dryer & Horowitz, 1997). And we tend not to feel attracted to those who show our own worst traits (Schimel & others, 2000). But researcher David Buss (1985) doubts complementarity: "The tendency of opposites to marry, or mate . . . has never been reliably demonstrated, with the single exception of sex."

LIKING THOSE WHO LIKE US

With hindsight, the reward principle explains our conclusions so far:

- *Proximity* is rewarding. It costs less time and effort to receive friendship's benefits with someone who lives or works close by.
- We like *attractive* people because we perceive that they offer other desirable traits and because we benefit by associating with them.
- If others have *similar* opinions, we feel rewarded because we presume that they like us in return. Moreover, those who share our views help validate them. We especially like people if we have successfully converted them to our way of thinking (Lombardo & others, 1972; Riordan, 1980; Sigall, 1970).

If we like those whose behaviour is rewarding, then we ought to adore those who like and admire us. Are the best friendships mutual admiration societies? Indeed, one person's liking for another does predict the other's liking in return (Kenny & Nasby, 1980). Liking is usually mutual.

But does one person's liking another *cause* the other to return the appreciation? People's reports of how they fell in love suggest yes (Aron & others, 1989). Discovering that an appealing someone really likes you seems to awaken romantic feelings. Experiments confirm it: Those told that certain others like or admire them usually feel a reciprocal affection (Berscheid & Walster, 1978).

And consider this finding by Ellen Berscheid and her colleagues (1969): Students like another student who says eight positive things about them better than one who says seven positive things and one negative thing. We are sensitive to the slightest hint of criticism. Writer Larry L. King speaks for many in noting, "I have discovered over the years that good reviews strangely fail to make the author feel as good as bad reviews make him feel bad." Whether we are judging ourselves or others, negative information carries more weight because, being less usual, it grabs more attention (Yzerbyt & Leyens, 1991). People's votes are more influenced by their impressions of presidential candidates' weaknesses than by their impressions of strengths (Klein, 1991), a phenomenon that has not been lost on those who design negative campaigns.

That we like those we perceive as liking us was recognized long ago. Observers from the ancient philosopher Hecato ("If you wish to be loved, love") to Ralph Waldo Emerson ("The only way to have a friend is to be one") to Dale Carnegie ("Dole out praise lavishly") anticipated the findings. What they did not anticipate was the precise conditions under which the principle works.

Self-Esteem and Attraction

Elaine Hatfield (Walster, 1965) wondered if another's approval is especially rewarding after we have been deprived of approval, much as eating is most powerfully rewarding after fasting. To test this idea, she gave some Stanford University women either very favourable or very unfavourable analyses of their personalities, affirming some and wounding others. Then she asked them to evaluate several people, including an attractive male confederate who just before the experiment had struck up a warm conversation with each woman and had asked each for a date. (Not one turned him down.) Which women do you suppose most liked the man? It was those whose self-esteem had been temporarily shattered and who were presumably hungry for social approval. This helps explain why people sometimes fall passionately in love on the rebound, after an ego-bruising rejection.

Proximity, attractiveness, similarity, being liked—these are the factors known to influence our friendship formation. Sometimes friendship deepens into the passion and intimacy of love. What is love? And why does it sometimes flourish and sometimes fade? To these questions we turn next.

OUR NEED TO BELONG

We humans, whom Aristotle called "the social animal," have an intense **need to belong**—to connect with others in enduring, close relationships.

Social psychologists Roy Baumeister and Mark Leary (1995) illustrate the power of social attractions bred by our need to belong:

- For our ancestors, mutual attachments enabled group survival. When hunting game or erecting shelter, ten hands were better than two.

- For a woman and a man, the bonds of love can lead to children, whose survival chances are boosted by the nurturing of two bonded parents who support one another.

Need to belong
A motivation to bond with others in relationships that provide ongoing, positive interactions.

- For children and their caregivers, social attachments enhance survival. Unexplainably separated from one another, parent and toddler may each panic, until reunited in a tight embrace.

- For people everywhere, actual and hoped-for close relationships preoccupy thinking and colour emotions. Finding a supportive soul mate in whom we can confide, we feel accepted and prized. Falling in love, we feel irrepressible joy. Longing for acceptance and love, we spend billions on cosmetics, clothes, and diets.

- For the jilted, the widowed, and the sojourner in a strange place, the loss of social bonds triggers pain, loneliness, or withdrawal. Reared under extreme neglect or in institutions without belonging to anybody, children become withdrawn, anxious creatures. Losing a soul-mate relationship, adults feel jealous, distraught, or bereaved, as well as more mindful of death and the fragility of life.

- Reminders of death in turn heighten our need to belong, to be with others and hold close those we love (Mikulincer & others, 2003; Wisman & Koole, 2003). Facing the terror of 9/11, millions of North Americans called and connected with loved ones. Likewise, the shocking death of a classmate, co-worker, or family member brings people together, their differences no longer mattering.

We are, indeed, social animals. We need to belong. When we do belong—when we feel supported by close, intimate relationships—we tend to be healthier and happier.

Kipling Williams (2002) has explored what happens when our need to belong is thwarted by *ostracism* (acts of excluding or ignoring). Humans in all cultures, whether in schools, workplaces, prisons, or homes, use ostracism to regulate social behaviour. So what is it like to be shunned—to be avoided, met with averted eyes, or given the silent treatment? People (women especially) respond to ostracism with depressed mood, anxiety, hurt feelings, efforts to restore relationships, and eventual withdrawal. The silent treatment is "emotional abuse" and "a terrible, terrible weapon to use" say those who have experienced it from a family member or co-worker. In experiments, people who are left out of a simple game of ball tossing feel deflated and stressed.

Sometimes deflation turns nasty. In several studies, Jean Twenge and her collaborators (2001, 2002; Baumeister & others, 2002) gave some people an experience of being socially included. Others experienced exclusion: They were either told (based on a personality test) that they "were likely to end up alone later in life" or that others whom they'd met didn't want them in their group. Those led to feel excluded became more likely to disparage or deliver a blast of noise to someone who had insulted them. If a small laboratory experience could produce such aggression, noted the researchers, one wonders what aggressive tendencies "might arise from a series of important rejections or chronic exclusion."

Williams and his colleagues (2000) were surprised to discover that even "cyber-ostracism" by faceless people whom one will never meet takes a toll. (Perhaps you have experienced this when feeling ignored in a chat room or when having your e-mail messages go unanswered.) The researchers had 1,486 participants from

62 countries play a web-based game of throwing a flying disc with two others (actually computer-generated fellow players). Those ostracized by the other players experienced poorer moods and became more likely to conform to others' wrong judgments on a subsequent perceptual task. Williams and four of his colleagues (2000) even found ostracism stressful when each was ignored for an agreed-upon day by the unresponsive four others. Contrary to their expectations that this would be a laughter-filled role-playing game, the simulated ostracism disrupted work, interfered with pleasant social functioning, and "caused temporary concern, anxiety, paranoia, and general fragility of spirit." To thwart our deep need to belong is to unsettle our life.

CONCEPTS TO REMEMBER

Proximity   p. 253
Mere-exposure effect   p. 254
Matching phenomenon   p. 258

Physical-attractiveness stereotype   p. 259
Complementarity   p. 264
Need to belong   p. 265

Please visit the *Exploring Social Psychology* Online Learning Centre at **www.mcgrawhill.ca/college/myers** to participate in module activities, view module videos, access research and study tools, and test your knowledge with interactive quizzes, exercises, and scenarios.

Romantic Relationships

When asked what love means to them, people tend to list characteristics associated with both close friends and companions (e.g., warmth, intimacy, loyalty) and passionate relationships (e.g., euphoria, sexual attraction, obsessive thoughts). Which set of traits do you associate with love?

What is this thing called love? Can passionate love endure? If not, what can replace it? Loving is more complex than liking and thus more difficult to measure, more perplexing to study. People yearn for it, live for it, die for it. Yet, only in the last three decades has loving become a serious topic in social psychology.

Most attraction researchers have studied what is most easily studied—responses during brief encounters between strangers. The influences on our initial liking of another—proximity, attractiveness, similarity, being liked, and other rewarding traits—also influence our long-term, close relationships. The impressions that dating couples quickly form of each other therefore provide a clue to their long-term future (Berg, 1984; Berg & McQuinn, 1986). Indeed, if North American romances flourished *randomly*, without regard to proximity and similarity, then most Catholics (being a minority) would marry Protestants, most minorities would marry Whites, and postsecondary graduates would be as apt to marry high school dropouts as fellow graduates.

So first impressions are important. Nevertheless, long-term loving is not merely an intensification of initial liking. Social psychologists have therefore shifted their attention from the mild attraction experienced during first encounters to the study of enduring, close relationships.

PASSIONATE LOVE

The first step in scientifically studying romantic love, as in studying any variable, is to decide how to define and measure it. We have ways to measure aggression, altruism, prejudice, and liking—but how do we measure love? What does love mean to you? If we were to ask people what love is, what would they say? Dr. Beverley Fehr at the University of Winnipeg wanted to know as well (see Fehr, 1988). To test this, in one of her early studies, she asked University of British Columbia students to list what they perceived to be characteristics of love. Students listed features such as warmth, intimacy, concern for the other person's well being, loyalty, and caring—features we would expect to see in relationships with our best friends and companions. Students also listed characteristics we would see in passionate romantic relationships—obsessive thoughts, increased heart rate, euphoria, and sexual attraction. However, the "friendship" traits were consistently rated higher than the "love" traits by both men and women (see Fehr & Broughton, 2001).

Elizabeth Barret Browning asked a similar question: "How do I love thee? Let me count the ways." Social scientists have counted various ways. Psychologist Robert Sternberg (1998) views love as a triangle, whose three sides (of varying lengths) are passion, intimacy, and commitment (Figure 24-1). Drawing from ancient philosophy and literature, sociologist John Alan Lee (1988) and psychologists Clyde Hendrick and Susan Hendrick (1993) identify three primary love styles—*eros* (self-disclosing passion), *ludus* (uncommitted game playing), and *storge* (friendship)—which, like the

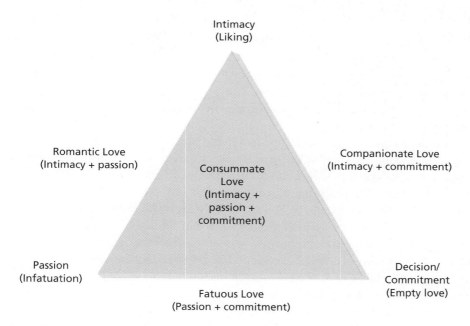

FIGURE 24–1
Robert Sternberg's (1988) conception of the kinds of loving as combinations of three basic components of love.

primary colours, combine to form secondary love styles. Some love styles, notably eros and storge, predict high relationship satisfaction; others, such as ludus, predict low satisfaction (Hendrick & Hendrick, 1997).

Some elements are common to all loving relationships, be they heterosexual, homosexual, or non-sexual friendships: mutual understanding, giving and receiving support, enjoying the loved one's company. Some elements are distinctive. If we experience passionate love, we express it physically, we expect the relationship to be exclusive, and we are intensely fascinated with our partner. You can see it in our eyes. Zick Rubin confirmed this. He administered a love scale to hundreds of University of Michigan dating couples. Later, from behind a one-way mirror in a laboratory waiting room, he clocked eye-contact among "weak-love" and "strong-love" couples. His result will not surprise you: The strong-love couples gave themselves away by gazing long into one another's eyes.

Passionate love is emotional, exciting, intense. Elaine Hatfield (1988) defined it as *"a state of intense longing for union with another"* (p. 193). If reciprocated, one feels fulfilled and joyous; if not, one feels empty or despairing. Like other forms of emotional excitement, passionate love involves a roller coaster of elation and gloom, tingling exhilaration and dejected misery. How passionately do you love? Visit the Online Learning Centre and complete Activity 24.1 to find out.

Passionate love A state of intense longing for union with another. Passionate lovers are absorbed in one another, feel ecstatic at attaining their partner's love, and are disconsolate on losing it.

OLC
Activity 24.1

A Theory of Passionate Love

To explain passionate love, Hatfield notes that a given state of arousal can be steered into any of several emotions, depending on how we attribute the arousal. An emotion involves both body and mind—both arousal and how we interpret and label the arousal. Imagine yourself with pounding heart and trembling hands: Are you experiencing fear, anxiety, joy? Physiologically, one emotion is quite similar to another. You may therefore experience the arousal as joy if you are in a euphoric situation, anger if your environment is hostile, and passionate love if the situation is romantic. In this view, passionate love is the psychological experience of being biologically aroused by someone we find attractive.

If indeed passion is a revved-up state that's labelled "love," then whatever revs one up should intensify feelings of love. In several experiments, college men aroused sexually by reading or viewing erotic materials had a heightened response to a woman (for example, by scoring much higher on a love scale when describing their girlfriend) (Carducci & others, 1978; Dermer & Pyszczynski, 1978; Stephan & others, 1971). The **two-factor theory of emotion** claims that emotional experience is a product of physiological arousal and how we cognitively label the arousal. Proponents of the two-factor theory of emotion, developed by Stanley Schachter and Jerome Singer (1962), argue that when the revved-up men responded to a woman, they easily misattributed some of their arousal to her.

Two-factor theory of emotion Arousal × label = emotion. (Emotional experience is a product of physiological arousal and how we cognitively label the arousal.)

According to this theory, being aroused by *any* source should intensify passionate feelings—providing the mind is free to attribute some of the arousal to a romantic stimulus. Donald Dutton and Arthur Aron (1974, 1989) invited University of British Columbia men to participate in a learning experiment. After meeting their attractive female partners, some were frightened with the news that they would be suffering some "quite painful" electric shocks. Before the experiment was to begin, the researcher gave a brief questionnaire "to get some information on your present feelings and reactions, since these often influence performance on the learning task." Asked how much they would like to date and kiss their female partners, the aroused (frightened) men expressed more intense attraction toward the women.

Does this phenomenon occur outside the laboratory? Recall the study you read about in Module 3 about misattribution of arousal. In this study, Dutton and Aron (1974) had an attractive, young woman approach individual young men as they crossed a narrow, wobbly, 137-metre-long suspension walkway hanging 70 metres above British Columbia's rocky Capilano River. The woman asked each man to help her fill out a class questionnaire. When he had finished, she scribbled her name and phone number and invited him to call if he wanted to hear more about the project. Most accepted the phone number, and half who did so called. By contrast, men approached by the woman on a low, solid bridge, and men approached on the high bridge by a *male* interviewer, rarely called. Once again, physical arousal accentuated romantic responses. As you perhaps have noticed after scary movies, roller-coaster rides, and physical exercise, adrenaline makes the heart grow fonder.

Variations in Love

Time and Culture

There is always a temptation to assume that most others share our feelings and ideas. People in Western cultures assume, for example, that love is a precondition for marriage. However, within cultures the very definition of marriage has been debated in recent years. In 2005, Canada became the fourth country in the world to formally recognize the right of homosexual couples to marry. Nonetheless, people's ideas about love seem to be fairly consistent across cultures. Most cultures—89 percent in one analysis of 166 cultures—do have a concept of romantic love, as reflected in flirtation or couples running off together (Jankowiak & Fischer, 1992). But in some cultures, notably those practising arranged marriages, love tends to follow rather than to precede marriage. Moreover, until recently in North America, marital choices, especially those by women, were strongly influenced by considerations of economic security, family background, and professional status.

Karen Dion and Kenneth Dion at the University of Toronto have been researching the role of culture on perceptions of love for a number of years (for example, Dion & Dion, 1993; Dion, 2001). In one study (1993), they surveyed students at the University of Toronto from a wide range of cultures—Chinese, Vietnamese, English, Irish, Spanish, and German, among others. They found that people from Asian cultures were more likely to prefer a style of love that is more focused on a companionate, friendship-based romance that can be integrated into their existing family relationships. Thus, culture definitely influences people's preferences and expectations around love.

Gender

Do males and females differ in how they experience passionate love? Studies of men and women falling in and out of love reveal some surprises. Most people suppose that women fall in love more readily. However, it is actually *men* who tend to fall more readily in love (Dion & Dion, 1985; Peplau & Gordon, 1985). Men also seem to fall out of love more slowly and are less likely than women to break up a premarital romance. Women in love, however, are typically as emotionally involved as their partners, or more so. They are more likely to report feeling euphoric and "giddy and carefree," as if they were "floating on a cloud." Women are also somewhat more likely than men to focus on the intimacy of the friendship and on their concern for their partner. Men are more likely than women to think about the playful and physical aspects of the relationship (Hendrick & Hendrick, 1995).

COMPANIONATE LOVE

Companionate love
The affection we feel for those with whom our lives are deeply intertwined.

OLC
Activity 24.2

Although passionate love burns hot, it inevitably simmers down. The longer a relationship endures, the fewer its emotional ups and downs (Berscheid & others, 1989). The high of romance may be sustained for a few months, even a couple of years. But no high lasts forever. The novelty, the intense absorption in the other, the thrill of the romance, the giddy "floating on a cloud" feeling, fades. After two years of marriage, spouses express affection about half as often as when they were newlyweds (Huston & Chorost, 1994). About four years after marriage, the divorce rate peaks in cultures worldwide and many gay and lesbian partnerships have likewise ended (Fisher, 1994). If a close relationship is to endure, it will settle to a steadier but still warm afterglow that Hatfield calls **companionate love**.

Unlike the wild emotions of passionate love, companionate love is lower key; it's a deep, affectionate attachment. And it is just as real. Even if one develops a tolerance for a drug, withdrawal can be painful. So it is with close relationships. Mutually dependent couples who no longer feel the flame of passionate love will often, upon divorce or death, discover that they have lost more than they expected. Having focused on what was not working, they stopped noticing what was (Carlson & Hatfield, 1992).

The cooling of passionate love over time and the growing importance of other factors, such as shared values, can be seen in the feelings of those who enter arranged versus love-based marriages in India. Usha Gupta and Pushpa Singh (1982) asked 50 couples in Jaipur, India, to complete a love scale. They found that those who married for love reported diminishing feelings of love if they had been married more than five years. By contrast, those in arranged marriages reported *more* love if they were not newlyweds (Figure 24-2).

The cooling of intense romantic love often triggers a period of disillusion, especially among those who regard such love as essential both for a marriage and for its continuation. Jeffry Simpson, Bruce Campbell, and Ellen Berscheid (1986) suspect "the sharp rise in the divorce rate in the past two decades is linked, at least in part,

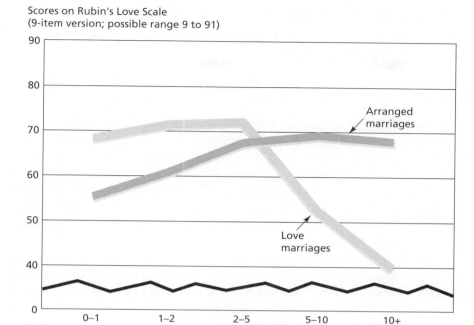

Scores on Rubin's Love Scale
(9-item version; possible range 9 to 91)

FIGURE 24–2
Romantic love between partners in arranged or love marriages in Jaipur, India.
Data from Gupta & Singh, 1982.

to the growing importance of intense positive emotional experiences (e.g., romantic love) in people's lives, experiences that may be particularly difficult to sustain over time." Compared to North Americans, Asians tend to focus less on personal feelings and more on the practical aspects of social attachments (Dion & Dion, 1988; Sprecher & others, 1994). Thus, they are less vulnerable to disillusionment. Asians are also less prone to the self-focused individualism that, in the long run, can undermine a relationship and lead to divorce (Dion & Dion, 1991, 1996; Triandis & others, 1988).

The decline in intense mutual fascination may be natural and adaptive for species survival. The result of passionate love frequently is children, whose survival is aided by the parents' waning obsession with one another (Kenrick & Trost, 1987). Nevertheless, for those married more than 20 years, some of the lost romantic feeling is often renewed as the family nest empties and the parents are once again free to focus their attention on each other (Hatfield & Sprecher, 1986). "No man or woman really knows what love is until they have been married a quarter of a century," said Mark Twain. If the relationship has been intimate and mutually rewarding, companionate love rooted in a rich history of shared experiences deepens. But what is intimacy? And what is mutually rewarding?

MAINTAINING CLOSE RELATIONSHIPS

What factors influence the ups and downs of our close relationships? Let's consider two: equity and intimacy (self-disclosure).

Equity

Equity A condition in which the outcomes people receive from a relationship are proportional to what they contribute to it. *Note*: Equitable outcomes needn't always be equal outcomes.

If both partners in a relationship pursue their personal desires willy-nilly, the friendship will die. Therefore, our society teaches us to exchange rewards by what Elaine Hatfield, William Walster, and Ellen Berscheid (1978) have called an **equity** principle of attraction: What you and your partner get out of a relationship should be proportional to what you each put into it. If two people receive equal outcomes, they should contribute equally; otherwise one or the other will feel it is unfair. If both feel their outcomes correspond to the assets and efforts each contributes, then both perceive equity.

Strangers and casual acquaintances maintain equity by exchanging benefits: You lend me your class notes; later, I'll lend you mine. I invite you to my party; you invite me to yours. Those in an enduring relationship, including roommates and those in love, do not feel bound to trade similar benefits—notes for notes, parties for parties (Berg, 1984). They feel freer to maintain equity by exchanging a variety of benefits ("When you drop by to lend me your notes, why don't you stay for dinner?") and eventually to stop keeping track of who owes whom.

Long-Term Equity

Is it crass to suppose that friendship and love are rooted in an equitable exchange of rewards? Don't we sometimes give in response to a loved one's need, without expecting any sort of return? Indeed, those involved in an equitable, long-term relationship are unconcerned with short-term equity. Margaret Clark and Judson Mills (1979, 1993; Clark, 1984, 1986) argue that people even take pains to *avoid* calculating any exchange benefits. When we help a good friend, we do not want instant repayment. If someone has us over for dinner we wait before reciprocating, lest the person attribute the motive for our return invitation to be merely paying off a social debt. True friends tune in to one another's needs even when reciprocation is impossible (Clark & others, 1986, 1989). As people observe their partners sacrificing self-interest, their sense of trust grows (Wieselquist & others, 1999). One clue that an acquaintance is becoming a close friend is that the person shares when sharing is unexpected (Miller & others, 1989). Happily married people tend *not* to keep score of how much they are giving and getting (Buunk & Van Yperen, 1991).

Previously we noted an equity rule at work in the matching phenomenon: People usually bring equal assets to romantic relationships. Recall that often they are matched for attractiveness, status, and so forth. If they are mismatched in one area, such as attractiveness, they tend to be mismatched in some other area, such as status. But in total assets, they are an equitable match. No one says, and few even think, "I'll trade you my good looks for your big income." But especially in relationships that last, equity is the rule.

Perceived Equity and Satisfaction

Those in an equitable relationship are more content (Fletcher & others, 1987; Hatfield & others, 1985; Van Yperen & Buunk, 1990). Those who perceive their relationship as *in*equitable feel discomfort: The one who has the better deal may feel guilty and the one who senses a raw deal may feel strong irritation. (Given the self-serving bias— most husbands perceive themselves as contributing more housework than their wives credit them for—the person who is "overbenefited" is less sensitive to the inequity.)

The Story Behind the Research

Do men and women differ in their memories for relationship events? Do our current relationship experiences shape our memories for past relationship events? Dr. Diane Holmberg and her colleagues wanted to know. Dr. Holmberg has been conducting research in this area since her undergraduate years at the University of Waterloo. Now at Acadia University in Wolfville, Nova Scotia, Dr. Holmberg became interested in this topic as an undergraduate research assistant working with Dr. Michael Ross. He was interested in how people's memories for the same event differed. Married couples were chosen as a convenient sample of people who would have shared memories. As soon as the researchers began to analyze the data, though, they realized that relationships are important when it comes to memory.

In an early study (Holmberg & Ross, 1992), they found that women tended to have much more vivid memories of important events that couples share—a first date, a vacation, or a recent argument. Furthermore, women tended to assign more importance to the situations, and they reported reminiscing about the events more frequently than their male partners. Holmberg decided to continue in this line of research for her undergraduate honours thesis, working with Dr. John Holmes, and later pursued it for her graduate research at the University of Michigan.

After completing her Ph.D., Dr. Holmberg began her current position at Acadia University and continued her research with her students there. They have continued to explore gender differences in relationship memories, and have shown that women's memories about relationship events are not only more vivid, but also more complete, detailed, and accurate than men's (Holmberg & others, 2006). Dr. Holmberg has also returned to those married couples, examining their interviews again in their seventh year of marriage (Holmberg & others, 2004). These studies noted that couples' relationship stories tend to change over time to more closely resemble the standard relationship "script." For example, in most couples the husband initiated the relationship, but in some the wife played a major role. Many of the latter group came to gloss over the wife's role in later years, though, simply saying "we both were interested." However, those who continued to emphasize the wife's role in relationship initiation in their stories had husbands who were less happy (on a standard scale) by the seventh year of marriage. In a related line of research (Holmberg and Mackenzie, 2002), dating couples' relationship well-being was higher if their relationship had developed, and continued to develop, as both partners expected typical relationships to develop (that is, the relationship is following the expected script), and if the partners shared similar scripts for how their relationship should develop over time.

In her most recent work, Dr. Holmberg and her students have been exploring why women seem to have better memories when it comes to relationships, and what implications these gender differences might have for relational well-being. Regardless, all of these studies show that people's memories, expectations, and beliefs have a strong impact on the quality, development, and maintenance of romantic relationships. ‖

Robert Schafer and Patricia Keith (1980) surveyed several hundred married couples of all ages, noting those who felt their marriages were somewhat unfair because one spouse contributed too little to the cooking, housekeeping, parenting, or providing. Inequity took its toll: Those who perceived inequity also felt more distressed and depressed. During the child-rearing years, when wives often feel underbenefited and husbands feel overbenefited, marital satisfaction tends to dip. During the honeymoon and empty-nest stages, spouses are more likely to perceive equity and to feel satisfaction with their marriages (Feeney & others, 1994). When both partners freely give and receive, and make decisions together, the odds of sustained, satisfying love are good.

Self-Disclosure

Deep, companionate relationships are intimate. They enable us to be known as we truly are and feel accepted. We discover this delicious experience in a good marriage or a close friendship—a relationship wherein trust displaces anxiety and we are therefore free to open ourselves without fear of losing the other's affection (Holmes & Rempel, 1989). Such relationships are characterized by what the late Sidney Jourard called self-disclosure (Derlega & others, 1993). As a relationship grows, **self-disclosing** partners reveal more and more of themselves to one another; their knowledge of one another penetrates to deeper and deeper levels until it reaches an appropriate depth.

Self-disclosure Revealing intimate aspects of oneself to others.

Experiments have probed both the *causes* and the *effects* of self-disclosure. When are people most willing to disclose intimate information concerning "what you like and don't like about yourself" or "what you're most ashamed and most proud of"? And what effects do such revelations have upon those who reveal and receive them?

The most reliable finding is the **disclosure reciprocity** effect: Disclosure begets disclosure (Berg, 1987; Miller, 1990; Reis & Shaver, 1988). We reveal more to those who have been open with us. But intimacy is seldom instant. (If it is, the person may seem indiscreet and unstable.) Appropriate intimacy progresses like a dance: I reveal a little, you reveal a little—but not too much. You then reveal more, and I reciprocate.

Disclosure reciprocity The tendency for one person's intimacy of self-disclosure to match that of a conversational partner.

Some people—most of them women—are especially skilled "openers"—they easily elicit intimate disclosures from others, even from those who normally don't reveal very much of themselves (Miller & others, 1983; Pegalis & others, 1994; Shaffer & others, 1996). Such people tend to be good listeners. During conversation they maintain attentive facial expressions and appear to be comfortably enjoying themselves (Purvis & others, 1984). They may also express interest by uttering supportive phrases while their conversational partner is speaking. They are what psychologist Carl Rogers (1980) called "growth-promoting" listeners—people who are *genuine* in revealing their own feelings, who are *accepting* of others' feelings, and who are *empathic*, sensitive, reflective listeners.

Intimate self-disclosure is one also of companionate love's delights. Dating and married couples who most reveal themselves to one another express most satisfaction with their relationship and are more likely to endure in it (Berg & McQuinn, 1986; Hendrick & others, 1988; Sprecher, 1987).

Researchers have also found that women are often more willing to disclose their fears and weaknesses than are men (Cunningham, 1981). As Kate Millett (1975) put it, "Women express, men repress." Nevertheless, men today, particularly men with egalitarian gender-role attitudes, seem increasingly willing to reveal intimate feelings and to enjoy the satisfactions that accompany a relationship of mutual trust and self-disclosure. And that, say Arthur Aron and Elaine Aron (1994), is the essence of love—two selves connecting, disclosing, and identifying with one another; two selves, each retaining their individuality, yet sharing activities, delighting in similarities, and mutually supporting.

Does the Internet Create Intimacy or Isolation?

As a reader of this textbook, you are almost surely one of the world's more than 600 million (as of 2002) Internet users. After taking the telephone seven decades to go from 1 percent to 75 percent penetration of North American households, Internet access reached 75 percent penetration in little more than seven years (Putnam, 2000). You—and soon a billion others—enjoy e-mail, web surfing, and perhaps lurking or participating in listservs, news groups, or chat rooms.

So what do you think: Is computer-mediated communication within virtual communities a poor substitute for in-person relationships? Or is it a wonderful way to widen our social circles? Does the Internet do more to connect people with new-found soul mates or to drain time from face-to-face relationships? Consider the emerging debate.

**OLC
Activity 24.3**

Point: The Internet, like the printing press and telephone, expands communication, and communication enables relationships. Printing reduced face-to-face story telling and the telephone reduced face-to-face chats, but both enable us to reach and be reached by people without limitations of time and distance. Social relations involve networking, and the Net is the ultimate network. It enables efficient networking with family, friends, and kindred spirits everywhere—including people we otherwise never could have found and befriended, be they fellow skin cancer patients, St. Nicholas collectors, or Harry Potter fans.

Counterpoint: True, but computer communication is impoverished. It lacks the nuances of eye-to-eye contact punctuated with nonverbal cues and physical touches. Except for simple emoticons—such as a :-) for an unnuanced smile—electronic messages are devoid of gestures, facial expressions, and tones of voice. No wonder it's so easy to misread them. The absence of expressive e-motion makes for ambiguous emotion.

For example, vocal nuances can signal whether a statement is serious, kidding, or sarcastic. Research by Justin Kruger and his colleagues (1999) shows that communicators often think their "just kidding" intent is equally clear, whether e-mailed or spoken, when it isn't. Thanks also to one's anonymity in virtual discussions, the occasional result is a hostile "flame war."

Moreover, the Internet, like television, diverts time from real relationships. Cyber-romances are not the developmental equivalent of real dating. Cyber-sex is artificial intimacy. Individualized cyber-entertainment displaces getting together for games of Bridge or Euchre. Such artificiality and isolation is regrettable, because our ancestral history predisposes our needing real-time relationships, replete with smirks, smiles, and smooches. No wonder that when Carnegie-Mellon University researchers followed 169 new Internet users for two years they found increased loneliness and depression and decreased social engagement (Kraut & others, 1998). And no wonder a Stanford University survey found that 25 percent of more than 4,000 adults surveyed reported that their time online had reduced time spent in person and on the phone with family and friends (Nie & Erbring, 2000).

Point: But most folks don't perceive the Internet to be isolating. Another national survey found that "Internet users in general—and online women in particular—believe that their use of e-mail has strengthened their relationships and increased their contact with relatives and friends" (Pew, 2000). Internet use may displace in-person intimacy, but it also displaces television watching. And if one-click cyber-shopping is bad for your local bookstore, it frees time for relationships. Telecommuting does the same, enabling many people to work from home and to have more time for their families.

What's more, why say that computer-formed relationships are unreal? On the Internet your looks and location cease to matter. Your appearance, age, and race don't deter people from relating to you based on what's more genuinely important—your shared interests and values. In workplace and professional networks, computer-mediated discussions are less influenced by status and are therefore more candid and equally participatory. Computer-mediated communication fosters more spontaneous self-disclosure than face-to-face conversation (Joinson, 2001).

By 2003, online dating sites were receiving 45 million visits per month (Harmon, 2003). Americans alone, in the first half of 2003, spent US$214 million on Internet dating sites—almost triple their spending in all of 2001 (Egan, 2003).

Most Internet flirtations go nowhere. "Everyone I know who has tried online dating . . . agrees that we loathe spending (wasting?) hours gabbing to someone and then meeting him and realizing that he is a creep," observed one Toronto woman (Dicum, 2003). But friendships and romantic relationships that form on the Internet are *more* likely to last for at least two years, report Katelyn McKenna and John Bargh, and their colleagues (Bargh & others, 2002; McKenna & Bargh, 1998, 2000; McKenna & others, 2002). In one experiment, they found that people disclosed more, with greater honesty and less posturing, when they met people online. They also felt more liking for people whom they conversed with online for 20 minutes than for those met for the same time face-to-face. This was even true when they unknowingly met the *same* person in both contexts. People surveyed similarly feel that Internet friendships are as real, important, and close as offline relationships.

Counterpoint: The Internet allows people to be who they really are, but also to feign who they really aren't, sometimes in the interests of sexual exploitation. And Internet sexual media, like other forms of pornography, likely serve to distort people's perceptions of sexual reality, decrease the attractiveness of their real-life partner, prime men to perceive women in sexual terms, make sexual coercion seem more trivial, provide mental scripts for how to act in sexual situations, increase arousal, and lead to disinhibition and imitation of loveless sexual behaviours.

Finally, suggests Robert Putnam (2000), the social benefits of computer-mediated communication are constrained by two other realities: The "digital divide" accentuates social and educational inequalities between the world's haves and have-nots. And, while "cyber-balkanization" enables BMW owners to network, it also, as we noted in Module 14, enables White supremacists to find and feed each other. The first reality may be remedied with lowering prices and increasing public access locations. The second is intrinsic to the medium.

As the debate over the Internet's social consequences continues, "the most important question," says Putnam (p. 180), will be "not what the Internet will do to us, but what we will do with it? . . . How can we harness this promising technology for thickening community ties? How can we develop the technology to enhance social presence, social feedback, and social cues? How can we use the prospect of fast, cheap communication to enhance the now fraying fabric of our real communities?"

ENDING RELATIONSHIPS

Often, love dies. What factors predict marital dissolution? How do couples typically detach or renew their relationships?

In 1971, a man wrote a love poem to his bride, slipped it into a bottle, and dropped it into the Pacific Ocean between Seattle and Hawaii. A decade later, a jogger found it on a Guam beach:

> If, by the time this letter reaches you, I am old and gray, I know that our love will be as fresh as it is today.
>
> It may take a week or it may take years for this note to find you. . . . If this should never reach you, it will still be written in my heart that I will go to extreme means to prove my love for you. Your husband, Bob.

The woman to whom the love note was addressed was reached by phone. When the note was read to her she burst out laughing. And the more she heard, the harder she laughed. "We're divorced," she finally said, and slammed down the phone.

So it often goes. Comparing their unsatisfying relationship with the support and affection they imagine is available elsewhere, people are divorcing. Indeed, sometimes divorce seems inevitable. Headlines scream "Two-thirds of marriages end in divorce!" However, are these really accurate statements? It turns out that the statistics are a little more complicated. Using the most up-to-date numbers (from 2004), Statistics Canada reports that 38 percent of all Canadian marriages will end in divorce. Although perceptions are that divorce rates are increasing (and, indeed, they are five times higher than prior to the reform of the Marriage Act in 1968), the divorce rate has been relatively steady for approximately 20 years. Enduring relationships are rooted in enduring love and satisfaction, but also in inattention to possible alternative partners, fear of the termination cost, and a sense of moral obligation (Adams & Jones, 1997; Miller, 1997).

A 1988 national survey conducted by the Gallup Organization offers a dismal conclusion: Two out of three 35- to 54-year-olds had divorced, separated, or been close to separation (Colasanto & Shriver, 1989). If this pattern continues, "our nation will soon reach the point where the dominant experience of adults will have been marital instability."

Britain's royal House of Windsor knows well the hazards of modern marriage. The fairy-tale marriages of Princess Margaret, Princess Anne, Prince Charles, and Prince Andrew all crumbled, smiles replaced with stony stares. Shortly after her 1986 marriage to Prince Andrew, Sarah Ferguson gushed, "I love his wit, his charm, his looks. I worship him." Andrew reciprocated her euphoria: "She is the best thing in my life." Six years later, Andrew, having decided her friends were "philistines," and Sarah, having derided Andrew's boorish behaviour as "terribly gauche," called it quits (*Time*, 1992).

Who Divorces?

Divorce rates vary widely by country, ranging from .01 percent of the population in Bolivia, the Philippines, and Spain to 4.7 percent annually in the world's most divorce-prone country, the United States. To predict a culture's divorce rates, it helps to know its values (Triandis, 1994). Individualistic cultures (where love is a feeling and people ask, "What does my heart say?") have more divorce than do communal cultures (where love entails obligation and people ask, "What will other people say?"). Individualists marry "for as long as we both shall love"; collectivists more often for life. Individualists expect more passion and personal fulfillment in a marriage, which puts greater pressure on the relationship (Dion & Dion, 1993). "Keeping romance alive" was rated as important to a good marriage by 78 percent of American women surveyed and 29 percent of Japanese women (*American Enterprise*, 1992).

Interestingly, divorce in Canada depends on what province or territory you live in. By far, the highest divorce rate in Canada (in 2003) was in Quebec. Ontario, British Columbia, and the Yukon cluster together as the next group. Lower are the Maritime Provinces (Nova Scotia, New Brunswick, and PEI), the Prairies (Manitoba and Saskatchewan), and Nunavut and the Northwest Territories, which all have a similar rate of divorce. Finally, Newfoundland and Labrador wins as the province with the lowest divorce rate in Canada. Why do these differences exist? Could this be the result of cultural or religious differences among provinces? Or might it be due to the availability of alternatives? To date, no study seems to have addressed this. However, the research provides some suggestions.

Risk of divorce also depends on who marries whom (Fergusson & others, 1984; Myers, 2000; Tzeng, 1992). If these factors vary by province, this might explain some of the differences in divorce rates. People usually stay married if they:

- Married after age 20;
- Both grew up in stable, two-parent homes;
- Dated for a long while before marriage;
- Are well and similarly educated;
- Enjoy a stable income from a good job;
- Live in a small town or on a farm;
- Did not cohabit or become pregnant before marriage;
- Are religiously committed; and
- Are of similar age, faith, and education.

None of these predictors, by itself, is essential to a stable marriage. But if none of these things is true for someone, marital breakdown is an almost sure bet. If all are true, they are *very* likely to stay together until death. This list of predictors of marriage success is particularly relevant to one of the authors of this textbook. While Steve was still a graduate student at Queen's University, Harry Reis, a renowned relationship researcher from the University of Rochester, visited the psychology department to give a guest lecture. During drinks afterward, Steve got to talking about his relationship with his then-fiancée, Isabel. Steve excitedly told Dr. Reis about his beautiful and charming fiancée, and at the end of the conversation Dr. Reis gave his prediction for their relationship. They differed in age, they had no stable income, they lived together before they were married, Isabel's parents were divorced, they were moving to a big city, and neither were religiously committed. Dr. Reis suggested that, according to the research, the relationship would not last. However, to date (seven years later) they are still happily married. Perhaps this is another example of correlation not necessarily indicating causation? However, perhaps this simply illustrates it is difficult to predict the outcome for an individual (or couple, in this case) from data based on a large group. Exceptions to the rule will always occur. Similarly, "anecdotal evidence" is not really evidence at all. We cannot use one example (or one couple) to prove (or disprove) the existence of a relationship between variables.

The Detachment Process

Severing bonds produces a predictable sequence of agitated preoccupation with the lost partner, followed by deep sadness and, eventually, the beginnings of emotional detachment and a return to normal living (Hazan & Shaver, 1994). Even newly separated couples who have long ago ceased feeling affection are often surprised at their desire to be near the former partner. Deep and longstanding attachments seldom break quickly; detaching is a process, not an event.

Among dating couples, the closer and longer the relationship and the fewer the available alternatives, the more painful the breakup (Simpson, 1987). Surprisingly, Roy Baumeister and Sara Wotman (1992) report that, months or years later, people recall more pain over spurning someone's love than over having been spurned. Their distress arises from guilt over hurting someone, from upset over the heartbroken lover's persistence, or from uncertainty over how to respond. Among married couples, breakup has additional costs: shocked parents and friends, guilt over broken vows, possibly restricted parental rights. Still, each year millions of couples are willing to pay such costs to extricate themselves from what they perceive as the greater costs of continuing a painful, unrewarding relationship. Such costs include, in one study of 328 married couples, a tenfold increase in depression symptoms when a marriage is marked by discord rather than satisfaction (O'Leary & others, 1994).

When relationships suffer, those without better alternatives or who feel invested in a relationship (through time, energy, mutual friends, possessions, and perhaps children) will seek alternatives to divorce. Caryl Rusbult and her colleagues (1986, 1987, 1998) have explored three other ways of coping with a failing relationship. Some people exhibit *loyalty*—by waiting for conditions to improve. The problems are too painful to speak of and the risks of separation are too great, so the loyal partner perseveres, hoping the good old days will return. Others (especially men) exhibit *neglect*; they ignore the partner and allow the relationship to deteriorate. When painful dissatisfactions are ignored, an insidious emotional uncoupling ensues as the partners talk less and begin redefining their lives without each other. Still others will *voice* their concerns and take active steps to improve the relationship by discussing problems, seeking advice, and attempting to change.

How does culture influence how we end relationships? Lisa Sinclair and Beverley Fehr at the University of Winnipeg asked the same question. Recall that people from Western cultures tend to have independent self-construals—perceiving themselves to be independent and unique. People from Eastern cultures tend to have more interdependent self-construals—perceiving themselves more in terms of their relationships with others. With this different focus on relationships, should we expect a different preference for ending a relationship? These researchers (see Sinclair & Fehr, 2005) conducted two studies (one where self-construal was measured and one where it was manipulated). Across both studies, the researchers found that people with an independent self-construal tended toward the more active, constructive response of *voice*—expressing their dissatisfaction with the relationship in an attempt to improve it; whereas people with an interdependent self-construal tended to exhibit the more passive, constructive response of *loyalty*—optimistically waiting for conditions to improve.

Study after study—in fact, 115 studies of 45,000 couples—reveal that unhappy couples disagree, command, criticize, and put down. Happy couples more often agree, approve, assent, and laugh (Karney & Bradbury, 1995; Noller & Fitzpatrick, 1990). After observing 2,000 couples, John Gottman (1994, 1998) noted that healthy marriages were not necessarily devoid of conflict. Rather, they were marked by an ability to reconcile differences and to overbalance criticism with affection. In successful marriages, positive interactions (smiling, touching, complimenting, laughing) outnumbered negative interactions (sarcasm, disapproval, insults) by at least a 5 to 1 ratio.

Successful couples have learned, sometimes aided by communication training, to restrain the cancerous putdowns and gut-level, fire-with-fire reactions, to fight fair (by stating feelings without insulting), and to depersonalize conflict with comments like, "I know it's not your fault" (Markman & others, 1988; Notarius & Markman, 1993; Yovetich & Rusbult, 1994). Would unhappy relationships get better if the partners agreed to *act* more as happy couples do—by complaining and criticizing less? By affirming and agreeing more? By setting times aside to voice their concerns? By praying or playing together daily? As attitudes trail behaviours, do affections trail actions?

Joan Kellerman, James Lewis, and James Laird (1989) wondered. They knew that among couples passionately in love, eye gazing is typically prolonged and mutual (Rubin, 1973). Would intimate eye gazing similarly stir feelings between those not in love? To find out, they asked unacquainted male–female pairs to gaze intently for two minutes either at one another's hands or in one another's eyes. When they separated, the eye gazers reported a tingle of attraction and affection toward each other. Simulating love had begun to stir it.

Researcher Robert Sternberg (1988) believes that by enacting and expressing love, the passion of initial romance can evolve into enduring love given the psychological ingredients of marital happiness—kindred minds, social and sexual intimacy, equitable giving and receiving of emotional and material resources. It does, however, become possible to contest the French saying, "Love makes the time pass and time makes love pass." But it takes effort to stem love's decay. It takes effort to carve out time each day to talk over the day's happenings. It takes effort to forgo nagging and bickering and instead to disclose and hear one another's hurts, concerns, and dreams. It takes effort to make a relationship into "a classless utopia of social equality" (Sarnoff & Sarnoff, 1989), in which both partners freely give and receive, share decision making, and enjoy life together.

CONCEPTS TO REMEMBER

Passionate love   p. 270
Two-factor theory of emotion   p. 270
Companionate love   p. 272

Equity   p. 274
Self-disclosure   p. 276
Disclosure reciprocity   p. 276

Please visit the *Exploring Social Psychology* Online Learning Centre at **www.mcgrawhill.ca/college/myers** to participate in module activities, view module videos, access research and study tools, and test your knowledge with interactive quizzes, exercises, and scenarios.

PART FIVE

Applying Social Psychology

By now, you may be asking yourself this question: "Theory is all good, but how does this social psychology stuff apply to the real world?" Throughout the previous sections of this book (on social thinking, social influence, and social relations), we have given many examples of how social psychology can be applied to the real world. However, there are some areas where the applied elements are more obvious.

Therefore, in this section of the text, we look at three areas where the roles of social psychology and social psychological processes have been extensively explored in order to better understand what is happening in our world: the media, the law, and the environment.

Media and Social Behaviour

D o the media influence people's behaviour? Can watching violence on TV or playing violent video games affect how we behave in the real world? The answer you get depends on whom you ask. The prevailing view among people in the entertainment industry is that violent people are violent—what they watch is a symptom, not the cause of the behaviour. The media are simply giving us what we want. Guy Paquette at l'Université Laval found that between 1993 and 2001, although there was significant pressure on broadcasters to reduce violence in their shows, the amount of violence depicted in the French- and English-language media has consistently increased in Canada (Paquette, 2004). Statistics Canada reports that although the overall crime rate has declined slightly since 1984, violent crime rates are 35 percent higher than 20 years ago. Is it just a coincidence that in the last 40 years violent behaviour in society has correlated with violence in the media?

In this module, we'll take a look at the social consequences of sexually explicit material, and the effects of modelling violence in movies, on television, and in video games.

The average child spends many hours per week engaged with media such as television and video games. Can exposure to violent content in media affect how children interact with others?

PORNOGRAPHY AND SEXUAL VIOLENCE

Repeated exposure to fictional eroticism has several effects. It can decrease one's attraction to one's less exciting, real-life partner (Kenrick & others, 1989). It can also increase one's acceptance of extramarital sex and of women's sexual submission to men (Zillmann, 1989b). Rock video images of macho men and sexually acquiescent women similarly colour viewers' perceptions of men and women (Hansen, 1989; Hansen & Hansen, 1988; St. Lawrence & Joyner, 1991). (This has prompted one comedian to observe that all this might change if male singers were required to have women their own age in their videos with them.)

Pornography has become big business. In the United States, more money is spent on pornography than professional football, baseball, and basketball combined—more than $10 billion per year. To date, there are more than 400,000 for-profit pornography websites (National Research Council, 2002; Rich, 2001; Schlosser, 2003). In one survey of university students, 57 percent of men and 35 percent of women reported having sought out sex-related websites, though only 6 percent of men and 1 percent of women did so "frequently" (Banfield & McCabe, 2001).

Social-psychological research on pornography has focused mostly on depictions of sexual violence. A typical, sexually violent episode finds a man forcing himself upon a woman. She at first resists and tries to fight off her attacker. Gradually she becomes sexually aroused, and her resistance melts. By the end she is in ecstasy, pleading for more. We have all viewed or read nonpornographic versions of this sequence: She resists, he persists. Dashing man grabs and forcibly kisses protesting woman. Within moments, the arms that were pushing him away are clutching him tight, her resistance overwhelmed by her unleashed passion. This theme has been consistent for years through movies as diverse as *Gone With the Wind* and *Indiana Jones*, and through TV shows as diverse as *Friends* and *Desperate Housewives*.

Social psychologists report that viewing such fictional scenes of a man overpowering and arousing a woman can (1) distort one's perceptions of how women actually respond to sexual coercion and (2) increase men's aggression against women, at least in laboratory settings.

Distorted Perceptions of Sexual Reality

Does viewing sexual violence reinforce the myth that some women would welcome sexual assault—that "no doesn't really mean no"? To find out, Neil Malamuth and James Check (1981) showed University of Manitoba men either two nonsexual movies or two movies depicting a man sexually overcoming a woman. A week later, when surveyed by a different experimenter, those who saw the films with mild sexual violence were more accepting of violence against women. Other studies confirm that exposure to pornography increases acceptance of the rape myth (Oddone-Paolucci & others, 2000).

Viewing slasher movies has much the same effect. Men shown films such as the *Texas Chainsaw Massacre* become desensitized to brutality and more likely to view rape victims unsympathetically (Linz & others, 1988, 1989). While spending three evenings watching sexually violent movies, male viewers in an experiment by Charles Mullin and Daniel Linz (1995) became progressively less bothered by the raping and slashing. Compared to others not exposed to the films, they also, three days later, expressed less sympathy for domestic violence victims and they rated the victims' injuries as less severe. In fact, said researchers Edward Donnerstein, Daniel Linz, and Steven Penrod (1987), what better way for an evil character to get people to react calmly to the torture and mutilation of women than to show a gradually escalating series of such films?

Aggression against Women

Evidence also suggests that pornography may contribute to men's actual aggression toward women. Correlational studies raise that possibility. John Court (1985) noted that across the world, as pornography became more widely available during the 1960s and 1970s, the rate of reported rapes sharply increased—except in countries and areas where pornography was controlled. (The examples that counter this trend, such as Japan, where violent pornography is available but the rape rate is low, remind us that other factors are also important.)

When interviewed, Canadian and American sexual offenders commonly acknowledge pornography use. For example, William Marshall at Queen's University (1989) reported that Ontario rapists and child molesters used pornography much more than men who were not sexual offenders. An FBI study also reports considerable exposure to pornography among serial killers, as does the Los Angeles Police Department among most child sex abusers (Bennett, 1991; Ressler & others, 1988). Of course, this *correlation* cannot prove that pornography is a contributing *cause* of rape. Maybe the offenders' use of pornography is merely a symptom and not a cause of their basic deviance. Moreover, the evidence is mixed: Some studies find prior pornography use (including childhood exposure to pornography) uncorrelated with sexual aggression (Bauserman, 1996).

Although limited to the sorts of short-term behaviours that can be studied in the laboratory, controlled experiments reveal cause and effect. A consensus statement by 21 leading social scientists sums up the results: "Exposure to violent pornography increases punitive behaviour toward women" (Koop, 1987).

If the ethics of conducting such experiments trouble you, rest assured that these researchers appreciate the controversial and powerful experience they are giving participants. Only after giving their knowing consent do people participate. Moreover, after the experiment, researchers debunk any myths the films communicated. One hopes that such debriefing sufficiently offsets the vivid image of a supposedly euphoric rape victim. Judging from studies with University of Manitoba and Winnipeg students by James Check and Neil Malamuth (1984; Malamuth & Check, 1984), it does. Those who read erotic rape stories and were then fully debriefed became *less* accepting of the "women-enjoy-rape" myth than students who had not seen the film.

Justification for this experimentation is not only scientific but also humanitarian. Statistics Canada reports that one in four Canadian women will be sexually assaulted

The Story Behind the Research

Dr. Robert Sinclair has had a long interest in how people's perceptions of social situations influence behaviour. Dr. Sinclair, who is now at Laurentian University in Sudbury, Ontario, conducted an interesting study on a group of University of Alberta undergraduates (see Sinclair & others, 1995). In one of his studies, he was interested in finding out if feedback after viewing an erotic or sexually aggressive film might mitigate any negative effect of the film on viewers.

Dr. Sinclair became interested in how social comparison might influence people's reactions to sexual content in movies shortly after an undergraduate, Theresa Lee, approached him about doing her honours thesis with him. He asked her what she was interested in and she replied, "sex." Theresa Lee, whose parents were from Hong Kong, was an aspiring actress and wanted to explore how people reacted to the depiction of women on film. Sinclair and Lee developed a research project to determine how men perceive and react to violent and nonviolent erotic films. If people are reminded that pornography is degrading to women, does that influence their response to the films?

They presented 70 male students with movies that either had strictly erotic content (*Night Trips*, a couples-oriented adult film), sexually violent content (rape scenes from *The Accused* and *A Clockwork Orange*), or violence toward women (scenes from *Extremities* and *Sleeping With the Enemy*). Participants watched one of these films with a confederate. Participants were randomly assigned to either a social comparison or control condition. In the social comparison condition, the confederate indicated that he felt the film was disgusting and degrading to women. In the control condition, nothing was said.

Students' sexual arousal, levels of affect, and perceptions of violence were then assessed. Later, in a purportedly separate study on punishment and learning, participants had the opportunity to punish women by administering electric shock. Results showed that in conditions where participants watched the erotic film and received feedback about the degrading nature of the movie, participants' sexual arousal and affect significantly reduced, and perceptions of violence increased. Further, in all film conditions, feedback led to a reduction in aggressiveness toward women as assessed by level and intensity of shock. Thus, feedback about the nature of films can influence people's interpretation of the film as well as later behaviour toward women. This suggests one way in which the negative effects of violence and pornography may be mitigated. (Interestingly, after graduating from the University of Alberta, Theresa Lee moved to Hong Kong and has become a well-known actress in the mainstream film industry there.) |

in their lifetime. Although rates of sexual assault have decreased in the last ten years, they are still high. Eighty-five percent of sexual assault victims are women and girls, and 60 percent of sexual offences reported to police involve people under 18 (Statistics Canada, 2005). In the U.S., in surveys of 6,200 college students nationwide and 2,200 Ohio working women, Mary Koss and her colleagues (1988, 1990, 1993) found that 28 percent of the women reported an experience that met the legal definition of rape or attempted rape. Surveys in other industrialized countries produce similar results. Three in four stranger rapes and nearly all acquaintance rapes went unreported to police. Careful surveys conducted by Statistics Canada estimate that upward of 90 percent of sexual assaults are never reported. Thus, the known rape rate *greatly* underestimates the actual rape rate. Moreover, many more women—half in one survey of college women (Sandberg & others, 1985)—report having suffered some form of sexual assault while on a date, and even more have experienced verbal sexual coercion or harassment (Craig, 1990; Pryor, 1987). Men who behave in sexually coercive, aggressive ways typically desire dominance, exhibit hostility toward women, and are sexually promiscuous (Anderson & others, 1997; Malamuth & others, 1995).

We must caution against oversimplifying the complex causes of rape—which is no more attributable to any one cause than is cancer. However, viewing violence, especially sexual violence, can have antisocial effects.

In the contest of individual versus collective rights, people in most Western nations typically side with individual rights. So, as an alternative to censorship, many psychologists favour "media awareness training." Recall that pornography researchers have successfully resensitized and educated participants to women's actual responses to sexual violence. Could educators similarly promote critical viewing skills? By sensitizing people to the view of women that predominates in pornography and to issues of sexual harassment and violence, it should be possible to counter the myth that women enjoy being coerced. Dr. Robert Sinclair's research (see The Story Behind the Research on p. 290) suggests one approach that might help.

OLC
Activity 25.1

Is such a hope naive? Consider: Without banning cigarettes, the number of smokers dropped from 50 percent in 1965 to 18 percent in 2003 (see Module 11). As public consciousness changed, script writers, producers, and media executives decided that exploitative images of ethnic and sexual minorities were not good. Will we one day look back with embarrassment on the time when movies entertained people with scenes of exploitation, mutilation, and sexual coercion?

OLC
Video 25.1

Picture this scene from one of Albert Bandura's experiments (Bandura & others, 1961). A Stanford nursery school child is put to work on an interesting art activity. An adult is in another part of the room, where there are Tinker Toys, a mallet, and a big, inflated "Bobo doll." After a minute of working with the Tinker Toys, the adult gets up and for almost 10 minutes attacks the inflated doll. She pounds it with the mallet, kicks it, and throws it, all the while yelling, "Sock him in the nose. . . . Knock him down. . . . Kick him."

After observing this outburst, the child goes to a different room with many very attractive toys. But after two minutes the experimenter interrupts, saying these are her best toys and she must "save them for the other children." The frustrated child now goes into another room with various toys for aggressive and nonaggressive play, two of which are a Bobo doll and a mallet.

Seldom did children who were not exposed to the aggressive adult model display any aggressive play or talk. Although frustrated, they nevertheless played calmly. Those who had observed the aggressive adult were many times more likely to pick up the mallet and lash out at the doll. Watching the adult's aggressive behaviour lowered their inhibitions. Moreover, the children often reproduced the model's acts and said her words. Observing aggressive behaviour had both lowered their inhibitions and taught them ways to aggress.

TELEVISION

We have seen that watching an aggressive model can unleash children's aggressive urges and teach them new ways to aggress. Would watching aggressive models on television similarly affect children? Does television have any similar effects?

Consider these few facts about watching television. Today 99 percent of households have a TV set, more than have bathtubs or telephones. Two-thirds of homes have three or more TV sets, which helps explain why parents' reports of what their children watch correlate minimally with children's reports of what they watch (Donnerstein, 1998). With music channels and news networks spanning the globe, and *Baywatch* and *CSI* having billions of viewers in more than 152 countries, television is creating a global pop culture.

In the average home, the TV is on seven hours a day, with individual household members averaging four hours. Women watch more than men, non-Whites more than Whites, preschoolers and retired people more than those in school or working, and the less educated more than the highly educated (Comstock & Scharrer, 1999).

During all those hours, what social behaviours are modelled? For a quarter century, George Gerbner and other TV watchers (1993, 1994) at the University of Pennsylvania sampled U.S. network prime-time and Saturday morning entertainment programs. From 1994 to 1997, bleary-eyed employees of the National Television Violence Study (1997) analyzed some 10,000 programs from the major networks and cable channels. Their findings? Six in ten programs contained violence ("physically compelling action that threatens to hurt or kill, or actual hurting or killing").

What does it add up to? By the end of elementary school, the average child views some 8,000 TV murders and 100,000 other violent acts (Huston & others, 1992). Reflecting on his 22 years of cruelty counting, Gerbner (1994) lamented: "Humankind has had more bloodthirsty eras but none as filled with *images* of violence as the present. We are awash in a tide of violent representations the world has never seen . . . drenching every home with graphic scenes of expertly choreographed brutality."

Does it matter? Does prime-time crime stimulate the behaviour it depicts? Or, as viewers vicariously participate in aggressive acts, do the shows drain off aggressive energy?

Catharsis Emotional release. The catharsis view of aggression is that the aggressive drive is reduced when one "releases" aggressive energy, either by acting aggressively or by fantasizing aggression.

The latter idea, a variation on the **catharsis** hypothesis, maintains that watching violent drama enables people to release their pent-up hostilities. Defenders of the media cite this theory frequently and remind us that violence predates television. However, as we saw in the module on aggression, support for the catharsis hypothesis is mixed, at best.

Television's Effects on Behaviour

Do viewers imitate violent models? Examples abound of people reenacting television crimes. There are anecdotal reports that criminals are learning new tricks from shows such as *CSI* and *Law & Order*. Indeed, one RCMP officer told the story of how a criminal, in trying to avoid leaving footprints at a crime scene, covered his shoes in duct tape (Patry & others, 2006). Unfortunately for the criminal, he left the duct tape roll at the crime scene—covered in easy-to-read fingerprints.

Correlating TV Viewing and Behaviour

Crime stories are not scientific evidence. Researchers therefore use correlational and experimental studies to examine the effects of viewing violence. One technique, commonly used with schoolchildren, asks whether their TV watching predicts their aggressiveness. To some extent it does. The more violent the content of the child's TV viewing, the more aggressive the child (Eron, 1987; Turner & others, 1986). The relationship is modest but consistently found in the United States, Europe, and Australia.

So can we conclude that a diet of violent TV fuels aggression? Perhaps you are already thinking that because this is a correlational study, the cause–effect relation could also work in the opposite direction. Maybe aggressive children prefer aggressive programs. Or maybe some underlying third factor, such as lower intelligence, predisposes some children both to prefer aggressive programs and to act aggressively.

Researchers have developed two ways to test these alternative explanations. They test the "hidden third factor" explanation by statistically pulling out the influence of some of these possible factors. For example, William Belson (1978; Muson, 1978) studied 1,565 London boys. Compared to those who watched little violence, those who watched a great deal (especially realistic rather than cartoon violence) admitted to 50 percent more violent acts during the preceding six months (for example, "I busted the telephone in a telephone box"). Belson also examined 22 likely third factors, such as family size. The heavy and light viewers still differed after equating them with respect to potential third factors. So Belson surmised that the heavy viewers were indeed more violent *because* of their TV exposure.

Similarly, Leonard Eron and Rowell Huesmann (1980, 1985) found that violence viewing among 875 8-year-olds correlated with aggressiveness even after statistically pulling out several obvious, possible third factors. Moreover, when they restudied these individuals as 19-year-olds, they discovered that viewing violence at age 8 modestly predicted aggressiveness at age 19, but that aggressiveness at age 8 did *not* predict viewing violence at age 19. Aggression followed viewing, not the reverse. They confirmed these findings in follow-up studies of 758 Chicago-area and 220 Finnish youngsters (Huesmann & others, 1984). What is more, when Eron and Huesmann (1984) examined the later criminal conviction records of their initial sample of 8-year-olds, they found that, at age 30, those men who as children had watched a great deal of violent television were more likely to have been convicted of a serious crime (see Figure 25-1 on page 294).

Huesmann and his colleagues (1984, 2003) confirmed these findings in follow-up studies of Chicago-area youngsters. Boys who as 8-year-olds had been in the top 20 percent of violence watchers were, 15 years later, twice as likely as others to acknowledge pushing, grabbing, or shoving their wives, and their violence-viewing female counterparts were twice as likely, as young women, to have thrown something at their husbands.

Adolescent viewing also clues us to future adult behaviours, as Jeffrey Johnson and his co-workers (2002) found when they followed more than 700 lives through time. Among 14-year-olds who watched less than an hour of TV daily, 6 percent were involved in aggressive acts (such as assault, robbery, or threats of injury) at ages 16 to

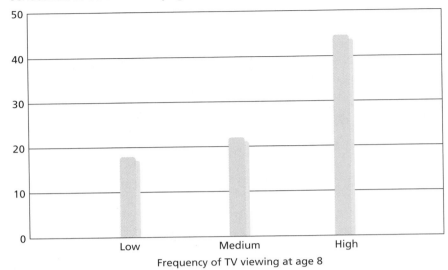

Seriousness of criminal acts by age 30

Frequency of TV viewing at age 8

FIGURE 25-1
Children's television viewing and later criminal activity. Violence viewing at age 8 was a predictor of a serious criminal offence by age 30.

Data from Eron & Huesmann, 1984.

22, as were five times as many—29 percent—of those who had watched more than three hours a day.

Another fact to ponder: Where television goes, increased violence follows. Even murder rates increase when and where television comes. In Canada and the United States, the homicide rate doubled between 1957 and 1974 as violent television spread. In census regions where television came later, the homicide rate jumped later, too. In White South Africa, where television was not introduced until 1975, a similar near doubling of the homicide rate did not begin until after 1975 (Centerwall, 1989). And in a closely studied rural Canadian town where television came late, playground aggression doubled soon after (Williams, 1986).

Notice that these studies illustrate how researchers are now using correlational findings to *suggest* cause and effect. Yet, an infinite number of possible third factors could be creating a merely coincidental relation between viewing violence and aggression. Fortunately, however, the experimental method can control these extraneous factors. If we randomly assign some children to watch a violent film and others a nonviolent film, any later aggression difference between the two groups will be due to the only factor that distinguishes them: what they watched.

TV Viewing Experiments

The trailblazing experiments by Albert Bandura and Richard Walters (1963) sometimes had young children view the adult pounding the inflated doll on film instead of observing it live—with much the same effect. Then Leonard Berkowitz and Russell Geen

(1966) found that angered college students who viewed a violent film acted more aggressively than did similarly angered students who viewed nonaggressive films. These laboratory experiments, coupled with growing public concern, were sufficient to prompt the U.S. Surgeon General to commission 50 new research studies during the early 1970s. By and large, these studies confirmed that viewing violence amplifies aggression (Anderson & Bushman, 2002) .

For example, research teams led by Ross Parke (1977) in the United States and Jacques Leyens (1975) in Belgium showed institutionalized American and Belgian delinquent boys a series of either aggressive or nonaggressive commercial films. Their consistent finding: "Exposure to movie violence . . . led to an increase in viewer aggression." Compared to the week preceding the film series, physical attacks increased sharply in cottages where boys were viewing violent films. Dolf Zillmann and James Weaver (1999) similarly exposed men and women, on four consecutive days, to violent or nonviolent feature films. When participating in a different project on the fifth day, those exposed to the violent films were more hostile to the research assistant.

The aggression provoked in these experiments is not assault and battery; it's more on the scale of a shove in the lunch line, a cruel comment, a threatening gesture. Nevertheless, the convergence of evidence is striking. "The irrefutable conclusion," said a 1993 American Psychological Association youth violence commission, is "that viewing violence increases violence." This is especially so among people with aggressive tendencies (Bushman, 1995). The violence viewing effect also is strongest when an attractive person commits justified, realistic violence that goes unpunished and that shows no pain or harm (Donnerstein, 1998).

All in all, conclude researchers Brad Bushman and Craig Anderson (2001), violence-viewing's effect on aggression surpasses the effect of passive smoking on lung cancer, calcium intake on bone mass, and homework on academic achievement. As with smoking and cancer, not everyone shows the effect—other factors matter as well. The cumulative long-term effects are what's worrisome, and corporate interests pooh-pooh the evidence. But the evidence is now "overwhelming," say Bushman and Anderson: "Exposure to media violence causes significant increases in aggression." The research base is large, the methods diverse, and the overall findings consistent, echo a National Institute of Mental Health task force of leading media violence researchers (Anderson & others, 2003). "Our in-depth review . . . reveals unequivocal evidence that exposure to media violence can increase the likelihood of aggressive and violent behaviour in both immediate and long-term contexts."

Why Does TV Viewing Affect Behaviour?

The conclusion drawn by these researchers is *not* that television and pornography are primary causes of social violence. Rather, they say television is *a* cause. Even if it is just one ingredient in a complex recipe for violence, it is one that, like cyclamates, is potentially controllable (see Broune & Hamilton-Griachrissis, 2005). Given the convergence of correlational and experimental evidence, researchers have explored *why* viewing violence has this effect.

Consider three possibilities (Geen & Thomas, 1986). One is that it is not the violent content itself that causes social violence but the *arousal* it produces (Mueller &

others, 1983; Zillmann, 1989a). As we noted earlier, arousal tends to spill over: One type of arousal energizes other behaviours.

Other research shows that viewing violence *disinhibits*. In Bandura's experiment, the adult's punching of the Bobo doll seemed to legitimate such outbursts and to lower the children's inhibitions. Viewing violence primes the viewer for aggressive behaviour by activating violence-related thoughts (Berkowitz, 1984; Bushman & Geen, 1990; Josephson, 1987). Listening to music with sexually violent lyrics seems to have a similar effect, predisposing younger males to accept the rape myth and to behave more aggressively (Barongan & Hall, 1995; Johnson & others, 1995; Pritchard, 1998).

Media portrayals also evoke *imitation*. The children in Bandura's experiments reenacted the specific behaviours they had witnessed. The commercial television industry is hard-pressed to dispute that television leads viewers to imitate what they have seen: Its advertisers model consumption.

Prosocial behaviour
Positive, constructive, helpful social behaviour; the opposite of antisocial behaviour.

If the ways of relating and problem solving modelled on television do trigger imitation, especially among young viewers, then modelling **prosocial behaviour** (see Module 22) should be socially beneficial. Happily, it is. Television's subtle influence can indeed teach children positive lessons in behaviour. Susan Hearold (1986) statistically combined 108 comparisons of prosocial programs with neutral programs or no program. She found that, on average, "if the viewer watched prosocial programs instead of neutral programs, he would [at least temporarily] be elevated from the 50th to the 74th percentile in prosocial behavior—typically altruism."

In one such study, researchers Lynette Friedrich and Aletha Stein (1973; Stein & Friedrich, 1972) showed preschool children episodes of *Mister Rogers' Neighborhood* each day for four weeks as part of their nursery school program. During this viewing period, children from less-educated homes became more cooperative, helpful, and likely to state their feelings. In a follow-up study, kindergartners who viewed four *Mister Rogers* programs were able to state its prosocial content, both on a test and in puppet play (Friedrich & Stein, 1975; see also Coates & others, 1976).

VIDEO GAMES

Do video games influence behaviour? Illegal street racing has become a major problem in Canada. There have been a number of deadly crashes in recent years. For example, in February 2006 in Vancouver, three men in their twenties died when their BMW split in half after colliding with a metal light standard during a street race. They had reached speeds of 160 km/h before the crash. The previous week, two 18-year-olds raced down a Toronto street at 140 km/h—90 km/h over the posted limit. At the end of the race, a taxi driver was killed when one of the cars struck his cab as he tried to turn on to the street on which the cars were racing. Police investigating the accident found a copy of the video game *Need for Speed* in the backseat of one of the cars.

"The scientific debate over *whether* media violence has an effect is basically over," contend Douglas Gentile and Craig Anderson (2003). Researchers are now shifting their attention to video games, which have exploded in popularity and are exploding with increasing brutality. Educational research shows that "video games are excellent teaching tools," note Gentile and Anderson. "If health video games can successfully teach health behaviors, and flight simulator video games can teach people how to fly, then what should we expect violent murder-simulating games to teach?"

The Games Kids Play

In 2002, the video game industry celebrated its 30th birthday. Since the first video game in 1972 we have moved from electronic Ping-Pong to splatter games (Anderson, 2004; Gentile & Anderson, 2003).

Today's mass murder simulators are not obscure games. By the turn of the twenty-first century some 200 million games a year were being purchased, and the average 2- to 17-year-old was playing video games seven hours a week. In one survey of fourth-graders, 59 percent of girls and 73 percent of boys reported their favourite games as violent ones (Anderson, 2003, 2004). Games rated "M" (mature) are supposedly intended for sale only to those 17 and older but often are marketed to those younger. The U.S. Federal Trade Commission found that in four out of five attempts, underage children could easily purchase them (Pereira, 2003).

Effects of the Games Kids Play

Concerns about violent video games heightened after teen assassins in Kentucky, Arkansas, and Colorado enacted the horrific violence they had so often played on-screen. People wondered: When youth role-play attacking and dismembering people, do they learn anything that stays with them?

Most smokers don't die of heart disease. Most abused children don't become abusive. And most people who spend hundreds of hours rehearsing human slaughter live gentle lives. This enables video game defenders, like tobacco and TV interests, to say their products are harmless. "There is absolutely no evidence, none, that playing a violent game leads to aggressive behavior," contended Doug Lowenstein (2000), president of the Interactive Digital Software Association. Gentile and Anderson nevertheless offer some reasons why violent game playing *might* have a more toxic effect than watching violent television. With game playing, players

- identify with, and play the role of, a violent character.
- actively rehearse violence, not just passively watch it.
- engage in the whole sequence of enacting violence—selecting victims, acquiring weapons and ammunition, stalking the victim, aiming the weapon, pulling the trigger.
- are engaged with continual violence and threats of attack.
- repeat violent behaviours over and over.
- are rewarded for effective aggression.

For such reasons, military organizations often prepare soldiers to fire in combat (which many in World War II reportedly were hesitant to do) by engaging them with attack simulation games.

But what does the available research actually find? Craig Anderson (2003, 2004; Anderson & others, 2004) offers statistical digests of three dozen available studies that reveal five consistent effects. Playing violent video games, more than playing nonviolent games

- *increases arousal*—heart rate and blood pressure rise.
- *increases aggressive thinking*—for example, Brad Bushman and Anderson (2002) found that after playing games such as *Duke Nukem* and *Mortal Kombat*, university students became more likely to guess that a man whose car was just rear-ended would respond aggressively, by using abusive language, kicking out a window, or starting a fight. Anderson and his colleagues (2003) find that violent music lyrics also prime aggressive thinking, making students more likely to complete "h_t" as "hit" rather than "hat."
- *increases aggressive feelings*—frustration levels rise, as does expressed hostility.
- *increases aggressive behaviours*—after violent game play, children and youth play more aggressively with their peers, get into more arguments with their teachers, and participate in more fights. The effect occurs inside and outside the laboratory, across self-reports, teacher reports, and parent reports, and for reasons illustrated in Figure 25-2.
- *decreases prosocial behaviours*—after violent video game playing, people become slower to help a person whimpering in the hallway outside and slower to offer help to peers.

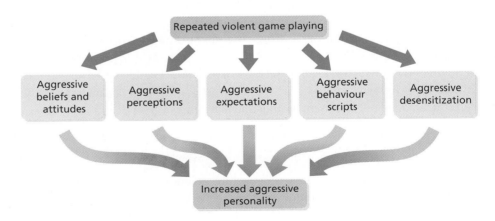

FIGURE 25-2
Violent video game influences on aggressive tendencies.

Adapted from Craig A. Anderson and Brad J. Bushman (2001).

- *increases physical injury*—Craig Emes at McGill University (1997) reviewed the existing literature on the impact of video games on children and concluded that although video games can have a positive impact on children (similar to findings about prosocial TV), playing video games can have negative physical effects (for example, causing seizures and tendonitis) and can lead to aggressive behaviour, particularly among younger children. Bartholow and his colleagues (2005) have found that, similar to TV viewing, exposure to video game violence *causes* increases in aggression.

Moreover, the more violent the games played, the bigger the effects. Video games *have* become more violent, which helps explain why newer studies find the biggest effects. Although much remains to be learned, these studies indicate that, contrary to the catharsis hypothesis, practising violence breeds rather than releases violence.

As a concerned scientist, Anderson (2003, 2004) therefore encourages parents to discover what their kids are ingesting and to ensure that their media diet, as least in their own home, is healthy. Parents may not be able to control what their child watches, plays, and eats in someone else's home, but they can oversee consumption in their own home and provide increased time for alternative activities. Networking with other parents can build a kid-friendly neighbourhood. And schools can help by providing media awareness education.

CONCEPTS TO REMEMBER

Catharsis   p. 292
Prosocial behaviour   p. 296

Please visit the *Exploring Social Psychology* Online Learning Centre at **www.mcgrawhill.ca/college/myers** to participate in module activities, view module videos, access research and study tools, and test your knowledge with interactive quizzes, exercises, and scenarios.

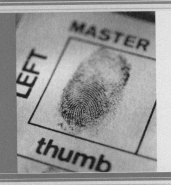

Social Psychology and the Law

Eyewitness testimony, police investigations, court judgments, and jury decision making are all areas in which the law intersects with aspects of social psychology. Can you think of factors for each of these areas that might help or hinder due legal process?

Think back to the Tom Sophonow case you read about in Module 1. Sophonow had been in Winnipeg at the time of a grisly murder. The murderer had entered a donut shop, locked the door, and proceeded to rob and murder the young woman working behind the counter. As he was leaving the crime scene, he ran into a man who was trying to enter the shop. He told the man the shop was closed. Nonetheless, the man soon discovered the dead teenager and ran outside to confront the murderer. The murderer threatened the witness with a knife and ran off. Later, the police interviewed Tom Sophonow and asked him if he would mind providing a photo to use in a lineup. Interestingly, the witness remembered that the man had worn a cowboy hat. Before police took a picture of Sophonow, they asked him to put on a cowboy hat.

If you had been in Sophonow's situation, what would you have done? Would you have let the police take your photo? Would you have believed that you had nothing to worry about because you were innocent? Of course you would. So did Sophonow. So do most innocent people (Kassin, 2005).

The police asked the witness from the coffee shop to try to identify the criminal from a photo lineup that included a picture of Sophonow in the cowboy hat. The witness was not able to do so. Nonetheless, police arrested Sophonow. After the witness saw Sophonow in custody and in handcuffs, he said he was "90 percent sure" Sophonow

Tom Sophnow leaving his retrial in 1985 and in 2000, at a press conference in which police apologized for his wrongful conviction in the grisly murder of Barbara Stoppel in 1981.

OLC
Activity 26.1

was the man he had seen leaving the crime scene. Sophonow was eventually convicted, based largely on the eyewitness testimony. Faced with a confident eyewitness would you have convicted Sophonow? Visit the Online Learning Centre and complete Activity 26.1 to submit your verdict. Then go back to Activity 1.1 and revisit the case.

EYEWITNESS TESTIMONY

We know now that Tom Sophonow is not alone. He was convicted in large part due to a mistaken eyewitness. There is little evidence that can be presented at trial that is more compelling than a confident eyewitness. Eyewitnesses are even believed when their evidence has been shown to be discredited (Whitley, 1987). Elizabeth Loftus, a pioneer in the eyewitness field (Loftus, 1974, 1979) conducted a study that shows the power of eyewitness testimony to influence trial outcomes. Students were presented with a hypothetical criminal case based on circumstantial evidence, or the same evidence and one eyewitness. When the case had only the circumstantial evidence, 18 percent of jurors voted for conviction. However, when there was a confident eyewitness, 72 percent voted for conviction. Interestingly, when the eyewitness was discredited (it turned out she had 20/400—extremely nearsighted—vision), 68 percent of jurors still voted for conviction.

How Many Eyewitnesses Are Wrong?

There are hundreds of documented cases where honest eyewitness mistakes have led to false imprisonment. Can jurors tell when an eyewitness is mistaken? Gary Wells and Rod Lindsay (see Wells & others, 1979) conducted studies at the University of Alberta and found that both correct and incorrect eyewitnesses are believed about 80 percent of the time.

OLC
Activity 26.2

Confidence–accuracy correlation The finding that the correlation between the confidence and accuracy of an eyewitness is weak to nonexistent.

Although it is impossible to know how often eyewitnesses make mistakes, we know that mistakes get made. For example, of approximately 8,000 sexual assault cases where DNA was tested by the U.S. Federal Bureau of Investigation, the suspect was exonerated approximately 25 percent of the time (Scheck & others, 2001). In most of those cases, eyewitness identification was the primary way in which suspects were identified. A group of lawyers out of a New York law school have developed what is called the Innocence Project. Students and professors investigate cases where DNA evidence is available but was not tested to determine if people who have been convicted of the crimes are actually innocent (testing of DNA was not common in all cases until 1993, when evidence rules changed). Of the (to date) 140 Innocence Project cases where people have been falsely imprisoned and subsequently exonerated, more than 80 percent involved mistaken eyewitness identification. Not surprisingly, improving the accuracy of eyewitness evidence has been a focus of social psychologists for many years. How good of an eyewitness would you make? Visit the Online Learning Centre and complete Activity 26.2 to find out.

Why are eyewitnesses so compelling? If an eyewitness has no reason to lie, and they say they saw someone commit a crime, juries will believe them. This is particularly true when the witness is confident (Luus & Wells, 1994). Indeed, in the United States, the *Neil v. Biggers* criteria, used to assess eyewitness accuracy, specifically say that an eyewitness's confidence in his or her identification should be used to determine accuracy. However, the **confidence–accuracy correlation** (Sporer & others, 1995) is notoriously low, even at the best of times. Although the confidence–accuracy correlation varies wildly from study to study, it is typically around .30 (a weak positive correlation). However, by the time a witness gets to trial, so many factors may have influenced their confidence that confidence is unlikely to predict accuracy at all (Wells & Bradfield, 1998).

Why Eyewitnesses Make Mistakes

Literally hundreds of studies have explored the accuracy of eyewitness identifications (see Wells, 1993; Wells & others, 2000). These researchers have found that there are a number of different factors that can affect eyewitness accuracy. An important distinction that can be made among these factors is the difference between *system variables*—factors the legal system can control, and *estimator variables*—factors the legal system cannot control. With system variables, one can construct the situation so that errors may be avoided.

An example of an estimator variable is the race of the criminal relative to the witness (see Bothwell & others, 1989; Smith & others, 2001, 2004). Research has shown a consistent decrease in eyewitness accuracy if the witness and the suspect are of different races. Because this decrement is greater when the majority group member identifies a minority, relative to when a minority attempts to identify a majority group member, some researchers have suggested familiarity with the other group may be the cause of the increased error (see Smith & others, 2004, for a review). Other researchers have suggested that different racial groups focus on different facial features. However, a definitive cause has thus far eluded researchers (Ng & Lindsay,

1994). Importantly, there is little the legal system can do to alleviate this problem. Thus, many researchers have argued it may be best to focus on system variables as these are the factors that the legal system will be able to change. Two important elements that can be controlled by the legal system are how eyewitnesses are interviewed and how police lineups are constructed.

Interviewing Eyewitnesses

Almost 2,500 years ago, Plato argued that memory was a "wax tablet" whereupon our everyday experiences left their impressions. An important consequence of this characterization, one that was accepted as truth for some time, is that once a memory is encoded it is set and unchangeable. Although a memory can be "forgotten" for some time, it could eventually be completely and accurately retrieved. The reality is much different. Memory is a constructive process. Memories change over time. They are influenced by our beliefs and expectations. You have probably all experienced this yourself—think of the last time you and a friend got into an argument. Would you give different versions of the story? Probably—and you would both believe you were telling the complete and accurate truth.

Recall the confirmation bias we talked about in Module 7. We ask questions in such a way that the answers we get will tend to confirm our expectations rather than disconfirm them—police do this as well. Not surprisingly, confirmation bias can have a significant effect on how we remember events. Elizabeth Loftus has demonstrated memory construction in a number of experiments. In one study (Loftus & others, 1978) she showed participants slides of a car accident. In one slide, a red Datsun is shown going through either a stop sign or a yield sign. Half of the participants were then asked if another car passed the Datsun while it was at the stop sign. The other half of participants were asked the same question, but with "yield sign" substituted for "stop sign." Next, participants were presented with pictures from the slide show and asked to choose the picture they saw—either a picture with a stop sign or one with a yield sign. Participants who received the leading question were more likely to "remember" the incorrect information.

At times this can go so far that witnesses may develop completely false memories of events—these memories can be held with just as much confidence as true memories. The Martensville daycare case is an excellent example (*Globe and Mail*, 2002). In 1991, the mother of one of the children being babysat by the Sterling family in the small Saskatchewan town found a suspicious rash on her child's bottom. She suspected her child had been abused and filed a complaint with Saskatchewan police, who began an investigation. Although there was no physical evidence of sexual abuse, the police eventually arrested 9 people, including a police officer, and charged them with more than 40 crimes against a number of children.

John Yuille, an eyewitness researcher from the University of British Columbia, was an expert witness in the case and testified that the police interview tactics were flawed: there were leading and suggestive questions, children were cajoled into giving certain answers, and children were rewarded when they gave the "right answer."

In the end, ten years later, all charges were dropped and the province was forced to pay compensation to those arrested.

Cognitive interview
An interview technique based in cognitive psychology, focusing on context reinstatement to enhance recall of events.

To combat these types of problems, Ron Fisher and his colleagues (for example, Fisher & others, 1987) have designed the **cognitive interview** (CI) technique. In their initial research, Fisher and his colleagues found that after asking an open-ended question to a witness police often interrupted with closed-ended and often misleading questions (questions that could lead to misinformation and changes in memory). They designed the CI to improve how police interviewed witnesses. The CI is based on principles of cognitive psychology that have to do with cues that can help people to recall specific events. Thus, law enforcement officials are encouraged to establish rapport with the witnesses; encourage them to mentally "go back" to the event by having them visualize what they were thinking and feeling at the time of the event; encourage witnesses to give complete answers; ask only open-ended, non-leading questions (for example, asking "What was the criminal wearing?" versus "Can you describe the guy in the black jacket?"); and caution people against guessing about what they had witnessed.

Fisher and his colleagues trained numerous groups of detectives on the CI technique and found that it elicited 50 percent more information from witnesses without increasing the rate of incorrect information recalled. Fisher & Geiselman (1996) report that many police agencies in North America and Great Britain have adopted the CI and now include the interview technique in their standard training package.

Police Lineup Procedures

Every year in North America at least 75,000 people are identified from police lineups and subsequently prosecuted. The most common police lineups used are called **simultaneous lineups**—where photos are shown all at one time (see Figure 26-1). In Canada, the police use 12-person lineups, and they are almost always photo rather than live lineups. The vast majority of police lineups are simultaneous, but is this the best way for police to identify criminals? The simultaneous lineup has some problems (see Lindsay & Wells, 1985; Lindsay & Bellinger, 1999). You can conceive of a simultaneous lineup as much like a multiple-choice test—the right answer (that is, the suspect) is there, all you have to do is choose the right person. However, if an innocent suspect is chosen, this false identification can lead to an innocent person being imprisoned. Nonetheless, when presented with a lineup witnesses often feel pressure to choose someone, and they will compare the photos and choose the one that looks most like what they remember. This is called a *relative judgment*, and it can lead to errors.

Simultaneous lineup A lineup type that presents photos together in one array.

Sequential lineup A lineup type where photos are presented individually.

A better approach is to use **sequential lineups**—where photos are shown one at a time and witnesses have to make a yes or no decision before moving on. Gary Wells (at Iowa State University) and Rod Lindsay (at Queen's University) (1985) have shown that using a sequential lineup procedure can dramatically reduce error rates compared to other types of lineups. These researchers have proposed that a sequential procedure forces people into *absolute judgment* strategies and reduces people's ability to compare among photos.

To further reduce errors during lineups, police should provide witnesses with unbiased instructions. For example, Roy Malpass and Patricia Devine (1984) have demonstrated that biased lineup instructions (for example, "The guy is in the lineup, all you have to do is pick him out") lead to more eyewitness errors (because people feel they have to choose someone) than unbiased instruction (for example, "The criminal may or may not be present in the lineup"). Thus, whenever police present a witness with a lineup, the witness should be advised of the possibility that the criminal may not be there (current RCMP procedures already include such an instruction).

FIGURE 26-1
A police photo lineup.

POLICE INVESTIGATIONS

Lie Detection

Being able to tell if a witness is lying is a skill police would very much like to have. For a number of decades psychologists have been trying to identify ways to determine whether people are lying. However, research has typically shown that people rarely perform at better than chance levels at detecting deception (DePaulo & others, 1982; Memon & Gabbert, 2003), that people cannot effectively be trained to detect deception (Bull, 1989), and that police, judges, psychiatrists, and other legal professionals perform no better than laypeople.

Therefore, police often turn to mechanical means to determine if someone is deceiving them. The polygraph is by far the most commonly used and economical of these instruments. The polygraph does not measure lying per se, but is used to assess a number of physiological indices that are supposed to be a response to the anxiety and discomfort lying produces—including breathing rate, galvanic skin response (sweating), heart rate, and blood pressure. Police use the polygraph to verify witnesses' and suspects' versions of events. These are also used quite frequently in the assessment of potential police officers (to test for criminal and drug-related experiences). But how accurate is the polygraph? Although controversial, polygraph tests can accurately identify guilty suspects as guilty in as high as 85 percent of cases (Patrick & Iacono, 1991). However, the polygraph can misclassify innocent suspects as guilty in up to 25 percent of cases. Thus, the polygraph is not considered reliable enough to be admissible in Canadian courts (*R v. Beland*, 1987).

Some researchers have argued that they may be able to detect deception far more accurately than the standard polygraph apparatus. In the last 15 years, a new method has been developed that measures *event-related brain potentials* (ERPs). When we encounter information that is infrequent or personally significant, there is activity in the cerebral cortex (that is, we show an ERP response). These electrical patterns in the brain can be measured by placing a series of electrodes on a person's scalp (see Allen & others, 1992; Rosenfeld & others, 1996). Presumably, when a guilty suspect is presented with information about the crime he or she will show an ERP response. However, an innocent person would not. In one study, Lawrence Farwell and his colleagues (for example, Farwell & Donchin, 1991) were able to classify 18 of 20 of guilty suspects and 17 of 20 not-guilty suspects correctly. Rosenfeld and his colleagues have found overall correct classification rates of 92 percent for guilty participants and 87 percent for not-guilty suspects—seemingly an improvement over other methods. However, more recently Rosenfeld and his colleagues (Rosenfeld & others, 2004) have suggested that people who are knowledgeable about ERPs may be able to fake the tests. Thus, no method of detecting deception is infallible.

Confessions

We have already pointed out how mistaken eyewitness identifications are a major cause of false convictions and imprisonment. However, false confessions are another serious problem. For example, of the Innocence Project cases cited above, 27 percent have involved a false confession given by a suspect. It is important to point out that these were legally obtained confessions—they were not beaten out of the suspect. Most of you are probably thinking, "If you confess, you must be guilty—I would never confess to a crime I didn't commit!" When teaching, Steven Smith regularly asks his classes to put up their hand if they think they would ever confess to a crime they did not commit. Only five or six out of a hundred will say they would. However, research by Saul Kassin (2005) suggests that easily half of people could confess to such crimes.

It is important to recognize the awesome power of the social situation when a suspect is being interrogated by police. During an interrogation police do everything they can (within the law) to extract a confession. Many people do not realize that the police are allowed to mislead people they are interviewing. Police can tell suspects that they have evidence (hair, fingerprints, DNA), say that there are witnesses to the crime, or tell suspects that they have failed a polygraph. As long as the police do not actually fabricate evidence, they are behaving within the law.

Police around the world are trained in the *Reid technique* (Inbau & others, 2001), an interview style designed to extract confessions from unwilling suspects. Saul Kassin and his colleagues (Kassin 2005; Kassin & Gudjonsson, 2004) have found that this type of interrogation can put substantial social pressure on a suspect to confess. Police generally believe that suspects are guilty, and that if they deny their guilt then they are lying. Indeed, one experienced police detective was quoted as saying, "You can tell if a suspect is lying by whether he is moving his lips" (Leo, 1996). As mentioned above, police are no more skilled at detecting deception than the average person, but police are very confident in their judgments (Kassin, 2005). Finally, the Reid technique itself (see the boxed feature on page 307) is specifically designed to overcome a suspect's assertions of innocence.

The Reid Technique

The Reid technique (Inbau & others, 2001) is specifically designed to get suspects to incriminate themselves through the application of three psychological processes: isolation of the witness from others; confrontation; and minimization.

The Reid technique prescribes a nine-step process:

1. Confront the suspect with assertions of guilt: This includes thinking about and visualizing the crime, which can lead to confusion.

2. Develop "themes" that justify or excuse the crime: Minimization gives suspects a way out and functions as the equivalent of a promise of leniency.

3. Interrupt all efforts at denial.

4. Overcome the suspect's factual, moral, and emotional objections.

5. Ensure that the passive suspect does not withdraw.

6. Show sympathy and understanding; urge the suspect to cooperate.

7. Offer a face-saving alternative view of the alleged guilty act: "It was an accident, provoked, spontaneous," and so on.

8. Get the suspect to recount the details of the crime: vivid, detailed accounts can seem real after a while.

9. Convert statements into a full written confession. I

The combination of seemingly overwhelming evidence with an aggressive and relentless interrogation technique results in a remarkable number of confessions (Kassin, 2005). Although this is an invaluable technique when the suspect is guilty, it is problematic if the suspect is innocent. This is particularly true because innocent people are also more likely than guilty suspects to waive their right to an attorney (Kassin & Norwick, 2004), and innocent suspects tend to elicit aggressive interrogation styles because their protests of innocence cause police officers to become frustrated (Kassin & others, 2003).

INFLUENCES ON COURT JUDGMENTS

Defendant Characteristics

When juries are deciding the outcome of a criminal case, do factors such as attractiveness and similarity of the defendant to the jurors play a role? When Paul Bernardo was arrested for the grisly murder of two teenage girls, people were shocked. How could such a good-looking and charming man be accused of such heinous crimes? In the OJ Simpson case, a shocking number of jurors believed that OJ could not have committed the murders because he was an excellent football player (Wrightsman & others, 2001). Why do people react this way? Remember the "what is beautiful is good" hypothesis. Can this really have an effect in court?

Michael Efran at the University of Toronto wanted to test this (1974). He gave students a description of a cheating case with the photo of the cheater attached. When the cheater was attractive, he was rated as less guilty and received a more lenient punishment. Other research has confirmed that attractiveness can influence trial outcomes, especially when the available evidence is ambiguous (Mazzela & Fiengold, 1994). However, in Canada fewer than 20 percent of trials are held in front of a jury. Surely judges are not subject to these biases. To test this, Chris Downs and Phillip Lyons (1991) obtained attractiveness ratings of 1,742 defendants in misdemeanour cases heard in front of 40 different judges. Regardless of the severity of the crime, judges gave more lenient bail amounts and fines to more attractive defendants (see Figure 26-2).

Judge's Instructions

At the end of every jury trial, judges provide instructions to the jury in terms of the relevant aspects of the law, as well as what information they should consider in rendering their decision. However, we have all seen TV shows—such as *Law & Order*—where one lawyer presents evidence he or she shouldn't have and opposing counsel shouts "I object!" The judge then quickly instructs the jury to "disregard that statement." Does this work? Evidence suggests the answer is no. For example, Stanley Sue and his colleagues (Sue & others, 1973) presented participants with a description of a crime and summaries of the defence and prosecution cases. Although the prosecu-

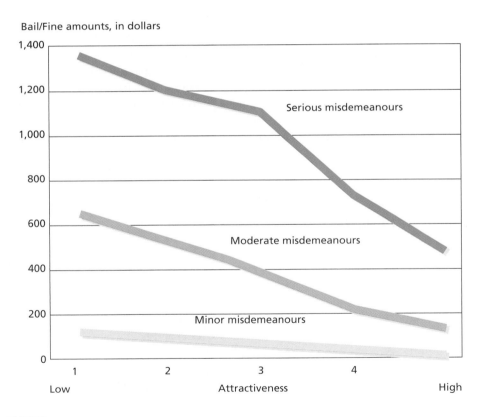

Bail/Fine amounts, in dollars

FIGURE 26-2

Attractiveness and legal judgments. Texas Gulf Coast judges set higher bails and fines for less attractive defendants.

Data from Downs & Lyons, 1991.

tion case was weak, in one condition participants heard a recording of an incriminating phone call made by the defendant. However, at the end of the trial the judge instructed jurors that this evidence was inadmissible. Nonetheless, jurors in this condition were just as likely to convict as if no such instruction were given.

This has been supported by more recent work on information processing—people are not very good at correcting for the influence of potentially biasing information, and indeed their attempts to correct for the biasing information can actually lead to an increase in bias (Wegener & others, 2000). Perhaps famed defence attorney Jim Perruto summed it up best when he said that giving instructions to disregard evidence is like "putting a drop of ink into a jug of milk, shaking it, and then trying to take the ink back out again." Once the information is out there, the jury and the trial outcome has already been tainted.

A second element of the judge's instructions revolves around guidelines for the verdict. In a murder case, for example, a defendant can be found guilty of premeditated murder or manslaughter, acquitted, or found to have been defending himself (that is, the murder was justified). Jurors must also understand statements such as "preponderance of evidence" and "beyond a reasonable doubt," which may have different meanings for legal professionals than for jurors (Kagehiro, 1990). Instructions can be quite complicated. Indeed, in order to avoid grounds for appeal, judges often read from legal texts that a typical juror will not necessarily understand. Vicki Smith (1991) reports that, in the end, jurors might convict based on their own definitions of the crime rather than the instructions provided by the judge. To combat this problem, instructions to the jury should be written in clear, non-technical language (Halverson & others, 1997), and jurors should be allowed to take notes and review trial transcripts so they do not have to rely on their memory for details (Bourgeois & others, 1993).

JURY DECISION MAKING

Jury Decision-Making Processes

Once a jury begins deliberating, how do they reach a verdict? Although it is legal in the United States, in Canada researchers are not allowed to question jurors about deliberations in specific cases. Jury decision-making research usually involves mock trials where every element of the deliberations can be observed. Typically, juries begin by having an initial vote. Although two-thirds of these juries will not agree on a verdict initially, eventually 95 percent will (Kalvern & Ziesel, 1966). But how are these final verdicts achieved? Some intriguing work by James Davis, Norbert Kerr, and their colleagues (for example, Davis & others, 1989; Kerr & others, 1976) tested a number of mathematical models to determine when juries would arrive at a verdict and when they would result in a hung jury. Although results varied depending specific circumstances, a "two-thirds rule" seemed to apply in most cases—if there was a two-thirds majority at the time of the initial vote, the final verdict was usually consistent with that initial vote. In addition, Kalven and Ziesel's work found that nine out of ten verdicts were consistent with the verdict of the majority in the initial vote.

A number of factors can affect the verdict, however. For example, as we saw in Module 15, when groups discuss an issue individuals in the group can arrive at a more extreme position than they initially held—a process called *polarization* (for example, Baron & Byrne, 1991). In the case of jury deliberations this could mean a guilty verdict when some of the jurors initially might have been leaning toward acquittal. On the other hand, juries can sometimes show leniency biases (for example, MacCoun & Kerr, 1988), whereby the jury may actually be more lenient once it has deliberated. As you might imagine, the outcomes of jury deliberations are not easy to predict.

The Story Behind the Research

Although research on eyewitness accuracy has been around for about 100 years, only recently have legal practitioners begun to embrace the findings and change their procedures in order to avoid errors. In 1999, the U.S. Department of Justice published a landmark set of recommendations on the treatment of eyewitness evidence entitled *Eyewitness Evidence: A Guide for Law Enforcement.*

The then–Attorney General of the United States, Janet Reno, called together the relevant stakeholder groups and asked them to come up with an empirically validated guide for law enforcement that the whole group could support. The final group comprised 33 members: 17 police officers, 4 district attorneys, 6 public defenders, and 6 eyewitness researchers (including two Canadians, Rod Lindsay at Queen's University and John Turtle at Ryerson University). This group of legal professionals met a number of times in various locations across the United States to develop the guidelines they eventually proposed. The *Guide* may represent the most comprehensive and potentially influential work of its type ever developed.

The purpose was to provide step-by-step procedures for law enforcement in dealing with eyewitnesses. These procedures were designed to minimize the risk of contaminating eyewitness evidence and reduce the likelihood of mistaken identifi-

cations. One recommendation is the use of the *cognitive interview* technique discussed earlier in this module, and describes in detail to police how to interview eyewitnesses to crimes. In terms of lineup procedures used by police, the *Guide* recommends the use of single-suspect lineups (that is, one suspect with all others being known innocent fillers); ensuring the use of unbiased lineup instructions; and avoiding post-identification feedback to witnesses.

In addition, researchers in the group wanted the *Guide* to recommend the sequential lineup procedure. Further, the researchers wanted to recommend double-blind procedures such that neither the officer conducting the lineup nor the witness are aware of the identity of the suspect—a procedure that further reduces false identifications. However, other members of the group were reluctant to include these two elements in the *Guide* as they might not be feasible for some police departments. Interestingly, many law-enforcement agencies that have adopted the *Guide* report little difficulty implementing these procedures (see Wells & others, 2000). Thus, it is clear that psychological research has had a great deal to contribute to the legal system. Indeed, the eyewitness area is an excellent example of how researchers and practitioners can work together to ensure a better outcome for society. ▌

Minority Influence

Many of you might remember Henry Fonda's portrayal in *12 Angry Men* of a man stead-fastly arguing for the acquittal of the defendant (if not, rent it—it is an excellent movie). In the film, Fonda's character is a minority of one who eventually convinces all 11 other members of the jury of the defendant's innocence. However, the work cited above sug-gests that such minorities will rarely prevail. Nonetheless, minorities can be effective. As with any group, some individuals will contribute more than others. Research by Reid Hastie and his colleagues (for example, Hastie & others, 1983) shows that if the minor-ity is consistent, vocal, and persistent, then it will eventually prevail.

CONCLUSIONS

The law and our legal system are constantly (if slowly) evolving. However, thousands of people every year rely on our legal system to protect them and to punish people who violate the rights of others. However, social-psychological research tells us that we must remain vigilant to the impact of our very human biases and expectations on how people are treated within that system. Due process tells us that it is better for ten guilty people to go free than for one innocent person to be convicted. However, it should be clear from what we have presented above that there are many opportuni-ties for innocent people to be falsely convicted. We must make sure that our legal sys-tem does its best to protect all of those with whom it comes into contact.

CONCEPTS TO REMEMBER

Confidence–accuracy correlation   p. 302
Cognitive interview   p. 304

Simultaneous lineup   p. 304
Sequential lineup   p. 304

Please visit the *Exploring Social Psychology* Online Learning Centre at **www.mcgrawhill.ca/college/myers** to participate in module activities, view module videos, access research and study tools, and test your knowl-edge with interactive quizzes, exercises, and scenarios.

The Social Psychology of the Environment

To combat climate change, many countries have started to consider—and implement—sources of renewable energy such as these windmills. What are some things you can do every day to minimize stress on the environment?

OLC
Activity 27.1

What would a typical day be for you in your ideal world? Perhaps the day starts with a nice hot shower, followed by a drive in the country in your Porsche convertible (or your SUV). Would you spend the day surfing waves in California, or surfing the Net in your home office? Many would be happy lounging in front of a big-screen TV watching new-release movies on a surround sound audio system. Life would be good. Indeed, compared to years past, life is good. Today we enjoy luxuries unknown even to royalty in centuries past—hot showers, flush toilets, microwave ovens, jet travel, flat panel televisions, e-mail, instant messaging, and Post-it Notes. But on the horizon beyond the sunny skies, dark clouds are gathering. In scientific gatherings hosted by the United Nations, the Royal Society, and the National Academy of Sciences, a consensus has emerged: Increasing population and increasing consumption have combined to overshoot the earth's ecological carrying capacity (Heap & Kent, 2000; Oskamp, 2000). We are spending our environmental capital, not just living off the interest.

In 1950, the earth carried 2.5 billion people and 50 million cars. As of February 2006, it has more than 6.5 billion people and 10 times as many cars. If world economic growth enabled all countries to match North Americans' present car ownership, the number of cars would multiply yet another 13 times over (N. Myers, 2000). These cars, along with the burning of coal and oil to generate electricity and heat homes, produce greenhouse gases that contribute to global warming (Hileman,

1999). The warmest 23 years on record have all occurred since 1975, with 2005 the hottest year ever. The polar icecaps are melting at an accelerating rate. So are mountain glaciers from the Alps to the Andes. Ski resorts in St. Moritz (the site of two Winter Olympic Games) are going as far as to place reflective blankets on the icecaps to slow down their rate of melting (*National Geographic*, 2006). Equatorial insects and vegetation are migrating toward the poles. The polar icecaps are also melting at an alarming rate—they are smaller now than ever in recorded history. January 2006 was the warmest January on record. The winter of 2005–2006 was the warmest winter since Environment Canada began keeping records (CBC, 2006). The *Times* newspaper of London reports that polar bears, already an at-risk species, are drowning because they cannot swim far enough to reach the sea ice. Indeed, the Canadian Wildlife Service has found that the polar bear population around Hudson Bay is down 22 percent in the last 20 years. With the changing climate, extreme atmospheric events, including heat waves, droughts, and floods, are becoming more common. As precipitation falls more as rain, and less as snow, the likely result will be more floods in rainy seasons and less melting snow and glaciers for rivers during dry seasons.

With world economic growth and population both destined to increase (even as birth rates fall), resource depletion and further global warming now seem inevitable. Ergo, the need for more sustainable consumption has taken on "urgency and global significance" (Heap & Kent, 2000). The simple, stubborn fact is that the earth cannot support our present consumption indefinitely, much less the expected increase in consumption. For our species to survive and flourish, some things must change.

Canadians do seem to care about environmental issues, rating the environment as the most important campaign issue in the 2004 federal election—edging out health care and improved federal/provincial cooperation. However, in the 2006 federal election the Green Party, which is dedicated to protecting the environment, received only 5 percent of the national vote (as a comparison, the NDP received 17 percent) and did not win a single seat in Parliament. If global warming is occurring (as most scientists believe), why are we not more concerned? It seems this is yet another example of an attitude–behaviour mismatch (see Module 8). Why does the federal Environment Minister call the Kyoto targets for the reduction of greenhouse gas emissions "unattainable"? Both American and Canadian politicians seem willing to sacrifice the future in order to satisfy current economic concerns.

Is it, as Gallup researcher Lydia Saad (2003) believes, because on a chilly winter day "'global warming' may sound, well, appealing"? Might people be more concerned about averting "global heating"? Recall from earlier modules that

There is debate about whether this type of large sport utility vehicle is appropriate for navigating urban settings such as this downtown residential neighbourhood in Toronto, Ontario. Moreover, in addition to requiring significant amounts of fuel, the size of these vehicles can make them dangerous when they are involved in collisions with pedestrians, cyclists, and smaller cars.

labels matter. Whether we call those resisting the foreign occupation of their country "terrorists," "the guerrilla resistance," or "freedom fighters" colours our attitudes. Whether we describe someone who responds to others as "conforming" or as "sensitive" and "open" shapes our perceptions. Language shapes thought.

Resource depletion will also affect the human future. Most of the world's original forest cover has been taken down, and what remains in the tropics is being cleared for agriculture, livestock grazing, logging, and settlements. With deforestation comes diminished absorption of greenhouse gases and sometimes flooding, soil erosion, changing rainfall and temperature, and the decimation of many animal species.

A growing population's appetite for fish, together with ecosystem destruction, has also led to decreasing annual catches in 11 of 15 major oceanic fishing areas and in 7 in 10 major fish species (Karavellas, 2000; McGinn, 1998). Due in part to overfishing, stocks of wild salmon, Atlantic cod, haddock, herring, and other species have suffered major depletion.

ENABLING SUSTAINABLE LIVING

So, what shall we do? Eat, drink, and be merry for tomorrow is doom? Behave as have so many participants in prisoners' dilemma games, by pursuing self-interest to our collective detriment? ("Heck, on a global scale, my consumption is infinitesimal; it provides me pleasure at but a nominal cost to the world.") Wring our hands and vow never to bring children into a hurting world? Must fertility plus prosperity produce calamity?

Those more optimistic about the future see two routes to sustainable lifestyles: (a) increasing technological efficiency and agricultural productivity, and (b) moderating consumption and decreasing population.

Increasing Efficiency and Productivity

One route to a sustainable future is through improving eco-technologies. Already we have replaced many incandescent bulbs with cool fluorescent bulbs, replaced printed and delivered letters and catalogues with e-mail and e-commerce, and developed environmentally friendlier cars. Today's middle-aged adults drive cars that get twice the mileage and produce a twentieth the pollution of their first cars.

Plausible future technologies include diodes that emit light for 20 years without bulbs; ultrasound washing machines that consume no water, heat, or soap; reusable and compostable plastics; cars running on fuel cells that combine hydrogen and oxygen and produce water exhaust; extra-light materials stronger than steel; and roofs and roads that double as solar energy collectors (N. Myers, 2000).

Given the speed of innovation—who could have imagined today's world a century ago?—the future will surely bring solutions that we aren't yet imagining. Surely, say the optimists, the future will bring increased material well-being for more people requiring many fewer raw materials and much less polluting waste.

Reducing Consumption

The second route to a sustainable future is through reduced consumption. Instead of more people consuming and polluting more, a stable population will need to consume and pollute less.

Thanks to family planning efforts, the world's population growth rate has decelerated, especially in developed nations. Where food security has improved and women have become educated and empowered, birthrates have fallen. But even if birthrates everywhere instantly fell to replacement levels, the lingering momentum of population growth, fed by the bulge of younger humans, would continue for years to come.

Given that we have already overshot the earth's carrying capacity, individual consumption must also moderate. With our material appetites continually swelling—as people seek more CDs, more air conditioning, more holiday travel—what can be done to moderate consumption?

One way is through public policies that harness the motivating power of incentives. As a general rule, what we tax we get less of, what we reward we get more of. If our highways are jammed and our air polluted, we can create fast lanes that reward carpooling and penalize driving solo. We can build bike lanes and subsidize mass transportation, thus encouraging alternatives to cars. We can shift taxes to petrol, and reward recycling with a refundable deposit on soda cans and bottles.

Robert Frank (1999), an economist well-versed in social psychology, suggests how a socially responsible market economy might reward achievement while promoting more sustainable consumption. He proposes a progressive consumption tax that encourages savings and investment while increasing the price on nonessential luxury goods, such as the $18,500 Range Rover child's toy car. His proposal is simple: Tax people not on what they earn but on what they spend—which is their earnings minus their savings and perhaps their charity. The tax could be made progressive with ample exemptions for dependants and higher tax rates for the big spenders. Frank argues that a progressive consumption tax (beginning, say, with a 20-percent tax rate on annual consumption beyond $30,000 for a family of four and rising to 70 percent for consumption over $500,000) promises to moderate consumption. People who would have bought a BMW may now adjust, with no less happiness, down to a Mazda.

Support for such policies will require a shift in public consciousness not unlike that occurring during the 1960s U.S. civil rights movement and the 1970s women's movement. As the atmosphere warms and oil and other resources become scarce, such a shift is inevitable, eventually. Is there any hope that, before the crisis becomes acute, human priorities might shift from accumulating money to finding meaning, and from aggressive consumption to nurturing connections? Perhaps social psychology can help, by exposing our *materialism*, by informing people of the disconnect between *economic growth and human morale*, and by helping people understand *why materialism and money fail to satisfy*.

The Story Behind the Research

Dr. Luc Pelletier, a psychology professor at the University of Ottawa, has been interested for the last 20 years in how psychology can contribute to the protection of the environment. His interest in the topic began in 1987, in the aftermath of the Chernobyl disaster (where the Russian nuclear power plant had a catastrophic accident resulting in a meltdown). The toxic clouds that resulted from this accident (and other accidents in Bhopal, India, and Three-Mile Island in the U.S.) dispersed across the globe and damaged ecosystems throughout the world. At the same time there was growing realization that midwestern power plants in the United States were causing acid rain in Ontario and Quebec, killing trees (particularly maple trees), poisoning waterways, and destroying wildlife habitats.

Interestingly (as a lifelong fan of maple syrup), Dr. Pelletier became particularly motivated to understand the links between human behaviours and environmental conditions, and what could be the best strategies to increase people's pro-environmental motivations and behaviours. In 1989, when he took his position at the University of Ottawa, he started a line of research looking at how people's motivations influence their environmental behaviours. Most approaches to environmental protection have aimed to change people's behaviours by using punishments (such as fines) and rewards (such as returns on can deposits), or by warning people of the health threats of a poor environment. However, the same research has shown that if these rewards, punishments, or heath concerns are removed, peo-

ple's pro-environmental behaviours also decline. Thus, Dr. Pelletier and his colleagues began to examine ways in which pro-environmental behaviours can be sustained over time.

In his most recent work (see Pelletier & Sharp, 2006), the researchers looked at three different communities in the Ottawa region: one that had curbside recycling, one that had a local recycling centre but no curbside recycling, and one that had no recycling program at all. As we would expect, effort required to recycle predicted recycling behaviour, but only for those people with low self-determined motivation. Highly motivated people recycled in their homes regardless of the difficulty. In addition, people with high self-determined motivation also recycled outside the home (for example, when camping or on vacation). People with low self-determined motivation recycled only when they had a curbside recycling program (that is, when recycling was easy), and they recycled much less when the behaviour was more difficult or when they were outside their home. Furthermore, people with high self-determined motivation are also more satisfied with the environment and feel their behaviours are contributing positively relative to people with low self-determined motivation. Thus, they are more likely to continue in their pro-environmental behaviours. This suggests that increasing people's self-determined motivation may be a more fruitful approach than trying to change people's behaviours directly. If we can change motivations, the behaviours will follow. ∎

OLC
Activity 27.2

INCREASING MATERIALISM

Does money buy happiness? No? Ah, but would a *little* more money make us a *little* happier? Many of us smirk and nod. There is, we believe, *some* connection between fiscal fitness and feeling fantastic. Indeed, the 2003 General Social Survey found that Canadians' happiness is related to their income; see Table 27-1 (Statistics Canada, 2004). Three in four American students entering college—nearly double the 1970 proportion—now consider it "very important" or "essential" that they become "very well off financially" (Figure 27-1). It's not just collegians. Money matters. "Whoever said money can't buy happiness isn't spending it right," proclaimed a Lexus ad. No wonder many people hunger to know the secrets of "the millionaire mind."

Ironically, however, those who most ardently seek after money tend to live with lower well-being, a finding that "comes through very strongly in every culture I've looked at," reports research psychologist Richard Ryan (1999). Ryan's collaborator, Tim Kasser (2000), concludes from their studies that people who instead seek "intimacy, personal growth, and contribution to the community" experience greater quality of life. Their research, summarized in Kasser's *The High Price of Materialism* (2002),

TABLE 27-1 *Annual Income and Ratings of Happiness in Canada*

Annual Income	Very Happy	Somewhat Happy	Very or Somewhat Unhappy
< $20,000/year	36.1	53.4	10.4
$20–40,000/year	45.1	49.7	5.2
$40–60,000/year	50.4	46.0	3.6
$60–80,000/year	54.7	42.9	2.5
$80,000/year	57.6	40.2	2.2

Source: Adapted from Statistics Canada 2003 General Social Survey

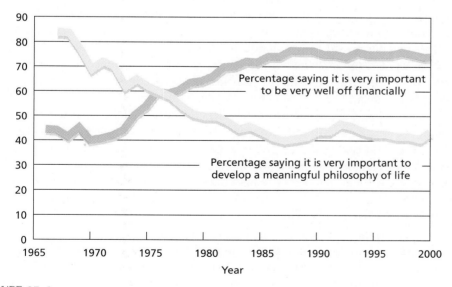

FIGURE 27-1
Changing materialism, from annual surveys of more than 200,000 U.S. students entering college (total sample nearly 7 million students).

Data from Dey, Astin, & Korn, 1991, and subsequent annual reports.

echoes an earlier finding that college alumni with "Yuppie values"—those preferring high income and vocational success to close friendships and marriage—were twice as likely as their former classmates to be "fairly" or "very" unhappy (Perkins, 1991).

Consider: What's been the most satisfying event for you in the past month? When Ken Sheldon and his colleagues (2001) put such questions to university students, and asked them also to rate how much 10 different needs were met by the satisfying event, the students were most likely to report that the event met their needs for self-esteem, relatedness to others, and autonomy. At the bottom of the list of satisfaction predictors were money and luxury.

ECONOMIC GROWTH AND HUMAN MORALE

Materialism—lusting for more—exacts ecological and psychic costs. But might actually getting more pay emotional dividends? Perhaps unsustainable consumption is bad for the planet but good for one's sense of well-being. Would people be happier if they could trade a simple lifestyle for one with a private chef, Aspen ski vacations, and travel on private jets? Would they be happier if they won a publishers' sweepstake and could decide among its suggested indulgences, including a 40-foot yacht, a deluxe motor home, and a luxury car?

We can observe the traffic between wealth and well-being by asking, first, if rich nations have more satisfied people. There is, indeed, some correlation between national wealth and well-being (indexed as self-reported happiness and life satisfaction). The Scandinavians have been mostly prosperous and satisfied; the Bulgarians are neither. But early 1990s data revealed that once nations reached about $10,000 GNP per person, which was roughly the economic level of Ireland, higher levels of national wealth were not predictive of increased well-being. Better to be Irish than Bulgarian. But whether one was an average Irish person or West German (with double the Irish purchasing power) hardly mattered (Inglehart, 1990, 1997).

We can ask, second, whether within any given nation rich people are happier. In poor countries—where low income threatens basic needs—being relatively well off does predict greater well-being (Argyle, 1999). In affluent countries, where most can afford life's necessities, affluence matters less. Income increases and windfalls temporarily boost happiness, and recessions create short-term psychic losses (Di Tella, MacCulloch, & Oswald, 2001; Gardner & Oswald, 2001). But over time the emotions wane. Once comfortable, more and more money produces diminishing long-term returns. World values researcher Ronald Inglehart (1990, p. 242) therefore found the income–happiness correlation to be "surprisingly weak." David Lykken (1999, p. 17) illustrates: "People who go to work in their overalls and on the bus are just as happy, on the average, as those in suits who drive to work in their own Mercedes." Even winning a lottery seems not to enduringly elevate well-being (Brickman, Coates, and Janoff-Bulman, 1978). Such jolts of joy have "a short half-life," notes Richard Ryan (1999).

We can ask, third, whether, over time, a culture's happiness rises with its affluence. Does our collective well-being float upward with a rising economic tide? Since 1960, we have seen the proportion of households with dishwashers rise from 7 to 50 percent, those with clothes dryers from 20 to 71 percent, and those with air conditioning from 15 to 73 percent. As we mentioned at the beginning of this module, 99 percent of homes have at least one phone line. However, in 2004, 21 percent of Canadian homes had two phone lines, and an additional 28 percent had three phones or more. Also in 2004, 52 percent of Canadian households had Internet access, double the 1999 rate. In 1987 there were 100,000 cell phones in use in Canada. Today, there are more than 15 million cell phones being used (out of 30 million Canadians).

So, believing that it's "very important" to "be very well-off financially," and having become better off financially, are people happier? Are we happier with espresso coffee, caller ID, and suitcases on wheels than we were before? Probably not. Since 1957, the number of Americans who say they are "very happy" has declined slightly, from 35 to 32 percent. These facts of life explode a bombshell underneath our society's materialism: *Economic growth has provided no boost to human morale.*

WHY MATERIALISM AND MONEY FAIL TO SATISFY

It is striking that economic growth in affluent countries has failed to satisfy. People who identify themselves with expensive possessions experience fewer positive moods, report Emily Solberg, Ed Diener, and Michael Robinson (2003). Such materialists tend to report a relatively large gap between what they want and what they have, and to enjoy fewer close, fulfilling relationships. The challenge for healthy nations, then, is to foster improving standards of living without encouraging a materialism and consumerism that displaces the deep need to belong. So, why have we not become happier?

Our Human Capacity for Adaptation

The **adaptation-level phenomenon** is our tendency to judge our experience (for example, of sounds, lights, or income) relative to a neutral level defined by our prior experience. We adjust our neutral levels—the points at which sounds seem neither loud nor soft, temperatures neither hot nor cold, events neither pleasant nor unpleasant—based on our experience. We then notice and react to up or down changes from these levels.

> **Adaptation-level phenomenon** The tendency to adapt to a given level of stimulation and thus to notice and react to changes from that level.

One of the authors of this textbook experienced this phenomenon when he took his family on a trip to Australia in 2003. It was May, entering Australia's winter. Steve and his family were in Newcastle, two hours north of Sydney, where Steve was working with a colleague at the University of Newcastle. When the colleague asked where his wife and children were, Steve replied that they were at the beach. "It's too bad you came at this time of year," said his colleague. "They won't be able to enjoy the beach—the water is far too cold!" Steve replied, "But the water is 23 degrees!" (The ocean in Nova Scotia rarely gets warmer than 19 degrees.) "I know!" said the colleague (who never swam in water colder than 25 degrees). Steve's kids spent hours frolicking in the surf in their bathing suits, metres away from Australian surfers wearing full wetsuits to ward off the chill. What you are used to affects what you are happy with.

Similarly, as our achievements rise above past levels we feel successful and satisfied. As our social prestige, income, or in-home technology surges, we feel pleasure. Before long, however, we adapt. What once felt good comes to register as neutral, and what formerly was neutral now feels like deprivation. As the good feelings wane, it takes a higher high to rejuice the joy.

So, could we ever create a social paradise? Donald Campbell (1975) answered no: If you woke up tomorrow to your utopia—perhaps a world with no bills, no ills, someone who loves you unreservedly—you would feel euphoric, for a time. Yet, before long, you would recalibrate your adaptation level and again sometimes feel gratified (when achievements surpass expectations), sometimes feel deprived (when they fall below), and sometimes feel neutral. That helps explain why, despite the realities of triumph and tragedy, million-dollar lottery winners and people who are paralyzed report roughly similar levels of happiness. We also sometimes "miswant." When first-year university students predicted their satisfaction with various housing possibilities shortly before entering their school's housing lottery, they focused on physical features. "I'll be happiest in a beautiful and well-located residence," many students seemed to think. But they were wrong. When contacted a year later, it was the social features, such as a sense of community, that predicted happiness, report Elizabeth Dunn and her colleagues (2003). When focused on the short-term and forgetting how quickly we adapt, we may think that the material features of our world predispose our happiness. Actually, report Leaf Van Boven and Thomas Gilovich (2003) from their surveys and experiments, positive *experiences* (often social experiences) leave us happier. The best things in life are not things.

Our Wanting to Compare

Social comparison
Evaluating one's abilities and opinions by comparing oneself to others.

Much of life revolves around **social comparison**. We are always comparing ourselves with others. And whether we feel good or bad depends on who those others are. We are slow-witted or clumsy only when others are smart or agile. Let one baseball player sign a new contract for $15 million a year and his $8-million teammate may now feel less satisfied. "Our poverty became a reality. Not because of our having less, but by our neighbors having more," recalled Will Campbell in *Brother to a Dragonfly*.

Social comparisons help us understand the modest income–happiness correlation. Middle- and upper-income people in a given country, who can compare themselves with the relatively poor, tend to be slightly more satisfied with life than their less-fortunate compatriots. Nevertheless, once people reach a moderate income level, further increases do little to increase their happiness. Why? Because we tend to compare upward as we climb the ladder of success or income (Gruder, 1977; Suls & Tesch, 1978). Beggars compare with more successful beggars, not millionaires, noted Bertrand Russell (1930). Thus, "Napoleon envied Caesar, Caesar envied Alexander, and Alexander, I daresay, envied Hercules, who never existed. You cannot, therefore, get away from envy by means of success alone, for there will always be in history or legend some person even more successful than you are" (pp. 68–69).

Rising income inequality, notes Michael Hagerty (2000), makes for more people markedly above us in our communities. And that helps explain why those living in communities with a large rich–poor gap tend to feel less satisfied. If you live in a 2,000-square-foot house in a community filled with other 2,000-square-foot houses, you likely are happier than if living in the same house amid 4,000-square-foot homes. Television modelling of the lifestyles of the wealthy also serves to accentuate feelings of "relative deprivation" and desires for more (Schor, 1998).

The adaptation-level and social comparison phenomena give us pause. They imply that the quest for happiness through material achievement requires continually expanding affluence. But the good news is that adaptation to simpler lives can also happen. If choice or necessity shrinks our consumption we will initially feel pain, but it will pass. Indeed, thanks to our capacity to adapt and to adjust comparisons, the emotional impact of significant life events—losing a job, or even a disabling accident—dissipates sooner than most people suppose (Gilbert & others, 1998).

TOWARD SUSTAINABILITY AND SURVIVAL

A shift to post-materialist values will gain momentum as people:

- face the implications of population and consumption growth for climate change, habitat destruction, and resource depletion;
- realize that materialist values mark less happy lives; and
- appreciate that economic growth has not bred increased well-being.

"If the world is to change for the better it must have a change in human consciousness," said Czech poet-president Vaclav Havel (1990). We must discover "a deeper sense of responsibility toward the world, which means responsibility toward something higher than self." If people came to believe that stacks of unplayed CDs, closets full of seldom-worn clothes, and garages with luxury cars do not define the good life, then might a shift in consciousness become possible? Instead of being an indicator of social status, might conspicuous consumption become gauche?

Social psychology's contribution to a sustainable and survivable future will come partly through its consciousness-transforming insights into adaptation and comparison. These insights also come from experiments that lower people's comparison standards and thereby cool luxury fever and renew contentment. In two such experiments, Marshall Dermer and his colleagues (1979) put university women through imaginative exercises in deprivation. After viewing depictions of the grimness of Milwaukee life in 1900, or after imagining and writing about being burned and disfigured, the women expressed greater satisfaction with their own lives.

In another experiment, Jennifer Crocker and Lisa Gallo (1985) found that people who five times completed the sentence "I'm glad I'm not a . . ." afterward felt less depressed and more satisfied with their lives than did those who completed sentences beginning "I wish I were a. . . ." Realizing that others have it worse helps us count our blessings. "I cried because I had no shoes," says a Persian proverb, "until I met a man who had no feet."

Social psychology also contributes to a sustainable and survivable future through its explorations of the good life. If materialism does not enhance life quality, what does? One ingredient of well-being is the satisfaction of our deep "need to belong." As social creatures, we are deeply motivated not only to eat, to procreate, and to achieve, but also to bond with important others. Our distant ancestors who formed attachments were more likely to reproduce and to stay together to nurture their off-spring to maturity. In solo combat, our ancestors were not the toughest predators. But as hunters they learned that six hands were better than two. Those who foraged in groups also gained protection from predators and enemies. The inevitable result: an innately social creature. That helps us understand why those supported by intimate friendships or a committed marriage are much likelier to declare themselves happy. The 1998 General Social Survey (Statistics Canada, 1999) found that people who spent a lot of time by themselves were less likely to be happy. For example, about 44 percent of people with a partner and children (and 48 percent of people with a partner alone) rated themselves as very happy, but only 30 percent of people without a partner rate themselves as very happy. Positive traits—self-esteem, internal locus of control, optimism, extraversion—also mark happy times and lives (Myers, 2000b).

So do leisure and work experiences that engage one's skills. Between the anxiety of being stressed and overwhelmed and the apathy of being bored lies a zone in which people experience "flow," notes Mihaly Csikszentmihalyi (1990, 1999). Flow is an optimal state of absorption during which we lose consciousness of time and self. When people's experience is sampled using electronic pagers, they report greatest enjoyment not when mindlessly passive, but when unself-consciously absorbed in a challenge. What's more, the *less* expensive (and usually more involving) a leisure activity is, the happier people are while engaged in it. Most of us are happier talking to friends than watching TV. Low-consumption recreations prove most satisfying.

And that is indeed good news. The things that make for genuinely good life— close, supportive relationships, a hope-filled faith community, positive traits, engaging activity—are enduringly sustainable.

CONCEPTS TO REMEMBER

Adaptation-level phenomenon   p. 319
Social comparison   p. 320

Please visit the *Exploring Social Psychology* Online Learning Centre at **www.mcgrawhill.ca/college/myers** to participate in module activities, view module videos, access research and study tools, and test your knowledge with interactive quizzes, exercises, and scenarios.

Glossary

A

Adaptation-level phenomenon The tendency to adapt to a given level of stimulation and thus to notice and react to changes from that level.

Aggression Physical or verbal behaviour intended to hurt. In laboratory experiments, this might mean delivering electric shocks or saying something likely to hurt another's feelings. By this social psychological definition, one can be socially assertive without being aggressive.

Altruism A motive to increase another's welfare without conscious regard for one's self-interests.

Arbitration Resolution of a conflict by a neutral third party who studies both sides and imposes a settlement.

Attitude A belief and feeling that can predispose our response to something or someone.

Attitude inoculation Exposing people to weak attacks on their attitudes so that when stronger attacks come, they will have refutations available.

Attractiveness Having qualities that appeal to an audience. An appealing communicator (often someone similar to the audience) is most persuasive on matters of subjective preference.

Availability heuristic An efficient but fallible rule of thumb that judges the likelihood of things in terms of their availability in memory. If instances of something come readily to mind, we presume it to be commonplace.

B

Bargaining Seeking an agreement through direct negotiation between parties to a conflict.

Behavioural confirmation A type of self-fulfilling prophecy whereby people's social expectations (based more on social beliefs than personal expectation) lead them to act in ways that cause others to confirm the expectations.

Bystander effect The finding that a person is less likely to provide help when there are other bystanders.

C

Catharsis Emotional release. The catharsis view of aggression is that aggressive drive is reduced when one "releases" aggressive energy, either by acting aggressively or by fantasizing aggression.

Central-route persuasion Persuasion that occurs when interested people focus on the arguments and respond with favourable thoughts.

Co-actors Co-participants working individually on a noncompetitive activity.

Cognitive dissonance theory Cognitive dissonance is tension that arises when one is simultaneously aware of two inconsistent cognitions, as when we realize that we have, with little justification, acted contrary to our attitudes. Cognitive dissonance theory proposes that we act to reduce such tension, as when we adjust our attitudes to correspond with our actions.

Cognitive interview An interview technique based in cognitive psychology, focusing on context reinstatement to enhance recall of events.

Collectivism Giving priority to the goals of one's groups (often one's extended family or work group) and defining one's identity accordingly.

Companionate love The affection we feel for those with whom our lives are deeply intertwined.

Complementarity The popularly supposed tendency, in a relationship between two people, for each to complete what is missing in the other.

Confidence–accuracy correlation The finding that the correlation between the confidence and accuracy of an eyewitness is weak to nonexistent.

Conflict A perceived incompatibility of actions or goals.

Correlational research The study of the naturally occurring relationships among variables.

Credibility Believability. A credible communicator is perceived as both expert and trustworthy.

Crowding A subjective feeling that there is not enough space per person.

Cult (also called new religious movement) A group typically characterized by (1) the distinctive rituals and beliefs related to its devotion to a god or a person, (2) isolation from the surrounding "evil" culture, and (3) a charismatic leader. (A sect, by contrast, is a spinoff from a major religion.)

Culture The enduring behaviours, ideas, attitudes, and traditions shared by a large group of people and transmitted from one generation to the next.

D

Deindividuation Loss of self-awareness and evaluation apprehension; occurs in group situations that foster responsiveness to group norms, good or bad.

Dependent variable The variable being measured, so called because it may *depend* on manipulations of the independent variable.

Disclosure reciprocity The tendency for one person's intimacy of self-disclosure to match that of a conversational partner.

Discrimination Unjustifiable negative behaviour toward a group or its members.

Displacement The redirection of aggression to a target other than the source of the frustration. Generally, the new target is a safer or more socially acceptable target.

E

Empathy The vicarious experience of another's feelings; putting oneself in another's shoes.

Equal-status contact Contact made on an equal basis. Just as a relationship between people of unequal status breeds attitudes consistent with their relationship, so do relationships between those of equal status. Thus, to reduce prejudice, interracial contact should be between persons equal in status.

Equity A condition in which the outcomes people receive from a relationship are proportional to what they contribute to it. *Note:* Equitable outcomes needn't always be equal outcomes.

Ethnocentrism A belief in the superiority of one's own ethnic and cultural group, and a corresponding disdain for all other groups.

Evaluation apprehension Concern for how others are evaluating us.

Experimental realism The degree to which an experiment absorbs and involves its participants.

Experimental research Studies that seek clues to cause–effect relationships by manipulating one or more factors (independent variables) while controlling others (holding them constant).

F

False consensus effect The tendency to overestimate the commonality of one's opinions and one's undesirable or unsuccessful behaviours.

False uniqueness effect The tendency to underestimate the commonality of one's abilities and one's desirable or successful behaviours.

Foot-in-the-door phenomenon The tendency for people who have first agreed to a small request to comply later with a larger request.

Free riders People who benefit from the group but give little in return.

Frustration The blocking of goal-directed behaviour.

Fundamental attribution error The tendency for observers to underestimate situational influences and overestimate dispositional influences on others' behaviour. (Also called *correspondence bias*, because we so often see behaviour as corresponding to a disposition.)

G

Gender In psychology, the characteristics, whether biological or socially influenced, by which people define male and female.

Gender role A set of behavioural expectations (norms) for males or females.

GRIT Acronym for "graduated and reciprocated initiatives in tension reduction"—a strategy designed to de-escalate international tensions.

Group polarization Group-produced enhancement of members' preexisting tendencies; a strengthening of the members' *average* tendency, not a split within the group.

Groupthink "The mode of thinking that persons engage in when concurrence-seeking becomes so dominant in a cohesive in-group that it tends to override realistic appraisal of alternative courses of action."—Irving Janis (1971)

H

Hindsight bias The tendency to exaggerate, after learning an outcome, one's ability to have foreseen how something turned out. Also known as the *I-knew-it-all-along phenomenon.*

Hypothesis A testable proposition that describes a relationship that might exist between events.

I

Illusion of control Perception of uncontrollable events as subject to one's control or as more controllable than they are.

Illusory correlation Perception of a relationship where none exists, or perception of a stronger relationship than actually exists.

Independent variable The experimental factor that a researcher manipulates.

Individualism The concept of giving priority to one's goals over group goals and defining one's identity in terms of personal attributes rather than group identifications.

Indoctrination A process, used by a number of social groups, to teach members a partisan and uncritical acceptance of the group's perspective on issues.

Informed consent An ethical principle requiring that research participants be told enough to enable them to decide whether they wish to participate.

Ingroup "Us"—a group of people who share a sense of belonging, a feeling of common identity.

Ingroup bias The tendency to favour one's own group.

Integrative agreements Win–win agreements that reconcile both parties' interests to their mutual benefit.

Interaction The effect of one factor (such as biology) depends on another factor (such as environment).

J

Just-world phenomenon The tendency of people to believe the world is just and that people therefore get what they deserve and deserve what they get.

L

Leadership The process by which certain group members motivate and guide the group.

Learned helplessness The hopelessness and resignation learned when a human or animal perceives no control over repeated bad events.

Locus of control The extent to which people perceive outcomes as internally controllable by their own efforts and actions, or as externally controlled by chance or outside forces.

Low-ball technique A tactic for getting people to agree to something. People who agree to an initial request will often still comply when the requester ups the ante. People who receive only the costly request are less likely to comply with it.

M

Matching phenomenon The tendency for men and women to choose as partners those who are a "good match" in attractiveness and other traits.

Mediation An attempt by a neutral third party to resolve a conflict by facilitating communication and offering suggestions.

Mere-exposure effect The tendency for novel stimuli to be liked more or rated more positively after the rater has been repeatedly exposed to them.

Mirror-image perceptions Reciprocal views of one another often held by parties in conflict; for example, each may view itself as moral and peace-loving and the other as evil and aggressive.

Mundane realism The degree to which an experiment is superficially similar to everyday situations.

N

Need to belong A motivation to bond with others in relationships that provide ongoing, positive interactions.

Non-zero-sum games Games in which outcomes need not sum to zero. With cooperation, both can win; with competition, both can lose. (Also called *mixed-motive situations.*)

O

Outgroup "Them"—a group that people perceive as distinctively different from or apart from their ingroup.

Outgroup homogeneity effect Perception of outgroup members as more similar to one another than are ingroup members. Thus "they are alike; we are diverse."

P

Passionate love A state of intense longing for union with another. Passionate lovers are absorbed in one another, feel ecstatic at attaining their partner's love, and are disconsolate on losing it.

Peripheral-route persuasion Persuasion that occurs when people are influenced by incidental cues, such as a speaker's attractiveness.

Personal space A portable bubble or buffer zone that we like to maintain between ourselves and others.

Physical-attractiveness stereotype The presumption that physically attractive people possess other socially desirable traits as well: What is beautiful is good.

Prejudice A negative prejudgment of a group and its individual members.

Prosocial behaviour Positive, constructive, helpful social behaviour; the opposite of antisocial behaviour.

Proximity Geographical nearness. Proximity (more precisely, "functional distance") powerfully predicts liking.

R

Racism (1) An individual's prejudicial attitudes and discriminatory behaviour toward people of a given race, or (2) institutional practices (even if not motivated by prejudice) that subordinate people of a given race.

Random assignment The process of assigning participants to the conditions of an experiment such that all persons have the same chance of being in a given condition. (Note the distinction between random assignment in experiments and random sampling in surveys. Random *assignment* helps us infer cause and effect. Random *sampling* helps us generalize to a population.)

Reactance A motive to protect or restore one's sense of freedom. Reactance arises when someone threatens our freedom of action.

Realistic group conflict theory The theory that prejudice arises from competition among groups for scarce resources.

Reciprocity norm An expectation that people will help, not hurt, those who have helped them.

Regression toward the average The statistical tendency for extreme scores or extreme behaviour to return toward one's average.

Role A set of norms that define how people in a given social position ought to behave.

S

Self-concept A person's answers to the question, "Who am I?"

Self-disclosure Revealing intimate aspects of oneself to others.

Self-efficacy A sense that one is competent and effective. Distinguished from *self-esteem*, a sense of one's self-worth.

Self-fulfilling prophecy The tendency for one's expectations to evoke behaviour in others that confirms the expectations.

Self-perception theory The theory that when unsure of our attitudes, we infer them much as would someone observing us—by looking at our behaviour and the circumstances under which it occurs.

Self-presentation Wanting to present a desired image both to an external audience (other people) and an internal audience (ourselves).

Self-reference effect The tendency to process efficiently and remember well information related to oneself.

Self-schema Beliefs about self that organize and guide the processing of self-relevant information.

Self-serving bias The tendency to perceive and present oneself favourably.

Sequential lineup A lineup type where photos are presented individually.

Sexism (1) An individual's prejudicial attitudes and discriminatory behaviour toward people of a given gender, or (2) institutional practices (even if not motivated by prejudice) that subordinate people of a given gender.

Simultaneous lineup A lineup type that presents photos together in one array.

Sleeper effect A delayed impact of a message; occurs when we remember the message but forget the reason for discounting it.

Social comparison Evaluating one's abilities and opinions by comparing oneself to others.

Social-exchange theory The theory that human interactions are transactions that aim to maximize one's rewards and minimize one's costs.

Social facilitation (1) Original meaning—the tendency of people to perform simple or well-learned tasks better when others are present. (2) Current meaning—the strengthening of dominant (prevalent, likely) responses in the presence of others.

Social identity The "we" aspect of our self-concept. The part of our answer to "Who am I?" that comes from our group.

Social learning theory The theory that we learn social behaviour by observing and imitating and by being rewarded and punished.

Social loafing The tendency for people to exert less effort when they pool their efforts toward a common goal than when they are individually accountable.

Social psychology The scientific study of how people think about, influence, and relate to one another.

Social-responsibility norm An expectation that people will help those dependent upon them.

Stereotype A belief about the personal attributes of a group of people. Stereotypes are sometimes overgeneralized, inaccurate, and resistant to new information.

Stereotype threat A disruptive concern, when facing a negative stereotype, that one will be evaluated based on a negative stereotype. Unlike self-fulfilling prophecies that hammer one's reputation into one's self-concept, stereotype-threat situations have immediate effects.

Subliminal messages Messages presented in such a manner as to be below a person's threshold of conscious awareness.

Superordinate goal A shared goal that necessitates cooperative effort; a goal that overrides people's differences from one another.

T

Theory An integrated set of principles that explain and predict observed events.

Two-factor theory of emotion Arousal × label = emotion. (Emotional experience is a product of physiological arousal and how we cognitively label the arousal.)

References

ABRAMS, D. (1991). AIDS: What young people believe and what they do. Paper presented at the British Association for the Advancement of Science conference.

ABRAMS, D., WETHERELL, M., COCHRANE, S., HOGG, M. A., & TURNER, J. C. (1990). Knowing what to think by knowing who you are: Self-categorization and the nature of norm formation, conformity and group polarization. *British Journal of Social Psychology, 29,* 97–119.

ACITELLI, L. K., & ANTONUCCI, T. C. (1994). Gender differences in the link between marital support and satisfaction in older couples. *Journal of Personality and Social Psychology, 67,* 688–698.

ADAIR, J. G., DUSHENKO, T. W., & LINDSAY, R. C. L. (1985). Ethical regulations and their impact on research practice. *American Psychologist, 40,* 59–72.

ADAMS, J. M., & JONES, W. H. (1997). The conceptualization of marital commitment: An integrative analysis. *Journal of Personality and Social Psychology, 72,* 1177–1196.

ADLER, R. P., LESSER, G. S., MERINGOFF, L. K., ROBERTSON, T. S., & WARD, S. (1980). *The effects of television advertising on children.* Lexington, MA: Lexington Books.

ADORNO, T., FRENKEL-BRUNSWIK, E., LEVINSON, D., & SANFORD, R. N. (1950). *The authoritarian personality.* New York: Harper.

AIELLO, J. R., THOMPSON, D. E., & BRODZINSKY, D. M. (1983). How funny is crowding anyway? Effects of room size, group size, and the introduction of humor. *Basic and Applied Social Psychology, 4,* 193–207.

AJZEN, I. (1991). The theory of planned behavior. *Organizational Behavior and Human Decision Processes, 50,* 179–211.

ALLEE, W. C., & MASURE, R. M. (1936). A comparison of maze behavior in paired and isolated shell-parakeets (Melopsittacus undulatus Shaw) in a two-alley problem box. *Journal of Comparative Psychology, 22,* 131–155.

ALLEN, J. J., IACONO, W. G., & DANIELSON, K. D. (1992). The identification of concealed memories using the event-related potential and implicit behavioral measures: A methodology for prediction in the face of individual differences. *Psychophysiology, 29(5),* 504–22.

ALLISON, S. T., JORDAN, M. R., & YEATTS, C. E. (1992). A cluster-analytic approach toward identifying the structure and content of human decision making. *Human Relations, 45,* 49–72.

ALLISON, S. T., MESSICK, D. M., & GOETHALS, G. R. (1989). On being better but not smarter than others: The Muhammad Ali effect. *Social Cognition, 7,* 275–296.

ALLPORT, F. H. (1920). The influence of the group upon association and thought. *Journal of Experimental Psychology, 3,* 159–182.

ALLPORT, G. W. (1958). *The nature of prejudice (abridged).* Garden City, NY: Anchor Books.

ALTEMEYER, B. (1988). *Enemies of freedom: Understanding right-wing authoritarianism.* San Francisco: Jossey-Bass.

ALTEMEYER, B. (1992). Six studies of right-wing authoritarianism among American state legislators. Unpublished manuscript, University of Manitoba.

ALTEMEYER, R. (2004). Highly dominating, highly authoritarian personalities. *Journal of Social Psychology, 144,* 421–447.

AMABILE, T. M., & GLAZEBROOK, A. H. (1982). A negativity bias in interpersonal evaluation. *Journal of Experimental Social Psychology, 18,* 1–22.

AMERICAN ENTERPRISE. (1992, January/February). Women, men, marriages & ministers, p. 106.

AMIR, Y. (1969). Contact hypothesis in ethnic relations. *Psychological Bulletin, 71,* 319–342.

ANDERSON, C. A. (2003). Video games and aggressive behavior. In D. Ravitch and J. P. Viteritti (Eds.), *Kids stuff: Marking violence and vulgarity in the popular culture.* Baltimore: Johns Hopkins University Press.

ANDERSON, C. A. (2004). An update on the effects of violent video games. *Journal of Adolescence, 27,* 113–122.

ANDERSON, C. A., & ANDERSON, K. B. (1998). Temperature and aggression: Paradox, controversy, and a (fairly) clear picture. In R. G. Geen & E. Donnerstein (Eds.), *Human aggression: Theories, research, and implications for social policy.* San Diego, CA: Academic Press.

ANDERSON, C. A., ANDERSON, K. B., DORR, N., DENEVE, K. M., & FLANAGAN, M. (2000). Temperature and aggression. In M. P. Zanna (Ed.), *Advances in experimental social psychology,* Vol. 32, pp. 63–133. San Diego: Academic Press.

ANDERSON, C. A., BENJAMIN, A. J., JR., & BARTHOLOW, B. D. (1998). Does the gun pull the trigger? Automatic priming effects of weapon pictures and weapon names. *Psychological Science, 9,* 308–314.

ANDERSON, C. A., & BUSHMAN, B. J. (2002). Media violence and the American public revisited. *American Psychologist, 57,* 448–450.

ANDERSON, C. A., CARNAGEY, N. L., & EUBANKS, J. (2003). Exposure to violent media: The effects of songs with violent lyrics on aggressive thoughts and feelings. *Journal of Personality and Social Psychology, 84,* 960–971.

ANDERSON, C. A., HOROWITZ, L. M., & FRENCH, R. D. (1983). Attributional style of lonely and depressed people. *Journal of Personality and Social Psychology, 45,* 127–136.

ANDERSON, C. A., LINDSAY, J. J., & BUSHMAN, B. J. (1999). Research in the psychological laboratory: Truth or triviality? *Current Directions in Psychological Science, 8,* 3–9.

ANDERSON, K. B., COOPER, H., & OKAMURA, L. (1997). Individual differences and attitudes toward rape: A meta-analytic review. *Personality and Social Psychology Review, 23,* 295–315.

ANDERSON, K. J., & LEAPER, C. (1998). Meta-analyses of gender effects on conversational interruption: Who, what, when, where, and how. *Sex Roles, 39,* 225–252.

AP. (1993, June 10). Walking past a dying man. *New York Times* (via Associated Press), 485.

ARCHER, D., & GARTNER, R. (1976). Violent acts and violent times: A comparative approach to postwar homicide rates. *American Sociological Review, 41,* 937–963.

ARCHER, J. (1991). The influence of testosterone on human aggression. *British Journal of Psychology, 82,* 1–28.

ARCHER, J. (2000). Sex differences in aggression between heterosexual partners: A meta-analytic review. *Psychological Bulletin, 126,* 651–680.

ARENDT, H. (1963). *Eichmann in Jerusalem: A report on the banality of evil.* New York: Viking Press.

ARGYLE, M. (1999). Causes and correlates of happiness. In D. Kahneman, E. Diener, & N. Schwartz (Eds.), *Foundations of hedonic psychology: Scientific perspectives on enjoyment and suffering.* New York: Russell Sage Foundation.

ARGYLE, M., SHIMODA, K., & LITTLE, B. (1978). Variance due to persons and situations in England and Japan. *British Journal of Social and Clinical Psychology, 17,* 335–337.

ARKIN, R. M., & BURGER, J. M. (1980). Effects of unit relation tendencies on interpersonal attraction. *Social Psychology Quarterly, 43,* 380–391.

ARKIN, R. M., COOPER, H., & KOLDITZ, T. (1980). A statistical review of the literature concerning the self-serving attribution bias in interpersonal influence situations. *Journal of Personality, 48,* 435–448.

ARKIN, R. M., & MARUYAMA, G. M. (1979). Attribution, affect, and college exam performance. *Journal of Educational Psychology, 71,* 85–93.

ARKIN, R. M., LAKE, E. A., & BAUMGARDNER, A. H. (1986). Shyness and self-presentation. In W. H. Jones, J. M. Cheek, & S. R. Briggs (Eds). *Shyness: Perspectives on Research and Treatment,* (p. 65). New York: Plenum.

ARMOR, D. A., & TAYLOR, S. E. (1996). Situated optimism: Specific outcome expectancies and self-regulation. In M. P. Zanna (Ed.), *Advances in experimental social psychology,* vol. 30. San Diego, CA: Academic Press.

ARMS, R. L., RUSSELL, G. W., & SANDILANDS, M. L. (1979). Effects on the hostility of spectators of viewing aggressive sports. *Social Psychology Quarterly, 42,* 275–279.

ARON, A., & ARON, E. (1989). *The heart of social psychology,* 2nd ed. Lexington, MA: Lexington Books.

ARON, A., & ARON, E. N. (1994). Love. In A. L. Weber & J. H. Harvey (Eds.), *Perspective on close relationships.* Boston: Allyn & Bacon.

ARON, A., DUTTON, D. G., ARON, E. N., & IVERSON, A. (1989). Experiences of falling in love. *Journal of Social and Personal Relationships, 6,* 243–257.

ARONSON, E. (1980). *The social animal.* New York: Freeman.

ARONSON, E. (2000). *Nobody left to hate: Teaching compassion after Columbine.* New York: Freeman/Worth.

ARONSON, E. (2002). Building empathy, compassion, and achievement in the jigsaw classroom. In J. Aronson (Ed.), *Improving academic achievement: Impact of psychological factors on education.* San Diego, CA: Academic Press.

ARONSON, E., BLANEY, N., STEPHAN, C., SIKES, J., & SNAPP, M. (1978). *The jigsaw classroom.* Beverly Hills, CA: Sage.

ARONSON, E., BREWER, M., & CARLSMITH, J. M. (1985). Experimentation in social psychology. In G. Lindzey & E. Aronson (Eds.), *Handbook of social psychology,* vol. 1. Hillsdale, NJ: Erlbaum.

ARONSON, E., & GONZALEZ, A. (1988). Desegregation, jigsaw, and the Mexican-American experience. In P. A. Katz & D. Taylor (Eds.), *Towards the elimination of racism: Profiles in controversy.* New York: Plenum.

ARONSON, E., & MILLS, J. (1959). The effect of severity of initiation on liking for a group. *Journal of Abnormal and Social Psychology, 59,* 177–181.

ASCH, S. E. (1955, November). Opinions and social pressure. *Scientific American,* pp. 31–35.

ASHER, J. (1987, April). Born to be shy? *Psychology Today,* pp. 56–64.

ATSB. (2005). Road deaths: Australia, 2004 statistical summary.

ATWELL, R. H. (1986, July 28). Drugs on campus: A perspective. *Higher Education and National Affairs,* p. 5.

AVERILL, J. R. (1983). Studies on anger and aggression: Implications for theories of emotion. *American Psychologist, 38,* 1145–1160.

AXELROD, R., & DION, D. (1988). The further evolution of cooperation. *Science, 242,* 1385–1390.

AXSOM, D., YATES, S., & CHAIKEN, S. (1987). Audience response as a heuristic cue in persuasion. *Journal of Personality and Social Psychology, 53,* 30–40.

AYRES, I. (1991). Fair driving: Gender and race discrimination in retail car negotiations. *Harvard Law Review, 104,* 817–872.

AZMIER, J. J. (2005, June). Gambling in Canada 2005: Statistics and context. *CanadaWest Foundation,* 1–12.

AZRIN, N. H. (1967, May). Pain and aggression. *Psychology Today,* pp. 27–33.

BABAD, E., HILLS, M., & O'DRISCOLL, M. (1992). Factors influencing wishful thinking and predictions of election outcomes. *Basic and Applied Social Psychology, 13,* 461–476.

BACHMAN, J. G., & O'MALLEY, P. M. (1977). Self-esteem in young men: A longitudinal analysis of the impact of educational and occupational attainment. *Journal of Personality and Social Psychology, 35,* 365–380.

BAILEY, J. M., GAULIN, S., AGYEI, Y., & GLADUE, B. A. (1994). Effects of gender and sexual orientation on evolutionary relevant aspects of human mating psychology. Journal of *Personality and Social Psychology, 66,* 1081–1093.

BAILEY, J. M., KIRK, K. M., ZHU, G., DUNNE, M. P., & MARTIN, N. G. (2000). Do individual differences in sociosexuality represent genetic or environmentally contingent strategies? Evidence from the Australian Twin Registry. *Journal of Personality and Social Psychology, 78,* 537–545.

BAILIS, D., FEIGENSON, N. R., & KLEIN, M. P. (2005). A cross-national comparison of perceived risks from terrorism and disease. Unpublished manuscripts, University of Manitoba, Quinnipiac University, and University of Pittsburgh.

BAIZE, H. R., JR., & SCHROEDER, J. E. (1995). Personality and mate selection in personal ads: Evolutionary preferences in a public mate selection process. *Journal of Social Behavior and Personality, 10,* 517–536.

BAKER, L. A., & EMERY, R. E. (1993). When every relationship is above average: Perceptions and expectations of divorce at the time of marriage. *Law and Human Behavior, 17,* 439–450.

BANAJI, M. R., & BHASKAR, R. (2000). Implicit stereotypes and memory: The bounded rationality of social beliefs. In D. L. Schacter & E. Scarry (Eds.), *Memory, brain, and belief.* Cambridge, MA: Harvard University Press.

BANDURA, A. (1979). The social learning perspective: Mechanisms of aggression. In H. Toch (Ed.), *Psychology of crime and criminal justice.* New York: Holt, Rinehart & Winston.

BANDURA, A. (1986). *Social foundations of thought and action: A social cognitive theory.* Englewood Cliffs, NJ: Prentice Hall.

BANDURA, A. (1997). *Self-efficacy: The exercise of control.* New York: Freeman.

BANDURA, A., & WALTERS, R. H. (1959). *Adolescent aggression.* New York: Ronald Press.

BANDURA, A., & WALTERS, R. H. (1963). *Social learning and personality development.* New York: Holt, Rinehart and Winston.

BANDURA, A., PASTORELLI, C., BARBARANELLI, C., & CAPRARA, G. V. (1999). Self-efficacy pathways to childhood depression. *Journal of Personality and Social Psychology, 76,* 258–269.

BANDURA, A., ROSS, D., & ROSS, S. A. (1961). Transmission of aggression through imitation of aggressive models. *Journal of Abnormal and Social Psychology, 63,* 575–582.

BANFIELD, S., & MCCABE, M. P. (2001). Extra relationship involvement among women: Are they different from men? *Archives of Sexual Behavior, 30,* 119–142.

BARGH, J. A., & CHARTRAND, T. L. (1999). The unbearable automaticity of being. *American Psychologist, 54,* 462–479.

BARGH, J. A., MCKENNA, K. Y. A., & FITZSIMONS, G. M. (2002). Can you see the real me? Activation and expression of the "true self" on the Internet. *Journal of Social Issues, 58,* 33–48.

BARON, R. A., & BRYNE, D. (1991). *Social psychology: Understanding human interaction* (6th ed.). Toronto: Allyn & Bacon.

BARON, R. M., MANDEL, D. R., ADAMS, C. A., & GRIFFEN, L. M. (1976). Effects of social density in university residential environments. *Journal of Personality and Social Psychology, 34,* 434–446.

BARON, R. S. (1986). Distraction-conflict theory: Progress and problems. In L. Berkowitz (Ed.), *Advances in experimental social psychology.* Orlando, FL: Academic Press.

BARON, R. S. (2000). Arousal, capacity, and intense indoctrination. *Personality and Social Psychology Review, 4,* 238–254.

BARON, R. S., DAVID, J. P., INMAN, M., & BRUNSMAN, B. M. (1997). Why listeners hear less than they are told: Attentional load and the teller-listener extremity effect. *Journal of Personality and Social Psychology, 72,* 826–838.

BARONGAN, C., & HALL, G. C. N. (1995). The influence of misogynous rap music on sexual aggression against women. *Psychology of Women Quarterly, 19,* 195–207.

BARRY, D. (1995, January). Bored stiff. *Funny Times,* p. 5.

BARTHOLOW, B. D. (2005). Correlates and consequences of exposure to video game violence: Hostile personality, empathy, and aggressive behavior. *Personality and Social Psychology Bulletin, 31,* 1573–1586.

BATSON, C. D. (1991). *The altruism question: Toward a social-psychological answer.* Hillsdale, NJ: Erlbaum.

BATSON, C. D., & MORAN, T. (1999). Empathy-induced altruism in a prisoner's dilemma. *European Journal of Social Psychology, 29,* 909–924.

BATSON, C. D., SYMPSON, S. C., HINDMAN, J. L., DECRUZ, P., TODD, R. M., JENNINGS, G., & BURRIS, C. T. (1996). "I've been there, too": Effect on empathy of prior experience with a need. *Personality and Social Psychology Bulletin, 22,* 474–482.

BAUMGARDNER, A. H. (1991). Claiming depressive symptoms as a self-handicap: A protective self-presentation strategy. *Basic and Applied Social Psychology, 12,* 97–113.

BAUMEISTER, R. (1996). Should schools try to boost self-esteem? Beware the dark side. *American Educator, 20,* 14–19, 43.

BAUMEISTER, R. F. (1991). *Meanings of life.* New York: Guilford.

BAUMEISTER, R. F., & ILKO, S. A. (1995). Shallow gratitude: Public and private acknowledgement of external help in accounts of success. *Basic and Applied Social Psychology, 16,* 191–209.

BAUMEISTER, R. F., & LEARY, M. R. (1995). The need to belong: Desire for interpersonal attachment as a fundamental human motivation. *Psychological Bulletin, 117*, 497–529.

BAUMEISTER, R. F., & SCHER, S. J. (1988). Self-defeating behavior patterns among normal individuals: Review and analysis of common self-destructive tendencies. *Psychological Bulletin, 104*, 3–22.

BAUMEISTER, R. F., & VOHS, K. (2004). Sexual economics: Sex as female resource for social exchange in heterosexual interactions. *Personality and Social Psychology Bulletin, 8*, 339–363.

BAUMEISTER, R. F., & WOTMAN, S. R. (1992). *Breaking hearts: The two sides of unrequited love.* New York: Guilford Press.

BAUMEISTER, R. F., CAMPBELL, J. D., KRUEGER, J. I., & VOHS, K. D. (2003). Does high self-esteem cause better performance, interpersonal success, happiness, or healthier lifestyles? *Psychological Science in the Public Interest, 4*, 1–44.

BAUMEISTER, R. F., CATANESE, K. R., & VOHS, K. D. (2001). Is there a gender difference in strength of sex drive? Theoretical views, conceptual distinctions, and a review of relevant evidence. *Personality and Social Psychology Review, 5*, 242–273.

BAUMEISTER, R. F., CATANESE, K. R., & WALLACE, H. M. (2002). Conquest by force: A narcissistic reactance theory of rape and sexual coercion. *Review of General Psychology, 6*, 92–135.

BAUSERMAN, R. (1996). Sexual aggression and pornography: A review of correlational research. *Basic and Applied Social Psychology, 18*, 405–427.

BAXTER, T. L., & GOLDBERG, L. R. (1987). Perceived behavioral consistency underlying trait attributions to oneself and another: An extension of the actor-observer effect. *Personality and Social Psychology Bulletin, 13*, 437–447.

BAYER, E. (1929). Beitrage zur zeikomponenten theorie des hungers. *Zeitschrift fur Psychologie, 112*, 1–54.

BAZERMAN, M. H. (1986, June). Why negotiations go wrong. *Psychology Today*, pp. 54–58.

BAZERMAN, M. H. (1990). *Judgment in managerial decision making*, 2nd ed. New York: Wiley.

BEAMAN, A. L., BARNES, P. J., KLENTZ, B., & McQUIRK, B. (1978). Increasing helping rates through information dissemination: Teaching pays. *Personality and Social Psychology Bulletin, 4*, 406–411.

BEAMAN, A. L., & KLENTZ, B. (1983). The supposed physical attractiveness bias against supporters of the women's movement: A meta-analysis. *Personality and Social Psychology Bulletin, 9*, 544–550.

BEAMAN, A. L., KLENTZ, B., DIENER, E., & SVANUM, S. (1979). Self-awareness and transgression in children: Two field studies. *Journal of Personality and Social Psychology, 37*, 1835–1846.

BEAUVOIS, J. L., & DUBOIS, N. (1988). The norm of internality in the explanation of psychological events. *European Journal of Social Psychology, 18*, 299–316.

BELL, P. A. (1980). Effects of heat, noise, and provocation on retaliatory evaluative behavior. *Journal of Social Psychology, 110*, 97–100.

BELSON, W. A. (1978). *Television violence and the adolescent boy.* Westmead, England: Saxon House, Teakfield Ltd.

BEM, D. J. (1972). Self-perception theory. In L. Berkowitz (Ed.), *Advances in experimental social psychology*, vol. 6. New York: Academic Press.

BENNETT, R. (1991, February). Pornography and extrafamilial child sexual abuse: Examining the relationship. Unpublished manuscript, Los Angeles Police Department Sexually Exploited Child Unit.

BENNIS, W. (1984). Transformative power and leadership. In T. J. Sergiovani & J. E. Corbally (Eds.), *Leadership and organizational culture.* Urbana: University of Illinois Press.

BEN-ZEEV, T., FEIN, S., & INZLICHT, M. (2005). Arousal and stereotype threat. *Journal of Experimental Social Psychology, 41*, 174–181.

BERG, J. H. (1984). Development of friendship between roommates. *Journal of Personality and Social Psychology, 46*, 346–356.

BERG, J. H. (1987). Responsiveness and self-disclosure. In V. J. Derlega & J. H. Berg (Eds.), *Self-disclosure: Theory, research, and therapy.* New York: Plenum.

BERG, J. H., & McQUINN, R. D. (1986). Attraction and exchange in continuing and noncontinuing dating relationships. *Journal of Personality and Social Psychology, 50*, 942–952.

BERKOWITZ, L. (1968, September). Impulse, aggression and the gun. *Psychology Today*, pp. 18–22.

BERKOWITZ, L. (1978). Whatever happened to the frustration-aggression hypothesis? *American Behavioral Scientists, 21*, 691–708.

BERKOWITZ, L. (1981, June). How guns control us. *Psychology Today*, pp. 11–12.

BERKOWITZ, L. (1983). Aversively stimulated aggression: Some parallels and differences in research with animals and humans. *American Psychologist, 38*, 1135–1144.

BERKOWITZ, L. (1984). Some effects of thoughts on anti- and prosocial influences of media events: A cognitive-neoassociation analysis. *Psychological Bulletin, 95*, 410–427.

BERKOWITZ, L. (1989). Frustration-aggression hypothesis: Examination and reformulation. *Psychological Bulletin, 106*, 59–73.

BERKOWITZ, L. (1995). A career on aggression. In G. G. Brannigan & M. R. Merrens (Eds.), *The social psychologists: Research adventures.* New York: McGraw-Hill.

BERKOWITZ, L. (1998). Affective aggression: The role of stress, pain, and negative affect. In R. G. Geen & E. Donnerstein (Eds.), *Human aggression: Theories, research, and implications for social policy*. San Diego, CA: Academic Press.

BERKOWITZ, L., & GEEN, R. G. (1966). Film violence and the cue properties of available targets. *Journal of Personality and Social Psychology, 3*, 525–530.

BERKOWITZ, L., & LEPAGE, A. (1967). Weapons as aggression-eliciting stimuli. *Journal of Personality and Social Psychology, 7*, 202–207.

BERRY J. W. (1997). Immigration, acculturation, and adaptation. *Applied Psychology, 46*, 5–34.

BERSCHEID, E. (1981). An overview of the psychological effects of physical attractiveness and some comments upon the psychological effects of knowledge of the effects of physical attractiveness. In W. Lucker, K. Ribbens, & J. A. McNamera (Eds.), *Logical aspects of facial form (craniofacial growth series)*. Ann Arbor: University of Michigan Press.

BERSCHEID, E. (1999). The greening of relationship science. *American Psychologist, 54*, 260–266.

BERSCHEID, E., BOYE, D., & WALSTER (HATFIELD), E. (1968). Retaliation as a means of restoring equity. *Journal of Personality and Social Psychology, 10*, 370–376.

BERSCHEID, E., DION, K., WALSTER (HATFIELD), E., & WALSTER, G. W. (1971). Physical attractiveness and dating choice: A test of the matching hypothesis. *Journal of Experimental Social Psychology, 7*, 173–189.

BERSCHEID, E., GRAZIANO, W., MONSON, T., & DERMER, M. (1976). Outcome dependency: Attention, attribution, and attraction. *Journal of Personality and Social Psychology, 34*, 978–989.

BERSCHEID, E., SNYDER, M., & OMOTO, A. M. (1989). Issues in studying close relationships: Conceptualizing and measuring closeness. In C. Hendrick (Ed.), *Review of personality and social psychology*, vol. 10. Newbury Park, CA: Sage.

BERSCHEID, E., & WALSTER (HATFIELD), E. (1978). *Interpersonal attraction*. Reading, MA: Addison-Wesley.

BERSCHEID, E., WALSTER, G. W., & HATFIELD (WAS WALSTER), E. (1969). Effects of accuracy and positivity of evaluation on liking for the evaluator. Unpublished manuscript. Summarized by E. Berscheid and E. Walster (Hatfield) (1978), *Interpersonal attraction*. Reading, MA: Addison-Wesley.

BETTENCOURT, B. A., DILL, K. E., GREATHOUSE, S. A., CHARLTON, K., & MULHOLLAND, A. (1997). Evaluations of ingroup and outgroup members: The role of category-based expectancy violation. *Journal of Experimental Social Psychology, 33*, 244–275.

BETTENCOURT, B. A., & MILLER, N. (1996). Gender differences in aggression as a function of provocation: A meta-analysis. *Psychological Bulletin, 119*, 422–447.

BEYER, L. (1990, Fall issue on women). Life behind the veil. *Time*, p. 37.

BIANCHI, S. M., MILKIE, M. A., SAYER, L. C., & ROBINSON, J. P. (2000). Is anyone doing the housework? Trends in the gender division of household labor. *Social Forces, 79*, 191–228.

BIBBY, R. (2004). *The Future Families Project: A survey of canadian hopes and dreams*. The Vanier Institute of the Family: Ottawa.

BIERBRAUER, G. (1979). Why did he do it? Attribution of obedience and the phenomenon of dispositional bias. *European Journal of Social Psychology 9*, 67–84.

BIERLY, M. M. (1985). Prejudice toward contemporary outgroups as a generalized attitude. *Journal of Applied Social Psychology, 15*, 189–199.

BIERNAT, M. (1991). Gender stereotypes and the relationship between masculinity and femininity: A developmental analysis. *Journal of Personality and Social Psychology, 61*, 351–365.

BIERNAT, M., & KOBRYNOWICZ, D. (1997). Gender- and race-based standards of competence: Lower minimum standards but higher ability standards for devalued groups. *Journal of Personality and Social Psychology, 72*, 544–557.

BIERNAT, M., & WORTMAN, C. B. (1991). Sharing of home responsibilities between professionally employed women and their husbands. *Journal of Personality and Social Psychology, 60*, 844–860.

BIERNAT, M., VESCIO, T. K., & GREEN, M. L. (1996). Selective self-stereotyping. *Journal of Personality and Social Psychology, 71*, 1194–1209.

BILLIG, M., & TAJFEL, H. (1973). Social categorization and similarity in intergroup behaviour. *European Journal of Social Psychology, 3*, 27–52.

BJÖRKQVIST, K. (1994). Sex differences in physical, verbal, and indirect aggression: A review of recent research. *Sex Roles, 30*, 177–188.

BLAKE, R. R., & MOUTON, J. S. (1962). The intergroup dynamics of win-lose conflict and problem-solving collaboration in union-management relations. In M. Sherif (Ed.), *Intergroup relations and leadership*. New York: Wiley.

BLAKE, R. R., & MOUTON, J. S. (1979). Intergroup problem solving in organizations: From theory to practice. In W. G. Austin & S. Worchel (Eds.), *The social psychology of intergroup relations*. Monterey, CA: Brooks/Cole.

BLISS, M. (2004). *Right honorable men*. HarperCollins: Toronto.

BLOCK J., & FUNDER, D. C. (1986). Social roles and social perception: Individual differences in attribution and error. *Journal of Personality and Social Psychology, 51*, 1200–1207.

BOCHNER, S. (1994). Cross-cultural differences in the self-concept: A test of Hofstede's individualism/collectivism distinction. *Journal of Cross-Cultural Psychology, 25,* 273–283.

BODENHAUSEN, G. V. (1990). Stereotypes as judgmental heuristics: Evidence of circadian variations in discrimination. *Psychological Science, 1,* 319–322.

BODENHAUSEN, G. V. (1993). Emotions, arousal, and stereotypic judgments: A heuristic model of affect and stereotyping. In D. M. Mackie & D. L. Hamilton (Eds.), *Affect, cognition, and stereotyping: Interactive processes in group perception.* San Diego, CA: Academic Press.

BOND, C. F., JR., & TITUS, L. J. (1983). Social facilitation: A meta-analysis of 241 studies. *Psychological Bulletin, 94,* 265–292.

BORGIDA, E., & BREKKE, N. (1985). Psycholegal research on rape trials. In A. W. Burgess (Ed.), *Rape and sexual assault: A research handbook.* New York: Garland.

BORNSTEIN, G., & RAPOPORT, A. (1988). Intergroup competition for the provision of step-level public goods: Effects of preplay communication. *European Journal of Social Psychology, 18,* 125–142.

BORNSTEIN, G., RAPOPORT, A., KERPEL, L., & KATZ, T. (1989). Within- and between-group communication in intergroup competition for public goods. *Journal of Experimental Social Psychology, 25,* 422–436.

BOSSARD, J. H. S. (1932). Residential propinquity as a factor in marriage selection. *American Journal of Sociology, 38,* 219–224.

BOTHWELL, R. K., BRIGHAM, J. C., & MALPASS, R. S. (1989). Cross-racial identification. *Personality and Social Psychology Bulletin, 15,* 19–25.

BOTVIN, G. J., SCHINKE, S., & ORLANDI, M. A. (1995). School-based health promotion: Substance abuse and sexual behavior. *Applied & Preventive Psychology, 4,* 167–184.

BOTWIN, M. D., BUSS, D. M., & SHACKELFORD, T. K. (1997). Personality and mate preferences: Five factors in mate selection and marital satisfaction. *Journal of Personality, 65,* 107–136.

BOUAS, K. S., & KOMORITA, S. S. (1996). Group discussion and cooperation in social dilemmas. *Personality and Social Psychology Bulletin, 22,* 1144–1150.

BOURGEOIS, M. J., HOROWITZ, I. A., & LEE, L. F. (1993). Effects of technically and access to trial transcripts on verdicts and information processing in a civil trial. *Personality and Social Psychology Bulletin, 19,* 219–226.

BOYANOWSKY, E. (1999). Violence and aggression in the heat of passion and in cold blood: The Ecs-TC syndrome. *International Journal of Law & Psychiatry, 22,* 257–271.

BOYATZIS, C. J., MATILLO, G. M., & NESBITT, K. M. (1995). Effects of the "Mighty Morphin Power Rangers" on children's aggression with peers. *Child Study Journal, 25,* 45–55.

BRAY, S. R., LAW, J., & FOYLE, J. (2003). Team quality and game location effects in English professional soccer. *Journal of Sport Behavior, 26,* 319–334.

BREHM, S., & BREHM, J. W. (1981). *Psychological reactance: A theory of freedom and control.* New York: Academic Press.

BREWER, M. B. (1987). Collective decisions. *Social Science, 72,* 140–143.

BREWER, M. B., & MILLER, N. (1988). Contact and cooperation: When do they work? In P. A. Katz & D. Taylor (Eds.), *Towards the elimination of racism: Profiles in controversy.* New York: Plenum.

BREWER, M. B., & SILVER, M. (1978). In-group bias as a function of task characteristics. *European Journal of Social Psychology, 8,* 393–400.

BRICKMAN, P., COATES, D., & JANOFF-BULMAN, R. J. (1978). Lottery winners and accident victims: Is happiness relative? *Journal of Personality and Social Psychology, 36,* 917–927.

BROAD, W. J., & HULSE, C. (2003, February 3). NASA dismissed advisers who warned about safety. *New York Times.* (www.nytimes.com).

BROCKNER, J., & HULTON, A. J. B. (1978). How to reverse the vicious cycle of low self-esteem: The importance of attentional focus. *Journal of Experimental Social Psychology, 14,* 564–578.

BROCKNER, J., RUBIN, J. Z., FINE, J., HAMILTON, T. P., THOMAS, B., & TURETSKY, B. (1982). Factors affecting entrapment in escalating conflicts: The importance of timing. *Journal of Research in Personality, 16,* 247–266.

BRODT, S. E., & ROSS, L. D. (1998). The role of stereotyping in overconfident social prediction. *Social Cognition, 16,* 228–252.

BRONFENBRENNER, U. (1961). The mirror image in Soviet-American relations. *Journal of Social Issues, 17(3),* 45–56.

BROWN, D. E. (1991). *Human universals.* New York: McGraw-Hill.

BROWN, H. J., JR. (1990). *P.S. I love you.* Nashville, TN: Rutledge Hill.

BROWN, J. (2001, September 13). Anti-Arab passions sweep the U.S. Salon.com (www.salon.com/news/feature/2001/09/13/backlash/print.html).

BROWN, J. D., NOVICK, N. J., LORD, K. A., & RICHARDS, J. M. (1992). When Gulliver travels: Social context, psychological closeness, and self-appraisals. *Journal of Personality and Social Psychology, 62,* 717–727.

BROWN, R., MARAS, P., MASSER, B., VIVIAN, J., & HEWSTONE, M. (2001). Life on the ocean wave: Testing some intergroup hypotheses in a naturalistic setting. *Group Processes and Intergroup Relations, 4,* 81–97.

BROWN, R., VIVIAN, J., & HEWSTONE, M. (1999). Changing attitudes through intergroup contact: The effects of group membership salience. *European Journal of Social Psychology, 29,* 741–764.

BROWN, R., & WOOTTON-MILLWARD, L. (1993). Perceptions of group homogeneity during group formation and change. *Social Cognition, 11,* 126–149.

BROWN, R. P., CHARNSANGAVEJ, T., KEOUGH, K. A., NEWMAN, M. L., & RENTFROM, P. J. (2000). Putting the "affirm" into affirmative action: Preferential selection and academic performance. *Journal of Personality and Social Psychology, 79,* 736–747.

BROWNING, C. (1992). *Ordinary men: Reserve police battalion 101 and the final solution in Poland.* New York: HarperCollins.

BURGER, J. M. (1987). Increased performance with increased personal control: A self-presentation interpretation. *Journal of Experimental Social Psychology, 23,* 350–360.

BURGER, J. M. (1991). Changes in attributions over time: The ephemeral fundamental attribution error. *Social Cognition, 9,* 182–193.

BURGER, J. M., & BURNS, L. (1988). The illusion of unique invulnerability and the use of effective contraception. *Personality and Social Psychology Bulletin, 14,* 264–270.

BURGER, J. M., & PAVELICH, J. L. (1994). Attributions for presidential elections: The situational shift over time. *Basic and Applied Social Psychology, 15,* 359–371.

BURGER, J. M., SOROKA, S., GONZAGO, K., MURPHY, E., & SOMERVELL, E. (2001). The effect of fleeting attraction on compliance to requests. *Personality and Social Psychology Bulletin, 27,* 1578–1586.

BURKHOLDER, R. (2003, February 14). Unwilling coalition? Majorities in Britain, Canada oppose military action in Iraq. Gallup Poll Tuesday Briefing (www.gallup.com/poll).

BURN, S. M. (1992). Locus of control, attributions, and helplessness in the homeless. *Journal of Applied Social Psychology, 22,* 1161–1174.

BURNSTEIN, E., & KITAYAMA, S. (1989). Persuasion in groups. In T. C. Brock & S. Shavitt (Eds.), *The psychology of persuasion.* San Francisco: Freeman.

BURNSTEIN, E., & VINOKUR, A. (1977). Persuasive argumentation and social comparison as determinants of attitude polarization. *Journal of Experimental Social Psychology, 13,* 315–332.

BURNSTEIN, E., & WORCHEL, P. (1962). Arbitrariness of frustration and its consequences for aggression in a social situation. *Journal of Personality, 30,* 528–540.

BURR, W. R. (1973). *Theory construction and the sociology of the family.* New York: Wiley.

BUSHMAN, B. J. (1993). Human aggression while under the influence of alcohol and other drugs: An integrative research review. *Current Directions in Psychological Science, 2,* 148–152.

BUSHMAN, B. J. (1995). Moderating role of trait aggressiveness in the effects of violent media on aggression. *Journal of Personality and Social Psychology, 69,* 950–960.

BUSHMAN, B. J. (2002). Does venting anger feed or extinguish the flame? Catharsis, rumination, distraction, anger, and aggressive responding. *Personality and Social Psychology Bulletin, 28,* 724–731.

BUSHMAN, B. J., & ANDERSON, C. A. (2001). Media violence and the American public: Scientific facts versus media misinformation. *American Psychologist, 56,* 477–489.

BUSHMAN, B. J., & BAUMEISTER, R. (1998). Threatened egotism, narcissism, self-esteem, and direct and displaced aggression: Does self-love or self-hate lead to violence? *Journal of Personality and Social Psychology, 75,* 219–229.

BUSHMAN, B. J., & COOPER, H. M. (1990). Effects of alcohol on human aggression: An integrative research review. *Psychological Bulletin, 107,* 341–354.

BUSHMAN, B. J., & GEEN, R. G. (1990). Role of cognitive-emotional mediators and individual differences in the effects of media violence on aggression. *Journal of Personality and Social Psychology, 58,* 156–163.

BUSS, D. M. (1984). Toward a psychology of person-environment (PE) correlation: The role of spouse selection. *Journal of Personality and Social Psychology, 47,* 361–377.

BUSS, D. M. (1985). Human mate selection. *American Scientist, 73,* 47–51.

BUSS, D. M. (1989). Sex differences in human mate preferences: Evolutionary hypotheses tested in 37 cultures. *Behavioral and Brain Sciences, 12,* 1–49.

BUSS, D. M. (1994a). *The evolution of desire: Strategies of human mating.* New York: Basic Books.

BUSS, D. M. (1995b). Psychological sex differences: Origins through sexual selection. *American Psychologist, 50,* 164–168.

BUSS, D. M. (1999). Behind the scenes. In D. G. Myers, *Social psychology,* 6th ed. New York: McGraw-Hill.

BUTCHER, S. H. (1951). *Aristotle's theory of poetry and fine art.* New York: Dover.

BUTLER, J. L., & BAUMEISTER, R. F. (1998). The trouble with friendly faces: Skilled performance with a supportive audience. *Journal of Personality and Social Psychology, 75,* 1213–1230.

BUUNK, B. P., & VAN DER EIJNDEN, R. J. J. M. (1997). Perceived prevalence, perceived superiority, and relationship satisfaction: Most relationships are good, but ours is the best. *Personality and Social Psychology Bulletin, 23,* 219–228.

BUUNK, B. P., & VAN YPEREN, N. W. (1991). Referential comparisons, relational comparisons, and exchange orientation: Their relation to marital satisfaction. *Personality and Social Psychology Bulletin, 17,* 709–717.

BYRNE, D. (1971). *The attraction paradigm.* New York: Academic Press.

BYRNE, D., & WONG, T. J. (1962). Racial prejudice, interpersonal attraction, and assumed dissimilarity of attitudes. *Journal of Abnormal and Social Psychology, 65,* 246–253.

BYRNES, J. P., MILLER, D. C., & SCHAFER, W. D. (1999). Gender differences in risk taking: A meta-analysis. *Psychological Bulletin, 125,* 367–383.

BYTWERK, R. L. (1976). Julius Streicher and the impact of Der Stürmer. *Wiener Library Bulletin, 29,* 41–46.

CACIOPPO, J. T., PETTY, R. E., FEINSTEIN, J. A., & JARVIS, W. B. G. (1996). Dispositional differences in cognitive motivation: The life and times of individuals varying in need for cognition. *Psychological Bulletin, 119,* 197–253.

CACIOPPO, J. T., PETTY, R. E., & MORRIS, K. J. (1983). Effects of need for cognition on message evaluation, recall, and persuasion. *Journal of Personality and Social Psychology, 45,* 805–818.

CAIRNS, E., & HEWSTONE, M. (2002). The impact of peacemaking in Northern Ireland on intergroup behavior. In S. Gabi & B. Nevo (Eds.), *Peace education: The concept, principles, and practices around the world.* Mahwah, NJ: Erlbaum.

CALHOUN, J. B. (1962, February). Population density and social pathology. *Scientific American,* 139–148.

CAMERON, J. E. (2004). A three-factor model of social identity. *Self & Identity, 3,* 239–262.

CAMERON, J. E., & LALONDE, R. N. (2001). Social identification and gender-related ideology in women and men. *British Journal of Social Psychology, 40,* 59–77.

CAMPBELL, D. T. (1975). The conflict between social and biological evolution and the concept of original sin. *Zygon, 10,* 234–249.

CAMPBELL, W. K., & SEDIKIDES, C. (1999). Self-threat magnifies the self-serving bias: A meta-analytic integration. *Review of General Psychology, 3,* 23–43.

CANADIAN CENTRE ON SUBSTANCE ABUSE. (1997). *Canadian profile: Alcohol, tobacco, and other drugs.* Ottawa: Canadian Centre on Substance Abuse.

CARDUCCI, B. J., COSBY, P. C., & WARD, D. D. (1978). Sexual arousal and interpersonal evaluations. *Journal of Experimental Social Psychology, 14,* 449–457.

CARLI, L. L. (1991). Gender, status, and influence. In E. J. Lawler & B. Markovsky (Eds.), *Advances in group processes: Theory and research,* vol. 8. Greenwich, CT: JAI Press.

CARLI, L. L. (1999). Cognitive reconstruction, hindsight, and reactions to victims and perpetrators. *Personality and Social Psychology Bulletin, 25,* 966–979.

CARLI, L. L., & LEONARD, J. B. (1989). The effect of hindsight on victim derogation. *Journal of Social and Clinical Psychology, 8,* 331–343.

CARLSON, J., & HATFIELD, E. (1992). *The psychology of emotion.* Fort Worth: Holt, Rinehart & Winston.

CARLSON, M., MARCUS-NEWHALL, A., & MILLER, N. (1990). Effects of situational aggression cues: A quantitative review. *Journal of Personality and Social Psychology, 58,* 622–633.

CARLSTON, D. E., & SHOVAR, N. (1983). Effects of performance attributions on others' perceptions of the attributor. *Journal of Personality and Social Psychology, 44,* 515–525.

CARTER, S. L. (1993). *Reflections of an affirmative action baby.* New York: Basic Books.

CARTWRIGHT, D. S. (1975). The nature of gangs. In D. S. Cartwright, B. Tomson, & H. Schwartz (Eds.), *Gang delinquency.* Monterey, CA: Brooks/Cole.

CASH, T. F., & JANDA, L. H. (1984, December). The eye of the beholder. *Psychology Today,* pp. 46–52.

CASPI, A., & HERBENER, E. S. (1990). Continuity and change: Assortative marriage and the consistency of personality in adulthood. *Journal of Personality and Social Psychology, 58,* 250–258.

CBC. (2006, March 13). *Yes, it's been the warmest Canadian winter on record.* Retrieved from http://www.cbc.ca/story/canada/national/2006/03/13/warm-winter060313.html.

CBC NEWS ONLINE. (2005, June 23). Indepth: Forces of nature. Retrieved 2 June 2006 from http://www.cbc.ca/news/background/forceofnature/.

CBC NEWS ONLINE. (2006, June 15). Indepth: Iraq, casualties in Iraq war. Retrieved 19 June 2006 from http://www.cbc.ca/printablestory.jsp.

CENTERWALL, B. S. (1989). Exposure to television as a risk factor for violence. *American Journal of Epidemiology, 129,* 643–652.

CHAIKEN, S. (1979). Communicator physical attractiveness and persuasion. *Journal of Personality and Social Psychology, 37,* 1387–1397.

CHAIKEN, S. (1980). Heuristic versus systematic information processing and the use of source versus message cues in persuasion. *Journal of Personality and Social Psychology, 39,* 752–766.

CHANCE, J. E., & GOLDSTEIN, A. G. (1981). Depth of processing in response to own- and other-race faces. *Personality and Social Psychology Bulletin, 7,* 475–480.

CHANCE, J. E., & GOLDSTEIN, A. G. (1996). The other-race effect and eyewitness identification. In S. L. Sporer (Ed.), *Psychological issues in eyewitness identification* (pp. 153–176) Mahwah, NJ: Erlbaum.

CHECK, J., & MALAMUTH, N. (1984). Can there be positive effects of participation in pornography experiments? *Journal of Sex Research, 20,* 14–31.

CHEN, H. C., REARDON, R., & REA, C. (1992). Forewarning of content and involvement: Consequences for persuasion and resistance to persuasion. *Journal of Experimental Social Psychology, 28,* 523–541.

CHEN, L-H., BAKER, S. P., BRAVER, E. R., & LI, G. (2000). Carrying passengers as a risk factor for crashes fatal to 16- and 17-year-old drivers. *Journal of the American Medical Association, 283,* 1578–1582.

CHEN, S. C. (1937). Social modification of the activity of ants in nest-building. *Physiological Zoology, 10,* 420–436.

CHODOROW, N. J. (1978). *The reproduction of mother: Psychoanalysis and the sociology of gender.* Berkeley: University of California Press.

CHODOROW, N. J. (1989). *Feminism and psychoanalytic theory.* New Haven, CT: Yale University Press.

CHOI, I., NISBETT, R. E., & NORENZAYAN, A. (1999). Causal attribution across cultures: Variation and universality. *Psychological Bulletin, 125,* 47–63.

CHRISTIAN, J. J., FLYGER, V., & DAVIS, D. E. (1960). Factors in the mass mortality of a herd of sika deer, Cervus Nippon. *Chesapeake Science, 1,* 79–95.

CHUA-EOAN, H. (1997, April 7). *Imprisoned by his own passions.* Time, pp. 40–42.

CHURCH, G. J. (1986, January 6). China. *Time,* pp. 6–19.

CIALDINI, R. B. (1988). *Influence: Science and practice.* Glenview, IL: Scott, Foresman/Little, Brown.

CIALDINI, R. B., CACIOPPO, J. T., BASSETT, R., & MILLER, J. A. (1978). Lowball procedure for producing compliance: Commitment then cost. *Journal of Personality and Social Psychology, 36,* 463–476.

CIALDINI, R. B., DEMAINE, L. J., BARRETT, D. W., SAGARIN, B. J., & RHOADS, K. L. V. (2003). The poison parasite defense: A strategy for sapping a stronger opponent's persuasive strength. Unpublished manuscript, Arizona State University.

CIALDINI, R. B., & RICHARDSON, K. D. (1980). Two indirect tactics of image management: Basking and blasting. *Journal of Personality and Social Psychology, 39,* 406–415.

CIALDINI, R. B., WOSINSKA, W., DABUL, A. J., WHETSTONE-DION, R., & HESZEN, I. (1998). When social role salience leads to social role rejection: Modest self-presentation among women and men in two cultures. *Personality and Social Psychology Bulletin, 24,* 473–481.

CICERELLO, A., & SHEEHAN, E. P. (1995). Personal advertisements: A content analysis. *Journal of Social Behavior and Personality, 10,* 751–756.

CLANCY, S. M., & DOLLINGER, S. J. (1993). Photographic depictions of the self: Gender and age differences in social connectedness. *Sex Roles, 29,* 477–495.

CLARK, M. S. (1984). Record keeping in two types of relationships. *Journal of Personality and Social Psychology, 47,* 549–557.

CLARK, M. S. (1986). Evidence for the effectiveness of manipulations of desire for communal versus exchange relationships. *Personality and Social Psychology Bulletin, 12,* 414–425.

CLARK, M. S., & BENNETT, M. E. (1992). Research on relationships: Implications for mental health. In D. Ruble P. Costanzo (Eds.), *The social psychology of mental health.* New York: Guilford Press.

CLARK, M. S., & MILLS, J. (1979). Interpersonal attraction in exchange and communal relationships. *Journal of Personality and Social Psychology, 37,* 12–24.

CLARK, M. S., MILLS, J., & CORCORAN, D. (1989). Keeping track of needs and inputs of friends and strangers. *Personality and Social Psychology Bulletin, 15,* 533–542.

CLARK, M. S., MILLS, J., & POWELL, M. C. (1986). Keeping track of needs in communal and exchange relationships. *Journal of Personality and Social Psychology, 51,* 333–338.

CLARK, R. D., III. (1995). A few parallels between group polarization and minority influence. In S. Moscovici, H. Mucchi-Faina, & A. Maass (Eds.), *Minority influence.* Chicago: Nelson-Hall.

CLARK, R. D., III, & MAASS, A. (1990). The effects of majority size on minority influence. *European Journal of Social Psychology, 20,* 99–117.

CLARKE, A. C. (1952). An examination of the operation of residual propinquity as a factor in mate selection. *American Sociological Review, 27,* 17–22.

CLIFFORD, M. M., & WALSTER, E. H. (1973). The effect of physical attractiveness on teacher expectation. *Sociology of Education, 46,* 248–258.

CLORE, G. L., BRAY, R. M., ITKIN, S. M., & MURPHY, P. (1978). Interracial attitudes and behavior at a summer camp. *Journal of Personality and Social Psychology, 36,* 107–116.

CNN.COM. (2001, September 17). Hate crimes reports up in wake of terrorist attacks. cnn.com/U.S. (www.cnn.com/2001/US/09/16/gen.hate.crimes/).

COATES, B., PUSSER, H. E., & GOODMAN, I. (1976). The influence of "Sesame Street" and "Mister Rogers' Neighborhood" on children's social behavior in the preschool. *Child Development, 47,* 138–144.

COATS, E. J., & FELDMAN, R. S. (1996). Gender differences in nonverbal correlates of social status. *Personality and Social Psychology Bulletin, 22,* 1014–1022.

CODOL, J.-P. (1976). On the so-called superior conformity of the self behavior: Twenty experimental investigations. *European Journal of Social Psychology, 5,* 457–501.

COHEN, M., & DAVIS, N. (1981). *Medication errors: Causes and prevention.* Philadelphia: G. F. Stickley Co. Cited by R. B. Cialdini (1989). Agents of influence: Bunglers, smugglers, and sleuths. Paper presented at the American Psychological Association convention.

COHEN, S. (1980). Training to understand TV advertising: Effects and some policy implications. Paper presented at the American Psychological Association convention.

COLASANTO, D., & SHRIVER, J. (1989, May). Mirror of America: Middle-aged face marital crisis. *Gallup Report* (No. 284), pp. 34–38.

COLVIN, C. R., BLOCK, J., & FUNDER, D. C. (1995). Overly-positive self evaluations and personality: Negative implications for mental health. *Journal of Personality and Social Psychology, 68,* 1152–1162.

COMER, D. R. (1995). A model of social loafing in real work group. *Human Relations, 48,* 647–667.

COMSTOCK, G., & SCHARRER, E. (1999). *Television: What's on, who's watching and what it means.* San Diego, CA: Academic Press.

CONWAY, L. G., & SCHALLER, M. (2005). When authorities' commands backfire: Attributions about consensus and effects on deviant decision making. *Journal of Personality and Social Psychology, 89,* 311–326.

COOK, T. D., & FLAY, B. R. (1978). The persistence of experimentally induced attitude change. In L. Berkowitz (Ed.), *Advances in experimental social psychology,* vol. 11. New York: Academic Press.

COOPER, H. (1983). Teacher expectation effects. In L. Bickman (Ed.), *Applied social psychology annual,* vol. 4. Beverly Hills, CA: Sage.

COREY, S. M. (1937). Professed attitudes and actual behavior. *Journal of Educational Psychology, 28,* 271–280.

CORRELL, J., PARK, B., JUDD, C. M., & WITTENBRINK, B. (2002). The police officer's dilemma: Using ethnicity to disambiguate potentially threatening individuals. *Journal of Personality and Social Psychology, 83,* 1314–1329.

COTA, A. A., & DION, K. L. (1986). Salience of gender and sex composition of ad hoc groups: An experimental test of distinctiveness theory. *Journal of Personality and Social Psychology, 50,* 770–776.

COTTON, J. L. (1981). Ambient temperature and violent crime. Paper presented at the Midwestern Psychological Association convention.

COTTRELL, N. B., WACK, D. L., SEKERAK, G. J., & RITTLE, R. M. (1968). Social facilitation of dominant responses by the presence of an audience and the mere presence of others. *Journal of Personality and Social Psychology, 9,* 245–250.

COURT, J. H. (1985). Sex and violence: A ripple effect. In N. M. Malamuth & E. Donnerstein (Eds.), *Pornography and sexual aggression.* New York: Academic Press.

CRAIG, M. E. (1990). Coercive sexuality in dating relationships: A situational model. *Clinical Psychology Review, 10,* 395–423.

CRANDALL, C. S. (1994). Prejudice against fat people: Ideology and self-interest. *Journal of Personality and Social Psychology, 66,* 882–894.

CRIC. (2005). *Portraits of Canada 2004.* Ottawa: Centre for Research and Information on Canada. CROCKER, J. (1981). Judgment of covariation by social perceivers. *Psychological Bulletin, 90,* 272–292.

CROCKER, J. (1994, October 14). Who cares what they think? Reflected and deflected appraisal. Presentation to the Society of Experimental Social Psychology meeting.

CROCKER, J. (2002). The costs of seeking self-esteem. *Journal of Social Issues, 58,* 597–615.

CROCKER, J., & GALLO, L. (1985). The self-enhancing effect of downward comparison. Paper presented at the American Psychological Association convention.

CROCKER, J., & LUHTANEN, R. (2003). Level of self-esteem and contingencies of self-worth: Unique effects on academic, social, and financial problems in college students. *Personality and Social Psychology Bulletin, 29,* 701–712.

CROCKER, J., & MCGRAW, K. M. (1984). What's good for the goose is not good for the gander: Solo status as an obstacle to occupational achievement for males and females. *American Behavioral Scientist, 27,* 357–370.

CROCKER, J., & PARK, L. E. (2004). The costly pursuit of self-esteem. *Psychological Bulletin, 130,* 392–414.

CROCKER, J., THOMPSON, L. L., MCGRAW, K. M., & INGERMAN, C. (1987). Downward comparison, prejudice, and evaluations of others: Effects of self-esteem and threat. *Journal of Personality and Social Psychology, 52,* 907–916.

CROIZET, J. C., DESPRES, G., GAUZINS, M. E., HUGUET, P., LEYENS, J. P., & MEOT, A. (2004). Stereotype threat undermines intellectual performance by triggering a disruptive mental load. *Personality and Social Psychology Bulletin, 30,* 721–731.

CROSBY, F., BROMLEY, S., & SAXE, L. (1980). Recent unobtrusive studies of black and white discrimination and prejudice: A literature review. *Psychological Bulletin, 87,* 546–563.

CROSBY, F. J., PUFALL, A., SNYDER, R. C., O'CONNELL, M., & WHALEN, P. (1989). The denial of personal disadvantage among you, me, and all the other ostriches. In M. Crawford & M. Gentry (Eds.), *Gender and thought.* New York: Springer-Verlag.

CROSS, S. E., LIAO, M-H., & JOSEPHS, R. (1992). A cross-cultural test of the self-evaluation maintenance model. Paper presented at the American Psychological Association convention.

CROWLEY, G. (1996, June 3). The biology of beauty. *Newsweek,* pp. 61–69.

CROXTON, J. S., & MILLER, A. G. (1987). Behavioral disconfirmation and the observer bias. *Journal of Social Behavior and Personality, 2,* 145–152.

CROXTON, J. S., & MORROW, N. (1984). What does it take to reduce observer bias? *Psychological Reports, 55,* 135–138.

CSIKSZENTMIHALYI, M. (1990). *Flow: The psychology of optimal experience.* New York: Harper & Row.

CSIKSZENTMIHALYI, M. (1999). If we are so rich, why aren't we happy? *American Psychologist, 54,* 821–827.

CUNNINGHAM, J. D. (1981). Self-disclosure intimacy: Sex, sex-of-target, cross-national, and generational differences. *Personality and Social Psychology Bulletin, 7,* 314–319.

DABBS, J. M., JR. (1992). Testosterone measurements in social and clinical psychology. *Journal of Social and Clinical Psychology, 11,* 302–321.

DABBS, J. M., JR. (2000). *Heroes, rogues, and lovers: Testosterone and behavior.* New York: McGraw-Hill.

Dabbs, J. M., Jr., Carr, T. S., Frady, R. L., & Riad, J. K. (1995). Testosterone, crime, and misbehavior among 692 male prison inmates. *Personality and Individual Differences, 18,* 627–633.

Dabbs, J. M., Jr., & Janis, I. L. (1965). Why does eating while reading facilitate opinion change? An experimental inquiry. *Journal of Experimental Social Psychology, 1,* 133–144.

Dabbs, J. M., Jr., & Morris, R. (1990). Testosterone, social class, and antisocial behavior in a sample of 4,462 men. *Psychological Science, 1,* 209–211.

Dabbs, J. M., Jr., Strong, R., & Milun, R. (1997). Exploring the mind of testosterone: A beeper study. *Journal of Research in Personality, 31,* 577–588.

Daly, M., & Wilson, M. (1989). Killing the competition: Female/female and male/male homicide. *Human Nature, 1,* 81–107.

Damon, W. (1995). *Greater expectations: Overcoming the culture of indulgence in America's Homes and schools.* New York: Free Press.

Darley, J. M., & Berscheid, E. (1967). Increased liking as a result of the anticipation of personal contact. *Human Relations, 20,* 29–40.

Darley, J. M., & Latané, B. (1968). Bystander intervention in emergencies: Diffusion of responsibility. *Journal of Personality and Social Psychology, 8,* 377–383.

Darley, S., & Cooper, J. (1972). Cognitive consequences of forced noncompliance. *Journal of Personality and Social Psychology, 24,* 321–326.

Das, E. H. H. J., de Wit, J. B. F., & Stroebe, W. (2003). Fear appeals motivate acceptance of action recommendations: Evidence for a positive bias in the processing of persuasive messages. Personality and *Social Psychology Bulletin, 29,* 650–664.

Dashiell, J. F. (1930). An experimental analysis of some group effects. *Journal of Abnormal and Social Psychology, 25,* 190–199.

Davidson, R. J., Putnam, K. M., & Larson, C. L. (2000). Dysfunction in the neural circuitry of emotion regulation—A possible prelude to violence. *Science, 289,* 591–594.

Davies, P. G., Spencer, S. J., & Steele, C. M. (2005). Clearing the air: Identity safety moderates the effects of stereotype threat on woman's leadership aspirations. *Journal of Personality and Social Psychology, 88,* 1–19.

Davis, B. M., & Gilbert, L. A. (1989). Effect of dispositional and situational influences on women's dominance expression in mixed-sex dyads. *Journal of Personality and Social Psychology, 57,* 294–300.

Davis, K. E., & Jones, E. E. (1960). Changes in interpersonal perception as a means of reducing cognitive dissonance. *Journal of Abnormal and Social Psychology, 61,* 402–410.

Davis, J. H., Kameda, T., Parks, C., Stasson, M., & Zimmerman, S. (1989). Some social mechanics of group decision making: The distribution of opinion, polling sequence, and implications fro consensus. *Journal of Personality and Social Psychology, 57,* 1000–1012.

Davis, L., & Greenlees, C. (1992). Social loafing revisited: Factors that mitigate—and reverse—performance loss. Paper presented at the Southwestern Psychological Association convention.

Davis, M. H. (1979). The case for attributional egotism. Paper presented at the American Psychological Association convention.

Davis, M. H., & Stephan, W. G. (1980). Attributions for exam performance. *Journal of Applied Social Psychology, 10,* 235–248.

Dawes, R. M. (1990). The potential nonfalsity of the false consensus effect. In R. M. Hogarth (Ed.), *Insights in decision making: A tribute to Hillel J. Einhorn.* Chicago: University of Chicago Press.

Dawes, R. M. (1991). Social dilemmas, economic self-interest, and evolutionary theory. In D. R. Brown & J. E. Keith Smith (Eds.), *Frontiers of mathematical psychology: Essays in honor of Clyde Coombs.* New York: Springer-Verlag.

Dawes, R. M. (1994). *House of cards: Psychology and psychotherapy built on myth.* New York: Free Press.

Dawson, N. V., Arkes, H. R., Siciliano, C., Blinkhorn, R., Lakshmanan, M., & Petrelli, M. (1988). Hindsight bias: An impediment to accurate probability estimation in clinicopathologic conferences. *Medical Decision Making, 8,* 259–264.

Deaux, K., & LaFrance, M. (1998). Gender. In D. Gilbert, S. Fiske, & G. Lindzey (Eds.), *The handbook of social psychology,* 4th ed. Hillsdale, NJ: Erlbaum.

Deci, E. L., & Ryan, R. M. (1987). The support of autonomy and the control of behavior. *Journal of Personality and Social Psychology, 53,* 1024–1037.

Della Cava, M. R. (2003, April 2). Iraq gets sympathetic press around the world. *USA Today* (www.usatoday.com).

Dengerink, H. A., & Myers, J. D. (1977). Three effects of failure and depression on subsequent aggression. *Journal of Personality and Social Psychology, 35,* 88–96.

Department of Justice. (2004). Pay equity: A new approach to a fundamental right. *Pay Equity Task Force Final Report.* Ottawa: Her Majesty the Queen in Right in Canada.

DePaulo, B. M., Lassiter, G. D., & Stone, J. I. (1982). Attentional determinants of success at detecting deception and truth. *Personality and Social Psychology Bulletin, 8,* 273–279.

Derlega, V., Metts, S., Petronio, S., & Margulis, S. T. (1993). *Self-disclosure.* Newbury Park, CA: Sage.

Dermer, M., Cohen, S. J., Jacobsen, E., & Anderson, E. A. (1979). Evaluative judgments of aspects of life as a function of vicarious exposure to hedonic extremes. *Journal of Personality and Social Psychology, 37,* 247–260.

DERMER, M., & PYSZCZYNSKI, T. A. (1978). Effects of erotica upon men's loving and liking responses for women they love. *Journal of Personality and Social Psychology, 36,* 1302–1309.

DESFORGES, D. M., LORD, C. G., PUGH, M. A., SIA, T. L., SCARBERRY, N. C., & RATCLIFF, C. D. (1997). Role of group representativeness in the generalization part of the contact hypothesis. *Basic and Applied Social Psychology, 19,* 183–204.

DESFORGES, D. M., LORD, C. G., RAMSEY, S. L., MASON, J. A., VAN LEEUWEN, M. D., WEST, S. C., & LEPPER, M. R. (1991). Effects of structured cooperative contact on changing negative attitudes toward stigmatized social groups. *Journal of Personality and Social Psychology, 60,* 531–544.

DESMARAIS, S., & CURTIS, J. (2001). Gender and perceived income entitlement among full-time workers: Analyses for Canadian national samples, 1984 and 1994. *Basic and Applied Social Psychology, 23,* 157–168.

DESTENO, D. A., & SALOVEY, P. (1996). Jealousy and the characteristics of one's rival: A self-evaluation maintenance perspective. *Personality and Social Psychology Bulletin, 22,* 920–932.

DEUTSCH, M. (1985). *Distributive justice: A social psychological perspective.* New Haven, CT: Yale University Press.

DEUTSCH, M. (1993). Educating for a peaceful world. *American Psychologist, 48,* 510–517.

DEUTSCH, M. (1994). Constructive conflict resolution: Principles, training, and research. *Journal of Social Issues, 50,* 13–32.

DEUTSCH, M. (1999). Behind the scenes. In D. G. Myers, *Social psychology* 6th ed., p. 519. New York: McGraw-Hill.

DEUTSCH, M., & KRAUSS, R. M. (1960). The effect of threat upon interpersonal bargaining. *Journal of Abnormal and Social Psychology, 61,* 181–189.

DEVINE, P. G. (1989). Stereotypes and prejudice: Their automatic and controlled components. *Journal of Personality and Social Psychology, 56,* 5–18.

DEVINE, P. G., PLANT, E. A., & BUSWELL, B. N. (2000). Breaking the prejudice habit: Progress and obstacles. In S. Oskamp (Ed.), *Reducing prejudice and discrimination.* Mahwah, NJ: Erlbaum.

DEVOS-COMBY, L., & SALOVEY, P. (2002). Applying persuasion strategies to alter HIV-relevant thoughts and behavior. *Review of General Psychology, 6,* 287–304.

DEY, E. L., ASTIN, A. W., & KORN, W. S. (1991). *The American freshman: Twenty-five year trends.* Los Angeles: Higher Education Research Institute, UCLA.

DHAWAN, M., ROSEMAN, I. J., NAIDU, R. K., THAPA, K., & RETTEK, S. I. (1995). Self-concepts across two cultures: India and the United States. *Journal of Cross-Cultural Psychology, 26,* 606–621.

DI TELLA, R., MACCULLOH, R. J., OSWALD, A. J. (2001). Preferences over inflation and unemployment: Evidence from surveys of happiness. *The American Economic Review, 91,* 335.

DICUM, J. (2003, November 11). Letter to the editor. *New York Times,* p. A20.

DIENER, E. (1976). Effects of prior destructive behavior, anonymity, and group presence on deindividuation and aggression. *Journal of Personality and Social Psychology, 33,* 497–507.

DIENER, E. (1979). Deindividuation, self-awareness, and disinhibition. *Journal of Personality and Social Psychology, 37,* 1160–1171.

DIENER, E. (1980). Deindividuation: The absence of self-awareness and self-regulation in group members. In P. Paulus (Ed.), *The psychology of group influence.* Hillsdale, NJ: Erlbaum.

DIENER, E., & CRANDALL, R. (1979). An evaluation of the Jamaican anticrime program. *Journal of Applied Social Psychology, 9,* 135–146.

DIENER, E., & WALLBOM, M. (1976). Effects of self-awareness on antinormative behavior. *Journal of Research in Personality, 10,* 107–111.

DIENSTBIER, R. A., ROESCH, S. C., MIZUMOTO, A., HEMENOVER, S. H., LOTT, R. C., & CARLO, G. (1998). Effects of weapons on guilt judgments and sentencing recommendations for criminals. *Basic and Applied Social Psychology, 20,* 93–102.

DINDIA, K., & ALLEN, M. (1992). Sex differences in self-disclosure: A meta-analysis. *Psychological Bulletin, 112,* 106–124.

DION, K. (2002). Facial attractiveness: Evolutionary, cognitive, and social perspectives. In G. Rhodes & L. A. Zebrowitz (Eds.), *Advances in visual cognition* (pp. 239–259). Westport, CT: Ablex Publishing.

DION, K. K. (1972). Physical attractiveness and evaluations of children's transgressions. *Journal of Personality and Social Psychology, 24,* 207–213.

DION, K. K. (1973). Young children's stereotyping of facial attractiveness. *Developmental Psychology, 9,* 183–188.

DION, K. K. (1979). Physical attractiveness and interpersonal attraction. In M. Cook & G. Wilson (Eds.), *Love and attraction.* New York: Pergamon Press.

DION, K. K., & BERSCHEID, E. (1974). Physical attractiveness and peer perception among children. *Sociometry, 37,* 1–12.

DION, K. K., & DION, K. L. (1985). Personality, gender, and the phenomenology of romantic love. In P. R. Shaver (Ed.), *Review of personality and social psychology,* vol. 6. Beverly Hills, CA: Sage.

DION, K. K., & DION, K. L. (1991). Psychological individualism and romantic love. *Journal of Social Behavior and Personality, 6,* 17–33.

DION, K. K., & DION, K. L. (1993). Individualistic and collectivistic perspectives on gender and the cultural context of love and intimacy. *Journal of Social Issues, 49,* 53–69.

DION, K. K., & DION, K. L. (1996). Cultural perspectives on romantic love. *Personal Relationships, 3,* 5–17.

DION, K. K., & STEIN, S. (1978). Physical attractiveness and interpersonal influence. *Journal of Experimental Social Psychology, 14,* 97–109.

DION, K. L. (1975). Women's reactions to discrimination from members of the same or opposite sex. *Journal of Research in Personality, 9,* 294–306.

DION, K. L. (2001). Gender and relationships. In *Handbook of the psychology of women and gender* (p. 256–274). John Wiley.

DION, K. L. (2002a). The social psychology of perceived prejudice and discrimination. *Canadian Psychology, 43,* 1–10.

DION, K. L., & DION, K. K. (1988). Romantic love: Individual and cultural perspectives. In R. J. Sternberg & M. L. Barnes (Eds.), *The psychology of love.* New Haven, CT: Yale University Press.

DION, K. L., & KAWAKAMI, K. (1996). Ethnicity and perceived discrimination: Another look at the personal/group discrimination discrepancy. *Canadian Journal of Behavioral Science, 28,* 203–213.

DION, K. L., DION, K. K., & KEELAN, J. P. (1990). Appearance anxiety as a dimension of social-evaluative anxiety: Exploring the ugly duckling syndrome. *Contemporary Social Psychology, 14* (4), 220–224.

DISHION, T. J., McCORD, J., & POULIN, F. (1999). When interventions harm: Peer groups and problem behavior. *American Psychologist, 54,* 755–764.

DIXON, J., & DURRHEIM, K. (2003). Contact and the ecology of racial division: Some varieties of informal segregation. *British Journal of Social Psychology, 42,* 1–23.

DIXON, J., DURRHEIM, K., & TREDOUX, C. (2005). Beyond the optimal contact strategy: A reality check for the contact hypothesis. *American Psychologist, 60,* 697–711.

DOLLARD, J., DOOB, L., MILLER, N., MOWRER, O. H., & SEARS, R. R. (1939). *Frustration and aggression.* New Haven, CT: Yale University Press.

DOLNIK, L., CASE, T. I., & WILLIAMS, K. D. (2003). Stealing thunder as a courtroom tactic revisited: Processes and boundaries. *Law and Human Behavior, 27,* 265–285.

DONNERSTEIN, E. (1998). Why do we have those new ratings on television? Invited address to the National Institute on the Teaching of Psychology.

DONNERSTEIN, E., LINZ, D., & PENROD, S. (1987). *The question of pornography.* London: Free Press.

DOOB, A. N., & ROBERTS, J. (1988). Public attitudes toward sentencing in Canada. In N. Walker & M. Hough (Eds.), *Sentencing and the public.* London: Gower.

DOTY, R. M., PETERSON, B. E., & WINTER, D. G. (1991). Threat and authoritarianism in the United States, 1978–1987. *Journal of Personality and Social Psychology, 61,* 629–640.

DOVIDIO, J. R., BRIGHAM, J. C., JOHNSON, B. T., & GAERTNER, S. L. (1996). Stereotyping, prejudice, and discrimination: Another look. In N. Macrae, M. Hewstone, & C. Stangor (Eds.), *Stereotypes and stereotyping.* New York: Guilford.

DOWNS, A. C., & LYONS, P. M. (1991). Natural observations of the links between attractiveness and initial legal judgments. *Personality and Social Psychology Bulletin, 17,* 541–547.

DROLET, A. L., & MORRIS, M. W. (2000). Rapport in conflict resolution: Accounting for how face-to-face contact fosters mutual cooperation in mixed-motive conflicts. *Journal of Experimental Social Psychology, 36,* 26–50.

DRYER, D. C., & HOROWITZ, L. M. (1997). When do opposites attract? Interpersonal complementarity versus similarity. *Journal of Personality and Social Psychology, 72,* 592–603.

DUFFY, M. (2003, June 9). Weapons of mass disappearance. *Time,* pp. 28–33.

DUGGER, C. W. (2001, April 22). Abortion in India spurred by sex text skew the ratio against girls. *New York Times,* Late edition, p. 12.

DUNCAN, B. L. (1976). Differential social perception and attribution of intergroup violence: Testing the lower limits of stereotyping of blacks. *Journal of Personality and Social Psychology, 34,* 590–598.

DUNN, E. W., WILSON, T. D., & GILBERT, D. T. (2003). Location, location, location: The misprediction of satisfaction in housing lotteries. *Personality and Social Psychology Bulletin, 29,* 1421–1432.

DUNNING, D. (1995). Trait importance and modifiability as factors influencing self-assessment and self-enhancement motives. *Personality and Social Psychology Bulletin, 21,* 1297–1306.

DUNNING, D., & HAYES, A. F. (1996). Evidence for egocentric comparison in social judgment. *Journal of Personality and Social Psychology, 71,* 213–229.

DUNNING, D., MEYEROWITZ, J. A., & HOLZBERG, A. D. (1989). Ambiguity and self-evaluation. *Journal of Personality and Social Psychology, 57,* 1082–1090.

DUNNING, D., PERIE, M., & STORY, A. L. (1991). Self-serving prototypes of social categories. *Journal of Personality and Social Psychology, 61,* 957–968.

DUTTON, D. G. (1974). Some evidence for heightened sexual attraction under conditions of high anxiety. *Journal of Personality and Social Psychology, 30,* 510–517.

DUTTON, D. G., & ARON, A. P. (1974). Some evidence for heightened sexual attraction under conditions of high anxiety. *Journal of Personality and Social Psychology, 30,* 510–517.

DUTTON, D. G., & ARON, A. (1989). Romantic attraction and generalized liking for others who are sources of conflict-based arousal. *Canadian Journal of Behavioural Science, 21,* 246–257.

EAGLY, A. H. (1987). *Sex differences in social behavior: A social-role interpretation.* Hillsdale, NJ: Erlbaum.

EAGLY, A. H. (1994). Are people prejudiced against women? Donald Campbell Award invited address, American Psychological Association convention.

EAGLY, A. H. (1997). *Sex differences in social behavior: Social psychology meets evolutionary psychology.* Midwestern Psychological Association invited address.

EAGLY, A. H., & CHAIKEN, S. (1993). *The psychology of attitudes.* San Diego, CA: Harcourt Brace Jovanovich.

EAGLY, A. H., & CROWLEY, M. (1986). Gender and helping behavior: A meta-analytic review of the social psychological literature. *Psychological Bulletin, 100,* 283–308.

EAGLY, A. H., & JOHNSON, B. T. (1990). Gender and leadership style: A meta-analysis. *Psychological Bulletin, 108,* 233–256.

EAGLY, A. H., & KARAU, S. J. (2000). Few women at the top: Is prejudice a cause? Unpublished manuscript, Northwestern University.

EAGLY, A. H., ASHMORE, R. D., MAKHIJANI, M. G., & LONGO, L. C. (1991). What is beautiful is good, but . . . : A meta-analytic review of research on the physical attractiveness stereotype. *Psychological Bulletin, 110,* 109–128.

EAGLY, A. H., DIEKMAN, A. B., SCHNEIDER, M., & KULESA, P. (2003). Experimental tests of an attitudinal theory of the gender gap in voting. *Personality and Social Psychology Bulletin, 29,* 1245–1258.

EAGLY, A. H., KARAU, S. J., & MAKHIJANI, M. G. (1995). Gender and the effectiveness of leaders: A meta-analysis. *Psychological Bulletin, 117,* 125–145.

EAGLY, A. H., MAKHIJANI, M. G., & KLONSKY, B. G. (1992). Gender and the evaluation of leaders: A meta-analysis. *Psychological Bulletin, 111,* 3–22.

EAGLY, A. H., MLADINIC, A., & OTTO, S. (1991). Are women evaluated more favorably than men? *Psychology of Women Quarterly, 15,* 203–216.

EARN, B., & ADAIR, J. G. (2005). Kenneth Lucien Dion (1944–2004). *Canadian Psychology, 46,* 61–63.

EBBESEN, E. B., DUNCAN, B., & KONECNI, V. J. (1975). Effects of content of verbal aggression on future verbal aggression: A field experiment. *Journal of Experimental Social Psychology, 11,* 192–204.

EDWARDS, C. P. (1991). Behavioral sex differences in children of diverse cultures: The case of nurturance to infants. In M. Pereira & L. Fairbanks (Eds.), *Juveniles: Comparative socioecology.* Oxford: Oxford University Press.

EFRAN, M. G. (1974). The effect of physical appearance on the judgment of guilt, interpersonal attraction and severity of recommended punishment in a simulated jury task. *Journal of Research in Personality, 8,* 45–54.

EGAN, J. (2003, November 23). Love in the time of no time. *New York Times* (www.nytimes.com).

EISENBERG, N., & LENNON, R. (1983). Sex differences in empathy and related capacities. *Psychological Bulletin, 94,* 100–131.

EISER, J. R., SUTTON, S. R., & WOBER, M. (1979). Smoking, seat-belts, and beliefs about health. *Addictive Behaviors, 4,* 331–338.

ELDER, G. H., JR., & CLIPP, E. C. (1988). Wartime losses and social bonding: Influences across 40 years in men's lives. *Psychiatry, 51,* 177–197.

ELLEMERS, N., VAN RIJSWIJK, W., ROEFS, M., & SIMONS, C. (1997). Bias in intergroup perceptions: Balancing group identity with social reality. *Personality and Social Psychology Bulletin, 23,* 186–198.

ELLICKSON, P. L., & BELL, R. M. (1990). Drug prevention in junior high: A multi-site longitudinal test. *Science, 247,* 1299–1305.

ELLIS, B. J., & SYMONS, D. (1990). Sex difference in sexual fantasy: An evolutionary psychological approach. *Journal of Sex Research, 27,* 490–521.

ELLIS, H. D. (1981). Theoretical aspects of face recognition. In G. H. Davies, H. D. Ellis, & J. Shepherd (Eds.), *Perceiving and remembering faces.* London: Academic Press.

ELLYSON, S. L., DOVIDIO, J. F., & BROWN, C. E. (1991). The look of power: Gender differences and similarities in visual dominance behavior. In C. Ridgeway (Ed.), *Gender and interaction: The role of microstructures in inequality.* New York: Springer-Verlag.

EMES, C. E. (1997). Is Mr. Pac Man eating our children? A review of the effect of video games on children. *Canadian Journal of Psychiatry, 42,* 404–414.

ENGS, R., & HANSON, D. J. (1989). Reactance theory: A test with collegiate drinking. *Psychological Reports, 64,* 1083–1086.

ENNIS, B. J., & VERRILLI, D. B., JR. (1989). Motion for leave to file brief *amicus curiae* and brief of Society for the Scientific Study of Religion, American Sociological Association, and others. U.S. Supreme Court Case No. 88–1600, Holy Spirit Association for the Unification of World Christianity, et al., v. David Molko and Tracy Leal. On petition for write of certiorari to the Supreme Court of California. Washington, DC: Jenner & Block, 21 Dupont Circle NW.

ENNIS, R., & ZANNA, M. P. (1991). Hockey assault: Constitutive versus normative violations. Paper presented at the Canadian Psychological Association convention.

EPLEY, N., & HUFF, C. (1998). Suspicion, affective response, and educational benefit as a result of deception in psychology research. *Personality and Social Psychology Bulletin, 24,* 759–768.

ERICKSON, B., HOLMES, J. G., FREY, R., WALKER, L., & THIBAUT, J. (1974). Functions of a third party in the resolution of conflict: The role of a judge in pretrial conferences. *Journal of Personality and Social Psychology, 30,* 296–306.

ERON, L. D. (1987). The development of aggressive behavior from the perspective of a developing behaviorism. *American Psychologist, 42,* 425–442.

ERON, L. D., & HUESMANN, L. R. (1980). Adolescent aggression and television. *Annals of the New York Academy of Sciences, 347,* 319–331.

ERON, L. D., & HUESMANN, L. R. (1984). The control of aggressive behavior by changes in attitudes, values, and the conditions of learning. In R. J. Blanchard & C. Blanchard (Eds.), *Advances in the study of aggression,* vol. 1. Orlando, FL: Academic Press.

ERON, L. D., & HUESMANN, L. R. (1985). The role of television in the development of prosocial and antisocial behavior. In D. Olweus, M. Radke-Yarrow, & J. Block (Eds.), *Development of antisocial and prosocial behavior.* Orlando, FL: Academic Press.

ESSER, J. K., & LINDOERFER, J. S. (1989). Groupthink and the space shuttle Challenger accident: Toward a quantitative case analysis. *Journal of Behavioral Decision Making, 2,* 167–177.

ESSES, V. M., & ZANNA, M. P. (1995). Mood and the expression of ethnic stereotypes. *Journal of Personality and Social Psychology, 69,* 1052–1068.

ESSES, V. M, DIETZ, J., & BHARDWAJ, A. (2005). *The Role of prejudice in the discounting of immigrant skills.* (In press). London, ON: University of Western Ontario.

ESSES, V. M., HADDOCK, G., & ZANNA, M. P. (1993). The role of mood in the expression of intergroup stereotypes. In M. P. Zanna & J. M. Olson (Eds.), *The psychology of prejudice: The Ontario symposium,* vol. 7. Hillsdale, NJ: Erlbaum.

EVANS, G. W. (1979). Behavioral and physiological consequences of crowding in humans. *Journal of Applied Social Psychology, 9,* 27–46.

EVANS, R. I., SMITH, C. K., & RAINES, B. E. (1984). Deterring cigarette smoking in adolescents: A psychosocial-behavioral analysis of an intervention strategy. In A. Baum, J. Singer, & S. Taylor (Eds.), *Handbook of psychology and health: Social psychological aspects of health,* vol. 4. Hillsdale, NJ: Erlbaum.

FABRIGAR, L. R., DAVIDSON, M., BONNEY, J. J., & DAVIDSON-HARDEN, J. (2002). Examining the self-perception explanation for the foot-in-the-door compliance technique. Unpublished manuscript.

FARWELL, L., & WEINER, B. (2000). Bleeding hearts and the heartless: Popular perceptions of liberal and conservative ideologies. *Personality and Social Psychology Bulletin, 26,* 845–852.

FARWELL, L. A., & DONCHIN, E. (1991). The truth will out: Interrogative polygraphy ("lie detection") with event-related brain potentials. *Psychophysiology, 28,* 531–547.

FAULKNER, S. L., & WILLIAMS, K. D. (1996). A study of social loafing in industry. Paper presented to the Midwestern Psychological Association convention.

FAZIO, R. H., JACKSON, J. R., DUNTON, B. C., & WILLIAMS, C. J. (1995). Variability in automatic activation as an unobtrusive measure of racial attitudes: A bona fide pipeline? *Journal of Personality and Social Psychology, 69,* 1013–1027.

FEENEY, J., PETERSON, C., & NOLLER, P. (1994). Equity and marital satisfaction over the family life cycle. *Personality Relationships, 1,* 83–99.

FEHR, B. (1988). Prototype analysis of the concepts of love and commitment. *Journal of Personality and Social Psychology, 55,* 557–579.

FEHR, B., & BROUGHTON, R. (2001). Gender and personality differences in conceptions of love: An interpersonal theory analysis. *Personal Relationships, 8,* 115–136.

FEIN, S., & SPENCER, S. J. (1997). Prejudice as self-image maintenance: Affirming the self through derogating others. *Journal of Personality and Social Psychology, 73,* 31–44.

FEIN, S., HILTON, J. L., & MILLER, D. T. (1990). Suspicion of ulterior motivation and the correspondence bias. *Journal of Personality and Social Psychology, 58,* 753–764.

FEINGOLD, A. (1988). Matching for attractiveness in romantic partners and same-sex friends: A meta-analysis and theoretical critique. *Psychological Bulletin, 104,* 226–235.

FEINGOLD, A. (1990). Gender differences in effects of physical attractiveness on romantic attraction: A comparison across five research paradigms. *Journal of Personality and Social Psychology, 59,* 981–993.

FEINGOLD, A. (1991). Sex differences in the effects of similarity and physical attractiveness on opposite-sex attraction. *Basic and Applied Social Psychology, 12,* 357–367.

FEINGOLD, A. (1992a). Gender differences in mate selection preferences: A test of the parental investment model. *Psychological Bulletin, 112,* 125–139.

FEINGOLD, A. (1992b). Good-looking people are not what we think. *Psychology Bulletin, 111,* 304–341.

FELSON, R. B. (1984). The effect of self-appraisals of ability on academic performance. *Journal of Personality and Social Psychology, 47,* 944–952.

FENIGSTEIN, A. (1984). Self-consciousness and the overperception of self as a target. *Journal of Personality and Social Psychology, 47,* 860–870.

FERGUSSON, D. M., HORWOOD, L. J., & SHANNON, F. T. (1984). A proportional hazards model of family breakdown. *Journal of Marriage and the Family, 46,* 539–549.

FESHBACH, N. D. (1980). The child as "psychologist" and "economist": Two curricula. Paper presented at the American Psychological Association convention.

FESHBACH, S. (1980). Television advertising and children: Policy issues and alternatives. Paper presented at the American Psychological Association convention.

FESTINGER, L. (1954). A theory of social comparison processes. *Human Relations, 7,* 117–140.

FESTINGER, L. (1957). *A theory of cognitive dissonance.* Stanford, CA: Stanford University Press.

FESTINGER, L., & CARLSMITH, J. M. (1959). Cognitive consequences of forced compliance. *Journal of Abnormal & Social Psychology, 58,* 203–210.

FESTINGER, L., & MACCOBY, N. (1964). On resistance to persuasive communications. *Journal of Abnormal and Social Psychology, 68,* 359–366.

FESTINGER, L., PEPITONE, A., & NEWCOMB, T. (1952). Some consequences of deindividuation in a group. *Journal of Abnormal and Social Psychology, 47,* 382–389.

FIEDLER, F. E. (1987, September). When to lead, when to stand back. *Psychology Today,* pp. 26–27.

FIEDLER, K., SEMIN, G. R., & KOPPETSCH, C. (1991). Language use and attributional biases in close personal relationships. *Personality and Social Psychology Bulletin, 17,* 147–155.

FINCHAM, F. D., & JASPARS, J. M. (1980). Attribution of responsibility: From man the scientist to man as lawyer. In L. Berkowitz (Ed.), *Advances in experimental social psychology* (Vol. 13). New York: Academic Press.

FINDLEY, M. J., & COOPER, H. M. (1983). Locus of control and academic achievement: A literature review. *Journal of Personality and Social Psychology, 44,* 419–427.

FINEBERG, H. V. (1988). Education to prevent AIDS: Prospects and obstacles. *Science, 239,* 592–596.

FISCHHOFF, B., & BAR-HILLEL, M. (1984). Focusing techniques: A shortcut to improving probability judgments? *Organizational Behavior & Human Performance, 34,* 174–194.

FISHBEIN, D., & THELEN, M. H. (1981a). Husband-wife similarity and marital satisfaction: A different approach. Paper presented at the Midwestern Psychological Association convention.

FISHBEIN, D., & THELEN, M. H. (1981b). Psychological factors in mate selection and marital satisfaction: A review (Ms. 2374). *Catalog of Selected Documents in Psychology, 11,* 84.

FISHBEIN, M., & AJZEN, I. (1975). *Belief, attitude, intention, and behavior: An introduction to theory and research.* Reading, MA: Addison-Wesley.

FISHER, H. (1994, April). The nature of romantic love. *Journal of NIH Research,* pp. 59–64.

FISHER, M. (2005). *Dissertation Abstracts International: Section B: The Sciences and Engineering, 66,* 597.

FISHER, R. J. (1994). Generic principles for resolving intergroup conflict. *Journal of Social Issues, 50,* 47–66.

FISHER, R. P., & GEISELMAN, R. E. (1992). *Memory enhancing technique for investigative interviewing: The cognitive interview.* Springfield, IL: Charles C. Thomas.

FISHER, R. P., GEISELMAN, R. E., & RAYMOND, D. S. (1987). Critical analysis of police interviewing techniques. *Journal of Police Science and Administration, 15,* 177–185.

FISKE, S. T. (2002, June). Envy, contempt, pity, and pride: Dangerous intergroup emotions on September 11th. Talk given at the APS symposium "Psychological science perspectives on September 11th."

FLAY, B. R., RYAN, K. B., BEST, J. A., BROWN, K. S., KERSELL, M. W., d'AVERNAS, J. R., & ZANNA, M. P. (1985). Are social-psychological smoking prevention programs effective? The Waterloo study. *Journal of Behavioral Medicine, 8,* 37–59.

FLEMING, I., BAUM, A., & WEISS, L. (1987). Social density and perceived control as mediators of crowding stress in high-density residential neighborhoods. *Journal of Personality and Social Psychology, 52,* 899–906.

FLETCHER, G. J. O., FINCHAM, F. D., CRAMER, L., & HERON, N. (1987). The role of attributions in the development of dating relationships. *Journal of Personality and Social Psychology, 53,* 481–489.

FOLEY, L. A. (1976). Personality and situational influences on changes in prejudice: A replication of Cook's railroad game in a prison setting. *Journal of Personality and Social Psychology, 34,* 846–856.

FOLLETT, M. P. (1940). Constructive conflict. In H. C. Metcalf & L. Urwick (Eds.), *Dynamic administration: The collected papers of Mary Parker Follett.* New York: Harper.

FORGAS, J. P., & FIEDLER, K. (1996a). Mood effects on intergroup discrimination: The role of affect in reward allocation decisions. *Journal of Personality and Social Psychology, 70,* 28–40.

FORGAS, J. P., & FIEDLER, K. (1996b). Us and them: Mood effects on intergroup discrimination. *Journal of Personality and Social Psychology, 70,* 28–40.

FORSYTH, D. R., BERGER, R. E., & MITCHELL, T. (1981). The effects of self-serving vs. other-serving claims of responsibility on attraction and attribution in groups. *Social Psychology Quarterly, 44,* 59–64.

FOWLER, S. P., WILLIAMS, K., HUNT, K. J., RESENDEZ, G. R., HAZUDA, H. P., & STERN, M. P. (2005, June 10–14). Diet soft drink consumption is associated with increased incidence of overweight and obesity in The San Antonio Heart Study. Slide show presented at the 65th Annual Scientific Sessions, American Diabetes Association.

FRANK, M. G., & GILOVICH, T. (1988). The dark side of self and social perception: Black uniforms and aggression in professional sports. *Journal of Personality and Social Psychology, 54,* 74–85.

FRANK, M. G., & GILOVICH, T. (1989). Effect of memory perspective on retrospective causal attributions. *Journal of Personality and Social Psychology, 57,* 399–403.

FRANK, R. (1999). *Luxury fever: Why money fails to satisfy in an era of excess.* New York: Free Press.

FREEDMAN, J. L., & FRASER, S. C. (1966). Compliance without pressure: The foot-in-the-door technique. *Journal of Personality and Social Psychology, 4,* 195–202.

FREEDMAN, J. L., & PERLICK, D. (1979). Crowding, contagion, and laughter. *Journal of Experimental Social Psychology, 15,* 295–303.

FREEDMAN, J. L., & SEARS, D. O. (1965). Warning, distraction, and resistance to influence. *Journal of Personality and Social Psychology, 1,* 262–266.

FREEDMAN, J. S. (1965). Long-term behavioral effects of cognitive dissonance. *Journal of Experimental Social Psychology, 1,* 145–155.

FRENCH, J. R. P. (1968). The conceptualization and the measurement of mental health in terms of self-identity theory. In S. B. Sells (Ed.), *The definition and measurement of mental health.* Washington, DC: Department of Health, Education, and Welfare. (Cited by M. Rosenberg, 1979, Conceiving the self. New York: Basic Books.)

FRIEDMAN, T. L. (2003a, April 9). Hold your applause. *New York Times* (www.nytimes.com).

FRIEDMAN, T. L. (2003b, June 4). Because we could. *New York Times* (www.nytimes.com).

FRIEDRICH, L. K., & STEIN, A. H. (1973). Aggressive and prosocial television programs and the natural behavior of preschool children. *Monographs of the Society of Research in Child Development, 38* (4, Serial No. 151).

FRIEDRICH, L. K., & STEIN, A. H. (1975). Prosocial television and young children: The effects of verbal labeling and role playing on learning and behavior. *Child Development, 46,* 27–38.

FRIEZE, I. H., OLSON, J. E., & RUSSELL, J. (1991). Attractiveness and income for men and women in management. *Journal of Applied Social Psychology, 21,* 1039–1057.

FTC. (2003, June 12). Federal Trade Commission cigarette report for 2001 (www.ftc.gov/opa/2003/06/2001cigrpt.htm).

FURNHAM, A. (1982). Explanations for unemployment in Britain. *European Journal of Social Psychology, 12,* 335–352.

FURNHAM, A., & GUNTER. B. (1984). Just world beliefs and attitudes towards the poor. *British Journal of Social Psychology, 23,* 265–269.

GABRENYA, W. K., JR., WANG, Y.-E., & LATANÉ, B. (1985). Social loafing on an optimizing task: Cross-cultural differences among Chinese and Americans. *Journal of Cross-Cultural Psychology, 16,* 223–242.

GABRIEL, S., & GARDNER, W. L. (1999). Are there "his" and "hers" types of interdependence? The implications of gender differences in collective versus relational interdependence for affect, behavior, and cognition. *Journal of Personality and Social Psychology, 77,* 642–655.

GAERTNER, L., SEDIKIDES, C., & GRAETZ, K. (1999). In search of self-definition: Motivational primacy of the individual self, motivational primacy of the collective self, or contextual primacy? *Journal of Personality and Social Psychology, 76,* 5–18.

GAERTNER, S. L., DOVIDIO, J. F., ANASTASIO, P. A., BACHMAN, B. A., & RUST, M. C. (1993). The Common Ingroup Identity Model: Recategorization and the reduction of intergroup bias. In W. Stroebe & M. Hewstone (Eds.), *European Review of Social Psychology,* vol. 4. London: Wiley.

GAERTNER, S. L., DOVIDIO, J. F., NIER, J. A., BANKER, B. S., WARD, C. M., HOULETTE, M., & LOUX, S. (2000). The common ingroup identity model for reducing intergroup bias: Progress and challenges. In D. Capozza & R. Brown (Eds.), *Social identity processes: Trends in theory and research.* London: Sage.

GALANTER, M. (1989). *Cults: Faith, healing, and coercion.* New York: Oxford University Press.

GALANTER, M. (1990). Cults and zealous self-help movements: A psychiatric perspective. *American Journal of Psychiatry, 147,* 543–551.

GALINSKY, A. D., & MOSKOWITZ, G. B. (2000). Perspective-taking: Decreasing stereotype expression, stereotype accessibility, and in-group favoritism. *Journal of Personality and Social Psychology, 78,* 708–724.

GALIZIO, M., & HENDRICK, C. (1972). Effect of musical accompaniment on attitude: The guitar as a prop for persuasion. *Journal of Applied Social Psychology, 2,* 350–359.

GALLUP ORGANIZATION. (1990). April 19–22 survey reported in *American Enterprise,* September/October, 1990, p. 92.

GALLUP ORGANIZATION. (2003, June 10). American public opinion about Iraq. Gallup Poll News Service (www.gallup.com/poll/focus/sr030610.asp).

GANGESTAD, S. W., & THORNHILL, R. (1997). Human sexual selection and developmental stability. In J. A. Simpson & D. T. Kenrick (Eds.), *Evolutionary social psychology.* Mahwah, NJ: Erlbaum.

GARDNER, J., & OSWALD, A. (2001). Does money buy happiness? A longitudinal study using data on windfalls. Working paper, Department of Economics, Cambridge University.

GARDNER, M. (1997, July/August). Heaven's Gate: The UFO cult of Bo and Peep. *Skeptical Inquirer,* pp. 15–17.

GASTORF, J. W., SULS, J., & SANDERS, G. S. (1980). Type A coronary-prone behavior pattern and social facilitation. *Journal of Personality and Social Psychology, 8,* 773–780.

GATES, D. (1993, March 29). White male paranoia. *Newsweek,* pp. 48–53.

GATES, M. F., & ALLEE, W. C. (1933). Conditioned behavior of isolated and grouped cockroaches on a simple maze. *Journal of Comparative Psychology, 15,* 331–358.

GECAS, V. (1989). The social psychology of self-efficacy. *Annual Review of Sociology, 15,* 291–316.

GEEN, R. G. (1998). Aggression and antisocial behavior. In D. Gilbert, S. Fiske, & G. Lindzey (Eds.), *Handbook of social psychology,* 4th ed. New York: McGraw-Hill.

GEEN, R. G., & GANGE, J. J. (1983). Social facilitation: Drive theory and beyond. In H. H. Blumberg, A. P. Hare, V. Kent, & M. Davies (Eds.), *Small groups and social interaction,* vol. 1. London: Wiley.

GEEN, R. G., & QUANTY, M. B. (1977). The catharsis of aggression: An evaluation of a hypothesis. In L. Berkowitz (Ed.), *Advances in experimental social psychology,* (vol. 10). New York: Academic Press.

GEEN, R. G., & THOMAS, S. L. (1986). The immediate effects of media violence on behavior. *Journal of Social Issues, 42,* 7–28.

GENTILE, D. A., & ANDERSON, C. A. (2003). Violent video games: The newest media violence hazard. In D. A. Gentile (Ed.), *Media violence and children.* Westport, CT: Ablex.

GERARD, H. B., & MATHEWSON, G. C. (1966). The effects of severity of initiation on liking for a group: A replication. *Journal of Experimental Social Psychology, 2,* 278–287.

GERBNER, G. (1994). The politics of media violence: Some reflections. In C. Hamelink & O. Linne (Eds.), *Mass communication research: On problems and policies.* Norwood, NJ: Ablex.

GERRIG, R. J., & PRENTICE, D. A. (1991, September). The representation of fictional information. *Psychological Science, 2,* 336–340.

GIBBONS, F. X., EGGLESTON, T. J., & BENTHIN, A. C. (1997). Cognitive reactions to smoking relapse: The reciprocal relation between dissonance and self-esteem. *Journal of Personality and Social Psychology, 72,* 184–195.

GIFFORD, R., & HINE, D. W. (1997). Toward cooperation in commons dilemmas. *Canadian Journal of Behavioural Science, 29,* 167–179.

GIFFORD, R., & PEACOCK, J. (1979). Crowding: More fearsome than crime-provoking? Comparison of an Asian city and a North American city. *Psychologia, 22,* 79–83.

GIGONE, D., & HASTIE, R. (1993). The common knowledge effect: Information sharing and group judgment. *Journal of Personality and Social Psychology, 65,* 959–974.

GILBERT, D. T., & EBERT, J. E. J. (2002). Decisions and revisions: The affective forecasting of escapable outcomes. Unpublished manuscript, Harvard University.

GILBERT, D. T., & HIXON, J. G. (1991). The trouble of thinking: Activation and application of stereotypic beliefs. *Journal of Personality and Social Psychology, 60,* 509–517.

GILBERT, D. T., & JENKINS, J. E. (2001). Decisions and revisions: The affective forecasting of escapable outcomes. Unpublished manuscript, Harvard University.

GILBERT, D. T., MCNULTY, S. E., GIULIANO, T. A., & BENSON, J. E. (1992). Blurry words and fuzzy deeds: The attribution of obscure behavior. *Journal of Personality and Social Psychology, 62,* 18–25.

GILBERT, D. T., PELHAM, B. W., & KRULL, D. S. (1988). On cognitive busyness: When person perceivers meet persons perceived. *Journal of Personality and Social Psychology, 54,* 733–740.

GILBERT, D. T., PINEL, E. C., WILSON, T. D., BLUMBERG, S. J., & WHEATLEY, T. P. (1998). Immune neglect: A source of durability bias in affective forecasting. *Journal of Personality and Social Psychology, 75,* 617–638.

GILBERT, D. T., & WILSON, T. D. (2000). Miswanting: Some problems in the forecasting of future affective states. In J. Forgas (Ed.), *Feeling and thinking: The role of affect in social cognition.* Cambridge: Cambridge University Press.

GILLIGAN, C. (1982). *In a different voice: Psychological theory and women's development.* Cambridge, MA: Harvard University Press.

GILLIGAN, C., LYONS, N. P., & HANMER, T. J. (EDS.). (1990). *Making connections: The relational worlds of adolescent girls at Emma Willard School.* Cambridge, MA: Harvard University Press.

GILLIS, J. S., & AVIS, W. E. (1980). The male-taller norm in mate selection. *Personality and Social Psychology Bulletin, 6,* 396–401.

GILMOR, T. M., & REID, D. W. (1979). Locus of control and causal attribution for positive and negative outcomes on university examinations. *Journal of Research in Personality, 13,* 154–160.

GILOVICH, T. (1987). Secondhand information and social judgment. *Journal of Experimental Social Psychology, 23,* 59–74.

GILOVICH, T., MEDVEC, V. H., & SAVITSKY, K. (2000). The spotlight effect in social judgment: An egocentric bias in estimates of the salience of one's own actions and appearance. *Journal of Personality and Social Psychology, 78,* 211–222.

GINSBURG, B., & ALLEE, W. C. (1942). Some effects of conditioning on social dominance and subordination in inbred strains of mice. *Physiological Zoology, 15,* 485–506.

GLASS, D. C. (1964). Changes in liking as a means of reducing cognitive discrepancies between self-esteem and aggression. *Journal of Personality, 32,* 531–549.

GLENN, N. D. (1980). Aging and attitudinal stability. In O. G. Brim, Jr. & J. Kagan (Eds.), *Constancy and change in human development.* Cambridge, MA: Harvard University Press.

GLENN, N. D. (1981). Personal communication.

GLOBE AND MAIL. (2002, June 19). *Saskatchewan to pay officer $1.3-million to settle Martensville lawsuit.* By C. Wong.

GOETHALS, G. R., MESSICK, D. M., & ALLISON, S. T. (1991). The uniqueness bias: Studies of constructive social comparison. In J. Suls & T. A. Wills (Eds.), *Social comparison: Contemporary theory and research.* Hillsdale, NJ: Erlbaum.

GOETHALS, G. R., & ZANNA, M. P. (1979). The rold of social comparison in choice shifts. *Journal of Personality and Social Psychology, 37,* 1469–1476.

GOLDHAGEN, D. J. (1996). *Hitler's willing executioners.* New York: Knopf.

GOLDMAN, J. (1967). A comparison of sensory modality preference of children and adults. Dissertation: Thesis (Ph.D.). Ferkauf Graduate School of Humanities and Social Sciences, Yeshiva University.

GOLDMAN, W., & LEWIS, P. (1977). Beautiful is good: Evidence that the physically attractive are more socially skillful. *Journal of Experimental Social Psychology, 13,* 125–130.

GOLDSMITH, C. (2003, March 25). World media turn wary eye on U.S. *Wall Street Journal,* p. A12.

GOLDSTEIN, A. P., & GLICK, B. (1994). Aggression replacement training: Curriculum and evaluation. *Simulation and Gaming, 25,* 9–26.

GOLDSTEIN, J. H. (1982). Sports violence. *National Forum, 62,* 9–11.

GOLDSTEIN, J. H., & ARMS, R. L. (1971). Effects of observing athletic contests on hostility. *Sociometry, 34,* 83–90.

GOODHART, D. E. (1986). The effects of positive and negative thinking on performance in an achievement situation. *Journal of Personality and Social Psychology, 51,* 117–124.

GORTMAKER, S. L., MUST, A., PERRIN, J. M., SOBOL, A. M., & DIETZ, W. H. (1993). Social and economic consequences of overweight in adolescence and young adulthood. *New England Journal of Medicine, 329,* 1008–1012.

GOTTMAN, J. (WITH N. SILVER). (1994). *Why marriages succeed or fail.* New York: Simon & Schuster.

GOTTMAN, J. M. (1998). Psychology and the study of marital processes. *Annual Review of Psychology, 49,* 169–197.

GOVERNMENT OF CANADA. (N.D.). Tri-Council Policy Statement: Ethical Conduct for Research Involving Humans. Retrieved 27 May 2006 from http://www.pre.ehthics.gc.ca/english/policystatement/policystatement.

GRAHAM, K., & WELLS, S. (2001). Aggression among young adults in the social context of the bar. *Addiction Research & Theory, 9,* 193–219.

GRAHAM, K., & WELLS, S. (2003). "Somebody's gonna get their head kicked in tonight!" Aggression among young males in bars— A question of values? *British Journal of Criminology, 42,* 546–566.

GRAHAM, K., LAROCQUE, L., YETMAN, R., ROSS, T. J., & GUISTRA, E. (1980). Aggression and barroom environments. *Journal of Studies on Alcohol, 41,* 468–485.

GRAHAM, K., OSGOOD, D. W., WELLS, S., & STOCKWELL, T. (2005). To what extent is intoxication associated with aggression in bars? A multilevel analysis: Social factors and prevention interventions. *Centre for Addiction and Mental Health.*

GRAHAM, K., OSGOOD, D. W., ZIBROWSKI, E., PURCELL, J., GLIKSMAN, L., LEONARD, K., PEMANEN, K., SALTZ, R. F., & TOOMEY, T. L. (2004). The effect of the Safer Bars program on physical aggression in bars: Results of a randomized controlled trial. *Drug and Alcohol Review, 23,* 31–41.

GRAY, J. D., & SILVER, R. C. (1990). Opposite sides of the same coin: Former spouses' divergent perspectives in coping with their divorce. *Journal of Personality and Social Psychology, 59,* 1180–1191.

GREELEY, A. M., & SHEATSLEY, P. B. (1971). Attitudes toward racial integration. *Scientific American, 225(6),* 13–19.

GREENBERG, J. (1986). Differential intolerance for inequity from organizational and individual agents. *Journal of Applied Social Psychology, 16,* 191–196.

GREENBERG, J., PYSZCZYNSKI, T., SOLOMON, S., ROSENBLATT, A., VEEDER, M., KIRKLAND, S., & LYON, D. (1990). Evidence for terror management theory: II. The effects of mortality salience on reactions to those who threaten or bolster the cultural worldview. *Journal of Personality and Social Psychology, 58,* 308–318.

GREENBERG, J., PYSZCZYNSKI, T., SOLOMON, S., SIMON, L., & BREUS, M. (1994). Role of consciousness and accessibility of death-related thoughts in mortality salience effects. *Journal of Personality and Social Psychology, 67,* 627–637.

GREENBERG, J., SOLOMON, S., & PYSZCZYNSKI, T. (1997). Terror management theory of self-esteem and cultural worldviews: Empirical assessments and conceptual refinements. *Advances in Experimental Social Psychology, 29,* 61–142.

GREENWALD, A. G., BANAJI, M. R., RUDMAN, L. A., FARNHAM, S. D., NOSEK, B. A., & ROSIER, M. (2000). Prologue to a unified theory of attitudes, stereotypes, and self-concept. In J. P. Forgas (Ed.), *Feeling and thinking: The role of affect in social cognition and behavior.* New York: Cambridge University Press.

GREENWALD, A. G., CARNOT, C. G., BEACH, R., & YOUNG, B. (1987). Increasing voting behavior by asking people if they expect to vote. *Journal of Applied Psychology, 72,* 315–318.

GREENWALD, A. G., MCGHEE, D. E., & SCHWARTZ, J. L. K. (1998). Measuring individual differences in implicit cognition: The implicit association test. *Journal of Personality and Social Psychology, 74,* 1464–1480.

GREENWALD, A. G., NOSEK, B. A., & BANAJI, M. R. (2003). Understanding and using the implicit association test: I. An improved scoring algorithm. *Journal of Personality and Social Psychology, 85,* 197–216.

GRIFFIN, B. Q., COMBS, A. L., LAND, M. L., & COMBS, N. N. (1983). Attribution of success and failure in college performance. *Journal of Psychology, 114,* 259–266.

GRIFFITT, W. (1970). Environmental effects on interpersonal affective behavior. Ambient effective temperature and attraction. *Journal of Personality and Social Psychology, 15,* 240–244.

GRIFFITT, W. (1987). Females, males, and sexual responses. In K. Kelley (Ed.), *Females, males, and sexuality: Theories and research.* Albany: State University of New York Press.

GRIFFITT, W., & VEITCH, R. (1971). Hot and crowded: Influences of population density and temperature on interpersonal affective behavior. *Journal of Personality and Social Psychology, 17,* 92–98.

GRIFFITT, W., & VEITCH, R. (1974). Preacquaintance attitude similarity and attraction revisited: Ten days in a fallout shelter. *Sociometry, 37,* 163–173.

GROENENBOOM, A., WILKE, H. A. M., & WIT, A. P. (2001). Will we be working together again? The impact of future interdependence on group members' task motivation. *European Journal of Social Psychology, 31,* 369–378.

GROSS, A. E., & CROFTON, C. (1977). What is good is beautiful. *Sociometry, 40,* 85–90.

GROVE, J. R., HANRAHAN, S. J., & MCINMAN, A. (1991). Success/failure bias in attributions across involvement categories in sport. *Personality and Social Psychology Bulletin, 17,* 93–97.

GRUDER, C. L. (1977). Choice of comparison persons in evaluating oneself. In J. M. Suls & R. L. Miller (Eds.), *Social comparison processes.* Washington: Hemisphere Publishing.

GRUDER, C. L., COOK, T. D., HENNIGAN, K. M., FLAY, B., ALESSIS, C., & KALAMAJ, J. (1978). Empirical tests of the absolute sleeper effect predicted from the discounting cue hypothesis. *Journal of Personality and Social Psychology, 36,* 1061–1074.

GRUMAN, J. C., & SLOAN, R. P. (1983). Disease as justice: Perceptions of the victims of physical illness. *Basic and Applied Social Psychology, 4,* 39–46.

GRUSH, J. E., & GLIDDEN, M. V. (1987). *Power and satisfaction among distressed and nondistressed couples.* Paper presented at the Midwestern Psychological Association convention.

GUDYKUNST, W. B. (1989). Culture and intergroup processes. In M. H. Bond (Ed.), *The cross-cultural challenge to social psychology.* Newbury Park, CA: Sage.

GUERIN, B. (1993). *Social facilitation.* Paris: Cambridge University Press.

GUERIN, B. (1994). What do people think about the risks of driving? Implications for traffic safety interventions. *Journal of Applied Social Psychology, 24,* 994–1021.

GUERIN, B. (1999). Social behaviors as determined by different arrangements of social consequences: Social loafing, social facilitation, deindividuation, and a modified social loafing. *The Psychological Record, 49,* 565–578.

GUERIN, B., & INNES, J. M. (1982). Social facilitation and social monitoring: A new look at Zajonc's mere presence hypothesis. *British Journal of Social Psychology, 21,* 7–18.

GUPTA, U., & SINGH, P. (1982). Exploratory study of love and liking and type of marriages. *Indian Journal of Applied Psychology, 19,* 92–97.

HACKMAN, J. R. (1986). The design of work teams. In J. Lorsch (Ed.), *Handbook of organizational behavior.* Englewood Cliffs, NJ: Prentice-Hall.

HADDOCK, G., & ZANNA, M. P. (1994). Preferring "housewives" to "feminists." *Psychology of Women Quarterly, 18,* 25–52.

HAFER, C. L., REYNOLDS, K. L., & OBERTYNSKI, M. A. (1996). Message comprehensibility and persuasion: Effects of complex language in counter-attitudinal appeals of laypeople. *Social Cognition, 14,* 317–337.

HAGERTY, M. R. (2000). Social comparisons of income in one's community: Evidence from national surveys of income and happiness. *Journal of Personality and Social Psychology, 78,* 764–771.

HALBERSTADT, J., & RHODES, G. (2000). The attractiveness of nonface averages: Implications for an evolutionary explanation of the attractiveness of average faces. *Psychological Science, 11,* 285–289.

HALL, J. A. (1984). *Nonverbal sex differences: Communication accuracy and expressive style.* Baltimore: Johns Hopkins University Press.

HALL, J. A., & CARTER, J. D. (1999). Gender-stereotype accuracy as an individual difference. *Journal of Personality and Social Psychology, 77,* 350–359.

HALVERSON, A. M., HALLAHAN, M., HART, A. J., & ROSENTHAL, R. (1997). Reducing the biasing effects of judges' non-verbal behavior with simplified jury instruction. *Journal of Applied Psychology, 82,* 590–598.

HAMBERGER, J., & HEWSTONE, M. (1997). Inter-ethnic contact as a predictor of blatant and subtle prejudice: Tests of a model in four West European nations. *British Journal of Social Psychology, 36,* 173–190.

HAMBLIN, R. L., BUCKHOLDT, D., BUSHELL, D., ELLIS, D., & FERITOR, D. (1969, January). Changing the game from get the teacher to learn. *Transaction,* pp. 20–25, 28–31.

HANEY, C., & ZIMBARDO, P. (1998). The past and future of U.S. prison policy: Twenty-five years after the Stanford Prison Experiment. *American Psychologist, 53,* 709–727.

HANSEN, C. H. (1989). Priming sex-role stereotypic event schemas with rock music videos: Effects on impression favorability, trait inferences, and recall of a subsequent male/female interaction. *Basic and Applied Social Psychology, 10,* 371–391.

HANSEN, C. H., & HANSEN, R. D. (1988). Priming stereotypic appraisal of social interactions: How rock music videos can change what's seen when boy meets girl. *Sex Roles, 19,* 287–316.

HARDIN, G. (1968). The tragedy of the commons. *Science, 162,* 1243–1248.

HARDY, C., & LATANÉ, B. (1986). Social loafing on a cheering task. *Social Science, 71,* 165–172.

HARITOS-FATOUROS, M. (1988). The official torturer: A learning model for obedience to the authority of violence. *Journal of Applied Social Psychology, 18,* 1107–1120.

HARITOS-FATOUROS, M. (2002). *Psychological origins of institutionalized torture.* New York: Routledge.

HARKINS, S. G. (1981). Effects of task difficulty and task responsibility on social loafing. Presentation to the First International Conference on Social Processes in Small Groups, Kill Devil Hills, North Carolina.

HARKINS, S. G., & JACKSON, J. M. (1985). The role of evaluation in eliminating social loafing. *Personality and Social Psychology Bulletin, 11,* 457–465.

HARKINS, S. G., LATANÉ, B., & WILLIAMS, K. (1980). Social loafing: Allocating effort or taking it easy? *Journal of Experimental Social Psychology, 16,* 457–465.

HARKINS, S. G., & PETTY, R. E. (1981). Effects of source magnification of cognitive effort on attitudes: An information-processing view. *Journal of Personality and Social Psychology, 40,* 401–413.

HARKINS, S. G., & PETTY, R. E. (1982). Effects of task difficulty and task uniqueness on social loafing. *Journal of Personality and Social Psychology, 43,* 1214–1229.

HARKINS, S. G., & PETTY, R. E. (1987). Information utility and the multiple source effect. *Journal of Personality and Social Psychology, 52,* 260–268.

HARKINS, S. G., & SZYMANSKI, K. (1989). Social loafing and group evaluation. *Journal of Personality and Social Psychology, 56,* 934–941.

HARMON, A. (2003, June 29). Online dating sheds its stigma as Losers.com. *New York Times* (www.nytimes.com).

HARMON-JONES, E., BREHM, J. W., GREENBERG, J., SIMON, L., & NELSON, D. E. (1996). Evidence that the production of aversive consequences is not necessary to create cognitive dissonance. *Journal of Personality and Social Psychology, 70,* 5–16.

HARRIS, J. R. (1998). *The nurture assumption.* New York: Free Press.

HARRIS, M. J., & ROSENTHAL, R. (1985). Mediation of interpersonal expectancy effects: 31 meta-analyses. *Psychological Bulletin, 97,* 363–386.

HARRIS, M. J., & ROSENTHAL, R. (1986). Four factors in the mediation of teacher expectancy effects. In R. S. Feldman (Ed.), *The social psychology of education.* New York: Cambridge University Press.

HARRISON, A. A. (1977). Mere exposure. In L. Berkowitz (Ed.), *Advances in experimental social psychology,* (vol. 10). New York: Academic Press.

HARVEY, J. H., TOWN, J. P., & YARKIN, K. L. (1981). How fundamental is the fundamental attribution error? *Journal of Personality and Social Psychology, 40,* 346–349.

HASTIE, R., PENROD, S. D., & PENNINGTON, N. (1983). *Inside the jury.* Cambridge, MA: Harvard University Press.

HATFIELD, E. (1988). Passionate and compassionate love. In R. J. Sternberg & M. L. Barnes (Eds.), *The psychology of love.* New Haven, CT: Yale University Press.

HATFIELD, E., & SPRECHER, S. (1986). *Mirror, mirror: The importance of looks in everyday life.* Albany: State University of New York Press.

HATFIELD, E., TRAUPMANN, J., SPRECHER, S., UTNE, M., & HAY, J. (1985). Equity and intimate relations: Recent research. In W. Ickes (Ed.), *Compatible and incompatible relationships.* New York: Springer-Verlag.

HATFIELD (WALSTER), E., ARONSON, V., ABRAHAMS, D., & ROTTMAN, L. (1966). Importance of physical attractiveness in dating behavior. *Journal of Personality and Social Psychology, 4,* 508–516.

HATFIELD (WALSTER), E., WALSTER, G. W., & BERSCHEID, E. (1978). *Equity: Theory and research.* Boston: Allyn & Bacon.

HAVEL, V. (1990). *Disturbing the peace.* New York: Knopf.

HAY, D., & ROSS, H. S. (1982). The social nature of early conflict. *Child Development, 53,* 105–114.

HAZAN, C., & SHAVER, P. R. (1994). Attachment as an organizational framework for research on close relationships. *Psychological Inquiry, 5,* 1–22.

HEADEY, B., & WEARING, A. (1987). The sense of relative superiority—central to well-being. *Social Indicators Research, 20,* 497–516.

HEAP, B., & KENT, J. (EDS.). (2000). *Towards sustainable consumption: A European perspective.* London: The Royal Society.

HEAROLD, S. (1986). A synthesis of 1043 effects of television on social behavior. In G. Comstock (Ed.), *Public communication and behavior* (Vol. 1). Orlando, FL: Academic Press.

HEBL, M. R., & HEATHERTON, T. F. (1998). The stigma of obesity in women: The difference is black and white. *Personality and Social Psychology Bulletin, 24,* 417–426.

HEDLEY, A. (1994). Review essay, identity: Sense of self & nation. *Canadian Review of Sociology and Anthropology, 31,* 200–214.

HEILMAN, M. E. (1976). Oppositional behavior as a function of influence attempt intensity and retaliation threat. *Journal of Personality and Social Psychology, 33,* 574–578.

HEINE, S. J., LEHMAN, D. R., MARKUS, H. R., & KITAYAMA, S. (1999). Is there a universal need for positive self-regard? *Psychological Review, 106,* 766–794.

HENDERSON-KING, E. I., & NISBETT, R. E. (1996). Anti-black prejudice as a function of exposure to the negative behavior of a single black person. *Journal of Personality and Social Psychology, 71,* 654–664.

HENDRICK, C., & HENDRICK, S. (1993). *Romantic love.* Newbury Park, CA: Sage.

HENDRICK, S. S., & HENDRICK, C. (1995). Gender differences and similarities in sex and love. *Personal Relationships, 2,* 55–65.

HENDRICK, S. S., & HENDRICK, C. (1997). Love and satisfaction. In R. J. Sternberg & M. Hojjat (Eds.), *Satisfaction in close relationships.* New York: Guilford Press.

HENDRICK, S. S., HENDRICK, C., & ADLER, N. L. (1988). Romantic relationships: Love, satisfaction, and staying together. *Journal of Personality and Social Psychology, 54,* 980–988.

HENRY, W. A., III. (1994, June 27). Pride and prejudice. *Time,* pp. 54–59.

HEPWORTH, J. T., & WEST, S. G. (1988). Lynchings and the economy: A time-series reanalysis of Hovland and Sears (1940). *Journal of Personality and Social Psychology, 55,* 239–247.

HERADSTVEIT, D. (1979). The Arab-Israeli conflict: Psychological obstacles to peace, (vol. 28). Oslo, Norway: Universitetsforlaget. Distributed by Columbia University Press. Reviewed by R. K. White (1980), *Contemporary Psychology, 25,* 11–12.

HEREK, G. (1993). Interpersonal contact and heterosexuals' attitudes toward gay men: Results from a national survey. *Journal of Sex Research, 30,* 239–244.

HERMAN, C. P., ROTH, D. A., & POLIVY, J. (2003). Effects of the presence of others on food intake: A normative interpretation. *Psychological Bulletin, 129,* 873–886.

HESS, U., ADAMS, R. B. JR., & KELECK, R. E. (2004). Facial appearance, gender, and emotion expression. *Emotion, 4,* 378–388.

HEWSTONE, M. (2003). Intergroup contact: Panacea for prejudice? *The Psychologist, 16,* 352–355.

HEWSTONE, M., HANTZI, A., & JOHNSTON, L. (1991). Social categorisation and person memory: The pervasiveness of race as an organizing principle. *European Journal of Social Psychology, 21,* 517–528.

HIGBEE, K. L., MILLARD, R. J., & FOLKMAN, J. R. (1982). Social psychology research during the 1970s: Predominance of experimentation and college students. *Personality and Social Psychology Bulletin, 8,* 180–183.

HIGGINS, E. T., & BARGH, J. A. (1987). Social cognition and social perception. *Annual Review of Psychology, 38,* 369–425.

HIGGINS, E. T., & MCCANN, C. D. (1984). Social encoding and subsequent attitudes, impressions and memory: "Context-driven" and motivational aspects of processing. *Journal of Personality and Social Psychology, 47,* 26–39.

HIGGINS, E. T., & RHOLES, W. S. (1978). Saying is believing: Effects of message modification on memory and liking for the person described. *Journal of Experimental Social Psychology, 14,* 363–378.

HIGGINS, N. C., & BHATT, G. (2001). Culture moderates the self-serving bias: Etic and emic features of causal attributes in India and in Canada. *Social Behavior and Personality, 29,* 49–61.

HILEMAN, B. (1999, August 9). Case grows for climate change. *Chemical and Engineering News,* pp. 16–23.

HILL, T., SMITH, N. D., & LEWICKI, P. (1989). The development of self-image bias: A real-world demonstration. *Personality and Social Psychology Bulletin, 15,* 205–211.

HINE, D. W., & GIFFORD, R. (1996). Attributions about self and others in commons dilemmas. *European Journal of Social Psychology, 26,* 429–445.

HINSZ, V. B., TINDALE, R. S., & VOLLRATH, D. A. (1997). The emerging conceptualization of groups as information processors. *Psychological Bulletin, 121,* 43–64.

HIRSCHMAN, R. S., & LEVENTHAL, H. (1989). Preventing smoking behavior in school children: An initial test of a cognitive-development program. *Journal of Applied Social Psychology, 19,* 559–583.

HOAKEN, P. N. S., PIHL, R. O. (2000). The effects of alcohol intoxication on aggressive responses in men and women. *Alcohol and Alcoholism, 35,* 471–477.

HOFFMAN, C., & HURST, N. (1990). Gender stereotypes: Perception or rationalization? *Journal of Personality and Social Psychology, 58,* 197–208.

HOFFMAN, L. W. (1977). Changes in family roles, socialization, and sex differences. *American Psychologist, 32,* 644–657.

HOFFRAGE, U., HERTWIG, R., & GIGERENZER, G. (2000, May). Hindsight bias: A by-product of knowledge updating? *Journal of Experimental Psychology: Learning, Memory, and Cognition, 26,* 566–581.

HOFLING, C. K., BROTZMAN, E., DAIRYMPLE, S., GRAVES, N., & PIERCE, C. M. (1966). An experimental study in nurse-physician relationships. *Journal of Nervous and Mental Disease, 143,* 171–180.

HOGAN, R., CURPHY, G. J., & HOGAN, J. (1994). What we know about leadership: Effectiveness and personality. *American Psychologist, 49,* 493–504.

HOGG, M. A. (1992). *The social psychology of group cohesiveness: From attraction to social identity.* London: Harvester Wheatsheaf.

HOGG, M. A. (1996). Intragroup processes, group structure and social identity. In W. P. Robinson (Ed.), *Social groups and identities: Developing the legacy of Henri Tajfel.* Oxford: Butterworth Heinemann.

HOGG, M. A. (2003). Social identity. In M. R. Leary & J. P. Tangey (Eds.), *Handbook of self and identity.* New York: Guilford Press.

HOGG, M. A., HAINS, S. C., & MASON, I. (1998). Identification and leadership in small groups: Salience, frame of reference, and leader stereotypicality effects on leader evaluations. *Journal of Personality and Social Psychology, 75,* 1248–1263.

HOGG, M. A., TURNER, J. C., & DAVIDSON, B. (1990). Polarized norms and social frames of reference: A test of the self-categorization theory of group polarization. *Basic and Applied Social Psychology, 11,* 77–100.

HOLMBERG D., & MACKENZIE, S. (2002). So far so good: Scripts for romantic relationship development as predictors of relational well-being. *Journal of Social and Personal Relationships, 19,* 777–796.

HOLMBERG, D., ORBUCH, T. L., & VEROFF, J. (2004). *Thrice-told tales: Married couples tell their stories.* Mahwah, NJ: Lawrence Erlbaum Associates.

HOLMBERG, D., PRINGLE, J. D., SHEA, S. L., & DODGE, D. (2006). She remembers it well: evidence for superior female relationship memory. Unpublished manuscript. Wolfville: Acadia University.

HOLMBERG, D., & ROSS, M. (1992). Are wives' memories for events more vivid than their husbands memories? *Journal of Social and Personal Relationships, 9,* 585–604.

HOLMES, J. G., & REMPEL, J. K. (1989). Trust in close relationships. In C. Hendrick (Ed.), *Review of personality and social psychology,* vol. 10. Newbury Park, CA: Sage.

HOLMES, J. G., MILLER, D. T., & LERNER, J. M. (2002). Committing altruism under the cloak of self-interest: The exchange fiction. *Journal of Experimental Social Psychology, 38,* 144–151.

HOLTGRAVES, T. (1997). Styles of language use: Individual and cultural variability in conversational indirectness. *Journal of Personality and Social Psychology, 73,* 624–637.

HOLTGRAVES, T., & SRULL, T. K. (1989). The effects of positive self-descriptions on impressions: General principles and individual differences. *Personality and Social Psychology Bulletin, 15,* 452–462.

HONEYMAN, J. C., & OGLOFF, J. (1996). Capital punishment: Arguments for life and death. *Canadian Journal of Behavioral Science, 28,* 27–35.

HOORENS, V. (1993). Self-enhancement and superiority biases in social comparison. In W. Stroebe & M. Hewstone (Eds.), *European review of social psychology,* vol. 4. Chichester, England: Wiley.

HOORENS, V., & NUTTIN, J. M. (1993). Overvaluation of own attributes: Mere ownership or subjective frequency? *Social Cognition, 11,* 177–200.

HOORENS, V., NUTTIN, J. M., HERMAN, I. E., & PAVAKANUN, U. (1990). Mastery pleasure versus mere ownership: A quasi-experimental cross-cultural and cross-alphabetical test of the name letter effect. *European Journal of Social Psychology, 20,* 181–205.

HOUSE, R. J., & SINGH, J. V. (1987). Organizational behavior: Some new directions for I/O psychology. *Annual Review of Psychology, 38,* 669–718.

HOUSTON, V., & BULL, R. (1994). Do people avoid sitting next to someone who is facially disfigured? *European Journal of Social Psychology, 24,* 279–284.

HOVLAND, C. I., LUMSDAINE, A. A., & SHEFFIELD, F. D. (1949). Experiments on mass communication. *Studies in social psychology in World War II,* vol. 3. Princeton, NJ: Princeton University Press.

HOVLAND, C. I., & SEARS, R. (1940). Minor studies of aggression: Correlation of lynchings with economic indices. *Journal of Psychology, 9,* 301–310.

HUDDY, L., & VIRTANEN, S. (1995). Subgroup differentiation and subgroup bias among Latinos as a function of familiarity and positive distinctiveness. *Journal of Personality and Social Psychology, 68,* 97–108.

HUESMANN, L. R., LAGERSPETZ, K., & ERON, L. D. (1984). Intervening variables in the TV violence-aggression relation: Evidence from two countries. *Developmental Psychology, 20,* 746–775.

HUESMANN, L. R., MOISE-TITUS, J., PODOLSKI, C-L., & ERON, L. D. (2003). Longitudinal relations between children's exposure to TV violence and their aggressive and violent behavior in young adulthood: 1977–1992. *Developmental Psychology, 39,* 201–222.

HUGENBERG, K., & BODENHAUSEN, G. V. (2003). Facing prejudice: Implicit prejudice and the perception of facial threat. *Psychological Science, 14,* 640–643.

HULL, J. G., & BOND, C. F., JR. (1986). Social and behavioral consequences of alcohol consumption and expectancy: A meta-analysis. *Psychological Bulletin, 99,* 347–360.

HULL, J. G., LEVENSON, R. W., YOUNG, R. D., & SHER, K. J. (1983). Self-awareness-reducing effects of alcohol consumption. *Journal of Personality and Social Psychology, 44,* 461–473.

HUNT, M. (1990). *The compassionate beast: What science is discovering about the humane side of human kind.* New York: William Morrow.

HUNT, M. (1993). *The story of psychology.* New York: Doubleday.

HUNT, P. J., & HILLERY, J. M. (1973). Social facilitation in a location setting: An examination of the effects over learning trials. *Journal of Experimental Social Psychology, 9,* 563–571.

HUNTER, J. A., STRINGER, M., & WATSON, R. P. (1991). Intergroup violence and intergroup attributions. *British Journal of Social Psychology, 30,* 261–266.

HUNTER, J. D. (2002, June 21–22). "To change the world." Paper presented to the Board of Directors of The Trinity Forum, Denver, Colorado.

HURTADO, S., DEY, E. L., & TREVINO, J. G. (1994). Exclusion or self-segregation? Interaction across racial/ethnic groups on college campuses. Paper presented at the American Educational Research Association annual meeting.

HUSTON, A. C., DONNERSTEIN, E., FAIRCHILD, H., FESHBACH, N. D., KATZ, P. A., & MURRAY, J. P. (1992). *Big world, small screen: The role of television in American society.* Lincoln: University of Nebraska Press.

HUSTON, T. L. (1973). Ambiguity of acceptance, social desirability, and dating choice. *Journal of Experimental Social Psychology, 9,* 32–42.

HUSTON, T. L., & CHOROST, A. F. (1994). Behavioral buffers on the effect of negativity on marital satisfaction: A longitudinal study. *Personal Relationships, 1,* 223–239.

ICKES, B. (1980). On disconfirming our perceptions of others. Paper presented at the American Psychological Association convention.

ICKES, W., LAYDEN, M. A., & BARNES, R. D. (1978). Objective self-awareness and individuation: An empirical link. *Journal of Personality, 46,* 146–161.

ICKES, W., SNYDER, M., & GARCIA, S. (1997). Personality influences on the choice of situations. In R. Hogan, J. Johnson, & S. Briggs (Eds.), *Handbook of personality psychology.* San Diego, CA: Academic Press.

ILO. (1997, December 11). Women's progress in workforce improving worldwide, but occupation segregation still rife. International Labor Association press release (www.ilo.org/public/english/bureau/inf/pr/1997/35.htm).

IMAI, Y. (1994). Effects of influencing attempts on the perceptions of powerholders and the powerless. *Journal of Social Behavior and Personality, 9,* 455–468.

INBAU, F. E., REID, J. E., BUCKLEY, J. P., & JAYNE, B. C. (2001). *Criminal interrogation and confessions* (4th ed.). Gaithersburg, MD: Aspen.

INGHAM, A. G., LEVINGER, G., GRAVES, J., & PECKHAM, V. (1974). The Ringelmann effect: Studies of group size and group performance. *Journal of Experimental Social Psychology, 10,* 371–384.

INGLEHART, R. (1990). *Culture shift in advanced industrial society.* Princeton, NJ: Princeton University Press.

INGLEHART, R. (1997). *Modernization and postmodernization.* Princeton, NJ: Princeton University Press.

INTERNATIONAL CIVIL AVIATION ORGANIZATION (ICAO). (2005). From http://www.icao.int/cgi/goto_m.pl?/icao/en/jr/jr.cfm.

IPU. (2005). *Women in politics 1945–2005.* Inter-Parliamentary Union: Geneva.

ISLAM, M. R., & HEWSTONE, M. (1993). Dimensions of contact as predictors of intergroup anxiety, perceived out-group variability, and out-group attitude: An integrative model. *Personality and Social Psychology Bulletin, 19,* 700–710.

ISOZAKI, M. (1984). The effect of discussion on polarization of judgments. *Japanese Psychological Research, 26,* 187–193.

ISR NEWSLETTER. (1975). Institute for Social Research, University of Michigan, 3, 4–7.

ITO, T. A., MILLER, N., & POLLOCK, V. E. (1996). Alcohol and aggression: A meta-analysis on the moderating effects of inhibitory cues, triggering events, and self-focused attention. *Psychological Bulletin, 120,* 60–82.

IYENGAR, S. S., & LEPPER, M. R. (2000). When choice is demotivating: Can one desire too much of a good thing? *Journal of Personality and Social Psychology, 79,* 995–1006.

IYER, P. (1993, Fall). The global village finally arrives. *Time,* pp. 86–87.

JACKMAN, M. R., & SENTER, M. S. (1981). Beliefs about race, gender, and social class different, therefore unequal: Beliefs about trait differences between groups of unequal status. In D. J. Treiman & R. V. Robinson (Eds.), *Research in stratification and mobility,* vol. 2. Greenwich, CT: JAI Press.

JACKS, J. Z., & CAMERON, K. A. (2003). Strategies for resisting persuasion. *Basic and Applied Social Psychology, 25,* 145–161.

JACKSON, J. M., & LATANÉ, B. (1981). All alone in front of all those people: Stage fright as a function of number and type of co-performers and audience. *Journal of Personality and Social Psychology, 40,* 73–85.

JACKSON, L. A. (1989). Relative deprivation and the gender wage gap. *Journal of Social Issues, 45,* 117–133.

JACKSON, L. A., HUNTER, J. E., & HODGE, C. N. (1995). Physical attractiveness and intellectual competence: A meta-analytic review. *Social Psychology Quarterly, 58,* 108–123.

JACOBY, S. (1986, December). When opposites attract. *Reader's Digest,* pp. 95–98.

JAMIESON, D. W., LYDON, J. E., STEWART, G., & ZANNA, M. P. (1987). Pygmalion revisited: New evidence for student expectancy effects in the classroom. *Journal of Educational Psychology, 79,* 461–466.

JANIS, I. L. (1971, November). Groupthink. *Psychology Today,* pp. 43–46.

JANIS, I. L. (1982). Counteracting the adverse effects of concurrence-seeking in policy-planning groups: Theory and research perspectives. In H. Brandstatter, J. H. Davis, & G. Stocker-Kreichgauer (Eds.), *Group decision making.* New York: Academic Press.

JANIS, I. L., KAYE, D., & KIRSCHNER, P. (1965). Facilitating effects of eating while reading on responsiveness to persuasive communications. *Journal of Personality and Social Psychology, 1,* 181–186.

JANIS, I. L., & MANN, L. (1977). *Decision-making: A psychological analysis of conflict, choice and commitment.* New York: Free Press.

JANKOWIAK, W. R., & FISCHER, E. F. (1992). A cross-cultural perspective on romantic love. *Ethnology, 31,* 149–155.

JELLISON, J. M., & GREEN, J. (1981). A self-presentation approach to the fundamental attribution error: The norm of internality. *Journal of Personality and Social Psychology, 40,* 643–649.

JENNINGS, D. L., AMABILE, T. M., & ROSS, L. (1982). Informal covariation assessment: Data-based vs theory-based judgments. In D. Kahneman, P. Slovic, & A. Tversky (Eds.), *Judgment under uncertainty: Heuristics and biases.* New York: Cambridge University Press.

JOHNSON, B. T., & EAGLY, A. H. (1989). Effects of involvement on persuasion: A meta-analysis. *Psychological Bulletin, 106,* 290–314.

JOHNSON, B. T., & EAGLY, A. H. (1990). Involvement and persuasion: Types, traditions, and the evidence. *Psychological Bulletin, 107,* 375–384.

JOHNSON, D. J., & RUSBULT, C. E. (1989). Resisting temptation: Devaluation of alternative partners as a means of maintaining commitment in close relationships. *Journal of Personality and Social Psychology, 57,* 967–980.

JOHNSON, D. W., MARUYAMA, G., JOHNSON, R., NELSON, D., & SKON, L. (1981). Effects of cooperative, competitive, and individualistic goal structures on achievement: A meta-analysis. *Psychological Bulletin, 89,* 47–62.

JOHNSON, J. D., JACKSON, L. A., & GATTO, L. (1995). Violent attitudes and deferred academic aspirations: Deleterious effects of exposure to rap music. *Basic and Applied Social Psychology, 16,* 27–41.

JOHNSON, J. G., COHEN, P., SMAILES, E. M., KASEN, S., & BROOK, J. S. (2002). Television viewing and aggressive behavior during adolescence and adulthood. *Science, 295,* 2468–2471.

JOHNSON, J. T., JEMMOTT, J. B., III., & PETTIGREW, T. F. (1984). Causal attribution and dispositional inference: Evidence of inconsistent judgments. *Journal of Experimental Social Psychology, 20,* 567–585.

JOHNSON, R. D., & DOWNING, L. L. (1979). Deindividuation and valence of cues: Effects of prosocial and antisocial behavior. *Journal of Personality and Social Psychology, 37,* 1532–1538.

JOINSON, A. N. (2001). Self-disclosure in computer-mediated communication: The role of self-awareness and visual anonymity. *European Journal of Social Psychology, 31,* 177–192.

JONES, E. E. (1976). How do people perceive the causes of behavior? *American Scientist, 64,* 300–305.

JONES, E. E., & HARRIS, V. A. (1967). The attribution of attitudes. *Journal of Experimental Social Psychology, 3,* 2–24.

JONES, E. E., & NISBETT, R. E. (1971). *The actor and the observer: Divergent perceptions of the cases of behavior.* Morristown, NJ: General Learning Press.

JOSEPHSON, W. L. (1987). Television violence and children's aggression: Testing the priming, social script, and disinhibition predictions. *Journal of Personality and Social Psychology, 53,* 882–890.

JOURDEN, F. J., & HEATH, C. (1996). The evaluation gap in performance perceptions: Illusory perceptions of groups and individuals. *Journal of Applied Psychology, 81,* 369–379.

JUDD, C. M., BLAIR, I. V., & CHAPLEAU, K. M. (2004). Automatic stereotypes vs. automatic prejudice: Sorting out the possibilities in the Payne (2001) weapon paradigm. *Journal of Experimental Social Psychology, 40,* 75–81.

JUDD, C. M., RYAN, C. S., & PARK, B. (1991). Accuracy in the judgment of in-group and out-group variability. *Journal of Personality and Social Psychology, 61,* 366–379.

JUSSIM, L. (1986). Self-fulfilling prophecies: A theoretical and integrative review. *Psychological Review, 93,* 429–445.

KAGEHIRO, D. K. (1990). Defining the standard of proof injuring instructions. *Psychological Science, 1,* 194–200.

KAGAN, J. (1989). Temperamental contributions to social behavior. *American Psychologist, 44,* 668–674.

KAHN, M. W. (1951). The effect of severe defeat at various age levels on the aggressive behavior of mice. *Journal of Genetic Psychology, 79,* 117–130.

KAHNEMAN, D., & SNELL, J. (1992). Predicting a changing taste: Do people know what they will like? *Journal of Behavioral Decision Making, 5,* 187–200.

KAHNEMAN, D., & TVERSKY, A. (1995). Conflict resolution: A cognitive perspective. In K. Arrow, R. Mnookin, L. Ross, A. Tversky, & R. Wilson (Eds.), *Barriers to the negotiated resolution of conflict.* New York: Norton.

KALICK, S. M. (1977). Plastic surgery, physical appearance, and person perception. Unpublished doctoral dissertation, Harvard University. Cited by E. Berscheid in An overview of the psychological effects of physical attractiveness and some comments upon the psychological effects of knowledge of the effects of physical attractiveness. In W. Lucker, K. Ribbens, & J. A. McNamera (Eds.), *Logical aspects of facial form (craniofacial growth series).* Ann Arbor: University of Michigan Press, 1981.

KALVERN, H., & ZEISEL, H. (1966). *The American jury.* Boston: Little, Brown.

KAMEDA, T., & SUGIMORI, S. (1993). Psychological entrapment in group decision making: An assigned decision rule and a groupthink phenomenon. *Journal of Personality and Social Psychology, 65*, 282–292.

KAMMER, D. (1982). Differences in trait ascriptions to self and friend: Unconfounding intensity from variability. *Psychological Reports, 51*, 99–102.

KANDEL, D. B. (1978). Similarity in real-life adolescent friendship pairs. *Journal of Personality and Social Psychology, 36*, 306–312.

KAPLAN, M. F., WANSHULA, L. T., & ZANNA, M. P. (1993). Time pressure and information integration in social judgment: The effect of need for structure. In O. Svenson & J. Maule (Eds.), *Time pressure and stress in human judgment and decision making.* Cambridge: Cambridge University Press.

KARAU, S. J., & WILLIAMS, K. D. (1993). Social loafing: A meta-analytic review and theoretical integration. *Journal of Personality and Social Psychology, 65*, 681–706.

KARAU, S. J., & WILLIAMS, K. D. (1997). The effects of group cohesiveness on social loafing and compensation. *Group Dynamics: Theory, Research, and Practice, 1*, 156–168.

KARAVELLAS, D. (2000). Sustainable consumption and fisheries. In B. Heap & J. Kent (Eds.), *Towards sustainable consumption: A European perspective.* London: The Royal Society.

KARNEY, B. R., & BRADBURY, T. N. (1995). The longitudinal course of marital quality and stability: A review of theory, method, and research. *Psychological Bulletin, 118*, 3–34.

KASSER, T. (2000). Two versions of the American dream: Which goals and values make for a high quality of life? In E. Diener & D. Rahtz (Eds.), *Advances in quality of life: Theory and research.* Dordrecht, Netherlands: Kluwer.

KASSER, T. (2002). *The high price of materialism.* Cambridge, MA: MIT Press.

KASSIN, S. M. (2005). On the psychology of confessions: Does innocence put innocents at risk? *American Psychologist, 60*, 215–228.

KASSIN, S. M., & GUDJONSSON, G. H. (2004). The psychology of confessions: A review of the literature and issues. *Psychological Science in the Public Interest, 5*, 33–67.

KASSIN, S. M., GOLDSTEIN, C. C., & SAVITSKY, K. (2003). Behavioral confirmation in the interrogation room: On the dangers of presuming guilt. *Law and Human Behavior, 27*, 187–203.

KASSIN S. M., & NORWICK, R. L. (2004). Why people waive their Miranda Rights: The power of innocence. *Law and Human Behavior, 28*, 211–221.

KATZ, A. M., & HILL, R. (1958). Residential propinquity and marital selection: A review of theory, method, and fact. *Marriage and Family Living, 20*, 237–335.

KAUFMAN, J., & ZIGLER, E. (1987). Do abused children become abusive parents? *American Journal of Orthopsychiatry, 57*, 186–192.

KAWAKAMI, K., DOVIDIO, J. F., MOLL, J., HERMSEN, S., & RUSSIN, A. (2000). Just say no (to stereotyping): Effects of training in the negation of stereotypic associations on stereotype activation. *Journal of Personality and Social Psychology, 78*, 871–888.

KEATING, J. P., & BROCK, T. C. (1974). Acceptance of persuasion and the inhibition of counterargumentation under various distraction tasks. Journal of *Experimental Social Psychology, 10*, 301–309.

KELLER, J., & DAUENHEIMER, D. (2003). Stereotype threat in the classroom: Dejection mediates the disrupting threat effect on women's math per-formance. *Personality and Social Psychology Bulletin, 29*, 371–381.

KELLERMAN, J., LEWIS, J., & LAIRD, J. D. (1989). Looking and loving: The effects of mutual gaze on feelings of romantic love. *Journal of Research in Personality, 23*, 145–161.

KELLEY, H. H., & STAHELSKI, A. J. (1970). The social interaction basis of cooperators' and competitors' beliefs about others. *Journal of Personality and Social Psychology, 16*, 66–91.

KELMAN, H. C. (1997). Group processes in the resolution of international conflicts: Experiences from the Israeli-Palestinian case. *American Psychologist, 52*, 212–220.

KELMAN, H. C. (1998). Building a sustainable peace: The limits of pragmatism in the Israeli-Palestinian negotiations. Address to the American Psychological Association convention.

KELTNER, D., & ROBINSON, R. J. (1996). Extremism, power, and the imagined basis of social conflict. *Current Directions in Psychological Science, 5*, 101–105.

KENNY, D. A., & NASBY, W. (1980). Splitting the reciprocity correlation. *Journal of Personality and Social Psychology, 38*, 249–256.

KENRICK, D. T., & CIALDINI, R. B. (1977). Romantic attraction: Misattraction versus reinforcement explanations. *Journal of Personality and Social Psychology, 35*, 381–391.

KENRICK, D. T. (1987). Gender, genes, and the social environment: A biosocial interactionist perspective. In P. Shaver & C. Hendrick (Eds.), *Sex and gender: Review of personality and social psychology*, vol. 7. Beverly Hills, CA: Sage.

KENRICK, D. T., & CIALDINI, R. B. (1977). Romantic attraction: Misattraction versus reinforcement explanations. *Journal of Personality and Social Psychology, 35*, 381–391.

KENRICK, D. T., & GUTIERRES, S. E. (1980). Contrast effects and judgments of physical attractiveness: When beauty becomes a social problem. *Journal of Personality and Social Psychology, 38*, 131–140.

KENRICK, D. T., GUTIERRES, S. E., & GOLDBERG, L. L. (1989). Influence of popular erotica on judgments of strangers and mates. *Journal of Experimental Social Psychology, 25,* 159–167.

KENRICK, D. T., & MACFARLANE, S. W. (1986). Ambient temperature and horn-honking: A field study of the heat/aggression relationship. *Environment and Behavior, 18,* 179–191.

KENRICK, D. T., & TROST, M. R. (1987). A biosocial theory of heterosexual relationships. In K. Kelly (Ed.), *Females, males, and sexuality.* Albany: State University of New York Press.

KERNIS, M. H. (2003). High self-esteem: A differentiated perspective. In E. C. Chang & L. J. Sanna (Eds.), *Virtue, vice, and personality: The complexity of behavior.* Washington, DC: APA Books.

KERR, N. L. (1983). Motivation losses in small groups: A social dilemma analysis. *Journal of Personality and Social Psychology, 45,* 819–828.

KERR, N. L. (1989). Illusions of efficacy: The effects of group size on perceived efficacy in social dilemmas. *Journal of Experimental Social Psychology, 25,* 287–313.

KERR, N. L., & BRUUN, S. E. (1981). Ringelmann revisited: Alternative explanations for the social loafing effect. *Personality and Social Psychology Bulletin, 7,* 224–231.

KERR, N. L., & BRUUN, S. E. (1983). Dispensibility of member effort and group motivation losses: Free-rider effects. *Journal of Personality and Social Psychology, 44,* 78–94.

KERR, N. L., & KAUFMAN-GILLILAND, C. M. (1994). Communication, commitment, and cooperation in social dilemmas. *Journal of Personality and Social Psychology, 66,* 513–529.

KERR, N. L., & KAUFMAN-GILLILAND, C. M. (1997). ". . . and besides, I probably couldn't have made a difference anyway": Justification of social dilemma defection via perceived self-inefficacy. *Journal of Experimental Social Psychology, 33,* 211–230.

KERR, N. L., ATKIN, R. S., STASSER, G., MEEK, D., HOLT, R. W., & DAVIS, J. H. (1976). Guilt beyond a reasonable doubt: Effects of concept definition and assigned decision rule on the judgments of mock jurors. *Journal of Personality and Social Psychology, 34,* 282–294.

KERR, N. L., GARST, J., LEWANDOWSKI, D. A., & HARRIS, S. E. (1997). That still, small voice: Commitment to cooperate as an internalized versus a social norm. *Personality and Social Psychology Bulletin, 23,* 1300–1311.

KERR, N. L., HARMON, D. L., & GRAVES, J. K. (1982). Independence of multiple verdicts by jurors and juries. *Journal of Applied Social Psychology, 12,* 12–29.

KIDD, J. B., & MORGAN, J. R. (1969). A predictive information system for management. *Operational Research Quarterly, 20,* 149–170.

KIESLER, C. A. (1971). *The psychology of commitment: Experiments linking behavior to belief.* New York: Academic Press.

KIHLSTROM, J. F., & CANTOR, N. (1984). Mental representations of the self. In L. Berkowitz (Ed.), *Advances in experimental social psychology,* vol. 17. New York: Academic Press.

KIM, H., & MARKUS, H. R. (1999). Deviance of uniqueness, harmony or conformity? A cultural analysis. *Journal of Personality and Social Psychology, 77,* 785–800.

KIMMEL, A. J. (1998). In defense of deception. *American Psychologist, 53,* 803–805.

KINDER, D. R., & SEARS, D. O. (1985). Public opinion and political action. In G. Lindzey & E. Aronson (Eds.), *The handbook of social psychology,* 3rd ed. New York: Random House.

KIRMEYER, S. L. (1978). Urban density and pathology: A review of research. *Environment and Behavior, 10,* 257–269.

KITAYAMA, S., & KARASAWA, M. (1997). Implicit self-esteem in Japan: Name letters and birthday numbers. *Personality and Social Psychology Bulletin, 23,* 736–742.

KITAYAMA, S., & MARKUS, H. R. (1995). Culture and self: Implications for internationalizing psychology. In N. R. Goldberger & J. B. Veroff (Eds.), *The culture and psychology reader.* New York: New York University Press.

KITE, M. E. (2001). Changing times, changing gender roles: Who do we want women and men to be? In R. K. Unger (Ed.), *Handbook of the psychology of women and gender.* New York: Wiley.

KLAAS, E. T. (1978). Psychological effects of immoral actions: The experimental evidence. *Psychological Bulletin, 85,* 756–771.

KLECK, R. E., & STRENTA, A. (1980). Perceptions of the impact of negatively valued physical characteristics on social interaction. *Journal of Personality and Social Psychology, 39,* 861–873.

KLEIN, J. G. (1991). Negative effects in impression formation: A test in the political arena. *Personality and Social Psychology Bulletin, 17,* 412–418.

KLEIN, W. M., & KUNDA, Z. (1992). Motivated person perception: Constructing justifications for desired beliefs. *Journal of Experimental Social Psychology, 28,* 145–168.

KLEINKE, C. L. (1977). Compliance to requests made by gazing and touching experimenters in field settings. *Journal of Experimental Social Psychology, 13,* 218–223.

KLENTZ, B., BEAMAN, A. L., MAPELLI, S. D., & ULLRICH, J. R. (1987). Perceived physical attractiveness of supporters and nonsupporters of the women's movement: An attitude-similarity-mediated error (AS-ME). *Personality and Social Psychology Bulletin, 13,* 513–523.

KLOPFER, P. H. (1958). Influence of social interaction on learning rates in birds. *Science, 128,* 903.

KNIGHT, G. P., FABES, R. A., & HIGGINS, D. A. (1996). Concerns about drawing causal inferences from meta-analyses: An example in the study of gender differences in aggression. *Psychological Bulletin, 119,* 410–421.

KNIGHT, J. A., & VALLACHER, R. R. (1981). Interpersonal engagement in social perception: The consequences of getting into the action. *Journal of Personality and Social Psychology, 40,* 990–999.

KNOWLES, E. S. (1983). Social physics and the effects of others: Tests of the effects of audience size and distance on social judgment and behavior. *Journal of Personality and Social Psychology, 45,* 1263–1279.

KNUDSON, R. M., SOMMERS, A. A., & GOLDING, S. L. (1980). Interpersonal perception and mode of resolution in marital conflict. *Journal of Personality and Social Psychology, 38,* 751–763.

KOESTNER, R., & WHEELER, L. (1988). Self-presentation in personal advertisements: The influence of implicit notions of attraction and role expectations. *Journal of Social and Personal Relationships, 5,* 149–160.

KOESTNER, R. F. (1993). False consensus effects for the 1992 Canadian referendum. Paper presented at the American Psychological Association Convention.

KOMORITA, S. S., & BARTH, J. M. (1985). Components of reward in social dilemmas. *Journal of Personality and Social Psychology, 48,* 364–373.

KOMORITA, S. S., PARKS, C. D., & HULBERT, L. G. (1992). Reciprocity and the introduction of cooperation in social dilemmas. *Journal of Personality and Social Psychology, 62,* 607–617.

KONRAD, A. M., RITCHIE, J. E., JR., LIEB, P., & CORRIGALL, E. (2000). Sex differences and similarities in job attribute preferences: A meta-analysis. *Psychological Bulletin, 126,* 593–641.

KOOMEN, W., & DIJKER, A. J. (1997). Ingroup and outgroup stereotypes and selective processing. *European Journal of Social Psychology, 27,* 589–601.

KOOP, C. E. (1987). Report of the surgeon general's workshop on pornography and public health. *American Psychologist, 42,* 944–945.

KORN, J. H., & NICKS, S. D. (1993). The rise and decline of deception in social psychology. Poster presented at the American Psychological Society convention.

KOSS, M. P. (1990, August 29). *Rape incidence: A review and assessment of the data.* Testimony on behalf of the American Psychological Association before the U.S. Senate Judiciary Committee.

KOSS, M. P., DINERO, T. E., SEIBEL, C. A., & COX, S. L. (1988). Stranger and acquaintance rape. *Psychology of Women, 12,* 1–24.

KRACKOW, A., & BLASS, T. (1995). When nurses obey or defy inappropriate physician orders: Attributional differences. *Journal of Social Behavior and Personality, 10,* 585–594.

KRAUT, R., PATTERSON, M., LUNDMARK, V., KIESLER, S., MUKOPADHYAY, T., & SCHERLIS, W. (1998). Internet paradox: A social technology that reduces social involvement and psychological well-being? *American Psychologist, 53,* 1017–1031.

KRAVITZ, D. A., & MARTIN, B. (1986). Ringelmann rediscovered: The original article. *Journal of Personality and Social Psychology, 50,* 936–941.

KREBS, D., & ADINOLFI, A. A. (1975). Physical attractiveness, social relations, and personality style. *Journal of Personality and Social Psychology, 31,* 245–253.

KROSNICK, J. A., & ALWIN, D. F. (1989). Aging and susceptibility to attitude change. *Journal of Personality and Social Psychology, 57,* 416–425.

KROSNICK, J. A., & PETTY, R. E. (1995). Attitude strength: Antecedents and consequences. *Ohio State University Series on Attitudes and Persuasion, 4,* 1–24.

KRUEGER, J. (1996). Personal beliefs and cultural stereotypes about racial characteristics. *Journal of Personality and Social Psychology, 71,* 536–548.

KRUEGER, J., & CLEMENT, R. W. (1994). The truly false consensus effect: An ineradicable and egocentric bias in social perception. *Journal of Personality and Social Psychology, 67,* 596–610.

KRUGER, J., EPLEY, N., & GILOVICH, T. (1999). Egocentrism over email. Paper presented to the American Psychological Society meeting.

KRUGER, J., & GILOVICH, T. (1999). "I cynicism" in everyday theories of responsibility assessment: On biased assumptions of bias. *Journal of Personality and Social Psychology, 76,* 743–753.

KRUGLANSKI, A. W., & WEBSTER, D. M. (1991). Group members' reactions to opinion deviates and conformists at varying degrees of proximity to decision deadline and of environmental noise. *Journal of Personality and Social Psychology, 61,* 212–225.

KRUGMAN, P. (2003, February 18). *Behind the great divide.* New York Times (www.nytimes.com).

KRULL, D. S., LOY, M. H-M., LIN, J., WANG, C-F., CHEN, S., & ZHAO, X. (1999). The fundamental attribution error: Correspondence bias in individualist and collectivist cultures. *Personality and Social Psychology Bulletin, 25,* 1208–1219.

KUBANY, E. S., BAUER, G. B., PANGILINAN, M. E., MUROKA, M.Y., & ENRIQUEZ, V. G. (1995). Impact of labeled anger and blame in intimate relationships. *Journal of Cross-Cultural Psychology, 26,* 65–83.

KUGIHARA, N. (1999). Gender and social loafing in Japan. *Journal of Social Psychology, 139,* 516–526.

KUIPER, N. A., & ROGERS, T. B. (1979). Encoding of personal information: Self-other differences. *Journal of Personality and Social Psychology, 37,* 499–514.

KWAN, V. S.Y., BOND, M. H., & SINGELIS, T. M. (1997). *Journal of Personality and Social Psychology, 73,* 1038–1051.

LADOUCEUR, R., & SEVEGNY, S. (2005). Structural characteristics of video lotteries: Effects of a stopping device on illusion of control and gambling persistence. *Journal of Gambling Studies, 21,* 117–131.

LAGERSPETZ, K. (1979). Modification of aggressiveness in mice. In S. Feshbach & A. Fraczek (Eds.), *Aggression and behavior change.* New York: Praeger.

LALONDE, R. N. (1992). The dynamics of group differentiation in the face of defeat. *Personality and Social Psychology Bulletin, 18,* 336–342.

LALONDE, R. N. (2002). Testing the social indentity–intergroup differentiation hypothesis: "We're not American eh!" *British Journal of Social Psychology, 41,* 611–631.

LANDERS, A. (1969, April 8). Syndicated newspaper column. Cited by L. Berkowitz in The case for bottling up rage. *Psychology Today,* September 1973, pp. 24–31.

LANER, M. R., & VENTRONE, N. A. (1998). Egalitarian daters/traditionalist dates. *Journal of Family Issues, 19,* 468–477.

LANER, M. R., & VENTRONE, N. A. (2000). Dating scripts revised. *Journal of Family Issues, 21,* 488–500.

LANGER, E. J., & IMBER, L. (1980). The role of mindlessness in the perception of deviance. *Journal of Personality and Social Psychology, 39,* 360–367.

LANGER, E. J., JANIS, I. L., & WOFER, J. A. (1975). Reduction of psychological stress in surgical patients. *Journal of Experimental Social Psychology, 11,* 155–165.

LANGER, E. J., & RODIN, J. (1976). The effects of choice and enhanced personal responsibility for the aged: A field experiment in an institutional setting. *Journal of Personality and Social Psychology, 334,* 191–198.

LANGLOIS, J., KALAKANIS, L., RUBENSTEIN, A., LARSON, A., HALLAM, M., & SMOOT, M. (1996). Maxims and myths of beauty: A meta-analytic and theoretical review. Paper presented to the American Psychological Society convention.

LANGLOIS, J. H., KALAKANIS, L., RUBENSTEIN, A. J., LARSON, A., HALLAM, M., & SMOOT, M. (2000). Maxims or myths of beauty? A meta-analytic and theoretical review. *Psychological Bulletin, 126,* 390–423.

LANGLOIS, J. H., & ROGGMAN, L. A. (1990). Attractive faces are only average. *Psychological Science, 1,* 115–121.

LANGLOIS, J. H., ROGGMAN, L. A., CASEY, R. J., RITTER, J. M., RIESER-DANNER, L. A., & JENKINS, V.Y. (1987). Infant preferences for attractive faces: Rudiments of a stereotype? *Developmental Psychology, 23,* 363–369.

LANGLOIS, J. H., ROGGMAN, L. A., & MUSSELMAN, L. (1994). What is average and what is not average about attractive faces? *Psychological Science, 5,* 214–220.

LANZETTA, J. T. (1955). Group behavior under stress. *Human Relations, 8,* 29–53.

LARSEN, R. J., & DIENER, E. (1987). Affect intensity as an individual difference characteristic: A review. *Journal of Research in Personality, 21,* 1–39.

LARSON, J. R., JR., FOSTER-FISHMAN, P. G., & KEYS, C. B. (1994). Discussion of shared and unshared information in decision-making groups. *Journal of Personality and Social Psychology, 67,* 446–461.

LARSSON, K. (1956). *Conditioning and sexual behavior in the male albino rat.* Stockholm: Almqvist & Wiksell.

LARWOOD, L. (1978). Swine flu: A field study of self-serving biases. *Journal of Applied Social Psychology, 18,* 283–289.

LARWOOD, L., & WHITTAKER, W. (1977). Managerial myopia: Self-serving biases in organizational planning. *Journal of Applied Psychology, 62,* 194–198.

LASSITER, G. D., & DUDLEY, K. A. (1991). The a priori value of basic research: The case of videotaped confessions. *Journal of Social Behavior and Personality, 6,* 7–16.

LASSITER, G. D., & IRVINE, A. A. (1986). Videotaped confessions: The impact of camera point of view on judgments of coercion. *Journal of Applied Social Psychology, 16,* 268–276.

LATANÉ, B., & DABBS, J. M., JR. (1975). Sex, group size and helping in three cities. *Sociometry, 38,* 180–194.

LATANÉ, B., & DARLEY, J. M. (1968). Group inhibition of bystander intervention in emergencies. *Journal of Personality and Social Psychology, 10,* 215–221.

LATANÉ, B., & DARLEY, J. M. (1970). *The unresponsive bystander: Why doesn't he help?* New York: Appleton-Century-Crofts.

LATANÉ, B., & NIDA, S. (1981). Ten years of research on group size and helping. *Psychological Bulletin, 89,* 308–324.

LATANÉ, B., WILLIAMS, K., & HARKINS. S. (1979). Many hands make light the work: The causes and consequences of social loafing. *Journal of Personality and Social Psychology, 37,* 822–832.

LAUMANN, E. O., GAGNON, J. H., MICHAEL, R. T., & MICHAELS, S. (1994). *The social organization of sexuality: Sexual practices in the United States.* Chicago: University of Chicago Press.

LAZARSFELD, P. F. (1949). The American soldier—an expository review. *Public Opinion Quarterly, 13,* 377–404.

LEAPER, C., & SMITH, T. E. (2004). A meta-analytic review of gender variations in children's language use. *Developmental Psychology, 40,* 993–1027.

LEARY, M. R. (1998). The social and psychological importance of self-esteem. In R. M. Kowalski & M. R. Leary (Eds.), *The social psychology of emotional and behavioral problems.* Washington, DC: American Psychological Association.

LEARY, M. R. (1999). Making sense of self-esteem. *Current Directions in Psychology, 8,* 32–35.

LEARY, M. R., NEZLEK, J. B., DOWNS, D. (1994). Self-presentation in everyday interactions: Effects of target familiarity and gender composition. *Journal of Personality and Social Psychology, 67,* 664–673.

LEE, F., HALLAHAN, M., & HERZOG, T. (1996). Explaining real-life events: How culture and domain shape attributions. *Personality and Social Psychology Bulletin, 22,* 732–741.

LEE, J. A. (1988). Love-styles. In R. J. Sternberg & M. L. Barnes (Eds.), *The psychology of love.* New Haven, CT: Yale University Press.

LEFCOURT, H. M. (1982). *Locus of control: Current trends in theory and research.* Hillsdale, NJ: Erlbaum.

LEIPPE, M. R., & ELKIN, R. A. (1987). Dissonance reduction strategies and accountability to self and others: Ruminations and some initial research. Presentation to the Fifth International Conference on Affect, Motivation, and Cognition, Nags Head Conference Center.

LEMYRE, L., & SMITH, P. M. (1985). Intergroup discrimination and self-esteem in the minimal group paradigm. *Journal of Personality and Social Psychology, 49,* 660–670.

LEO, R. A. (1996). Inside the interrogation room. *The Journal of Criminal Law and Criminology, 86,* 266–303.

LEON, D. (1969). The Kibbutz: A new way of life. London: Pergamon Press. Cited by B. Latané, K. Williams, & S. Harkins (1979), Many hands make light the work: The causes and consequences of social loafing. *Journal of Personality and Social Psychology, 37,* 822–832.

LERNER, M. J. (1980). *The belief in a just world: A fundamental delusion.* New York: Plenum.

LERNER, M. J., & MILLER, D. T. (1978). Just world research and the attribution process: Looking back and ahead. *Psychological Bulletin, 85,* 1030–1051.

LERNER, M. J., & SIMMONS, C. H. (1966). Observer's reaction to the "innocent victim": Compassion or rejection? *Journal of Personality and Social Psychology, 4,* 203–210.

LEVENTHAL, H. (1970). Findings and theory in the study of fear communications. In L. Berkowitz (Ed.), *Advances in experimental social psychology,* vol. 5. New York: Academic Press.

LEVER, J. (1978). Sex differences in the complexity of children's play and games. *American Sociological Review, 43,* 471–483.

LEVIN, D. T. (2000). Race as a visual feature: Using visual search and perceptual discrimination tasks to understand face categories and the cross-race recognition deficit. *Journal of Experimental Psychology: General, 129,* 559–574.

LEVINE, J. M. (1989). Reaction to opinion deviance in small groups. In P. Paulus (Ed.), *Psychology of group influence: New perspectives.* Hillsdale, NJ: Erlbaum.

LEVINE, J. M., & MORELAND, R. L. (1985). Innovation and socialization in small groups. In S. Moscovici, G. Mugny, & E. Van Avermaet (Eds.), *Perspectives on minority influence.* Cambridge: Cambridge University Press.

LEVINE, J. M., & RUSSO, E. M. (1987). Majority and minority influence. In C. Hendrick (Ed.) *Group processes: Review of personality and social psychology* (Vol. 8). Newbury Park, CA: Sage.

LEVINE, R. (2003). *The power of persuasion: How we're bought and sold.* New York: Wiley.

LEVINSON, H. (1950). *The science of chance: From probability to statistics.* New York: Rinehart.

LEVY, S. R., STROESSNER, S. J., & DWECK, C. S. (1998). Stereotype formation and endorsement: The role of implicit theories. *Journal of Personality and Social Psychology, 74,* 1421–1436.

LEVY-LEBOYER, C. (1988). Success and failure in applying psychology. *American Psychologist, 43,* 779–785.

LEWIS, C. S. (1952). *Mere Christianity.* New York: Macmillan.

LEYENS, J-P., CAMINO, L., PARKE, R. D., & BERKOWITZ, L. (1975). Effects of movie violence on aggression in a field setting as a function of group dominance and cohesion. *Journal of Personality and Social Psychology, 32,* 346–360.

LICHACZ, F. M., & PARTINGTON, J. T. (1996). Collective efficacy and true group performance. *International Journal of Sport Psychology, 27,* 146.

LICHTBLAU, E. (2003, March 18). U.S. seeks $289 billion in cigarette makers' profits. *New York Times* (www.nytimes.com).

LICKLITER, R., & HONEYCUTT, H. (2003). Developmental dynamics: Toward a biologically plausible evolutionary psychology. *Psychological Bulletin, 129,* 819–835.

LINDSAY, R. C. L., & BELLINGER, K. (1998). Alternatives to the sequential lineup: The importance of controlling the pictures. *Journal of Applied Psychology, 84,* 315–321.

LINDSAY, R. C. L., & WELLS, G. L. (1985). Improving eyewitness identification from lineups: Simultaneous versus sequential lineup presentations. *Journal of Applied Psychology, 70,* 556–564.

LINVILLE, P. W., GISCHER, W. G., & SALOVEY, P. (1989). Perceived distributions of the characteristics of in-group and out-group members: Empirical evidence and a computer simulation. *Journal of Personality and Social Psychology, 57,* 165–188.

LINZ, D. G., DONNERSTEIN, E., & ADAMS, S. M. (1989). Physiological desensitization and judgments about female victims of violence. *Human Communication Research, 15,* 509–522.

LINZ, D. G., DONNERSTEIN, E., & PENROD, S. (1988). Effects of long term exposure to violent and sexually degrading depictions of women. *Journal of Personality and Social Psychology, 55,* 758–768.

LIPSITZ, A., KALLMEYER, K., FERGUSON, M., & ABAS, A. (1989). Counting on blood donors: Increasing the impact of reminder calls. *Journal of Applied Social Psychology, 19,* 1057–1067.

LITTLE, A., & PERRETT, D. (2002). Putting beauty back in the eye of the beholder. *The Psychologist, 15,* 28–32.

LIVINGSTON, R. W. (2001). What you see is what you get: Systematic variability in perceptual-based social judgment. *Personality and Social Psychology Bulletin, 27,* 1086–1096.

LOCKE, E. A., & LATHAM, G. P. (1990). Work motivation and satisfaction: Light at the end of the tunnel. *Psychological Science, 1,* 240–246.

LOCKSLEY, A., ORTIZ, V., & HEPBURN, C. (1980). Social categorization and discriminatory behavior: Extinguishing the minimal intergroup discrimination effect. *Journal of Personality and Social Psychology, 39,* 773–783.

LOCKWOOD, P., & KUNDA, Z. (1997). Superstars and me: Predicting the impact of role models on self. *Journal of Personality and Social Psychology, 73,* 91–103.

LOCKWOOD, P., & KUNDA, Z. (1999). Increasing the salience of one's best selves can undermine inspiration by outstanding role models. *Journal of Personality and Social Psychology, 76,* 214–228.

LOCKWOOD, P., & KUNDA, Z. (2000). Outstanding role models: Do they inspire or demoralize us? *Psychological Perspectives on Self and Indentity, 69,* 147–171.

LOEWENSTEIN, G., & SCHKADE, D. (1999). Wouldn't it be nice? Predicting future feelings. In D. Kahneman, E. Diener, & N. Schwarz (Eds.), *Understanding well-being: Scientific perspectives on enjoyment and suffering.* New York: Russell Sage Foundation.

LOFLAND, J., & STARK, R. (1965). Becoming a worldsaver: A theory of conversion to a deviant perspective. *American Sociological Review, 30,* 862–864.

LOFTIN, C., McDOWALL, D., WIERSEMA, B., & COTTEY, T. J. (1991). Effects of restrictive licensing of handguns on homicide and suicide in the District of Columbia. *New England Journal of Medicine, 325,* 1615–1620.

LOFTUS, E. F. (1974, December). Reconstructing memory: The incredible eyewitness. *Psychology Today,* 117–119.

LOFTUS, E. F. (1979). *Eyewitness testimony.* Cambridge, MA: Harvard University Press.

LOFTUS, E. G., MILLER, D. G., & BURNS, H. J. (1978). Semantic integration of verbal information into a visual memory. *Journal of Experimental Psychology, Human Learning and Memory, 4,* 19–31.

LOMBARDO, J. P., WEISS, R. F., & BUCHANAN, W. (1972). Reinforcing and attracting functions of yielding. *Journal of Personality and Social Psychology, 21,* 359–368.

LORD, C. G., ROSS, L., & LEPPER, M. (1979). Biased assimilation and attitude polarization: The effects of prior theories on subsequently considered evidence. *Journal of Personality and Social Psychology, 37,* 2098–2109.

LORENZ, K. (1976). *On aggression.* New York: Bantam Books.

LOUIS, W. R., & TAYLOR, D. M. (2002). Understanding the September 11 terrorist attack on America: The role of intergroup theories of normative influence. *Analysis of Social Issues and Public Policy 1,* 87–100.

LOWE, R. H., & WITTIG, M. A. (1989). Comparable worth: Individual, interpersonal, and structural considerations. *Journal of Social Issues, 45,* 223–246.

LOWENSTEIN, D. (2000 May 20). Interview. The World (www.cnn.com/TRANSCRIPTS/0005/20/stc.00.html).

LUEPTOW, L. B., GAROVICH, L., & LUEPTOW, M. B. (1995). The persistence of gender stereotypes in the face of changing sex roles: Evidence contrary to the sociocultural model. *Ethology and Sociobiology, 16,* 509–530.

LUUS, C. A. E., & WELLS, G. L. (October, 1994). The malleability of eyewitness confidence: Co-witness and perseverance effects. *Journal of Applied Psychology, 79,* 714–723.

LYDON, J., & DUNKEL-SCHETTER, C. (1994). Seeing is committing: A longitudinal study of bolstering commitment in amniocenesis patients. *Personality and Social Psychology Bulletin, 20,* 218–227.

LYKKEN, D. T. (1997). The American crime factory. *Psychological Inquiry, 8,* 261–270.

LYKKEN, D. T. (1999). *Happiness.* New York: Golden Books.

LYNCH, B. S., & BONNIE, R. J. (1994). Toward a youth-centered prevention policy. In B. S. Lynch & R. J. Bonnie (Eds.), *Growing up tobacco free: Preventing nicotine addiction in children and youths.* Washington, DC: National Academy Press.

LYNN, M., & OLDENQUIST, A. (1986). Egoistic and nonegoistic motives in social dilemmas. *American Psychologist, 41,* 529–534.

LYONS, L. (2003, September 23). Oh, boy: Americans still prefer sons. Gallup Poll Tuesday Briefing (www.gallup.com).

LYTTLE, J. (2001). The effectiveness of humor in persuasion: The case of business ethics training. *Journal of General Psychology, 128,* 206–216.

MA, V., & SCHOENEMAN, T. J. (1997). Individualism versus collectivism: A comparison of Kenyan and American self-concepts. *Basic and Applied Social Psychology, 19,* 261–273.

MAASS, A. (1998). Personal communication from Universita degli Studi di Padova.

MAASS, A., & CLARK, R. D., III. (1984). Hidden impact of minorities: Fifteen years of minority influence research. *Psychological Bulletin, 95,* 428–450.

MAASS, A., & CLARK, R. D., III. (1986). Conversion theory and simultaneous majority/minority influence: Can reactance offer an alternative explanation? *European Journal of Social Psychology, 16,* 305–309.

MAASS, A., VOLPARO, C., & MUCCHIFAINA, A. (1996). Social influence and the verifiability of the issue under discussion: Attitudinal versus objective items. *British Journal of Social Psychology, 35,* 15–26.

MACCOBY, E. E. (2002). Gender and group process: A developmental perspective. *Current Directions in Psychological Science, 11,* 54–58.

MacCoun, R. J., & Kerr, N. L. (1988). Asymmetric influence in mock deliberation: Jurors' bias for leniency. *Journal of Personality and Social Psychology, 54,* 21–33.

MacDonald, D. J., & Standing, L. G. (2002). Does self-serving bias cancel the Barnum effect in self-perception? *Social Behavior and Personality, 30,* 625–630.

MacDonald, G., Zanna, M. P., & Holmes, J. G. (2000). An experimental test of the role of alcohol in relationship conflict. *Journal of Experimental Social Psychology, 36,* 182–193.

MacDonald, J., & McKelvie, S. (1992). Playing safe: Helping rates for a dropped mitten and a box of condoms. *Psychological Reports, 71,* 113–114

MacDonald, M., & Perrier, J. (2004). Gambling households in Canada. *Journal of Gambling Studies, 20,* 187–236.

MacDonald, T. K., & Ross, M. (1999). Assessing the accuracy of predictions about dating relationships: How and why do lovers' predictions differ from those made by observers? *Society for Personality and Social Psychology, 25,* 1417–1429.

MacGregor, R. M. (2003). I am Canadian: National identity in beer commercials. *The Journal of Popular Culture.*

Mack, D., & Rainey, D. (1990). Female applicants' grooming and personnel selection. *Journal of Social Behavior and Personality, 5,* 399–407.

Mackie, D. (1987). Systematic and nonsystematic processing of majority and minority persuasive communications. *Journal of Personality and Social Psychology, 53,* 41–52.

MacLeod, C., & Campbell, L. (1992). Memory accessibility and probability judgments: An experimental evaluation of the availability heuristic. *Journal of Personality and Social Psychology, 63,* 890–902.

Macrae, C. N., & Bodenhausen, G. V. (2000). Social cognition: Thinking categorically about others. *Annual Review of Psychology, 51,* 93–120.

Macrae, C. N., Bodenhausen, G. V., Milne, A. B., & Jetten, J. (1994). Out of mind but back in sight: Stereotypes on the rebound. *Journal of Personality and Social Psychology, 67,* 808–817.

Maddux, J. E. (1991). Personal efficacy. In V. Derlega, B. Winstead, & W. Jones (Eds.), *Personality: Contemporary theory and research* (2nd ed.). New York: Nelson-Hall.

Maddux, J. E., & Gosselin, J. T. (2003). Self-efficacy. In M. R. Leary & J. P. Tangney (Eds.), *Handbook of self and identity* (pp. 218–238). New York: Guilford Press.

Maddux, J. E., & Rogers, R. W. (1983). Protection motivation and self-efficacy: A revised theory of fear appeals and attitude change. *Journal of Experimental Social Psychology, 19,* 469–479.

Madon, S., Jussim, L., & Eccles, J. (1997). In search of the powerful self-fulfilling prophecy. *Journal of Personality and Social Psychology, 72,* 791–809.

Magnuson, E. (1986, March 10). "A serious deficiency": The Rogers Commission faults NASA's "flawed" decision-making process. *Time* [international ed.], pp. 40–42.

Major, B. (1989). Gender differences in comparisons and entitlement: Implications for comparable worth. *Journal of Social Issues, 45,* 99–116.

Major, B. (1993). Gender, entitlement, and the distribution of family labor. *Journal of Social Issues, 49,* 141–159.

Malamuth, N. M., & Check, J. V. P. (1981). The effects of media exposure on acceptance of violence against women: A field experiment. *Journal of Research in Personality, 15,* 436–446.

Malamuth, N. M., Linz, D., Heavey, C. L., Barnes, G., & Acker, M. (1995). Using the confluence model of sexual aggression to predict men's conflict with women: A 10-year follow-up study. *Journal of Personality and Social Psychology, 69,* 353–369.

Malpass, R. S., & Devine, P. G. (1981). Eyewitness identification: Lineup instructions and the absence of the offender. *Journal of Applied Psychology, 66,* 482–489.

Mann, L. (1981). The baiting crowd in episodes of threatened suicide. *Journal of Personality and Social Psychology, 41,* 703–709.

Marcus, D. K., & Miller, R. S. (2003). Sex differences in judgments of physical attractiveness: A social relations analysis. *Personality and Social Psychology Bulletin, 29,* 325–335.

Marcus, S. (1974). Review of Obedience to authority. *New York Times Book Review,* January 13, pp. 1–2.

Marcus-Newhall, A., Pedersen, W. C., Carlson, M., & Miller, N. (2000). Displaced aggression is alive and well: A meta-analytic review. *Journal of Personality and Social Psychology, 78,* 670–689.

Markman, H. J., Floyd, F. J., Stanley, S. M., & Storaasli, R. D. (1988). Prevention of marital distress: A longitudinal investigation. *Journal of Consulting and Clinical Psychology, 56,* 210–217.

Marks, G., & Miller, N. (1987). Ten years of research on the false-consensus effect: An empirical and theoretical review. *Psychological Bulletin, 102,* 72–90.

Markus, H., & Kitayama, S. (1991). Culture and the self: Implications for cognition, emotion, and motivation. *Psychological Review, 98,* 224–253.

Markus, H., & Wurf, E. (1987). The dynamic self-concept: A social psychological perspective. *Annual Review of Psychology, 38,* 299–337.

Marsh, H. W., & Young, A. S. (1997). Causal effects of academic self-concept on academic achievement: Structural equation models of longitudinal data. *Journal of Educational Psychology, 89,* 41–54.

Marshall, W. L. (1989). Pornography and sex offenders. In D. Zillmann & J. Bryant (Eds.), *Pornography: Research advances and policy considerations.* Hillsdale, NJ: Erlbaum.

Martin, C. L. (1987). A ratio measure of sex stereotyping. *Journal of Personality and Social Psychology, 52,* 489–499.

Maruyama, G., Rubin, R. A., & Kingbury, G. (1981). Self-esteem and educational achievement: Independent constructs with a common cause? *Journal of Personality and Social Psychology, 40,* 962–975.

Marvelle, K., & Green, S. (1980). Physical attractiveness and sex bias in hiring decisions for two types of jobs. Journal of the National Association of Women Deans, Administrators, and Counselors, 44, 3–6.

Marx, G. (1960). *Groucho and me.* New York: Dell.

Masuda, T., & Kitayama, S. (2004). Perceiver-induced constraint and attitude attribution in Japan and the U.S.: A case for culture-dependence of corre-spondence bias. *Journal of Experimental Social Psychology, 40,* 409–416.

Matheson, K., & Zanna, M. P. (1988). The impact of computer-mediated communication on self-awareness. *Computers in Human Behavior, 4,* 221–233.

Matheson, K., & Zanna, M. P. (1990). Computer-mediated communications: The focus is on me. *Social Science Computer Review, 8,* 1–12.

Mazzella, R., & Feingold, A. (1994). The effects of physical attractiveness, race, socioeconomic status, and gender of defendants and victims on judgments of mock jurors: A recta-analysis. *Journal of Applied Social Psychology, 24,* 1315–1344.

McAlister, A., Perry, C., Killen, J., Slinkard, L. A., & Maccoby, N. (1980). Pilot study of smoking, alcohol and drug abuse prevention. *American Journal of Public Health, 70,* 719–721.

McCann, C. D., & Hancock, R. D. (1983). Self-monitoring in communicative interactions: Social cognitive consequences of goal-directed message modification. *Journal of Experimental Social Psychology, 19,* 109–121.

McCarthy, J. F., & Kelly, B. R. (1978a). Aggressive behavior and its effect on performance over time in ice hockey athletes: An archival study. *International Journal of Sport Psychology, 9,* 90–96.

McCarthy, J. F., & Kelly, B. R. (1978b). Aggression, performance variables, and anger self-report in ice hockey players. *Journal of Psychology, 99,* 97–101.

McCauley, C. (1989). The nature of social influence in groupthink: Compliance and internalization. *Journal of Personality and Social Psychology, 57,* 250–260.

McCauley, C. R. (2002). Psychological issues in understanding terrorism and the response to terrorism. In C. E. Stout (Ed.), *The psychology of terrorism,* vol. 3. Westport, CT: Praeger/Greenwood.

McCauley, C. R., & Segal, M. E. (1987). Social psychology of terrorist groups. In C. Hendrick (Ed.), *Group processes and intergroup relations: Review of personality and social psychology,* vol. 9. Newbury Park, CA: Sage.

McConahay, J. B. (1981). Reducing racial prejudice in desegregated schools. In W. D. Hawley (Ed.), *Effective school desegregation.* Beverly Hills, CA: Sage.

McCullough, J. L., & Ostrom, T. M. (1974). Repetition of highly similar messages and attitude change. *Journal of Applied Psychology, 59,* 395–397.

McFarland, C., & Miller, D. (1990). Judgments of self–other similarity: Just like other people, only more so. *Personality and Social Psychology Bulletin, 16,* 475–484.

McFarland, S. G., Ageyev, V. S., & Abalakina-Paap, M. A. (1992). Authoritarianism in the former Soviet Union. *Journal of Personality and Social Psychology, 63,* 1004–1010.

McFarland, S. G., Ageyev, V. S., & Djintcharadze, N. (1996). Russian authoritarianism two years after communism. *Personality and Social Psychology Bulletin, 22,* 210–217.

McGillicuddy, N. B., Welton, G. L., & Pruitt, D. G. (1987). Third-party intervention: A field experiment comparing three different models. *Journal of Personality and Social Psychology, 53,* 104–112.

McGinn, A. P. (1998, June 20). Hidden forces mask crisis in world fisheries. Worldwatch Institute (www.worldwatch.org).

McGuire, A. (2002, August 19). Charity calls for debate on adverts aimed at children. *The Herald* (Scotland), p. 4.

McGuire, W. J. (1964). Inducing resistance to persuasion: Some contemporary approaches. In L. Berkowitz (Ed.), *Advances in experimental social psychology,* vol. 1. New York: Academic Press.

McGuire, W. J., & McGuire, C. V. (1986). Differences in conceptualizing self versus conceptualizing other people as manifested in contrasting verb types used in natural speech. *Journal of Personality and Social Psychology, 51,* 1135–1143.

McGuire, W. J., McGuire, C. V., & Winton, W. (1979). Effects of household sex composition on the salience of one's gender in the spontaneous self-concept. *Journal of Experimental Social Psychology, 15,* 77–90.

McGuire, W. J., & Padawer-Singer, A. (1978). Trait salience in the spontaneous self-concept. *Journal of Personality and Social Psychology, 33,* 743–754.

McKelvie, S. J. (1995). Bias in the estimated frequency of names. *Perceptual and Motor Skills, 81,* 1331–1338.

McKelvie, S. J. (1997). The availability heuristic: Effects of fame and gender on the estimated frequency of male and female names. *Journal of Social Psychology, 137,* 63–78.

McKenna, F. P., & Myers, L. B. (1997). Illusory self-assessments—Can they be reduced? *British Journal of Psychology, 88,* 39–51.

McKenna, K. Y. A., & Bargh, J. A. (1998). Coming out in the age of the Internet: Identity demarginalization through virtual group participation. *Journal of Personality and Social Psychology, 75,* 681–694.

McKenna, K. Y. A., & Bargh, J. A. (2000). Plan 9 from cyberspace: The implications of the Internet for personality and social psychology. *Personality and Social Psychology Review, 4,* 57–75.

McKenna, K. Y. A., Green, A. S., & Gleason, M. E. J. (2002). What's the big attraction? Relationship formation on the Internet. *Journal of Social Issues, 58,* 9–31.

McNeel, S. P. (1980). *Tripling up: Perceptions and effects of dormitory crowding.* Paper presented at the American Psychological Association convention.

Mealey, L., Bridgstock, R., & Townsend, G. C. (1999). Symmetry and perceived facial attractiveness: A monozygotic co-twin comparison. *Journal of Personality and Social Psychology, 76,* 151–158.

Meindl, J. R., & Lerner, M. J. (1984). Exacerbation of extreme responses to an out-group. *Journal of Personality and Social Psychology, 47,* 71–84.

Meissner, C. A., & Brigham, J. C. (2001). Thirty years of investigating the own-race bias in memory for faces: A meta-analytic review. *Psychology, Public Policy, and Law, 7,* 3–35.

Memon, A., & Gabbert, G. (2003). Improving the identification accuracy of senior witnesses: Do prelineup questions and sequential testing help? *Journal of Applied Psychology, 88,* 341–347.

Messé, L. A., & Sivacek, J. M. (1979). Predictions of others' responses in a mixed-motive game: Self-justification or false consensus? *Journal of Personality and Social Psychology, 37,* 602–607.

Messick, D. M., & Sentis, K. P. (1979). Fairness and preference. *Journal of Experimental Social Psychology, 15,* 418–434.

Mewhinney, D. M., Herald, E. S., & Maticka-Tyndale, E. (1995). Sexual scripts and risk-taking of Canadian university students on spring break in Daytona Beach, Florida. *Canadian Journal of Human Sexuality, 4,* 273–288.

Michaels, J. W., Blommel, J. M., Brocato, R. M., Linkous, R. A., & Rowe, J. S. (1982). Social facilitation and inhibition in a natural setting. *Replications in Social Psychology, 2,* 21–24.

Mikula, G. (1984). Justice and fairness in interpersonal relations: Thoughts and suggestions. In H. Taijfel (Ed.), *The social dimension: European developments in social psychology,* vol. 1. Cambridge: Cambridge University Press.

Mikulincer, M., Florian, V., & Hirschberger, G. (2003). The existential function of close relationships: Introducing death into the science of love. *Personality and Social Psychology Review, 7,* 20–40.

Milgram, A. (2000). My personal view of Stanley Milgram. In T. Blass (Ed.), *Obedience to authority: Current perspectives on the Milgram paradigm.* Mahwah, NJ: Erlbaum.

Milgram, S. (1965). Some conditions of obedience and disobedience to authority. *Human Relations, 18,* 57–76.

Milgram, S. (1974). *Obedience to authority.* New York: Harper and Row.

Milgram, S., & Sabini, J. (1983). On maintaining social norms: A field experiment in the subway. In H. H. Blumberg, A. P. Hare, V. Kent, & M. Davies (Eds.), *Small groups and social interaction,* vol. 1. London: Wiley.

Miller, A. G. (1986). *The obedience experiments: A case study of controversy in social science.* New York: Praeger.

Miller, A. G. (2004). What can the Milgram obedience experiments tell us about the Holocaust? Generalizing from the social psychological laboratory. In A. G. Miller (Ed.), *The social psychology of good and evil.* New York: Guilford Press.

Miller, A. G., Ashton, W., & Mishal, M. (1990). Beliefs concerning the features of constrained behavior: A basis for the fundamental attribution error. *Journal of Personality and Social Psychology, 59,* 635–650.

Miller, A. G., Gillen, G., Schenker, C., & Radlove, S. (1973). Perception of obedience to authority. *Proceedings of the 81st Annual Convention of the American Psychological Association, 8,* 127–128.

Miller, D. T., Downs, J. S., & Prentice, D. A. (1998). Minimal conditions for the creation of a unit relationship: The social bond between birthdaymates. *European Journal of Social Psychology, 28,* 475.

Miller, J. B. (1986). *Toward a new psychology of women,* 2nd ed. Boston: Beacon Press.

Miller, J. G. (1984). Culture and the development of everyday social explanation. *Journal of Personality and Social Psychology, 46,* 961–978.

Miller, K. I., & Monge, P. R. (1986). Participation, satisfaction, and productivity: A meta-analytic review. *Academy of Management Journal, 29,* 727–753.

Miller, L. C. (1990). Intimacy and liking: Mutual influence and the role of unique relationships. *Journal of Personality and Social Psychology, 59,* 50–60.

Miller, L. C., Berg, J. H., & Archer, R. L. (1983). Openers: Individuals who elicit intimate self-disclosure. *Journal of Personality and Social Psychology, 44,* 1234–1244.

Miller, L. C., Berg, J. H., & Rugs, D. (1989). Selectivity and sharing: Needs and norms in developing friendships. Unpublished manuscript, Scripps College.

Miller, N., & Marks, G. (1982). Assumed similarity between self and other: Effect of expectation of future interaction with that other. *Social Psychology Quarterly, 45,* 100–105.

Miller, N., Pedersen, W. C., Earleywine, M., & Pollock, V. E. (2003). A theoretical model of triggered displaced aggression. *Personality and Social Psychology Review, 7,* 75–97.

MILLER, N. E., & BUGELSKI, R. (1948). Minor studies of aggression: II. The influence of frustrations imposed by the in-group on attitudes expressed toward out-groups. *Journal of Psychology, 25,* 437–442.

MILLER, P. A., & EISENBERG, N. (1988). The relation of empathy to aggressive and externalizing/antisocial behavior. *Psychological Bulletin, 103,* 324–344.

MILLER, P. C., LEFCOURT, H. M., HOLMES, J. G., WARE, E. E., & SALEY, W. E. (1986). Marital locus of control and marital problem solving. *Journal of Personality and Social Psychology, 51,* 161–169.

MILLER, R. L., BRICKMAN, P., & BOLEN, D. (1975). Attribution versus persuasion as a means for modifying behavior. *Journal of Personality and Social Psychology, 31,* 430–441.

MILLER, R. S. (1997). Inattentive and contented: Relationship commitment and attention to alternatives. *Journal of Personality and Social Psychology, 73,* 758–766.

MILLER, R. S., & SIMPSON, J. A. (1990). Relationship satisfaction and attentiveness to alternatives. Paper presented at the American Psychological Association convention.

MILLETT, K. (1975, January). The shame is over. *Ms.,* pp. 26–29.

MITA, T. H., DERMER, M., & KNIGHT, J. (1977). Reversed facial images and the mere-exposure hypothesis. *Journal of Personality and Social Psychology, 35,* 597–601.

MONSON, T. C., & SNYDER, M. (1977). Actors, observers, and the attribution process: Toward a reconceptualization. *Journal of Experimental Social Psychology, 13,* 89–111.

MOODY, K. (1980). *Growing up on television: The TV effect.* New York: Times Books.

MOORE, D. L., & BARON, R. S. (1983). Social facilitation: A physiological analysis. In J. T. Cacioppo & R. Petty (Eds.), *Social psychophysiology.* New York: Guilford Press.

MOORE, D. W. (2003a, March 11). Half of young people expect to strike it rich: But expectations fall rapidly with age. Gallup News Service (www.gallup.com/poll/releases/pr030311.asp).

MOORE, D. W. (2003b, March 18). Public approves of Bush ultimatum by more than 2-to-1 margin. Gallup News Service (www.gallup.com), p. 202.

MORIER, D., & SEROY, C. (1994). The effect of interpersonal expectancies on men's self-presentation of gender role attitudes to women. *Sex Roles, 31,* 493–504.

MORRISON, D. M. (1989). Predicting contraceptive efficacy: A discriminant analysis of three groups of adolescent women. *Journal of Applied Social Psychology, 19,* 1431–1452.

MORRY, M. M. (2003). Perceived locus of control and satisfaction in same-sex friendships. *Personal Relationships, 10,* 495–509.

MORRY, M. M. (2005). Relationship satisfaction as a predictor of perceived similarity among cross-sex friends: A test of the attraction–similarity model. Manuscript under review.

MOSCOVICI, S. (1985). Social influence and conformity. In G. Lindzey & E. Aronson (Eds.), *The handbook of social psychology,* 3rd ed. Hillsdale, NJ: Erlbaum.

MOSCOVICI, S., LAGE, S., & NAFFRECHOUX, M. (1969). Influence of a consistent minority on the responses of a majority in a color perception task. *Sociometry, 32,* 365–380.

MOSCOVICI, S., & ZAVALLONI, M. (1969). The group as a polarizer of attitudes. *Journal of Personality and Social Psychology, 12,* 124–135.

MOSKOWITZ, D. S., SUH, E. J., & DESAULNIERS, J. (1994). Situational influences on gender differences in agency and communion. *Journal of Personality and Social Psychology, 66,* 753–761.

MOYER, K. E. (1976). *The psychobiology of aggression.* New York: Harper & Row.

MOYER, K. E. (1983). The physiology of motivation: Aggression as a model. In C. J. Scheier & A. M. Rogers (Eds.), *G. Stanley Hall Lecture Series,* vol. 3. Washington, DC: American Psychological Association.

MUELLER, C. W., DONNERSTEIN, E., & HALLAM, J. (1983). Violent films and prosocial behavior. *Personality and Social Psychology Bulletin, 9,* 83–89.

MULLEN, B. (1986a). Atrocity as a function of lynch mob composition: A self-attention perspective. *Personality and Social Psychology Bulletin, 12,* 187–197.

MULLEN, B. (1986b). Stuttering, audience size, and the other-total ratio: A self-attention perspective. *Journal of Applied Social Psychology, 16,* 139–149.

MULLEN, B., & BAUMEISTER, R. F. (1987). Group effects on self-attention and performance: Social loafing, social facilitation, and social impairment. In C. Hendrick (Ed.), *Group processes and intergroup relations: Review of personality and social psychology,* vol. 9. Newbury Park, CA: Sage.

MULLEN, B., BROWN, R., & SMITH, C. (1992). Ingroup bias as a function of salience, relevance, and status: An integration. *European Journal of Social Psychology, 22,* 103–122.

MULLEN, B., BRYANT, B., & DRISKELL, J. E. (1997). Presence of others and arousal: An integration. *Group Dynamics: Theory, Research, and Practice, 1,* 52–64.

MULLEN, B., & COPPER, C. (1994). The relation between group cohesiveness and performance: An integration. *Psychological Bulletin, 115,* 210–227.

MULLEN, B., & GOETHALS, G. R. (1990). Social projection, actual consensus and valence. *British Journal of Social Psychology, 29,* 279–282.

MULLEN, B., & RIORDAN, C. A. (1988). Self-serving attributions for performance in naturalistic settings: A meta-analytic review. *Journal of Applied Social Psychology, 18,* 3–22.

MULLEN, B., SALAS, E., & DRISKELL, J. E. (1989). Salience, motivation, and artifact as contributions to the relation between participation rate and leadership. *Journal of Experimental Social Psychology, 25,* 545–559.

MULLER, S., & JOHNSON, B. T. (1990). Fear and persuasion: A linear relationship? Paper presented to the Eastern Psychological Association convention.

MULLIN, C. R., & LINZ, D. (1995). Desensitization and resensitization to violence against women: Effects of exposure to sexually violent films on judgments of domestic violence victims. *Journal of Personality and Social Psychology, 69,* 449–459.

MURPHY, C. (1990, June). New findings: Hold on to your hat. *The Atlantic,* pp. 22–23.

MURRAY, S. L., GELLAVIA, G. M., ROSE, P., & GRIFFIN, D. W. (2003). Once hurt, twice hurtful: How perceived regard regulates daily marital interactions. *Journal of Personality and Social Psychology, 84,* 126–147.

MURRAY, S. L., HOLMES, J. G., GELLAVIA, G., GRIFFIN, D. W., & DOLDERMAN, D. (2002). Kindred spirits? The benefits of egocentrism in close relationships. *Journal of Personality and Social Psychology, 82,* 563–581.

MURRAY, S. L., HOLMES, J. G., & GRIFFIN, D. W. (1996). The self-fulfilling nature of positive illusions in romantic relationships: Love is not blind, but prescient. *Journal of Personality and Social Psychology, 71,* 1155–1180.

MURRAY, S. L., HOLMES, J. G., & GRIFFIN, D. W. (2000). Self-esteem and the quest for felt security: How perceived regard regulates attachment processes. *Journal of Personality and Social Psychology, 78,* 478–498.

MURRAY, S. L., HOLMES, J. G., MACDONALD, G., & ELLSWORTH, P. C. (1998). Through the looking glass darkly? When self-doubts turn into relationship insecurities. *Journal of Personality and Social Psychology, 75,* 1459–1480.

MURSTEIN, B. L. (1986). *Paths to marriage.* Newbury Park, CA: Sage.

MUSON, G. (1978, March). Teenage violence and the telly. *Psychology Today,* pp. 50–54.

MYERS, D. G. (2000). *The American paradox: Spiritual hunger in an age of plenty.* New Haven, CT: Yale University Press.

MYERS, D. G., & BISHOP, G. D. (1970). Discussion effects on racial attitudes. *Science, 169,* 778–789.

MYERS, N. (2000). Sustainable consumption: The meta-problem. In B. Heap & J. Kent (Eds.), *Towards sustainable consumption: A European perspective.* London: The Royal Society.

MYERS, T., ALLMAN, D., CALZAVARA, L., MAXWELL, J., REMIS, R., SWANTEE, C., & TRAVERS, R. (2004). *Ontario men's survey final report.* Toronto: University of Toronto Press.

NADLER, A., GOLDBERG, M., & JAFFE, Y. (1982). Effect of self-differentiation and anonymity in group on deindividuation. *Journal of Personality and Social Psychology, 42,* 1127–1136.

NAGAR, D., & PANDEY, J. (1987). Affect and performance on cognitive task as a function of crowding and noise. *Journal of Applied Social Psychology, 17,* 147–157.

NAIL, P. R., MACDONALD, G., & LEVY, D. A. (2000). Proposal of a four-dimensional model of social response. *Psychological Bulletin, 126,* 454–470.

NAPOLITAN, D. A., & GOETHALS, G. R. (1979). The attribution of friendliness. *Journal of Experimental Social Psychology, 15,* 105–113.

NATIONAL CENTER FOR HEALTH STATISTICS. (1991). Family structure and children's health: United States, 1988, Vital and Health Statistics, Series 10, No. 178, CHHS Publication No. PHS 91–1506 by Deborah A. Dawson.

NATIONAL COUNCIL FOR RESEARCH ON WOMEN. (1994). Women and philanthropy fact sheet. Issues Quarterly, 1(2), 9.

NATIONAL GEOGRAPHIC. (2006, February). *Meltdown: The Alps under pressure.* By Erla Zwingle.

NATIONAL RESEARCH COUNCIL. (2002). *Youth, pornography, and the Internet.* Washington, DC: National Academy Press.

NATIONAL TELEVISION VIOLENCE STUDY. (1997). Thousand Oaks, CA: Sage.

NAYLOR, T. H. (1990). Redefining corporate motivation, Swedish style. *Christian Century, 107,* 566–570.

NELSON, L. J., & MILLER, D. T. (1997). The distinctiveness effect in social categorization: You are what makes you unusual. *Psychological Science, 6,* 246.

NEMETH, C. (1979). The role of an active minority in intergroup relations. In W. G. Austin & S. Worchel (Eds.), *The social psychology of intergroup relations.* Monterey, CA: Brooks/Cole.

NEMETH, C., & WACHTLER, J. (1974). Creating the perceptions of consistency and confidence: A necessary condition for minority influence. *Sociometry, 37,* 529–540.

NEMETH, C. J. (1999). Behind the scenes. In D. G. Myers, *Social psychology,* 6th ed. New York: McGraw-Hill.

NEWCOMB, T. M. (1961). *The acquaintance process.* New York: Holt, Rinehart and Winston.

NEWELL, B., & LAGNADO, D. (2003). Think-tanks, or think tanks. *The Psychologist, 16,* 176.

NEWMAN, A. (2001, February 4). Rotten teeth and dead babies. *New York Times Magazine* (www.nytimes.com).

NEWMAN, H. M., & LANGER, E. J. (1981). Post-divorce adaptation and the attribution of responsibility. *Sex Roles, 7,* 223–231.

NEWMAN, L. S. (1993). How individualists interpret behavior: Idiocentrism and spontaneous trait inference. *Social Cognition, 11,* 243–269.

NEWPORT, F., MOORE, D. W., JONES, J. M., & SAAD, L. (2003, March 21). Special release: American opinion on the war. Gallup Poll Tuesday Briefing (www.gallup.com/poll/ tb/goverpubli/s0030325.asp), p. 202.

NG, W., & LINDSAY, R. C. L. (1994). Cross-race facial recognition: Failure of the contact hypothesis. *Journal of Cross-Cultural Psychology, 25,* 217–232.

NIAS, D. K. B. (1979). Marital choice: Matching or complementation? In M. Cook & G. Wilson (Eds.), *Love and attraction.* Oxford: Pergamon.

NICHOLS, J. (2003, February 9). Man overdoses online as chatters watch him die. *Grand Rapids Press,* p. A20.

NIE, N. H., & ERBRING, L. (2000, February 17). *Internet and society: A preliminary report.* Stanford, CA: Stanford Institute for the Quantitative Study of Society.

NISBETT, R. E., & ROSS, L. (1991). *The person and the situation.* New York: McGraw-Hill.

NISBETT, R. E., & WILSON, T. D. (1977). Telling more than we can know: Verbal reports on mental processes. *Psychological Review, 84,* 231–259.

NOLLER, P., & FITZPATRICK, M. A. (1990). Marital communication in the eighties. *Journal of Marriage and the Family, 52,* 832–843.

NOREM, J. K. (2000). Defensive pessimism, optimism, and pessimism. In E. C. Chang (Ed.), Optimism and pessimism. Washington, DC: APA Books.

NOREM, J. K., & CANTOR, N. (1986). Defensive pessimism: Harnessing anxiety as motivation. *Journal of Personality and Social Psychology, 51,* 1208–1217.

NOSEK, B. A., GREENWALD, A. G., & BANAJI, M. R. (2005). Understanding and using the implicit association test II: Method variables and construct validity. *Personality and Social Psychology Bulletin, 31,* 166–180.

NOTARIUS, C., & MARKMAN, H. J. (1993). *We can work it out.* New York: Putnam.

NOWAK, M., & SIGMUND, K. (1993). A strategy of win-stay, lose-shift that outperforms tit-for-tat in the Prisoner's Dilemma game. *Nature, 364,* 56–58.

NUTTIN, J. M., JR. (1987). Affective consequences of mere ownership: The name letter effect in twelve European languages. *European Journal of Social Psychology, 17,* 318–402.

O'BRIEN, L. T., & CRANDALL, C. S. (2003). Stereotype threat and arousal: Effects on women's math performance. Personality and *Social Psychology Bulletin, 29,* 782–789.

ODDONE-PAOLUCCI, E., GENUIS, M., & VIOLATO, C. (2000). A meta-analysis of the published research on the effects of pornography. In C. Violata (Ed.), *The changing family and child development.* Aldershot, England: Ashgate Publishing.

O'DEA, T. F. (1968). Sects and cults. In D. L. Sills (Ed.), *International encyclopedia of the social sciences,* vol. 14. New York: Macmillan.

OHBUCHI, K., & KAMBARA, T. (1985). Attacker's intent and awareness of outcome, impression management, and retaliation. *Journal of Experimental Social Psychology, 21,* 321–330.

O'LEARY, K. D., CHRISTIAN, J. L., & MENDELL, N. R. (1994). A closer look at the link between marital discord and depressive symptomatology. *Journal of Social and Clinical Psychology, 13,* 33–41.

OLSON, J. M., ROESE, N. J., & ZANNA, M. P. (1996). Expectancies. In E. T. Higgins & A. W. Kruglanski (Eds.), *Social psychology: Handbook of basic principles.* New York: Guilford Press, pp. 211–238.

OLSON, J. M., ZANNA, M. P. (1982). Repression-sensitization differences in responses to a decision. *Journal of Personality, 50,* 46–57.

OLSON, M. A., & FAZIO, R. H. (2004). Reducing the influence of extra-personal associations on the Implicit Association Test: Personalizing the IAT. Journal of *Personality and Social Psychology, 86,* 653–667.

OLWEUS, D. (1979). Stability of aggressive reaction patterns in males: A review. *Psychological Bulletin, 86,* 852–875.

OLWEUS, D., MATTSSON, A., SCHALLING, D., & LOW, H. (1988). Circulating testosterone levels and aggression in adolescent males: A causal analysis. *Psychosomatic Medicine, 50,* 261–272.

ORBELL, J. M., VAN DE KRAGT, A. J. C., & DAWES, R. M. (1988). Explaining discussion-induced cooperation. *Journal of Personality and Social Psychology, 54,* 811–819.

ORIVE, R. (1984). Group similarity, public self-awareness, and opinion extremity: A social projection explanation of deindividuation effects. *Journal of Personality and Social Psychology, 47,* 727–737.

ORNSTEIN, R. (1991). *The evolution of consciousness: Of Darwin, Freud, and cranial fire: The origins of the way we think.* New York: Prentice-Hall.

ORTNER, C. N. M., MacDONALD, T. K., OLMSTEAD, M. C. (2003). Alcohol intoxication reduces impulsivity in the delay-discounting paradigm. *Alcohol and Alcoholism, 38,* 151–156.

OSBERG, T. M., & SHRAUGER, J. S. (1986). Self-prediction: Exploring the parameters of accuracy. *Journal of Personality and Social Psychology, 51,* 1044–1057.

OSGOOD, C. E. (1962). *An alternative to war or surrender.* Urbana: University of Illinois Press.

OSGOOD, C. E. (1980). GRIT: A strategy for survival in mankind's nuclear age? Paper presented at the Pugwash Conference on New Directions in Disarmament, Racine, Wis.

OSKAMP, S. (2000). A sustainable future for humanity? How can psychology help? *American Psychologist, 55,* 496–508.

OSTERHOUSE, R. A., & BROCK, T. C. (1970). Distraction increases yielding to propaganda by inhibiting counterarguing. *Journal of Personality and Social Psychology, 15,* 344–358.

OSTROM, T. M., & SEDIKIDES, C. (1992). Out-group homogeneity effects in natural and minimal groups. *Psychological Bulletin, 112,* 536–552.

OZER, E. M., & BANDURA, A. (1990). Mechanisms governing empowerment effects: A self-efficacy analysis. *Journal of Personality and Social Psychology, 58,* 472–486.

PADGETT, V. R. (1989). Predicting organizational violence: An application of 11 powerful principles of obedience. Paper presented at the American Psychological Association Convention.

PAK, A. W., DION, K. L., & DION, K. K. (1991). Social-psychological correlates of experienced discrimination: Test of the double jeopardy hypothesis. *International Journal of Intercultural Relations, 15,* 243–254.

PALLAK, S. R., MURRONI, E., & KOCH, J. (1983). Communicator attractiveness and expertise, emotional versus rational appeals, and persuasion: A heuristic versus systematic processing interpretation. *Social Cognition, 2,* 122–141.

PALMER, D. L. (1996). Determinants of Canadian attitudes toward immigration: More than just racism? In R. C. Gardner & V. M. Esses (Eds.), *Canadian Journal of Behavioral Science, 28,* 180–192.

PALMER, E. L., & DORR, A. (EDS.). (1980). *Children and the faces of television: Teaching, violence, selling.* New York: Academic Press.

PANDEY, J., SINHA, Y., PRAKASH, A., & TRIPATHI, R. C. (1982). Right-left political ideologies and attribution of the causes of poverty. *European Journal of Social Psychology, 12,* 327–331.

PAPASTAMOU, S., & MUGNY, G. (1990). Synchronic consistency and psychologization in minority influence. *European Journal of Social Psychology, 20,* 85–98.

PAQUETTE, G. (2004). Violence on Canadian television networks. *Canadian Child and Adolescent Psychiatry Review, 13,* 13–15.

PARK, B., & ROTHBART, M. (1982). Perception of out-group homogeneity and levels of social categorization: Memory for the subordinate attributes of in group and out-group members. *Journal of Personality and Social Psychology, 42,* 1051–1068.

PARKE, R. D., BERKOWITZ, L., LEYENS, J. P., WEST, S. G., & SEBASTIAN, J. (1977). Some effects of violent and nonviolent movies on the behavior of juvenile delinquents. In L. Berkowitz (Ed.), *Advances in experimental social psychology,* vol. 10. New York: Academic Press.

PARKIN, A., & MENDELSOHN, M. (October, 2005). Centre for Research and Information on Canada (CRIC). *A New Canada: An Identity Shaped by Diversity,* 1–19.

PARKS, J., KONOPASKY, R., FLEMING, M. T., & SMITH, S. M. (2005). Giving 158 percent: How authors judge the amount and type of contribution to academic journal articles. Poster presented at the 67th annual conference of the Canadian Psychology Association, Montreal.

PASCARELLA, E. T., & TERENZINI, P. T. (1991). *How college affects students: Findings and insights from twenty years of research.* San Francisco: Jossey-Bass.

PATRICK, C. J., & IACONO, W. G. (1991). Validity of the control question polygraph test: The problem of sampling bias. *Journal of Applied Social Psychology, 76,* 229–238.

PATRY, M. W., STINSON, V., & SMITH, S. M. (in press). CSI Effect: Is popular television transforming Canadian society? In Greenberg & Elliott (Eds.), *Communications in Question: Canadian Perspectives on Controversial Issues in Communication Studies.*

PATTERSON, G. R., CHAMBERLAIN, P., & REID, J. B. (1982). A comparative evaluation of parent training procedures. *Behavior Therapy, 13,* 638–650.

PATTERSON, G. R., LITTMAN, R. A., & BRICKER, W. (1967). Assertive behavior in children: A step toward a theory of aggression. *Monographs of the Society for Research in Child Development, 32,* (Serial No. 113), 5.

PATTERSON, T. E. (1980). *The role of the mass media in presidential campaigns: The lessons of the 1976 election.* Items, 34, 25–30. Social Science Research Council, 605 Third Avenue, New York, NY 10016.

PAYNE, B. K. (2001). Prejudice and perception: The role of automatic and controlled processes in misperceiving a weapon. *Journal of Personality and Social Psychology, 81,* 181–192.

PEDERSEN, W. C., GONZALES, C., & MILLER, N. (2000). The moderating effect of trivial triggering provocation on displaced aggression. *Journal of Personality and Social Psychology, 78,* 913–927.

PEGALIS, L. J., SHAFFER, D. R., BAZZINI, D. G., & GREENIER, K. (1994). On the ability to elicit self-disclosure: Are there gender-based and contextual limitations on the opener effect? *Personality and Social Psychology Bulletin, 20,* 412–420.

PELLETIER, L. G., & SHARP, E. C. (2006). How easy is it to recycle? The influence of recycling level of difficulty and level of self-determined motivation on recycling, pro-environmental behaviours, and satisfaction with environmental policies. Manuscript in preparation. University of Ottawa.

PENTON-VOAK, I. S., JONES, B. C., LITTLE, A. C., BAKER, S., TIDDEMAN, B., BURT, D. M., & PERRETT, D. I. (2001). Symmetry, sexual dimorphism in facial proportions and male facial attractiveness. *Proceedings of the Royal Society of London, 268,* 1–7.

PEOPLE. (2003, September 1). Nipped, tucked, talking, pp. 102–111.

PEPLAU, L. A., & GORDON, S. L. (1985). Women and men in love: Gender differences in close heterosexual relationships. In V. E. O'Leary, R. K. Unger, & B. S. Wallston (Eds.), *Women, gender, and social psychology.* Hillsdale, NJ: Erlbaum.

PEREIRA, J. (2003, January 10). Just how far does First Amendment protection go? *Wall Street Journal,* pp. B1, B3.

PERKINS, H. W. (1991). Religious commitment, yuppie values, and well-being in post-collegiate life. *Review of Religious Research, 32,* 244–51.

PERLOFF, L. S. (1987). Social comparison and illusions of invulnerability. In C. R. Snyder & C. R. Ford (Eds.), *Coping with negative life events: Clinical and social psychological perspectives.* New York: Plenum.

PERLS, F. S. (1973). *Ego, hunger and aggression: The beginning of Gestalt therapy.* Random House, 1969. Cited by Berkowitz in The case for bottling up rage. *Psychology Today,* July, pp. 24–30.

PESSIN, J. (1933). The comparative effects of social and mechanical stimulation on memorizing. *American Journal of Psychology, 45,* 263–270.

PESSIN, J., & HUSBAND, R. W. (1933). Effects of social stimulation on human maze learning. *Journal of Abnormal and Social Psychology, 28,* 148–154.

PETERSON, B. E., DOTY, R. M., & WINTER, D. G. (1993). Authoritarianism and attitudes toward contemporary social issues. *Personality and Social Psychology Bulletin, 19,* 174–184.

PETERSON, C., SCHWARTZ, S. M., & SELIGMAN, M. E. P. (1981). Self-blame and depression symptoms. *Journal of Personality and Social Psychology, 41,* 253–259.

PETTIGREW, T. F. (1958). Personality and socio-cultural factors in intergroup attitudes: A cross-national comparison. *Journal of Conflict Resolution, 2,* 29–42.

PETTIGREW, T. F. (1969). Racially separate or together? *Journal of Social Issues, 2,* 43–69.

PETTIGREW, T. F. (1986). The intergroup contact hypothesis reconsidered. In M. Hewstone & R. Brown (Eds.), *Contact and conflict in intergroup encounters.* Oxford: Basil Blackwell.

PETTIGREW, T. F. (1988). Advancing racial justice: Past lessons for future use. Paper for the University of Alabama Conference: "Opening Doors: An Appraisal of Race Relations in America."

PETTIGREW, T. F. (1997). Generalized intergroup contact effects on prejudice. *Personality and Social Psychology Bulletin, 23,* 173–185.

PETTIGREW, T. F. (1998). Intergroup contact theory. *Annual Review of Psychology, 49,* 65–85.

PETTIGREW, T. F., & TROPP, L. R. (2000). Does intergroup contact reduce prejudice: Recent meta-analytic findings. In S. Oskamp, (Ed.), *Reducing prejudice and discrimination.* Mahwah, NJ: Erlbaum, pp. 93–114.

PETTY, R. E., & CACIOPPO, J. T. (1977). Forewarning cognitive responding, and resistance to persuasion. *Journal of Personality and Social Psychology, 35,* 645–655.

PETTY, R. E., & CACIOPPO, J. T. (1979). Effects of forewarning of persuasive intent and involvement on cognitive response and persuasion. *Personality and Social Psychology Bulletin, 5,* 173–176.

PETTY, R. E., & CACIOPPO, J. T. (1986). *Communication and persuasion: Central and peripheral routes to attitude change.* New York: Springer-Verlag.

PETTY, R. E., CACIOPPO, J. T., & GOLDMAN, R. (1981). Personal involvement as a determinant of argument-based persuasion. *Journal of Personality and Social Psychology, 41,* 847–855.

PETTY, R. E., & KROSNICK, J. A. (EDS.). (1995). *Attitude strength: Antecedents and consequences.* Hillsdale, NJ: Erlbaum.

PETTY, R. E., SCHUMANN, D. W., RICHMAN, S. A., & STRATHMAN, A. J. (1993). Positive mood and persuasion: Different roles for affect under high and low elaboration conditions. *Journal of Personality and Social Psychology, 64,* 5–20.

PETTY, R. E., & WEGENER, D. T. (1999). The elaboration likelihood model: Current status and controversies. In S. Chaiken & Y. Trope (Eds.), *Dual-process theories in social psychology,* pp. 41–72. New York: Guilford press.

PETTY, R. E., WHEELER, S. C., & BIZER, G. Y. (2000). Attitude functions and persuasion: An elaboration likelihood approach to matched versus mismatched messages. In G. R. Maio & J. M. Olson (Eds.), *Why we evaluate: Functions of attitudes,* pp. 133–162. Mahwah, NJ: Erlbaum.

PEW. (2003). *Views of a changing world 2003. The Pew Global Attitudes Project.* Washington, DC: Pew Research Center for the People and the Press (people-press. org/reports/pdf/185.pdf).

PFEIFER, J. E. (1992). The psychological framing of cults: Schematic representations and cult evaluations. *Journal of Applied Social Psychology, 22,* 531–544.

PFEIFER, J. E. (1999). Perceptual biases and mock juror decision making: Minority religions in court. *Social Justice Research, 4,* 409–419.

PFEIFER, J. E. (2006). *Satanic cult membership and child custody decisions.* Unpublished manuscript.

PHILLIPS, S. T., & ZILLER, R. C. (1997). Toward a theory and measure of the nature of nonprejudice. *Journal of Personality and Social Psychology, 72,* 420–434.

PINGITORE, R., DUGONI, B. L., TINDALE, R. S., & SPRING, B. (1994). Bias against overweight job applicants in a simulated employment interview. *Journal of Applied Psychology, 79,* 909–917.

PINKER, S. (1997). *How the mind works.* New York: Norton.

PLAKS, J. E., & HIGGINS, E. T. (2000). Pragmatic use of stereotyping in teamwork: Social loafing and compensation as a function of inferred partner-situation fit. *Journal of Personality and Social Psychology, 79,* 962–974.

PLATZ, S. J., & HOSCH, H. M. (1988). Cross-racial/ethnic eyewitness identification: A field study. *Journal of Applied Social Psychology, 18,* 972–984.

PLINER, P., HART, H., KOHL, J., & SAARI, D. (1974). Compliance without pressure: Some further data on the foot-in-the-door technique. *Journal of Experimental Social Psychology, 10,* 17–22.

POLIVY, J., HERMAN, C. P., YOUNGER, J. C., & ERSKINE, B. (1979). Effects of a model on eating behavior: The induction of a restrained eating style. *Journal of Personality, 47,* 100–117.

POMERLEAU, O. F., & RODIN, J. (1986). Behavioral medicine and health psychology. In S. L. Garfield & A. E. Bergin (Eds.), *Handbook of psychotherapy and behavior change,* 3rd ed. New York: Wiley.

PORTER, N., GEIS, F. L., & JENNINGS (WALSTEDT), J. (1983). Are women invisible as leaders? *Sex Roles, 9,* 1035–1049.

POSTMES, T., & SPEARS, R. (1998). Deindividuation and antinormative behavior: A meta-analysis. *Psychological Bulletin, 123,* 238–259.

POWELL, J. (1989). *Happiness is an inside job.* Valencia, CA: Tabor.

PRAGER, I. G., & CUTLER, B. L. (1990). Attributing traits to oneself and to others: The role of acquaintance level. *Personality and Social Psychology Bulletin, 16,* 309–319.

PRATKANIS, A. R., GREENWALD, A. G., LEIPPE, M. R., & BAUMGARDNER, M. H. (1988). In search of reliable persuasion effects: III. The sleeper effect is dead. Long live the sleeper effect. *Journal of Personality and Social Psychology, 54,* 203–218.

PRATTO, F. (1996). Sexual politics: The gender gap in the bedroom, the cupboard, and the cabinet. In D. M. Buss & N. M. Malamuth (Eds.), *Sex, power, conflict: Evolutionary and feminist perspectives.* New York: Oxford University Press.

PRATTO, F., LIU, J. H., LEVIN, S., SIDANIUS, J., SHIH, M., BACHRACH, H., & HEGARTY, P. (2000). Social dominance orientation and the legitimization of inequality across cultures. *Journal of Cross-Cultural Psychology, 31,* 369–409.

PRATTO, F., SIDANIUS, J., STALLWORTH, L. M., & MALLE, B. F. (1994). Social dominance orientation: A personality variable predicting social and political attitudes. *Journal of Personality and Social Psychology, 67,* 741–763.

PRATTO, F., STALLWORTH, L. M., & SIDANIUS, J. (1997). The gender gap: Differences in political attitudes and social dominance orientation. *British Journal of Social Psychology, 36,* 49–68.

PRENTICE-DUNN, S., & ROGERS, R. W. (1980). Effects of deindividuating situational cues and aggressive models on subjective deindividuation and aggression. *Journal of Personality and Social Psychology, 39,* 104–113.

PRENTICE-DUNN, S., & ROGERS, R. W. (1989). Deindividuation and the self-regulation of behavior. In P. B. Paulus (Ed.), *Psychology of group influence,* 2nd ed. Hillsdale, NJ: Erlbaum.

PRICE, G. H., DABBS, J. M., JR., CLOWER, B. J., & RESIN, R. P. (1974). At first glance—Or, is physical attractiveness more than skin deep? Paper presented at the Eastern Psychological Association convention. Cited by K. L. Dion & K. K. Dion (1979). Personality and behavioral correlates of romantic love. In M. Cook & G. Wilson (Eds.), *Love and attraction.* Oxford: Pergamon.

PRIESTER, J. R., & PETTY, R. E. (1995). Source attributions and persuasion: Perceived honesty as a determinant of message scrutiny. *Personality and Social Psychology Bulletin, 21,* 637–654.

PRITCHARD, I. L. (1998). The effects of rap music: On aggressive attitudes toward women. Master's thesis, Humboldt State University.

PROHASKA, V. (1994). "I know I'll get an A": Confident overestimation of final course grades. *Teaching of Psychology, 21,* 141–143.

PRUITT, D. G. (1986). Achieving integrative agreements in negotiation. In R. K. White (Ed.), *Psychology and the prevention of nuclear war.* New York: New York University Press.

PRUITT, D. G. (1998). Social conflict. In D. Gilbert, S. T. Fiske, & G. Lindzey (Eds.), *Handbook of social psychology,* 4th ed. New York: McGraw-Hill.

PRUITT, D. G., & KIMMEL, M. J. (1977). Twenty years of experimental gaming: Critique, synthesis, and suggestions for the future. *Annual Review of Psychology, 28,* 363–392.

PRUITT, D. G., & LEWIS, S. A. (1975). Development of integrative solutions in bilateral negotiation. *Journal of Personality and Social Psychology, 31,* 621–633.

PRUITT, D. G., & LEWIS, S. A. (1977). The psychology of integrative bargaining. In D. Druckman (Ed.), *Negotiations: A social-psychological analysis.* New York: Halsted.

PRUITT, D. G., & RUBIN, J. Z. (1986). *Social conflict.* San Francisco: Random House.

PRYOR, J. B. (1987). Sexual harassment proclivities in men. *Sex Roles, 17,* 269–290.

PRYOR, J. B., & REEDER, G. D. (1993). *The social psychology of HIV infection.* Hillsdale, NJ: Erlbaum.

PUBLIC OPINION. (1984, August/September). *Vanity fare,* p. 22.

PURVIS, J. A., DABBS, J. M., JR., & HOPPER, C. H. (1984). The "opener": Skilled user of facial expression and speech pattern. *Personality and Social Psychology Bulletin, 10,* 61–66.

PUTNAM, R. (2000). *Bowling alone.* New York: Simon & Schuster.

QUARTZ, S. R., & SEJNOWSKI, T. J. (2002). *Liars, lovers, and heroes: What the new brain science reveals about how we become who we are.* New York: William Morrow.

QUATTRONE, G. A. (1982). Behavioral consequences of attributional bias. *Social Cognition, 1,* 358–378.

QUATTRONE, G. A., & JONES, E. E. (1980). The perception of variability within in-groups and out-groups: Implications for the law of small numbers. *Journal of Personality and Social Psychology, 38,* 141–152.

RAINE, A., LENCZ, T., BIHRLE, S., LACASSE, L., & COLLETTI, P. (2000). Reduced prefrontal gray matter volume and reduced autonomic activity in antisocial personality disorder. *Archives of General Psychiatry, 57,* 119–127.

RAINE, A., STODDARD, J., BIHRLE, S., & BUCHSBAUM, M. (1998). Prefrontal glucose deficits in murderers lacking psychosocial deprivation. *Neuropsychiatry, Neuropsychology, & Behavioral Neurology, 11,* 1–7.

RAJECKI, D. W., BLEDSOE, S. B., & RASMUSSEN, J. L. (1991). Successful personal ads: Gender differences and similarities in offers, stipulations, and outcomes. *Basic and Applied Social Psychology, 12,* 457–469.

RAM, A. (2004). "We go to figure out": Factors influencing siblings' negotiations of conflicts of interests. *Dissertation Abstracts International: The Sciences and Engineering, 64,* 8–13.

RANK, S. G., & JACOBSON, C. K. (1977). Hospital nurses' compliance with medication overdose orders: A failure to replicate. *Journal of Health and Social Behavior, 18,* 188–193.

RAPOPORT, A. (1960). *Fights, games, and debates.* Ann Arbor: University of Michigan Press.

RCAGENDA (1979, November–December). p. 11. 475 Riverside Drive, New York, NY 10027.

REGAN, D. T., & CHENG, J. B. (1973). Distraction and attitude change: A resolution. *Journal of Experimental Social Psychology, 9,* 138–147.

REICHER, S., SPEARS, R., & POSTMES, T. (1995). A social identity model of deindividuation phenomena. In W. Storebe & M. Hewstone (Eds.), *European review of social psychology,* vol. 6. Chichester, England: Wiley.

REIFMAN, A. S., LARRICK, R. P., & FEIN, S. (1991). Temper and temperature on the diamond: The heat-aggression relationship in major league baseball. *Personality and Social Psychology Bulletin, 17,* 580–585.

REIS, H. T., NEZLEK, J., & WHEELER, L. (1980). Physical attractiveness in social interaction. *Journal of Personality and Social Psychology, 38,* 604–617.

REIS, H. T., & SHAVER, P. (1988). Intimacy as an interpersonal process. In S. Duck (Ed.), *Handbook of personal relationships: Theory, relationships and interventions.* Chichester, England: Wiley.

REIS, H. T., WHEELER, L., SPIEGEL, N., KERNIS, M. H., NEZLEK, J., & PERRI, M. (1982). Physical attractiveness in social interaction: II. Why does appearance affect social experience? *Journal of Personality and Social Psychology, 43,* 979–996.

RESSLER, R. K., BURGESS, A. W., & DOUGLAS, J. E. (1988). *Sexual homicide patterns.* Boston: Lexington Books.

RHODES, G., SUMICH, A., & BYATT, G. (1999). Are average facial configurations attractive only because of their symmetry. *Psychological Science, 10,* 52–58.

RHODEWALT, F., SALTZMAN, A. T., & WITTMEN, J. (1984). Self-handicapping among competitive athletes: The role of practice in self-esteem protection. *Basic and Applied Social Psychology, 12,* 197–209.

RHOLES, W. S., NEWMAN, L. S., & RUBLE, D. N. (1990). Understanding self and other: Developmental and motivational aspects of perceiving persons in terms of invariant dispositions. In E. T. Higgins & R. M. Sorrentino (Eds.), *Handbook of motivation and cognition: Foundations of social behavior,* vol. 2. New York: Guilford Press.

RICE, B. (1985, September). Performance review: The job nobody likes. *Psychology Today,* pp. 30–36.

RICH, F. (2001, May 20). Naked capitalists: There's no business like porn business. *New York Times* (www.nytimes.com).

RICHARDSON, L. F. (1960). Generalized foreign policy. British Journal of Psychology Monographs Supplements, 23. Cited by A. Rapoport in *Fights, games, and debates.* Ann Arbor: University of Michigan Press, 1960, p. 15.

RIORDAN, C. A. (1980). Effects of admission of influence on attributions and attraction. Paper presented at the American Psychological Association convention.

ROBBERSON, M. R., & ROGERS, R. W. (1988). Beyond fear appeals: Negative and positive persuasive appeals to health and self-esteem. *Journal of Applied Social Psychology, 18,* 277–287.

ROBERTSON, I. (1987). Sociology. New York: Worth. Robins, R. W., & Beer, J. S. (2001). Positive illusions about the self: Short-term benefits and long-term costs. *Journal of Personality and Social Psychology, 80,* 340–352.

ROBINS, R. W., SPRANCA, M. D., & MENDELSOHN, G. A. (1996). The actor-observer effect revisited: Effects of individual differences and repeated social interactions on actor and observer attributions. *Journal of Personality and Social Psychology, 71,* 375–389.

ROBINSON, M. D., & RYFF, C. D. (1999). The role of self-deception in perceptions of past, present, and future happiness. *Personality and Social Psychology Bulletin, 25,* 595–606.

ROBINSON, R. J., KELTNER, D., WARD, A., & ROSS, L. (1995). Actual versus assumed differences in construal: "Naive realism" in intergroup perception and conflict. *Journal of Personality and Social Psychology, 68,* 404–417.

ROBINSON, T. N., WILDE, M. L., NAVRACRUZ, L. C., HAYDEL, F., & VARADY, A. (2001). Effects of reducing children's television and video game use on aggressive behavior. *Archives of Pediatric and Adolescent Medicine, 155,* 17–23.

ROEHLING, M. V. (2000). Weight-based discrimination in employment: Psychological and legal aspects. *Personnel Psychology, 52,* 969–1016.

ROESE, N. J., & OLSON, J. M. (1996). Counterfactuals, causal attributions, and the hindsight bias: A conceptual integration. *Journal of Experimental Social Psychology, 32,* 197–227.

ROGERS, C. R. (1958). Reinhold Niebuhr's The self and the dramas of history: A criticism. *Pastoral Psychology, 9,* 15–17.

ROGERS, C. R. (1980). *A way of being.* Boston: Houghton Mifflin.

ROGERS, R. W., & MEWBORN, C. R. (1976). Fear appeals and attitude change: Effects of a threat's noxiousness, probability of occurrence, and the efficacy of coping responses. *Journal of Personality and Social Psychology, 34,* 54–61.

ROGERS, R. W., & PRENTICE-DUNN, S. (1981). Deindividuation and anger-mediated interracial aggression: Unmasking regressive racism. *Journal of Personality and Social Psychology, 41,* 63–73.

ROKEACH, M., & MEZEI, L. (1966). Race and shared beliefs as factors in social choice. *Science, 151,* 167–172.

ROSENFELD, J. P., SOSKINS, M., BOSH, G., & RYAN, A. (2004). Simple, effective countermeasures to P300-based tests of detection of concealed information. *Psychophysiology, 41,* 205–219.

ROSENFELD, J. P., SWEET, J. L., CHUANG, J., ELLWANGER, J., & SONG, L. (1996). Detection of simulated malingering using forced choice recognition enhanced with event related potential recording. *Neurophysiology, 120,* 163–179.

ROSENTHAL, R. (1985). From unconscious experimenter bias to teacher expectancy effects. In J. B. Dusek, V. C. Hall, & W. J. Meyer (Eds.), *Teacher expectancies.* Hillsdale, NJ: Erlbaum.

ROSENTHAL, R. (1991). Teacher expectancy effects: A brief update 25 years after the Pygmalion experiment. *Journal of Research in Education, 1,* 3–12.

ROSENTHAL, R. (2003). Covert communication in laboratories, classrooms, and the truly real world. *Current Directions in Psychological Science, 12,* 151–154.

ROSS, L. (1977). The intuitive psychologist and his shortcomings: Distortions in the attribution process. In L. Berkowitz (Ed.), *Advances in experimental social psychology,* vol. 10. New York: Academic Press.

ROSS, L. (1981). The "intuitive scientist" formulation and its developmental implications. In J. H. Havell & L. Ross (Eds.), *Social cognitive development: Frontiers and possible futures.* Cambridge, England: Cambridge University Press.

ROSS, L. (1988). Situationist perspectives on the obedience experiments. Review of A. G. Miller's The obedience experiments. *Contemporary Psychology, 33,* 101–104.

ROSS, L., AMABILE, T. M., & STEINMETZ, J. L. (1977). Social roles, social control, and biases in social-perception processes. *Journal of Personality and Social Psychology, 35,* 485–494.

ROSS, L., & WARD, A. (1995). Psychological barriers to dispute resolution. In M. P. Zanna (Ed.), *Advances in experimental social psychology,* vol. 27. San Diego, CA: Academic Press.

ROSS, M., & SICOLY, F. (1979). Egocentric biases in availability and attribution. *Journal of Personality and Social Psychology, 37,* 322–336.

ROSS, M., HILDY, S., SIDDIQUI, A., RAM, A., & WARD, L. (2004). Perspectives on self and other children's representations of sibling conflict. *International Journal of Behavioral Development, 128,* 37–47.

ROSS, M., THIBAUT, J., & EVENBECK, S. (1971). Some determinants of the intensity of social protest. *Journal of Experimental Social Psychology, 7,* 401–418.

ROSSI, A. S., & ROSSI, P. H. (1990). *Of human bonding: Parent-child relations across the life course.* Hawthorne, NY: Aldine de Gruyter.

ROSZELL, P., KENNEDY, D., & GRABB, E. (1990). Physical attractiveness and income attainment among Canadians. *Journal of Psychology, 123,* 547–559.

ROTHBART, M., FULERO, S., JENSEN, C., HOWARD, J., & BIRRELL, P. (1978). From individual to group impressions: Availability heuristics in stereotype formation. *Journal of Experimental Social Psychology, 14,* 237–255.

ROTHBART, M., & TAYLOR, M. (1992). Social categories and social reality. In G. R. Semin & K. Fielder (Eds.), *Language, interaction and social cognition.* London: Sage.

ROTTON, J., & FREY, J. (1985). Air pollution, weather, and violent crimes: Concomitant time-series analysis of archival data. *Journal of Personality and Social Psychology, 49,* 1207–1220.

ROUHANA, N. N., & BAR-TAL, D. (1998). Psychological dynamics of intractable ethnonational conflicts: The Israeli-Palestinian case. *American Psychologist, 53,* 761–770.

ROWE, D. C., ALMEIDA, D. M., & JACOBSON, K. C. (1999). School context and genetic influences on aggression in adolescence. *Psychological Science, 10,* 277–280.

RUBACK, R. B., CARR, T. S., & HOPER, C. H. (1986). Perceived control in prison: Its relation to reported crowding, stress, and symptoms. *Journal of Applied Social Psychology, 16,* 375–386.

RUBIN, J. Z. (1986). Can we negotiate with terrorists: Some answers from psychology. Paper presented at the American Psychological Association convention.

RUBIN, L. B. (1985). *Just friends: The role of friendship in our lives.* New York: Harper & Row.

RUITER, R. A. C., KOK, G., VERPLANKEN, B., & BRUG, J. (2001). Evoked fear and effects of appeals on attitudes to performing breast self-examination: An information-processing perspective. *Health Education Research, 16,* 307–319.

RULE, B. G., TAYLOR, B. R., & DOBBS, A. R. (1987). Priming effects of heat on aggressive thoughts. *Social Cognition, 5,* 131–143.

RUSBULT, C. E., JOHNSON, D. J., & MORROW, G. D. (1986). Impact of couple patterns of problem solving on distress and nondistress in dating relationships. *Journal of Personality and Social Psychology, 50,* 744–753.

RUSBULT, C. E., MARTZ, J. M., & AGNEW, C. R. (1998). The investment model scale: Measuring commitment level, satisfaction level, quality of alternatives, and investment size. *Personal Relationships, 5,* 357–391.

RUSBULT, C. E., MORROW, G. D., & JOHNSON, D. J. (1987). Self-esteem and problem-solving behaviour in close relationships. *British Journal of Social Psychology, 26,* 293–303.

RUSHTON, J. P., FULKER, D. W., NEALE, M. C., NIAS, D. K. B., & EYSENCK, H. J. (1986). Altruism and aggression: The heritability of individual differences. *Journal of Personality and Social Psychology, 50,* 1192–1198.

RUSSELL, B. (1930/1980). *The conquest of happiness.* London: Unwin Paperbacks.

RUSSELL, G. W. (1983). Psychological issues in sports aggression. In J. H. Goldstein (Ed.), *Sports violence.* New York: Springer-Verlag.

RUSSELL, G. W. (1992). Response of the macho male to viewing a combatant sport. *Journal of Social Behavior and Personality, 7,* 631–638.

RYAN, R. (1999, February 2). Quoted by A. Kohn, In pursuit of affluence, at a high price. *New York Times* (via www.nytimes.com).

SAAD, L. (2003, April 22). *Giving global warming the cold shoulder.* The Gallup Organization (www.gallup.com).

SAGARIN, B. J., RHOADS, K. v. L., & CIALDINI, R. B. (1998). Deceiver's distrust: Denigration as a consequence of undiscovered deception. *Personality and Social Psychology Bulletin, 24,* 1167–1176.

SALES, S. M. (1972). Economic threat as a determinant of conversion rates in authoritarian and nonauthoritarian churches. *Journal of Personality and Social Psychology, 23,* 420–428.

SALES, S. M. (1973). Threat as a factor in authoritarianism: An analysis of archival data. *Journal of Personality and Social Psychology, 28,* 44–57.

SANDBERG, G. G., JACKSON, T. L., & PETRETIC-JACKSON, P. (1985). *Sexual aggression and courtship violence in dating relationships.* Paper presented at the Midwestern Psychological Association convention.

SANDE, G. N., GOETHALS, G. R., & RADLOFF, C. E. (1988). Perceiving one's own traits and others': The multifaceted self. *Journal of Personality and Social Psychology, 54,* 13–20.

SANDERS, G. S. (1981a). Driven by distraction: An integrative review of social facilitation and theory and research. *Journal of Experimental Social Psychology, 17,* 227–251.

SANDERS, G. S. (1981b). Toward a comprehensive account of social facilitation: Distraction/conflict does not mean theoretical conflict. *Journal of Experimental Social Psychology, 17,* 262–265.

SANDERS, G. S., & BARON, R. S. (1977). Is social comparison irrelevant for producing choice shifts? *Journal of Experimental Social Psychology, 13,* 303–314.

SANDERS, G. S., BARON, R. S., & MOORE, D. L. (1978). Distraction and social comparison as mediators of social facilitation effects. *Journal of Experimental Social Psychology, 14,* 291–303.

SANITIOSO, R., KUNDA, Z., & FONG, G. T. (1990). Motivated recruitment of autobiographical memories. *Journal of Personality and Social Psychology, 59,* 229–241.

SAPADIN, L. A. (1988). Friendship and gender: Perspectives of professional men and women. *Journal of Social and Personal Relationships, 5,* 387–403.

SARTRE, J-P. (1946/1948). *Anti-Semite and Jew.* New York: Schocken Books.

SATTERFIELD, A. T., & MUEHLENHARD, C. L. (1997). Shaken confidence: The effects of an authority figure's flirtatiousness on women's and men's self-rated creativity. *Psychology of Women Quarterly, 21,* 395–416.

SAVITSKY, K., EPLEY, N., & GILOVICH, T. (2001). Do others judge us as harshly as we think? Overestimating the impact of our failures, shortcomings, and mishaps. *Journal of Personality and Social Psychology, 81,* 44–56.

SAX, L. J., ASTIN, A. W., KORN, W. S., & MAHONEY, K. M. (1999). *The American freshman: National norms for Fall 1999.* Los Angeles: Higher Education Research Institute, UCLA.

SAX, L. J., LINDHOLM, J. A., ASTIN, A. W., KORN, W. S., & MAHONEY, K. M. (2002). *The American freshman: National norms for Fall, 2002.* Los Angeles: Cooperative Institutional Research Program, UCLA.

SCHACHTER, S. (1951). Deviation, rejection and communication. *Journal of Abnormal and Social Psychology, 46,* 190–207.

SCHACHTER, S., & SINGER, J. E. (1962). Cognitive, social and physiological determinants of emotional state. *Psychological Review, 69,* 379–399.

SCHAFER, R. B., & KEITH, P. M. (1980). Equity and depression among married couples. *Social Psychology Quarterly, 43,* 430–435.

SCHAFFNER, P. E., WANDERSMAN, A., & STANG, D. (1981). Candidate name exposure and voting: Two field studies. *Basic and Applied Social Psychology, 2,* 195–203.

SCHECK, B., NEUFELD, P., & DWYER, J. (2000). *Actual innocence.* Garden City, NY: Doubleday.

SCHEIER, M. F., & CARVER, C. S. (1992). Effects of optimism on psychological and physical well-being: Theoretical overview and empirical update. *Cognitive Therapy and Research, 16,* 201–228.

SCHIFFENBAUER, A., & SCHIAVO, R. S. (1976). Physical distance and attraction: An intensification effect. *Journal of Experimental Social Psychology, 12,* 274–282.

SCHIMEL, J., ARNDT, J., PYSZCZYNSKI, T., & GREENBERG, J. (2001). Being accepted for who we are: Evidence that social validation of the intrinsic self reduces general defensiveness. *Journal of Personality and Social Psychology, 80,* 35–52.

SCHIMEL, J., PYSZCZYNSKI, T., GREENBERG, J., O'MAHEN, H., & ARNDT, J. (2000). Running from the shadow: Psychological distancing from others to deny characteristics people fear in themselves. *Journal of Personality and Social Psychology, 78,* 446–462.

SCHIMEL, J., SIMON, L., GREENBERG, J., PYSZCZYNSKI, T., SOLOMON, S., & WAXMONSKY, J. (1999). Stereotypes and terror management: Evidence that mortality salience enhances stereotypic thinking and preferences. *Journal of Personality and Social Psychology, 77,* 905–926.

SCHLENKER, B. R. (1976). *Egocentric perceptions in cooperative groups: A conceptualization and research review.* Final Report, Office of Naval Research Grant NR 170–797.

SCHLENKER, B. R., & MILLER, R. S. (1977a). Egocentrism in groups: Self-serving biases or logical information processing? *Journal of Personality and Social Psychology, 35,* 755–764.

SCHLENKER, B. R., & MILLER, R. S. (1977b). Group cohesiveness as a determinant of egocentric perceptions in cooperative groups. *Human Relations, 30,* 1039–1055.

SCHLESINGER, A., JR. (1949). The statistical soldier. *Partisan Review, 16,* 852–856.

SCHLOSSER, E. (2003, March 10). Empire of the obscene. *New Yorker,* pp. 61–71.

SCHMADER, T., & JOHNS, M. (2003). Converging evidence that stereotype threat reduces working memory capacity. *Journal of Personality and Social Psychology, 85,* 440–451.

SCHMITT, D. P. (2003). Universal sex differences in the desire for sexual variety; tests from 52 nations, 6 continents, and 13 islands. *Journal of Personality and Social Psychology, 85,* 85–104.

SCHOENFELD, B. (1995, May 14). The loneliness of being white. *New York Times Magazine,* 34–37.

SCHOR, J. B. (1998). *The overworked American.* New York: Basic Books.

SCHULZ, J. W., & PRUITT, D. G. (1978). The effects of mutual concern on joint welfare. *Journal of Experimental Social Psychology, 14,* 480–492.

SCHWARTZ, B. (2000). Self-determination: The tyranny of freedom. *American Psychologist, 55,* 79–88.

SCHWARTZ, B. (2004). *The tyranny of choice.* New York: Ecco/HarperCollins.

SCHWARTZ, S. H., & GOTTLIEB, A. (1981). Participants' post-experimental reactions and the ethics of bystander research. *Journal of Experimental Social Psychology, 17,* 396–407.

SCHWARZ, N., BLESS, H., & BOHNER, G. (1991). Mood and persuasion: Affective states influence the processing of persuasive communications. In M. Zanna (Ed.), *Advances in experimental social psychology,* vol. 24. New York: Academic Press.

SCOTT, J. P., & MARSTON, M. V. (1953). Nonadaptive behavior resulting from a series of defeats in fighting mice. *Journal of Abnormal and Social Psychology, 48,* 417–428.

SEARS, D. O. (1979). Life stage effects upon attitude change, especially among the elderly. Manuscript prepared for Workshop on the Elderly of the Future, Committee on Aging, National Research Council, Annapolis, MD, May 3–5.

SEARS, D. O. (1986). College sophomores in the laboratory: Influences of a narrow data base on social psychology's view of human nature. *Journal of Personality and Social Psychology, 51,* 515–530.

SEDIKIDES, C. (1993). Assessment, enhancement, and verification determinants of the self-evaluation process. *Journal of Personality and Social Psychology, 65,* 317–338.

SEGALL, M. H., DASEN, P. R., BERRY, J. W., & POORTINGA, Y. H. (1990). *Human behavior in global perspective: An introduction to cross-cultural psychology.* New York: Pergamon.

SEIBT, B., & FORSTER, J. (2004). Stereotype threat and performance: How self-stereotypes influence processing by inducing regulatory foci. *Journal of Personality and Social Psychology, 87,* 38–56.

SELIGMAN, M. (1994). *What you can change and what you can't.* New York: Knopf.

SELIGMAN, M. E. P. (1975). *Helplessness: On depression, development and death.* San Francisco: W. H. Freeman.

SELIGMAN, M. E. P. (1991). *Learned optimism.* New York: Knopf.

SENTYRZ, S. M., & BUSHMAN, B. J. (1998). Mirror, mirror, on the wall, who's the thinnest one of all? Effects of self-awareness on consumption of fatty, reduced-fat, and fat-free products. *Journal of Applied Psychology, 83,* 944–949.

SETA, C. E., & SETA, J. J. (1992). Increments and decrements in mean arterial pressure levels as a function of audience composition: An averaging and summation analysis. *Personality and Social Psychology Bulletin, 18,* 173–181.

SHACKELFORD, T. K., & LARSEN, R. J. (1997) tor of psychological, emotional, and physiological distress. *Journal of Personality and Social Psychology, 72,* 456–466.

SHAFFER, D. R., PEGALIS, L. J., & BAZZINI, D. G. (1996). When boy meets girls (revisited): Gender, gender-role orientation, and prospect of future interaction as determinants of self-disclosure among same- and opposite-sex acquaintances. *Personality and Social Psychology Bulletin, 22,* 495–506.

SHARMA, N. (1981). Some aspect of attitude and behaviour of mothers. Indian *Psychological Review, 20,* 35–42.

SHAVITT, S. (1990). The role of attitude objects in attitude functions. *Journal of Experimental Social Psychology, 26,* 124–148.

SHELDON, K. M., ELLIOT, A. J., YOUNGMEE, K., & KASSER, T. (2001). What is satisfying about satisfying events? Testing 10 candidate psychological needs. *Journal of Personality and Social Psychology, 80,* 325–339.

SHEPPERD, J. A., & ARKIN, R. M. (1991). Behavioral other-enhancement: Strategically obscuring the link between performance and evaluation. *Journal of Personality and Social Psychology, 60,* 79–88.

SHEPPERD, J. A., & WRIGHT, R. A. (1989). Individual contributions to a collective effort: An incentive analysis. *Personality and Social Psychology Bulletin, 15,* 141–149.

SHERIF, M. (1966). *In common predicament: Social psychology of intergroup conflict and cooperation.* Boston: Houghton Mifflin.

SHERMAN, D. K., NELSON, L. D., & ROSS, L. D. (2003). Naive realism and affirmative action: Adversaries are more similar than they think. *Basic and Applied Social Psychology, 25,* 275–289.

SHERMAN, J. W. (1996). Development and mental representation of stereotypes. *Journal of Personality and Social Psychology, 70,* 1126–1141.

SHERMAN, J. W., LEE, A. Y., BESSENOFF, G. R., & FROST, L. A. (1998). Stereotype efficiency reconsidered: Encoding flexibility under cognitive load. *Journal of Personality and Social Psychology, 75,* 589–606.

SHERMAN, S. J., CIALDINI, R. B., SCHWARTZMAN, D. F., & REYNOLDS, K. D. (1985). Imagining can heighten or lower the perceived likelihood of contracting a disease: The mediating effect of ease of imagery. *Personality and Social Psychology Bulletin, 11,* 118–127.

SHIH, M., PITTINSKY, T. L., & AMBADY, N. (1999). Stereotype susceptibility: Identity salience and shifts in quantitative performance. *Psychological Science, 10,* 80–83.

SHORT, J. F., JR. (ED.). (1969). *Gang delinquency and delinquent subcultures.* New York: Harper & Row.

SHOWERS, C., & RUBEN, C. (1987). Distinguishing pessimism from depression: Negative expectations and positive coping mechanisms. Paper presented at the American Psychological Association convention.

SHRAUGER, J. S. (1983). The accuracy of self-prediction: How good are we and why? Paper presented at the Midwestern Psychological Association convention.

SHRAUGER, J. S., RAM, D., GRENINGER, S. A., & MARIANO, E. (1996). Accuracy of self-predictions versus judgments by knowledgeable others. *Personality and Social Psychology Bulletin, 22,* 1229–1243.

SIDANIUS, J., & PRATTO, F. (1999). *Social dominance: An intergroup theory of social hierarchy and oppression.* New York: Cambridge University Press.

SIDANIUS, J., PRATTO, F., & BOBO, L. (1994). Social dominance orientation and the political psychology of gender: A case of invariance? *Journal of Personality and Social Psychology, 67,* 998–1011.

SIDANIUS, J., PRATTO, F., & BOBO, L. (1996). Racism, conservatism, affirmative action, and intellectual sophistication: A matter of principled conservatism or group dominance? *Journal of Personality and Social Psychology, 70,* 476–490.

SIDDIQUI, A., ROSS, H. S., RAM, A., & WARD, L. (2004). Perspectives on self and other in children's representations of sibling conflict. *International Journal of Behavioral Development, 28,* 37–48.

SIEFF, E. M., DAWES, R. M., & LOEWENSTEIN, G. F. (1999). Anticipated versus actual responses to HIV test results. *American Journal of Psychology, 112,* 297–311.

SIGALL, H. (1970). Effects of competence and consensual validation on a communicator's liking for the audience. *Journal of Personality and Social Psychology, 16,* 252–258.

SILKE, A. (2003). Deindividuation, anonymity, and violence: Findings from Northern Ireland. *Journal of Social Psychology, 143,* 493–499.

SILVERMAN, C. (2004, March/April). Canadian Cults: Blind Faith or New Religion? *The New Canadian Magazine,* 1–4. Retrieved 1 June 2006, from http://ordinary.blogs.com/clips/Cults.pdf.

SIMMONS, W. W. (2000, December). When it comes to having children, Americans still prefer boys. *The Gallup Poll Monthly,* pp. 63–64.

SIMONTON, D. K. (1994). *Greatness: Who makes history and why.* New York: Guilford Press.

SIMPSON, J. A. (1987). The dissolution of romantic relationships: Factors involved in relationship stability and emotional distress. *Journal of Personality and Social Psychology, 53,* 683–692.

SIMPSON, J. A., CAMPBELL, B., & BERSCHEID, E. (1986). The association between romantic love and marriage: Kephart (1967) twice revisited. *Personality and Social Psychology Bulletin, 12,* 363–372.

SIMPSON, J. A., GANGESTAD, S. W., & LERMA, M. (1990). Perception of physical attractiveness: Mechanisms involved in the maintenance of romantic relationships. *Journal of Personality and Social Psychology, 59,* 1192–1201.

SINCLAIR, L., & FEHR, B. (2005). Voice versus loyalty: Self-construal and responses to dissatisfaction in romantic relationships. *Journal of Experimental Psychology, 41,* 298–304.

SINCLAIR, L., & KUNDA, Z. (1999). Reactions to a Black professional: Motivated inhibition and activation of conflicting stereotypes. *Journal of Personality and Social Psychology, 77,* 885–904.

SINCLAIR, L., & KUNDA, Z. (2000). Motivated stereotyping of women: She's fine if she praised me but incompetent if she criticized me. *Personality and Social Psychology Bulletin, 26,* 1329–1342.

SINCLAIR, R. C., LEE, T., & JOHNSON, T. E. (1995). The effect of social-comparison feedback on aggressive responses to erotic and aggressive film. *Journal of Applied Social Psychology, 25,* 818–837.

SINGER, M. (1979). *Cults and cult members.* Address to the American Psychological Association convention.

SKAALVIK, E. M., & HAGTVET, K. A. (1990). Academic achievement and self-concept: An analysis of causal predominance in a developmental perpsective. *Journal of Personality and Social Psychology, 58,* 292–307.

SKITKA, L. J. (1999). Ideological and attributional boundaries on public compassion: Reactions to individuals and communities affected by a natural disaster. *Personality and Social Psychology Bulletin, 25,* 793–808.

SLAVIN, R. E. (1990, December/January). Research on cooperative learning: Consensus and controversy. *Educational Leadership,* pp. 52–54.

SLOAN, J. H., KELLERMAN, A. L., REAY, D. T., FERRIS, J. A., KOEPSELL, T., RIVARA, F. P., RICE, C., GRAY, L., & LOGERFO, J. (1988). Handgun regulations, crime, assaults, and homicide: A tale of two cities. *New England Journal of Medicine, 319,* 1256–1261.

SLOVIC, P. (1972). From Shakespeare to Simon: Speculations—and some evidence—about man's ability to process information. *Oregon Research Institute Research Bulletin, 12*(2).

SLOVIC, P., & FISCHHOFF, B. (1977). On the psychology of experimental surprises. *Journal of Experimental Psychology: Human Perception and Performance, 3,* 455–551.

SMITH, A. (1976). *The wealth of nations. Book 1.* Chicago: University of Chicago Press. (Originally published 1776.)

SMITH, D. E., GIER, J. A., & WILLIS, F. N. (1982). Interpersonal touch and compliance with a marketing request. *Basic and Applied Social Psychology, 3,* 35–38.

SMITH, H. (1976). The Russians. New York: Balantine Books. Cited by B. Latané, K. Williams, & S. Harkins in Many hands make light the work. *Journal of Personality and Social Psychology, 37,* 1979, pp. 822–832.

SMITH, H. J., & TYLER, T. R. (1997). Choosing the right pond: The impact of group membership on self-esteem and group-oriented behavior. *Journal of Experimental Social Psychology, 33,* 146–170.

SMITH, H. W. (1981). Territorial spacing on a beach revisited: A cross-national exploration. *Social Psychology Quarterly, 44,* 132–137.

SMITH, J. L., BERRY, N. J., WHITELEY, P. (1997). The effect of interviewer-guise upon gender self-report responses as a function of interviewee's self-monitoring position. *European Journal of Social Psychology, 27,* 237–243.

SMITH, P. B., & TAYEB, M. (1989). Organizational structure and processes. In M. Bond (Ed.), *The cross-cultural challenge to social psychology.* Newbury Park, CA: Sage.

SMITH, S. M., STINSON, V., & PROSSER, M. A. (2004). Do they all look alike? An exploration of decision making strategies in cross-race identifications. *Canadian Journal of Behavioral Science, 36,* 146–154.

SMITH, T. W. (1998, December). *American sexual behavior: Trends, socio-demographic differences, and risk behavior.* National Opinion Research Center GSS Topical Report No. 25.

SMITH, V. L. (1991). Impact of pretrial instruction on jurors' information processing and decision making. *Journal of Applied Psychology, 76,* 220–228.

SNYDER, C. R. (1978). The "illusion" of uniqueness. *Journal of Humanistic Psychology, 18,* 33–41.

SNYDER, C. R. (1980, March). The uniqueness mystique. *Psychology Today,* pp. 86–90.

SNYDER, C. R., & FROMKIN, H. L. (1980). *Uniqueness: The human pursuit of difference.* New York: Plenum.

SNYDER, C. R., & HIGGINS, R. L. (1988). Excuses: Their effective role in the negotiation of reality. *Psychological Bulletin, 104,* 23–35.

SNYDER, M. (1983). The influence of individuals on situations: Implications for understanding the links between personality and social behavior. *Journal of Personality, 51,* 497–516.

SNYDER, M. (1984). When belief creates reality. In L. Berkowitz (Ed.), *Advances in experimental social psychology,* vol. 18. New York: Academic Press.

SNYDER, M., & DEBONO, K. G. (EDS.). (1989). Understanding the functions of attitudes: Lessons from personality and social behavior. In *Attitude structure and function.* Lawrence Erlbaum Associates, Inc.

SNYDER, M., & ICKES, W. (1985). Personality and social behavior. In G. Lindzey & E. Aronson (Eds.), *Handbook of social psychology,* 3rd ed. New York: Random House.

SNYDER, M., SIMPSON, J. A. (1987). Orientations toward romantic relationships. In M. Snyder and J. A. Simpson (Eds.), *Intimate relationships: Development, dynamics, and deterioration.* Sage Publications, Inc.

SNYDER, M., TANKE, E. D., & BERSCHEID, E. (1977). Social perception and interpersonal behavior: On the self-fulfilling nature of social stereotypes. *Journal of Personality and Social Psychology, 35,* 656–666.

SOKOLL, G. R., & MYNATT, C. R. (1984). Arousal and free throw shooting. Paper presented at the Midwestern Psychological Association convention, Chicago.

SOLBERG, E. C., DIENER, E., & ROBINSON, M. D. (2003). Why are materialists less satisfied? In T. Kasser & A. D. Kanner (Eds.), *Psychology and consumer culture: The struggle for a good life in a materialistic world.* Washington, DC: APA Books.

SOLOMON, S., GREENBERG, J., & PYSZCZYNSKI, T. (2000). Pride and prejudice: Fear of death and social behavior. *Current Directions in Psychological Science, 9,* 200–203.

SOMMER, R. (1969). *Personal space.* Englewood Cliffs, NJ: Prentice-Hall.

SPARRELL, J. A., & SHRAUGER, J. S. (1984). Self-confidence and optimism in self-prediction. Paper presented at the American Psychological Association convention.

SPECTOR, P. E. (1986). Perceived control by employees: A meta-analysis of studies concerning autonomy and participation at work. *Human Relations, 39,* 1005–1016.

SPENCER, S., FEIN, S., WOLFE, C., FONG, C., & DUNN, M. A. (1998). Automatic activation of stereotypes: The role of self-image threat. *Personality and Social Psychology Bulletin, 24,* 1139–152.

SPENCER, S. J., STEELE, C. M., & QUINN, D. M. (1999). Stereotype threat and women's math performance. *Journal of Experimental Social Psychology, 3,* 4–28.

SPIVAK, J. (1979, June 6). *Wall Street Journal.*

SPIVEY, C. B., & PRENTICE-DUNN, S. (1990). Assessing the directionality of deindividuated behavior: Effects of deindividuation, modeling, and private self-consciousness on aggressive and prosocial responses. *Basic and Applied Social Psychology, 11,* 387–403.

SPORER, S. L., PENROD, S., READ, D., & CUTLER, B. (1995). Choosing confidence and accuracy: A meta-analysis of the confidence-accuracy relation in eyewitness identification studies. *Psychological Bulletin, 118,* 315–327.

SPRECHER, S. (1987). The effects of self-disclosure given and received on affection for an intimate partner and stability of the relationship. *Journal of Personality and Social Psychology, 4,* 115–127.

SPRECHER, S., ARON, A., HATFIELD, E., CORTESE, A., POTAPOVA, E., & LEVITSKAYA, A. (1994). Love: American style, Russian style, and Japanese style. *Personal Relationships, 1,* 349–369.

SPRECHER, S., SULLIVAN, Q., & HATFIELD, E. (1994). Mate selection preferences: Gender differences examined in a national sample. *Journal of Personality and Social Psychology, 66,* 1074–1080.

ST. LAWRENCE, J. S., & JOYNER, D. J. (1991). The effects of sexually violent rock music on males' acceptance of violence against women. *Psychology of Women Quarterly, 15* (1), 49–63.

STANDING, L. G. (2002). Modeling effects in students drinking and smoking, revisited after 24 years. *Social Behavior and Personality, 30,* 435–442.

STANGOR, C., JONAS, K., STROEBE, W., & HEWSTONE, M. (1996). Influence of student exchange on national stereotypes, attitudes and perceived group variability. *European Journal of Social Psychology, 26,* 663–675.

STANGOR, C., LYNCH, L., DUAN, C., & GLASS, B. (1992). Categorization of individuals on the basis of multiple social features. *Journal of Personality and Social Psychology, 62,* 207–218.

STARK, R., & BAINBRIDGE, W. S. (1980). Networks of faith: Interpersonal bonds and recruitment of cults and sects. *American Journal of Sociology, 85,* 1376–1395.

STASSER, G. (1991). Pooling of unshared information during group discussion. In S. Worchel, W. Wood, & J. Simpson (Eds.), *Group process and productivity.* Beverly Hills, CA: Sage.

STATISTICS CANADA (2000). Youths and adults charged in criminal incidents, criminal code and federal statutes, by sex (www.statcan.ca/english/pgdb/state/justice/legal14.htm).

STATISTICS CANADA. (2004). Results of 2003 General Social Survey.

STATISTICS CANADA. *The Daily.* (2005, July 21). Crime Statistics. Retrieved on 20 June 2006, from http://www.statcan.ca/Daily/English/050721/d050721a.htm.

STAUB, E. (1989). *The roots of evil: The origins of genocide and other group violence.* Cambridge: Cambridge University Press.

STAUB, E. (2003). *The psychology of good and evil: Why children, adults, and groups help and harm others.* New York: Cambridge University Press.

STAUB, E., & PEARLMAN, L. A. (2004). Advancing healing and reconciliation. *Journal of Genocide Studies, 24,* 297–334.

STEELE, C. M. (1997). A threat in the air: How stereotypes shape intellectual identity and performance. *American Psychologist, 52,* 613–629.

STEELE, C. M., & ARONSON, J. (1995). Stereotype threat and the intellectual test performance of African Americans. *Journal of Personality and Social Psychology, 69,* 797–811.

STEELE, C. M., & SOUTHWICK, L. (1985). Alcohol and social behavior I: The psychology of drunken excess. *Journal of Personality and Social Psychology, 48,* 18–34.

STEELE, C. M., SPENCER, S. J., & ARONSON, J. (2002). Contending with group image: The psychology of stereotype and social identity threat. In M. P. Zanna (Ed.), *Advances in experimental social psychology,* pp. 34, 379–440. San Diego, CA: Academic Press.

STEIN, A. H., & FRIEDRICH, L. K. (1972). Television content and young children's behavior. In J. P. Murray, E. A. Rubinstein, & G. A. Comstock (Eds.), *Television and social learning.* Washington, DC: Government Printing Office.

STEIN, D. D., HARDYCK, J. A., & SMITH, M. B. (1965). Race and belief: An open and shut case. *Journal of Personality and Social Psychology, 1,* 281–289.

STEPHAN, W. G. (1986). The effects of school desegregation: An evaluation 30 years after Brown. In R. Kidd, L. Saxe, & M. Saks (Eds.), *Advances in applied social psychology.* New York: Erlbaum.

STEPHAN, W. G. (1987). The contact hypothesis in intergroup relations. In C. Hendrick (Ed.), *Group processes and intergroup relations.* Newbury Park, CA: Sage.

STEPHAN, W. G. (1988). School desegregation: Short-term and long-term effects. Paper presented at the national conference "Opening doors: An appraisal of race relations in America," University of Alabama.

STEPHAN, W. G., BERSCHEID, E., & WALSTER, E. (1971). Sexual arousal and heterosexual perception. *Journal of Personality and Social Psychology, 20,* 93–101.

STERNBERG, R. J. (1988). Triangulating love. In R. J. Sternberg & M. L. Barnes (Eds.), *The psychology of love.* New Haven, CT: Yale University Press.

STERNBERG, R. J. (2003). A duplex theory of hate and its development and its application to terrorism, massacres, and genocide. *Review of General Psychology, 7,* 299–328.

STILLINGER, C., EPELBAUM, M., KELTNER, D., & ROSS, L. (1991). The "reactive devaluation" barrier to conflict resolution. Unpublished manuscript, Stanford University.

STOCKDALE, J. E. (1978). Crowding: Determinants and effects. In L. Berkowitz (Ed.), *Advances in experimental social psychology,* vol. 11. New York: Academic Press.

STONE, A. A., HEDGES, S. M., NEALE, J. M., & SATIN, M. S. (1985). Prospective and cross-sectional mood reports offer no evidence of a "blue Monday" phenomenon. *Journal of Personality and Social Psychology, 49,* 129–134.

STONE, J. (2000, November 6). Quoted by Sharon Begley, The stereotype trap. *Newsweek.*

STONE, J., LYNCH, C. I., SJOMELING, M., & DARLEY, J. M. (1999). Stereotype threat effects on Black and White athletic performance. *Journal of Personality and Social Psychology, 77,* 1213–1227.

STONER, J. A. F. (1961). A comparison of individual and group decisions involving risk. Unpublished master's thesis, Massachusetts Institute of Technology, 1961. Cited by D. G. Marquis in Individual responsibility and group decisions involving risk. *Industrial Management Review, 3,* 8–23.

STORMS, M. D. (1973). Videotape and the attribution process: Reversing actors' and observers' points of view. *Journal of Personality and Social Psychology, 27,* 165–175.

STORMS, M. D., & THOMAS, G. C. (1977). Reactions to physical closeness. *Journal of Personality and Social Psychology, 35,* 412–418.

STRAHAN, E. J., SPENCER, S. J., & ZANNA, M. P. (2002). Subliminal priming and persuasion: Striking while the iron is hot. *Journal of Experimental Social Psychology, 38,* 556–568.

STRAHAN, E. J., SPENCER, S. J., & ZANNA, M. P. (2005). Subliminal priming and persuasion: How motivation affects the activation of goals and persuasiveness of messages. In F. R. Kardes, P. M. Herr, & J. Nantel (Eds.), *Applying social cognition to consumer-focused strategy.* Mahwah, NJ: Lawrence Erlbaum Associates.

STRAUS, M. A., & GELLES, R. J. (1980). *Behind closed doors: Violence in the American family.* New York: Anchor/Doubleday.

STROEBE, W., INSKO, C. A., THOMPSON, V. D., & LAYTON, B. D. (1971). Effects of physical attractiveness, attitude similarity, and sex on various aspects of interpersonal attraction. *Journal of Personality and Social Psychology, 18,* 79–91.

STROESSNER, S. J., HAMILTON, D. L., & LEPORE, L. (1990). Intergroup categorization and intragroup differentiation: Ingroup-outgroup differences. Paper presented at the American Psychological Association convention.

STROESSNER, S. J., & MACKIE, D. M. (1993). Affect and perceived group variability: Implications for stereotyping and prejudice. In D. M. Mackie & D. L. Hamilton (Eds.), *Affect, cognition, and stereotyping: Interactive processes in group perception.* San Diego, CA: Academic Press.

SUE, S., SMITH, R. E., & CALDWELL, C. (1973). Effects of inadmissible evidence on the decisions of simulated jurors: A moral dilemma. *Journal of Applied Social Psychology, 3,* 345–353.

SUH, E. J., MOSKOWITZ, D. S., FOURNIER, M. A., & ZUROFF, D. C. (2004). Gender and relationships: Influences on a genetic and communal behaviors. *Personal Relationships, 11,* 41–59.

SULS, J., & TESCH, F. (1978). Students' preferences for information about their test performance: A social comparison study. *Journal of Applied Social Psychology, 8,* 189–197.

SULS, J., WAN, C. K., & SANDERS, G. S. (1988). False consensus and false uniqueness in estimating the prevalence of health-protective behaviors. *Journal of Applied Social Psychology, 18,* 66–79.

SUMMERS, G., & FELDMAN, N. S. (1984). Blaming the victim versus blaming the perpetrator: An attributional analysis of spouse abuse. *Journal of Social and Clinical Psychology, 2,* 339–347.

SUNDSTROM, E., DE MEUSE, K. P., & FUTRELL, D. (1990). Work teams: Applications and effectiveness. *American Psychologist, 45,* 120–133.

SVENSON, O. (1981). Are we all less risky and more skillful than our fellow drivers? *Acta Psychologica, 47,* 143–148.

SWANN, W. B., JR. (1996). *Self-traps: The elusive quest for higher self-esteem.* New York: Freeman.

SWANN, W. B., JR. (1997). The trouble with change: Self-verification and allegiance to the self. *Psychological Science, 8,* 177–180.

SWAP, W. C. (1977). Interpersonal attraction and repeated exposure to rewarders and punishers. *Personality and Social Psychology Bulletin, 3,* 248–251.

SWEENEY, J. (1973). An experimental investigation of the free rider problem. *Social Science Research, 2,* 277–292.

SWIM, J. K. (1994). Perceived versus meta-analytic effect sizes: An assessment of the accuracy of gender stereotypes. *Journal of Personality and Social Psychology, 66,* 21–36.

SWIM, J. K., AIKIN, K. J., HALL, W. S., & HUNTER, B. A. (1995). Sexism and racism: Old-fashioned and modern prejudices. *Journal of Personality and Social Psychology, 68,* 199–214.

SWIM, J. K., & COHEN, L. L. (1997). Overt, covert, and subtle sexism. *Psychology of Women Quarterly, 21,* 103–118.

SWIM, J. K., & HYERS, L. L. (1999). Excuse me—What did you just say?!: Women's public and private reactions to sexist remarks. *Journal of Experimental Social Psychology, 35,* 68–88.

SWIM, J. K., & STANGOR, C. (EDS.). (1998). *Prejudice: The target's perspective.* San Diego, CA: Academic Press.

SYMONS, C. S., & JOHNSON, B. T. (1997). The self-reference effect in memory: A meta-analysis. *Psychological Bulletin, 121,* 371–394.

TAFARODI, R. W., KANG, J., MILNE, A. B. (2002). When different becomes similar: Compensatory conformity in bicultural visible minorities. *Personality and Social Psychology Bulletin, 28,* 1131–1142.

TAJFEL, H. (1970, November). Experiments in intergroup discrimination. *Scientific American,* pp. 96–102.

TAJFEL, H. (1981). *Human groups and social categories: Studies in social psychology.* London: Cambridge University Press.

TAJFEL, H. (1982). Social psychology of intergroup relations. *Annual Review of Psychology, 33,* 1–39.

TAJFEL, H., & BILLIG, M. (1974). Familiarity and categorization in intergroup behavior. *Journal of Experimental Social Psychology, 10,* 159–170.

TAJFEL, H., & TURNER, J. C. (1979). An integrative theory of intergroup conflict. In S. Worchel & W. G. Austin (Eds.), *Psychology of intergroup relations.* Monterey, CA: Brooks-Cole.

TAMRES, L. K., JANICKI, D., & HELGESON, V. S. (2002). Sex differences in coping behavior: A meta-analytic review and an examination of relative coping. *Personality and Social Psychology Review, 6,* 2–30.

TANNEN, D. (1990). *You just don't understand: Women and men in conversation.* New York: William Morrow.

TARMANN, A. (2002, May/June). Out of the closet and onto the Census long form. *Population Today, 30,* 1, 6.

TAYLOR, D. M., & DORIA, J. R. (1981). Self-serving and group-serving bias in attribution. *Journal of Social Psychology, 113,* 201–211.

TAYLOR, D. M., & LOUIS, W. R. (2004). Terrorism and the quest for identity. In Fathali M. Moghaddam (Ed.), *Understanding terrorism: Psychosocial roots, consequences, and interventions.* American Psychological Association.

TAYLOR, D. M., WRIGHT, S. C., MOGHADDAM, F. M., & LALONDE, R. N. (1990). The personal/group discrepancy: Perceiving my group, but not myself, to be a target of discrimination. *Personality and Social Psychology Bulletin, 16,* 254–262.

TAYLOR, K. M., & SHEPPERD, J. A. (1998). Bracing for the worst: Severity, testing, and feedback timing as moderators of the optimistic bias. *Personality and Social Psychology Bulletin, 24,* 915–926.

TAYLOR, S. E. (1979). Remarks at symposium on social psychology and medicine, American Psychological Association convention.

TAYLOR, S. E. (1981). A categorization approach to stereotyping. In D. L. Hamilton (Ed.), *Cognitive processes in stereotyping and intergroup behavior.* Hillsdale, NJ: Erlbaum.

TAYLOR, S. E., CROCKER, J., FISKE, S. T., SPRINZEN, M., & WINKLER, J. D. (1979). The generalizability of salience effects. *Journal of Personality and Social Psychology, 37,* 357–368.

TAYLOR, S. E., & FISKE, S. T. (1978). Salience, attention, and attribution: Top of the head phenomena. In L. Berkowitz (Ed.), *Advances in experimental social psychology,* vol. 11. New York: Academic Press.

TAYLOR, S. E., FISKE, S. T., ETCOFF, N. L., & RUDERMAN, A. J. (1978). Categorical and contextual bases of person memory and stereotyping. *Journal of Personality and Social Psychology, 36,* 778–793.

TAYLOR, S. P., & CHERMACK, S. T. (1993). Alcohol, drugs and human physical aggression. *Journal of Studies on Alcohol,* Supplement No. 11, 78–88.

TAYLOR, S. P., & PISANO, R. (1971). Physical aggression as a function of frustration and physical attack. *Journal of Social Psychology, 84,* 261–267.

TEGER, A. I. (1980). *Too much invested to quit.* New York: Pergamon Press.

TELCH, M. J., KILLEN, J. D., McALISTER, A. L., PERRY, C. L., & MACCOBY, N. (1981). Long-term follow-up of a pilot project on smoking prevention with adolescents. Paper presented at the American Psychological Association convention.

TESTA, M. (2002). The impact of men's alcohol consumption on perpetration of sexual aggression. *Clinical Psychology Review, 22,* 1239–1263.

TETLOCK, P. E. (1985). Integrative complexity of American and Soviet foreign policy rhetoric: A time-series analysis. *Journal of Personality and Social Psychology, 49,* 1565–1585.

TGM. (2000, May 30). Canadian teens forsaking television for the Internet (an Angus Reid poll reported by the Toronto *Globe and Mail*). Grand Rapids Press.

THOMAS, K. W., & PONDY, L. R. (1977). Toward an "intent" model of conflict management among principal parties. *Human Relations, 30,* 1089–1102.

THOMPSON, L. (1990a). An examination of naive and experienced negotiators. *Journal of Personality and Social Psychology, 59,* 82–90.

THOMPSON, L. (1990b). The influence of experience on negotiation performance. *Journal of Experimental Social Psychology, 26,* 528–544.

THOMPSON, L. (1998). *The mind and heart of the negotiator.* Upper Saddle River, NJ: Prentice-Hall.

THOMPSON, L., VALLEY, K. L., & KRAMER, R. M. (1995). The bittersweet feeling of success: An examination of social perception in negotiation. *Journal of Experimental Social Psychology, 31,* 467–492.

THOMPSON, L. L., & CROCKER, J. (1985). Prejudice following threat to the self-concept. Effects of performance expectations and attributions. Unpublished manuscript, Northwestern University.

THORNTON, B., & MAURICE, J. (1997). Physique contrast effect: Adverse impact of idealized body images for women. *Sex Roles, 37,* 433–439.

TICE, D. M., BUTLER, J. L., MURAVEN, M. B. (1995). When modesty prevails: Deferential favorability of self-presentation to friends and strangers. *Journal of Personality and Social Psychology, 69,* 1120–1138.

TIME. (1992, March 30). The not so merry wife of Windsor, pp. 38–39.

TIMKO, C., & MOOS, R. H. (1989). Choice, control, and adaptation among elderly residents of sheltered care settings. *Journal of Applied Social Psychology, 19,* 636–655.

TOMORROW, T. (2003, April 30). Passive tense verbs deployed before large audience; stories remain unclear (www240.pair.com/tomtom/pages/ ja/ja_fr.html).

TORMALA, Z. L., & PETTY, R. E. (2002). What doesn't kill me makes me stronger: The effects of resisting persuasion on attitude change. *Journal of Personality and Social Psychology, 83,* 1298–1313.

TRAVIS, L. E. (1925). The effect of a small audience upon eye-hand coordination. *Journal of Abnormal and Social Psychology, 20,* 142–146.

TRIANDIS, H. C. (1981). Some dimensions of intercultural variation and their implications for interpersonal behavior. Paper presented at the American Psychological Association convention.

TRIANDIS, H. C. (1994). *Culture and social behavior.* New York: McGraw-Hill.

TRIANDIS, H. C., BONTEMPO, R., VILLAREAL, M. J., ASAI, M., & LUCCA, N. (1988). Individualism and collectivism: Cross-cultural perspectives on self-ingroup relationships. *Journal of Personality and Social Psychology, 54,* 323–338.

TRIPLETT, N. (1898). The dynamogenic factors in pacemaking and competition. *American Journal of Psychology, 9,* 507–533.

TROLIER, T. K., & HAMILTON, D. L. (1986). Variables influencing judgments of correlational relations. *Journal of Personality and Social Psychology, 50,* 879–888.

TROPP, L. R., & PETTIGREW, T. F. (2004). Intergroup contact and the central role of affect in intergroup prejudice. In C. W. Leach & L. Tiedens (Eds.), *The social life of emotion.* Cambridge: Cambridge University Press.

TROST, M. R., MAASS, A., & KENRICK, D. T. (1992). Minority influence: Personal relevance biases cognitive processes and reverses private acceptance. *Journal of Experimental Social Psychology, 28,* 234–254.

TSANG, J-A. (2002). Moral rationalization and the integration of situational factors and psychological processes in immoral behavior. *Review of General Psychology, 6,* 25–50.

TSUI, L., NICOLADIS, E. (2004). Losing it: Similarities and differences in first intercourse experiences of men and women. *Canadian Journal of Human Sexuality, 13,* 95–106.

TURNER, C. W., HESSE, B. W., & PETERSON-LEWIS, S. (1986). Naturalistic studies of the long-term effects of television violence. *Journal of Social Issues, 42*(3), 51–74.

TURNER, J. C. (1981). The experimental social psychology of intergroup behaviour. In J. Turner & H. Giles (Eds.), *Intergroup behavior.* Oxford, England: Basil Blackwell.

TURNER, J. C. (1987). *Rediscovering the social group: A self-categorization theory.* New York: Basil Blackwell.

TURNER, J. C. (1991). *Social influence.* Milton Keynes, England: Open University Press.

TURNER, M. E., & PRATKANIS, A. R. (1994). Social identity maintenance prescriptions for preventing groupthink: Reducing identity protection and enhancing intellectual conflict. *International Journal of Conflict Management, 5,* 254–270.

TURNER, M. E., PRATKANIS, A. R., PROBASCO, P., & LEVE, C. (1992). Threat cohesion, and group effectiveness: Testing a social identity maintenance perspective on groupthink. *Journal of Personality and Social Psychology, 63,* 781–796.

TVERSKY, A., & KAHNEMAN, D. (1973). Availability: A neuristic for judging frequency and probability. *Cognitive Psychology, 5,* 207–302.

TVERKSY, A., & KAHNEMAN, D. (1974). Judgment under uncertainty: Heuristics and biases. *Science, 185,* 1123–1131.

TWENGE, J. M., BAUMEISTER, R. F., TICE, D. M., & STUCKE, T. S. (2001). If you can't join them, beat them: Effects of social exclusion on aggressive behavior. *Journal of Personality and Social Psychology, 81,* 1058–1069.

TWENGE, J. M., CATANESE, K. R., & BAUMEISTER, R. F. (2002). Social exclusion causes self-defeating behavior. *Journal of Personality and Social Psychology, 83,* 606–615.

TZENG, M. (1992). The effects of socioeconomic heterogamy and changes on marital dissolution for first marriages. *Journal of Marriage and the Family, 54,* 609–619.

UMBERSON, D., & HUGHES, M. (1987). The impact of physical attractiveness on achievement and psychological well-being. *Social Psychology Quarterly, 50,* 227–236.

UNITED NATIONS. (1991). *The world's women 1970–1990: Trends and statistics.* New York: United Nations.

UPI. (1970/1967). September 23, 1967. Cited by P. G. Zimbardo in The human choice: Individuation, reason, and order versus deindividuation, impulse, and chaos. In W. J. Arnold & D. Levine (Eds.), *Nebraska symposium on motivation, 1969.* Lincoln: University of Nebraska Press.

VALLONE, R. P., ROSS, L., & LEPPER, M. R. (1985). The hostile media phenomenon: Biased perception and perceptions of media bias in coverage of the "Beirut Massacre." *Journal of Personality and Social Psychology, 49,* 577–585.

VAN BOVEN, L., & GILOVICH, T. (2003). To do or to have? That is the question. *Journal of Personality and Social Psychology, 85,* 1193–1202.

VAN KNIPPENBERG, D., & WILKE, H. (1992). Prototypicality of arguments and conformity to ingroup norms. *European Journal of Social Psychology, 22,* 141–155.

VAN LANGE, P. A. M. (1991). Being better but not smarter than others: The Muhammad Ali effect at work in interpersonal situations. *Personality and Social Psychology Bulletin, 17,* 689–693.

VAN LANGE, P. A. M., TARIS, T. W., & VONK, R. (1997). Dilemmas of academic practice: Perceptions of superiority among social psychologists. *European Journal of Social Psychology, 27,* 675–685.

VAN LANGE, P. A. M., & VISSER, K. (1999). Locomotion in social dilemmas: How people adapt to cooperative, tit-for-tat, and noncooperative partners. *Journal of Personality and Social Psychology, 77,* 762–773.

VAN VUGT, M., VAN LANGE, P. A. M., & MEERTENS, R. M. (1996). Commuting by car or public transportation? A social dilemma analysis of travel mode judgements. *European Journal of Social Psychology, 26,* 373–395.

VAN YPEREN, N. W., & BUUNK, B. P. (1990). A longitudinal study of equity and satisfaction in intimate relationships. *European Journal of Social Psychology, 20,* 287–309.

VANDERSLICE, V. J., RICE, R. W., & JULIAN, J. W. (1987). The effects of participation in decision-making on worker satisfaction and productivity: An organizational simulation. *Journal of Applied Social Psychology, 17,* 158–170.

VEYSEY, B. M., & MESSNER, S. F. (1999). Further testing of social disorganization theory: An elaboration of Sampson and Groves's "Community structure and crime." *Journal of Research in Crime and Delinquency, 36,* 156–174.

VISSER, P. S., & KROSNICK, J. A. (1998). Development of attitude strength over the life cycle: Surge and decline. *Journal of Personality and Social Psychology, 75,* 1389–1410.

VITELLI, R. (1988). The crisis issue assessed: An empirical analysis. *Basic and Applied Social Psychology, 9,* 301–309.

VORAUER, J., & KUMHYR, S. M. (2001). Is this about you or me? Self- versus other-directed judgments and feelings in response to intergroup interaction. *Personality and Social Psychology Bulletin, 27,* 706–719.

VORAUER, J. D., & ROSS, M. (1999). Self-awareness and feeling transparent: Failing to suppress one's self. *Journal of Experimental Social Psychology, 35,* 415–440.

VORAUER, J. D., MAIN, K. J., & O'CONNELL, G. B. (1998). How do individuals expect to be viewed by members of lower status groups? Content and implications of meta-stereotypes. *Journal of Personality and Social Psychology, 75,* 917–937.

WAGSTAFF, G. F. (1983). Attitudes to poverty, the Protestant ethic, and political affiliation: A preliminary investigation. *Social Behavior and Personality, 11,* 45–47.

WALFISH, D. (2001). National count reveals major societal changes. *Science, 292,* 1823.

WALLACE, C. P. (2000, May 8). Germany's glass ceiling. *Time,* p. B8.

WALLER, J. (2002). *Becoming evil: How ordinary people commit genocide and mass killing.* New York: Oxford University Press.

WALSTER (HATFIELD), E. (1965). The effect of self-esteem on romantic liking. *Journal of Experimental Social Psychology, 1,* 184–197.

WALSTER (HATFIELD), E., ARONSON, V., ABRAHAMS, D., & ROTTMAN, L. (1966). Importance of physical attractiveness in dating behavior. *Journal of Personality and Social Psychology, 4,* 508–516.

WALSTER (HATFIELD), E., WALSTER, G. W., & BERSCHEID, E. (1978). *Equity: Theory and research.* Boston: Allyn & Bacon.

WATSON, D. (1982, November). The actor and the observer: How are their perceptions of causality divergent? *Psychological Bulletin, 92,* 682–700.

WATSON, R. I., JR. (1973). Investigation into deindividuation using a cross-cultural survey technique. *Journal of Personality and Social Psychology, 25,* 342–345.

WEBSTER, D. M. (1993). Motivated augmentation and reduction of the overattribution bias. *Journal of Personality and Social Psychology, 65,* 261–271.

WEGENER, D. T., KERR, N., FLEMING, M., & PETTY, R. E. (2000). Flexible corrections of juror judgments: Implications for jury instructions. *Psychology, Public Policy, and Law, 6,* 629–654.

WEGNER, D. M., & ERBER, R. (1992). The hyperaccessibility of suppressed thoughts. *Journal of Personality and Social Psychology, 63,* 903–912.

WEHR, P. (1979). *Conflict regulation.* Boulder, CO: Westview Press.

WEIGEL, R. H., & NEWMAN, L. S. (1976). Increasing attitude–behavior correspondence by broadening the scope of the behavioral measure. *Journal of Personality and Social Psychology, 33,* 793–802.

WEINER, B. (1981). The emotional consequences of causal ascriptions. Unpublished manuscript, UCLA.

WEINSTEIN, N. D. (1980). Unrealistic optimism about future life events. *Journal of Personality and Social Psychology, 39,* 806–820.

WEINSTEIN, N. D. (1982). Unrealistic optimism about susceptibility to health problems. *Journal of Behavioral Medicine, 5,* 441–460.

WEISS, J., & BROWN, P. (1976). Self-insight error in the explanation of mood. Unpublished manuscript, Harvard University.

WELLS, G. L., LINDSAY, R. C. L., & FERGUSON, T. (1979). Accuracy, confidence, and juror perceptions in eyewitness identification. *Journal of Applied Psychology, 64,* 440–448.

WELLS, G. L. (1993). What do we know about eyewitness identification? *American Psychologist, 48,* 553–571.

WELLS, G. L., & BRADFIELD, A. L. (1998). "Good, you identified the suspect": Feedback to eyewitnesses distorts their reports of the witnessing experience. *Journal of Applied Psychology, 83,* 360–376.

WELLS, G. L, MALPASS, R. S., LINDSAY, R. C. L., FISHER, R. P., TURTLE, J. W., & FULERO, S. M. (2000). From the lab to the police station: A successful application of eyewitness research. *American Psychologist, 55,* 581–598

WENER, R., FRAZIER, W., & FARBSTEIN, J. (1987, June). Building better jails. *Psychology Today,* pp. 40–49.

WHEELER, L., & KIM, Y. (1997). What is beautiful is culturally good: The physical attractiveness stereotype has different content in collectivistic cultures. *Personality and Social Psychology Bulletin, 23,* 795–800.

WHITE, G. L. (1980). Physical attractiveness and courtship progress. *Journal of Personality and Social Psychology, 39,* 660–668.

WHITE, H. R., BRICK, J., & HANSELL, S. (1993). A longitudinal investigation of alcohol use and aggression in adolescence. *Journal of Studies on Alcohol,* Supplement No. 11, 62–77.

WHITE, J. A., & PLOUS, S. (1995). Self-enhancement and social responsibility: On caring more, but doing less, than others. *Journal of Applied Social Psychology, 25,* 1297–1318.

WHITE, J. W., & KOWALSKI, R. M. (1994). Deconstructing the myth of the nonaggressive woman. *Psychology of Women Quarterly, 18,* 487–508.

WHITE, P. A., & YOUNGER, D. P. (1988). Differences in the ascription of transient internal states to self and other. *Journal of Experimental Social Psychology, 24,* 292–309.

WHITE, R. K. (1996). Why the Serbs fought: Motives and misperceptions. *Peace and Conflict: Journal of Peace Psychology, 2,* 109–128.

WHITE, R. K. (1998). American acts of force: Results and misperceptions. *Peace and Conflict, 4,* 93–128.

WHITLEY, B.E., JR. (1987). The effects of discredited eyewitness testimony: A meta-analysis. *Journal of Social Psychology, 127,* 209–214.

WHITLEY, B. E., JR. (1999). Right-wing authoritarianism, social dominance orientation, and prejudice. *Journal of Personality and Social Psychology, 77,* 126–134.

WHITMAN, D. (1996, December 16). I'm OK, you're not. *U.S. News and World Report,* p. 24.

WHYTE, G. (1993). Escalating commitment in individual and group decision making: A prospect theory approach. *Organizational Behavior and Human Decision Processes, 54,* 430–455.

WICKER, A. W. (1971). An examination of the "other variables" explanation of attitude-behavior inconsistency. *Journal of Personality and Social Psychology, 19,* 18–30.

WIDOM, C. S. (1989). Does violence beget violence? A critical examination of the literature. *Psychological Bulletin, 106,* 3–28.

WIEGMAN, O. (1985). Two politicians in a realistic experiment: Attraction, discrepancy, intensity of delivery, and attitude change. *Journal of Applied Social Psychology, 15,* 673–686.

WIESELQUIST, J., RUSBULT, C. E., FOSTER, C. A., & AGNEW, C. R. (1999). Commitment, pro-relationship behavior, and trust in close relationships. *Journal of Personality and Social Psychology, 77,* 942–966.

WILDER, D. A. (1978). Perceiving persons as a group: Effect on attributions of causality and beliefs. *Social Psychology, 41,* 13–23.

WILDER, D. A. (1981). Perceiving persons as a group: Categorization and intergroup relations. In. D. L. Hamilton (Ed.), *Cognitive processes in stereotyping and intergroup behavior.* Hillsdale, NJ: Erlbaum.

WILDER, D. A. (1990). Some determinants of the persuasive power of in-groups and out-groups: Organization of information and attribution of independence. *Journal of Personality and Social Psychology, 59,* 1202–1213.

WILDER, D. A., & SHAPIRO, P. N. (1984). Role of out-group cues in determining social identity. *Journal of Personality and Social Psychology, 47,* 342–348.

WILDSCHUT, T., PINTER, B., VEVEA, J., INSKO, G., & SCHOPLER, J. (2003). Beyond the group mind: A quantitative review of the interindividual-intergroup discontinuity effect. *Psychological Bulletin, 129,* 698–722.

WILLIAMS, J. E., & BEST, D. L. (1990a). *Measuring sex stereotypes: A multination study.* Newbury Park, CA: Sage.

WILLIAMS, J. E., & BEST, D. L. (1990b). *Sex and psyche: Gender and self viewed cross-culturally.* Newbury Park, CA: Sage.

WILLIAMS, J. E., SATTERWHITE, R. C., & BEST, D. L. (1999). Pancultural gender stereotypes revisited: The Five Factor model. *Sex Roles, 40,* 513–525.

WILLIAMS, J. E., SATTERWHITE, R. C., & BEST, D. L. (2000). Five-factor gender stereotypes in 27 countries. Paper presented at the XV Congress of the International Association for Cross-Cultural Psychology, Pultusk, Poland.

WILLIAMS, K. D. (2002). *Ostracism: The power of silence.* New York: Guilford Press.

WILLIAMS, K. D., CHEUNG, C. K. T., & CHOI, W. (2000). Cyberostracism: Effects of being ignored over the Internet. *Journal of Personality and Social Psychology, 79,* 748–762.

WILLIAMS, K. D., HARKINS, S., & LATANÉ, B. (1981). Identifiability as a deterrent to social loafing: Two cheering experiments. *Journal of Personality and Social Psychology, 40,* 303–311.

WILLIAMS, K. D., & KARAU, S. J. (1991). Social loafing and social compensation: The effects of expectations of coworker performance. *Journal of Personality and Social Psychology, 61,* 570–581.

WILLIAMS, K. D., NIDA, S. A., BACA, L. D., & LATANÉ, B. (1989). Social loafing and swimming: Effects of identifiability on individual and relay performance of intercollegiate swimmers. *Basic and Applied Social Psychology, 10,* 73–81.

WILLIAMS, T. M. (ED.). (1986). *The impact of television: A natural experiment in three communities.* Orlando, FL: Academic Press.

WILLIS, F. N., & HAMM, H. K. (1980). The use of interpersonal touch in securing compliance. *Journal of Nonverbal Behavior, 5,* 49–55.

WILSON, G. (1994, March 25). *Equal, but different.* The Times Higher Education Supplement, Times of London.

WILSON, R. S., & MATHENY, A. P., JR. (1986). Behavior-genetics research in infant temperament: The Louisville twin study. In R. Plomin & J. Dunn (Eds.), *The study of temperament: Changes, continuities, and challenges.* Hillsdale, NJ: Erlbaum.

WILSON, T. D., LASER, P. S., & STONE, J. I. (1982). Judging the predictors of one's mood: Accuracy and the use of shared theories. *Journal of Experimental Social Psychology, 18,* 537–556.

WINCH, R. F. (1958). *Mate selection: A study of complementary needs.* New York: Harper & Row.

WINTER, F. W. (1973). A laboratory experiment of individual attitude response to advertising exposure. *Journal of Marketing Research, 10,* 130–140.

WISMAN, A., & KOOLE, S. L. (2003). Hiding in the crowd: Can mortality salience promote affiliation with others who oppose one's worldviews? *Journal of Personality and Social Psychology, 84,* 511–526.

WOHL, M. J. A., & ENZLE, M. E. (2002). The deployment of personal luck: Illusory control in games of pure chance. *Personality and Social Psychology Bulletin, 28,* 1388–1397.

WOHL, M. J. A., & ENZLE, M. E. (2003). The effects of near wins and losses on self-perceived personal luck and subsequent gambling behavior. *Journal of Experimental Social Psychology, 39,* 184–191.

WOLF, S. (1987). Majority and minority influence: A social impact analysis. In M. P. Zanna, J. M. Olson, & C. P. Herman (Eds.), *Social influence: The Ontario symposium on personality and social psychology,* vol. 5. Hillsdale, NJ: Erlbaum.

WOLF, S., & LATANÉ, B. (1985). Conformity, innovation and the psycho-social law. In S. Moscovici, G. Mugny, & E. Van Avermaet (Eds.), *Perspectives on minority influence.* Cambridge: Cambridge University Press.

WOOD, J. V., HEIMPEL, S. A., & MICHELA, J. L. (2003). Savoring versus dampening: Self-esteem differences in regulating positive affect. *Journal of Personality and Social Psychology, 85,* 566–580.

WOOD, J. V., MICHELA, J. L., & GIORDANO, C. (2000). Downward comparison in everyday life reconciling self-enhancement models with mood-cognition priming model. *Journal of Personality and Social Psychology, 35,* 563–579.

WOOD, J. V., TAYLOR, S. E., & LICHTMAN, R. R. (1985). Social comparison in adjustment to breast cancer. *Journal of Personality and Social Psychology, 79,* 1169–1183.

WOOD, W., & EAGLY, A. H. (2000). A cross-cultural analysis of the behavior of women and men: Implications for the origins of sex differences. Unpublished manuscript, Texas A&M University.

WOOD, W., & RHODES, N. (1991). Sex differences in interaction style in task groups. In C. Ridgeway (Ed.), *Gender and interaction: The role of microstructures in inequality.* New York: Springer-Verlag.

WOOD, W., & QUINN, J. M. (2003). Forewarned and forewarmed? Two meta-analytic syntheses of forewarnings of influence appeals. *Psychological Bulletin, 129,* 119–138.

WOOD, W., LUNDGREN, S., OUELLETE, J. A., BUSCEME, S., & BLACKSTONE, T. (1994). Minority influence: A meta-analytic review of social influence processes. *Psychological Bulletin, 115,* 323–345.

WOOD, W., POOL, G. J., LECK, K., & PURVIS, D. (1996). Self-definition, defensive processing, and influence: The normative impact of majority and minority groups. *Journal of Personality and Social Psychology, 71,* 1181–1193.

WOOD, W., WONG, F. Y., & CHACHERE, J. G. (1991). Effects of media violence on viewers' aggression in unconstrained social interaction. *Psychological Bulletin, 109,* 371–383.

WORCHEL, S., & BROWN, E. H. (1984). The role of plausibility in influencing environmental attributions. *Journal of Experimental Social Psychology, 20,* 86–96.

WORCHEL, S., ROTHGERBER, H., DAY, E. A., HART, D., & BUTEMEYER, J. (1998). Social identity and individual productivity within groups. *British Journal of Social Psychology, 37,* 389–413.

WORD, C. O., ZANNA, M. P., & COOPER, J. (1974). The nonverbal mediation of self-fulfilling prophecies in interracial interaction. *Journal of Experimental Social Psychology, 10,* 109–120.

WORRINGHAM, C. J., & MESSICK, D. M. (1983). Social facilitation of running: An unobtrusive study. *Journal of Social Psychology, 121,* 23–29.

WRIGHT, D. B., BOYD, C. E., & TREDOUX, C. G. (2001). A field study of own-race bias in South Africa and England. *Psychology, Public Policy, & Law, 7,* 119–133.

WRIGHT, R. (1998, February 2). Politics made me do it. *Time,* p. 34.

WRIGHT, R. (2003, June 29). Quoted by Thomas L. Friedman, "Is Google God?" *New York Times* (www.nytimes.com).

WRIGHT, S. C., ARON, A., McLAUGHLIN-VOLPE, T., & ROPP, S. A. (1997). The extended contact effect: Knowledge of cross-group friendships and prejudice. *Journal of Personality and Social Psychology, 73,* 73–90.

WRIGHTSMAN, L. S. (2001). *Forensic psychology.* Belmont, CA: Wadsworth.

WYLIE, R. C. (1979). *The self-concept Theory and research on selected topics,* vol. 2. Lincoln: University of Nebraska Press.

YBARRA, O. (1999). Misanthropic person memory when the need to self-enhance is absent. *Personality and Social Psychology Bulletin, 25,* 261–269.

YOVETICH, N. A., & RUSBULT, C. E. (1994). Accommodative behavior in close relationships: Exploring transformation of motivation. *Journal of Experimental Social Psychology, 30,* 138–164.

YUKL, G. (1974). Effects of the opponent's initial offer, concession magnitude, and concession frequency on bargaining behavior. *Journal of Personality and Social Psychology, 30,* 323–335.

YZERBYT, V., ROCHER, S., & SCHADRON, G. (1997). Stereotypes as explanations: A subjective essentialistic view of group perception. In R. Spears, P. J. Oakes, N. Ellemers, & S. A. Haslam (Eds.), *The social psychology of stereotyping and group life.* Oxford: Basil Blackwell.

YZERBYT, V. Y., & LEYENS, J-P. (1991). Requesting information to form an impression: The influence of valence and confirmatory status. *Journal of Experimental Social Psychology, 27,* 337–356.

ZAJONC, R. B. (1965). Social facilitation. *Science, 149,* 269–274.

ZAJONC, R. B. (1968). Attitudinal effects of mere exposure. *Journal of Personality and Social Psychology, 9,* Monograph Suppl. No. 2, part 2.

ZAJONC, R. B. (1970, February). Brainwash: Familiarity breeds comfort. *Psychology Today,* pp. 32–35, 60–62.

ZAJONC, R. B. (1998). Emotions. In D. Gilbert, S. T. Fiske, & G. Lindzey (Eds.), *Handbook of social psychology,* 4th ed. New York: McGraw-Hill.

ZAJONC, R. B. (2000). Massacres: Mass murders in the name of moral imperatives. Unpublished manuscript, Stanford University.

ZAJONC, R. B., & SALES, S. M. (1966). Social facilitation of dominant and subordinate responses. *Journal of Experimental Social Psychology, 2,* 160–168.

ZANNA, M. P., & PACK, S. J. (1975). On the self-fulfilling nature of apparent sex differences in behavior. *Journal of Experimental Social Psychology, 11,* 583–591.

ZANNA, M. P., OLSON, J. M, & FAZIO, R. H. (1980). Attitude–behavior consistency: An individual difference perspective. *Journal of Personality and Social Psychology, 38,* 432–440.

ZEBROWITZ-McARTHUR, L. (1988). Person perception in cross-cultural perspective. In M. H. Bond (Ed.), *The cross-cultural challenge to social psychology.* Newbury Park, CA: Sage.

ZILLMANN, D. (1989a). Aggression and sex: Independent and joint operations. In H. L. Wagner & A. S. R. Manstead (Eds.), *Handbook of psychophysiology: Emotion and social behavior.* Chichester, England: Wiley.

ZILLMANN, D. (1989b). Effects of prolonged consumption of pornography. In D. Zillmann & J. Bryant (Eds.), *Pornography: Research advances and policy considerations.* Hillsdale, NJ: Erlbaum.

ZILLMANN, D., & PAULUS, P. B. (1993). Spectators: Reactions to sports events and effects on athletic performance. In R. N. Singer, N. Murphey, & L. K. Tennant (Eds.), *Handbook of research on sport psychology.* New York: Macmillan.

ZILLMANN, D., & WEAVER, J. B., III. (1999). Effects of prolonged exposure to gratuitous media violence on provoked and unprovoked hostile behavior. *Journal of Applied Social Psychology, 29,* 145–165.

ZILLMER, E. A., HARROWER, M., RITZLER, B. A., & ARCHER, R. P. (1995). *The quest for the Nazi personality: A psychological investigation of Nazi war criminals.* Hillsdale, NJ: Erlbaum.

ZIMBARDO, P. G. (1970). The human choice: Individuation, reason, and order versus deindividuation, impulse, and chaos. In W. J. Arnold & D. Levine (Eds.), *Nebraska symposium on motivation, 1969.* Lincoln: University of Nebraska Press.

ZIMBARDO, P. G. (1971). The psychological power and pathology of imprisonment. A statement prepared for the U.S. House of Representatives Committee on the Judiciary, Subcommittee No. 3: Hearings on Prison Reform, San Francisco, CA, October 25.

ZIMBARDO, P. G. (1972). The Stanford prison experiment. A slide/tape presentation produced by Philip G. Zimbardo, Inc., P. O. Box 4395, Stanford, CA. 94305.

ZIMBARDO, P. G. (2002, April). Nurturing psychological synergies. *APA Monitor*, pp. 5, 38.

ZIMBARDO, P. G. (2004). A situationist perspective on the psychology of evil: Understanding how good people are transformed into perpetrators. In A. G. Miller (Ed.), *The social psychology of good and evil.* New York: Guilford Press.

ZUCKER, G. S., & WEINER, B. (1993). Conservatism and perceptions of poverty: An attributional analysis. *Journal of Applied Social Psychology, 23,* 925–943.

Figure and Table Credits

Page 23, From H. Markus & S. Kitayama, "Culture and the Self: Implications for Cognition, Emotion, and Motivation," *Psychological Review*, 98, 1991, pp. 224–253. © 1991 by the American Psychological Association. Reprinted with permission.

Page 48, Adapted from E. E. Jones & V. A. Harris, "The Attribution of Attitudes," in *Journal of Experimental Social Psychology*, 3, 1967, pp. 2–24. © 1967 by Academic Press. Adapted by permission of Academic Press and Prof. Edward E. Jones.

Page 55, © Esbin-Anderson/The Image Works.

Page 58, Adapted from R. P. Vallone, L. D. Ross, & M. R. Lepper, "The Hostile Media Phenomenon: Biased perception and perceptions of media bias in coverage of the 'Beruit massacre,'" in *Journal of Personality and Social Psychology*, 49, 1985, pp. 577–585. © 1985. Used by permission of Prof. Lee D. Ross.

Page 93, Reprinted with permission of the Pew Research Center for the People and the Press.

Page 94, From Eagly & Wood (eds.), "Explaining sex differences in social behaviour," in Personality and Social Psychology Bulletin, 17, 1991, pp. 306–315. © 1991 by Sage Publications, Inc. Reprinted by permission of Sage Publications, Inc.

Page 100, From *Obedience to Authority* by Stanley Milgram (NY: Harper Collins).

Page 101, From S. Milgram, "some conditions of obedience and disobedience to authority," in Human Relations, 18(1), 1965, p. 73. © 1965 by Plenum Press, renewed 1993 by Alexandra Milgram.

Page 140, Courtesy Alan G. Ingham.

Page 142, (top) © Royalty-free/Corbis; (bottom) © David Young-Wolff/PhotoEdit.

Page 192, Adapted from Statistics Canada, 2001 Census.

Page 226, Adapted from Canadian Human Rights Commission, 2004 Employment Equity Annual Report.

Page 232, Courtesy John Dixon, Lancaster University, and Kevin Durrheim of KwaZulu-Natal.

Page 247, From J. M. Darley & B. Latané, "Bystander Intervention in Emergencies: Diffusion of Responsibility," *Journal of Personality and Social Psychology*, 8, 1968, pp. 337–383. © 1968 by the American Psychological Association. Reprinted with permission.

Page 248, After J. M Darley & B. Latané, "Group Inhibition of Bystander Intervention in Emergencies," *Journal of Personality and Social Psychology*, 10, 1968, pp. 215–221. © 1968 by the American Psychological Association. Reprinted with permission.

Page 255, From R. B. Zajonc, "Attitudinal effects of mere exposure," *Journal of Personality and Social Psychology*, Monograph Suppl. No. 2, part 2. © 1968 by the American Psychological Association. Reprinted with permission.

Page 269, From Robert J. Sternberg, "Triangulating Love," *The Psychology of Love*, edited by Robert J. Sternberg and M. L. Barnes, 1988. © 1988 by Yale University Press. Reprinted with permission.

Page 294, After L. D. Eron & L. R. Huesmann, "The control of aggressive behavior by changes in attitude, values, and the conditions of learning," in *Advances in the Study of Aggression*, 1, Figure 5, pp. 139–168. (R. J. Blanchard & C. Blanchard, eds.) © 1984 Academic Press. Adapted by permission of Academic Press and L. D. Eron.

Page 305, © Reuters/Corbis.

Page 317, Adapted from Statistics Canada, 2003 General Social Survey.

Photo Credits

Name Index

Abalakina-Papp, M. A., 210
Abas, A., 73
Abrahams, D., 256–257
Abrams, D., 34, 158
Acitelli, L. K., 84
Adair, 195
Adair, J. G., 9
Adams, C. A., 186
Adams, J. M., 279
Adinolfi, A. A., 256
Adler, N. L., 276
Adler, R. P., 130
Adorno, T., 210
Ageyev, V. S., 210
Agnew, C. R., 274, 281–282
Agyei, Y., 87
Aiello, J. R., 137
Aikin, K. J., 199
Ajzen, I., 69
Alessis, C., 112
Allee, W. C., 133, 182
Allen, 306
Allen, M., 83
Allison, S. T., 34, 61, 488
Allport, F. H., 133
Allport, G. W., 202–203, 208
Altemeyer, B., 210–211
Amabile, T. M., 49, 50f, 62, 209
Ambady, N., 205
Amir, Y., 231
Amundsen, R., 170
Anastasio, P. A., 235
Anderson, C. A., 13, 38, 85, 181, 185, 291, 295, 296, 297, 298, 299
Anderson, D. C., 185
Anderson, E. A., 321
Antonucci, T. C., 84
Applewhite, M., 122, 125
Archer, D., 186
Archer, J., 86, 180
Archer, R. L., 276
Archer, R. P., 108
Arendt, H., 108
Argyle, M., 164, 318
Arkes, H. R., 17
Arkin, R. M., 29, 33, 253
Armor, D. A., 35
Arms, R. L., 186
Arndt, J., 45, 264
Aron, A., 97, 224, 232, 257, 264, 270–271, 273, 277
Aron, E., 277
Aron, E. N., 97, 264

Aronson, E., 10, 123, 233, 235
Aronson, J., 204, 205
Aronson, V., 256, 257
Asai, M., 273
Asch, S. E., 97–98, 105
Asher, J., 178
Ashton, W., 48
Astin, A. W., 83, 86, 317
Atkins, R. S., 309
ATSB, 61
Atwell, 166
Averill, J. R., 181
Avis, W. E., 94
Axelrod, R., 241
Axsom, D., 117
Ayres, I., 199
Azmier, J. J., 62
Azrin, N., 184

Babad, E., 35
Baca, L. D., 141
Bachman, B. A., 235
Bachman, J. G., 7
Bailey, J. M., 86, 87
Bailis, D., 42, 61
Bainbridge, W., 125
Bainbridge, W. S., 124
Baize, H. R., Jr., 258
Baker, L. A., 35
Baker, S. P., 154
Banaji, M. R., 196
Bandura, A., 40, 44, 183, 291, 294
Banfield, S., 288
Bar-Hillel, M., 60
Bar-Tal, D., 227
Barbaranelli, C., 40
Bargh, J. A., 22, 156, 196, 278
Barnes, P. J., 250
Barnes, R. D., 151
Baron, R. A., 310
Baron, R. M., 186
Baron, R. S., 53, 125, 136, 138, 158
Barongan, C., 296
Barrett, D. W., 128
Barry, D., 87
Barth, J. M., 223, 241
Bartholow, B. D., 181, 299
Bassett, R., 73
Batson, C. D., 84, 239, 244
Bauer, G. B., 187
Baum, A., 186
Baumeister, R. F., 7, 29, 38, 45, 87, 136, 138, 141, 166, 265, 266, 281

Baumgardner, A. H., 29
Baumgardner, M. H., 112
Bauserman, 289
Baxter, T. L., 53
Bayer, E., 133
Bazerman, M. H., 240
Bazzini, G., 276
Beach, R., 73
Beaman, A. L., 151, 250, 262
Bell, 128
Bell, P. A., 185
Bellinger, K., 304
Belson, W., 293
Bem, D., 77
Ben-Zeev, T., 205
Benjamin, A. J., Jr., 181
Bennett, M., 37
Bennett, R., 289
Bennis, W., 172
Benson, J. E., 55
Berg, J. H., 268, 274, 276
Berger, R. E., 30
Berkowitz, L., 181, 184, 294, 296
Berry, J., 206
Berry, J. W., 87, 193
Berry, N. J., 30
Berscheid, E., 52, 66, 74, 225, **254**, **256**, 257, 258, 264–265, 270, **272**, **274**
Bertuzzi, T., 175
Bessenoff, G. R., 211
Best, D., 85, 202
Best, D. L., 198
Best, J. A., 128
Bettencourt, B. A., 86, 214
Beyer, L., 199
Bhardwaj, A., 195
Bhaskar, R., 196
Bhatt, G., 34
Bianchi, S. M., 929
Bibby, 13
Bierbrauer, G., 108
Bierly, M. M., 210
Biernat, M., 39, 92, 211, 214
Bihrle, S., 177
Biko, S., 69
Billig, M., 207
Birrell, P., 215
Bishop, G. D., 155
Bizer, G. Y., 110
Björkqvist, K., 86
Blair, I. V., 196
Blake, R. R., 235, 240
Blass, T., 104

385

Subject Index

absolute judgment, 304
abusive parents, learned aggression and, 183
academic achievement
  self-esteem and, 7–8
  teacher expectations and, 64
accentuation phenomenon, 156
acculturation, 193
actor-observer bias, 51, 53
adaptation, human capacity for, 319–320
adaption-level phenomenon, 319–320, 321
adaptive traits
  anticipatory liking, 254
  self-serving bias and, 38–39
adolescence
  formative experiences in, 116
  Western cultures, in, 22–23
adult relationships. *See* relationships
advertising
  antismoking, 128–129
  fear arousing messages in, 115
  inoculating children against influence of, 129–130
affect, attitudes and, 189
African Americans. *See also* racial prejudice; racial stereotypes
  ethnic pride in, 202
  prejudices among, 194
age of audience
  cult indoctrination, for, 123
  persuasion, for, 116
aggression, 83, 175–188
  blood chemistry and, 178–180
  defined, 95, 176, 188
  deindividuation and, 149–150
  displaced, 180–188, 208
  environmental influences on, 184–188
  frustration and, 180–182
  gender differences in, 86
  genetic influences on, 178
  guns and, 181–182
  instinct, as an, 177
  instrumental, 176
  learning of, 182–184
  neural influences on, 177–178
  psychological influences on, 180–188
  reducing, 186–187
  rewards of, 182–183
  social learning theory of, 183–185
  source of prejudice in, 208–209
  television and, 293–294, 295–296
  television's effect on, 9–11
  testosterone, 88–89
  theories of, 177–180
  video games and, 298
  weapons and, 181–182

women, against, 289–290
aggressive cues, 181–182
alcohol use
  aggression and, 178–180
  underage drinking, reactance and, 165
altruism, 223
  See also helping behaviour
  defined, 244, 251
  foot-in-the-door phenomenon and, 72–73
American Council on Education, 86
American Psychological Association, 11, 180, 295
anger, and aggression, 181
animal research, on feelings of control, 41
anonymity
  deindividuation and, 147–150
  effect of, on behaviour, 5–6
  anti-Semitism, 210
  See also Nazi Holocaust
anticipation of interaction, 253–254
anticipatory liking, 254
anticonformity, 165
antismoking advertising, 128–129
antismoking programs, 128–130
antisocial cues, 149
anxiety, self-serving bias and, 38
Arab Americans, 190
arbitration, 236, 240, 242
arousal. *See also* social arousal
  deindividuation and, 150
  facilitating dominant responses, 133–134
  group influence and, 144–145
  passionate love and, 270–271
arrogance, hindsight bias and, 16–17
assertiveness training, 117–118
attacks, aggression and, 185
attitude inoculation, 127–130
  against influence of advertising, 129–130
  against smoking, 128–130
  defined, 131
  developing counterarguments, 127
  implications of, 131
  programs for, 128–130
  stimulating commitment, 127–128
attitude(s)
  adjust to behaviour, 201–203
  being conscious of, 69
  cognitive dissonance theory and, 76–78
  defined, 68, 77
  desegregation's impact on racial, 230–233
  dual, 196
  evil acts and, 74–75
  foot-in-the-door phenomenon and, 72–74

gender, 199–200
  influence of behaviour on, 69–78
  influence on behaviour, 68–70
  interracial behaviour and racial, 75
  prejudice and, 189, 190
  role-playing and, 70–71
  self-perception theory and, 76
  specificity, 69
  speech and, 71
  strength, 69
  theories of, 69
attitudes-follow-behaviour principle
  cult indoctrination and, 122–123
  evil acts and, 74–75
  theories explaining, 75–78
attraction
  equity principle of, 274
  evolution and, 261
  influence of, on long-term relationships, 268
  likeness-leads-to-liking effect on, 263
  need to belong and, 265–267
  opposites, to, 263–264
  physical attractiveness and, 256–262
  proximity and, 253–256
  reward theory of, 252
  self-esteem and, 264–265
  those who like us, to, 264–265
  what is associated with oneself, to, 254–256
attractiveness. *See* physical attractiveness
attribution bias, 54–55
attributions, prejudice and, 216–217
  See also fundamental attribution error
audience
  age of, 116
  arousing emotions in, 115–116
  counterarguing by, 117
  cult indoctrination and, 123
  cult indoctrination, for, 123
  distracting, 117
  involvement by, 117–118
  persuasion, for, 116–118
authoritarian personality, 210–211
authority
  closeness and legitimacy of the, 102–104
  institutional, 104
automatic information processing, 19
automatic prejudice, 196–197
automatic stereotyping, 196
automatic thinking. *See also* intuition
availability heuristic, 60–61, 67
average
  physical attractiveness and, 259–260
  regression toward, 63–64, 67

Questions for Keep:

? Cost of text per x 150
? cost of etextbook x 150

? cover change to reflect student interest

? istudy psychology. ca

    quizzes ?

? instructors manual
? computerized test bank
? PPT ?
? Blackboard management.

www.mcgrawhill.ca/olc/myers.